LAND AND WATER
1900-1970

CONSERVATION IN THE UNITED STATES

A Documentary History

General Editor: **Frank E. Smith**

LAND AND WATER
1900-1970

Frank E. Smith
Member, Board of Directors
Tennessee Valley Authority

New York
CHELSEA HOUSE PUBLISHERS
In association with
VAN NOSTRAND REINHOLD CO.
New York, Cincinnati, Toronto, London, Melbourne
1971

EDITORIAL STAFF:

Editor-In-Chief: **Fred L. Israel**

Project Editor: **Kim Siegel**

Managing Editor: **William P. Hansen**

Associate Editors: **Joan Tapper**
Nina Flannery

Editorial Assistants: **Jane Fuller**
Maxine Krasnow
Jaffray Cuyler

Copyright © 1971 by Chelsea House Publishers
A Division of Chelsea House Educational Communications, Inc.
Library of Congress Catalogue Card Number: 71-93813

Printed in the United States of America

THE PUBLIC DOMAIN AND INTERNAL IMPROVEMENTS
Conservation Development 1900–1970

Conservation philosophy became active political doctrine at the turn of the century, when Theodore Roosevelt, by a combination of political accidents, came to the Presidency. He was the movement's ideal champion, in the right place at the right time. His legislative achievements in the field were limited, but he dramatized conservation in ways that demonstrate their impact even today.

Perhaps this fortuitous circumstance existed in part because the end of the nineteenth century also marked a distinct change in the growth of America. Frederick Jackson Turner had already noted the end of the traditional type frontier. Most of the accessible and desirable areas had already been opened up, homesteaded, or set aside in the forest reserves established by Presidents Harrison and Cleveland. The new principles of efficient and scientific management of resources were being accepted among the better educated elements of the population, and some business leaders were beginning to comprehend their value. The general public, however, was still disgusted with the waste and exploitation which seemed the by-products of government public land policy. The railroad land grant scandals were still vivid memories, and reaction against them bolstered the reformist movement which was the eastern counterpart of the Populist revolt on the plains and in the South. The muckraker movement in journalism was about to reach its peak of influence, and the very intensity of feeling about conservation gave the muckrakers a chance to translate many of its issues into crusades.

When Theodore Roosevelt became President in 1901, Gifford Pinchot was already well established as his conservation adviser, a relationship that dated back to initial consultation with Roosevelt when he was Governor of New York. Pinchot was regarded as the unofficial "minister of conservation" in the Roosevelt administration, and he played an important role in every major resource decision during T. R.'s seven years in the White House. Despite his influence, however, Pinchot's official position remained Chief Forester of the United States—"The Forester" was the title at that time.

Roosevelt and Pinchot jointly gave the movement its name—Conservation—adopting a suggestion from W J McGee. The full-fledged philosophy to which they gave allegiance for the rest of their lives developed as they went along. It was the most exciting development of the period, and consequently attracted some of the best minds in the country, to whom Roosevelt gave unstinting credit for their advice. Pinchot was their leader, and usually their emissary to Roosevelt, but the scientific background and training of the new breed of conservationists bore the brand of John Wesley Powell.

[v]

"They actually did the job that I and the others talked about," Roosevelt recalled later. "I know what they did because it was something in which I intensely believed, and yet it was something about which I did not have enough practical knowledge to work except through them. . . ."

All of T. R.'s conservationists came with some background of special interest and training in a single-purpose aspect of conservation or resource development, but most of them naturally supported adherence to a coordinated policy. They all instinctively abhorred waste, and waste was the inevitable result of uncoordinated development. Most of them were tinged with some reformist characteristics, Henry George being a chief example. They believed that the nation's resources had to be protected from waste and exploitation, and at the same time preserved and developed for the best use of all the people. They joined in the popular reaction against monopoly, which to them meant selfish control of resources.

At the urging of Pinchot and F. H. Newell, chief hydrographer of the Geological Survey, President Roosevelt, in his first message to Congress, endorsed a program of federal irrigation. The bill was enacted and Newell installed as the first chief of the Reclamation Service, a name more suitable as well as more psychologically persuasive. Reclamation was to be the major program achievement of Roosevelt's seven years in office, but his inability to bring other programs to equal success should not becloud T. R.'s contributions to American conservation.

The author of the irrigation bill which Roosevelt endorsed was a Democrat, Representative Francis G. Newlands of Nevada. In response to the cries of anguish from the Republican Party for his cooperation with a Democrat, T. R. in election years disparaged Newlands' contributions to reclamation and conservation, but in less political circumstances he unhesitatingly praised the Nevadan. Newlands later advanced to the Senate, where water conservation has never had a more dedicated or altruistic champion. Representing a state where the only major water problem was water for irrigation, Newlands worked until his death for a national water program designed to coordinate the needs of navigation, flood control, power, and irrigation. Roosevelt endorsed the same ideas before he went out of office. The Newlands plan in modified form was adopted in 1917, was never tried in actuality, and was repealed in 1920 when Newlands' death removed the major force behind its support.

Like his later national water program, Newlands' reclamation plan proposed to turn its back on the pork-barrel system of authorizing and allocating projects, but Roosevelt found he had to depart from this ideal in the early days of the program, to achieve adequate congressional support from the western states to which the program was limited. Although there have been major changes in the system of financing reclamation projects, as well as in the system of repayment for water and the power later authorized, the Bureau of Reclamation today is in good measure the Reclamation Service laid out by Roosevelt, Newlands, and Newell in 1903.

For Pinchot, T. R.'s greatest program achievement was the transfer of the forest reserves from the Interior Department to the Department of Agriculture, where the Bureau of Forestry had been established in 1900. Pinchot believed that the vast reserves now permanently claimed by the Federal Government must be scientifically managed if they were to make a proper contribution to the nation's economy and to the economic development of the western states.

Naturally he believed that his Bureau was the one organization equipped to handle the responsibility. Pinchot, the pioneer conservationist, was no preservationist in the current definition of that word. His concept of sustained-yield management was the natural forerunner of the current doctrine of multiple-use of forests.

The vested interests which benefited from Interior Department management of the forests, plus the patronage system of the departmental bureaucracy, were difficult to overcome. Pinchot secured transfer of the reserves to Agriculture only by mobilizing the American Forestry Association and a good segment of the lumber industry in support of the Roosevelt proposal.

Despite the progress Pinchot made in converting lumbermen to his forest policy, federal forest ownership continued to be a political bugaboo in the West, where it could be opposed—if nothing else—as contrary to western states' rights. In 1907 the western congressmen attached a rider to the Agriculture appropriation bill barring any addition to the reserves in Colorado, Idaho, Montana, Oregon, Washington, and Wyoming. Roosevelt signed the bill, but before he did so he signed an Executive order creating or enlarging thirty-two national forests within six states. He also proclaimed national monuments of historic or scientific interest be preserved by signing the Antiquities Act of 1906.

Water policy began to move slowly toward multipurpose development during the Roosevelt years. Giving first attention to congressional watchdogs like Theodore Burton of Ohio, the Corps of Engineers resisted the idea of new responsibilities. Burton's vision was not broad enough to encompass full development of the resource potential of the nation's rivers, but he firmly resisted their control for monopolistic private power generation at the expense of other possible uses. Burton's stand bolstered Roosevelt's firm resolve to protect the public interest in waterways, and helped uphold several vetoes. Perhaps the most important of these vetoes killed a bill to give to a private promotional firm the right to build a dam on the Tennessee River at Muscle Shoals, Alabama, thus preserving to public priority what was to become the most significant of government river valley development programs.

W J McGee and Pinchot were the leaders in persuading the President to take the most dramatic step of his administration toward a unified conservation policy. The President appointed an Inland Waterways Commission to review and recommend national policy in the field. The ideas of Newlands and McGee prevailed in the report, which proposed that navigation improvement include plans for the purification of waters, development of power, control of floods, reclamation of lands, and "all other uses of the waters or benefits to be derived from their control."

Despite a valiant try by Newlands, the Commission plan failed to pass the Congress. Roosevelt then called a Governors' Conference on Conservation, which endorsed some general Roosevelt concepts, and specifically asked for a national conservation inventory. When Congress failed to act on this proposal, the President appointed a National Conservation Commission to report on waters, forests, lands, and minerals. This report also went unheeded, and the Congress even refused to pay for its printing. To emphasize the point that the Congress wanted no more conservation advice from Roosevelt, an appropriation rider was adopted forbidding any federal administrative official from assisting in any way the work of any executive commission not authorized by Congress.

William Howard Taft, T. R.'s choice as his successor, gave only perfunctory allegiance to the conservation principles of his mentor. His indifference to the conduct of the programs, and his lack of devotion to the concept, gave rise to the first great public conservation crusade, marred the Taft administration with allegations of scandal and corruption, and probably was the major factor in producing the party split which denied him reelection.

Taft's Secretary of the Interior was Richard A. Ballinger, a Seattle lawyer who had served previously as Commissioner of Public Lands. The conservation group who had dominated executive policy under Roosevelt became suspicious of Ballinger when he began to slow down the reclamation program in favor of private irrigation schemes. Their antagonism was heightened when he joined the Corps of Engineers in urging perpetual, unlimited franchises for the construction of dams on navigable streams.

In this atmosphere Louis R. Glavis, a Bureau of Public Lands employee in Portland, Oregon, was ordered by Secretary Ballinger to suspend an investigation of some coal land claims in Alaska which Glavis suspected were fraudulent. Convinced that the claims were being protected by someone higher up in the Department, Glavis went to Washington and told the story to Roosevelt's Interior Secretary, James A. Garfield (son of the assassinated President). When Garfield recalled that Ballinger had been interested in the claims as a private attorney, he told Pinchot, who took the story to Taft, convinced that the Secretary would be immediately dismissed.

Instead it was Glavis who was fired. Taft supported Ballinger's conduct, and stirred up a storm of protest from the eastern press, which convicted Ballinger in headlines like "Ballinger—Shyster Lawyer." Pinchot, still Chief Forester, helped keep the issue alive, and Ballinger claimed that the Forest Service was the source of all the attacks made upon him. When Pinchot answered this charge with an unauthorized letter to Senator Jonathan P. Dolliver of Iowa, Taft fired him for insubordination.

The immediate result was a joint congressional investigation which attracted more national attention than any other before that time. A party-line report cleared Ballinger, but the Democratic minority, joined by Republican Representative E. H. Madison of Kansas, demanded that he resign.

Despite this predictable outcome, Taft had allowed Pinchot and his friends to convert the incident into a great crusade for morality in the administration of natural resources. In spite of some of the ugly implications at the time of the dispute, no evidence of bribery or corruption was presented; the judgment rested on the convictions of the conservationists that it was dishonest and thus immoral to give away a natural resource that was the property of the people of the country.

Taft's inept political handling of the Ballinger affair has obscured some important conservation achievements during the remainder of his administration. Ballinger's successor, Walter L. Fisher, did a satisfactory job, and gained the approbation of both Garfield and Pinchot. Taft's Secretary of War, Henry L. Stimson, forced upon the Corps of Engineers a brief adherence to the Roosevelt waterway development doctrines.

Taft's choice as Pinchot's successor to the post of Chief Forester was a Pinchot disciple, Henry L. Graves, who carried forward the same programs with probably greater attention to detail. The great achievement of Graves and Taft was their support of the Weeks Act (1911), which authorized federal financial aid to any state which would establish fire prevention programs for timberlands at the head of navigable streams. More importantly, it gave the Federal Government authority to buy timberland and establish national forests where the timber was at the headwaters of a navigable stream.

The link of the timberlands to navigable streams in both major provisions of the bill was necessary to alleviate any doubt about the constitutionality of the new law. The navigable stream basis could and would be used in the future for virtually any type of conservation or resource development program, although repeated judicial tests would be made before the last doubter was convinced. Congress and the Corps of Engineers had for generations been fearful of expanding water activity beyond navigation improvement, yet the Weeks Act was to pave the way for justifying any water conservation program on the basis of its indirect benefit to navigation. The Weeks Act was not to be implemented on a broad scale until the New Deal period, but it was a major benefit to forestry in spreading the program throughout the country.

Conservation's major advance during the administrations of President Woodrow Wilson was the establishment of the National Park Service, which is dealt with in the *Recreation* volume of this series. For southerners of the lower Mississippi Valley, the presence of a fellow Democrat in the White House gave them a chance to pursue their fight for federal flood control on the Mississippi. Senator Newlands had established close liaison with the southerners as possible allies in his fight to enact his Newlands plan for coordinated national waterway development. For a time the prospects looked bright for success, but most of the lower Mississippi Valley leaders deserted when they became convinced that they could secure more funds and authority for the Mississippi River Commission through the assistance of elements in the Congress who were fearful of the cost of the Newlands program. Officers of the Corps of Engineers who still believed in the "levees only" doctrine helped stir the opposition to Newlands.

In 1916, President Wilson endorsed the Newlands plan, now modified to be called the Waterways Commission—River Regulation Bill. His new Secretary of War, Newton D. Baker, was personally committed to the plan, and forced official acceptance by the Corps. Even with this lineup, a bill to authorize only assistance in the construction of levees on the Mississippi was passed in the House. By gathering together every influence he could mobilize in the Senate, Newlands managed a new compromise which enacted both the levee bill and the modified Newlands plan.

The Newlands Waterways Commission plan became law on August 8, 1917. For the next few months, in the midst of war preparations, Newlands and his old opponents sparred over the composition of the Commission, which the Nevada Senator wanted to be dominated by members of the Cabinet, to insure national coordination. The Commission was still not appointed when Newlands died on Christmas Eve, 1917, and it never was appointed. Not having been acted on, the whole plan was repealed in 1920. The "levees only" plan continued during the next ten years, but its ineffectiveness was made all too clear by the 1927 flood which devastated the lower Mississippi Valley.

Renewed efforts to grant private power companies control of prime hydro-generation sites on the Tennessee River prompted the Wilson administration to seek a system of federal control and licensing of power sites. In 1920, a favorable bill passed the House, establishing a Federal Power Commission, and making clear the federal control of power sites on navigable streams. Senator John K. Shields of Tennessee, supporting private power control, diluted the House bill in conference with a definition of navigability which resulted in the Tennessee River's being declared non-navigable.

The old Roosevelt conservation forces entered the fray at this point, led by Pinchot and the National Conservation Association which he headed after leaving government. There were not enough votes to defeat the Shields bill, but the issue was dramatic enough to convince Senator Robert LaFollette of Wisconsin that it was worth a full-scale filibuster. LaFollette had to stop four appropriation bills in the course of his dramatic effort on March 4, 1919, but he managed to kill the Shields bill with the end of that term of Congress.

The Republican landslide in the 1920 election installed Senator Wesley Jones of Washington as the new chairman of the Commerce Committee. Jones brought out a bill endorsed by Pinchot and his Conservation Association, although opposed by progressives like George Norris of Nebraska, who objected to the authority of the new Power Commission to grant private monopolies over public waters. The Jones bill did establish federal jurisdiction, however, and contained the historic preference clause, giving preference to public bodies in the case of conflicting applications, as well as first preference in buying the power generated.

During the 1920's conservation programs generally marked time—marked, if anything, by retrogression in some public policy concepts. The important examples of limited progress were in forestry programs and broader recognition of the multipurpose concept of water development. The most important event, however, was another scandal involving a Cabinet officer.

The congressional investigation of Secretary of the Interior Albert B. Fall and the Teapot Dome oil leases (given more treatment in the *Minerals* volume of this series) was no whitewash. Fall went to jail, even though the oil company executives who had paid him off escaped. The most important result of Teapot Dome, however, was that it generated another conservation crusade. The crusade met with no real success until the election of Franklin D. Roosevelt in 1932, but it did prevent new scandals and helped establish an atmosphere that led to minor concessions from the reluctant Republican administrations which were characterized by a general retreat from all types of federal activity.

During the twenties the Forest Service made substantial progress in promoting the management-for-use concept for federal forest lands. Much of the progress was made possible by the presence in the Republican legislative hierarchy of Senator Charles McNary of Oregon, a state with one of the largest percentages of federal forests. McNary's name is listed on laws which authorized cooperative fire control programs (without even the limitation to navigable streams) and cooperative planting of seedlings with the states, expanded research in all aspects of forestry, and expanded purchase authority for national forests.

The reclamation program during this period was subjected to a great deal of talk about shifting toward state control, but little was done about it. The most spectacular achievement was the authorization of the first major multipurpose dam. The Boulder Canyon project was first nourished by Reclamation Chief A. P. Davis, a protege and successor of F. H. Newell in the Bureau of Reclamation. After Davis was ousted with the return to normalcy, the idea seemed headed toward a quiet death at the hands of the private power companies. Secretary of Commerce Herbert Hoover learned of the proposal after President Harding assigned him to referee a dispute between the states over apportionment of Colorado River irrigation water. Without Hoover's support, the bill authorizing Boulder Dam might never have been signed by President

Coolidge, who agreed to accept it in 1928, after plans had been modified to allow private power companies to acquire most of the dam's power output.

Today Boulder Dam is Hoover Dam, and it is still a multipurpose showcase. In addition to providing power to return a substantial share of its cost, the structure controls spring floods in the Imperial Valley, is a major source of water supply for the city of Los Angeles, and provides irrigation of approximately one million acres of agricultural land in the surrounding states.

In 1927 flood devastation on the lower Mississippi shocked the nation. Even the reluctant Coolidge administration was willing to accept full federal responsibility for flood control in the valley—the U.S. Chamber of Commerce even voted for such a principle by a margin of 2,619 to 156. The flood finally converted the Mississippi River Commission to a plan calling for tributary reservoirs and channel cutoffs and diversions, in addition to higher and stronger levees; but instead of submitting the commission plan, the administration backed the much less expensive proposal of General Edgar Jadwin, Chief of Engineers, which was basically the old "levees only" theory.

In 1928 Congress passed what was essentially the inadequate Jadwin plan, but in 1936 Mississippi Valley Congressmen modified it to include the River Commission proposals after Franklin Roosevelt became President.

Like his cousin Theodore, Franklin Roosevelt came to the Presidency already a committed and knowledgeable conservationist. His own experiences as a forest farmer at Hyde Park, as chairman of the state legislative Forest, Fish and Game Commission, and as Governor struggling to establish the New York State Power Authority to generate and distribute Niagara River power, were added to that of a Democratic politician seeking to make capital of the Republican inadequacies of the past three administrations.

Conservation measures were important during the honeymoon of the New Deal, and F. D. R. continued to push for them until World War II absorbed most of his energies. Unlike Theodore, Franklin Roosevelt had no conservation minister similar to Gifford Pinchot, although the aging Pinchot was active among his supporters and advisers on conservation issues. Other more immediately compelling and dramatic issues dominated F. D. R.'s twelve years in the White House, but no administration compares with his in conservation achievements.

As Francis Newlands dominated the conservation legislative scene during the early years of the century, George Norris of Nebraska was the dominant figure during the New Deal days. When Roosevelt came to office, Norris had already prepared for his first great conservation goal—the Tennessee Valley Authority.

The accident of his chairmanship of the Senate Agriculture Committee and the capacity to convert a World War I chemical plant at Muscle Shoals, Alabama, to the manufacture of fertilizers brought Norris into sponsorship of the TVA concept of a multipurpose coordinated resource development for an entire river valley. The munitions plant had been located where a major dam could be built at Muscle Shoals to supply its power. Neither facility had been finished before the end of the war, but the very fact that they were underway had enabled munitions czar Bernard Baruch to cut by millions the cost of nitrate supplies from South America.

When the War Department began evaluating plans to dispose of the dam and the chemical plant as war surplus property, automobile tycoon Henry Ford entered the negotiations with a plan to buy the property and use it as the base for a vast but nebulous economic development plan for the Tennessee River area of north Alabama. Norris led the fight in the Congress against the Ford offer. In the process he developed a plan for government development of the entire Tennessee River and its tributaries, as well as operation of the chemical plant to provide low-cost fertilizer for farmers.

Gradually building a plan for an independent government corporation to generate power, operate the chemical plant, and develop the other resource potentials of the valley, Norris constructed a coalition of support from southern and western farm areas, old-line Roosevelt conservationists, and scattered liberals and progressives from throughout the country. Twice he managed to secure congressional approval of his plan, to be vetoed first by Coolidge and then by Hoover.

Franklin Roosevelt endorsed the proposal during his campaign in 1932. He worked out with Norris an even broader authority for the government corporation, and the Tennessee Valley Authority was established by law on May 18, 1933. The basic plan is still in effect, and many conservationists and historians alike consider the TVA the major storybook success of the New Deal.

Another F. D. R. accomplishment was the Civilian Conservation Corps, a highly imaginative plan to offer employment of permanent value for idle young men. Within a few months after Roosevelt was in office, the plan had taken 300,000 boys off street corners and rural crossroads and into rural camps where they worked under semi-military discipline in planting trees, terracing gullies, and other practical conservation measures. Before World War II ended the program, two and one-half million unemployed youths had spent a healthful period in the "3-C's." Present-day estimates of the long-range economic values of the work performed indicate that the actual cost of the program has been dwarfed by the increased yields and values of the forest lands and parks which benefited from the Conservation Corps work.

F. D. R., the Hyde Park forester, kept close to forestry programs throughout his time in the Presidency. Vast purchases of private land to become public forests were made in the 1930's, thanks to his interest and the fact that the depression made the acreage available at reasonable prices. The Shelterbelt forest across the Great Plains was kept alive through his persistence, despite congressional neglect and opposition.

The emergency system of farm relief established by the New Deal was geared to improvement of land through improvement of agricultural practices. When the Supreme Court outlawed the original Agricultural Adjustment Act, it was replaced by the Soil Conservation and Domestic Allotment Act of 1936. All farm programs designed to curb surpluses or support the price of commodities have been based in part upon the 1936 act. Other major Department of Agriculture programs since that time have included a conservation theme as part of their justification.

One of the major conservation programs now in the Agriculture Department originated when Harold Ickes, Roosevelt's Secretary of the Interior, took a long-time Agriculture Department geologist, Hugh Hammond Bennett, away from that Department and set him up as head of the Soil Erosion Service (SES) in the Interior Department. The federal soil conservation program is the child of Bennett, who nourished it in a long struggle reminiscent of the career of John Wesley Powell, but it would never have been brought to flourishing prosperity without the attention of Roosevelt and the congressional patrons Bennett cultivated.

In its early days the Soil Conservation Service was bitterly opposed by the established hierarchy of the Department of Agriculture, but today it is a fundamental part of that establishment. Broadening the base of the soil conservation programs to include small watershed system reservoirs was one of the relatively few conservation advances made during the Eisenhower administration twenty years later. In the current generation the watershed program offers strikingly imaginative possibilities for meeting both urban and rural recreation, water supply, and open space problems if congressional and budget limitations can be surmounted.

When Ickes came to Interior, he faced a major problem of shaking the agency loose from inaction based on a philosophy of "state control" and "returning land to the tax rolls." For the first time since the first Roosevelt, there was a frank facing up to the necessity of government land policy being tied to a more general government policy of development and preservation for public use. Meaningful additions to the national park system were made east of the Mississippi, and the Reclamation Service was shifted to adaptation for major multipurpose projects in the framework of Grand Coulee.

Unfortunately for Ickes' record of conservation achievement, a major part of his energy and effectiveness was dissipated in unsuccessful efforts to transfer to the Interior Department all conservation agencies and all conservation responsibilities. If the reorganization could have been achieved in laboratory or textbook fashion, it would have been worthwhile. The net effect of all the activity, however, was little change in organization, and enormous waste of energies in peripheral infighting which might have been devoted to persuading the public and Congress to accept conservation goals instead of theoretical departmental charts.

Ickes failed in his attempt to have the Forest Service transferred back to Interior, but the passage of the Taylor Grazing Act in 1934, regulating grazing on the public domain, was a major achievement.

F. D. R. left squabbles about organizational procedure to his subordinates, but most of the struggles over public power and regulation of the utility industry were made in his name. The Rural Electrification Administration, (REA), established by his Executive order in 1935, ranks with TVA as a frontrank contribution. After Congress, led by Senator Norris and Representative Sam Rayburn of Texas, joined in authorizing the program by law in 1936, cooperatives were established across the country, financed with low-interest government loans, to supply farms and rural homes with electric service. No other activity of the New Deal brought such a change in everyday life.

The fight to eliminate utility holding companies was directly related to Roosevelt's conservation policies. The legislation was designed to eliminate the massive financial superstructure which the relatively new private power companies had to support as part of a financing system that offered greater profits in organizing and financing power companies than in generating and selling electricity. The bitter fight to pass the "death sentence" for the holding companies probably drew as clear a line as any of Roosevelt's fights with the business community.

Grand Coulee, the country's largest dam, which F. D. R. started during his first 100 days of 1933, was the foremost of a number of massive multipurpose projects which became identified with the President. The great structure in the State of Washington became a reality in F. D. R.'s time. Another landmark achievement was the 1936 Omnibus Flood Control Act which provided for surveys and improvements of watersheds and basins, and which placed both the Corps of Engineers and the Department of Agriculture in the picture for flood control work, initiating decades of controversy on big dams versus little dams and land treatment. Other projects, such as the St. Lawrence Seaway, were lost causes until picked up by a successor. Still another category, such as the Passamaquoddy tidal hydro-generating plan, still remains in the planning stage.

Harry Truman never wavered in his acceptance of the Roosevelt conservation doctrine, although he gained few victories on major issues during the years when he was without majority support in the Congress. He actively fought to secure for the Missouri and Columbia basins the establishment of valley authorities patterned after TVA, but could never even bring the issues to a vote. Perhaps his most noteworthy action was a courageous veto, in 1946, of legislation to give the states title to offshore oil reserves.

The administration of Dwight D. Eisenhower was marked by a determined effort to cut back water development programs, and resistance to congressional pressure for federal action to abate water pollution. Political reality made it necessary for Eisenhower to support several major development programs with important Republican sponsorship, and, consequently, landmarks such as the St. Lawrence Seaway and the Upper Colorado project came into being under his aegis. The Small Watershed Program for the Soil Conservation Service ranks as an important achievement of his administration, as does the support of the Multiple-Use Act of 1960, the first important amendments to public forest management since the Pettigrew-McRae legislation of 1897. The Outdoor Recreation Resources Review Commission was set up under Eisenhower in 1958 and has served to focus national attention on the new and voracious uses of land and water. However, the Eisenhower approval of a new version of the tidelands oil legislation earned him no conservation credits.

John F. Kennedy made a campaign issue of the Republican administration's neglect of conservation programs and its favoritism toward private power. The most important Kennedy administration contribution was the stimulation of action in areas where he had promised action, such as pollution abatement. And, for the first time, recreation was included as a full and legitimate partner in the justification of water development programs. The Bureau of Outdoor Recreation was created and established in 1962.

Lyndon B. Johnson gave active support to new conservation concepts, and an impressive list of legislative achievements followed the election of 1964. The Water Resources Research Act, the Wilderness Bill, and the Air Pollution Abatement Act are examples. The Highway Beautification Act was a halting start toward awareness of the conservation values of aesthetics, and credit is due Mrs. Johnson for the current respectability of the phrase "natural beauty." Both Kennedy and Johnson, and their appointees to various departments and agencies, began to relate natural resource and conservation problems to the basic principle that conservation also means developing human resources. There are still major gaps in coordinated governmental action on conservation issues, but there is far greater emphasis on coordinated planning than ever before.

Inevitably, the war in Vietnam drew a sharp line between the promise and the performance of the Johnson administration on conservation, as on most other domestic problems. The years that stretch before us will properly measure the progress which survives the long haul.

Frank E. Smith
Tennessee Valley Authority
Knoxville, Tennessee

CONTENTS

Attempts to Coordinate National Water Policy

The Public Domain

Establishing Federal Policy for Water Power

The Dust Bowl

The Tennessee Valley Authority

Flood Control and Water Development Programs

THE ST. LAWRENCE SEAWAY

LAND AND WATER
1900-1970

THEODORE ROOSEVELT

LETTER FROM THEODORE ROOSEVELT ON
FOREST RESERVATIONS*
August 24, 1897

This excerpt from a letter by Theodore Roosevelt makes clear his interest in assuring credit to a Republican President, William McKinley, for the role he had to play in preserving forest reservations in the opening days of his Presidency. It is one of the few discussions of directly related conservation issues found in Roosevelt's pre-presidential correspondence.

TO GEORGE BIRD GRINNELL

Washington, August 24, 1897

My dear Grinnell:

Beyond one or two slight verbal changes I have nothing serious to suggest about the preface, excepting on one point. This is in reference to the forestry business. I wish to say in substance exactly what you have said, but I think there should be a more just division of praise. It was a serious matter taking this great mass of forest reservations away from the settlers. That it needed to be done admits of no question, but the great bulk of the people themselves strongly objected to its being done; and a great deal of nerve and a good deal of tact were needed in accomplishing it. I am exceedingly glad that President Cleveland issued the order; but none of the trouble came on him at all. He issued the order at the very end of his administration, practically to take effect in the next administration. In other words he issued an order which it was easy to issue, but difficult to execute, and which had to be executed by his successor. This is a perfectly common thing; in civil service matters, for instance, I have seen it done by Presidents Arthur, Harrison and Cleveland; in fact by every outgoing President since the civil service law went into effect. At present it seems to be about the only way we can get ahead on certain lines; for the President who is not willing to do the thing himself, is glad enough to direct that his successor shall

*The Letters of Theodore Roosevelt, Vol. 1, Elting E. Morison, ed. (Cambridge: Harvard University Press, 1951), 657–58.

do it; and the latter, who probably would not have the nerve to do it, in his turn makes the excuse to the foes of the reform that he can't go back on what his predecessor did. I think that credit should be given the man who issues the order, but I think it should be just as strongly given to the man who enforces it. Cleveland had issued the order without consulting the Senators and Congressmen who were all powerful in the matter of legislation, and if he had stayed in power the order would have been promptly nullified. President McKinley and Secretary Bliss took the matter up, and by great resolution finally prevented its complete overthrow. It was impossible to expect its going into effect at once. Not a dozen men in the Senate were for it, and all of these were from the far west. Now, the point I want to make is that quite as much is owing to McKinley as to Cleveland in the matter, and I think that either we should not mention either of them, or we should mention both. What Cleveland did was very easy to do; for it is not at all difficult to say that your successor must be virtuous. McKinley had to encounter real opposition. If this country could be ruled by a benevolent czar we would doubtless make a good many changes for the better, but as things are, if we want to accomplish anything, we have got to get the best work we can out of the means that are available. All of this is a needless homily. The only point is that I wish you would revise the sentence about that reservation, so as either to make it more general or more fully specific.

* * *

LETTER FROM GOVERNOR ROOSEVELT ON
CONSERVATION PERSONNEL*
June 5, 1900

As Governor of New York, Roosevelt found that the civil service regulations sometimes had to be circumvented in order to get the best qualified men for the state's conservation program. The Governor's previous major experience in government had been as a federal Civil Service Commissioner. These letters were addressed to state civil service commissioners. Note the reference to Gifford Pinchot as having "no more to do with politics than the astronomers of the Harvard Observatory."

TO SILAS WRIGHT BURT

Albany, June 5, 1900

My dear Col. Burt:

I inclose you a copy of a letter I have sent to Mr. McAneny. You probably know Mr. Austin Wadsworth personally and some of the other members of the Forest, Fish & Game Commission, at least by reputation. You probably know Mr. Gifford Pinchot by reputation. This Commission is simply trying to get the best results that can be obtained. Such positions as that of Chief Fire Warden, Special Agent, Oyster Protector and Forester cannot be filled from the competitive examinations as they are now fixed, and they must be filled at once. We cannot afford to have the work of the Commission hampered, and it is hampered just as much by inaction and delay as in any other way. I hope that Mr. Collier and yourself can arrange to see one or more members of the Forest, Fish & Game Commission at once. Wherever the positions can be filled by promotion, of course I desire them so to be filled.

Sincerely yours

TO GEORGE McANEY

Albany, June 5, 1900

My dear Mr. McAneny:

First, as to your letter: Wheeler is a most admirable man and I believe would make an excellent member of the Commission. I am also considering Cuthbert W. Pound and McKinstry. Each of them has points in which he is inferior to

---

*The Letters of Theodore Roosevelt, Vol. 2, Elting E. Morison, ed. (Cambridge: Harvard University Press, 1951), 1320–22.

Wheeler and points in which he would be more useful. Probably Pound would be on the whole the best man, owing to his legislative experience.

Just at present what I am concerned with is the effort to make the Commission and the Civil Service Law a help instead of a hindrance in getting good results in certain departments. I send you a copy of a letter I have sent to Col. Burt, whom Collier wants to have made President of the Commission. You will see from this that the Forest, Fish & Game Commission are seriously hampered by the present rules. They have appointed a couple of Foresters on the suggestion of Gifford Pinchot whom you probably know. Pinchot is the best authority on forestry in the country. He is at the head of the Forestry Division in the National Government. The Commission want to work with the Forestry Division and took Pinchot's men. Pinchot has no more to do with politics than the astronomers of the Harvard Observatory have. All he is interested in is his forestry work. A great deal of this work is technical and I do not know how examinations for the positions could be held. Perhaps you know Mr. Austin Wadsworth, the President of the Forest, Fish & Game Commission. If you do you will probably know he has never been active in politics, and is certainly not approaching this work of the Forest, Fish & Game Commission from the political side. I do not believe that any of the members of that Commission are so approaching it. I think they all realize that the best service that the Commission can render the party is by making a good commission, and I certainly do not believe that they are trying to get any position exempted save with an idea of getting the right man to fill it. In most places I do not believe they take the political element into consideration at all, and I am certain that they will always subordinate it entirely to the good of the service. If not, I shall stop them with a rough hand. But they must be able to choose good men and they must be able to choose them *now*. They do not want to let the season go by while they are held up in the effort to procure the right men. Mr. Wadsworth, for instance, wants to appoint a Special Agent—that is, he wants someone whom he can send anywhere he desires on any kind of secret and confidential work, who will oversee things and report exactly what is up. He does not believe he can fill the place by promotion, and he believes that he could not get, and would not know how to get, the type of man he wants from a competitive examination. He is going to find out if he cannot promote somebody in the present force, but if he cannot, I fail to see how it is possible to avoid excepting the place.

So when it comes to an Oyster Protector. The man appointed to this position should of course have some literary knowledge, some scholarly attainment, but he must know practically about oysters and be able to row and sail and handle himself on the mud flats. Above all he must have executive capacity. So it is with several other positions. For instance, the Chief Fire Warden must to my thinking be an excepted place. This is one of the most important positions under the Commission, and I should be quite as irritated as you could possibly be if the

Commission chose such a man for political reasons. They ought to get a thoroughly competent administrator and woodsman. It is essentially an executive place and should be filled by an active man who can get around all through the north country, see to the putting out of fires, the establishing of fire guards and all the rest of the work himself. I cannot conceive of any useful competitive examination for such a place. If the place can be filled by promotion, well and good, but if there is not just the right man in the force below, it will have to be exempted from examination.

I wish to call your attention to the fact that great delay is itself a very serious evil, especially when the new Commission has come in and is trying to administer the work of the Commission on an improved basis.

After our late correspondence I have taken up the matter to see whether we could not diminish the excepted places. I think perhaps it can be done, but I am also convinced that until very great improvement in the system of examinations is worked out, good administration will demand a considerable number of excepted places. I never want the Commission to except a place when the exception is demanded because of a desire to put in anyone for political reasons; but neither do I wish to see the public service hampered by a sacrifice of the spirit to the letter of the law. In civil service reform competitive examinations are merely a means to an end. I am thoroughly convinced that if the Association spent more time in trying to perfect the system of examinations and secure better results from them instead of trying to widen the scope, it would for the time being be much more useful work.

Sincerely yours

LETTER FROM PRESIDENT ROOSEVELT ON MANAGEMENT*
October 18, 1901

Gifford Pinchot wanted management of the national forest reserves under his control in the Department of Agriculture. The counter proposition was for his forestry division to be transferred to the Interior Department, which had the forests before and after their reservation.

This letter from the President soon after he took office was obviously written before he had accepted Pinchot's view.

TO GIFFORD PINCHOT

Personal   Washington, October 18, 1901

My dear Mr. Pinchot:

I have just had a conversation with Secretary Hitchcock about the Forestry Division in the Land Office. He informs me that he has had an explicit understanding with Mr. Hermann, that Mr. Hermann absolutely and without reservation acquiesces in the Secretary's determination that if you come over you will have an absolutely free hand, and that what you say as to the policies to be pursued, the men to be appointed, etc., etc., shall be done without question so far as Mr. Hermann is concerned. In other words, you will have exactly the same freedom as though you were the independent head of the bureau. There will not be one shadow of difference. Under these circumstances it seems to me utterly unimportant that you should merely put your initials on a letter instead of signing it yourself. What you and I and the Secretary are after is to get results. It is of no more consequence to you from a personal standpoint that your name should be there than that the Secretary's name should be there, or mine. We all of us have a common object. It seems to me to be to the last degree unwise to refuse to take advantage of the chance to do such excellent work because of anything so unimportant as having your initials on a letter instead of signing it. The condition of affairs is not expected to be permanent. It is expected to be a transition stage, which shall itself develop conditions which will enable us in the future to make a permanent establishment. As long as the Secretary and I are here you will have precisely as much liberty of action, precisely as good a chance to do your work, as if you signed your name instead of your initials. From my point of view it is perfectly obvious that where the matter is really trivial you should not hesitate for a moment in acceding to the Secretary's wishes. He pre-

The Letters of Theodore Roosevelt, Vol. 3, Elting E. Morison, ed. (Cambridge: Harvard University Press, 1951), 177–78.

sents what seems to me good reasons against such an entire innovation as having you sign your own name. It would create a precedent that would certainly plague us, and cause in all probability real disorganization of the service.

If you choose, you might show this to Secretary Wilson.

Faithfully yours

PRESIDENT ROOSEVELT'S STATE OF THE UNION MESSAGE*
December 3, 1901

Theodore Roosevelt specified his special interest in conservation measures in his first message to Congress. He devoted far more space to conservation-related issues than had any previous President, as the following excerpt indicates.

Wise forest protection does not mean the withdrawal of forest resources, whether of wood, water, or grass, from contributing their full share to the welfare of the people, but, on the contrary, gives the assurance of larger and more certain supplies. The fundamental idea of forestry is the perpetuation of forests by use. Forest protection is not an end of itself; it is a means to increase and sustain the resources of our country and the industries which depend upon them. The preservation of our forests is an imperative business necessity. We have come to see clearly that whatever destroys the forest, except to make way for agriculture, threatens our well being.

The practical usefulness of the national forest reserves to the mining, grazing, irrigation, and other interests of the regions in which the reserves lie has led to a widespread demand by the people of the West for their protection and extension. The forest reserves will inevitably be of still greater use in the future than in the past. Additions should be made to them whenever practicable, and their usefulness should be increased by a thoroughly business-like management.

At present the protection of the forest reserves rests with the General Land Office, the mapping and description of their timber with the United States Geological Survey, and the preparation of plans for their conservative use with the Bureau of Forestry, which is also charged with the general advancement of practical forestry in the United States. These various functions should be united in the Bureau of Forestry, to which they properly belong. The present diffusion of responsibility is bad from every standpoint. It prevents that effective co-operation between the Government and the men who utilize the resources of the reserves, without which the interests of both must suffer. The scientific bureaus generally should be put under the Department of Agriculture. The President should have by law the power of transferring lands for use as forest reserves to the Department of Agriculture. He already has such power in the case of lands needed by the Departments of War and the Navy.

The wise administration of the forest reserves will be not less helpful to the interests which depend on water than to those which depend on wood and grass.

*The State of the Union Messages of the Presidents, Vol. 2, Fred L. Israel, ed. (New York: Chelsea House, 1967), 2028–33.

The water supply itself depends upon the forest. In the arid region it is water, not land, which measures production. The western half of the United States would sustain a population greater than that of our whole country to-day if the waters that now run to waste were saved and used for irrigation. The forest and water problems are perhaps the most vital internal questions of the United States.

Certain of the forest reserves should also be made preserves for the wild forest creatures. All of the reserves should be better protected from fires. Many of them need special protection because of the great injury done by live stock, above all by sheep. The increase in deer, elk, and other animals in the Yellowstone Park shows what may be expected when other mountain forests are properly protected by law and properly guarded. Some of these areas have been so denuded of surface vegetation by overgrazing that the ground breeding birds, including grouse and quail, and many mammals, including deer, have been exterminated or driven away. At the same time the water-storing capacity of the surface has been decreased or destroyed, thus promoting floods in times of rain and diminishing the flow of streams between rains.

In cases where natural conditions have been restored for a few years, vegetation has again carpeted the ground, birds and deer are coming back, and hundreds of persons, especially from the immediate neighborhood, come each summer to enjoy the privilege of camping. Some at least of the forest reserves should afford perpetual protection to the native fauna and flora, safe havens of refuge to our rapidly diminishing wild animals of the larger kinds, and free camping grounds for the ever-increasing numbers of men and women who have learned to find rest, health, and recreation in the splendid forests and flower-clad meadows of our mountains. The forest reserves should be set apart forever for the use and benefit of our people as a whole and not sacrificed to the short-sighted greed of a few.

The forests are natural reservoirs. By restraining the streams in flood and replenishing them in drought they make possible the use of waters otherwise wasted. They prevent the soil from washing, and so protect the storage reservoirs from filling up with silt. Forest conservation is therefore an essential condition of water conservation.

The forests alone cannot, however, fully regulate and conserve the waters of the arid region. Great storage works are necessary to equalize the flow of streams and to save the flood waters. Their construction has been conclusively shown to be an undertaking too vast for private effort. Nor can it be best accomplished by the individual States acting alone. Far-reaching interstate problems are involved; and the resources of single States would often be inadequate. It is properly a national function, at least in some of its features. It is as right for the National Government to make the streams and rivers of the arid region useful by engineering works for water storage as to make useful the rivers and harbors of the humid region by engineering works of another kind. The storing of the floods in reservoirs at the headwaters of our rivers is but an enlargement of our present policy of river control, under which levees are built on the lower reaches of the same streams.

The Government should construct and maintain these reservoirs as it does other public works. Where their purpose is to regulate the flow of streams, the water should be turned freely into the channels in the dry season to take the same course under the same laws as the natural flow.

The reclamation of the unsettled arid public lands presents a different problem. Here it is not enough to regulate the flow of streams. The object of the Government is to dispose of the land to settlers who will build homes upon it. To accomplish this object water must be brought within their reach.

The pioneer settlers on the arid public domain chose their homes along streams from which they could themselves divert the water to reclaim their holdings. Such opportunities are practically gone. There remain, however, vast areas of public land which can be made available for homestead settlement, but only by reservoirs and main-line canals impracticable for private enterprise. These irrigation works should be built by the National Government. The lands reclaimed by them should be reserved by the Government for actual settlers, and the cost of construction should so far as possible be repaid by the land reclaimed. The distribution of the water, the division of the streams among irrigators, should be left to the settlers themselves in conformity with State laws and without interference with those laws or with vested rights. The policy of the National Government should be to aid irrigation in the several States and Territories in such manner as will enable the people in the local communities to help themselves, and as will stimulate needed reforms in the State laws and regulations governing irrigation.

The reclamation and settlement of the arid lands will enrich every portion of our country, just as the settlement of the Ohio and Mississippi valleys brought prosperity to the Atlantic States. The increased demand for manufactured articles will stimulate industrial production, while wider home markets and the trade of Asia will consume the larger food supplies and effectually prevent Western competition with Eastern agriculture. Indeed, the products of irrigation will be consumed chiefly in upbuilding local centers of mining and other industries, which would otherwise not come into existence at all. Our people as a whole will profit, for successful home-making is but another name for the upbuilding of the nation.

The necessary foundation has already been laid for the inauguration of the policy just described. It would be unwise to begin by doing too much, for a great deal will doubtless be learned, both as to what can and what cannot be safely attempted, by the early efforts, which must of necessity be partly experimental in character. At the very beginning the Government should make clear, beyond shadow of doubt, its intention to pursue this policy on lines of the broadest public interest. No reservoir or canal should ever be built to satisfy selfish personal or local interests; but only in accordance with the advice of trained experts, after long investigation has shown the locality where all the conditions combine to make the work most needed and fraught with the greatest usefulness to the community as a whole. There should be no extravagance, and the believers in the need of irrigation will most benefit their cause by seeing to it that it is free from the least taint of excessive or reckless expenditure of the public moneys.

Whatever the nation does for the extension of irrigation should harmonize with, and tend to improve, the condition of those now living on irrigated land. We are not at the starting point of this development. Over two hundred millions of private capital has already been expended in the construction of irrigation works, and many million acres of arid land reclaimed. A high degree of enterprise and ability has been shown in the work itself; but as much cannot be said in reference to the laws relating thereto. The security and value of the homes created depend largely on the stability of titles to water; but the majority of these rest on the uncertain foundation of court decisions rendered in ordinary suits at law. With a few creditable exceptions, the arid States have failed to provide for the certain and just division of streams in times of scarcity. Lax and uncertain laws have made it possible to establish rights to water in excess of actual uses or necessities, and many streams have already passed into private ownership, or a control equivalent to ownership.

Whoever controls a stream practically controls the land it renders productive, and the doctrine of private ownership of water apart from land cannot prevail without causing enduring wrong. The recognition of such ownership, which has been permitted to grow up in the arid regions, should give way to a more enlightened and larger recognition of the rights of the public in the control and disposal of the public water supplies. Laws founded upon conditions obtaining in humid regions, where water is too abundant to justify hoarding it, have no proper application in a dry country.

In the arid States the only right to water which should be recognized is that of use. In irrigation this right should attach to the land reclaimed and be inseparable therefrom. Granting perpetual water rights to others than users, without compensation to the public, is open to all the objections which apply to giving away perpetual franchises to the public utilities of cities. A few of the Western States have already recognized this, and have incorporated in their constitutions the doctrine of perpetual State ownership of water.

The benefits which have followed the unaided development of the past justify the nation's aid and co-operation in the more difficult and important work yet to be accomplished. Laws so vitally affecting homes as those which control the water supply will only be effective when they have the sanction of the irrigators; reforms can only be final and satisfactory when they come through the enlight-

[13]

enment of the people most concerned. The larger development which national aid insures should, however, awaken in every arid State the determination to make its irrigation system equal in justice and effectiveness that of any country in the civilized world. Nothing could be more unwise than for isolated communities to continue to learn everything experimentally, instead of profiting by what is already known elsewhere. We are dealing with a new and momentous question, in the pregnant years while institutions are forming, and what we do will affect not only the present but future generations.

Our aim should be not simply to reclaim the largest area of land and provide homes for the largest number of people, but to create for this new industry the best possible social and industrial conditions; and this requires that we not only understand the existing situation, but avail ourselves of the best experience of the time in the solution of its problems. A careful study should be made, both by the Nation and the States, of the irrigation laws and conditions here and abroad. Ultimately it will probably be necessary for the Nation to co-operate with the several arid States in proportion as these States by their legislation and administration show themselves fit to receive it.

AN ACT TO TRANSFER FOREST RESERVES TO THE DEPARTMENT OF AGRICULTURE*
February 1, 1905

Gifford Pinchot's long effort to secure the transfer of the forest reserves from the Interior Department to the Department of Agriculture was achieved by this law. This brought the trained foresters who were in Agriculture together with the 60 forest reserves aggregating some 56 million acres. The present Forest Service really dates from the Agricultural Appropriation Bill of two months later. Two years later the name "forest reserves" was changed to "national forests."

An Act providing for the transfer of forest reserves from the Department of the Interior to the Department of Agriculture.

Be it enacted by the Senate and House of Representatives of the United States of America in Congress assembled, That the Secretary of the Department of Agriculture shall, from and after the passage of this Act, execute or cause to be executed all laws affecting public lands heretofore or hereafter reserved under the provisions of section twenty-four of the Act entitled "An Act to repeal the timber-culture laws, and for other purposes," approved March third, eighteen hundred and ninety-one, and Acts supplemental to and amendatory thereof, after such lands have been so reserved, excepting such laws as affect the surveying, prospecting, locating, appropriating, entering, relinquishing, reconveying, certifying, or patenting of any of such lands.

SEC. 2. That pulp wood or wood pulp manufactured from timber in the district of Alaska may be exported therefrom.

SEC. 3. That forest supervisors and rangers shall be selected, when practicable, from qualified citizens of the States or Territories in which the said reserves, respectively, are situated.

SEC. 4. That rights of way for the construction and maintenance of dams, reservoirs, water plants, ditches, flumes, pipes, tunnels, and canals, within and across the forest reserves of the United States, are hereby granted to citizens and corporations of the United States for municipal or mining purposes, and for the purposes of the milling and reduction of ores, during the period of their beneficial use, under such rules and regulations as may be prescribed by the Secretary of the Interior, and subject to the laws of the State or Territory in which said reserves are respectively situated.

SEC. 5. That all money received from the sales of any products or the use of any land or resources of said forest reserves shall be covered into the Treasury

*33 *Statutes at Large,* 628.

of the United States and for a period of five years from the passage of this Act shall constitute a special fund available, until expended, as the Secretary of Agriculture may direct, for the protection, administration, improvement, and extension of Federal forest reserves.

Approved, February 1, 1905.

LETTER FROM PRESIDENT ROOSEVELT ON THE LOS ANGELES
WATER SUPPLY BILL*
June 25, 1906

This letter–memorandum to Ethan Allen Hitchock shows how the President himself was brought into decisions about western water supply.

Washington, June 25, 1906

My dear Mr. Secretary:

As I think it best that there should be a record of our attitude in the Los Angeles water supply bill, I am dictating this letter to you in your presence, and that of Senator Flint on behalf of the California Delegation, of Director Walcott of the Geological Survey, and of Chief Forester Pinchot. The question is whether the city of Los Angeles should be prohibited from using the water it will obtain under this bill for irrigation purposes. Your feeling is that it should be so prohibited because the passage of the bill without the prohibition might establish a monopoly in the municipality of Los Angeles as regards irrigation, by permitting the municipality to use the surplus of the water thus acquired, beyond the amount actually used for drinking purposes, for some irrigation scheme.

Senator Flint states that under the proposed law Los Angeles will be seeking to provide its water supply for the next half century, which will mean that at first there will be a large surplus, and that in order to keep their rights they will have to from the beginning draw the full amount of water (otherwise the water will be diverted to other uses and could not be obtained by the city); and while if the city did not need the water it would be proper that the other users should have it, yet it is a hundred or a thousandfold more important to the State and more valuable to the people as a whole if used by the city than if used by the people of Owens Valley; Senator Flint further says that the same water that is used for drinking and washing is also used on innumerable little plots of land in and around Los Angeles for gardening and similar purposes, and that to prohibit this would so nearly destroy the value of the bill as to make it an open question whether the city either could or would go on with the project; it being open to doubt whether the words "domestic use" would cover irrigation of this kind.

Mr. Walcott and Mr. Pinchot state that there is no objection to permitting Los Angeles to use the water for irrigating purposes so far as there is a surplusage after the city's drinking, washing, fire and other needs have been met.

*The Letters of Theodore Roosevelt, Vol. 5, Elting E. Morison, ed. (Cambridge: Harvard University Press, 1952), 315–16.

They feel that no monopoly in an offensive sense is created by municipal owner-ship of the water as obtained under this bill, and that as a matter of fact to attempt to deprive the city of Los Angeles of the right to use the water for irrigation would mean that for many years no use whatever could be made by it of the surplus water beyond that required for drinking and similar purposes.

I am informed by Senator Flint that the law of California provides that if a municipality sells water to people outside the municipality, it must be at the same rate that it sells it to those within the municipality.

I am also impressed by the fact that the chief opposition to this bill, aside from the opposition of the few settlers in Owens Valley (whose interest is genuine, but whose interest must unfortunately be disregarded in view of the infinitely greater interest to be served by putting the water in Los Angeles) comes from certain private power companies whose object evidently is for their own pecu-niary interest to prevent the municipality from furnishing its own water. The people at the head of these power companies are doubtless respectable citizens, and if there is no law they have the right to seek their own pecuniary advantage in securing the control of this necessary of life for the city. Nevertheless, their opposition seems to me to afford one of the strongest arguments for passing the law, inasmuch as it ought not to be within the power of private individuals to control such a necessary of life as against the municipality itself.

Under the circumstances I decide, in accordance with the recommendations of the Director of the Geological Survey and the Chief of the Forestry Serivce, that the bill be approved, with the prohibition against the use of the water by the municipality for irrigation struck out. I request, however, that there be put in the bill a prohibition against the city of Los Angeles ever selling or letting to any corporation or individual except a minicipality, the right for that corporation or that individual itself to sell or sublet the water given to it or him by the city for irrigation purposes.

Sincerely yours

[*President Roosevelt*]

P.S. Having read the above aloud I now find that everybody agrees to it—you, Mr. Secretary, as well as Senator Flint, Director Walcott, and Mr. Pinchot; and therefore I [finish] with a far more satisfied heart than when I started to dic-tate this letter.

GIFFORD PINCHOT ON NAMING THE MOVEMENT*
1907

The conservation movement was a culmination of many forces in American political, economic, and cultural life. During the administration of Theodore Roosevelt it first became a viable philosophy, expressing the concept of the close relationship between all natural resource development and preservation.

Gifford Pinchot, Roosevelt's "conservation minister" and the great activist of the movement, explains in his autobiography, Breaking New Ground, *how the movement was given a name.*

It was my great good luck that I had more to do with the work of more bureaus than any other man in Washington. This was partly because the Forest Service was dealing not only with trees but with public lands, mining, agriculture, irrigation, stream flow, soil erosion, fish, game, animal industry, and a host of other matters with which other bureaus also were concerned. The main reason, however, was that much of T.R.'s business with the natural resources bureaus was conducted through me.

It was therefore the most natural thing in the world that the relations of forests, waters, lands, and minerals, each to each, should be brought strongly to my mind. But for a long time my mind stopped there. Then at last I woke up. And this is how it happened:

In the gathering gloom of an expiring day, in the moody month of February, some forty years ago, a solitary horseman might have been observed pursuing his silent way above a precipitous gorge in the vicinity of the capital city of America. Or so an early Victorian three-volume novelist might have expressed it.

In plain words, a man by the name of Pinchot was riding a horse by the name of Jim on the Ridge Road in Rock Creek Park near Washington. And while he rode, he thought. He was a forester, and he was taking his problems with him, on that winter's day of 1907, when he meant to leave them behind.

The forest and its relation to streams and inland navigation, to water power and flood control; to the soil and its erosion; to coal and oil and other minerals; to fish and game; and many another possible use or waste of natural resources— these questions would not let him be. What had all these to do with Forestry? And what had Forestry to do with them?

Here were not isolated and separate problems. My work had brought me into touch with all of them. But what was the basic link between them?

Suddenly the idea flashed through my head that there was a unity in this

*Gifford Pinchot, *Breaking New Ground* (New York: Harcourt, Brace & Co., Inc., 1947), 322–26.

[19]

complication—that the relation of one resource to another was not the end of the story. Here were no longer a lot of different, independent, and often antagonistic questions, each on its own separate little island, as we had been in the habit of thinking. In place of them, here was one single question with many parts. Seen in this new light, all these separate questions fitted into and made up the one great central problem of the use of the earth for the good of man.

To me it was a good deal like coming out of a dark tunnel. I had been seeing one spot of light ahead. Here, all of a sudden, was a whole landscape. Or it was like lifting the curtain on a great new stage.

There was too much of it for me to take it all in at once. As always, my mind worked slowly. From the first I thought I had stumbled on something really worth while, but that day in Rock Creek Park I was far from grasping the full reach and swing of the new idea.

It took time for me to appreciate that here were the makings of a new policy, not merely nationwide but world-wide in its scope—fundamentally important because it involved not only the welfare but the very existence of men on the earth. I did see, however, that something ought to be done about it.

But, you may say, hadn't plenty of people before that day seen the value of Forestry, of irrigation, of developing our streams, and much besides? Hadn't plenty pointed out the threat of erosion, the shame and pity of the destruction of wild life, and the reasons against man's vandalism of many kinds? Hadn't plenty pointed out that forests, for example, affect floods, and many other cases in which one natural resource reacts upon another?

Certainly they had. But so far as I knew then or have since been able to find out, it had occurred to nobody, in this country or abroad, that here was one question instead of many, one gigantic single problem that must be solved if the generations, as they came and went, were to live civilized, happy, useful lives in the lands which the Lord their God had given them.

But, you might go on, after the new idea was born, wasn't the situation just as it had been before? Shouldn't each Government bureau go on dealing with its same old subject in its same old way?

Not by a jugful, as they say in the backwoods.

The ancient classic simile of the bundle of twigs, which the Fascists have perverted and made known throughout the world, might point the moral and adorn the tale I am trying to tell. In union there is strength. But perhaps we can find a better illustration in the birth of our own Government.

The American colonies, like the Government bureaus which have to do with the various natural resources, were founded at different times, for different reasons, and by different kinds of people. Each colony, from Georgia to New Hampshire, dealt with nature in a somewhat different form. Each had to face a problem unlike the problems of all the others, and each was itself unlike all the other colonies.

Before the Declaration of Independence they were so many weak and separate twigs. Could we have become what we are today if the thirteen colonies had remained independent, self-sufficient little nationlets, quarreling among themselves over rights, boundaries, jurisdictions, instead of merging into a single nation with a single federal purpose?

The mere fact of union produced something different and unknown before. Here were new purpose and new power, and a future infinitely greater than anything thirteen separated colonies could ever have lived to see. Union did not wipe out the thirteen separate characters of the thirteen separate states, but it did bind them together into the strength of the new nation.

E Pluribus Unum is the fundamental fact in our political affairs. *E Pluribus Unum* is and always must be the basis in dealing with the natural resources. Many problems fuse into one great policy, just as many states fuse into one great Union. When the use of all the natural resources for the general good is seen to be a common policy with a common purpose, the chance for the wise use of each of them becomes infinitely greater than it had ever been before.

The Conservation of natural resources is the key to the future. It is the key to the safety and prosperity of the American people, and all the people of the world, for all time to come. The very existence of our Nation, and of all the rest, depends on conserving the resources which are the foundations of its life. That is why Conservation is the greatest material question of all.

Moreover, Conservation is a foundation of permanent peace among the nations, and the most important foundation of all. But more of that in another place.

It is not easy for us moderns to realize our dependence on the earth. As civilization progresses, as cities grow, as the mechanical aids to human life increase, we are more and more removed from the raw materials of human existence, and we forget more easily that natural resources must be about us from our infancy or we cannot live at all.

What do you eat, morning, noon, and night? Natural resources, transformed and processed for your use. What do you wear, day in and day out—your coat, your hat, your shoes, your watch, the penny in your pocket, the filling in your tooth? Natural resources changed and adapted to your necessity.

What do you work with, no matter what your work may be? What are the desk you sit at, the book you read, the shovel you dig with, the machine you operate, the car you drive, the light you see by when the sunlight fails? Natural resources in one form or another.

What do you live in and work in, but in natural resources made into dwellings and shops and offices? Wood, iron, rock, clay, sand, in a thousand different shapes, but always natural resources. What are the living you earn, the medicine you take, the movie you watch, but things derived from nature?

What are railroads and good roads, ocean liners and birch canoes, cities and summer camps, but natural resources in other shapes?

What does agriculture produce? Natural resources. What does industry manufacture? What does commerce deal in? What is science concerned with? Natural resources.

What is your own body but natural resources constantly renewed—your body, which would cease to be yours to command if the natural resources which keep it in health were cut off for so short a time as 1 or 2 per cent of a single year?

There are just two things on this material earth—people and natural resources.

From all of which I hope you have gathered, if you did not realize it before, that a constant and sufficient supply of natural resources is the basic human problem.

But to return to the newborn idea. The first man I carried it to was Overton Price. Within a few days I told him the story as we rode our horses together on the Virginia side of the Potomac, and asked what he thought of it. He saw it as I did. I was glad of that, for my reliance on his judgment was very great.

After Overton, I discussed my brain child not only with my Father and Mother, whose interest in my work never flagged, but with McGee, Newell, Gannett, Shipp, Beveridge, and others. It was McGee who grasped it best. He sensed its full implication even more quickly than I had done, and saw its future more clearly.

McGee became the scientific brains of the new movement. With his wide general knowledge and highly original mind we developed, as I never could have done alone, the breadth and depth of meaning which lay in the new idea. McGee had constructive imagination.

It was McGee, for example, who defined the new policy as the use of the natural resources for the greatest good of the greatest number for the longest time. It was McGee who made me see, at long last and after much argument, that monopoly of natural resources was only less dangerous to the public welfare than their actual destruction.

Very soon after my own mind was clear enough to state my proposition with confidence, I took it to T.R. And T.R., as I expected, understood, accepted, and adopted it without the smallest hesitation. It was directly in line with everything he had been thinking and doing. It became the heart of his Administration.

Launching the Conservation movement was the most significant achievement of the T.R. Administration, as he himself believed. It seems altogether probable that it will also be the achievement for which he will be longest and most gratefully remembered.

Having just been born, the new arrival was still without a name. There had to be a name to call it by before we could even attempt to make it known, much less give it a permanent place in the public mind. What should we call it?

Both Overton and I knew that large organized areas of Government forest lands in British India were named Conservancies, and the foresters in charge of them Conservators. After many other suggestions and long discussions, either Price or I (I'm not sure which and it doesn't matter) proposed that we apply a new meaning to a word already in the dictionary, and christen the new policy Conservation.

During one of our rides I put the name up to T.R., and he approved it instantly. So the child was named, and that bridge was behind us.

Today, when it would be hard to find an intelligent man in the United States who hasn't at least some conception of what Conservation means, it seems incredible that the very word, in the sense in which we use it now, was unknown less than forty years ago.

FINAL MESSAGE FROM PRESIDENT ROOSEVELT
ON CONSERVATION*
January 22, 1909

The outgoing President used the transmittal of the report of the National Conservation Commission to give the Congress his final recommendations on conservation issues. The message is interesting for the broad expressions of Roosevelt's political philosophy as related to the conservation issue.

SPECIAL MESSAGE OF THE PRESIDENT TRANSMITTING THE REPORT OF THE NATIONAL CONSERVATION COMMISSION

To the Senate and House of Representatives:

I transmit herewith a report of the National Conservation Commission, together with the accompanying papers. This report, which is the outgrowth of the conference of governors last May, was unanimously approved by the recent joint conference held in this city between the National Conservation Commission and governors of States, state conservation commissions, and conservation committees of great organizations of citizens. It is therefore in a peculiar sense representative of the whole nation and all its parts.

With the statements and conclusions of this report I heartily concur, and I commend it to the thoughtful consideration both of the Congress and of our people generally. It is one of the most fundamentally important documents ever laid before the American people. It contains the first inventory of its natural resources ever made by any nation. In condensed form it presents a statement of our available capital in material resources, which are the means of progress, and calls attention to the essential conditions upon which the perpetuity, safety, and welfare of this nation now rest and must always continue to rest. It deserves, and should have, the widest possible distribution among the people.

The facts set forth in this report constitute an imperative call to action. The situation they disclose demands that we, neglecting for a time, if need be, smaller and less vital questions, shall concentrate an effective part of our attention upon the great material foundations of national existence, progress and prosperity.

This first inventory of natural resources prepared by the National Conservation Commission is undoubtedly but the beginning of a series which will be indispensable for dealing intelligently with what we have. It supplies as close

*Sen. Doc. 676, 60th Cong., 2nd sess., 1–9.

an approximation to the actual facts as it was possible to prepare with the knowledge and time available. The progress of our knowledge of this country will continually lead to more accurate information and better use of the sources of national strength. But we can not defer action until complete accuracy in the estimates can be reached, because before that time many of our resources will be practically gone. It is not necessary that this inventory should be exact in every minute detail. It is essential that it should correctly describe the general situation; and that the present inventory does. As it stands it is an irrefutable proof that the conservation of our resources is the fundamental question before this nation, and that our first and greatest task is to set our house in order and begin to live within our means.

The first of all considerations is the permanent welfare of our people; and true moral welfare, the highest form of welfare, can not permanently exist save on a firm and lasting foundation of material well-being. In this respect our situation is far from satisfactory. After every possible allowance has been made, and when every hopeful indication has been given its full weight, the facts still give reason for grave concern. It would be unworthy of our history and our intelligence, and disastrous to our future, to shut our eyes to these facts or attempt to laugh them out of court. The people should and will rightly demand that the great fundamental questions shall be given attention by their representatives. I do not advise hasty or ill-considered action on disputed points, but I do urge, where the facts are known, where the public interest is clear, that neither indifference and inertia, nor adverse private interests, shall be allowed to stand in the way of the public good.

The great basic facts are already well known. We know that our population is now adding about one-fifth to its numbers in ten years, and that by the middle of the present century perhaps one hundred and fifty million Americans, and by its end very many millions more, must be fed and clothed from the products of our soil. With the steady growth in population and the still more rapid increase in consumption, our people will hereafter make greater and not less demands per capita upon all the natural resources for their livelihood, comfort, and convenience. It is high time to realize that our responsibility to the coming millions is like that of parents to their children, and that in wasting our resources we are wronging our descendants.

We know now that our rivers can and should be made to serve our people effectively in transportation, but that the vast expenditures for our waterways have not resulted in maintaining, much less in promoting, inland navigation. Therefore, let us take immediate steps to ascertain the reasons and to prepare and adopt a comprehensive plan for inland-waterway navigation that will result in giving the people the benefits for which they have paid but which they have not yet received. We know now that our forests are fast disappearing, that less than one-fifth of them are being conserved, and that no good purpose can be met by failing to provide the relatively small sums needed for the protection, use, and improvement of all forest still owned by the Government, and to enact laws to check the wasteful destruction of the forests in private hands. There are differences of opinion as to many public questions; but the American people stand nearly as a unit for waterway development and for forest protection.

We know now that our mineral resources once exhausted are gone forever, and that the needless waste of them costs us hundreds of human lives and nearly $300,000,000 a year. Therefore, let us undertake without delay the investigations necessary before our people will be in position, through state action or otherwise, to put an end to this huge loss and waste, and conserve both our mineral resources and the lives of the men who take them from the earth.

I desire to make grateful acknowledgment to the men, both in and out of the government service, who have prepared the first inventory of our natural resources. They have made it possible for this nation to take a great step forward. Their work is helping us to see that the greatest questions before us are not partisan questions, but questions upon which men of all parties and all shades of opinion may be united for the common good. Among such questions on the material side, the conservation of natural resources stands first. It is the bottom round of the ladder on our upward progress toward a condition in which the nation as a whole, and its citizens as individuals, will set national efficiency and the public welfare before personal profit.

The policy of conservation is perhaps the most typical example of the general policies which this Government has made peculiarly its own during the opening years of the present century. The function of our Government is to insure to all its citizens, now and hereafter, their rights to life, liberty, and the pursuit of happiness. If we of this generation destroy the resources from which our children would otherwise derive their livelihood, we reduce the capacity of our land to support a population, and so either degrade the standard of living or deprive the coming generations of their right to life on this continent. If we allow great industrial organizations to exercise unregulated control of the means of production and the necessaries of life, we deprive the Americans of to-day and of the future of industrial liberty, a right no less precious and vital than political freedom. Industrial liberty was a fruit of political liberty, and in turn has become one of its chief supports, and exactly as we stand for political democracy so we must stand for industrial democracy.

The rights to life and liberty are fundamental, and like other fundamental necessities, when once acquired, they are little dwelt upon. The right to the pursuit of happiness is the right whose presence or absence is most likely to be felt in daily life. In whatever it has accomplished, or failed to accomplish, the administration which is just drawing to a close has at least seen clearly the fundamental need of freedom of opportunity for every citizen. We have realized that the right of every man to live his own life, provide for his family, and endeavor, according to his abilities, to secure for himself and for them a fair share of the good things of existence, should be subject to one limitation and to no other. The freedom of the individual should be limited only by the present and future rights, interests, and needs of the other individuals who make up the community. We should do all in our power to develop and protect individual liberty, individual initiative, but subject always to the need of preserving and promoting the general good. When necessary, the private right must yield, under due process of law and with proper compensation to the welfare of the commonwealth. The man who serves the community greatly should be greatly rewarded by the community; as there is great inequality of service, so there must be great inequality of reward; but no man and no set of men should be allowed to play the game of competition with loaded dice.

All this is simply good common sense. The underlying principle of conservation has been described as the application of common sense to common problems for the common good. If the description is correct, then conservation is the great fundamental basis for national efficiency. In this stage of the world's history, to be fearless, to be just, and to be efficient are the three great requirements of national life. National efficiency is the result of natural resources well handled, of freedom of opportunity for every man, and of the inherent capacity, trained ability, knowledge, and will, collectively and individually, to use that opportunity.

This administration has achieved some things; it has sought, but has not been able, to achieve others; it has doubtless made mistakes; but all it has done or attempted has been in the single, consistent effort to secure and enlarge the rights and opportunities of the men and women of the United States. We are trying to conserve what is good in our social system, and we are striving toward this end when we endeavor to do away with what is bad. Success may be made too hard for some if it is made too easy for others. The rewards of common industry and thrift may be too small if the rewards for other, and on the whole less valuable, qualities, are made too large, and especially if the rewards for qualities which are really, from the public standpoint, undesirable are permitted to become too large. Our aim is so far as possible to provide such conditions that there shall be equality of opportunity where there is equality of energy, fidelity, and intelligence; when there is a reasonable equality of opportunity the distribution of rewards will take care of itself.

The unchecked existence of monopoly is incompatible with equality of opportunity. The reason for the exercise of government control over great monopolies is to equalize opportunity. We are fighting against privilege. It was made unlawful for corporations to contribute money for election expenses in order to abridge the power of special privilege at the polls. Railroad-rate control is an attempt to secure an equality of opportunity for all men affected by rail transportation; and that means all of us. The great anthracite coal strike was settled, and the pressing danger of a coal famine averted, because we recognized that the control of a public necessity involves a duty to the people, and that public intervention in the affairs of a public-service corporation is neither to be resented as usurpation nor permitted as a privilege by the corporations, but on the contrary to be accepted as a duty and exercised as a right by the Government in the interest of all the people. The efficiency of the army and the navy has been increased so that our people may follow in peace the great work of making this country a better place for Americans to live in, and our navy was sent round the world for the same ultimate purpose. All the acts taken by the Government during the last seven years, and all the policies now being pursued by the Government, fit in as parts of a consistent whole.

Our public-land policy has for its aim the use of the public land so that it will promote local development by the settlement of home makers; the policy we champion is to serve all the people legitimately and openly, instead of permitting the lands to be converted, illegitimately and under cover, to the private benefit of a few. Our forest policy was established so that we might use the public forests for the permanent public good, instead of merely for temporary private gain. The reclamation act, under which the desert parts of the public domain are converted to higher uses for the general benefit, was passed so that more Americans might have homes on the land.

These policies were enacted into law and have justified their enactment. Others have failed, so far, to reach the point of action. Among such is the attempt to secure public control of the open range, and thus to convert its benefits to the use of the small man, who is the home maker, instead of allowing it to be controlled by a few great cattle and sheep owners.

The enactment of a pure-food law was a recognition of the fact that the public welfare outweighs the right to private gain, and that no man may poison the people for his private profit. The employers' liability bill recognized the controlling fact that while the employer usually has at stake no more than his profit, the stake of the employee is a living for himself and his family.

We are building the Panama Canal; and this means that we are engaged in the giant engineering feat of all time. We are striving to add in all ways to the habitability and beauty of our country. We are striving to hold in the public hands the remaining supply of unappropriated coal, for the protection and benefit of all the people. We have taken the first steps toward the conservation of our natural resources, and the betterment of country life, and the improvement of our waterways. We stand for the right of every child to a childhood free from grinding toil, and to an education; for the civic responsibility and decency of every citizen; for prudent foresight in public matters, and for fair play in every relation of our national and economic life. In international matters we apply a system of diplomacy which puts the obligations of international morality on a level with those that govern the actions of an honest gentleman in dealing with his fellow-men. Within our own border we stand for truth and honesty in public and in private life, and war sternly against wrongdoers of every grade. All these efforts are integral parts of the same attempt, the attempt to enthrone justice and righteousness, to secure freedom of opportunity to all of our citizens, now and hereafter, and to set the ultimate interest of all of us above the temporary interest of any individual, class or group.

The nation, its government, and its resources exist, first of all, for the American citizen, whatever his creed, race, or birthplace, whether he be rich or poor, educated or ignorant, provided only that he is a good citizen, recognizing his obligations to the nation for the rights and opportunities which he owes to the nation.

The obligations, and not the rights, of citizenship increase in proportion to the increase of a man's wealth or power. The time is coming when a man will be judged, not by what he has succeeded in getting for himself from the common store, but by how well he has done his duty as a citizen, and by what the ordinary citizen has gained in freedom of opportunity because of his service for the common good. The highest value we know is that of the individual citizen, and the highest justice is to give him fair play in the effort to realize the best there is in him.

The tasks this nation has to do are great tasks. They can only be done at all by our citizens acting together, and they can be done best of all by the direct and simple application of homely common sense. The application of common sense to common problems for the common good, under the guidance of the principles upon which this republic was based, and by virtue of which it exists, spells perpetuity for the nation, civil and industrial liberty for its citizens, and freedom of opportunity in the pursuit of happiness for the plain American, for whom this nation was founded, by whom it was preserved, and through whom alone it can be perpetuated. Upon this platform—larger than party differences, higher than class prejudice, broader than any question of profit and loss—there is room for every American who realizes that the common good stands first.

The National Conservation Commission wisely confined its report to the statement of facts and principles, leaving the Executive to recommend the specific steps to which these facts and principles inevitably lead. Accordingly, I call your attention to some of the larger features of the situation disclosed by the report, and to the action thereby clearly demanded for the general good.

WATERS

The report says:

Within recent months it has been recognized and demanded by the people, through many thousand delegates from all States assembled in convention in different sections of the country, that the waterways should and must be improved promptly and effectively as a means of maintaining national prosperity.

The first requisite for waterway improvement is the control of the waters in such manner as to reduce floods and regulate the regimen of the navigable rivers. The second requisite is development of terminals and connections in such manner as to regulate commerce.

Accordingly, I urge that the broad plan for the development of our waterways recommended by the Inland Waterways Commission be put in effect without delay. It provides for a comprehensive system of waterway improvement extending to all the uses of the waters and benefits to be derived from their control, including navigation, the development of power, the extension of irrigation, the drainage of swamp and overflow lands, the prevention of soil wash, and the purification of streams for water supply. It proposes to carry out the work by coordinating agencies in the federal departments through the medium of an administrative commission or board, acting in cooperation with the States and other organizations and individual citizens.

The work of waterway development should be undertaken without delay. Meritorious projects in known conformity with the general outlines of any comprehensive plan should proceed at once. The cost of the whole work should be met by direct appropriation if possible, but if necessary by the issue of bonds in small denominations.

It is especially important that the development of water power should be guarded with the utmost care both by the National Government and by the States in order to protect the people against the upgrowth of monopoly and to insure to them a fair share in the benefits which will follow the development of this great asset which belongs to the people and should be controlled by them.

FORESTS

I urge that provision be made for both protection and more rapid development of the national forests. Otherwise, either the increasing use of these forests by the people must be checked or their protection against fire must be dangerously weakened. If we compare the actual fire damage on similar areas on private and national forest lands during the past year, the government fire patrol saved commercial timber worth as much as the total cost of caring for all national forests at the present rate for about ten years.

I especially commend to the Congress the facts presented by the commission as to the relation between forests and stream flow in its bearing upon the importance of the forest lands in national ownership. Without an understanding of this intimate relation the conservation of both these natural resources must largely fail.

The time has fully arrived for recognizing in the law the responsibility to the community, the State, and the nation which rests upon the private owners of private lands. The ownership of forest land is a public trust. The man who would so handle his forest as to cause erosion and to injure stream flow must be not only educated, but he must be controlled.

The report of the National Conservation Commission says:

> Forests in private ownership can not be conserved unless they are protected from fire. We need good fire laws, well enforced. Fire control is impossible without an adequate force of men whose sole duty is fire patrol during the dangerous season.

I hold as first among the tasks before the States and the nation in their respective shares in forest conservation the organization of efficient fire patrols and the enactment of good fire laws on the part of the States.

The report says further:

> Present tax laws prevent reforestation of cut-over land and the perpetuation of existing forests by use. An annual tax upon the land itself, exclusive of the timber, and a tax upon the timber when cut is well adapted to actual conditions of forest investment and is practicable and certain. It is far better that forest land should pay a moderate tax permanently than that it should pay an excessive revenue temporarily and then cease to yield at all.

Second only in importance to good fire laws well enforced is the enactment of tax laws which will permit the perpetuation of existing forests by use.

LANDS

With our increasing population the time is not far distant when the problem of supplying our people with food will become pressing. The possible additions to our arable area are not great, and it will become necessary to obtain much larger crops from the land, as is now done in more densely settled countries. To do this, we need better farm practice and better strains of wheat, corn, and other crop plants, with a reduction in losses from soil erosion and from insects, animals, and other enemies of agriculture. The United States Department of Agriculture is doing excellent work in these directions, and it should be liberally supported.

The remaining public lands should be classified and the arable lands disposed of to home makers. In their interest the timber and stone act and the commutation clause of the homestead act should be repealed, and the desert-land law should be modified in accordance with the recommendations of the Public Lands Commission.

The use of the public grazing lands should be regulated in such ways as to improve and conserve their value.

Rights to the surface of the public land should be separated from rights to forests upon it and to minerals beneath it, and these should be subject to separate disposal.

The coal, oil, gas, and phosphate rights still remaining with the Government should be withdrawn from entry and leased under conditions favorable for economic development.

MINERALS

The accompanying reports show that the consumption of nearly all of our mineral products is increasing more rapidly than our population. Our mineral waste is about one-sixth of our product, or nearly $1,000,000 for each working day in the year. The loss of structural materials through fire is about another million a day. The loss of life in the mines is appalling. The larger part of these losses of life and property can be avoided.

Our mineral resources are limited in quantity and can not be increased or reproduced. With the rapidly increasing rate of consumption the supply will be exhausted while yet the nation is in its infancy unless better methods are devised or substitutes are found. Further investigation is urgently needed in order to improve methods and to develop and apply substitutes.

It is of the utmost importance that a bureau of mines be established in accordance with the pending bill to reduce the loss of life in mines and the waste of mineral resources and to investigate the methods and substitutes for prolonging the duration of our mineral supplies. Both the need and the public demand for such a bureau are rapidly becoming more urgent. It should cooperate with the States in supplying data to serve as a basis for state mine regulations. The establishment of this bureau will mean merely the transfer from other bureaus of work which it is agreed should be transferred and slightly enlarged and reorganized for these purposes.

CONCLUSIONS

The joint conference already mentioned adopted two resolutions to which I call your special attention. The first was intended to promote cooperation between the States and the nation upon all of the great questions here discussed. It is as follows:

> Resolved, That a joint committee be appointed by the chairman, to consist of six members of state conservation commissions and three members of the National Conservation Commission, whose duty it shall be to prepare and present to the state and national commissions, and through them to the governors and the President, a plan for united action by all organizations concerned with the conservation of natural resources.
>
> (On motion of Governor Noel, of Mississippi, the chairman and secretary of the conference were added to and constituted a part of this committee.)

The second resolution of the joint conference to which I refer calls upon the Congress to provide the means for such cooperation. The principle of the community of interest among all our people in the great natural resources runs through the report of the National Conservation Commission and the proceedings of the joint conference. These resources, which form the common basis of our welfare, can be wisely developed, rightly used, and prudently conserved only by the common action of all the people, acting through their representatives in State and nation. Hence the fundamental necessity for cooperation. Without it we shall accomplish but little, and that little badly. The resolution follows:

> We also especially urge on the Congress of the United States the high desirability of maintaining a national commission on the conservation of the resources of the country, empowered to cooperate with state commissions to the end that every sovereign commonwealth and every section of the country may attain the high degree of prosperity and the sureness of perpetuity naturally arising in the abundant resources and the vigor, intelligence, and patriotism of our people.

In this recommendation I most heartily concur, and I urge that an appropriation of at least $50,000 be made to cover the expenses of the National Conservation Commission for necessary rent, assistance, and traveling expenses. This is a very small sum. I know of no other way in which the appropriation of so small a sum would result in so large a benefit to the whole nation.

Theodore Roosevelt

The White House
January 22, 1909

RECLAMATION

LETTER FROM PRESIDENT ROOSEVELT ENDORSING THE NEWLANDS BILL*
June 13, 1902

This letter from Roosevelt to Joe Cannon shows the precedent that Roosevelt set in pushing for passage of the Newlands bill. Cannon was the Republican Speaker of the House, but was not impressed by the program of the Republican President. He opposed the plan for the Reclamation Service because it would involve new government expenditures and because it was sponsored by a Democratic Member of the House. Despite Cannon's opposition, Roosevelt's espousal of the Newlands bill was sufficient to bring enough Republican support to secure its passage.

TO JOSEPH GURNEY CANNON

Personal   Washington, June 13, 1902

My dear Mr. Cannon:

I do not believe that I have ever before written to an individual legislator in favor of an individual bill, but I break through my rule to ask you as earnestly as I can not to oppose the Irrigation measure. Believe me this is something of which I have made a careful study, and great and real though my deference is for your knowledge of legislation, and for your attitude in stopping expense, I yet feel from my acquaintance with the far West that it would be a genuine and rankling injustice for the Republican party to kill this measure. I believe in it with all my heart from every standpoint. I am just about to sign the River and Harbor bill. It is a large bill, but I feel it is justified by the great commercial interests at stake. Now this is a measure for the material benefit of your State and mine and of the other states with harbors and navigable rivers. Surely it is but simple justice for us to give to the arid regions a measure of relief, the financial burden of which will be but trifling, while the benefit to the country involved is far greater than under the River and Harbor bill. I cannot too strongly express my feeling upon this matter.

Faithfully yours

*The Letters of Theodore Roosevelt, Vol. 3, Elting E. Morison, ed. (Cambridge: Harvard University Press, 1951), 272–73.

THE RECLAMATION ACT*
June 17, 1902

Representative Francis G. Newlands (Nevada) had sponsored for some time a bill to establish a federal irrigation program. The Newlands bill had been drafted with the help of F. H. Newell, who was to become the first chief of the Reclamation Service.

Roosevelt endorsed the Newlands bill after he succeeded to the Presidency, and the reclamation law which resulted is one of the major achievements of his administration.

An Act appropriating the receipts from the sale and disposal of public lands in certain States and Territories to the construction of irrigation works for the reclamation of arid lands.

Be it enacted by the Senate and House of Representatives of the United States of America in Congress assembled, That all moneys received from the sale and disposal of public lands in Arizona, California, Colorado, Idaho, Kansas, Montana, Nebraska, Nevada, New Mexico, North Dakota, Oklahoma, Oregon, South Dakota, Utah, Washington, and Wyoming, beginning with the fiscal year ending June thirtieth, nineteen hundred and one, including the surplus of fees and commissions in excess of allowances to registers and receivers, and excepting the five per centum of the proceeds of the sales of public lands in the above States set aside by law for educational and other purposes, shall be, and the same are hereby, reserved, set aside, and appropriated as a special fund in the Treasury to be known as the "reclamation fund," to be used in the examination and survey for and the construction and maintenance of irrigation works for the storage, diversion, and development of waters for the reclamation of arid and semiarid lands in the said States and Territories, and for the payment of all other expenditures provided for in this Act: *Provided,* That in case the receipts from the sale and disposal of public lands other than those realized from the sale and disposal of lands referred to in this section are insufficient to meet the requirements for the support of agricultural colleges in the several States and Territories, under the Act of August thirtieth, eighteen hundred and ninety, entitled "An Act to apply a portion of the proceeds of the public lands to the more complete endowment and support of the colleges for the benefit of agriculture and the mechanic arts, established under the provisions of an Act of Congress approved July second, eighteen hundred and sixty-two," the deficiency, if any, in the sum necessary for the support of the said colleges shall be provided for from any moneys in the Treasury not otherwise appropriated.

SEC. 2. That the Secretary of the Interior is hereby authorized and directed

*32 *Statutes at Large,* 388–90.

to make examinations and surveys for, and to locate and construct, as herein provided, irrigation works for the storage, diversion, and development of waters, including artesian wells, and to report to Congress at the beginning of each regular session as to the results of such examinations and surveys, giving estimates of cost of all contemplated works, the quantity and location of the lands which can be irrigated therefrom, and all facts relative to the practicability of each irrigation project; also the cost of works in process of construction as well as of those which have been completed.

SEC. 3. That the Secretary of the Interior shall, before giving the public notice provided for in section four of this Act, withdraw from public entry the lands required for any irrigation works contemplated under the provisions of this Act, and shall restore to public entry any of the lands so withdrawn when, in his judgment, such lands are not required for the purposes of this Act; and the Secretary of the Interior is hereby authorized, at or immediately prior to the time of beginning the surveys for any contemplated irrigation works, to withdraw from entry, except under the homestead laws, any public lands believed to be susceptible of irrigation from said works: *Provided,* That all lands entered and entries made under the homestead laws within areas so withdrawn during such withdrawal shall be subject to all the provisions, limitations, charges, terms, and conditions of this Act; that said surveys shall be prosecuted diligently to completion, and upon the completion thereof, and of the necessary maps, plans, and estimates of cost, the Secretary of the Interior shall determine whether or not said project is practicable and advisable, and if determined to be impracticable or unadvisable he shall thereupon restore said lands to entry; that public lands which it is proposed to irrigate by means of any contemplated works shall be subject to entry only under the provisions of the homestead laws in tracts of not less than forty nor more than one hundred and sixty acres, and shall be subject to the limitations, charges, terms, and conditions herein provided: *Provided,* That the commutation provisions of the homestead laws shall not apply to entries made under this Act.

SEC. 4. That upon the determination by the Secretary of the Interior that any irrigation project is practicable, he may cause to be let contracts for the construction of the same, in such portions or sections as it may be practicable to construct and complete as parts of the whole project, providing the necessary funds for such portions or sections are available in the reclamation fund, and thereupon he shall give public notice of the lands irrigable under such project, and limit of area per entry, which limit shall represent the acreage which, in the opinion of the Secretary, may be reasonably required for the support of a family upon the lands in question; also of the charges which shall be made per acre upon the said entries, and upon lands in private ownership which may be irrigated by the waters of the said irrigation project, and the number of annual installments, not exceeding ten, in which such charges shall be paid and the time when such payments shall commence. The said charges shall be determined with a view of returning to the reclamation fund the estimated cost of construction of the project, and shall be apportioned equitably: *Provided,* That in all construction work eight hours shall constitute a day's work, and no Mongolian labor shall be employed thereon.

SEC. 5. That the entryman upon lands to be irrigated by such works shall, in addition to compliance with the homestead laws, reclaim at least one-half of the total irrigable area of his entry for agricultural purposes, and before receiving patent for the lands covered by his entry shall pay to the Government the charges apportioned against such tract, as provided in section four. No right to the use of water for land in private ownership shall be sold for a tract exceeding one hundred and sixty acres to any one landowner, and no such sale shall be made to any landowner unless he be an actual bona fide resident on such land, or occupant thereof residing in the neighborhood of said land, and no such right shall permanently attach until all payments therefor are made. The annual installments shall be paid to the receiver of the local land office of the district in which the land is situated, and a failure to make any two payments when due shall render the entry subject to cancellation, with the forfeiture of all rights under this Act, as well as of any moneys already paid thereon. All moneys received from the above sources shall be paid into the reclamation fund. Registers and receivers shall be allowed the usual commissions on all moneys paid for lands entered under this Act.

SEC. 6. That the Secretary of the Interior is hereby authorized and directed to use the reclamation fund for the operation and maintenance of all reservoirs and irrigation works constructed under the provisions of this Act: *Provided,* That when the payments required by this Act are made for the major portion of the lands irrigated from the waters of any of the works herein provided for, then the management and operation of such irrigation works shall pass to the owners of the lands irrigated thereby, to be maintained at their expense under such forms of organization and under such rules and regulations as may be acceptable to the Secretary of the Interior: *Provided,* That the title to and the management and operation of the reservoirs and the works necessary for their protection and operation shall remain in the Government until otherwise provided by Congress.

SEC. 7. That where in carrying out the provisions of this Act it becomes necessary to acquire any rights or property, the Secretary of the Interior is hereby authorized to acquire the same for the United States by purchase or by condemnation under judicial process, and to pay from the reclamation fund the sums which may be needed for that purpose, and it shall be the duty of the Attorney-General of the United States upon every application of the Secretary of the Interior, under this Act, to cause proceedings to be commenced for condemnation within thirty days from the receipt of the application at the Department of Justice.

[37]

SEC. 8. That nothing in this Act shall be construed as affecting or intended to affect or to in any way interfere with the laws of any State or Territory relating to the control, appropriation, use, or distribution of water used in irrigation, or any vested right acquired thereunder, and the Secretary of the Interior, in carrying out the provisions of this Act, shall proceed in conformity with such laws, and nothing herein shall in any way affect any right of any State or of the Federal Government or of any landowner, appropriator, or user of water in, to, or from any interstate stream or the waters thereof: *Provided,* That the right to the use of water acquired under the provisions of this Act shall be appurtenant to the land irrigated, and beneficial use shall be the basis, the measure, and the limit of the right.

SEC. 9. That it is hereby declared to be the duty of the Secretary of the Interior in carrying out the provisions of this Act, so far as the same may be practicable and subject to the existence of feasible irrigation projects, to expend the major portion of the funds arising from the sale of public lands within each State and Territory hereinbefore named for the benefit of arid and semiarid lands within the limits of such State or Territory: *Provided,* That the Secretary may temporarily use such portion of said funds for the benefit of arid or semiarid lands in any particular State or Territory hereinbefore named as he may deem advisable, but when so used the excess shall be restored to the fund as soon as practicable, to the end that ultimately, and in any event, within each ten-year period after the passage of this Act, the expenditures for the benefit of the said States and Territories shall be equalized according to the proportions and subject to the conditions as to practicability and feasibility aforesaid.

SEC. 10. That the Secretary of the Interior is hereby authorized to perform any and all acts and to make such rules and regulations as may be necessary and proper for the purpose of carrying the provisions of this Act into full force and effect.

Approved, June 17, 1902.

LETTER FROM PRESIDENT ROOSEVELT
ON DIVIDING THE WORK*
July 2, 1902

Newlands had hoped to make the reclamation program less subject to the traditional pork-barrel pressures by leaving selection of projects to the Reclamation Service, without the necessity of spreading out among the states to assure general support. However, with this letter of instruction to Secretary of the Interior Hitchcock, Roosevelt immediately began to abandon Newlands' idea. It is not known whether T. R.'s directive resulted from private commitments in getting the bill passed, or from concern for future political effect in the West or in the Congress.

TO ETHAN ALLEN HITCHCOCK

Personal   Washington, July 2, 1902

To the Secretary of the Interior:

In the irrigation business, instead of starting on a few large enterprises, I should think it would be best to divide up the work among the different States as fairly as possible; and be sure we can carry out whatever we undertake. This irrigation business is most important. We must not make any slips at the outset.

---

*The Letters of Theodore Roosevelt, Vol. 3, Elting E. Morison, ed. (Cambridge: Harvard University Press, 1951), 284.

LETTERS FROM PRESIDENT ROOSEVELT ON CREDIT
FOR THE IRRIGATION BILL*
July 2; August 20, 1902

After the Newlands bill had become law, Republicans were still complaining about Roosevelt's support of a Democrat's legislation. These letters to Secretary of Agriculture Wilson and to a western publisher were the President's reaction.

When he published his autobiography in 1913, however, Theodore Roosevelt wrote:

> *On the day the message was read, a committee of Western Senators and Congressmen was organized to prepare a Reclamation Bill in accordance with the recommendations. By far the most effective of the Senators in drafting and passing the bill, which became known by his name, was Newlands. . . . my active interference was necessary to prevent it being made unworkable by an undue insistence upon States Rights, in accordance with the efforts of Mr. Mondell and other Congressmen, who consistently fought for local and private interests as against the interests of the people as a whole.*

TO JAMES WILSON

Personal   Washington, July 2, 1902

My dear Secretary Wilson:

Interviews that I am sure are faked have appeared in which you are represented as stating that Mr. Newlands was entitled to the credit of passing the irrigation measure. Now, as a matter of fact, I never consulted with him or said a thing to him about my message, although I did consult Senators Stewart and Warren and Congressmen Mondell, Long, and Burkett. If the interviews are not true, I should think that a brief statement from you to that effect might be good, as Newlands is evidently trying to use your interviews as a campaign document.

Sincerely yours

TO CHARLES FLETCHER LUMMIS

Confidential   Oyster Bay, August 20, 1902

My dear Mr. Lummis:

One word confidentially. I do not like your paper[1] to be used to boom Newlands, as in your last piece about irrigation. The bill is not the Newlands' bill

---

*The Letters of Theodore Roosevelt, Vol. 3, Elting E. Morison, ed. (Cambridge: Harvard University Press, 1951), 284, 317.
[1] The magazine, Out West.

[40]

at all. He had for instance, far less to do with preparing it than Senator Stewart of Nevada, or Congressman Mondell of Wyoming; and I consulted him far less than I did Senator Gibson of Montana and especially Senator Warren of Wyoming. Mr. Newlands had absolutely nothing to do with getting the bill through, but he has since industriously worked a newspaper bureau to give him the credit. This bureau has gone so far as to publish fake interviews with the Secretary of the Interior and the Secretary of Agriculture. The chief work that has been done was not by the western people at all. I had to devote myself to the easterners, and all that I had to do with Newlands was to make it evident that I would not back the extreme scheme with which he had been identified, the backing of which meant that nothing whatever would be accomplished. As soon as we got the westerners to agree upon a moderate bill, and could show that we were not going to do anything like what Mr. Newlands had originally proposed, then it only remained to bring the easterners in line, and that caused hard work, but we finally did it.

I write you thus at length because I have been convinced that Mr. Newlands had sought to exploit this bill for his own political purposes.

Of course, treat this letter as entirely confidential and for your own information.

I thank you for sending me the typewritten copy of the report, and I return it to you herewith.

Is the action of the Interior Department satisfactory? I stirred them up instantly after hearing from you.

Sincerely yours

THE FIRST ANNUAL REPORT OF
THE RECLAMATION SERVICE*
1903

The first annual report of the Reclamation Service reviews the history of government activity related to irrigation. The section presented below details the laws recognizing irrigation. Certain portions of this document also appear in the first volume of this series, but are reprinted here since the report itself is an important reclamation document.

The first project under the Reclamation Act was the Salt River project in Arizona, the construction of which began in August 1903.

LAWS RECOGNIZING IRRIGATION

Before discussing the reclamation law, reference should be made to the acts of Congress which may be said in one sense to lead up to it, or which have resulted in creating conditions which must be met in putting the reclamation law into effect. Most of these laws appertain to the rights of individuals who have sought to obtain possession of the public lands or of waters flowing across or over them. The most notable exception to this is the so-called Carey Act, which first recognizes the importance of State or Government action in reclaiming the arid land. This law, while not as yet effective in reclaiming any considerable body of land, has served a useful purpose in satisfying some persons who have held that the States should take charge of the matter. The law is given in full on a later page, and also a discussion of the conditions resulting from it.

RIGHTS TO USE OF WATER

The first recognition by Congress of the peculiar conditions of water supply existing in the arid regions is found in section 9 of the act of July 26, 1866 (Stat. L., vol. 14, p. 253), now incorporated in the Revised Statutes of the United States as section 2339. This section was part of a general act relating to mineral lands, the passage of which was due largely to the efforts of Senator Stewart, of Nevada, and resulted from the necessity of providing for an adjustment of the conditions arising from the enormous development of the mining industry, in connection with which the use of water in hydraulic mining had gained great importance, while its use in agriculture by the Mexicans had already attracted some attention. This section of the law, although primarily intended to relate to the rights to water required in mining operations, was very broadly drawn,

*H. Doc. 79, 57th Cong., 2nd sess., 45–61, 63–75.

so as to include agriculture and other uses. It was, as held by the United States Supreme Court, a recognition of the rules and regulations that had grown up in the West, as declared by the local laws, customs, and decisions of the courts. Its language is as follows:

> SEC. 2339. Whenever, by priority of possession, rights to the use of water for mining, agricultural, manufacturing, or other purposes have vested and accrued, and the same are recognized and acknowledged by the local customs, laws, and the decisions of courts, the possessors and owners of such vested rights shall be maintained and protected in the same; and the right of way for the construction of ditches and canals for the purposes herein specified is acknowledged and confirmed; but whenever any person, in the construction of any ditch or canal, injures or damages the possession of any settler on the public domain, the party committing such injury or damage shall be liable to the party injured for such injury or damage.

This law was supplemented in July, 1870, by a provision authorizing the reservation of the rights so recognized in all patents issued for the public lands. This additional legislation was originally section 17 of the act of July 9, 1870 (Stat. L., vol. 16, p. 218). It is now section 2340 of the Revised Statutes, as follows:

> SEC. 2340. All patents granted, or preemption or homesteads allowed, shall be subject to any vested and accrued water rights, or rights to ditches and reservoirs used in connection with such water rights, as may have been acquired under or recognized by the preceding section.

DESERT-LAND LAW

The conditions arising from the aridity of the Western country soon forced themselves upon the attention of Congress, and by act of March 3, 1875 (Stat. L., vol. 18, p. 497), special provision was made for the sale of desert lands in Lassen County, Cal., requiring the entryman to irrigate and reclaim them in somewhat the same manner as under the present desert-land act. It reads as follows:

> An Act to provide for the sale of desert lands in Lassen County, California.
>
> *Be it enacted by the Senate and House of Representatives of the United States of America in Congress assembled,* That it shall be lawful for any citizen of the United States, or any person of requisite age who may be entitled to become a citizen, and who has filed his declaration of intention to become such, to file a declaration with the register and the receiver of the proper land district for the county of Lassen, California, in which any desert land is situated, that he intends to reclaim a tract of desert land situated in said county, not exceeding one section, by conducting water upon the same, so as to reclaim all of said land within the period of two years thereafter; and said declaration shall be under oath and shall describe particularly said section of land, if surveyed, and if unsurveyed shall describe the same as nearly as possible without a survey; which said declaration shall be supported by the affidavit of at least two credible witnesses, establishing to the satisfaction of the register or receiver the fact that said lands are of the character described in this act. And at any time within the period of two years after filing said declaration, and upon making satisfactory proof of the reclamation of said tract of land in the manner aforesaid, before the register and receiver of said land office, such person shall be entitled to enter or locate the reclaimed section, or any part thereof, in the same manner as in cases where public lands of the United States are subject to entry, at a price not exceeding one dollar and twenty-five cents per acre, and shall receive a patent therefor.

SEC. 2. That all lands within said county of Lassen, exclusive of timber lands and of mineral lands, which do not produce grass, or which will not, without such reclamation, produce some agricultural crop, shall be deemed desert lands within the meaning of this act.

This act, which was applicable to only one county of the State of California, paved the way two years later for a general act covering a number of States and Territories in the arid region, which provided for the taking of desert lands by individuals. This is known as "The Desert-Land Act," and was approved March 3, 1877 (Stat. L., vol. 19, p. 377). Its language is as follows:

An Act to provide for the sale of desert lands in certain States and Territories.

Be it enacted by the Senate and House of Representatives of the United States of America in Congress assembled, That it shall be lawful for any citizen of the United States, or any person of requisite age "who may be entitled to become a citizen, and who has filed his declaration to become such," and upon payment of twenty-five cents per acre, to file a declaration under oath with the register and the receiver of the land district in which any desert land is situated, that he intends to reclaim a tract of desert land, not exceeding one section; by conducting water upon the same within the period of three years thereafter, *Provided however,* That the right to the use of water by the person so conducting the same, on or to any tract of desert land of six hundred and forty acres shall depend upon bona fide prior appropriation; and such right shall not exceed the amount of water actually appropriated and necessarily used for the purpose of irrigation and reclamation; and all surplus water over and above such actual appropriation and use, together with the water of all lakes, rivers, and other sources of water supply upon the public lands, and not navigable, shall remain and be held free for the appropriation and use of the public for irrigation, mining, and manufacturing purposes subject to existing rights. Said declaration shall describe particularly said section of land if surveyed, and if unsurveyed shall describe the same as nearly as possible without a survey. At any time within the period of three years after filing said declaration, upon making satisfactory proof to the register and receiver of the reclamation of said tract of land in the manner aforesaid, and upon the payment to the receiver of the additional sum of one dollar per acre for a tract of land not exceeding six hundred and forty acres to any one person, a patent for the same shall be issued to him: *Provided,* That no person shall be permitted to enter more than one tract of land, and not to exceed six hundred and forty acres, which shall be in compact form.

SEC. 2. That all lands exclusive of timber lands and mineral lands which will not, without irrigation, produce some agricultural crop, shall be deemed desert lands within the meaning of this act, which fact shall be ascertained by proof of two or more credible witnesses under oath, whose affidavits shall be filed in the land-office in which said tract of land may be situated.

SEC. 3. That this act shall only apply to and take effect in the States of California, Oregon, and Nevada, and the Territories of Washington, Idaho, Montana, Utah, Wyoming, Arizona, New Mexico, and Dakota, and the determination of what may be considered desert land shall be subject to the decision and regulation of the Commissioner of the General Land Office.

IRRIGATION INVESTIGATION

This law requires the irrigation and reclamation of lands by individual effort. The need, however, for action on a larger scale by the General Government was first prominently set before the public by Maj. John W. Powell, formerly Director of the Geological Survey. His report, issued in 1879, dealt largely with the arid region and the problems presented. He recognized clearly and stated definitely that the General Government must of necessity deal directly with the irrigation question. The report was much discussed by those who were interested in the development of the West, and the subject attracted more and more attention from year to year, until after a lapse of ten years a thorough investigation of the water resources of the arid region was authorized by joint resolution of March 20, 1888 (Stat. L., vol. 25, p. 618):

> Joint resolution directing the Secretary of the Interior by means of the Director of the Geological Survey to investigate the practicability of constructing reservoirs for the storage of water in the arid region of the United States, and to report to Congress.
>
> Whereas a large portion of the unoccupied public lands of the United States is located within what is known as the arid region, and now utilized only for grazing purposes, but much of which, by means of irrigation, may be rendered as fertile and productive as any land in the world, capable of supporting a large population, thereby adding to the national wealth and prosperity;
>
> Whereas all the water flowing during the summer months in many of the streams of the Rocky Mountains, upon which chiefly the husbandman of the plains and the mountain valleys chiefly depends for moisture for his crops, has been appropriated and is used for the irrigation of lands contiguous thereto, whereby a comparatively small area has been reclaimed; and
>
> Whereas there are many natural depressions near the sources and along the courses of these streams which may be converted into reservoirs for the storage of the surplus water which during the winter and spring seasons flows through the streams; from which reservoirs the water there stored can be drawn and conducted through properly constructed canals, at the proper season, thus bringing large areas of land into cultivation and making desirable much of the public land for which there is now no demand: Therefore, be it
>
> *Resolved by the Senate and House of Representatives of the United States of America in Congress assembled,* That the Secretary of the Interior, by means of the Director of the Geological Survey, be, and he is hereby, directed to make an examination of that portion of the arid regions of the United States where agriculture is carried on by means of irrigation, as to the natural advantages for the storage of water for irrigating purposes, with the practicability of constructing reservoirs, together with the capacity of the streams and the cost of construction and capacity of reservoirs, and such other facts as bear on the question of storage of water for irrigating purposes; and that he be further directed to report to Congress as soon as practicable the result of such investigation.

October 2 of the same year an appropriation of $100,000 was made for the purpose of investigating the extent to which the arid region could be redeemed by irrigation. (Stat. L., vol. 25, p. 526.) This act provided also for the segregation of the land needed for sites for reservoirs, ditches, or canals, and enacted in addition that all the lands made susceptible of irrigation by such works should be reserved from sale, and should not thereafter be subject to entry, settlement, or occupation until further provided by law. The language of the act is as follows:

> For the purpose of investigating the extent to which the arid region of the United States can be redeemed by irrigation, and the segregation of the irrigable lands in such arid region, and for the selection of sites for reservoirs and other hydraulic works necessary for the storage and utilization of water for irrigation and the prevention of floods and overflows, and to make the necessary maps, including the pay of employees in field and in office, the cost of all instruments, apparatus, and materials, and all other necessary expenses connected therewith, the work to be performed by the Geological Survey, under the direction of the Secretary of the Interior, the sum of one hundred thousand dollars, or so much thereof as

may be necessary. And the Director of the Geological Survey, under the supervision of the Secretary of the Interior, shall make a report to Congress on the first Monday in December of each year, showing in detail how the said money has been expended, the amount used for actual survey and engineer work in the field in locating sites for reservoirs, and an itemized account of the expenditure under this appropriation. And all the lands which may hereafter be designated or selected by such United States surveys for sites for reservoirs, ditches, or canals for irrigation purposes and all the lands made susceptible of irrigation by such reservoirs, ditches, or canals are from this time henceforth hereby reserved from sale as the property of the United States, and shall not be subject after the passage of this act to entry, settlement, or occupation until further provided by law: *Provided,* That the President may at any time in his discretion by proclamation open any portion or all of the lands reserved by this provision to settlement under the homestead laws.

In pursuance of this law there was a general withdrawal from entry of all the lands in the arid region. In the next year an appropriation of $250,000 was made for carrying on the work, act of March 2, 1889 (Stat. L., vol. 25, p. 960). This general withdrawal of lands caused objection. Accordingly, in the act of August 30, 1890 (Stat. L., vol. 26, p. 391), the withdrawal from entry of the lands susceptible of irrigation under the act of October 2, 1888, was revoked and appropriation for irrigation surveys was omitted. The work of segregating reservoir sites, however, was maintained. The act contained also a special provision reserving right of way over lands thereafter sold west of the one hundredth meridian for ditches and canals constructed by authority of the United States, thus foreshadowing the present needs of the reclamation service. Such general reservation will be found valuable when, in the development of work under the reclamation act, it is found necessary to extend canals or other irrigation works over lands previously disposed of by the United States. The language of the law is as follows:

So much of the act of October second, eighteen hundred and eighty-eight, entitled "An act making appropriations for sundry civil expenses of the Government for the fiscal year ending June thirtieth, eighteen hundred and eighty-nine, and for other purposes," as provides for the withdrawal of the public lands from entry, occupation, and settlement is hereby repealed, and all entries made or claims initiated in good faith and valid but for said act shall be recognized and may be perfected in the same manner as if said law had not been enacted, except that reservoir sites heretofore located or selected shall remain segregated and reserved from entry or settlement as provided by said act until otherwise provided by law, and reservoir sites hereafter located or selected on public lands shall in like manner be reserved from the date of the location or selection thereof.

No person who shall, after the passage of this act, enter upon any of the public lands with a view to occupation, entry, or settlement under any of the land laws shall be permitted to acquire title to more than three hundred and twenty acres in the aggregate, under all of said laws, but this limitation shall not operate to curtail the right of any person who has heretofore made entry or settlement on the public lands, or whose occupation, entry, or settlement is validated by this act: *Provided,* That in all patents for lands hereafter taken up under any of the land laws of the United States, or on entries or claims validated by this act, west of the one hundredth meridian, it shall be expressed that there is reserved from the lands in said patent described a right of way thereon for ditches or canals constructed by the authority of the United States.

While this act makes no appropriation for surveys especially related to irrigation, the topographic surveys authorized by the general appropriation for the Geological Survey were of great value in the investigations relating to the irrigation of public lands. The survey and segregation of reservoir sites, as therein provided, has proceeded from time to time, as noted in the various annual reports of the Geological Survey. The authority to continue the examination of the water supply of the arid region still remained as provided by existing laws.

MODIFICATION OF DESERT-LAND LAW

The subject of individual effort now claimed attention, and by section 2 of the act of March 3, 1891 (Stat. L., vol. 26, p. 1095), the original desert-land law of 1877 was modified in several important particulars, its application being extended to the State of Colorado in addition to the States and Territories named in the original act. The provisions are as follows:

SEC. 2. That an act to provide for the sale of desert lands in certain States and Territories, approved March third, eighteen hundred and seventy-seven, is hereby amended by adding thereto the following sections:

"SEC. 4. That at the time of filing the declaration hereinbefore required the party shall also file a map of said land, which shall exhibit a plan showing the mode of contemplated irrigation, and which plan shall be sufficient to thoroughly irrigate and reclaim said land, and prepare it to raise ordinary agricultural crops, and shall also show the source of the water to be used for irrigation and reclamation. Persons entering or proposing to enter separate sections, or fractional parts of sections, of desert lands may associate together in the construction of canals and ditches for irrigating and acclaiming all of said tracts, and may file a joint map or maps showing their plan of internal improvements.

"SEC. 5. That no lands shall be patented to any person under this act unless he or his assignors shall have expended in the necessary irrigation, reclamation, and cultivation thereof, by means of main canals and branch ditches, and in permanent improvements upon the land, and in the purchase of water rights for the irrigation of the same, at least three dollars per acre of whole tract reclaimed and patented in the manner following: Within one year after making entry for such tract of desert land as aforesaid, the party so entering shall expend not less than one dollar per acre for the purposes aforesaid; and he shall in like manner expend the sum of one dollar per acre during the second and also during the third year thereafter, until the full sum of three dollars per acre is so expended. Said party shall file during each year with the register, proof, by the affidavits of two or more credible witnesses, that the full sum of one dollar per acre has been expended in such necessary improvements during such year, and the manner in which expended, and at the expiration of the third year a map or plan showing the character and extent of such improvement. If any party who has made such application shall fail during any year to file the testimony aforesaid, the lands shall revert to the United States, and the twenty-five cents advanced payment shall be forfeited to the United States, and the entry shall be canceled. Nothing herein contained shall prevent a claimant from making his final entry and receiving his patent at an earlier date than hereinbefore prescribed, provided that he then makes the required proof of reclamation to the aggregate extent of three dollars per acre: *Provided,* That proof be further required of the cultivation of one-eighth of the land.

"SEC. 6. That this act shall not affect any valid rights heretofore accrued under said act of March third, eighteen hundred and seventy-seven, but all bona fide claims heretofore lawfully initiated may be perfected, upon due compliance with the provisions of said act, in the same manner, upon the same terms and conditions, and subject to the same limitations, forfeitures, and contests as if this act had not been passed; or said claims, at the option of the claimant, may be perfected and patented under the provisions of said act, as amended by this act, so far as applicable; and all acts and parts of acts in conflict with this act are hereby repealed.

"SEC. 7. That at any time after filing the declaration, and within the period of four years thereafter, upon making satisfactory proof to the register and the receiver of the reclamation and cultivation of said land to the extent and cost and in the manner aforesaid, and substantially in accordance with the plans herein provided for, and that he or she is a citizen of the United States, and upon payment to the receiver of the additional sum of one dollar per acre for said land, a patent shall issue therefor to the applicant or his assigns; but no person or association of persons shall hold, by assignment or otherwise prior to the issue of patent, more than three hundred and twenty acres of such arid or desert lands; but this section shall not apply to entries made or initiated prior to the approval of this act: *Provided, however,* That additional proofs may be required at any time within the period prescribed by law, and that the claims or entries made under this or any preceding act shall be subject to contest, as provided by the law relating to homestead cases, for illegal inception, abandonment, or failure to comply with the requirements of law, and upon satisfactory proof thereof shall be canceled, and the lands and moneys paid therefor shall be forfeited to the United States.

"SEC. 8. That the provisions of the act to which this is an amendment, and the amendments thereto, shall apply to and be in force in the State of Colorado, as well as the States named in the original act; and no person shall be entitled to make entry of desert land except he be a resident citizen of the State or Territory in which the land sought to be entered is located."

RESERVOIR SITES

Section 17 of the same act provides that the reservoir sites located and selected under the acts of 1888 and 1890 shall be restricted to the land actually needed for the construction and maintenance of the reservoirs, excluding as far as practicable the land actually occupied by settlers. The section reads as follows:

SEC. 17. That reservoir sites located or selected and to be located and selected under the provisions of "An act making appropriations for sundry civil expenses of the Government for the fiscal year ending June thirtieth, eighteen hundred and eighty-nine, and for other purposes," and amendments thereto, shall be restricted to and shall contain only so much land as is actually necessary for the construction and maintenance of reservoirs; excluding so far as practicable lands occupied by actual settlers at the date of the location of said reservoirs, and that the provisions of "An act making appropriations for sundry civil expenses of the Government for the fiscal year ending June thirtieth, eighteen hundred and ninety-one, and for other purposes," which reads as follows, viz: "No person who shall after the passage of this act enter upon any of the public lands with a view to occupation, entry, or settlement under any of the land laws shall be permitted to acquire title to more than three hundred and twenty acres in the aggregate under all said laws," shall be construed to include in the maximum amount of lands the title to which is permitted to be acquired by one person only agricultural lands and not include lands entered or sought to be entered under mineral land laws.

RIGHTS OF WAY

In the same act, sections 18 to 21, inclusive, there is a provision under which grants were made to corporations and individuals for right of way for irrigation purposes, in order that they might be assured of such right of way prior to the actual construction, which was a requisite for the vesting of the rights recognized and confirmed by sections 2339 and 2340 of the Revised Statutes, hereinbefore referred to. These sections of the act read as follows:

SEC. 18. That the right of way through the public lands and reservations of the United States is hereby granted to any canal or ditch company formed for the purpose of irrigation and duly organized under the laws of any State or Territory, which shall have filed, or may hereafter file, with the Secretary of the Interior a copy of its articles of incorporation, and due proofs of its organization under the same, to the extent of the ground occupied by the water of the reservoir and of the canal and its laterals, and fifty feet on each side of the marginal limits thereof; also the right to take from the public lands adjacent to the line of the canal or ditch, material, earth and stone, necessary for the construction of such canal or ditch: *Provided,* That no such right of way shall be so located as to interfere with the proper occupation by the Government of any such reservation, and all maps of location shall be subject to the approval of the department of the Government having jurisdiction of such reservation, and the privilege herein granted shall not be construed to interfere with the control of water for irrigation and other purposes under authority of the respective States or Territories.

SEC. 19. That any canal or ditch company desiring to secure the benefits of this act shall, within twelve months after the location of ten miles of its canal, if the same be upon surveyed lands, and, if upon unsurveyed lands, within twelve months after the survey thereof by the United States, file with the register of the land office for the district where such land is located a map of its canal or ditch and reservoir; and upon the approval thereof by the Secretary of the Interior the same shall be noted upon the plats in said office, and thereafter all such lands over which such rights of way shall pass shall be disposed of subject to such right of way. Whenever any person or corporation, in the construction of any canal, ditch, or reservoir, injures or damages the possession of any settler on the public domain, the party committing such injury or damage shall be liable to the party injured for such injury or damage.

SEC. 20. That the provisions of this act shall apply to all canals, ditches, or reservoirs, heretofore or hereafter constructed, whether constructed by corporations, individuals, or association of individuals, on the filing of the certificates and maps herein provided for. If such ditch, canal, or reservoir has been or shall be constructed by any individual or association of individuals, it shall be sufficient for such individual or association of individuals to file with the Secretary of the Interior and with the register of the land office where said land is located a map of the line of such canal, ditch, or reservoir, as in case of a corporation, with the name of the individual owner or owners thereof, together with the articles of association, if any there be. Plats heretofore filed shall have the benefits of this act from the date of their filing as though filed under it: *Provided,* That, if any section of said canal or ditch shall not be completed within five years after the location of said section, the rights herein granted shall be forfeited as to any uncompleted section of said canal, ditch, or reservoir, to the extent that the same is not completed at the date of the forfeiture.

SEC. 21. That nothing in this act shall authorize such canal or ditch company to occupy such right of way, except for the purpose of said canal or ditch, and then only so far as may be necessary for the construction, maintenance, and care of said canal or ditch.

Legislation for canals and reservoirs constructed for commercial purposes by individuals or corporations was passed January 21, 1895 (Stat. L., vol. 28, p. 635), providing for right of way for canals, reservoirs, and tramroads to be used in connection with mining, quarrying, cutting timber, and the manufacturing of lumber, as follows:

[49]

An Act to permit the use of right of way through the public lands for tramroads, canals, and reservoirs, and for other purposes.

Be it enacted by the Senate and House of Representatives of the United States of America in Congress assembled, That the Secretary of the Interior be, and hereby is, authorized and empowered, under general regulations to be fixed by him, to permit the use of the right of way through the public lands of the United States, not within the limits of any park, forest, military or Indian reservation, for tramroads, canals, or reservoirs to the extent of the ground occupied by the water of the canals and reservoirs and fifty feet on each side of the marginal limits thereof; or fifty feet on each side of the center of the tramroad, by any citizen or any association of citizens of the United States engaged in the business of mining or quarrying or of cutting timber and manufacturing lumber.

An extension of this act is found in the act of May 14, 1896 (Stat. L., vol. 29, p. 120), providing for right of way for electric-power purposes, viz:

An Act to amend the act approved March third, eighteen hundred and ninety-one, granting the right of way upon the public lands for reservoir and canal purposes.

Be it enacted by the Senate and House of Representatives of the United States of America in Congress assembled, That the act entitled "An act to permit the use of the right of way through the public lands for tramroads, canals, and reservoirs, and for other purposes," approved January twenty-first, eighteen hundred and ninety-five, be, and the same is hereby, amended by adding thereto the following:

"SEC. 2. That the Secretary of the Interior be, and hereby is, authorized and empowered, under general regulations to be fixed by him, to permit the use of right of way to the extent of twenty-five feet, together with the use of necessary ground, not exceeding forty acres, upon the public land and forest reservations of the United States, by any citizen or association of citizens of the United States, for the purposes of generating, manufacturing, or distributing electric power."

By the act of January 13, 1897 (Stat. L., vol. 29, p. 484), provision was made for the occupation of the public lands for reservoirs constructed for the purpose of watering live stock, as follows:

An Act providing for the location and purchase of public lands for reservoir sites.

Be it enacted by the Senate and House of Representatives of the United States of America in Congress assembled, That any person, live-stock company, or transportation corporation engaged in breeding, grazing, driving, or transporting live stock may construct reservoirs upon unoccupied public lands of the United States, not mineral or otherwise reserved, for the purpose of furnishing water to such live stock, and shall have control of such reservoir, under regulations prescribed by the Secretary of the Interior, and the lands upon which the same is constructed, not exceeding one hundred and sixty acres; so long as such reservoir is maintained and water kept therein for such purposes: *Provided,* That such reservoir shall not be fenced and shall be open to the free use of any person desiring to water animals of any kind.

SEC. 2. That any person, live-stock company, or corporation desiring to avail themselves of the provisions of this act shall file a declaratory statement in the United States land office in the district where the land is situated, which statement shall describe the land where such reservoir is to be or has been constructed; shall state what business such corporation is engaged in; specify the capacity of the reservoir in gallons, and whether such company, person, or corporation has filed upon other reservoir sites within the same county; and if so, how many.

SEC. 3. That at any time after the completion of such reservoir or reservoirs which, if not completed at the date of the passage of this act, shall be constructed and completed within two years after filing such declaratory statement, such person, company, or corporation shall have the same accurately surveyed, as hereinafter provided, and shall file in the United States land office in the district in which such reservoir is located a map or plat showing the location of such reservoir, which map or plat shall be transmitted by the register and receiver of said United States land office to the Secretary of the Interior and approved by him, and thereafter such land shall be reserved from sale by the Secretary of the Interior so long as such reservoir is kept in repair and water kept therein.

SEC. 4. That Congress may at any time amend, alter, or repeal this act.

By the act of February 26, 1897 (Stat. L., vol. 29, p. 599), the reservoir sites segregated under the acts of 1888 and 1890, heretofore cited, were rendered subject to applications for right of way under sections 18 to 21 of the act of March 3, 1891, already quoted. The act of 1897 reads as follows:

An Act to provide for the use and occupation of reservoir sites reserved.

Be it enacted by the Senate and House of Representatives of the United States of America in Congress assembled, That all reservoir sites reserved or to be reserved shall be open to use and occupation under the right-of-way act of March third, eighteen hundred and ninety-one. And any State is hereby authorized to improve and occupy such reservoir sites to the same extent as an individual or private corporation, under such rules and regulations as the Secretary of the Interior may prescribe: *Provided,* That the charges for water coming in whole or part from reservoir sites used or occupied under the provisions of this act shall always be subject to the control and regulation of the respective States and Territories in which such reservoirs are in whole or part situate.

A paragraph of the forest-reserve act of June 4, 1897 (Stat. L., vol. 30, p. 34), provides as follows concerning the use of waters on such reservations:

All waters on such reservations may be used for domestic, mining, milling, or irrigation purposes, under the laws of the State wherein such forest reservations are situated, or under the laws of the United States and the rules and regulations established thereunder.

On May 11, 1898 (Stat. L., vol. 30, p. 404), the right-of-way acts of 1891 and 1895 were amended for the purpose of extending the application of their provisions, as follows:

An Act to amend an act to permit the use of the right of way through public lands for tramroads, canals, and reservoirs, and for other purposes.

Be it enacted by the Senate and House of Representatives of the United States of America in Congress assembled, That the act entitled "An act to permit the use of the right of way through the public lands for tramroads, canals, and reservoirs, and for other purposes," approved January twenty-first, eighteen hundred and ninety-five, be, and the same is hereby, amended by adding thereto the following:

"That the Secretary of the Interior be, and hereby is, authorized and empowered, under general regulations to be fixed by him, to permit the use of right of way upon the public lands of the United States, not within limits of any park, forest, military, or Indian reservations, for tramways, canals, or reservoirs, to the extent of the ground occupied by the waters of the canals and reservoirs, and fifty feet on each side of the marginal limits thereof, or fifty feet on each side of the center line of the tramroad, by any citizen or association of citizens of the United States, for the purposes of furnishing water for domestic, public, and other beneficial uses.

SEC. 2. That rights of way for ditches, canals, or reservoirs heretofore or hereafter approved under the provisions of sections eighteen, nineteen, twenty, and twenty-one of the act entitled 'An act to repeal timber-culture laws, and for other purposes,' approved March third, eighteen hundred and ninety-one, may be used for purposes of a public nature; and said rights of way may be used for purposes of water transportation, for domestic purposes, or for the development of power, as subsidiary to the main purpose of irrigation."

On February 15, 1901 (Stat. L., vol. 31, p. 790), a general act was passed providing for the use of the public lands for right of way for reservoirs, ditches, and other methods of conveying water, as follows:

An Act relating to rights of way through certain parks, reservations, and other public lands.

Be it enacted by the Senate and House of Representatives of the United States of America in Congress assembled, That the Secretary of the Interior be, and hereby is, authorized and empowered, under general regulations to be fixed by him, to permit the use of rights of way through the public lands, forest, and other reservations of the United States, and the Yosemite, Sequoia, and General Grant national parks, California, for electrical plants, poles, and lines for the generation and distribution of electrical power, and for telephone and telegraph purposes, and for canals, ditches, pipes and pipe lines, flumes, tunnels, or other water conduits, and for water plants, dams, and reservoirs used to promote irrigation or mining or quarrying, or the manufacturing or cutting of timber or lumber, or the supplying of water for domestic, public, or any other beneficial uses to the extent of the ground occupied by such canals, ditches, flumes tunnels, reservoirs, or other water conduits or water plants, or electrical or other works permitted hereunder, and not to exceed fifty feet on each side of the marginal limits thereof, or not to exceed fifty feet on each side of the center line of such pipes and pipe lines, electrical, telegraph, and telephone lines and poles, by any citizen, association, or corporation of the United States, where it is intended by such to exercise the use permitted hereunder, or any one or more of the purposes herein named: *Provided,* That such permits shall be allowed within or through any of said parks or any forest, military, Indian, or other reservation only upon the approval of the chief officer of the Department under whose supervision such park or reservation falls, and upon a finding by him that the same is not incompatible with the public interest: *Provided further,* That all permits given hereunder for telegraph and telephone purposes shall be subject to the provision of title sixty-five of the Revised Statutes of the United States, and amendments thereto, regulating rights of way for telegraph companies over the public domain: *And provided further,* That any permission given by the Secretary of the Interior under the provisions of this act may be revoked by him or his successor in his discretion, and shall not be held to confer any right, or easement, or interest in, to, or over any public land, reservation, or park.

This act has been held by the Department to supersede the previous acts of 1895, 1896, and section 1 of the act of 1898, except in so far as they relate to tramroad right of way.

CAREY ACT

On August 18, 1894 (Stat. L., vol. 28, pp. 372–422), Congress passed what is known as the Carey Act, which is section 4 of the act making appropriations for sundry civil expenses of the Government, and is as follows:

SEC. 4. That to aid the public-land States in the reclamation of the desert lands therein, and the settlement, cultivation, and sale thereof in small tracts to actual settlers, the Secretary of the Interior, with the approval of the President, be, and hereby is, authorized and empowered, upon proper application of the State to contract and agree, from time to time, with each of the States in which there may be situated desert lands as defined by the act entitled "An act to provide for the sale of desert land in certain States and Territories," approved March third, eighteen hundred and seventy-seven, and the act amendatory thereof, approved March third, eighteen hundred and ninety-one, binding the United States to donate, grant, and patent to the State free of cost for survey or price such desert lands, not exceeding one million acres in each State, as the State may cause to be irrigated, reclaimed, occupied, and not less than twenty acres of each one hundred and sixty acre tract cultivated by actual settlers, within ten years next after the passage of this act, as thoroughly as is required of citizens who may enter under the said desert-land law.

Before the application of any State is allowed or any contract or agreement is executed or any segregation of any of the land from the public domain is ordered by the Secretary of the Interior, the State shall file a map of the said land proposed to be irrigated which shall exhibit a plan showing the mode of the contemplated irrigation and which plan shall be sufficient to thoroughly irrigate and reclaim said land and to prepare it to raise ordinary agricultural crops, and shall also show the source of the water to be used for irrigation and reclamation, and the Secretary of the Interior may make necessary regulations for the reservation of the lands applied for by the State to date from the date of the filing of the map and plan of irrigation, but such reservation shall be of no force whatever if such map and plan of irrigation shall not be approved. That any State contracting under this section is hereby authorized to make all necessary contracts to cause the said lands to be reclaimed, and to induce their settlement and cultivation in accordance with and subject to the provisions of this section; but the State shall not be authorized to lease any of said lands or to use or dispose of the same in any way whatever except to secure their reclamation, cultivation, and settlement.

As fast as any State may furnish satisfactory proof, according to such rules and regulations as may be prescribed by the Secretary of the Interior, that any of said lands are irrigated, reclaimed, and occupied by actual settlers, patents shall be issued to the State or its assigns for said lands so reclaimed and settled: *Provided,* That said States shall not sell or dispose of more than one hundred and sixty acres of said lands to any one person, and any surplus of money derived by any State from the sale of said lands in excess of the cost of their reclamation shall be held as a trust fund for and be applied to the reclamation of other desert lands in such State.

This act inaugurated the plan of turning over lands to the States for irrigation by any means which they may choose to adopt. The act makes a donation of 1,000,000 acres of desert land to each of the States in the arid region, provided that they shall cause the same to be irrigated and reclaimed. It was amended by the act of June 11, 1896 (Stat. L., vol. 29, p. 434), authorizing the States to create a lien against the lands segregated for the purpose of reclamation, in the following language:

That under any law heretofore or hereafter enacted by any State, providing for the reclamation of arid lands, in pursuance and acceptance of the terms of the grant made in section four of an act entitled "An act making appropriations for the sundry civil expenses of the Government for the fiscal year ending June thirtieth, eighteen hundred and ninety-five," approved August eighteenth, eighteen hundred and ninety-four, a lien or liens is hereby authorized to be created by the State to which such lands are granted and by no other authority whatever, and when created shall be valid on and against the separate legal subdivisions of land reclaimed, for the actual cost and necessary expenses of reclamation and reasonable interest thereon from the date of reclamation until disposed of to actual settlers; and when an ample supply of water is actually furnished in a substantial ditch or canal, or by artesian wells or reservoirs, to reclaim a particular tract or tracts of such lands, then patents shall issue for the same to such State without regard to settlement or cultivation: *Provided,* That in no event, in no contingency, and under no circumstances shall the United States be in any manner directly or indirectly liable for any amount of any such lien or liability, in whole or in part.

On March 3, 1901 (Stat. L., vol. 31, p. 1188), Congress extended the terms of this law, which had been limited to ten years from the date of its original passage, so that it should remain in continued operation, allowing ten years for the reclamation of each body of land segregated thereunder. The law reads as follows:

SEC. 3. That section four of the act of August eighteenth, eighteen hundred and ninety-four, entitled "An act making appropriations for sundry civil expenses of the Government for the fiscal year ending June thirtieth, eighteen hundred and ninety-five, and for other purposes," is hereby amended so that the ten years' period within which any State shall cause the lands applied for under said act to be irrigated and reclaimed, as provided in said section as amended by the act of June eleventh, eighteen hundred and ninety-six, shall begin to run from the date of approval by the Secretary of the Interior of the State's application for the segregation of such lands; and if the State fails within said ten years to cause the whole or any part of the lands so segregated to be so irrigated and reclaimed, the Secretary of the Interior may, in his discretion, continue said segregation for a period of not exceeding five years, or may, in his discretion, restore such lands to the public domain.

The results of the Carey Act during the eight years of its operation are shown by the following table from page 248 of the Report of the Commissioner of the General Land Office for the year 1902, being a statement of the segregations applied for by the various States under the Carey Act, and showing the status of the applications on July 1, 1902.

Statement of segregations applied for under act of August 18, 1894 (28 Stat. L., pp. 372–422), and the acts amendatory thereof, with the action taken thereon, including all lists filed from the passage of the act to July 1, 1902 (areas in acres).

Applications filed and temporarily segregated:

	Acres.
Idaho	336,902.88
Montana	100,001.79
Nevada	10,402.22
Oregon	171,993.48
Utah	236,458.28
Washington	86,854.26
Wyoming	246,965.72
Total	1,189,578.63

Approved and patented:

Wyoming	11,321.00

Approved, not patented:

Idaho	301,732.49
Oregon	8,793.47
Montana	93,855.00
Wyoming	165,095.34
Total	569,476.30

Relinquished, rejected, and otherwise disposed of:
Idaho. 35,170.39
Montana. 2,472.51
Oregon. 159,407.11
Utah 236,458.28
Washington 86,854.26
Wyoming 52,540.89
    Total. 572,903.44
Pending before this office:
Montana 3,674.28
Nevada 10,402.22
Oregon 3,792.90
Wyoming 18,008.49
    Total 35,877.89
        Grand total (approved, disposed of, and pending) 1,189,578.63

It will be observed that in the eight years since the passage of the act applications have been filed for less than 1,200,000 acres by seven of the States out of the maximum of 7,000,000 which these States could have filed upon, while four other States which might have taken advantage of the act have done nothing toward making any filings under it.

Applications for less than 600,000 acres have been presented in such form as to receive the approval of the Department, and of this number only 11,321 acres have been patented, showing that for only this small amount have the proper proofs of reclamation been submitted.

Under the heading "Relinquished, rejected, and otherwise disposed of," amounting to 572,903.44 acres, the Commissioner of the General Land Office states that applications for about 155,000 acres were returned to the States for correction, the remainder, about 417,000 acres, having been relinquished by the States or rejected by the Department.

The Commissioner's report shows that applications for 217,310.36 acres were received during the last fiscal year; so that about 1,000,000 acres of these filings have been under consideration of the Department for a year or more, of which only about 555,000 acres are pending for action. It is understood that a large proportion have been under consideration for several years, the delay being due in many cases to the failure of the State authorities to submit them in such form as to comply with departmental requirements.

From this analysis of the table it appears that no extensive action has been taken in order to obtain the benefits which might be possible under the Carey Act.

During the last year or more very little activity has been displayed in the matter of construction of irrigation works for the reclamation of the lands which have been segregated under this act.

There have been a number of provisions for the investigation of water supply in Indian reservations, and for the construction of irrigation works thereon, to which extended reference is not necessary.

RECLAMATION LAW

After providing so thoroughly for individual and State effort in the reclamation of arid lands, it became evident that further action was required in order to utilize the large bodies of arid public land which remained unoccupied.

During the twenty-five years in which these various laws for the encouragement of individual and State effort in the reclamation of the arid lands have been in effect the results have been strikingly meager. These laws have been valuable in encouraging the use of water on the public lands and the study of the various problems connected with the proper methods of irrigation. Nearly all the land which is available for irrigation by individual effort or which affords profitable opportunities for comparatively small investments has been utilized, and existing conditions showed the need of adopting other methods to realize the enormous wealth which could be developed by systematic and more effective plans of reclamation. To allow any individual or corporation to obtain the control of the water, as distinct from the ownership of the land, was shown to be unsatisfactory. The Government was not willing to part with its ownership of the lands in the arid region as a whole, or in large compact areas, and without ownership of the lands the construction of expensive irrigation works was found to be in most cases an unsuccessful investment. There was no way open except for the Government itself to undertake the reclamation of its lands. Experience having shown that it is not profitable to invest large amounts in the development and storage of water without the ownership of the lands to be irrigated, it was decided that the owner of the lands, namely the United States, must supply the means. Instead, however, of providing for a specific appropriation from the Treasury for this purpose, Congress decided that the money for the reclamation of the lands should be furnished on condition that it should be returned by those who derived benefit from the expenditure, namely the settlers—in effect, a loan without interest.

Accordingly, by the act approved June 17, 1902 (Stat. L., vol. 32, p. 388), provision was made for the examination, survey, and construction of irrigation works required to reclaim the public lands, and for this purpose there were appropriated the receipts from the sale and disposal of the public lands in the sixteen States and Territories of the arid region, this money constituting what is known as the "reclamation fund." The act provides for the entry of the lands reclaimed in accordance with the provisions of the homestead law, which is modified in certain important particulars, among them the following: That the entryman must repay to the reclamation fund the cost of constructing the works necessary to reclaim the land he has taken; that the entry can not be commuted; and that the area of the entry must be limited to an amount not less than 40 nor more than 160 acres. The law applies to Arizona, California, Colorado, Idaho, Kansas, Montana, Nebraska, Nevada, New Mexico, North Dakota, Oklahoma, Oregon, South Dakota, Utah, Washington, and Wyoming.

* * *

SCOPE OF RECLAMATION LAW

As preliminary to a discussion of the reclamation act of June 17, 1902, it would be well to consider the procedure pointed out by its provisions.

The first step is a request from the engineers of the Reclamation Service, made through the head of the organization, the Director of the Geological Survey, to the Secretary of the Interior, for the withdrawal of certain specified lands with a vew to their examination in the field, in order to determine the practicability of irrigation works for reclaiming them. When this request is approved by the Secretary of the Interior the proper steps are taken, by the General Land Office, for the withdrawal of the lands through the local land office for the district in which they are located. Thereafter no entries will be allowed, except under the provisions of the homestead law, as modified by the limitations and conditions of the act. In accordance therewith they may be limited to an area as small as 40 acres, and will not be subject to the commutation provisions of the homestead law. The entryman may, therefore, be required to reduce the area of his entry to such limit as in the opinion of the Secretary of the Interior may be reasonably required for the support of a family, and will be called upon to pay the charges per acre which may be determined on in not more than ten annual installments.

As soon as possible after such withdrawal, engineers are instructed to make the survey of the lands and of proposed canals and reservoirs; also to conduct necessary engineering investigations concerning the water supply and the conditions under which the construction will be carried on. Upon the completion of this work the results are to be summarized and submitted to the Secretary of the Interior, with such recommendations as may be deemed advisable by the Director of the Geological Survey, together with maps, plans, and estimates of cost.

It will then be the duty of the Secretary of the Interior to determine whether or not such project is practicable and advisable. If determined to be impracticable or inadvisable, he will restore to the public domain the lands withdrawn, and they will become subject to the public-land laws, as if such withdrawal had never been made. If the project is approved by the Secretary of the Interior, he may cause contracts to be let for the construction of the proposed works, either as a whole or for such portion or section as will constitute a complete system, if it should be deemed best not to undertake the entire project at that time. He will thereupon give public notice of the land which may be reclaimed thereunder, and of the particular limitations contemplated by the law as to area, cost, number of installments, date of payments, etc.

As soon as it shall be possible to furnish water for the irrigation of any particular portion of the lands involved, the entrymen thereon will be allowed to take the water; and as construction progresses additional lands will be supplied from time to time.

When payments have been made in full for the major portion of the lands irrigable under any system, the management and operation of the irrigation works shall pass to the owners of the land irrigated therefrom, to be maintained at their expense, under such form of organization and under such rules and regulations as may be acceptable to the Secretary of the Interior. It is provided, however, that the title to the reservoirs and the works necessary for their protection and operation shall remain in the Government, and that they shall continue under the control and management of the Government unless otherwise provided by Congress. Subject to such management and control as may be necessary under the regulations provided, the direct connection of the Government with the lands irrigated will thereupon cease.

DETAILS OF THE LAW

In order to carry out the above procedure, the reclamation act provides in detail as follows:

FUNDS FOR RECLAMATION

Section 1 sets aside for the reclamation fund the moneys received from the sale and disposal of the public lands in sixteen of the States and Territories in the arid and semiarid regions, namely, Arizona, California, Colorado, Idaho, Kansas, Montana, Nebraska, Nevada, New Mexico, North Dakota, Oklahoma, Oregon, South Dakota, Utah, Washington, and Wyoming. The sums so set aside include also the surplus of the fees and commissions of the registers and receivers in excess of the amounts allowed for their salaries. A deduction is made, however, of 5 per cent of the proceeds of the sale of the public lands, in all of the above States except California and in the Territory of New Mexico, for a fund which had been heretofore set aside by law for educational and other purposes. The moneys so provided for the purposes of the act constitute a special fund in the Treasury, known as the "reclamation fund," and it is to be used in the examination and survey for and the construction and maintenance of irrigation works for the storage, diversion, and development of waters for the reclamation of arid and semiarid lands in the States and Territories named, and for the payment of all other expenditures provided for in the act.

The accumulation of this fund begins with the fiscal year running from July

1, 1900, to June 30, 1901, known officially as the fiscal year 1901. The Treasury Department has furnished a report of the proceeds for the said year for each of the States and Territories named. It is as follows:

Official statement of the reclamation fund, fiscal year 1901.

Arizona	$42,586.16
California	205,030.40
Colorado	254,889.88
Idaho	206,645.36
Kansas	20,188.78
Montana	367,342.31
Nebraska	102,963.24
Nevada	9,183.47
New Mexico	75,203.06
North Dakota	449,474.96
Oklahoma	370,464.93
Oregon	364,988.62
South Dakota	113,274.20
Utah	98,416.00
Washington	257,180.95
Wyoming	206,989.59
Total	3,144,821.91

The amount of this fund for the fiscal year ending June 30, 1902, has not yet been determined by the Treasury Department, because the reports relating to the 5 per cent educational fund are not received until near the end of the calendar year. A preliminary statement, which is submitted as an approximation, has been compiled for the year 1902, as follows:

Approximate statement of the reclamation fund, fiscal year 1902.

Arizona	$39,200
California	298,600
Colorado	374,400
Idaho	301,700
Kansas	29,100
Montana	407.400
Nebraska	133,500
Nevada	14,600
New Mexico	72,100
North Dakota	780,600
Oklahoma	640,900
Oregon	547,400
South Dakota	194,500
Utah	48,200
Washington	541,500
Wyoming	176,300
Total	4,600,000

From these two tables it appears that the amount available to July 1, 1902, for the reclamation fund is about $7,774,000. A part of the moneys now set aside for the reclamation fund had been heretofore applied to the support of agricultural colleges in the several States and Territories, in pursuance of an act approved July 2, 1862, and amended August 30, 1890. In order to prevent a deficiency for these purposes, section 1 of the act provides that any deficiency in the sums necessary for the support of said colleges shall be supplied from any moneys in the Treasury not otherwise appropriated.

EXAMINATIONS AND SURVEYS

The provisions of section 2 comprise a statement of the duties of the Secretary of the Interior under the act. He is authorized and directed to make examination and surveys for appropriate irrigation works, and to locate and construct them. The section provides for the works necessary for the storage, diversion, and development of waters, making special mention of artesian wells. The Secretary is required to report to Congress at the beginning of each regular session the results of such examinations and surveys, with estimates of cost of all contemplated works, the quantity and location of the land irrigated therefrom, and other facts relative to the practicability of each irrigation project. He is required also to report the progress of works in process of construction, as well as those which have been completed.

A brief general description of the several projects examined since the organization of the Reclamation Service in July, 1902, follows; a more detailed report in each case will be found in paragraphs devoted to the State in which the work is located.

The work on the Milk River project in Montana included the investigation of the proposed dam sites at St. Mary Lakes, the examination of canal lines east to the Milk River, and thence to an additional tract of land to be developed in connection therewith, in the vicinity of Malta. A reconnaissance survey was made in the drainage basins of the Yellowstone and Musselshell rivers for the discovery of possible storage sites as a basis of study for the utilization of the waters of those rivers.

In Wyoming examinations have been made of the possibility of storing waters in the Bighorn Mountains for use along their eastern slopes, and at the proposed dam site for the Sweetwater reservoir, on the river of that name, a tributary of the North Platte.

In Colorado work has been prosecuted in the vicinity of Sterling, in connection with the possible utilization of the Pawnee Pass reservoir site, with a view to the irrigation of lands on the north bank of South Platte River. Surveys have also been made by way of examining the proposed plans for diverting the waters of the Gunnison River through a tunnel into the Uncompahgre Valley, where the waters can be applied for irrigation.

The Grand River project, involving the use of the waters of the Grand River on the plains west of Grand Junction in Colorado and Utah, has also been the subject of surveys and examinations.

Parties have been at work in Nevada, in the Truckee-Carson basin, with a view to the utilization of the waters of these rivers and examining the storage possibilities of Lake Tahoe and other lakes in the Sierra Nevada. Investigations have also been made in the valley of the Walker River, Nevada.

In Arizona and California an examination of the Colorado River from the Needles to Yuma has been begun for the study of plans for the reclamation of the low lands along both sides of the river. The practicability of storing the flood waters of the Salt River has also been investigated.

SEGREGATION OF LANDS

Section 3 covers various operations which are preliminary to the survey of the lands. It authorizes the Secretary of the Interior to withdraw from entry the public lands which may be required for any system of irrigation works, and also the land which may be irrigated from said system. To provide for these two purposes, withdrawals of two characters are authorized. First, for irrigation works (reservoirs, canals, etc.), the lands being withdrawn from entry of any kind. Second, for lands susceptible of irrigation, which remain, however, subject to homestead entries under the conditions specified in the act.

Among these conditions is the limitation of the homestead entry to tracts of not less than 40 nor more than 160 acres. Throughout the greater part of the arid region the consensus of opinion seems to be that 40 acres of good land, with ample water, are sufficient for a homestead. It seems advisable, therefore, at the outset, or until such time as the plans are prepared, to limit the entries to 40 acres. If at that time it is found that the tracts are not taken up in 40-acre entries, it will be possible to increase the size of the homestead without inconvenience. On the other hand, if entries are made of larger extent, it will be found difficult to reduce these to the minimum.

The entries thus made preliminary to the preparation of final plans are subject to all the provisions, limitations, charges, terms, and conditions of the act.

These entries will be subject to the charges necessary to refund the cost of reclamation and also to the other conditions prescribed by the law. An important limitation on these entries is that the usual commutation provisions of the homestead laws are not applicable. This section requires that the survey shall be diligently prosecuted to completion and that the practicability of the project shall be determined by the Secretary of the Interior. In case it should be decided that

[61]

any project is not feasible, the lands withdrawn are to be restored to entry under the public-land laws.

CONSTRUCTION

Section 4 provides that the Secretary of the Interior, upon deciding that any project is practicable, may cause contracts to be let for the construction of the same. He is likewise authorized to construct the necessary works in such portion or section as will constitute a complete system in itself. It is provided that no contract shall be entered into unless the necessary funds are available in the reclamation fund.

COST PER ACRE

After determining upon construction the Secretary of the Interior is required to give public notice of the lands to be irrigated under the project and of the limitation of area per entry which he may deem advisable and which shall be such as may be reasonably required for the support of a family upon the particular lands involved. This notice will also prescribe the charges which are to be made per acre upon the said entries and upon land in private ownership which may be irrigated by the waters supplied from the said works. He will also prescribe at this time the number of annual installments, not exceeding ten, in which such charges shall be paid and the time when the payments shall commence. It is provided that in fixing the charges per acre the sum shall be determined with a view to returning to the reclamation fund the estimated cost of the project, and the same is to be apportioned equitably.

REFUNDING THE COST

The operation of these provisions will result in making this fund a permanent one, inasmuch as the settlers on these lands and the users of water on lands in private ownership will repay into the fund the cost of constructing the works for the irrigation of their lands. Accordingly the money expended in the construction of any given system will in ten years or less be returned to the reclamation fund and will be available for new construction. Meanwhile the sales of public lands aside from those withdrawn will be added to this fund, so that for a number of years the fund will continue to increase by a sum which will be about the same as the present average annual returns from the sales of lands in these States and Territories. While the reclamation of these lands will tend to diminish the number of homestead entries made in other parts of the public domain, the general stimulation of industry caused by the influx of settlers will have a beneficial effect in increasing the sales of lands for other than agricultural purposes, so that, for some years at least, the increase in the fund should be maintained. By the time a serious diminution becomes apparent, if such decrease should occur, the annual returns from the moneys already invested in reclamation work will furnish a fund for continued operations under this act.

This section provides that the charges on the lands shall be apportioned equitably. This is evidently directed to the considerations that in many cases some of the lands will be less favorably situated for cultivation than others, that the soil in some places will be less capable of raising valuable crops than in others, and that the water supply will be more regular or more abundant in some parts of the reclamation area than in others. These considerations will involve a careful balancing of the possibilities in cultivating the land, and they require a thorough investigation of the location of the lands and a careful study of the various soils found in different parts of the irrigable area reclaimed by each project.

A further provision of section 4 is that in all construction work eight hours shall constitute a day's work, and that no Mongolian labor shall be employed thereon.

Section 5 deals with the requirements of entries made upon these lands. The entryman, in addition to complying with the homestead law, must reclaim for agricultural purposes at least one-half of the total irrigable area of his entry, and pay the charges apportioned against the tract, before receiving a patent for the land. He is required to pay the annual installment to the receiver of the local land office in the district in which the land is situated, and failure to make any two payments when due shall render the entry subject to cancellation, with the forfeiture of all rights under the act, as well as of any moneys paid thereunder.

It is probable that there will not be many cases in which the settler will fail to pay for the cost of reclamation, inasmuch as that charge will be small compared with the actual value of the land with water applied to it. If, however, such failure should occur, it is reasonable to suppose that a contest will be promptly entered against the settler, and that the contestant will, upon obtaining a decision in his favor, and upon the cancellation of the entry, promptly exercise his preference right to enter the same in his own name. In this way the important question of failure to pay installments when due should settle itself with a minimum amount of friction.

RECLAIMING PRIVATE LANDS

Recognizing the fact that there is scarcely a section of country in the United States, even in the most sparsely settled regions of the West, where an irrigation project would not involve the reclamation of lands in private ownership, as well as those belonging to the United States, this section authorizes the sale of the right to use water for land in private ownership, to be limited, however, to the amount required for a tract not exceeding 160 acres. A further limitation upon this provision is that no such sale shall be made unless the landowner is an actual bona fide resident upon the land, or occupant thereof, residing in the neighborhood. In this case, as in the case of one who takes up public land, the right to the use of water does not permanently attach until all the payments required have been made.

The provisions of this section, that no right to the use of water shall be sold for a tract exceeding 160 acres to any one landowner, would clearly apply to the amounts purchased under different projects. That is to say, the owner of lands irrigated in two or more different projects would be limited, in the total amount of water which he could purchase, by that needed to irrigate 160 acres. This is plainly evident from the further provision in the same sentence of the act—the requirement that the landowner shall be a bona fide resident on the land, or an occupant thereof, residing in the neighborhood. The act accordingly does not contemplate the condition that a man residing in the neighborhood of one tract of land irrigated under the act may acquire water sufficient for 160 acres of land there and later change his residence so as to become qualified to acquire water for another 160 acres under a different project. Therefore the regulations on the subject of acquiring water would very properly include a provision to limit the amount of water sold under this act to that which is needed to irrigate 160 acres of land for any individual, and to exclude application under any additional project after having acquired a right to use water to the extent indicated. The moneys derived from these sales are to be covered into the reclamation fund.

It is apparent that very carefully drawn, stringent regulations must be enforced in order to bring about the obvious intent of the reclamation law. It was asserted by the opponents of the measure during its passage that vast areas of the public lands had already been acquired fraudulently, or by violation of the spirit of the homestead law, and that now the owners of these lands were making an effort to increase the value of the lands by inducing the Government to provide water for them. This is recognized to be a real danger, and many persons who are possessed of areas of land of 1,000 acres or upward have asked, and are evidently seriously considering, how to evade the provisions of the law limiting the area of the water rights to 160 acres. The most obvious method is that similar to the so-called dummy or hobo homestead, in which men make filings, commute payments, and transfer the land at once to a single owner or corporation. This well-proved expedient will doubtless be tried many times in the acquisition of water rights under the reclamation law. It is extremely difficult to distinguish between bona fide and fictitious landowners, but if actual residence and cultivation of the soil is required for a long period, say five years, and total payment and passage of title to the use of the water are not made before the expiration of such period, it is probable that the abuse will be comparatively slight.

The man who is actually living on or near an irrigated tract, and who is earning his subsistence from the soil, can not object to the payments extending through-out a long period—even ten years. A man who is endeavoring to speculate in real estate can not afford, usually, to wait several years for the completion of the title to his right to use the water. The law very plainly is intended to discriminate against such speculation, and to inure to the benefit of the man who is making a permanent home.

OPERATION OF WORKS

Section 6 provides that the Secretary of the Interior is to use the reclamation fund for the operation and maintenance of the reservoirs and irrigation works constructed under the provisions of the act. When, however, the payments required by the act have been made for the major portion of the lands irrigated therefrom the management and operation of the works are to pass to the owners of the land irrigated thereby, to be maintained at their expense, under such form of organization and under such rules and regulations as may be acceptable to the Secretary of the Interior, except, however, that the title to the reservoirs and the works necessary for their protection and operation shall remain in the Government and that they shall continue under the management of the Government until otherwise provided by Congress.

The particular form of association under which the settlers shall combine when they are required to undertake the operation and maintenance of the irrigation works (except for the reservoirs) can not well be prescribed in detail for all parts of the country. The general principles to govern such associations should be prescribed for the guidance of the settlers, leaving it to them, however, to adopt such rules in regard to the details as may be most in harmony with the conditions of the particular section in which they live and with the customs which prevail. Nothing has as yet been done toward the formulation of such rules, inasmuch as there will be no need for them for some time, and it is desir-able that there be opportunity for a careful study of the methods now pursued by the various irrigation associations controlling reservoirs and ditches and the use of water before the Department adopts any special line of procedure for this phase of its work under the act.

In regard to the annual payments to be made by settlers and others using the water from the irrigation works constructed under this act, it would be much more convenient and satisfactory to all concerned if they should be made on behalf of the settlers by associations of the character described in this section of the act. The association, acting as agent for each of its members, could make these collections and pay over the sums to the local land office before the water is furnished, regulating by their own officers the distribution of the water in accordance with the payments made. The results under such a system would be much more satisfactory to the settlers, as well as to the Department, than if special officers should be appointed to represent the Government in this particular work. It will be sufficient if there is a general inspector to supervise the disposition of the water and safeguard the interests of the Government, by keeping in close touch with the work of distributing the water supply.

PURCHASE OF PROPERTY

In section 7 authority is given to acquire by purchase or condemnation any rights or property that may be needed to carry out the provisions of the act, and to pay from the reclamation fund the sums that may be necessary for that purpose. The power given by this section is extremely important to the successful management of the Reclamation Service. It will enable the Department to avoid the expensive litigation which might frequently arise from the attempts of individuals and corporations to gain possession of controlling points of an irrigation system and demand exorbitant prices for the rights which they might have acquired. This section provides for prompt action by the Attorney-General of the United States when requested to bring suit for condemnation by the Secretary of the Interior. When, therefore, it is found impossible to come to an agreement with the owners of lands or other property needed for the proposed works, the power of eminent domain may be exercised in order to acquire title to such property or rights.

WATER RIGHTS

Section 8 deals with the question of water rights, and provides that nothing in the act shall be construed as interfering with the laws of any State or Territory relating to water used in irrigation or with the vested rights acquired thereunder, and the Secretary of the Interior is required to proceed in conformity with such laws. Nothing in the act is to affect in any way any right of the Federal Government or of any State or of any landowner, appropriator or user of water in, to, or from any interstate stream or the waters thereof. It is further provided that the right to the use of water acquired under the provisions of the act shall be appurtenant to the lands irrigated, and that beneficial use shall be the basis, the measure, and the limit of the right.

In issuing patent for the lands taken under this act it will be necessary to include therein a conveyance of the water right for the irrigation of the land, and the patent should include, among the clauses conveying this right, an announcement of the above principles, namely, that the water right shall be appurtenant to the lands patented; that beneficial use shall be the basis, the measure, and the limit of the right; and, further, that it shall fail of itself upon violation of the conditions, the extent of the right being always dependent upon the application of the water to beneficial use.

These provisions are of great importance in carrying out the spirit of the act, inasmuch as they will prevent the use, for speculative purposes, of the water rights developed under this law. Moreover, they are an announcement of the fundamental principles of the laws relating to water rights and irrigation as generally administered in the arid region.

APPORTIONMENT OF FUNDS

Section 9 declares it to be the duty of the Secretary of the Interior to expend the major portion of the funds arising from the sale of public lands within the limits of the State or Territory in which they are collected, subject, however, to the existence of feasible irrigation projects and to his judgment as to whether such action is practicable. It is provided further, however, that when such portion derived from the sale of lands in one State is used in another, the excess shall be restored to the fund as soon as practicable, so that within each ten-year period after the passage of this act the expenditures in each State shall be equalized according to the proportion provided above, subject, however, to the rule of practicability and feasibility, as stated. . . . In a general way it may be said that the receipts in the various States and Territories are not in proportion to their needs in irrigation construction. Nevada, Arizona, and Utah contain probably the largest proportion of arid area compared with their total extent, and the sales therein produce the smallest amounts for the reclamation fund. The general authority given to the Secretary of the Interior by this section will enable him to consider the needs of the various States without being too closely bound by the proportion in which the sales of lands therein contribute to the reclamation fund, and will thus enable the Department to take up some of the projects most urgently needed in those States without awaiting the collection of sufficient funds to cover the expense of construction. In doing this there can be no reason to doubt that a surplus so expended in a particular State or Territory will be promptly returned to the fund; consequently, at the end of ten years the equalization contemplated by this section will be brought about.

The provisions of section 9 divide the reclamation fund into two portions, one designated "the major portion," which is to be expended eventually in the States or Territories in which it originated, subject to the existence therein of feasible irrigation projects; and the other, the minor portion, without such restriction.

"The major portion," which, of course, may be defined as anything more than half, may be regarded as represented by 51 per cent, leaving 49 per cent of the fund without restriction. Thus analyzed into general and special portions, the amount available in the reclamation fund is as follows:

Analysis of reclamation fund for years 1901 and 1902

	1901, official.	1902, estimated.	Total.	Restricted, 51 per cent.	Unrestricted, 49 per cent.
Arizona	$42,586.16	$39,200	$81,786.16	$41,710.94	$40,075.22
California	205,030.40	298,600	503,630.40	256,851.50	246,778.90
Colorado	254,889.88	374,400	629,289.88	320,937.84	308,352.04
Idaho	206,645.36	301,700	508,345.36	259,256.13	249,089.23
Kansas	20,188.78	29,100	49,288.78	25,137.28	24,151.50
Montana	367,342.31	407,400	774,742.31	395,118.58	379,623.73
Nebraska	102,963.24	133,500	236,463.24	120,596.25	115,866.99
Nevada	9,183.47	14,600	23,783.47	12,129.57	11,653.90
New Mexico	75,203.06	72,100	147,303.06	75,124.56	72,178.50
North Dakota	449,474.96	780,600	1,230,074.96	627,338.23	602,736.73
Oklahoma	370,464.93	640,900	1,011,364.93	515,796.11	495,568.82
Oregon	364,988.62	547,400	912,388.62	465,318.20	447,070.42
South Dakota	113,274.20	194,500	307,774.20	156,964.84	150,809.36
Utah	98,416.00	48,200	146,616.00	74,774.16	71,841.84
Washington	257,180.95	541,500	798,680.95	407,327.28	391,353.67
Wyoming		176,300	383,289.59	195,477.69	187,811.90
Total	3,144,821.91	4,600,000	7,744,821.91	3,949,859.16	3,794,962.75

RULES AND REGULATIONS

Section 10 gives to the Secretary of the Interior the authority to make the necessary rules and regulations for carrying the provisions of the act into full force and effect. This important power will, it is assumed, be exercised from time to time as subjects for regulation come up for consideration.

ARIZONA

The reclamation of arid land in this Territory is dependent mainly upon the construction of large storage reservoirs. The irrigable lands are for the most part in the southern half of the Territory and within the drainage basin of Gila River and its principal tributary, Salt River. Irrigation has already been developed to such an extent that there is not sufficient water in ordinary seasons for the lands now under partial cultivation. It is urged by the citizens of the Territory that first attention should be given to providing an adequate supply of water for the small farms whose owners are now suffering for lack of water or who are on the point of moving away because of their inability to cultivate the lands. The situation in this respect, while not peculiar, is most extreme as regards the entire West, the fluctuations of flow of the rivers being most marked and the effect upon the population most disastrous.

[68]

ATTEMPTS TO COORDINATE
NATIONAL WATER POLICY

SPEECH BY REPRESENTATIVE FRANCIS G. NEWLANDS
ON WATER POLICY*
January 9, 1901

Francis G. Newlands is today best known as the author of the bill establishing the Reclamation Service, but no member of Congress has contributed more to the general knowledge of water development programs than this man who represented the relatively arid state of Nevada. This excerpt from a speech in the House of Representatives in 1901 illustrates how his views were developing on water policy at that time.

. . . What improvements are required in our rivers? In the first place the navigable rivers are subject to floods, and we seek to prevent the overflow by constructing levees. Immense sums have been expended on the lower part of the Mississippi in an effort to confine the stream and to prevent overflow of the adjoining land. Another character of improvement is the dredging of the rivers for the purpose of meeting the period of drought in the summer when the rivers are low and when bars and shallows obstruct navigation. The flow of the lower Mississippi is increased by the flow of the rivers tributary to it. Some of them, like the Ohio, taking their source in the humid regions, and others, like the Missouri, the Arkansas, and the Platte, taking their source in the arid regions from the snows of the mountain; and it is contended that by storing the flood waters in the mountains regions, caused by the rapid melting of the snows in the spring, a large proportion of the flood in the Missouri and the Mississippi rivers can be prevented and a more equal and sustained flow of the rivers thus promoted.

It should be remembered that the waters stored in these reservoirs are not the only waters which will be held back during the flood seasons. The character of all the mountain streams in the arid region is that they are torrential during April, May, and June, and that they are reduced to almost nothing in the follow-

The Public Papers of Francis G. Newlands, Vol. 1, Arthur B. Darling, ed. (Boston: Houghton Mifflin Co., 1932), 58–65.

ing months. Large areas of arid land lie within reach of these streams, but the condition of the flow during the hot months of July, August, and September limits the area of reclamation; for whilst the waters of the early spring and summer months is sufficient for the requirements of vast areas of land, yet, if the waters were diverted over them and crops were planted, they would lack water at the period of greatest want when the crops were ripening for harvest.

The storage of water above enables a larger utilization of the flood waters which are unstored, and storage insures a supply during the period of greatest drought. The result would be that for every acre-foot of flood water stored there would be four or five acre-feet of flood water taken out over the arid lands, thus diminishing the flow of the streams tributary to the Missouri and Mississippi during the torrential period, and these great plains, now arid, would themselves be made the storage reservoirs of vast quantities of flood waters which would otherwise rush down to the Mississippi, so that the effectual storage will not be confined simply to the artificial reservoirs, but will be extended to these large areas of land which will be reclaimed and which will absorb annually a volume of water at least two feet deep over the entire surface. The diversion and overflow of flood waters over the arid lands above would diminish the overflow in the lower Mississippi and would diminish the cost of the levees intended for protection of the adjoining lands. The water carried over the arid lands above would penetrate the soil and would seep gradually back to the rivers and keep the streams below fuller during the hot months than they would be had not this water been diverted or stored. . . .

We contend that, by the construction of storage reservoirs at the head waters of these rivers in the Rocky Mountains, a large proportion of the expenditures for levees on the lower Mississippi will be saved and that a more equal flow of the main river will be maintained, and thus the expense of dredging during the hot season will be greatly diminished. Navigation, like irrigation, requires that the streams should maintain an equal flow; that they should not be torrents at one season and attenuated threads at another.

The evils which attach to both navigation and irrigation are the same. The streams are overflowing at a time when the water is not needed and they are attenuated threads at a time when the water is most in demand. We of the arid regions contend that both navigation and irrigation can be promoted by the storing of these waters at the sources of these mountain streams which are tributary to the great navigable rivers.

We also contend, even assuming that the river and harbor bill should be confined to improvements essential to navigation, that the proper place for appropriations for storage reservoirs on the rivers tributary to our navigable rivers is in the river and harbor bill, as they tend to promote navigation, although having a very much larger value in the promotion of irrigation.

But all the rivers in the arid regions are not tributaries to navigable rivers.

Upon what theory, then, should the Government proceed to store water on such rivers? Our contention is that irrigation is a public use, just as navigation is; that it is subject to the control of the law, and that the Congress of the United States, under the "general welfare" clause of the Constitution, can do anything in the way of internal improvement that is calculated to promote the general welfare, and that the general welfare is promoted by maintaining an equal and sustained flow of a stream for irrigation as well as by maintaining it for navigation.

Besides this, the United States Government is the owner of 600,000,000 acres of land in the arid region, of which 100,000,000 acres can be reclaimed by a gradual process of storage extending over fifty or one hundred years. The reclamation of these lands will make more valuable the remaining pastoral lands, which are now used in common by all the stock-raising interests in the West. The Government undoubtedly has the power to look after its own property—to survey it, to mark it by section posts, and to put it in condition for settlement and sale; and if the maintenance of an equal flow in the rivers running through its lands is essential in order to enable its lands to be reclaimed by settlers, it can take such measures as it deems advisable for the purpose of making the waters available to settlers.

Large areas of lands along these rivers have already been taken up by settlers, and they have been able to solve the easy problems of irrigation, consisting simply in the diversion of the waters over the adjoining lands, but they are not able to control the torrential flow which has its source perhaps hundreds of miles away from those settlements, nor have they been able to store the water so as to maintain the supply during the hot season of July and August, when water is essential to the ripening of the crops. The limit of reclamation and settlement has been reached unless the Federal Government, acting, as it can, without regard to state lines, makes a scientific study of each river and its tributaries and so stores the water as to prevent the torrential flow in the spring and to increase the scanty flow in the summer. By doing this its arid lands will be made available for settlers, and it can, if it chooses, secure compensation by a charge upon the lands.

It is estimated that there are about 600,000,000 acres of arid public lands in the West, and of this about 100,000,000 acres can be reclaimed if storage is afforded. It is also estimated that the storage of water will cost from two dollars to ten dollars per acre-foot; the average probably would be about five dollars per acre-foot. The cheaper forms of storage would doubtless be attempted first, and the more expensive forms of storage would only be taken up years hence, when the pressure of population and the increased value of the lands would warrant the expenditure.

A convenient argument against the immediate prosecution of this work is that we have no estimate of its ultimate cost. Our answer is that if the Government had halted at the threshold of any great public work for inquiry as to what the prosecution of like work would cost within one hundred years, the estimate would probably have paralyzed the action of congressional bodies. For instance, when the first river and harbor bill was introduced, suppose some captious member of Congress had demanded a halt until it could be ascertained what the total cost over a period of one hundred years would be. I imagine that the statement, verified subsequently by events, that in one hundred years nearly $400,000,000 would be expended on the river and harbor bill would have staggered the imagination, and yet this amount has been expended and the country has not felt it.

It is impossible to forecast the future and state exactly what the storage in the arid regions will cost; but assuming that 100,000,000 acres of land are to be reclaimed; that this land on an average will require annually 200,000,000 acre-feet of water, and that at least four-fifths of this will be supplied by the flood stream, and that one-fifth will be supplied by the stored water, we will require within the next fifty or one hundred years a storage capacity equal to 40,000,000 acre-feet of water—that is to say, a storage equal to covering 40,000,000 acres one foot deep, or 1,000,000 acres forty feet deep. Assuming that the average cost of this would be five dollars per acre-foot, the total cost would be within a period of fifty or one hundred years about $200,000,000.

Expenditures of the settlers upon their lands would far exceed this; it would probably average from ten dollars to forty or fifty dollars per acre, dependent upon the cost of the main canals, the level or broken character of the ground, and the difficulty in leading out the water from the river. But one thing is assured, and that is that every acre of land reclaimed would be worth at least fifty dollars, and, as 100,000,000 acres are to be reclaimed, we would have a total increase in the wealth of the country in land alone, without improvements, of $5,000,000,000 by the expenditure upon the part of the Government of $200,-000,000, and we would have a country opened up for the surplus population of the East and the Middle Western states.

There are two ways of legislating upon this work. One is to pass annually a bill similar to the river and harbor bill, providing, first, for the construction of projects which have been surveyed, estimated, and reported favorably, and, second, making appropriations for surveys, estimates, and reports as to projects that are contemplated. Such appropriations would come out of the National Treasury and would be raised from general taxation, just as the appropriations in the river and harbor bill are.

Another method would be to fasten the cost of the government work of storage upon the public lands susceptible of reclamation. Such a plan would involve the creation of an arid-land reclamation fund in the Treasury, into which all moneys received from the sales of public lands in the arid and semi-arid states would go. The receipts from the sales of public lands last year amounted to about $3,000,000, and including commissions and fees, to $4,000,000. So the sum available for the first year would be about $4,000,000. Provision should be made for investigation, surveys, estimates, and reports by the Geological Survey of various projects, and upon approval of a project by the Secretary of the Interior he should be authorized to withdraw from entry the lands in the reservoir sites and to withdraw from entry, except under the homestead act, all land susceptible of irrigation by reason of such project. He should then be given power to contract for the work; no contract to be made unless the money is in the fund. When the project is completed, the total cost should be ascertained, and the price of the lands susceptible of irrigation and of the water rights attached thereto should be so fixed as to compensate the fund in ten annual installments, thus maintaining the perpetuity of the fund for progressive work.

If the report should show that lands already settled required stored water, power should be given the Secretary of the Interior to sell water rights to such settlers upon the same terms as to new settlers. Right of entry under the law should be limited to eighty acres, and the sale of the water right to existing settlers should be limited to an amount sufficient for eight acres; the purpose of this being not only to prevent the creation of monopoly in the lands now belonging to the Government, but to break up existing land monopoly in the West by making it to the interest of the owner of a large tract of land made more valuable by the possibility of securing stored water to divide up his land and sell to actual settlers. The bill should be so framed as to make its operation automatic, progressive, and complete, to guard against improvident projects, to prevent land monopoly, to secure homes for actual settlers, and to promote the division of the large tracts of land which, under the unfortunate administration of state and national laws, have been created in the West.

Under this plan the West would reclaim itself without calling upon the general taxpayers for a dollar.

It has been suggested that the cession of the arid lands to the states would produce the same results, and would relieve the Federal Government of a great work. My answer to this is that the Government has no right to abdicate the great trust imposed upon it by the ownership of 600,000,000 acres of land, upon which the homes of unborn millions are to be made. It cannot afford to intrust these lands either to the ignorance, the improvidence, or the dishonesty of local legislatures. The experience of all the Western states has been that the grants of land made by the Federal Government to the states for the purpose of education or local improvement have been maladministered and have resulted in the concentration of immense holdings of land in single ownership.

This country has today 70,000,000 of people; within one hundred years it will have 300,000,000 people. The pressure for land will be great. Imagine the discontent and disturbance which will result from an improvident administration of these great areas easily capable of supporting 100,000,000 people.

Besides this, the physical conditions are such as to prevent states from dealing with this question. The arid region must be considered as a unit, regardless of state lines. Each unit should be a main river and all its tributaries. The plains to be watered may be in one state; the sources of the river which is to water them, and the only available sites for reservoirs, may be in an adjoining state. No state can act outside of its own boundaries, nor can it clothe its citizens with sufficient power so to do.

The National Government, by reason of its national character, is alone capable of taking hold of this interstate question and solving it. Nor can this undertaking be intrusted to private or corporate enterprise. Storage enterprises are of such magnitude as to require immense capital. Their purpose is to bring about a union of the water with the land, and no corporation can successfully operate unless it has a grant of an immense area of land. This involves all the evils of land monopoly or subjects the enterprise to all the expenses connected with promotion, bond selling, and so forth. The speculative element must be entirely eliminated; the purpose is to create homes for the people, to make the waters of the West available for the reclamation of arid lands by actual settlers, and to eliminate entirely the speculator and the capitalist. . . .

Now, I ask, who should undertake this work? Who can undertake the work? The view of the people of the arid region is that this is a public work of internal improvement which ought to be undertaken by the Government of the United States. It resembles in character the old canals that were constructed years ago, or the interstate roads that were constructed by the general government, or those improvements that have been made for a number of years in dredging our rivers and improving our harbors—public improvements intended for the general welfare; improvements from which the Government does not expect a direct reimbursement, but simply the general advantage that comes to the entire country and the general welfare from the promotion of enterprises of this kind. And inasmuch as the rivers of the arid region as a rule are not navigable rivers, and the only public use to which we can put them is irrigation, not navigation, we claim that a fair and equitable distribution of the benefits of government requires that these streams should be maintained in equal flow by the system of reservoirs to which I have alluded.

But we also claim that this is not simply a governmental matter in the ordinary sense, but that the Government itself occupies the position of proprietor of the public lands of that vast region, and as proprietor, pursuing the usual obligations of land proprietors, it is its right and its duty to put these lands in condition for settlement. By so doing it can continue the traditional policy of the country, which has been to open up the public lands for settlement, restricting the number of acres to be granted to each individual, the purpose being to promote home-building amongst a free people. And these arid lands have particular advantages for that kind of settlement; for if you will only see to it that moisture is applied to them by these artificial methods, you have the most scientific system of agriculture that can be conceived. . . .

THE WATERWAYS COMMISSION BILL*
December 4, 1907

Newlands was elected to the Senate in 1902 and spent most of his three terms in the upper chamber working for a coordinated national water policy. His bill for a national waterways commission, adopting the recommendations made by Roosevelt's Inland Waterways Commission, was the primary vehicle for this effort.

Be it enacted . . . That a special fund shall be established in the Treasury, to be known as the "inland waterway fund," to be used in the examination and survey for and the development of the inland waterways of the country; and the sum of $50,000,000 is hereby reserved, set aside, and appropriated as such fund.

Sec. 2. That the President of the United States is hereby authorized to cause to be made examinations and surveys for the development of the inland waterways of the country, including the Great Lakes, the Mississippi River and its tributaries, the navigable rivers of the Gulf of Mexico and their tributaries, the navigable rivers of the Atlantic Coast and their tributaries, the navigable rivers of the Pacific Coast and their tributaries, and for the connection of such rivers with each other, wherever practicable and desirable, by connecting canals and by coastal canals, with a view to the promotion of transportation between such rivers by vessels of a standard draft; and to investigate all questions relating to the development and improvement of the inland waterways of the country, with a view to the promotion of transportation; and to consider and coördinate the questions of irrigation, swamp-land reclamation, clarification of streams, utilization of water power, prevention of soil waste, protection of forests, regulation of flow, control of floods, transfer facilities and sites and the regulation and control thereof, and such other questions regarding waterways as are related to the development of rivers, lakes, and canals for the purposes of commerce.

Sec. 3. That in order to enable the President to make such examinations, surveys, and investigations and to construct the works provided for by this act he is authorized to appoint an inland waterways commission, to be composed of _____ members, and to bring in coördination therewith the Corps of Engineers of the Army, the Bureau of Soils, the Forest Service, the Bureau of Corporations, the Reclamation Service, and other branches of the public service related to waterways, and to appoint such experts and other persons and create such board or boards in connection therewith as the work may require, and to fix the salaries of all commissioners, experts, and other persons employed under

The Public Papers of Francis G. Newlands, Vol. 2, Arthur B. Darling, ed. (Boston: Houghton Mifflin Co., 1932), 194–96.

this act until the same have been fixed by Congress, the official salary of any official appointed or employed under this act to be deducted from the amount of salary or compensation fixed under the terms of this act.

SEC. 4. That such commission shall make to the President annually, and at such other periods as may be required either by law or by the order of the President, full and complete reports of all their acts and doings and of all the moneys received and expended in the construction of works and in the performance of their duties in connection therewith, which reports shall be by the President transmitted to Congress; and such commission shall furthermore give to either house of Congress such information as may at any time be required either by act of Congress or by order of either house of Congress. . . .

SEC. 5. That if after such examination, survey, and estimate such commission shall determine that any project for the improvement or construction of an inland waterway or coastal waterway is practicable and desirable, it may, with the approval of the President and through the appropriate service, construct or execute, or cause to be let, contracts for the construction or execution of the same, in such portions or sections as it may be practicable to construct and execute as parts of the whole project: *Provided,* That the necessary moneys therefor are available in the inland waterway fund.

SEC. 6. That such projects may include such collateral works for the irrigation of arid lands, for the reclamation of swamp lands, for the conservation or replacement of forests, for the clarification of streams, and for the utilization of water power as may be deemed advisable in connection with the development of a channel for navigation or as aiding in a compensatory way in the diminution of the cost of such project.

SEC. 7. That such commission is authorized, with the approval of the President, to enter into coöperation with states, municipalities, communities, corporations, and individuals in such collateral works, and to make arrangements for the proportionate payment of the cost thereof out of the inland waterway fund and by the states, municipalities, communities, corporations, and individuals benefited thereby, in such manner as to secure an equitable distribution of the costs and benefits: *Provided,* That the cost of such collateral works shall be paid, if practicable, out of funds provided therefor by Congress, but if sufficient provision therefor is not specially made by Congress, such commission is authorized to pay for the same out of the inland waterway fund, but the total payments made on account of such collateral works from such inland waterway fund shall not exceed ten per cent thereof, and provision shall be made, as far as practicable, for the reimbursement to such fund of such payments by the states, municipalities, communities, corporations, or individuals benefited thereby: *And provided also,* That the inland waterways developed shall remain free for all the uses of navigation.

SEC. 8. That such commission shall make, with the approval of the President, rules and regulations governing the coöperation and compensation to the fund, wherever practicable, by the conveyance of reclamation rights, the lease of water power, and such other means as may be beneficial to the United States and the several states, municipalities, communities, corporations, and individuals entering into such coöperation.

SEC. 9. That in carrying out the provisions of this act regard must be had, as far as practicable, to the equitable apportionment and contemporaneous execution of the projects contemplated under this act among the several waterway systems of the country.

SEC. 10. That the President is authorized, whenever the inland waterway fund is reduced below $20,000,000 to make up the deficiency in such fund by the issue and sale of bonds in such amount and for such time as he shall deem advisable, bearing interest at a rate not exceeding _____ per cent per annum; but the amount of bonds issued shall not at any time exceed the difference between the cash on hand in such fund and $50,000,000.

LETTER FROM PRESIDENT ROOSEVELT ON WATERWAYS*
February 26, 1908

This is the letter President Roosevelt submitted to the Congress with the preliminary report of the National Waterways Commission, important for its emphasis upon coordinated, multipurpose development of the waterways.

To the Senate and House of Representatives:

I transmit herewith a preliminary report from the Inland Waterways Commission, which was appointed by me last March in response to a widespread interest and demand from the people. The basis of this demand lay in the general and admitted inability of the railroads to handle promptly the traffic of the country, and especially the crops of the previous fall.

This report is well worth your attention. It is thorough, conservative, sane, and just. It represents the mature judgment of a body of men exceptionally qualified, by personal experience and knowledge of conditions throughout the United States, to understand and discuss the great problem of how best to use our waterways in the interest of all the people. Unusual care has been taken to secure accuracy and balance of statement. If the report errs at all it is by over-conservatism. It contains findings or statements of fact, a number of specific recommendations, and an account of inquiries still in progress, and it is based in part on statistics and other information contained in a voluminous appendix. The subject with which it deals is of critical importance both to the present and the future of our country.

Our river systems are better adapted to the needs of the people than those of any other country. In extent, distribution, navigability, and ease of use, they stand first. Yet the rivers of no other civilized country are so poorly developed, so little used, or play so small a part in the industrial life of the nation as those of the United States. In view of the use made of rivers elsewhere, the failure to use our own is astonishing, and no thoughtful man can believe that it will last. The accompanying report indicates clearly the reasons for it and the way to end it.

The Commission finds that it was unregulated railroad competition which prevented or destroyed the development of commerce on our inland waterways. The Mississippi, our greatest natural highway, is a case in point. At one time the traffic upon it was without a rival in any country. The report shows that commerce was driven from the Mississippi by the railroads. While production was limited, the railways, with their convenient terminals, gave quicker and more satisfactory service than the waterways. Later they prevented the restora-

Sen. Doc. 325, 60th Cong., 1st sess., iii–vii.

tion of river traffic by keeping down their rates along the rivers, recouping themselves by higher charges elsewhere. They also acquired water fronts and terminals to an extent which made water competition impossible. Throughout the country the railways have secured such control of canals and steamboat lines that to-day inland waterway transportation is largely in their hands. This was natural and doubtless inevitable under the circumstances, but it should not be allowed to continue unless under careful Government regulation.

Comparatively little inland freight is carried by boat which is not carried a part of its journey by rail also. As the report shows, the successful development and use of our interstate waterways will require intelligent regulation of the relations between rail and water traffic. When this is done the railways and waterways will assist instead of injuring each other. Both will benefit, but the chief benefit will accrue to the people in general through quicker and cheaper transportation.

The report rests throughout on the fundamental conception that every waterway should be made to serve the people as largely and in as many different ways as possible. It is poor business to develop a river for navigation in such a way as to prevent its use for power, when by a little foresight it could be made to serve both purposes. We can not afford needlessly to sacrifice power to irrigation, or irrigation to domestic water supply, when by taking thought we may have all three. Every stream should be used to the utmost. No stream can be so used unless such use is planned for in advance. When such plans are made we shall find that, instead of interfering, one use can often be made to assist another. Each river system, from its headwaters in the forest to its mouth on the coast, is a single unit and should be treated as such. Navigation of the lower reaches of a stream can not be fully developed without the control of floods and low waters by storage and drainage. Navigable channels are directly concerned with the protection of source waters and with soil erosion, which takes the materials for bars and shoals from the richest portions of our farms. The uses of a stream for domestic and municipal water supply, for power, and in many cases for irrigation, must also be taken into full account.

The development of our inland waterways will have results far beyond the immediate gain to commerce. Deep channels along the Atlantic and Gulf coasts and from the Gulf to the Great Lakes will have high value for the national defense. The use of water power will measurably relieve the drain upon our diminishing supplies of coal, and transportation by water instead of rail only will tend to conserve our iron. Forest protection, without which river improvement can not be permanent, will at the same time help to postpone the threatened timber famine, and will secure us against a total dearth of timber by providing for the perpetuation of the remaining woodlands. Irrigation will create the means of livelihood for millions of people, and supplies of pure water will powerfully promote the public health. If the policy of waterway improvement here recom-

[79]

mended is carried out, it will affect for good every citizen of the Republic. The National Government must play the leading part in securing the largest possible use of our waterways; other agencies can assist and should assist, but the work is essentially national in its scope.

The various uses of waterways are now dealt with by Bureaus scattered through four Federal Departments. At present, therefore, it is not possible to deal with a river system as a single problem. But the Commission here recommends a policy under which all the commercial and industrial uses of the waterways may be developed at the same time. To that end, Congress should provide some administrative machinery for coordinating the work of the various Departments so far as it relates to waterways. Otherwise there will not only be delay, but the people as a whole will fail to get from our streams the benefits to which they are justly entitled.

The Commission recognizes that the cost of improving our inland waterways will be large, but far less than would be required to relieve the congestion of traffic by railway extension. The benefits of such improvement will be large also, and they will touch the daily life of our people at every point, uniting the interests of all the States and sections of our country. The cost and the benefits should be equitably distributed, by cooperation with the States and the communities, corporations, and individuals beneficially affected. I heartily concur in the Commission's recommendation to this end. Such cooperation should result in united effort in carrying out the great duty of improving our inland waterways. While we delay our rivers remain unused, our traffic is periodically congested, and the material wealth and natural resources of the country related to waterways are being steadily absorbed by great monopolies.

Among these monopolies, as the report of the Commission points out, there is no other which threatens, or has ever threatened, such intolerable interference with the daily life of the people as the consolidation of companies controlling water power. I call your special attention to the attempt of the power corporations, through bills introduced at the present session, to escape from the possibility of Government regulation in the interests of the people. These bills are intended to enable the corporations to take possession in perpetuity of national forest lands for the purposes of their business, where and as they please, wholly without compensation to the public. Yet the effect of granting such privileges, taken together with rights already acquired under State laws, would be to give away properties of enormous value. Through lack of foresight we have formed the habit of granting without compensation extremely valuable rights amounting to monopolies on navigable streams and on the public domain. The repurchase at great expense of water rights thus carelessly given away without return has already begun in the East, and before long will be necessary in the West also. No rights involving water power should be granted to any corporations in perpetuity, but only for a length of time sufficient to allow them to conduct their business profitably. A reasonable charge should of course be made for valuable rights and privileges which they obtain from the National Government. The values for which this charge is made will ultimately, through the natural growth and orderly development of our population and industries, reach enormous amounts. A fair share of the increase should be safeguarded for the benefit of the people, from whose labor it springs. The proceeds thus secured, after the cost of administration and improvement has been met, should naturally be devoted to the development of our inland waterways.

The report justly calls attention to the fact that hitherto our national policy has been one of almost unrestricted disposition and waste of natural resources, and emphasizes the fundamental necessity for conserving these resources upon which our present and future success as a nation primarily rests. Running water is a most valuable natural asset of the people, and there is urgent need for conserving it for navigation, for power, for irrigation, and for domestic and municipal supply.

The Commission was appointed to obtain information concerning our waterways as related to the general welfare. Much work was done, but more remains to be done before a plan for their development can be prepared in detail. We need additional information on the flow of our streams, the condition of channels, the amount and cost of water traffic, the requirements for terminals, the area in each watershed which should be kept under forest, and the means of preventing soil waste and the consequent damage to our rivers. But it is neither necessary nor desirable to postpone the beginning of the work until all the facts are obtained. We have suffered heavily in the past from the lack of adequate transportation facilities, and unless a beginning is made promptly we shall suffer still more heavily in the future.

Being without funds or an expert staff, the Commission has confined itself to principles affecting the whole problem and the entire country. Its report is a plea, in the light of actual facts, for simplicity and directness in dealing with the great problem of our inland waterways in the interest of the people. It submits no specific plans or recommendations concerning even the most important projects. The first of these of course concerns the Mississippi and its tributaries, whose commercial development will directly affect half our people. The Mississippi should be made a loop of the sea and work upon it should be begun at the earliest possible moment. Only less important is the Atlantic inner passage, parts of which are already under way. The inner passages along the Gulf coast should be extended and connected with the Atlantic waters. The need for the developing of the Pacific coast rivers is not less pressing. Our people are united in support of the immediate adoption of a progressive policy of inland waterway development.

Hitherto our national policy of inland waterway development has been largely negative. No single agency has been responsible under the Congress for making

[81]

the best use of our rivers, or for exercising foresight in their development. In the absence of a comprehensive plan, the only safe policy was one of repression and procrastination. Frequent changes of plan and piecemeal execution of projects have still further hampered improvement. A channel is no deeper than its shallowest reach, and to improve a river short of the point of effective navigability is a sheer waste of all it costs. In spite of large appropriations for their improvement, our rivers are less serviceable for interstate commerce to-day than they were half a century ago and in spite of the vast increase in our population and commerce they are on the whole less used.

The first condition of successful development of our waterways is a definite and progressive policy. The second is a concrete general plan, prepared by the best experts available, covering every use to which our streams can be put. We shall not succeed until the responsibility for administering the policy and executing and extending the plan is definitely laid on one man or group of men who can be held accountable. Every portion of the general plan should consider and so far as practical secure to the people the use of water for power, irrigation, and domestic supply as well as for navigation. No project should be begun until the funds necessary to complete it promptly are provided, and no plan once under way should be changed except for grave reasons. Work once begun should be prosecuted steadily and vigorously to completion. We must make sure that projects are not undertaken except for sound business reasons, and that the best modern business methods are applied in executing them. The decision to undertake any project should rest on actual need ascertained by investigation and judgment of experts and on its relation to great river systems or to the general plan, and never on mere clamor.

The improvement of our inland waterways can and should be made to pay for itself so far as practicable from the incidental proceeds from water power and other uses. Navigation should of course be free. But the greatest return will come from the increased commerce, growth, and prosperity of our people. For this we have already waited too long. Adequate funds should be provided, by bond issue, if necessary, and the work should be delayed no longer. The development of our waterways and the conservation of our forests are the two most pressing physical needs of the country. They are interdependent, and they should be met vigorously, together, and at once. The questions of organization, powers, and appropriations are now before the Congress. There is urgent need for prompt and decisive action.

Theodore Roosevelt

The White House
February 26, 1908

REPORT FROM THE INLAND WATERWAYS COMMISSION*
February 26, 1908

This preliminary report of the Inland Waterways Commission was the only formal report which it presented. It represents the first effort to coordinate waterways planning and development by the Federal Government and to set a national policy for multipurpose development.

Despite the approval of the report by the congressional leaders who were members of the commission, the refusal to sign by General Alexander Mac-Kenzie, the Chief of Engineers, was indicative of the opposition to the coordinated program.

PROCEEDINGS

After conference and correspondence between the chairman and other Commissioners, a meeting for organization was held in the United States Capitol beginning April 29 and ending May 3. A second meeting and inspection trip on the Mississippi from St. Louis to the Passes took place May 13 to May 23. A third meeting and inspection trip, first on the Great Lakes from Cleveland to Duluth, next on the Mississippi from St. Paul to Memphis, and then on the Missouri from Kansas City to St. Louis, took place September 21 to October 13. A fourth meeting was held in the United States Capitol beginning on November 25, 1907, for the purpose of preparing a preliminary report; it ended February 3, 1908.

At the first session of the meeting for organization (on April 29), the Commission expressed concurrence in the designation by the President of Mr. Burton as chairman; and by viva voce votes Senator Newlands and Mr. McGee were elected vice-chairman and secretary, respectively.

During the organization and two inspecting meetings, 30 formal sessions were held in addition to informal meetings and conferences. At several of these sessions the entire Commission were present; at no session were there fewer than five Commissioners; the average attendance was over 7. During the meeting for the preparation of this report there were 27 sessions, with an average attendance of 7.

While provision was not made for formal hearings, experts on matters entrusted to the Commission were present by invitation at 24 sessions; of these experts there were 24 (of whom several attended two or more sessions), a majority being now or formerly attachés of the Corps of Engineers, United States Army.

In addition to the formal sessions, the Commissioners devoted much time to

*Sen. Doc. 325, 60th Cong., 1st sess., 17–27, 30–31.

the consideration of the waterways and related matters; two or three Commissioners jointly inspected the upper Missouri, the Columbia and Snake, the Sacramento and San Joaquin, and their leading tributaries; several employed agencies under their direction in collating and digesting data relating to canals, water transportation, etc.; and most of the Commissioners attended conventions and other meetings connected with the development of waterways and related interests.

A journal was kept, including brief minutes of the sessions and itineraries of inspection trips, with stenographic reports of the statements and deliberations of the second and third meetings; and in addition correspondence was conducted and a number of useful manuscript and printed statements were brought together and used in the deliberations of the Commission.

At the eighteenth session a special committee of one was appointed to prepare a list of statutes, etc., relating to water power. Pursuant to action at the twenty-third session (the President of the United States presiding) a letter requesting a conference on the conservation of natural resources was framed and presented to the President on October 4; and at the twenty-fifth session a committee of three was appointed to communicate further with the President on this matter, and also to prepare a preliminary draft of report. The former committee prepared an exhaustive digest of statutes, and the latter held a number of sessions; both committees reported at the fourth meeting.

RESULTS

The investigations and discussions have resulted in certain statements of fact connected with navigation and other uses of the inland waterways set forth hereinafter as *Findings,* with certain conclusions set forth as *Recommendations,* and also certain matters still under discussion which are set forth as *Inquiries in progress.*

The Commission is fully aware that its creation was due to a demand of the people, and that there exists an expectation in certain localities that the report here presented will include plans extending in detail to the principal waterways of the country. To prepare and consider such plans would require extended study at large expense by engineers and other experts whose services were not available. Under the instructions from the President, and in the absence of funds and of the men and time required for such study, the Commission was necessarily confined in preparing this preliminary report to the more general features of "a comprehensive plan designed for the benefit of the entire country," viz, a statement of principles and an outline of policy, coupled with recommendations which, if adopted, will insure the continuation of the work and the practical application of the principles and policy.

FINDINGS

1. The possibilities of inland navigation are indicated by the fact that there are in mainland United States some 25,000 miles of navigated rivers and at least an equal amount which are navigable or might be made so by improvement; there are also some 2,500 miles of navigable canals, and over 2,500 miles of sounds, bays, and bayous readily connectable by canals aggregating less than 1,000 miles in length to form inner passages paralleling the Atlantic and Gulf coasts—these being additional to some thousands of miles (reckoned between leading ports) of regularly navigated waters in lakes and land-locked bays. These waterways lie in or along the borders of Alabama, Arkansas, California, Connecticut, Delaware, Florida, Georgia, Idaho, Illinois, Indiana, Iowa, Kansas, Kentucky, Louisiana, Maine, Maryland, Massachusetts, Michigan, Minnesota, Mississippi, Missouri, Montana, Nebraska, New Hampshire, New Jersey, New York, North Carolina, North Dakota, Ohio, Oklahoma, Oregon, Pennsylvania, Rhode Island, South Carolina, South Dakota, Tennessee, Texas, Vermont, Virginia, Washington, West Virginia, and Wisconsin, i. e., 42 States; while the development of rivers for irrigation, power, and other purposes will also render navigable certain waterways in Arizona, Colorado, Nevada, New Mexico, Utah, and Wyoming. Although it is not probable that any considerable share of this vast mileage of navigable waterways will be improved to a high standard of efficiency at least at an early date, yet the assured growth of the country and the capacity of these waters not only for navigation but for other uses render imperative the necessity for their control and utilization as an asset of almost unlimited value. It is desirable that these waterways, of which portions have been surveyed or improved for purposes of navigation, should be further investigated with a view to the systematic development of interstate commerce in coordination with all other uses of the waters and benefits to be derived from them.

2. While the railways of mainland United States have been notably efficient in extending and promoting the production and commerce of the country, it is clear that at seasons recurring with increasing frequency they are unable to keep pace with production or to meet the requirements of transportation.

3. While navigation of the inland waterways declined with the increase in rail transportation during the later decades of the past century, it has become clear that the time is at hand for restoring and developing such inland navigation and water transportation as upon expert examination may appear to confer a benefit commensurate with the cost, to be utilized both independently and as a necessary adjunct to rail transportation.

4. While the decline of navigation in the inland waterways was largely due to the natural growth and legitimate competition attending railway extension,

it is also clear that railway interests have been successfully directed against the normal maintenance and development of water traffic by control of water-fronts and terminals, by acquisition or control of competing canals and vessels, by discriminating tariffs, by rebates, by adverse placement of tracks and structures, and by other means.

5. Any complete or practically successful plan for the general improvement of waterways must eventually provide for satisfactory adjustment of the relation of rail lines to such waterways. Since present and prospective railways reach all parts of the country while navigable waterways are confined to certain natural lines, it is clear that railways can so control transportation as to leave the waterways insufficient traffic to support the requisite vessels and terminals. The railways have accordingly, save in certain exceptional cases, substantially absorbed the traffic of the country, and unless the present unrestricted and short-sighted competition between the two systems is intelligently adjusted they will continue to do so. So large a portion of railway traffic is free from water competition that railways can readily afford to so reduce rates on those portions affected by such competition as to destroy the profits of the water lines without appreciably affecting the profits of the rail systems which recoup these reductions by higher rates elsewhere. This has been the case with most of the great inland waterways, excepting the Great Lakes where the conditions of water and traffic approach those of open seas. In spite of the great increase of traffic and the continued improvement of waterways, the total river traffic of the country has steadily decreased both proportionately and absolutely, with the result that few rivers are used to anything approaching their full capacity. It will not relieve traffic congestion to improve our waterways unless the improved waterways are used; hence it is obvious that relief from the existing congestion by waterway improvement can be made permanently effective only through such coordination of rail and water facilities as will insure harmonious cooperation rather than injurious opposition.

6. Existing data as to the nature and amount of the internal commerce of the country are extremely meager and incomplete. Such information is essential to the intelligent treatment of the inland waterways, and it is desirable that means be employed to obtain it.

7. Improvements of navigation in inland waterways in the main affect favorably the purity of the waters and the regularity of the supply, and these objects should be carefully kept in mind. The increasing pollution of streams by soil wash and other waste substances connected with a growing population reduces the value of the water for manufacturing purposes, and renders the water supply for communities injurious to and often destructive of human life. The prevention of these evils should be considered in any scheme of inland waterway improvement.

8. Engineering works designed to improve navigation affect favorably the regimen of the streams, including floods and low waters. The annual floods of the United States occasion loss of property reaching many millions of dollars with considerable loss of life, while the low water of late summer involves large loss in diminished water supply, in reduced power, and in the fouling of streams with consequent disease and death. It has been claimed that in specific cases the cost of works required both to control floods and meet the needs of commerce would be less than the amount of this loss. It is desirable that more detailed information be collected concerning the effects of floods and low waters and their prevention by engineering works and other devices.

9. The annual soil wash in mainland United States is estimated at about 1,000,000,000 tons, of which the greater part is the most valuable portion of the soil; it is carried into the rivers where it pollutes the waters, necessitates frequent and costly dredging, and reduces the efficiency of works designed to facilitate navigation and afford protection from floods. The direct and indirect losses from this source have not been measured, but are exceedingly large; and it is desirable that definite determinations be made with the view of devising means for reducing the loss to the land and preventing the impairment of the streams for purposes of commerce.

10. Both the regimen of streams and the purity and clarity of waters are affected by forests and other natural growth, and by farming, mining, and other industrial operations over the watersheds in which they gather. Millions of acres in mainland United States have been deforested unnecessarily, and the floods and low waters ascribed to this cause have in some localities occasioned losses commensurate with the value of the timber. Means should be devised and applied for coordinating forestry, farming, mining, and related industries with the uses of streams for commerce and for other purposes.

11. The effect of wide variations in the level of navigable streams is to render difficult the establishment of necessary terminals for the handling of traffic, and thus to interfere seriously with the utilization of our inland waterways. The prevention or mitigation of such variations would be most helpful to the revival of river traffic, and means to this end should be adopted in plans for waterway improvement.

12. The storage of flood waters combined with the diversion of streams to arid and semiarid lands for purposes of reclamation by irrigation creates canals and also tends to clarify the waters and increase the seepage or return waters during times of drought. There have already been put under irrigation over 10,000,000 acres of fertile land, adding a quarter of a million homes and several hundred million dollars of taxable wealth; and it is estimated that by fully conserving the waters and by utilizing the water power developed in connection with storage and other works, fully three times as much land can be reclaimed in the western

[87]

half of the United States. It is desirable to continue the collection of data with a view to so adjusting irrigation and power development with navigation and other uses of the streams as to secure the highest value of the water to the greatest number of people.

13. Locks and certain other works designed to improve navigation commonly produce head and store water in such manner as to develop power available for industrial purposes, while works designed to develop power on navigable and source streams affect the navigation and other uses of river systems; and these uses must necessarily be considered together. Information concerning water power in the several States and sections is incomplete, yet it is known to be a vast and intrinsically permanent asset which should be utilized for the benefit of the people of the country, in whose interests it should be administered with careful regard for present and prospective conditions. The facts ascertained in certain specific cases furnish a basis for the claim that the value of the power would pay the cost of all engineering and other works required in such cases to control the streams for navigation and other uses. In the light of recent progress in electrical application, it is clear that over wide areas the appropriation of water power offers an unequaled opportunity for monopolistic control of industries. Wherever water is now or will hereafter become the chief source of power, the monopolization of electricity produced from running streams involves monopoly of power for the transportation of freight and passengers, for manufacturing, and for supplying light, heat, and other domestic, agricultural, and municipal necessities, to such an extent that unless regulated it will entail monopolistic control of the daily life of our people in an unprecedented degree. There is here presented an urgent need for prompt and vigorous action by State and Federal governments.

14. Any comprehensive system of improvement of inland waterways will necessarily affect the drainage or reclamation of swamp and overflow lands, which are mainly rich alluvial tracts largely along or near waterways. The construction of dikes and levees or bank-protective works and the deepening of channels are often closely connected with means of control both of overflow and of underflow by drainage. It is estimated that there are 77,000,000 acres of such land, now unproductive, but which with drainage and protection from overflow will have an exceptionally high agricultural value; if divided into 40-acre farms these lands will furnish homes for some 10,000,000 people.

15. The control of waterways on which successful navigation depends is so intimately connected with the prevention of floods and low waters, and works designed for these purposes; with the protection and reclamation of overflow lands, and works designed therefor; with the safeguarding of banks and maintenance of channels, and works employed therein; with the purification and clarification of water supply, and works designed therefor in conjunction with interstate commerce; with control and utilization of power developed in

connection with works for the improvement of navigation; with the standardizing of methods and facilities and the coordinating of waterway and railway instrumentalities; and throughout the larger area of the country with reclamation by irrigation and drainage, and works designed primarily for these purposes—that local and special questions concerning the control of waterways should be treated as a general question of national extent, while local or special projects should be considered as parts of a comprehensive policy of waterway control in the interests of all the people.

16. Governmental agencies whose work is related to the use and control of streams are now in existence in the Federal Departments of War, Interior, Agriculture, and Commerce and Labor; and it is desirable in order to prevent duplication of work and function and to avoid unnecessary delays in the development of the inland waterways that means should be provided for coordinating all such agencies.

17. While precise figures are not now obtainable, it is safe to say that the current value of our inland transportation facilities (of which railways form all but a small percentage) exceeds one-eighth of our national wealth; yet these facilities are so far inadequate that production is impaired and the growth of the country is retarded. While trustworthy estimates can not be made without further data, it is reasonable to anticipate that congestion of interstate commerce can be obviated in large measure by judicious improvement of waterways adapted to barge and boat traffic, at a figure much less than that estimated by competent authorities for so increasing railway facilities as to meet present needs. It is desirable that additional data be obtained by requisite expert investigation.

18. It is conservative to estimate that judicious improvement of the waterways of the country will confer direct benefits through increased transportation facilities which will exceed the cost, while the collateral benefits will be at least comparable with the gain to commerce. Under a coordinated plan, such collateral benefits as the enhanced value of lands reclaimed by irrigation and drainage, the value of water power developed, the increased values due to the prevention of floods and low waters, and the great benefits of purified and clarified water, will more than balance the cost of the works.

19. In a comprehensive system of waterway improvement and control designed to meet present and future needs, the practicability of any project will depend not alone on local and general demands of commerce, but measurably on attendant natural and industrial conditions, including nature of banks and bed, suitability of the ground as a foundation for works, volume of water and liability to floods and low stages, configuration of the watershed and its susceptibility to control by judicious agriculture and forestry or by reservoirs and other means, local and general demand for pure water supply, amount and value of available water power incident to the works, proximity and cost of structural

materials, relations to existing and prospective projects on the same and neighboring waterways, and all other physical and economic factors entering into or tending to counterbalance the cost; and the local surveys or plans for any project should take account of all such natural and industrial conditions and be adapted to the attainment of maximum benefits at the minimum cost.

20. Existing data concerning the volume, regimen, and other physical features of most streams are meager and imperfect. Since plans for improving and controlling the waterways and utilizing the waters must rest on these facts, it is desirable that means be employed to extend and perfect physical data relating to the navigable and source streams of the country.

21. The benefits of a comprehensive system of waterway improvement will extend to all the people in the several sections and States of the country; and the means employed should be devised so far as possible to distribute the cost equitably through cooperation between Federal agencies, States, municipalities, communities, corporations, and individuals.

22. In order to improve the inland waterways for navigation and at the same time coordinate the agencies and means of transportation, develop the collateral benefits of waterway improvement, adapt all natural and industrial conditions related with waterways to the attainment of maximum benefits at the minimum cost, and perfect means for distributing the cost equitably between Federal agencies, States, municipalities, communities, corporations, and individuals in a prompt and efficient and economical manner, it is desirable to maintain an administrative agency with large powers for the investigation and elaboration of projects under suitable legislative regulation.

23. The immediate use of natural resources in the rapid development of the country are often allowed to stand in the way of more beneficient and permanent utilization. This is especially true of all resources connected with running waters, the substantial value of which has not been adequately appreciated. It is clearly practicable, without undue expense or interference with current use, to carry out broad plans for the complete development of the resources of the country, and thus assure to the greatest number of people the greatest good for both the present and the future; while if this is not done the temporary or partial development of these resources will prevent their full utilization for the general benefit. Steps should be taken without delay to outline and initiate the more pressing projects of conservation, and to apply practically the principle of conservation before it is too late.

24. Our unsurpassed natural wealth and the eagerness of our people for immediate results regardless of future needs have led to a policy of extravagant consumption of national resources and to an encouragement of monopoly, whereby an excessive share of such resources has been diverted to the enrichment of the few rather than preserved for the equitable benefit of the many. Monopolistic tendencies have appeared (a) in the extensive control of mineral fuels on

public lands, whereby large values essential to the development of the country have passed beyond public regulation; (*b*) in the acquisition and needless destruction of forests, whose preservation is a public necessity for stream control, for timber supply, and for other purposes; (*c*) in the acquisition of controlling sites on waterways and the appropriation of valuable waterpowers with their segregation from public use without adequate compensation, whereby indispensable utilities escape public regulation in the interests of the people; (*d*) in the segregation of lands, especially in the semiarid regions, whereby development is retarded so that the lands remain without benefit to commerce or advantage to the growth of the country; (*e*) in the control of products and of transportation to disturb the normal values and natural channels of trade, thereby imposing undue burdens on producers and consumers; and (*f*) in various interferences with the production and commerce of the country, whereby prosperity is curtailed and progress impeded. While such monopolistic tendencies have been conspicuous in connection with the agencies of transportation, they are now in many cases opposing the best utilization of streams by diverting their control from State and Federal jurisdiction in the public interests to personal and corporate means of excessive and burdensome profit. Since transportation is a primary factor in the existence and development of any people, and is increasingly important with the growth of population, it is essential that its means should be regulated in the public interests; and any plans for relieving congestion of transportation in the United States should be so framed as to employ all proper State, Federal, and municipal agencies in protecting from monopolistic control not only the agencies and avenues but also the materials of interstate commerce.

RECOMMENDATIONS

A. We recommend that hereafter plans for the improvement of navigation in inland waterways, or for any use of these waterways in connection with interstate commerce, shall take account of the purification of the waters, the development of power, the control of floods, the reclamation of lands by irrigation and drainage, and all other uses of the waters or benefits to be derived from their control.

B. We recommend that hereafter both local and general benefits to the people shall be fully considered in any such plans for the improvement of navigation in inland waterways, or for any use of these waterways in connection with interstate commerce; and that whereever practicable Federal agencies shall cooperate with States, municipalities, communities, corporations, and individuals with a view to an equitable distribution of costs and benefits.

C. We recommend that hereafter any plans for the navigation or other use of inland waterways in connection with interstate commerce shall take full account of transfer facilities and sites, and of the location of tracks, grades, bridges, dams, depots, and other works on navigable and source streams with a view to equitable cooperation between waterway and railway facilities for the promotion of commerce and the benefit of the people.

D. We recommend that any plans for improving the inland waterways shall take account of the present and prospective relation of rail lines to such waterways, and shall ascertain so far as may be whether such waterways when improved will be effectively used in the face of railway competition; and that the relations between railways and waterways be further examined with the purpose of devising means of rendering the two systems complementary and harmonious and making such fair division of traffic that rates and management may be coordinated economically and with benefit to the country.

E. We recommend the adoption of means for ascertaining regularly all facts related to traffic on the inland waterways, and for publishing the same in a form suitable for general use.

F. We recommend the adoption of means for ascertaining and rendering available, at such rate as to meet public necessities, all requisite data related to the physical character and general utility of the navigable and source streams of the country.

G. We recommend that hereafter any plans for the use of inland waterways in connection with interstate commerce shall regard the streams of the country as an asset of the people, shall take full account of the conservation of all resources connected with running waters, and shall look to the protection of these resources from monopoly and to their administration in the interests of the people.

H. We recommend that the Congress be asked to make suitable provision for improving the inland waterways of the United States at a rate commensurate with the needs of the people as determined by competent authority; and we suggest that such provision meet these requisites, viz: expert framing of a definite policy; certainty of continuity and coordination of plan and work; expert initiative in the choice of projects and the succession of works; freedom in selection of projects in accordance with terms of cooperation; and the widest opportunity for applying modern business methods.

I. We recommend that the Congress be asked to authorize the coordination and proper development of existing public services connected with waterways; and we suggest that such enactment might provide that the President of the United States be authorized, with the advice and consent of the Senate, to appoint and organize a National Waterways Commission to bring into coordination the Corps of Engineers of the Army, the Bureau of Soils, the Forest Service, the Bureau of Corporations, the Reclamation Service, and other branches of the public service in so far as their work relates to inland waterways, and that he be authorized to make such details and require such duties from these branches of the public service in connection with navigable and source streams as are not inconsistent with law; *the said Commission* to continue the investigation of all questions relating to the development and improvement and utilization of the inland waterways of the country and the conservation of its natural resources related thereto, and *to consider and* coordinate therewith all matters of irrigation, swamp and overflow land reclamation, clarification and purification of streams, prevention of soil waste, utilization of *water power,* preservation and extension of forests, regulation of flow and control of floods, transfer facilities and sites and the regulation and control thereof, and the relations between waterways and railways; and that the Commission be empowered to frame and recommend plans for developing the waterways and utilizing the waters, and as authorized by Congress to carry out the same, through established agencies when such are available, in cooperation with States, municipalities, communities, corporations, and individuals, in such manner as to secure an equitable distribution of costs and benefits.

* * *

SUPPLEMENTARY REPORT OF COMMISSIONER GENERAL ALEXANDER MACKENZIE

1. As a member of the Inland Waterways Commission, I am in accord with the general principles enunciated as proper for consideration in connection with the preparation of plans for improvement and control of inland waterways; and with recommendations which advise suitable provision for continuing the improvement of inland waterways at a rate commensurate with the requirements of commerce; and, so far as justifiable, with cooperation between Federal agencies and States, municipalities, and communities with a view to a distribution of costs and benefits; and I am in accord with a suggestion that in carrying out of examinations and surveys and in the making of plans of improvement of inland waterways, such consideration be given by the War Department to the subject of water power, floods and low water, drainage, and such other related subjects as may have a bearing upon the improvement of navigation and such as Congress, in its wisdom, may provide for.

2. I am in the fullest accord with recommendations looking to the protection to the greatest extent of the natural resources of the country, both in their relation to the interests of navigation and in the interest of multiplying prosperous homes; and I am in accord with the thought of utilizing such resources in every legal and proper way with a view to recompensing the Government for expenditures made in carrying out improvements.

3. I am not fully in accord, however, with the thought that all the related subjects mentioned, important and worthy of consideration by the Government as they may be, are as clearly and necessarily associated with the subject of channel improvement and interstate commerce as is assumed in the report, or that such assumptions can properly be made in all cases without further investigation, including, possibly, some legal questions.

4. I am in accord with the desire of this Commission to continue its inves-

tigations and discussions with a view to further consideration of interior-water-way improvements after consultation with transportation experts, and a more detailed consideration of the conservation of natural resources and coordination between the General Government and States after the conference on conservation to be held in May.

5. I can not, however, agree with the recommendation for the establishment at this time of a permanent inland-waterways commission, vested with the authority indicated, in addition to or as a substitute for the existing Commission. Until this Commission shall have fully carried out the duties allotted to it and prepared a comprehensive plan for the improvement and control of the river systems of the United States, or at least until such work is more advanced and results more thoroughly considered, I believe a recommendation for so radical a departure in the methods of planning and executing the improvement of waterways as that proposed is at least premature.

6. Moreover, it is my belief that further investigation will demonstrate that when this Commission shall have completed its labors all necessary cooperation can be secured, and all work proposed for the permanent commission can be equally well provided for by the existing agencies of the Government, and that through such agencies, without the interposition of a permanent commission, improvement of waterways and attention to allied subjects will be more promptly accomplished. While fully appreciating the importance of having general principles and schemes considered and recommended by a commission, as is now being done and as will continue to be done, I have grave fear that the scheme of operations recommended in connection with the proposed permanent commission would be found to be impracticable.

A. Mackenzie
Brigadier-General, Chief of Engineers

SUPPLEMENTARY REPORT OF COMMISSIONER SENATOR FRANCIS G. NEWLANDS

I concur in the report of the Commission, but desire to emphasize my belief that it is of the highest importance that in dealing with subjects relating to the respective powers, rights, and interests of the Nation, States, municipalities, corporations, and individuals, large powers and a comparatively free hand should be given to an administrative body of experts in the full development of projects, lest the complexity of the transactions, the time necessary to secure Congressional approval, and difference of view as to purpose or method, may result in indecision and delay, the worst enemies of effective development.

REPORT FROM THE NATIONAL CONSERVATION COMMISSION*
December 7, 1908

After Newlands' bill to establish a permanent Inland Waterways Commission was stalled in the Congress, Roosevelt called a Governors' Conference on Conservation. The governors proposed that Congress authorize a national conservation inventory. When Congress failed to act immediately on this proposal, Roosevelt appointed a National Conservation Commission to report on waters, forests, lands, and minerals. Gifford Pinchot was named general chairman of the commission, with various congressmen designated to head the four subject committees. However, experts, such as W J McGee on waters, were named secretaries for each section and did the actual work of the report.

Congress refused to appropriate funds for the commission, and Roosevelt's friends in the Senate had considerable difficulty in even getting the report printed.

The duty of man to man, on which the integrity of nations must rest, is no higher than the duty of each generation to the next; and the obligation of the nation to each actual citizen is no more sacred than the obligation to the citizen to be, who, in turn, must bear the nation's duties and responsibilities.

In this country, blessed with natural resources in unsurpassed profusion, the sense of responsibility to the future has been slow to awaken. Beginning without appreciation of the measure or the value of natural resources other than land with water for commercial uses, our forefathers pushed into the wilderness and, through a spirit of enterprise which is the glory of the nation, developed other great resources. Forests were cleared away as obstacles to the use of the land; iron and coal were discovered and developed, though for years their presence added nothing to the price of the land; and through the use of native woods and metals and fuels, manufacturing grew beyond all precedent, and the country became a power among the nations of the world.

Gradually the timber growing on the ground and the iron and coal within the ground came to have a market value and were bought and sold as sources of wealth. Meanwhile, vast holdings of these resources were acquired by those of greater foresight than their neighbors before it was generally realized that they possessed value in themselves; and in this way large interests, assuming monopolistic proportions, grew up, with greater enrichment to their holders than the world had seen before, and with the motive of immediate profit, with no concern for the future or thought of the permanent benefit of country and people, a wasteful and profligate use of the resources began and has continued.

*Sen. Doc. 676, 60th Cong., 2nd sess., 13–26.

[95]

The waters, at first recognized only as aids to commerce in supplying transportation routes, were largely neglected. In time this neglect began to be noticed, and along with it the destruction and approaching exhaustion of the forests. This, in turn, directed attention to the rapid depletion of the coal and iron deposits and the misuse of the land.

The public conscience became awakened. Seeing the increased value and noting the destructive consumption and waste of the natural resources, men began to realize that the permanent welfare of the country as well as the prosperity of their offspring were at stake.

The newly awakened sense of duty found expression in a call by the President upon the governors of the States to meet him in conference, and in the declaration of this conference at its sessions in the White House in May, 1908. The action of the conference led to the appointment of the National Conservation Commission, with authority to collect information and cooperate with similar commissions appointed by the States in the great work of conserving the natural resources of the country.

In the growth of the country and gradual development of the natural resources there have been three noteworthy stages. The first stage was that of individual enterprise for personal and family benefit. It led to the conquest of the wilderness.

The next stage was that of collective enterprise, either for the benefit of communities or for the profit of individuals forming the communities. It led to the development of cities and States, and too often to the growth of great monopolies.

The third stage is the one we are now entering. Within it the enterprise is collective and largely cooperative, and should be directed toward the larger benefit of communities, States, and the people generally.

In the first stage the resources received little thought. In the second, they were wastefully used. In the stage which we are entering wise and beneficial uses are essential, and the checking of waste is absolutely demanded.

Although the natural resources are interrelated they are unlike, and each class requires distinct treatment. The land is a fixed quantity which can not be materially increased, though its productivity and availability for the uses of man may be greatly augmented; the forests are variable in quantity and may be destroyed by fire, waste, and improvident use, or protected and improved in such way as to meet human necessities. Together the lands and the forests are improvable resources.

The minerals are limited in quantity and can not be increased or improved by anything which man may do. They are expendable resources.

The fresh waters are limited in quantity, though the supply is permanent. They form a naturally renewable resource which man may do nothing to increase, but may do much in the way of conservation and better utilization.

The treatment applied to each class should be adapted to its own fullest development and best utilization and to those of the other classes of resources.

The wastes which most urgently require checking vary widely in character and amount. The most reprehensible waste is that of destruction, as in forest fires, uncontrolled flow of gas and oil, soil wash, and abandonment of coal in the mines. This is attributable, for the most part, to ignorance, indifference, or false notions of economy, to rectify which is the business of the people collectively.

Nearly as reprehensible is the waste arising from misuse, as in the consumption of fuel in furnaces and engines of low efficiency, the loss of water in floods, the employment of ill-adapted structural materials, the growing of ill-chosen crops, and the perpetuation of inferior stocks of plants and animals, all of which may be remedied.

Reprehensible in less degree is the waste arising from nonuse. Since the utilization of any one resource is necessarily progressive and dependent on social and industrial conditions and the concurrent development of other resources, nonuse is sometimes unavoidable. It becomes reprehensible when it affects the common welfare and entails future injury. Then, it should be rectified in the general interest.

For the prevention of waste the most effective means will be found in the increase and diffusion of knowledge, from which is sure to result an aroused public sentiment demanding prevention. The people have the matter in their own hands. They may prevent or limit the destruction of resources and restrain misuse through the enactment and enforcement of appropriate state and federal laws.

At every stage in the growth of our country, strong men grew stronger through the exercise of nation building, and their intelligence and patriotism grew with their strength. The spirit and vigor of our people are the chief glory of the republic. Yet even as we have neglected our national resources, so have we been thoughtless of life and health. Too long have we overlooked that grandest of our resources, human life. Natural resources are of no avail without men and women to develop them, and only a strong and sound citizenship can make a nation permanently great. We can not too soon enter on the duty of conserving our chief source of strength by the prevention of disease and the prolongation of life.

Wastes reduced and resources saved are the first but not the last object of conservation. The material resources have an additional value when their preservation adds to the beauty and habitability of the land. Ours is a pleasant land in which to dwell. To increase its beauty and augment its fitness can not but multiply our pleasure in it and strengthen the bonds of our attachment.

In the conservation of all the resources of the country the interest of the present and all future generations is concerned, and in this great work—involving the welfare of the citizen, the family, the community, the state, and the nation—our dual system of government, state and federal, should be brought into harmonious cooperation and collaboration.

MINERALS

The mineral production of the United States for 1907 exceeded $2,000,000,000, and contributed 65 per cent of the total freight traffic of the country. The waste in the extraction and treatment of mineral products during the same year was equivalent to more than $300,000,000.

The production for 1907 included 395,000,000 tons of bituminous and 85,000,000 tons of anthracite coal, 166,000,000 barrels of petroleum, 52,000,000 tons of iron ore, 2,500,000 tons of phosphate rock, and 869,000,000 pounds of copper. The values of other mineral products during the same year included clay products, $162,000,000; stone, $71,000,000; cement, $56,000,000; natural gas, $53,000,000; gold $90,000,000; silver, $37,000,000; lead, $39,000,000, and zinc, $26,000,000.

The available and easily accessible supplies of coal in the United States aggregate approximately 1,400,000,000,000 tons. At the present increasing rate of production this supply will be so depleted as to approach exhaustion before the middle of the next century.

The known supply of high-grade iron ores in the United States approximates 4,788,150,000 tons, which at the present increasing rate of consumption can not be expected to last beyond the middle of the present century. In addition to this, there are assumed to be 75,116,070,000 tons of lower grade iron ores which are not available for use under existing conditions.

The supply of stone, clay, cement, lime, sand, and salt is ample, while the stock of the precious metals and of copper, lead, zinc, sulphur, asphalt, graphite, quicksilver, mica, and the rare metals can not well be estimated but is clearly exhaustible within one to three centuries unless unexpected deposits be found.

The known supply of petroleum is estimated at 15,000,000,000 to 20,000,000,000 barrels, distributed through six separate fields having an aggregate area of 8,900 square miles. The production is rapidly increasing, while the wastes and the loss through misuse are enormous. The supply can not be expected to last be-beyond the middle of the present century.

The known natural-gas fields aggregate an area of 9,000 square miles, distributed through 22 States. Of the total yield from these fields during 1907, 400,000,000,000 cubic feet, valued at $62,000,000, were utilized, while an equal quantity was allowed to escape into the air. The daily waste of natural gas—the most perfect known fuel—is over 1,000,000,000 cubic feet, or enough to supply every city in the United States of over 100,000 population.

Phosphate rock, used for fertilizer, represents the slow accumulation of organic matter during past ages. In most countries it is scrupulously preserved; in this country it is extensively exported; and largely for this reason its production is increasing rapidly. The original supply can not long withstand the increasing demand.

The consumption of nearly all our mineral products is increasing far more rapidly than our population. In many cases the waste is increasing more rapidly than the number of our people. In 1776 but a few dozen pounds of iron were in use by the average family; now our annual consumption of high-grade ore is over 1,200 pounds per capita. In 1812 no coal was used; now the consumption is over 5 tons and the waste nearly 3 tons per capita.

While the production of coal is increasing enormously, the waste and loss in mining are diminishing. At the beginning of our mineral development the coal abandoned in the mine was two or three times the amount taken out and used. Now the mine waste averages little more than half the amount saved. The chief waste is in imperfect combustion in furnaces and fire boxes. Steam engines utilize on the average about 8 per cent of the thermal energy of the coal. Internal-combustion engines utilize less than 20 per cent, and in electric lighting far less than 1 per cent of the thermal energy is rendered available.

With increasing industries new mineral resources become available from time to time. Some lignites and other low-grade coals are readily gasified and, through the development of internal-combustion engines may be made to check the consumption of high-grade coals.

Peat is becoming important; it is estimated that 14,000,000,000 tons are available in the United States. Its value is enhanced because of distribution through States generally remote from the fields of coal, oil, and natural gas.

The uses of all our mineral resources are interdependent. This is especially true of coal and iron, of which neither can be produced or used without aid from the other, and in the production or reduction of all other minerals both coal and iron are employed. The same standard minerals are necessary to the development of power, of which the use is increasing more rapidly than that of any other commodity.

The building operations of the country now aggregate about $1,000,000,000 per year. The direct and indirect losses from fire in the United States during 1907 approximated $450,000,000, or one-half the cost of construction. Of this loss four-fifths or an average of $1,000,000 per day, could be prevented, as shown by comparison with the standards of construction and fire losses in the larger European countries.

So far as the ores are taken from the mines and reduced to metals, these resources are capitalized; but after thus being changed to a more valuable form they should be so used as to reduce to a minimum the loss by rust, electrolytic action, and other wastes.

There is urgent need for greater safety to the miner. The loss of life through mine accidents is appalling, and preventive measures can not be taken too soon.

The National Government should exercise such control of the mineral fuels and phosphate rocks now in its possession as to check waste and prolong our supply.

While the distribution and quantity of most of our important mineral substances are known in a general way, there is imperative need for further surveys and investigations and for researches concerning the less-known minerals.

LANDS

The total land area of continental United States is 1,920,000,000 acres. Of this but little more than two-fifths is in farms, and less than one-half of the farm area is improved and made a source of crop production. We have nearly 6,000,000 farms; they average 146 acres each. The value of the farms is nearly one-fourth the wealth of the United States. There are more than 300,000,000 acres of public grazing land. The number of persons engaged in agricultural pursuits is more than 10,000,000.

We grow one-fifth of the world's wheat crop, three-fifths of its cotton crop, and four-fifths of its corn crop. We plant nearly 50,000,000 acres of wheat annually, with an average yield of about 14 bushels per acre; 100,000,000 acres of corn, yielding an average of 25 bushels per acre; and 30,000,000 acres of cotton, yielding about 12,000,000 bales.

We had on January 1, 1908, 71,000,000 cattle, worth $1,250,000,000; 54,000,000 sheep, worth $211,000,000; and 56,000,000 swine, worth $339,000,000. The census of 1900 showed $137,000,000 worth of poultry in this country, which produced in 1899, 293,000,000 dozen eggs.

There has been a slight increase in the average yield of our great staple farm products, but neither the increase in acreage nor the yield per acre has kept pace with our increase in population. Within a centry we shall probably have to feed three times as many people as now; and the main bulk of our food supply must be grown on our own soil.

The area of cultivated land may possibly be doubled. In addition to the land awaiting the plow, 75,000,000 acres of swamp land can be reclaimed, 40,000,000 acres of desert land irrigated, and millions of acres of brush and wooded land cleared. Our population will increase continuously, but there is a definite limit to the increase of our cultivated acreage. Hence we must greatly increase the yield per acre. The average yield of wheat in the United States is less than 14 bushels per acre, in Germany 28 bushels, and in England 32 bushels. We get 30 bushels of oats per acre, England nearly 45, and Germany more than 47. Our soils are fertile, but our mode of farming neither conserves the soil nor secures full crop returns. Soil fertility need not be diminished, but may be increased. The large yields now obtained from farms in Europe which have been cultivated for a thousand years prove this conclusively. Proper management will double our average yield per acre. The United States can grow the farm products needed by a population more than three times as great as our country now contains.

The greatest unnecessary loss of our soil is preventable erosion. Second only to this is the waste, nonuse, and misuse of fertilizer derived from animals and men.

The losses to farm products due to injurious mammals is estimated at $130,000,000 annually; the loss through plant diseases reaches several hundred million dollars; and the loss through insects is reckoned at $659,000,000. The damage by birds is balanced by their beneficent work in destroying noxious insects. Losses due to the elements are large, but no estimate has been made of them. Losses to live stock from these causes are diminishing because of protection and feeding during winter. The annual losses from disease among domestic animals are: Horses, 1.8 per cent; cattle, 2 per cent; sheep, 2.2 per cent, and swine, 5.1 per cent. Most of these farm losses are preventable.

There is a tendency toward consolidation of farm lands. The estimated area of abandoned farms is 16,000 square miles, or about 3 per cent of the improved land. The causes of abandonment differ in different parts of the country. Where most prevalent, it is caused principally by erosion and exhaustion of the soil.

The product of the fisheries of the United States has an annual value of $57,000,000. Fish culture is carried on by the nation and the States on an enormous scale. Most of the more important food species are propagated, and several species are maintained in that way. Fish from forest waters, furnish $21,000,000 worth of food yearly, a supply dependent on the preservation of the forests.

Our wild game and fur-bearing animals have been largely exterminated. To prevent their complete extinction the States and the United States have taken in hand their protection, and their numbers are now increasing. Forest game yields over $10,000,000 worth of food each year.

With game birds the story is much the same—wanton destruction until the number has been greatly reduced, followed in recent years by wise protection, which in some cases allows the remnant to survive and even to increase.

Each citizen of the United States owns an equal undivided interest in about 387,000,000 acres of public lands, exclusive of Alaska and the insular possessions. Besides this there are about 235,000,000 acres of national forests, national parks, and other lands devoted to public use.

Good business sense demands that a definite land policy be formulated. The National Conservation Commission believes that the following will serve as a basis therefor:

1. Every part of the public lands should be devoted to the use which will best subserve the interests of the whole people.

[101]

2. The classification of all public lands is necessary for their administration in the interests of the people.

3. The timber, the minerals, and the surface of the public lands should be disposed of separately.

4. Public lands more valuable for conserving water supply, timber and natural beauties or wonders than for agriculture should be held for the use of the people from all except mineral entry.

5. Title to the surface of the remaining nonmineral public lands should be granted only to actual home makers.

6. Pending the transfer of title to the remaining public lands they should be administered by the Government and their use should be allowed in a way to prevent or control waste and monopoly.

The present public-land laws as a whole do not subserve the best interests of the nation. They should be modified so far as may be required to bring them into conformity with the foregoing outline of policy.

FORESTS

Next to our need of food and water comes our need of timber.

Our industries which subsist wholly or mainly upon wood pay the wages of more than 1,500,000 men and women.

Forests not only grow timber, but they hold the soil and they conserve the streams. They abate the wind and give protection from excessive heat and cold. Woodlands make for the fiber, health, and happiness of the citizen and the nation.

Our forests now cover 550,000,000 acres, or about one-fourth of the United States. The original forests covered not less than 850,000,000 acres.

Forests publicly owned contain one-fifth of all our standing timber. Forests privately owned contain four-fifths of the standing timber. The timber privately owned is not only four times that publicly owned, but is generally more valuable.

Forestry is now practiced on 70 per cent of the forests publicly owned and on less than 1 per cent of the forests privately owned, or on only 18 per cent of the total area of forests.

The yearly growth of wood in our forests does not average more than 12 cubic feet per acre. This gives a total yearly growth of less than 7,000,000,000 cubic feet.

We have 200,000,000 acres of mature forests, in which yearly growth is balanced by decay; 250,000,000 acres partly cut over or burned over, but restocking naturally with enough young growth to produce a merchantable crop, and 100,000,000 acres cut over and burned over, upon which young growth is lacking or too scanty to make merchantable timber.

[102]

We take from our forests yearly, including waste in logging and in manu-facture, 23,000,000,000 cubic feet of wood. We use each year 100,000,000 cords of firewood; 40,000,000,000 feet of lumber; more than 1,000,000,000 posts, poles, and fence rails; 118,000,000 hewn ties; 1,500,000,000 staves; over 133,000,000 sets of heading; nearly 500,000,000 barrel hoops; 3,000,000 cords of native pulp wood; 165,000,000 cubic feet of round mine timbers, and 1,250,000 cords of wood for distillation.

Since 1870 forest fires have destroyed a yearly average of 50 lives and $50,000,000 worth of timber. Not less than 50,000,000 acres of forest is burned over yearly. The young growth destroyed by fire is worth far more than the merchantable timber burned.

One-fourth of the standing timber is lost in logging. The boxing of long-leaf pine for turpentine has destroyed one-fifth of the forests worked. The loss in the mill is from one-third to two-thirds of the timber sawed. The loss of mill product in seasoning and fitting for use is from one-seventh to one-fourth.

Of each 1,000 feet which stood in the forest, an average of only 320 feet of lumber is used.

We take from our forests each year, not counting the loss by fire, three and a half times their yearly growth. We take 40 cubic feet per acre for each 12 cubic feet grown; we take 260 cubic feet per capita, while Germany uses 37 and France 25 cubic feet.

We tax our forests under the general property tax, a method abandoned long ago by every other great nation. Present tax laws prevent reforestation of cut-over land and the perpetuation of existing forests by use.

Great damage is done to standing timber by injurious forest insects. Much of this damage can be prevented at small expense.

To protect our farms from wind and to reforest land best suited for forest growth will require tree planting on an area larger than Pennsylvania, Ohio, and West Virginia combined. Lands so far successfully planted make a total area smaller than Rhode Island; and year by year, through careless cutting and fires, we lower the capacity of existing forests to produce their like again, or else totally destroy them.

In spite of substitutes we shall always need more wood. So far our use of it has steadily increased. The condition of the world's supply of timber makes us already dependent upon what we produce. We send out of our country one and a half times as much timber as we bring in. Except for finishing woods, rela-tively small in amount, we must grow our own supply or go without. Until we pay for our lumber what it costs to grow it, as well as what it costs to log and saw, the price will continue to rise.

The preservation by use, under the methods of practical forestry, of all public forest lands, either in state or federal ownership, is essential to the per-manent public welfare. In many forest States the acquirement of additional forest lands as state forests is necessary to the best interests of the States themselves.

The conservation of our mountain forests, as in the Appalachian system, is a national necessity. These forests are required to aid in the regulation of streams used for navigation and other purposes. The conservation of these forests is impracticable through private enterprise alone, by any State alone, or by the Federal Government alone. Effective and immediate cooperation between these three agencies is essential. Federal ownership of limited protective areas upon important watersheds, effective state fire patrol, and the cooperation of private forest owners are all required.

The true remedy for unwise tax laws lies not in laxity in their application nor in special exemptions, but in a change in the method of taxation. An annual tax upon the land itself, exclusive of the value of the timber, and a tax upon the timber when cut, is well adapted to actual conditions of forest investment, and is practicable and certain. It is far better that forest land should pay a moderate tax permanently than that it should pay an excessive revenue temporarily and then cease to pay at all.

Forests in private ownership can not be conserved unless they are protected from fire. We need good fire laws, well enforced. Fire control is impossible without an adequate force of men whose sole duty is fire patrol during the dangerous season.

The conservative use of the forest and of timber by American citizens will not be general until they learn how to practice forestry. Through a vigorous national campaign in education, forestry has taken root in the great body of American citizenship. The basis already exists upon which to build a structure of forest conservation which will endure. This needs the definite commitment of state governments and the Federal Government to their inherent duty of teaching the people how to care for their forests. The final responsibility, both for investigative work in forestry and for making its results known, rests upon the States and upon the nation.

By reasonable thrift, we can produce a constant timber supply beyond our present need, and with it conserve the usefulness of our streams for irrigation, water supply, navigation, and power.

Under right management our forests will yield over four times as much as now. We can reduce waste in the woods and in the mill at least one-third, with present as well as future profit. We can perpetuate the naval-stores industry. Preservative treatment will reduce by one-fifth the quantity of timber used in the water or in the ground. We can practically stop forest fires at a cost yearly of one-fifth the value of the merchantable timber burned.

We shall suffer for timber to meet our needs until our forests have had time to grow again. But if we act vigorously and at once we shall escape permanent timber scarcity.

WATERS

The sole source of our fresh water is rainfall, including snow. From this source all running, standing, and ground waters are derived. The habitability of the country depends on these waters. Our mean annual rainfall is about 30 inches; the quantity about 215,000,000,000,000 cubic feet per year, equivalent to ten Mississippi rivers.

Of the total rainfall, over half is evaporated; about a third flows into the sea; the remaining sixth is either consumed or absorbed. These portions are sometimes called, respectively, the fly-off, the run-off, and the cut-off. They are partly interchangeable. About a third of the run-off, or a tenth of the entire rainfall, passes through the Mississippi. The run-off is increasing with deforestation and cultivation.

Of the 70,000,000,000,000 cubic feet annually flowing into the sea, less than 1 per cent is retained and utilized for municipal and community supply; less than 2 per cent (or some 10 per cent of that in the arid and semiarid regions) is used for irrigation; perhaps 5 per cent is used for navigation, and less than 5 per cent for power.

For municipal and community water supply there are protected catchment areas aggregating over 1,000,000 acres, and over $250,000,000 are invested in waterworks, with nearly as much more in the appurtenant catchment areas and other lands. The population so supplied approaches 10,000,000, and the annual consumption is about 37,500,000,000 cubic feet. The better managed systems protect the catchment areas by forests and grass; the water is controlled and the storm product used, but there is large waste after the water enters the mains.

For irrigation it is estimated that there are $200,000,000 invested in dams, ditches, reservoirs, and other works for the partial control of the waters, and that 1,500,000,000,000 cubic feet are annually diverted to irrigable lands, aggregating some 20,000 square miles. Except in some cases through forestry, few catchment areas are controlled, and few reservoirs are large enough to hold the storm waters. The waste in the public and private projects exceeds 60 per cent, while no more than 25 per cent of the water actually available for irrigation of the arid lands is restrained and diverted.

There are in continental United States 287 streams navigated for an aggregate of 26,226 miles, and as much more navigable if improved. There are also 45 canals, aggregating 2,189 miles, besides numerous abandoned canals. Except through forestry in recent years, together with a few reservoirs and canal locks and movable dams, there has been little effort to control headwaters or catchment areas in the interests of navigation, and none of our rivers are navigated to more than a small fraction even of their effective low-water capacity.

The water power now in use is 5,250,000 horsepower; the amount running over government dams and not used is about 1,400,000 horsepower; the amount reasonably available equals or exceeds the entire mechanical power now in use, or enough to operate every mill, drive every spindle, propel every train and boat, and light every city, town, and village in the country. While the utilization of water power ranks among our most recent and most rapid industrial developments, little effort has been made to control catchment areas or storm waters in any large way for power, though most plants effect local control through reservoirs and other works. Nearly all the freshet and flood water runs to waste, and the low waters which limit the efficiency of power plants are increasing in frequency and duration with the increasing flood run-off.

The practical utility of streams for both navigation and power is measured by the effective low-water stage. The volume carried when the streams rise above this stage is largely wasted and often does serious damage. The direct yearly damage by floods since 1900 has increased steadily from $45,000,000 to over $238,000,000. The indirect loss through depreciation of property is great, while a large loss arises in impeded traffic through navigation and terminal transfers.

The freshets are attended by destructive soil erosion. The soil matter annually carried into lower rivers and harbors or into the sea is computed at 783,000,000 tons. Soil wash reduces by 10 to 20 per cent the productivity of upland farms and increases channel cutting and bar building in the rivers. The annual loss to the farms alone is fully $500,000,000, and large losses follow the fouling of the waters and the diminished navigability of the streams.

Through imperfect control of the running waters lowlands are temporarily or permanently flooded. It is estimated that there are in mainland United States about 75,000,000 acres of overflow and swamp lands requiring drainage; that by systematic operation these can be drained at moderate expense, and that they would then be worth two or three times the present value and cost of drainage, and would furnish homes for 10,000,000 people.

It is estimated that the quantity of fresh water stored in lakes and ponds (including the American portion of the Great Lakes) is about 600,000,000,000,000 cubic feet, equivalent to three years' rainfall or eight years' run-off. Some 6,000,000 of our people draw their water supply from lakes.

A large part of that half of the annual rainfall not evaporated lodges temporarily in the soil and earth. It is estimated that the ground water to the depth of 100 feet averages 16⅔ per cent of the earth volume, or over 1,400,000,000,000,-000 cubic feet, equivalent to seven years' rainfall or twenty years' run-off. This subsurface reservoir is the essential basis of agriculture and other industries and is the chief natural resource of the country. It sustains forests and all other crops and supplies the perennial springs and streams and wells used by four-fifths of our population and nearly all our domestic animals. Its quantity is diminished by the increased run-off due to deforestation and injudicious farming. Although the volume of the available ground water is subject to control by suitable treatment of the surface, little effort has been made to retain or increase it, and it is probable that fully 10 per cent of this rich resource has been wasted since settlement began. The water of the strata below 100 feet supplies artesian and deep wells, large springs, and thermal and mineral waters. It can be controlled only through the subsurface reservoir.

Of the 35,000,000,000,000 cubic feet of cut-off, the chief share is utilized by natural processes or by agriculture and related industries. On an average the plant tissue of annual growths is three-fourths and of perennial growths three-eights water; of human and stock food over 80 per cent is water, and in animal tissue the ratio is about the same; and since water is the medium for organic circulation, the plants and animals of the country yearly require an amount many times exceeding their aggregate volume. Even in the more humid sections of the country the productivity of the soil and the possible human population would be materially increased by a greater rainfall, leaving a larger margin for organic and other chemical uses. Except through agriculture and forestry little general effort is made to control the annual cut-off, although some farmers in arid regions claim to double or triple the crop from given soil by supplying water just when needed and withholding it when not required.

Water is like other resources in that its quantity is limited. It differs from such mineral resources as coal and iron, which once used are gone forever, in that the supply is perpetual; and it differs from such resources as soils and forests, which are capable of renewal or improvement, in that it can not be augmented in quantity, though like all other resources it can be better utilized.

It is now recognized by statesmen and experts that navigation is interdependent with other uses of the streams; that each stream is essentially a unit from its source to the sea; and that the benefits of a comprehensive system of waterway improvement will extend to all the people in the several sections and States of the country.

It is also recognized, through the unanimous declaration of the governors of the States and Territories adopted in conference with the leading jurists and statesmen and experts of the country, that in the use of the natural resources the independent States are interdependent, and bound together by ties of mutual benefits, responsibilities, and duties.

It has recently been declared by a majority of our leading statesmen that it is an imperative duty to enter upon a systematic improvement, on a large and comprehensive plan, just to all portions of the country, of the waterways and harbors and Great Lakes, whose natural adaptability to the increasing traffic of the land is one of the greatest gifts of a benign Providence; while the minority indorsed the movement for control of the waterways still more specifically and in equally emphatic terms.

Within recent months it has been recognized and demanded by the people, through many thousand delegates from all States assembled in convention in different sections of the country, that the waterways should and must be improved promptly and effectively as a means of maintaining national prosperity.

The first requisite for waterway improvement is the control of the waters in such manner as to reduce floods and regulate the regimen of the navigable rivers. The second requisite is development of terminals and connections in such manner as to regulate commerce.

In considering the uses and benefits to be derived from the waters, the paramount use should be water supply; next should follow navigation in humid regions and irrigation in arid regions. The development of power on the navigable and source streams should be coordinated with the primary and secondary uses of the waters. Other things equal, the development of power should be encouraged, not only to reduce the drain on other resources, but because properly designed reservoirs and power plants retard the run-off and so aid in the control of the streams for navigation and other uses.

Broad plans should be adopted providing for a system of waterway improvement extending to all uses of the waters and benefits to be derived from their control, including the clarification of the water and abatement of floods for the benefit of navigation; the extension of irrigation; the development and application of power; the prevention of soil wash; the purification of streams for water supply; and the drainage and utilization of the waters of swamp and overflow lands.

To promote and perfect these plans scientific investigations, surveys, and measurements should be continued and extended, especially the more accurate determination of rainfall and evaporation, the investigation and measurement of ground water, the gauging of streams and determination of sediment, and topographic surveys of catchment areas and sites available for control of the waters for navigation and related purposes.

NATIONAL EFFICIENCY

Since the greatest of our national assets is the health and vigor of the American people, our efficiency must depend on national vitality even more than on the resources of the minerals, lands, forests, and waters.

The average length of human life in different countries varies from less than twenty-five to more than fifty years. This span of life is increasing wherever sanitary science and preventive medicine are applied. It may be greatly extended.

Our annual mortality from tuberculosis is about 150,000. Stopping three-fourths of the loss of life from this cause, and from typhoid and other prevalent and preventable diseases, would increase our average length of life over fifteen years.

There are constantly about 3,000,000 persons seriously ill in the United States of whom 500,000 are consumptives. More than half this illness is preventable.

If we count the value of each life at only $1,700 and reckon the average earning lost by illness as $700 per year for grown men, we find that the economic gain from mitigation of preventable disease in the United States would exceed $1,500,000,000 a year. In addition, we would decrease suffering and increase happiness and contentment among the people. This gain, or the lengthening and strengthening of life which it measures, can be secured through medical investigation and practice, school and factory hygiene, restriction of labor by women and children, the education of the people in both public and private hygiene, and through improving the efficiency of our health service—municipal, state, and national. The National Government has now several agencies exercising health functions which only need to be concentrated to become coordinated parts of a greater health service worthy of the nation.

The inventory of our natural resources made by your commission with the vigorous aid of all federal agencies concerned, of many States, and of a great number of associated and individual cooperators, furnishes a safe basis for general conclusions as to what we have, what we use and waste, and what may be the possible saving. But for none of the great resources of the farm, the mine, the forest, and the stream do we yet possess knowledge definite or wide enough to insure methods of use which will best conserve them.

In order to conserve a natural resource, we must know what that resource is by taking stock. We greatly need a more complete inventory of our natural resources; and this can not be made except through the active cooperation of the States with the nation.

The permanent welfare of the nation demands that its natural resources be conserved by proper use. To this end the States and the nation can do much by legislation and example. By far the greater part of these resources is in private hands. Private ownership of natural resources is a public trust; they should be administered in the interests of the people as a whole. The States and nation should lead rather than follow in the conservative and efficient use of property under their immediate control. But their first duty is to gather and distribute a knowledge of our natural resources and of the means necessary to insure their use and conservation, to impress the body of the people with the great importance of the duty, and to promote the cooperation of all. No agency, state, federal, corporate, or private, can do the work alone.

Finally, the conservation of our resources is an immediate and vital concern. Our welfare depends on conservation. The pressing need is for a general plan under which citizens, States, and nation may unite in an effort to achieve this great end. The lack of cooperation between the States themselves, between the States and the nation, and between the agencies of the National Government, is a potent cause of the neglect of conservation among the people. An organization through which all agencies—state, national, municipal, associate, and individual—may unite in a common effort to conserve the foundations of our prosperity is indispensable to the welfare and progress of the nation. To that end the immediate creation of a national agency is essential. Many States and associations of citizens have taken action by the appointment of permanent conservation commissions. It remains for the nation to do likewise, in order that the States and the nation, associations and individuals, may join in the accomplishment of this great purpose.

Accompanying this report, and transmitted as a part thereof, are detailed statements by the secretaries of the several sections, and many papers and illustrations prepared by experts at the request of your commission.

> *Gifford Pinchot*
> Chairman
>
> *W J McGee*
> Secretary, Section of Waters
>
> *Overton W. Price*
> Secretary, Section of Forests
>
> *George W. Woodruff*
> Secretary, Section of Lands
>
> *J. A. Holmes*
> Secretary, Section of Minerals

Attest: Thomas R. Shipp,
Secretary to the Commission
December 7, 1908

LETTER FROM SENATOR FRANCIS G. NEWLANDS
ON CONSERVATION*
January 3, 1910

This excerpt from a letter sent by Senator Newlands to a Democratic dinner at Reno is the best brief exposition of Newlands' philosophy of conservation.

The work of Bryan for the past thirteen years, supplemented by that of Roosevelt for the past eight years, together with the work of other leading men associated with them on the lines of wresting from monopoly and special interests the control of the people's government and restoring it to the people themselves, has culminated in a universal demand throughout the country for practical measures of gradual and progressive reform which will secure the action of the national sovereignty within its jurisdiction and of the state sovereignties within their jurisdiction, and the coöperation of both when necessary. The people realize that the complexity of our government, with its divided sovereignty, national and state, has hitherto confused reformers and prevented decisive action.

There is a demand for a constructive democracy, and a growing feeling that the people in their collective capacity can do things for the general good hitherto intrusted only to private interests. These ideas have developed themselves into the view that the collective ownership of the nation in the public domain, in its vast areas of coal, iron, and oil deposits, in forests and in farms, is a great public trust to be administered in such a way as to secure their highest development in the interest of all the people of present and future generations.

Hence the evolution of the so-called conservation policy, which found its most admirable expression in the Democratic national platforms of 1900, 1904, and 1908, on subjects relating to irrigation, forestry, the preservation of the public domain for home-seekers, the protection of the natural resources in timber, coal, iron, and oil against monopolistic control, and the development of our waterways for navigation and every other useful purpose, including the irrigation of arid lands, the reclamation of swamp lands, the clarification of streams, the development of water power and of hydro-electric power and their protection from the control of monopoly, and the exercise of all powers, national, state, and municipal, both separately and in coöperation, in these great works.

This policy does not necessarily involve the continued collective ownership of all of the public domain and the vast mineral treasures embraced within it;

The Public Papers of Francis G. Newlands, Vol. 1, Arthur B. Darling, ed. (Boston: Houghton Mifflin Co., 1932), 110–11.

but it means its careful study for the purpose of determining what shall be held in collective ownership, what shall be turned over to private ownership, and what restrictions shall be placed upon private ownership in order to prevent monopoly and oppressive charges for products of universal necessity.

SPEECH BY SENATOR JOSEPH DIXON ON A
CONSERVATION COMMISSION*
June 15, 1910

Senator Joseph M. Dixon (Montana) offered this idea for a conservation commission, which never became law, but indicates the developing concept of governmental planning to coordinate all activity in the conservation field.

Mr. JOSEPH DIXON. I offer the following amendment.

The VICE-PRESIDENT. The Senator from Montana offers an amendment to the amendment, which the Secretary will state.

The SECRETARY. It is proposed to add as new sections the following:

SEC.—. That the President of the United States be, and he is hereby, authorized to appoint a commission to serve, without salary, for a term of three years, not to exceed 15 in number, and to organize the same for the investigation of all questions relating to the conservation, use, and control of the water resources of the United States for navigation, irrigation, municipal supply, power, and swamp-land reclamation, to the prevention of floods and the maintenance of stream control, to the prevention of waste in the mining and extraction of coal, oil, gas, and other minerals, to the protection of human life in the mines, and to the prevention of erosion and soil wash; to the conservation of the forests, to the preservation of the public domain for home seekers, to the protection of the timber, coal, iron, and oil lands of the United States against absorption by monopoly; and for the investigation of all other questions relating to the conservation of the natural resources of the United States for the preservation of its beauty, healthfulness, and habitability.

SEC.—a. That such commission shall cooperate with commissions or boards appointed by the respective States for similar purposes, with a view to recommending suitable action relating to the conservation of the natural resources of the United States by Congress within the limits of and coextensive with national jurisdiction of the subject and complementary thereto by the legislatures of the several States within the limits of and coextensive with their jurisdiction.

SEC.—b. That such commission shall be known as the national commission for the conservation of natural resources.

SEC.—c. That such commission shall make to the President annually, and at such other periods as may be required either by law or by the order of the President, full and complete reports of all their acts, doings, recommendations, and expenditures, which reports shall be by the President transmitted to the Congress.

SEC.—d. That the President shall cause to be provided for the use of such commission and its employees under this act such offices in the District of Columbia and elsewhere, and such equipment, as may be necessary for the proper discharge of its duties.

SEC.—e. That in order to carry out the purposes of this act there is hereby appropriated, out of the funds in the Treasury not otherwise appropriated, the sum of $50,000, to be expended under the direction of the President.

Mr. DIXON. Mr. President, I at this time desire to make a brief statement regarding the amendment which I have just offered. Some days ago the Committee on Conservation of National Resources reported this amendment in the form of a bill, with one amendment, which I have inserted in this proposed amendment.

Cong. Rec., 61st Cong., 2nd sess., 8151.

[113]

For the past two or three years, I apprehend, there has been no question concerning which the people of this country have come as near agreeing on as on the general proposition of the conservation of natural resources. The trouble has been when the general principle was applied to specific conditions. Then serious differences have arisen as to what is practical and what is not. Two years ago President Roosevelt, on his own initiative, appointed what was known as the National Conservation Commission, composed of scientists and several members of the House and Senate. The work of the commission culminated in calling the conference of governors at the White House two years ago.

Since that time 33 States have organized conservation commissions for their own special interests. In the amendment I have offered it is simply provided that the President may appoint a commission of 15 men, and to insure against any salary proposition or any desire on the part of anyone merely to hold a job that pays some money we have expressly provided in the amendment that they shall serve without salary.

It was the intention of the committee that under this plan the President of the United States might possibly select 15 of the great men of this country to whom salary would not be an object. Their term is limited to three years. They are merely to meet and make recommendations. I do not believe they will solve the question, Mr. President, but I do believe it is possible, if conservative men of great capacity, of great experience in material affairs, are named on the commission, together with some of the experts of the Government, some great good will come out of it.

The amendment is most germane to the present withdrawal bill, known as the conservation bill. It involves no expense. No money is provided for except merely the expenses of stenographers and rent of an office here in Washington. I doubt whether any question before the people of the country has a more general accord than the proposition of a national conservation commission, such as is outlined in the present amendment, and I hope there will be no opposition to its adoption.

THE RIVER REGULATION AMENDMENT*
August 8, 1917

The waterways commission plan was repeatedly modified by Senator New-lands as he fought to gain support for the proposal through the years. Even after it had been endorsed by President Wilson, the Newlands plan became law only as a price for acceptance by the Senate of the Ransdell-Humphreys Mississippi River flood control bill.

One of the last modifications Newlands made was to call his plan "The River Regulation Amendment." It became law as an amendment to the Rivers and Harbors bill of 1917. The distractions of World War I delayed appointment of the commission created by the act. After Newlands died in December, no pressure developed to appoint the commission. The law itself was repealed in 1920.

SEC. 18. That a commission, to be known as the Waterways Commission, consisting of seven members to be appointed by the President of the United States, at least one of whom shall be chosen from the active or retired list of the Engineers Corps of the Army, at least one of whom shall be an expert hydraulic engineer from civil life, and the remaining five of whom may each be selected either from civil life or the public service, is hereby created and authorized, under such rules and regulations as the President may prescribe, and subject to the approval of the heads of the several executive departments concerned, to bring into coordination and cooperation the engineering, scientific, and constructive services, bureaus, boards, and commissions of the several governmental departments of the United States and commissions created by Congress that relate to study, development, or control of waterways and water resources and subjects related thereto, or to the development and regulation of interstate and foreign commerce, with a view to uniting such services in investigating, with respect to all watersheds in the United States, questions relating to the development, improvement, regulation, and control of navigation as a part of interstate and foreign commerce, including therein the related questions of irrigation, drainage, forestry, arid and swamp land reclamation, clarification of streams, regulation of flow, control of floods, utilization of water power, prevention of soil erosion and waste, storage, and conservation of water for agricultural, industrial, municipal, and domestic uses, cooperation of railways and waterways, and promotion of terminal and transfer facilities, to secure the necessary data, and to formulate and report to Congress, as early as practicable, a comprehensive plan or plans for the development of waterways and

*40 *Statutes at Large,* 269–70.

the water resources of the United States for the purposes of navigation and for every useful purpose, and recommendations for the modification or discontinuance of any project herein or heretofore adopted. Any member appointed from the retired list shall receive the same pay and allowances as he would if on the active list, and no member selected from the public service shall receive additional compensation for services on said commission, and members selected from civil life shall receive compensation of $7,500 per annum.

In all matters done, or to be done, under this section relating to any of the subjects, investigations, or questions to be considered hereunder, and in formulating plans, and in the preparation of a report or reports as herein provided, consideration shall be given to all matters which are to be undertaken, either independently by the United States or by cooperation between the United States and the several States, political subdivisions thereof, municipalities, communities, corporations, and individuals within the jurisdiction, powers, and rights of each, respectively, and with a view to assigning to the United States such portion of such development, promotion, regulation, and control as may be undertaken by the United States, and to the States, political subdivisions thereof, municipalities, communities, corporations, and individuals such portions as belong to their respective jurisdictions, rights, and interests.

The commission is authorized to employ, or retain, and fix the compensation for the services of such engineers, transportation experts, experts in water development and utilization, and constructors of eminence as it may deem necessary to make such investigations and to carry out the purposes of this section. And in order to defray the expenses made necessary by the provisions of this section there is hereby authorized to be appropriated such sums as Congress may hereafter determine, and the sum of $100,000 is hereby appropriated, available until expended, to be paid out upon warrants drawn on the Secretary of the Treasury by the Chairman of said commission.

The commission shall have power to make every expenditure requisite for and incident to its authorized work, and to employ in the District of Columbia and in the field such clerical, legal, engineering, artistic, and expert services as it may deem advisable, including the payment of per diem in lieu of subsistence for employees engaged in field work or traveling on official business, rent of offices in the District of Columbia and in the field, and the purchase of books, maps, and office equipment.

Nothing herein contained shall be construed to delay, prevent, or interfere with the completion of any survey, investigation, project, or work herein or heretofore or hereafter adopted or authorized upon or for the improvement of any of the rivers or harbors of the United States or with legislative action upon reports heretofore or hereafter presented.

Approved, August 8, 1917.

THE PUBLIC DOMAIN

THE KINKAID HOMESTEAD ACT*
April 28, 1904

The Kinkaid Homestead Act opened up to farming the western desert lands of Nebraska. It favored the farmer-homesteader in opposition to the grazing interests, and the experiment in Nebraska led to a new farm homestead revision. The long-range effect, however, was to help bring "the plow that broke the plains" and the dust bowls of less than a generation later.

An Act to amend the homestead laws as to certain unappropriated and unreserved lands in Nebraska.

Be it enacted by the Senate and House of Representatives of the United States of America in Congress assembled, That from and after sixty days after the approval of this Act entries made under the homestead laws in the State of Nebraska west and north of the following line, to wit: Beginning at a point on the boundary line between the States of South Dakota and Nebraska where the first guide meridian west of the sixth principal meridian strikes said boundary; thence running south along said guide meridian to its intersection with the fourth standard parallel north of the base line between the States of Nebraska and Kansas; thence west along said fourth standard parallel to its intersection with the second guide meridian west of the sixth principal meridian; thence south along said second guide meridian to its intersection with the third standard parallel north of the said base line; thence west along said third standard parallel to its intersection with the range line between ranges twenty-five and twenty-six west of the sixth principal meridian; thence south along said line to its intersection with the second standard parallel north of the said base line; thence west on said standard parallel to its intersection with the range line between ranges thirty and thirty-one west; thence south along said line to its intersection with the boundary line between the States of Nebraska and Kansas, shall not exceed in area six hundred and forty acres, and shall be as nearly compact in form as possible, and in no event over two miles in extreme length: *Provided,*

*33 *Statutes at Large,* 547–48.

[117]

That there shall be excluded from the provisions of this Act such lands within the territory herein described as in the opinion of the Secretary of the Interior it may be reasonably practicable to irrigate under the national irrigation law, or by private enterprise; and that said Secretary shall, prior to the date above mentioned, designate and exclude from entry under this Act the lands, particularly along the North Platte River, which in his opinion it may be possible to irrigate as aforesaid; and shall thereafter, from time to time, open to entry under this Act any of the lands so excluded, which, upon further investigation, he may conclude can not be practically irrigated in the manner aforesaid.

SEC. 2. That entrymen under the homestead laws of the United States within the territory above described who own and occupy the lands heretofore entered by them, may, under the provisions of this Act and subject to its conditions, enter other lands contiguous to their said homestead entry, which shall not, with the land so already entered, owned, and occupied, exceed in the aggregate six hundred and forty acres; and residence upon the original homestead shall be accepted as equivalent to residence upon the additional land so entered, but final entry shall not be allowed of such additional land until five years after first entering the same.

SEC. 3. That the fees and commissions on all entries under this Act shall be uniformly the same as those charged under the present law for a maximum entry at the minimum price. That the commutation provisions of the homestead law shall not apply to entries under this Act, and at the time of making final proof the entryman must prove affirmatively that he has placed upon the lands entered permanent improvements of the value of not less than one dollar and twenty-five cents per acre for each acre included in his entry: *Provided,* That a former homestead entry shall not be a bar to the entry under the provisions of this Act of a tract which, together with the former entry, shall not exceed six hundred and forty acres: *Provided,* That any former homestead entryman who shall be entitled to an additional entry under section two of this Act shall have for ninety days after the passage of this Act the preferential right to make additional entry as provided in said section.

Approved, April 28, 1904.

THE FOREST HOMESTEAD ACT*
June 11, 1906

Under this law some of the forest reserve lands were opened for homestead by farmers, if they were "chiefly valuable for agriculture." No commutation privilege was allowed as in the 1862 homestead act. This forest homestead act is in force at the present time, though it would be extremely difficult to find suitable land and make a claim.

An Act to provide for the entry of Agricultural lands within forest reserves.

Be it enacted by the Senate and House of Representatives of the United States of America in Congress assembled, That the Secretary of Agriculture may, in his discretion, and he is hereby authorized, upon application or otherwise, to examine and ascertain as to the location and extent of lands within permanent or temporary forest reserves, except the following counties in the State of California, Inyo, Tulare, Kern, San Luis Obispo, Santa Barbara, Ventura, Los Angeles, San Bernardino, Orange, Riverside, and San Diego; which are chiefly valuable for agriculture, and which, in his opinion, may be occupied for agricultural purposes without injury to the forest reserves, and which are not needed for public purposes, and may list and describe the same by metes and bounds, or otherwise, and file the lists and descriptions with the Secretary of the Interior, with the request that the said lands be opened to entry in accordance with the provisions of the homestead laws and this Act.

Upon the filing of any such list or description the Secretary of the Interior shall declare the said lands open to homestead settlement and entry in tracts not exceeding one hundred and sixty acres in area and not exceeding one mile in length, at the expiration of sixty days from the filing of the list in the land office of the district within which the lands are located, during which period the said list or description shall be prominently posted in the land office and advertised for a period of not less than four weeks in one newspaper of general circulation published in the county in which the lands are situated: *Provided,* That any settler actually occupying and in good faith claiming such lands for agricultural purposes prior to January first, nineteen hundred and six, and who shall not have abandoned the same, and the person, if qualified to make a homestead entry, upon whose application the land proposed to be entered was examined and listed, shall, each in the order named, have a preference right of settlement and entry: *Provided further,* That any entryman desiring to obtain patent to any lands described by metes and bounds entered by him under the

*34 *Statutes at Large,* 233–34.

provisions of this Act shall, within five years of the date of making settlement, file, with the required proof of residence and cultivation, a plat and field notes of the lands entered, made by or under the direction of the United States surveyor-general, showing accurately the boundaries of such lands, which shall be distinctly marked by monuments on the ground, and by posting a copy of such plat, together with a notice of the time and place of offering proof, in a conspicuous place on the land embraced in such plat during the period prescribed by law for the publication of his notice of intention to offer proof, and that a copy of such plat and field notes shall also be kept posted in the office of the register of the land office for the land district in which such lands are situated for a like period; and further, that any agricultural lands within forest reserves may, at the discretion of the Secretary, be surveyed by metes and bounds, and that no lands entered under the provisions of this Act shall be patented under the commutation provisions of the homestead laws, but settlers, upon final proof, shall have credit for the period of their actual residence upon the lands covered by their entries.

SEC. 2. That settlers upon lands chiefly valuable for agriculture within forest reserves on January first, nineteen hundred and six, who have already exercised or lost their homestead privilege, but are otherwise competent to enter lands under the homestead laws, are hereby granted an additional homestead right of entry for the purposes of this Act only, and such settlers must otherwise comply with the provisions of the homestead law, and in addition thereto must pay two dollars and fifty cents per acre for lands entered under the provisions of this section, such payment to be made at the time of making final proof on such lands.

SEC. 3. That all entries under this Act in the Black Hills Forest Reserve shall be subject to the quartz or lode mining laws of the United States, and the laws and regulations permitting the location, appropriation, and use of the waters within the said forest reserves for mining, irrigation, and other purposes; and no titles acquired to agricultural lands in said Black Hills Forest Reserve under this Act shall vest in the patentee any riparian rights to any stream or streams of flowing water within said reserve; and that such limitation of title shall be expressed in the patents for the lands covered by such entries.

SEC. 4. That no homestead settlements or entries shall be allowed in that portion of the Black Hills Forest Reserve in Lawrence and Pennington counties in South Dakota except to persons occupying lands therein prior to January first, nineteen hundred and six, and the provisions of this Act shall apply to the said counties in said reserve only so far as is necessary to give and perfect title of such settlers or occupants to lands chiefly valuable for agriculture therein occupied or claimed by them prior to the said date, and all homestead entries under this Act in said counties in said reserve shall be described by metes and bounds survey.

SEC. 5. That nothing herein contained shall be held to authorize any future settlement on any lands within forest reserves until such lands have been opened to settlement as provided in this Act, or to in any way impair the legal rights of any bona fide homestead settler who has or shall establish residence upon public lands prior to their inclusion within a forest reserve.

Approved, June 11, 1906.

MESSAGE FROM PRESIDENT ROOSEVELT
ON PUBLIC LAND LAWS*
December 17, 1906

This special message incorporates most of Theodore Roosevelt's recommendations on changes of the public land laws. The recommendations grew out of the report of the Public Lands Commission made in 1905.

To the Senate and House of Representatives:

PUBLIC-LAND LAWS

The developments of the past year emphasize with increasing force the need of vigorous and immediate action to recast the public-land laws and adapt them to the actual situation. The timber and stone act has demonstrated conclusively that its effect is to turn over the public timber lands to great corporations. It has done enormous harm. It is no longer needed, and it should be repealed.

The desert-land act results so frequently in fraud and so comparatively seldom in making homes on the land that it demands radical amendment. That provision which permits assignment before patent should be repealed, and the entryman should be required to live for not less than two years at home on the land before patent issues. Otherwise the desert-land law will continue to assist speculators and other large holders to get control of land and water on the public domain by indefensible means.

The commutation clause of the homestead act serves in a majority of cases to defeat the purpose of the homestead act itself, which is to facilitate settlement and create homes. In theory the commutation clause should assist the honest settler, and doubtless in some cases it does so. Far more often it supplies the means by which speculators and loan and mortgage companies secure possession of the land. Actual, not constructive, living at home on the land for three years should be required before commutation unless it should appear wiser to repeal the commutation clause altogether.

These matters are more fully discussed in the Report of the Public Lands Commission, to which I again call your attention.

I am gravely concerned at the extremely unsatisfactory condition of the public-land laws and at the prevalence of fraud under their present provisions. For much of this fraud the present laws are chiefly responsible. There is but one way by which the fraudulent acquisition of these lands can be definitely

*Sen. Doc. 141, 49th Cong., 2nd sess., 1–4.

stopped, and therefore I have directed the Secretary of the Interior to allow no patent to be issued to public land under any law until by an examination on the ground actual compliance with that law has been found to exist. For this purpose an increase of special agents in the General Land Office is urgently required. Unless it is given bona fide would-be settlers will be put to grave inconvenience or else the fraud will in large part go on. Further, the Secretary of the Interior should be enabled to employ enough mining experts to examine the validity of all mineral-land claims and to undertake the supervision and control of the use of the mineral fuels still belonging to the United States. The present coal law limiting the individual entry to 160 acres puts a premium on fraud by making it impossible to develop certain types of coal fields and yet comply with the law. It is a scandal to maintain laws which sound well, but which make fraud the key without which great natural resources must remain closed. The law should give individuals and corporations under proper government regulation and control (the details of which I shall not at present discuss) the right to work bodies of coal land large enough for profitable development. My own belief is that there should be provision for leasing coal, oil, and gas rights under proper restrictions. If the additional force of special agents and mining experts I recommend is provided and well used, the result will be not only to stop the land frauds, but to prevent delays in patenting valid land claims and to conserve the indispensable fuel resources of the nation.

RIGHTS OF WAY AND PRIVILEGES

Many of the existing laws affecting rights of way and privileges on public lands and reservations are illogical and unfair. Some work injustice by granting valuable rights in perpetuity without return. Others fail to protect the grantee in his possession of permanent improvements made at large expense. In fairness to the Government, to the holders of rights and privileges on the public lands, and to the people whom the latter serve, I urge the revision and reenactment of these laws in one comprehensive act, providing that the regulations and the charge now in force in many cases may be extended to all, to the end that unregulated or monopolistic control of great natural resources may not be acquired or misused for private ends.

PRIVATE HOLDINGS WITHIN NATIONAL FORESTS

The boundaries of the national forest reserves unavoidably include certain valuable timber lands not owned by the Government. Important among them are the land grants of various railroads. For more than two years negotiations with the land-grant railroads have been in progress looking toward an arrangement by which the forest on railroad lands within national forest reserves may be preserved by the removal of the present crop of timber under rules prescribed by the Forest Service, and its perpetuation may be assured by the transfer of the land to the Government without cost. The advantage of such an arrangement to the Government lies in the acquisition of lands whose protection is necessary to the general welfare. The advantage to the railroads is found in the proposal to allow them to consolidate their holdings of timber within forest reserves by exchange after deeding their lands to the Government and thus to cut within a limited time solid bodies of timber instead of alternate sections, although the amount of timber in each case would be the same. It is possible that legislation will be required to authorize this or a similar arrangement with the railroads and other owners. If so, I recommend that it be enacted.

WORKING CAPITAL FOR THE NATIONAL FORESTS

The money value of the national forests now reserved for the use and benefit of the people exceeds considerably the sum of one thousand millions of dollars. The stumpage value of the standing timber approaches seven hundred million dollars, and together with the range and timber lands, the water for irrigation and power, and the subsidiary values, reaches an amount equal to that of the national property now under the immediate control of the Army and Navy together. But this vast domain is withheld from serving the nation as freely and fully as it might by the lack of capital to develop it. The yearly running expenses are sufficiently met by the annual appropriation and the proceeds of the forests. Under the care of the Forest Service the latter are increasing at the rate of more than half a million dollars a year. The estimate of appropriation for the present year is less than for last year, and it is confidently expected that by 1910 the Forest Service will be entirely self-supporting. In the meantime there is the most urgent need for trails, fences, cabins for the rangers, bridges, telephone lines, and the other items of equipment without which the reserves can not be handled to advantage, can not be protected properly, and can not contribute as they should to the general welfare. Expenditures for such permanent improvements are properly chargeable to capital account. The lack of reasonable working equipment weakens the protection of the national forests and greatly limits their production. This want can not be supplied from the appropriation for running expenses. The need is urgent. Accordingly I recommend that the Secretary of the Treasury be authorized to advance to the Forest Service, upon the security of the standing timber, an amount, say $5,000,000, sufficient to provide a reasonable working capital for the national forests, to bear interest and to be repaid in annual installments beginning in ten years.

TRANSFER OF THE NATIONAL PARKS

The national parks of the West are forested, and they lie without exception within or adjacent to national forest reserves. Two years ago the latter were transferred to the care of the Secretary of Agriculture, with the most satisfactory results. The same reasons which led to this transfer make advisable a similar transfer of the national parks, now in charge of the Secretary of the Interior, and I recommend legislation to that end.

INDIAN LANDS

Within or adjoining national forests are considerable areas of Indian lands of more value under forest than for any other purpose. It would aid greatly in putting these lands to their best use if the power to create national forests by proclamation were extended to cover them. The Indians should be paid the full value of any land thus taken for public purposes from the proceeds of the lands themselves, but such land should revert to the Indians if it is excluded from national forest use before full payment has been made.

GOVERNMENT CONTROL OF GRAZING

The control of grazing in the national forests is an assured success. The condition of the range is improving rapidly, water is being developed, much feed formerly wasted is now saved and used, range controversies are settled, opposition to the grazing fee is practically at an end, and the stockmen are earnestly supporting the Forest Service and cooperating with it effectively for the improvement of the range.

The situation on the open Government range is strikingly different. Its carrying capacity has probably been reduced one-half by overgrazing and is still falling. Range controversies in many places are active and bitter, and life and property are often in danger. The interests both of the live-stock industry and of the Government are needlessly impaired. The present situation is indefensible from any point of view, and it should be ended.

I recommend that a bill be enacted which will provide for Government control of the public range through the Department of Agriculture, which alone is equipped for that work. Such a bill should insure to each locality rules for grazing specially adapted to its needs and should authorize the collection of a reasonable grazing fee. Above all, the rights of the settler and home maker should be absolutely guaranteed.

Much of the public land can only be used to advantage for grazing when fenced. Much fencing has been done for that reason, and also to prevent other

[125]

stock owners from using land to which they have an equal right under the law. Reasonable fencing, which promotes the use of the range and yet interferes neither with settlement nor with other range rights, would be thoroughly desirable if it were legal. Yet the law forbids it, and the law must and will be enforced. I will see to it that the illegal fences are removed unless Congress at the present session takes steps to legalize proper fencing by Government control of the range.

Theodore Roosevelt

The White House
December 17, 1906

SPEECH BY SENATOR WILLIAM BORAH ON WESTERN CONSERVATION SENTIMENT*
June 20, 1910

As Senator William E. Borah (Idaho) pointed out in this speech, everybody favored conserving the natural resources for the benefit of the "small man." He also contended, however, that the specific operation of conservation policies harmed the small-man-homesteader, who was "driven to other lands."

Senator Borah, whose long career gained him popular recognition as the typical western Senator in the first half of the twentieth century, here expresses the general anti-conservation argument presented by western lawmakers.

Mr. President, I recur to those old records in the hope of inducing some of our friends who are haunted with a dying faith in the integrity and intelligence of the common man to go back and read them. There were those in that day as in this who declared that the vast public domain belonged to "all the people;" who declared in effect that "all the people" were weak and incapable of taking care of this domain should it be parceled out among them. Therefore the plan was to retain title in the Government and make of this vast estate a revenue-producing proposition to pay taxes of the Government, to care in different ways for the people who were not able to take care of themselves. The Government, said they, will shield the faltering and protect the American citizen from the absent landlord, from monopoly, from avarice and greed. The Government was spoken of, as it is now, as some stranger, beneficent in purpose and all wise and wholly separated from the people who constitute it. It was a great political philosophy. It had two vices, however, which insured its sudden demise. It was built upon a false theory which has been the plaything of fools since the creation of the world, to wit: That the Government is better and more wise than the people who constitute it; and, secondly, it lacked faith in the self-governing, self-contained, and self-dependent manhood of the American citizen.

On the other hand, there were those with larger vision and saner views and stronger faith. They knew this Government could not exist for a decade after the American citizen had ceased to be able to take care of himself in the personal affairs of life. They said those natural resources should go to the people in their respective States in which they are situated, to make homes and independent, self-reliant American citizens. They said they are bravely taking care of those resources and utilizing them to the best purpose. The citizens upon whom we rely to protect the Government itself can protect their homes and best utilize those lands. Therefore the Hales and Houstons and Lincoln said: Give

*Cong. Rec., 61st Cong., 2nd sess. (June 20, 1910), 8511–12.

these resources, the wealth in the respective States, to those who will bona fide and in good faith utilize them, and let them become subject to the dominion and control and administration of the State. And the doubts and fears of the many gave way at last to the faith, the never-faltering faith, of Lincoln, and the public domain of America was devoted to home building.

In the more noted events of that day the struggle which fixed the land policy of the Government has been overlooked or forgotten. But to my mind the hand which attached its signature to the American homestead law was as true and faithful to the heart and mind which directed it as it was in any other instance of that noted career. I need only point you to the great Commonwealths which have grown up under this policy—those Commonwealths of homes and thrift filled with a people perfectly capable of taking care of their own and of guarding their heritage—those powerful and invincible States of the Middle West.

I need only say to you that the great monopolies of this country do not exist and have not been aided by reason of the fact that the titles to our natural resources passed into the hands of the individual citizen. Monopolies have been built up in different ways than that, and monopolies will be controlled, not by distrusting the individual citizen. Put your faith in the common citizen; give him the reins of government; make him the owner of his home; and let him grow to full stature of free citizenship and our institutions are safe. But distrust the citizen, take from him the responsibility of government, the responsibility of caring for the material beneath which is the basis of his Commonwealth's power, and you imperil the foundation stones of our whole free fabric—our entire scheme of representative government.

Sir, there is not an acre of public land in America capable of making a home that it is not an indefensible crime to withhold from the man who would so utilize it. The government which is spending its millions for war ships, its millions for standing armies, its millions for public buildings, its millions for additional offices and officers, its millions for display, and will not find and make homes upon and out of the public domain for its home hungry people may be a republic in name, but it is untrue to the great principles upon which is founded a republic in fact. Those who stand in the way of wise and speedy action in such a case may be friends of some who seek the favors of national legislation, but wittingly or unwittingly they are not the friends of the home builder or the people of the republic which they profess to serve.

Out on the desert in the West, struggling in every way which their ingenuity can devise to protect their homes until the water which they stand ready to pay for and which the Government promised to deliver reaches them are men and women from every State in the Union. There is not a Senator upon this floor who would not be able to find some of the best citizens of his State, connected with the best families of his Commonwealth, lately removed there. They are anxious to get a home. Gradually through delay of the Government they are

[128]

being forced into absolute need. To leave them in the situation of victims of the Government's invitation and dilatory methods when they offer to pay every dollar of expense would be a shameless betrayal of public duty which no Congress will do when it fully understands the situation. Not a dollar of expense will ever fall to the Government. The homesteader stands ready to have the entire burden put upon his land. He only asks that the Government fulfill its contract and that he be given a chance to secure a home at his own expense upon what is known as the American Desert. Turning the desert into a prosperous community at the expense and through the energy of the settlers alone looks to me like practical conservation. This ought to enlist the enthusiasm and support of those who are earnest and devoted believers in conserving our natural resources. If those who believe the principle of conservation to be the greatest question of to-day continue to "pass by on the other side" from the man engaged in the actual struggle for existence, the American people will come to believe after while that after all this is but an ostentatious and Pharisaical display of efforts that live only in dress parade. While conventions are being held and literature teems with plaintive platitudes about caring for the "small man," about looking after the interests of all the people, while speeches in Congress and out of Congress deal with "consecration to the cause of giving every man an equal chance," while we are being told that the first consideration of our Republic is to have a nation of homes, the real man in the case, the home builder, is marooned on the American desert, fighting the real battle of conservation.

I have no doubt, Mr. President, that as he looks out upon the burning desert, cleared for cultivation and waiting for four and five years for water, estimating how much longer he can possibly hold out, he is greatly moved by this discussion which is going on about scenic beauty and hunting parks and the fearful situation of generations yet unborn. While his wife and children suffer privations of pioneer life, deprived of schools; while he is threatened from day to day with cancellation of his title to his homestead upon which he has put his last dollar, he is no doubt cheered with the news that Andrew Carnegie has promised to deliver an address to the conservation congress on how to make home life on the farm pleasant. If he seems stolid to all other matters, if he is not moved by the eloquence of Mr. Carnegie, who has earnestly and energetically devoted his entire life to conserving all the natural resources in sight, he will certainly be unusually hopeful when he learns that by an extraordinary maneuver the Secretary of the Interior has withdrawn 10,000 acres of power sites in the Sawtooth Mountains, which will undoubtedly prevent some grinding monopoly from exacting exorbitant charges from the only inhabitants of that fertile region — the mountain goats. By this time the homesteader is ready for retirement to pleasant dreams, and he opens his family Bible and reads:

Ye hypocrites, well did Isaiah prophesy of you, saying this people draweth nigh unto me with their mouth and honoreth me with their lips, but their heart is far from me.

Mr. President, I presume that most of us have heard a good deal of late with reference to conserving the natural resources for the benefit of the "small man." I do not know of anyone who is opposed to that proposition. I do know that the only man who has suffered by reason of the present policy is the small man. I do know that where that policy has pinched it has been the small man. I do know that the advantages which have been derived from the policy have been with the large men. I do not mean to say for a moment that that is the intention or the purpose of those who are advancing that policy. I do say, however, that it is the result of it, and those who are in favor of conserving our natural resources for the benefit of the individual citizen must modify their policy which is at present obtaining with reference to this all-important question. Let them cease to deal with theories and take up the question of serving the "small man" and we will join them. But we have seen the "small man" driven from his homestead, driven to other lands, and we are no longer infatuated by lay sermons upon virtues which no sane man challenges.

I want to discuss for a time one phase of what is called the conservation movement, and that is the question of dealing with our power sites. What I shall say from this time forward in my speech relates largely or practically to the question as to what we should do with reference to the control and development of our power sites.

I believe in the regulation and control of power plants for the development of our power sites, and the only question which I desire to present is the question which sovereignty shall do the work, whether it shall be done by the Federal Government or by the state government. The State alone, in my judgment, can deal properly with the subject-matter both as a practical proposition and as a legal proposition.

In addition to the legal proposition it is essentially a local matter. It is one of those things which belongs peculiarly to the locality in which the power sites are physically located. I do not believe that I am outside of the doctrine of one who is generally styled as the author of the conservation movement and for whom I have a most profound respect when I advance that theory. The ex-President said in his message to the governors' congress:

> In matters that relate only to the people within the State, of course the State is to be sovereign and should have power to act. If the matter is such that the State itself can not act, then I wish, on behalf of the State, that the National Government should act.

When it is clear that it is a national proposition and the State can not deal with the subject-matter it will be sufficient time to discuss the proposition of the Federal Government taking hold of it. When it is clear that it is essentially a local matter with which the State can deal and with which the State can deal more successfully, both under the letter and the spirit of our Constitution, it should be dealt with by the State. We should give some consideration to the question of our Constitution in dealing with these questions of conservation.

Dr. Woodrow Wilson stated in a notable speech, which he delivered a few days ago, that while we should have regulation and control we should have such regulation and control as is provided for under the constitutions of our States and of our Federal Government, and that it is not necessary to proceed outside of the well-established legal principles in order to control entirely and completely the development of our great power plants and power sites and to dedicate them to the use of the people and to control them to their advantage.

In my opinion, federal control of our power sites means one thing, and that is a greater burden and higher charge for the ultimate consumer of the power. The Federal Government has, we will admit for the sake of the argument, the power to impose a license or a tax for the use of the physical property which it owns, and I am only admitting that for the purpose of the argument. But no one would contend that the Federal Government could follow that proposition as to a power proposition situated within a State and operated within a State, and fix the charge which the individual owner or consumer of the power should pay.

The rate which is to be charged to the ultimate consumer of the power is a thing within the control and jurisdiction of the State. If the burden is laid by the Federal Government upon the power plants, the power plants will pass it unquestionably to the ultimate consumer. The real object to be attained in dealing with this subject is a reasonable charge to the man who ultimately uses it or to the consumer in the respective States.

More than that, there can be, in my judgment, no national plan by reason of the different conditions prevailing in the public-land States from that which prevails in the older States.

For instance, Professor Gilmore, I think, of the Wisconsin University, has written, and there has been filed here his treatise upon the question of riparian rights. It is as clear, forceful, conclusive, and comprehensive of that subject as I have ever read in law books or elsewhere, and he reasons out to my mind to a correct conclusion, assuming his premises to be correct. But a national plan which should be based upon the facts which prevail in his State, and concerning which he was discussing, would have no application in the world in the State of Colorado or in the State of Idaho, and most of the public-land States, for the reason that riparian rights have been abolished in our State, and the doctrine of prior appropriation is made the rule. There will inhere in the beginning the difference in regard to that practice. In addition to that, the Government does not own any power sites except in five or six States in the Union. The Government would not have the hold to proceed in the State of Wisconsin or in any of the Middle States or in the Eastern States that it has in ours of the West.

[131]

As I said, we might admit that the Government by reason of owning the land could impose a license system, but when it was imposed the result would be that the five or six public-land States would be paying a tax which could not be imposed in the other States of the Union, and that I propose to discuss more at length in a few moments.

Mr. President, what is the relation of the National Government to the public lands and to the water in the respective States, including the water which flows over the public lands?

I shall not discuss that at great length, but I want to put enough in the RECORD to enable those who are interested in the subject to know where the source of authority is, whether I shall this day be able to convince them as to the correctness of my position or not.

In England and at common law the bed and shores of all navigable streams were vested at first in the Crown, and anciently it was in the power of the King to convey the title to private parties. But this power was taken away from the King by Magna Charta, and it now rests with Parliament. The sovereign right of Parliament with reference to this subject-matter was transferred to the respective States at the close of the American Revolution and the acquisition of independence on the part of American States.

The States had the same control, the same authority, over the subject-matter, the beds and shores of the navigable streams and the water as had Parliament prior to the independence of the States. I think I might submit here, without hazarding a successful contradiction or any contradiction that the States have never transferred any part or parcel of that sovereignty to the National Government, save and except the right to control the streams for the purpose of protecting navigation. Outside and except the proposition of the power of Congress to deal with the subject of interstate commerce, and to keep the streams open for the purpose of protecting interstate commerce, the Congress of the United States has no control over the streams of my State, or of your State, or of the beds and water or water courses and streams in the respective States. When Congress has kept those streams open and usable for interstate purposes in the way of commerce, it has exhausted its power, and in undertaking to control them under the guise of regulating commerce, which does not have the purpose and legitimate object of regulating commerce, is to undertake to accomplish under the guise of a constitutional provision that which does not legitimately belong to the power.

The water and the streams of the States belong to and are subject to the control of the States and are not subject to the control of the National Government except in so far as it is necessary to control them in the regulation of commerce.

The public lands which the National Government possesses within each State it holds by no other and greater power than that which belongs to a private proprietor.

It is almost impossible in general discussion and in common parlance, in dealing with this subject, to separate in the public mind the sovereign power of the National Government from its proprietary right as a holder of public lands. Those who insist that many things can be done by reason of the National Government owning public lands within the States, inevitably attach to the proprietary right a governmental or sovereign power. The fact is, Mr. President, that the Government, which we may, for the purpose of individualizing, more specifically refer to here as "Uncle Sam"—Uncle Sam is the owner of public lands in my State just the same as are John Jones and William Smith. He has his proprietary right, and he may sell the land if he chooses; he may hold it if he chooses; and he may attach such conditions to it as any other proprietor would attach to the sale of his land. But will anyone contend that if Jones or Smith owns a piece of land in the State of Idaho, in selling that land he can attach any condition to it which will embarrass, hinder, or disturb the State of Idaho in exercising its sovereign power as a State? Can the United States Government, in dealing with these public lands as a proprietor, attach any condition to the sale of those lands which interferes with, embarrasses, or impedes the State's sovereignty from exercising its full power as a sovereign State?

The National Government has no power to prescribe for its grantees any general rules of law concerning the use of either lands or streams to which they are adjacent binding upon its grantees to become operative after the Federal Government has parted with title.

The rule concerning the holding and disposition of real property and of the use of waters within a State belong exclusively to the jurisdiction of the State. In other words, over the public lands within a State the United States has only the rights of a proprietor, and as soon as it parts with its title the conditions attached to the title must become subject to the regulation and control of the police power of the State.

The National Government has no power to deal with the use of water flowing over its lands except such as any other proprietor would have, and it can not, in dealing with this subject of water within a State, join its sovereign power to its proprietary rights for the purpose of effecting objects which it could not effect as a proprietor.

THE WITHDRAWAL ACT*
June 25, 1910

President William Howard Taft carried forward some of the Roosevelt conservation policies, but often with significant concessions. He broadened the public lands withdrawal program to include oil reserves and water power sites, and asked the Congress to give him the power to withdraw mineral lands from entry. As part of this law, however, he accepted an amendment providing that no further forest reserves were to be created in the states of Oregon, Washington, Idaho, Montana, Colorado, or Wyoming, except by act of Congress. In 1912 a further amendment was approved opening withdrawn lands for exploration and purchase of metalliferous minerals.

An Act to authorize the President of the United States to make withdrawals of public lands in certain cases.

Be it enacted by the Senate and House of Representatives of the United States of America in Congress assembled, That the President may, at any time in his discretion, temporarily withdraw from settlement, location, sale, or entry any of the public lands of the United States including the District of Alaska and reserve the same for water-power sites, irrigation, classification of lands, or other public purposes to be specified in the orders of withdrawals, and such withdrawals or reservations shall remain in force until revoked by him or by an Act of Congress.

SEC. 2. That all lands withdrawn under the provisions of this Act shall at all times be open to exploration, discovery, occupation, and purchase, under the mining laws of the United States, so far as the same apply to minerals other than coal, oil, gas, and phosphates: *Provided,* That the rights of any person who, at the date of any order of withdrawal heretofore or hereafter made, is a bona fide occupant or claimant of oil or gas bearing lands, and who, as such date, is in diligent prosecution of work leading to discovery of oil or gas, shall not be affected or impaired by such order, so long as such occupant or claimant shall continue in diligent prosecution of said work: *And provided further,* That this Act shall not be construed as a recognition, abridgment, or enlargement of any asserted rights or claims initiated upon any oil or gas bearing lands after any withdrawal of such lands made prior to the passage of this Act: *And provided further,* That there shall be excepted from the force and effect of any withdrawal made under the provisions of this Act all lands which are, on the date of such withdrawal, embraced in any lawful homestead or desert-land entry theretofore made, or

*36 *Statutes at Large,* 847–48

upon which any valid settlement has been made and is at said date being maintained and perfected pursuant to law; but the terms of this proviso shall not continue to apply to any particular tract of land unless the entryman or settler shall continue to comply with the law under which the entry or settlement was made: *And provided further,* That hereafter no forest reserve shall be created, nor shall any additions be made to one heretofore created within the limits of the States of Oregon, Washington, Idaho, Montana, Colorado, or Wyoming, except by Act of Congress.

SEC. 3. That the Secretary of the Interior shall report all such withdrawals to Congress at the beginning of its next regular session after the date of the withdrawals.

Approved, June 25, 1910.

AN AMENDMENT AUTHORIZING LAND PATENTS
AFTER THREE YEARS' RESIDENCE*
June 6, 1912

This last major change in the homestead program was prompted largely by the desire to match the liberality of the Dominion Land Act of Canada. The Canadians required only three years' residence to secure title to a homestead. Senator Borah charged that 125,000 settlers left the United States for Canada in 1911 to take advantage of the more liberal land law, and to escape the supervision of Land Office officials whom he described as "lynx-eyed detectives [operating] upon the presumption that [the homesteader] is a criminal. . . ."

The new law provided that a land patent was to be issued at the end of three years' residence, allowing for a leave of absence of 5 months in each year. Commutation was to be allowed after 14 months of actual residence, which largely ended the old practice of cash commutation.

Final homestead entries under this law increased sharply during the next few years, especially in the untimbered areas where its chief application was intended. A provision which required at least one-sixteenth of the claim to be cultivated the second year and one-eighth in the third year proved often impossible to meet in timbered areas. As a result, there was continued migration to Canada from the Pacific Northwest.

An Act to amend section twenty-two hundred and ninety-one and section twenty-two hundred and ninety-seven of the Revised Statutes of the United States relating to homesteads.

Be it enacted by the Senate and House of Representatives of the United States of America in Congress assembled, That section twenty-two hundred and ninety-one and section twenty-two hundred and ninety-seven of the Revised Statutes of the United States be amended to read as follows:

"SEC. 2291. No certificate, however, shall be given or patent issued therefor until the expiration of three years from the date of such entry; and if at the expiration of such time, or at any time within two years thereafter, the person making such entry, or if he be dead his widow, or in case of her death his heirs or devisee, or in case of a widow making such entry her heirs or devisee, in case of her death, proves by himself and by two credible witnesses that he, she, or they have a habitable house upon the land and have actually resided upon and cultivated the same for the term of three years succeeding the time of filing the affidavit, and makes affidavit that no part of such land has been alienated, except as provided in section twenty-two hundred and eighty-eight,

* 37 *Statutes at Large,* 123–24.

and that he, she, or they will bear true allegiance to the Government of the United States, then in such case he, she, or they, if at that time citizens of the United States, shall be entitled to a patent, as in other cases provided by law: *Provided,* That upon filing in the local land office notice of the beginning of such absence, the entryman shall be entitled to a continuous leave of absence from the land for a period not exceeding five months in each year after establishing residence, and upon the termination of such absence the entryman shall file a notice of such termination in the local land office, but in case of commutation the fourteen months' actual residence as now required by law must be shown, and the person commuting must be at the time a citizen of the United States: *Provided,* That when the person making entry dies before the offer of final proof those succeeding to the entry must show that the entryman had complied with the law in all respects to the date of his death and that they have since complied with the law in all respects, as would have been required of the entryman had he lived, excepting that they are relieved from any requirement of residence upon the land: *Provided further,* That the entryman shall, in order to comply with the requirements of cultivation herein provided for, cultivate not less than one-sixteenth of the area of his entry, beginning with the second year of the entry, and not less than one-eighth, beginning with the third year of the entry, and until final proof, except that in the case of entries under section six of the enlarged-homestead law double the area of cultivation herein provided shall be required, but the Secretary of the Interior may, upon a satisfactory showing, under rules and regulations prescribed by him, reduce the required area of cultivation: *Provided,* That the above provision as to cultivation shall not apply to entries under the Act of April twenty-eighth, nineteen hundred and four, commonly known as the Kinkaid Act, or entries under the Act of June seventeenth, nineteen hundred and two, commonly known as the reclamation Act, and that the provisions of this section relative to the homestead period shall apply to all unperfected entries as well as entries hereafter made upon which residence is required: *Provided,* That the Secretary of the Interior shall, within sixty days after the passage of this Act, send a copy of the same to each homestead entryman of record who may be affected thereby, by ordinary mail to his last known address, and any such entryman may, by giving notice within one hundred and twenty days after the passage of this Act, by registered letter to the register and receiver of the local land office, elect to make proof upon his entry under the law under which the same was made without regard to the provisions of this Act."

"SEC. 2297. If, at any time after the filing of the affidavit as required in section twenty-two hundred and ninety and before the expiration of the three years mentioned in section twenty-two hundred and ninety-one, it is proved, after due notice to the settler, to the satisfaction of the register of the land office that the person having filed such affidavit has failed to establish residence within six months after the date of entry, or abandoned the land for more than six months at any time, then and in that event the land so entered shall revert to the Government: *Provided,* That the three years' period of residence herein fixed shall date from the time of establishing actual permanent residence upon the land: *And provided further,* That where there may be climatic reasons, sickness, or other unavoidable cause, the Commissioner of the General Land Office may, in his discretion, allow the settler twelve months from the date of filing in which to commence his residence on said land under such rules and regulations as he may prescribe."

Approved, June 6, 1912.

REPORT FROM REPRESENTATIVE EDWARD TAYLOR
ON THE WESTERN CONSERVATION CONFERENCE*
June 6, 1913

With new faces in Washington, including a western Secretary of the Interior, the "Western Conservation Conference" was held in Denver in 1913 to encourage disposal of public lands and the turnover to the states of many conservation functions.

The remarks incident to the introduction in the Congressional Record *of the resolutions passed at the conference are included because they were made by Representative Edward T. Taylor of Colorado. Twenty years later Taylor was to be the sponsor of the Taylor Grazing Act, which firmly ratified federal control of the public domain.*

Mr. [EDWARD] TAYLOR of Colorado. Mr. Speaker, on the 4th, 5th, and 6th of this month the governors of the Western States held a meeting in Salt Lake City, Utah, for the purpose of considering the question of conservation as it has been practiced by the Federal Government during the past few years.

The object of the governors was to thoroughly discuss, agree upon, and systematically show to this new administration and to Congress how and wherein the present public-land policy is seriously impeding and permanently retarding the settlement of the public-land States, and to earnestly urge upon this administration and this Congress the imperative necessity of opening the public domain to settlement, and of a more liberal and practical policy toward the public-land settlers, the miners, and the development of the West generally.

The meeting was attended by nearly all of the western governors. The First Assistant Secretary of the Interior and the Commissioner of the General Land Office were both present by special invitation, and there was a full and free three days' discussion of the Federal public-land policy. No other question was considered. The conference was perfectly harmonious, thoroughly businesslike, and most successful; and after an exhaustive presentation of the subject, representing all phases of the matter, the governors unanimously agreed upon a statement to the country in the form of a set of resolutions, which have been transmitted to me by the governor of Colorado, and I ask leave to extend my remarks by inserting those resolutions in the RECORD, and at some later time I will ask consent to discuss these various subjects more in detail.

*Cong. Rec., 63rd Cong., 1st sess. (June 17, 1913), 2054.

LAND AND WATER

State of Colorado, Executive Office,
Denver, June 12, 1913.

Hon. Edward T. Taylor,
House of Representatives, Washington, D.C.

Dear Ed.:

I send you herewith copy of resolutions unanimously agreed to by the governors' conference at Salt Lake City. No other subject was considered, and the full three days were spent considering this matter. I found that the sentiment from other States was as strong as that from Colorado. When the proceedings are published, I will send you copies.

Yours, sincerely,

E. M. Ammons,
Governor.

We, the governors of public-land States, in conference assembled, believing that upon the administration of the laws governing the disposal of the public lands in a very large measure depends the future prosperity of our States, do hereby agree to the following statement of what we believe should be the policy of the National Government in the administration of the public lands:

First. That the newer States, having been admitted in expressed terms on an equal footing in all respects whatever with the original States, no realization of that condition can be obtained until the State jurisdiction shall extend to all their territory, the taxing power to all their lands, and their political power and influence be thereby secured.

Second. That as rapidly as the States become prepared to take over the work of conservation the Federal Government withdraw its bureaus from the field and turn the work over to the States.

Third. The permanent withdrawal of any lands within our States from entry and sale we believe to be contrary to the spirit and letter of the ordinance of 1787, the policy of which was followed for over a century, and we urge that such lands be returned to entry and opened to sale as speedily as possible.

Fourth. Dilatory action on the part of executive departments of the Government in passing title to purchasers of public lands is unfair to the States, as it permits purchasers to occupy the lands indefinitely without the State having power to tax them.

Fifth. We believe that the best development of these States depends upon the disposal of the public land to citizens as rapidly as the laws can be complied with.

Sixth. Bona fide homestead entry within forest-reserve boundaries should be permitted in the same manner as on unreserved lands, subject only to protest where lands selected are heavily timbered with trees of commercial value or are known to contain valuable mineral deposits.

Seventh. That the Government grant to the public-land States 5 per cent of the public land remaining in each, to be administered by the States as the school lands are now administered, for the purpose of building national public highways.

Eighth. That liberal land grants be made for the purpose of establishing and maintaining forestry schools in the public-land States.

Ninth. That rights of way for all lawful purposes be granted without unwarranted hindrance or delay.

Tenth. That all mineral lands now withheld from entry or classified at prohibitive prices be reopened to entry at nominal prices under strict provision against monopolization.

Eleventh. That we express our appreciation of the splendid work done by the department at Washington in cooperation with the several States in experimentation and instruction. This assistance has been most valuable in the education of our children and the development of our States, and we commend the same principle to the administration at Washington as being the most feasible plan for the present advancement of true conservation.

Twelfth. We believe that the National Government should provide for expert experimental work in the solution of the mining problems of the mineral States in the same manner that the Agricultural Department now assists the farmers in solving the agricultural problems.

Thirteenth. We believe that the speedy settlement of these public lands constitutes the true and best interests of the Republic. The wealth and strength of the country are its land-owning population.

Fourteenth. The best and most economical development of this western territory was accomplished under those methods in vogue when the States of the Middle West were occupied and settled. In our opinion those methods have never been improved upon, and we advocate a return to these first principles of vested ownership with joint interest and with widely scattered individual responsibility.

"WHAT ABOUT OUR PUBLIC LAND?"*
December 1929

President Hoover proposed to solve part of the public land problem by disposing of most of the land to private owners by way of individual states. His Secretary of the Interior, Ray Lyman Wilbur, floated a trial balloon for this idea in an article in The Review of Reviews.

President Hoover's proposal to the Conference of Governors of the public land states held in Salt Lake City last August, indicating his desire for the appointment of a commission to study existing conditions in the public lands, and to make recommendations regarding the transfer of the unappropriated lands to the western states, has brought out for new discussion the most outstanding problem of the West. There is bound to be a wide difference of opinion as to the best course to pursue, but there can be no escape from the existing facts.

Former Secretary of the Interior James R. Garfield has recently been selected by the President as head of the National Commission to make a report to him and to Congress as to the wisest program for the future of the public domain. This was done after consultation with the chairmen of the Committees of the Senate and House on Public Lands, and on Agriculture, with the general understanding that legislation would be passed in the next Congress making provision for the commission and its financial support. Mr. Garfield's reputation as a conservationist, and his practical experience as Secretary of the Interior, make him the ideal chairman. The commission has representatives from all parts of the United States, and particularly from the eleven western states that are usually referred to as the public domain states.

Possible transfer of the custodianship of public lands is a conservation move of major significance. While, because of the political questions involved and the existing relations between the federal government and the states, it may take on a controversial aspect, if it results in bare-bone thinking and the facing of harsh realities it will be of great national significance.

Every informed person realizes that the lack of interest and of funds and of laws for proper control of the public domain has resulted in great if not irreparable damage to a considerable portion of our heritage.

The Public Lands Commission appointed by President Roosevelt in 1904 emphasized the fact that most of the then vacant public lands were unsuitable for cultivation under present conditions of agriculture, and so located that they could not be reclaimed by irrigation. It was brought out that their chief value

---

*Ray Lyman Wilbur, "What About Our Public Land?" *The Review of Reviews* (Dec., 1929), 56–58.

was for grazing. Since the lands were theoretically open common, free to all citizens, they were being over-grazed. The commission stated: "The general lack of control in the use of public grazing lands has resulted naturally and inevitably in over-grazing and the ruin of millions of acres of otherwise valuable grazing territory."

The conditions in 1904 and 1905 still prevail and are even more in evidence, except in those areas where there has been a degree of control through the grazing regulations of the National Forests. The deterioration of the public domain from the standpoint of its plant life has been persistent and steady. Since this has brought about increase in floods and erosion, decrease in the water-storage capacity of the soils, more rapid sedimentation of reservoirs, and the distinct decrease in the water-holding and water-carrying capacity of the great watersheds, it is a problem of primary importance to the welfare of the country.

Rain is looked upon by many as a gift of God. The geographers have discovered close relationships between population and the average annual rainfall in many parts of the world. Much of the western part of the United States is semi-arid. Not long ago it was called the Great American Desert in school geographies. Over this whole area water, and water alone, is the controlling factor in the establishment of homes, communities, and cities. The relationship of rainfall, of springs, and of stream flow to vegetation is not fully appreciated.

There is, unfortunately, much shallow thinking about mountain lands, so-called desert lands, and watershed lands. Many consider them of no value unless they are capable of furnishing homesteaders a living. As a matter of fact they are the basis of the life of the valleys. Without the mountains and their snow- and water-carrying capacities, the semi-arid regions would remain practically uninhabited. With the vegetation of the hills damaged, the water falling from the sky runs off as it would from a sharp roof. With the vegetation present, there is a considerable delay in the run-off of water and in the melting of snow which permits a steady supply to the springs, streams, and reservoirs. This applies in all sections of the country. In fact, industry must locate where there is a dependable water supply or regular stream flow. Cutting down forests to make farms and plowing up the prairies have both played a part in the increased danger of floods and in the constant soil erosion which is denuding this continent of the accumulated humus of millions of years.

The study made by the Geological Survey of Burnt Brook and Shoal Pond basins of the White Mountains in New Hampshire is of great significance in indicating the advantages of the increase in water-holding capacity due to the presence of vegetation. Continued experience has demonstrated that one of the greatest menaces from fires in the forests or on the plain is the uncovering of the soil to rain damage. Experiments conducted by the Forest Service show that proper care and seeding will bring much of this damaged area back into a more normal condition.

The plain and alarming fact is that, owing to many factors including the division between state and federal authority, outside of the National Parks and the National Forests, the twenty years since the public-land report under Roosevelt has shown persistent deterioration of the land. This is of more significance than the reduced carrying capacity of the range. It strikes at our future, which can be based only on the inherent values of the continent we occupy.

It is worth while to look at the present status of the public lands of the country. Since Continental days the Government has been passing its real property into the hands of its citizens. This process has been practically completed in the states east of the Missouri River. At present in the United States, exclusive of Alaska, there are roughly 190,000,000 acres under the general charge of the public land office without the slightest shadow of a program for its preservation as a range.

Unless some definite procedure is agreed upon this will be nibbled away gradually until that remnant which remains will be practically valueless. Either the federal government should have the laws and the funds properly to protect and administer the mountain tops, the deserts, and the public lands in general, or the states should assume this responsibility. Since the states live close to these problems of grazing, fires, floods, erosion, and the silting of reservoirs, and since there is in the states the opportunity for a political balance between the agriculturist of the valley and reclaimed area as opposed to the man using or abusing the watershed, there is more likelihood that real conservation and protection will result from local control and local management.

The fight in California between the farmers in the valley lands and the placer miners in the hills who were covering the farms with débris was won by the farmers. The political majorities are in the valleys and settled areas. When they realize the significance of the mountains, the public domain, and water in general, the best results are apt to follow.

It does not seem wise to me to have federal supervision over too much of an area of any state. This removes from the state the necessity of its taking care of many of its own problems. It is particularly apt to inhibit initiative in such matters as the development of state parks and forests. California, like other western states, satisfied with its National Parks and Forests, long neglected consideration of park problems. Finally she awoke to the fact that her almost thousand miles of seacoast had largely passed into private hands and that there was hardly a scrap of the great redwoods forests outside of private ownership. The citizens of the state had been dulled as to their responsibilities until the very pressure of numbers seeking recreation compelled attention.

The experience of several of the eastern states indicates how much can be done by wise state action in the control of plant life and watersheds. A study of the results in Pennsylvania indicates something of the possibilities in this direction. With the shift of the farm population into the more favored areas of the country the question of open spaces, cutover lands, abandoned farms, waste lands, and watersheds is demanding state action of a highly intelligent character, so that this problem is by no means confined to western states. Through the taxing power of the states a direct approach can be had to many of these important questions.

It is clear that we have drifted and stumbled across this great continent in our conquest of it, leaving change and destruction in our wake, without a well-worked-out strategy for handling the basic problems associated with rain and snowfall, stream flow, soil protection and erosion, and the preservation of wild plant life. With the increased spread of scientific training in the schools and that laboratory experience which is necessary in student life for evaluation of the facts of nature there is a better prospect of wise action in our democracy in the years ahead of us. It is imperative to realize that nature goes on her way following unchanging universal laws. We can deny them temporarily, but we cannot defeat them. We must conform our march with the orderly processes of nature or we are bound to fail.

Recreation has become of outstanding significance in the life of the nation. The mountains and the forests and the desert are the great open places for recreation, but recreation must be based on a proper conservation of the natural conditions prevailing in these regions. Few people realize the great value of mountains. They think of them as of no importance because for the most part people cannot live upon them. The truth is that the relationship of the mountains and hills to the precipitation and storage of water is fundamental to our valley and plains civilization as it exists today.

The storage of water is primary to all reclamation. Plans for the creation of water storage under federal control can readily be worked out in such a way as to free the states from the danger of the control of a distant bureaucracy. Water is the only key that will unlock the desert. The greatest achievement of the western pioneer has not been in detecting gold or releasing oil pools, but in conquest of water in its relationships to power and to irrigation. The citizen of an eastern state who has a dependable rain supply to guarantee him crops can never understand the water problem of the West. Enlightened local self-interest, it seems to me, is most likely to bring about the greatest protection of our valuable watersheds.

Absentee landlordism, whether it is that of an individual or of the national government, is not the ideal method for building a democratic commonwealth. It seems to me that the time has come for the states largely to absorb and manage their own local problems. There can be a degree of national help and considerable time can elapse as a period of adjustment, but in the long run state governments must accept responsibilities for the territory within their borders.

[145]

"Western states have long since passed from their swaddling clothes and are today more competent to manage much of these affairs than is the federal government," President Hoover has said.

The major question is the actual preservation of the plant life of the present public lands, and not what political unit or bureau shall have control. Trees, shrubs, and grasses do not know whether they are on fee lands, public domain, National Park, Indian reservation, or National Forest. They play their part or or fail to play it regardless of our present political units or ideas. The essential thing is that they be preserved.

"THE PUBLIC DOMAIN"*
August 6, 1930

An answer to the Hoover plan was summarized by Henry S. Graves in an article in The Nation. *Graves was a veteran of the Roosevelt-Pinchot conservation school and a former head of the Forest Service.*

The last chapter in the story of the federal public domain is about to be written. President Hoover has brought before the country, as a definite issue, the question of the disposal of the last remnants of the unreserved public lands, which are now without any semblance of supervision and control and are being rapidly ruined by abuse. On authority from Congress, he has appointed a commission to study the problem and to submit recommendations for its solution. He himself has proposed a tentative plan, namely, that the federal government should cede the remaining public lands to the several States in which they are located, with the reservation of certain mineral rights.

The President is to be highly commended for his insistence that some constructive steps be taken to provide for the right handling of the public lands. The appointment of a commission is an excellent method of dramatizing the situation and securing the advice of a group of well-informed citizens in formulating a new public-land policy. The tentative proposal for the transfer of lands to the States will, however, meet strong opposition. Many persons, including the writer of this article, believe that the plan to grant the lands to the States is not a real solution of the problems involved and that it would not be in the public interest from the standpoint either of the nation or of the States.

The public domain had its beginnings with the cession to the United States by the original States of their unsettled Western lands after the Revolutionary War. It was enormously increased by the acquisition of Florida, the Louisiana Purchase, the Oregon treaty, the accessions from Mexico, and the purchase of Alaska. There was no federal land in Texas, for upon the entry of that State into the Union it was stipulated that the public lands should remain in possession of the State.

The first public-land law was passed in 1785. It provided for a survey of the public properties and established a procedure for their sale. There has followed a long series of acts of Congress for the disposal of the federal lands, as changing conditions have called for new legislation. The early policy of selling the lands was replaced by one designed to encourage agricultural settlement, culminating in the free-homestead law of 1862. Subsequently, laws were passed for the disposal of arid lands requiring irrigation for cultivation, of so-called "dry-farming"

*Henry S. Graves, "The Public Domain," *The Nation,* Vol. 131, No. 3396 (Aug. 6, 1930), 147–49.

areas, and, more recently, of grazing lands. Special laws were passed for mineral lands, though, curiously enough, not until 1866. At the late date of 1878 an attempt was made to meet the special timberland problem, but the legislation was so faulty that it served chiefly as an instrument of fraud. There have also been large and numerous grants for education, for canals, highways, and railroads, for reclamation of arid lands, for reclamation of swamp lands, and for manifold other purposes.

The history of the public domain is intimately related to the industrial history of the country. The migration of a great population over the public lands, the establishment of millions of farms, the construction of the great system of railways, the development of industries depending on minerals, timber, forage, and other natural resources, the building of cities and towns, and the creation of independent States, all within a comparatively short period of time, constitute one of the most extraordinary epochs in all history. Unquestionably, the liberality of the government in its disposal of the public domain was a large factor in this economic and industrial expansion. Quick peopling of the land was accomplished. But the process was accompanied by many serious blunders, by a lax administration of the laws, resulting in speculation, fraud, and often corruption, by tremendous waste of valuable resources, by loss of control of lands which should have been retained in public ownership, by local social distress, much of which will never be known, and by other consequences that will fall as a burden upon generations to follow.

We often think of the public domain as a chapter that is closed. It is true that the public domain is no longer an important factor in our industrial expansion. The westward migration has ceased. The pressure for new lands for settlement has stopped because there are no more public lands fit for agricultural settlement. Moreover, the industrial and economic changes of the past fifty years have created new conditions which could not be met in the old ways even if we still had an expanse of public lands comparable to that of 1880. The problem of acquiring natural resources has now been replaced by the problem of using them.

Nevertheless, the nation still owns a large area of lands, the residue after more than a century of picking over by men seeking to acquire lands under the various laws. More than 340,000,000 acres in the United States are still owned by the government. In addition, there are about 20,000,000 acres upon which the mineral rights have been reserved though the ownership of the surface has passed to private individuals. This grand total includes about 140,000,000 acres in national forests and parks and about 12,000,000 acres in lands withdrawn for the control of coal, oil, potash, and phosphates. There remain about 190,000,000 acres of land, unreserved, unappropriated, awaiting constructive administration and development. Nearly all of it has no more protection and administration than on the day it was acquired, and because of abuse it has been steadily deteriorating in productive value. This is the land which the President has suggested should be transferred to the States.

The remaining open public domain is chiefly located in the arid and semi-arid portions of sixteen Western States. Seventy-five per cent of Nevada is still unreserved public domain, 50 per cent of Utah, 23 per cent of New Mexico, 22 per cent of Arizona, 18 per cent of California, 16 per cent of Idaho, 22 per cent of Oregon, 29 per cent of Wyoming, and smaller proportions of other Western States. Five or ten million acres are natural timberlands; several million acres are open woodlands or low scrub; the remaining lands are clothed with grass and other herbaceous vegetation or with dry-land shrubs. Some are virtual deserts.

About 15 per cent of the present public domain may be classed as unproductive desert owing to lack of water or to alkaline soil or both. The areas of real desert are situated in southern California in the Death Valley and the Salton Sea region, in Utah west of Salt Lake, and in southwestern Arizona. The remainder of the open public lands—about 160,000,000 acres—is naturally clothed with grass and other herbaceous vegetation, or with low woody plants such as sagebrush, creosote brush, mesquite, and other types of shrubs or small trees, many of which have some nutritious value as browse for live stock. The land has been used for grazing for more than fifty years and some of it for a much longer time. It is public land, unfenced and open, for the use of any or all who may be able to place their stock upon it. There has never been any control of its use by the government, no restrictions as to the number of stock or methods of grazing, and no efforts to prevent injury to the land.

For forty years or more these ranges have been overgrazed. The effect of overcrowding the land with live stock has been disastrous, a progressive march toward devastation. The first injury is the destruction of the more nutritious forage plants. The reduction in the density of the grass and other vegetation exposes the soil to sun and wind. The water-holding power is impaired and the remaining plants are less vigorous in growth. From year to year the carrying capacity of the land for live stock has declined. On an average, the productive power of the land has been reduced 50 to 75 per cent and in places 80 to 90 per cent.

A second consequence of overgrazing is the loss of the surface soil by erosion. It may seem odd to discuss erosion in connection with arid lands, where the lack of water is the most conspicuous characteristic. Erosion depends not only on topography and soil but on the character of precipitation. In the dry regions the storms are often cyclonic and the rain falls in heavy showers. A large part of the Western ranges is rolling, hilly, or actually mountainous. Under natural conditions the soil is held in place by the protective vegetation. Even the cactus plays its part. Under normal conditions the degradation of the hills and ridges is very gradual and violent surface changes occur only occasionally through unusually heavy storms. Overgrazing loosens the soil and every storm carries off large quantities of the upper surface. Great gullies are formed that change the whole character of the run-off of water. The more compact subsoil is exposed, less water enters the ground, and the general water table is lowered. In the rich valleys the agricultural lands are gullied out and great arroyos are formed, often ten feet deep and thirty feet or more in width. Irrigation ditches and reservoirs are filled and frequently tons of detritus are deposited on fertile farm lands in the valley bottoms.

The problem of instituting a reform in the handling of the public domain offers complexities because of the varying character of the lands, the extent of the damage by overgrazing, the present distribution of the lands, and their intimate relation to the local industrial development. Leaving out of consideration the areas of actual desert, there are about 160,000,000 acres of range lands which constitute the real public-land problem. These may be divided into three classes, as follows:

1. Very large areas which are chiefly in federal ownership. The most important areas in this category are the West Desert in western Utah and eastern Nevada, comprising some 16,000,000 acres; the Red Desert in Wyoming, covering about 7,000,000 acres; the Owyhee Desert in southeastern Oregon and southwestern Idaho, containing about 25,000,000 acres; the Ralston and Pahute Desert in southern Nevada, with perhaps 15,000,000 acres; and the Jornada Desert in New Mexico, comprising about 6,000,000 acres. It is probable that about 70 per cent of these lands is in public ownership.

2. Areas comprising more than 100,000 acres in a body, but far less extensive than those mentioned in the preceding paragraph. It is probable that this class aggregates nearly 30 per cent of the public range. The blocks of land are not compact bodies of government property but are interrupted by State holdings, railroad sections, and other private lands.

3. Areas varying in size from a few sections to 100,000 acres. A considerable portion of these lands is adjacent to the national forests and its development is closely dependent on the use of the forage in these public reservations.

The problem of the public domain cannot be met by the old methods of land disposal. The various homestead laws do not apply, except to a very limited extent. A general sale law would not be effective unless very large units were placed on the market, which would inevitably be embarrassing to small ranchers who now use the lands for grazing and which would give monopolistic control of the lands to large concerns. Moreover, a great deal of the land has been so depleted in productiveness that private owners cannot afford to hold it. The new policy to be adopted should make possible the handling of each portion of the public domain in a way adapted to the conditions prevailing on the land itself. Abuse by overgrazing not only destroys a natural resource which sustains one of the great industries of the semi-arid portions of the West, but it results also in erosion and in torrential conditions that have a far-reaching effect on stream flow, irrigation, and community welfare generally. Nearly all the public domain, outside the real desert areas, is situated on the watersheds of important river systems, including the Rio Grande, Gila, Salt, Arkansas, Snake, and Missouri rivers. The disturbance of the normal conditions of run-off on large masses of land inevitably affects the rivers and their beneficial service. The neglect of the public domain over the years is releasing natural forces that may be felt in increased irregularity of river flow, embarrassment in irrigation and power development, and public injury in many other ways.

An analogous situation was encountered more than thirty years ago in the forests on the public domain. They were being ruined by fire, overgrazing, and abuse. The solution was found in the establishment of the national forests. For twenty-five years about 160,000,000 acres of public property have been successfully administered and the forests and other resources protected and developed. The grazing lands within the national forests were brought under systematic control, erosion was checked, and the productive power of the land for grazing progressively restored. The handling of the national forests points the way for the administration of public domain.

The policy which, in the opinion of the writer of this article, should be followed by the government in handling the public domain is as follows:

1. To establish at once a system of control of grazing on all the public land analogous to that in successful operation in the national forests. This would involve a curtailment of the number of stock using the lands to the extent necessary to begin the restoration of the range.

2. To make a charge for the privilege of using the range for grazing, with provision for payment to the States of as liberal a proportion of the receipts from this source as Congress may deem appropriate.

3. To add to the national forests the areas of public grazing lands adjacent to them, where the grazing use may best be administered in conjunction with that in the national forests. The area of lands so situated is estimated to be about 16,000,000 acres.

4. To add to the national forests the lands in the public domain which are covered with forest growth and so located as to be best administered as permanent reservations. There are about 8,000,000 acres of such lands.

5. To establish permanent federal grazing reserves wherever conditions are such that the development and use of the lands and the protection of water resources can best be secured through this means.

6. To provide for the exchange of lands with States, railroads, and private owners in order to consolidate the federal and other holdings.

7. To provide for grants of lands to the States where this is desirable to round out existing holdings or to meet other special local problems.

8. To provide a procedure for the sale of land to individuals or companies

where it is clear that private ownership is the best means to promote the beneficial use of the property. Authority should be given to dispose of blocks of land large enough to meet the economic conditions of grazing but with clear limitations essential to prevent monopoly and interference with the interests of the small ranchmen. A very liberal proportion of the proceeds of such sales should be granted to the States.

9. To transfer the administration of the public ranges from the Department of the Interior to the Department of Agriculture, where there is a corps of men trained in problems of range control.

Such a program would involve extensive field study, and each step naturally would be subject to sanction by Congress on the basis of administrative recommendations. The plan has the advantage of an immediate check to the present abuse of the range. It provides a method of progressively disposing of all the land through the incorporation of a portion in permanent reservations and through transferring the balance in an orderly way to other ownership.

The restoration of the lands to productive condition will be a slow process. Generally speaking, it takes twenty years or more to rehabilitate a badly depleted range, and this is accomplished only through expert control and management. Improvements are also necessary, such as roads, water developments, drift fences, and the like, involving considerable capital outlay; and some engineering works must be constructed to prevent torrents and erosion which result from the past abuse of the land.

The proposal that the nation surrender to the States the responsibility of meeting the situation on the public domain is made presumably on the ground that the problem is a local one. There are, however, great national interests involved. First of all, the lands belong to the nation and the responsibility for handling the properties in the best interests of the public is in itself a national one. In the next place, watershed protection is an interstate problem of the first order. Still again, the problem of range control and use is interstate in character. On the great ranges immense numbers of stock are driven out of one State to graze on areas located in another State. The use of the public range has been a large factor in building up the existing live-stock industry, which involves large investments in stock and plant. The division of the jurisdiction over these lands would involve serious consequences for the industry if the several States should inaugurate different policies of land administration. Finally, the proper handling of the problems of the public domain is beyond the power of most of the States. The sheer magnitude of the undertaking places it in the category of a national problem.

Some persons entertain the belief that under State ownership the lands would pass to private ownership and thus increase the grand list. Some lands would doubtless be sold. The government, with appropriate authority from Congress, can also sell such lands as should not remain permanently under public control.

The States in the long run will gain far more from a liberal grant of the annual proceeds from grazing fees and other sources of income than by the effort to handle the lands themselves, especially if the States should undertake to restore them to productiveness and provide the improvements that are necessary.

The proposal to transfer the public lands to the States has been referred to as the new conservation. As yet I have been unable to find any evidence that the lands would be better handled by the States than by the government from the standpoint of conservation. The fact that the government has failed so far in administering the open ranges is not proof that it will continue to do so. The government has demonstrated that it is wholly competent to meet problems of this kind in its successful management of 160,000,000 acres of national forests. It can do as well on the public domain. The failure of the government in handling the open ranges may be charged to a number of causes. The chief responsibility lies in the lack of determined leadership by the Department of the Interior, which has charge of the public domain. This department is not organized and equipped for the administration of problems of soil production and land use. Formerly it had charge of the public forests and failed in exactly the same way that it has failed in the administration of the grazing problem on the public domain. The constructive handling of the national forests began when they were placed under the jurisdiction of the Department of Agriculture, where there was a corps of trained foresters. The administration of the grazing lands involves precisely the class of problems which the experts of the Department of Agriculture are qualified by their training and experience to handle.

The President has chosen an excellent commission to study the problems of the public domain. The chairman, Honorable James R. Garfield, was a leader in conservation when he served in President Roosevelt's Cabinet. Fifty thousand dollars has been provided by Congress for the expenses of the commission. It is hoped that a constructive plan will be developed, a plan which will not involve a shirking by the nation of its plain responsibilities.

THE TAYLOR GRAZING ACT*
June 28, 1934

Representative Edward T. Taylor came to Congress from Colorado in 1909 imbued with the standard western notions about conservation dictated from the East. He and his constituents saw so much deterioration of the public domain in twenty-five years, however, that Taylor undertook sponsorship of the bill to allow the Interior Department to regulate grazing on public lands and to collect fees for this use.

The Taylor Grazing Act is still the basis for administering the public domain. During the first twenty years of its life, conservationists had to mobilize several times to resist attempts to weaken it, but they won all the big fights. Thus, the act is an example of how the most rugged opponents of conservation programs can change when they see the light of intelligent self-interest.

An Act to stop injury to the public grazing lands by preventing over-grazing and soil deterioration, to provide for their orderly use, improvement, and development, to stabilize the livestock industry dependent upon the public range, and for other purposes.

Be it enacted by the Senate and House of Representatives of the United States of America in Congress assembled, That in order to promote the highest use of the public lands pending its final disposal, the Secretary of the Interior is authorized, in his discretion, by order to establish grazing districts or additions thereto and/or to modify the boundaries thereof, not exceeding in the aggregate an area of eighty million acres of vacant, unappropriated, and unreserved lands from any part of the public domain of the United States (exclusive of Alaska), which are not in national forests, national parks and monuments, Indian reservations, revested Oregon and California Railroad grant lands, or revested Coos Bay Wagon Road grant lands, and which in his opinion are chiefly valuable for grazing and raising forage crops: *Provided,* That no lands withdrawn or reserved for any other purpose shall be included in any such district except with the approval of the head of the department having jurisdiction thereof. Nothing in this Act shall be construed in any way to diminish, restrict, or impair any right which has been heretofore or may be hereafter initiated under existing law validly affecting the public lands, and which is maintained pursuant to such law except as otherwise expressly provided in this Act, nor to affect any land heretofore or hereafter surveyed which, except for the provisions of this Act, would be a part of any grant to any State, nor as limiting or restricting the power or authority of any State as to matters within its jur-

*48 *Statutes at Large,* 1269–75.

[154]

isdiction. Whenever any grazing district is established pursuant to this Act, the Secretary shall grant to owners of land adjacent to such district, upon application of any such owner, such rights-of-way over the lands included in such district for stock-driving purposes as may be necessary for the convenient access by any such owner to marketing facilities or to lands not within such district owned by such person or upon which such person has stock-grazing rights. Neither this Act nor the Act of December 29, 1916 (39 Stat. 862; U.S.C., title 43, secs. 291 and following), commonly known as the "Stock Raising Homestead Act", shall be construed as limiting the authority or policy of Congress or the President to include in national forests public lands of the character described in section 24 of the Act of March 3, 1891 (26 Stat. 1103; U.S.C., title 16, sec. 471), as amended, for the purposes set forth in the Act of June 4, 1897 (30 Stat. 35; U.S.C., title 16, sec. 475), or such other purposes as Congress may specify. Before grazing districts are created in any State as herein provided, a hearing shall be held in the State, after public notice thereof shall have been given, at such location convenient for the attendance of State officials, and the settlers, residents, and livestock owners of the vicinity, as may be determined by the Secretary of the Interior. No such district shall be established until the expiration of ninety days after such notice shall have been given, nor until twenty days after such hearing shall be held: *Provided, however,* That the publication of such notice shall have the effect of withdrawing all public lands within the exterior boundary of such proposed grazing districts from all forms of entry of settlement. Nothing in this Act shall be construed as in any way altering or restricting the right to hunt or fish within a grazing district in accordance with the laws of the United States or of any State, or as vesting in any permittee any right whatsoever to interfere with hunting or fishing within a grazing district.

SEC. 2. The Secretary of the Interior shall make provision for the protection, administration, regulation, and improvement of such grazing districts as may be created under the authority of the foregoing section, and he shall make such rules and regulations and establish such service, enter into such cooperative agreements, and do any and all things necessary to accomplish the purposes of this Act and to insure the objects of such grazing districts, namely, to regulate their occupancy and use, to preserve the land and its resources from destruction or unnecessary injury, to provide for the orderly use, improvement, and development of the range; and the Secretary of the Interior is authorized to continue the study of erosion and flood control and to perform such work as may be necessary amply to protect and rehabilitate the areas subject to the provisions of this Act, through such funds as may be made available for that purpose, and any willful violation of the provisions of this Act or of such rules and regulations thereunder after actual notice thereof shall be punishable by a fine of not more than $500.

SEC. 3. That the Secretary of the Interior is hereby authorized to issue or cause to be issued permits to graze livestock on such grazing districts to such bona fide settlers, residents, and other stock owners as under his rules and regulations are entitled to participate in the use of the range, upon the payment annually of reasonable fees in each case to be fixed or determined from time to time: *Provided,* That grazing permits shall be issued only to citizens of the United States or to those who have filed the necessary declarations of intention to become such, as required by the naturalization laws and to groups, associations, or corporations authorized to conduct business under the laws of the State in which the grazing district is located. Preference shall be given in the issuance of grazing permits to those within or near a district who are landowners engaged in the livestock business, bona fide occupants or settlers, or owners of water or water rights, as may be necessary to permit the proper use of lands, water or water rights owned, occupied, or leased by them, except that until July 1, 1935, no preference shall be given in the issuance of such permits to any such owner, occupant, or settler, whose rights were acquired between January 1, 1934, and December 31, 1934, both dates inclusive, except that no permittee complying with the rules and regulations laid down by the Secretary of the Interior shall be denied the renewal of such permit, if such denial will impair the value of the grazing unit of the permittee, when such unit is pledged as security for any bona fide loan. Such permits shall be for a period of not more than ten years, subject to the preference right of the permittees to renewal in the discretion of the Secretary of the Interior, who shall specify from time to time numbers of stock and seasons of use. During periods of range depletion due to severe drought or other natural causes, or in case of a general epidemic of disease, during the life of the permit, the Secretary of the Interior is hereby authorized, in his discretion to remit, reduce, refund in whole or in part, or authorize postponement of payment of grazing fees for such depletion period so long as the emergency exists: *Provided further,* That nothing in this Act shall be construed or administered in any way to diminish or impair any right to the possession and use of water for mining, agriculture, manufacturing, or other purposes which has heretofore vested or accrued under existing law validly affecting the public lands or which may be hereafter initiated or acquired and maintained in accordance with such law. So far as consistent with the purposes and provisions of this Act, grazing privileges recognized and acknowledged shall be adequately safeguarded, but the creation of a grazing district or the issuance of a permit pursuant to the provisions of this Act shall not create any right, title, interest, or estate in or to the lands.

SEC. 4. Fences, wells, reservoirs, and other improvements necessary to the care and management of the permitted livestock may be constructed on the public lands within such grazing districts under permit issued by the authority of the Secretary, or under such cooperative arrangement as the Secretary may approve. Permittees shall be required by the Secretary of the Interior to comply with the provisions of law of the State within which the grazing district is located with respect to the cost and maintenance of partition fences. No permit shall be issued which shall entitle the permittee to the use of such improvements constructed and owned by a prior occupant until the applicant has paid to such prior occupant the reasonable value of such improvements to be determined under rules and regulations of the Secretary of the Interior. The decision of the Secretary in such cases is to be final and conclusive.

SEC. 5. That the Secretary of the Interior shall permit, under regulations to be prescribed by him, the free grazing within such districts of livestock kept for domestic purposes; and provided that so far as authorized by existing law or laws hereinafter enacted, nothing herein contained shall prevent the use of timber, stone, gravel, clay, coal, and other deposits by miners, prospectors for mineral, bona fide settlers and residents, for firewood, fencing, buildings, mining, prospecting, and domestic purposes within areas subject to the provisions of this Act.

SEC. 6. Nothing herein contained shall restrict the acquisition, granting or use of permits or rights-of-way within grazing districts under existing law; or ingress or egress over the public lands in such districts for all proper and lawful purposes; and nothing herein contained shall restrict prospecting, locating, developing, mining, entering, leasing, or patenting the mineral resources of such districts under law applicable thereto.

SEC. 7. That the Secretary is hereby authorized, in his discretion, to examine and classify any lands within such grazing districts which are more valuable and suitable for the production of agricultural crops than native grasses and forage plants, and to open such lands to homestead entry in tracts not exceeding three hundred and twenty acres in area. Such lands shall not be subject to settlement or occupation as homesteads until after same have been classified and opened to entry after notice to the permittee by the Secretary of the Interior, and the lands shall remain a part of the grazing district until patents are issued therefor, the homesteader to be, after his entry is allowed, entitled to the possession and use thereof: *Provided,* That upon the application of any person qualified to make homestead entry under the public-land laws, filed in the land office of the proper district, the Secretary of the Interior shall cause any tract not exceeding three hundred and twenty acres in any grazing district to be classified, and such application shall entitle the applicant to a preference right to enter such lands when opened to entry as herein provided.

SEC. 8. That where such action will promote the purposes of the district or facilitate its administration, the Secretary is authorized and directed to accept on behalf of the United States any lands within the exterior boundaries of a district as a gift, or, when public interests will be benefited thereby, he is authorized and directed to accept on behalf of the United States title to any privately owned lands within the exterior boundaries of said grazing district, and in exchange therefor to issue patent for not to exceed an equal value of surveyed grazing district land or of unreserved surveyed public land in the same State or within a distance of not more than fifty miles within the adjoining State nearest the base lands: *Provided,* That before any such exchange shall be effected, notice of the contemplated exchange, describing the lands involved, shall be published by the Secretary of the Interior once each week for four successive weeks in some newspaper of general circulation in the county or counties in which may be situated the lands to be accepted, and in the same manner in some like newspaper published in any county in which may be situated any lands to be given in such exchange; lands conveyed to the United States under this Act shall, upon acceptance of title, become public lands and parts of the grazing district within whose exterior boundaries they are located: *Provided further,* That either party to an exchange may make reservations of minerals, easements, or rights of use, the values of which shall be duly considered in determining the values of the exchanged lands. Where reservations are made in lands conveyed to the United States, the right to enjoy them shall be subject to such reasonable conditions respecting ingress and egress and the use of the surface of the land as may be deemed necessary by the Secretary of the Interior. Where mineral reservations are made in lands conveyed by the United States, it shall be so stipulated in the patent, and any person who acquires the right to mine and remove the reserved mineral deposits may enter and occupy so much of the surface as may be required for all purposes incident to the mining and removal of the minerals therefrom, and may mine and remove such minerals, upon payment to the owner of the surface for damages caused to the land and improvements thereon. Upon application of any State to exchange lands within or without the boundary of a grazing district the Secretary of the Interior is authorized and directed, in the manner provided for the exchange of privately owned lands in this section, to proceed with such exchange at the earliest practicable date and to cooperate fully with the State to that end, but no State shall be permitted to select lieu lands in another State.

SEC. 9. The Secretary of the Interior shall provide, by suitable rules and regulations, for cooperation with local associations of stockmen, State land officials, and official State agencies engaged in conservation or propagation of wild life interested in the use of the grazing districts. The Secretary of the Interior shall provide by appropriate rules and regulations for local hearings on appeals from the decisions of the administrative officer in charge in a manner similar to the procedure in the land department. The Secretary of the Interior shall also be empowered to accept contributions toward the administration, protection, and improvement of the district, moneys so received to be covered into the Treasury as a special fund, which is hereby appropriated and made available until expended, as the Secretary of the Interior may direct, for payment of expenses incident to said administration, protection, and improvement, and for refunds to depositors of amounts contributed by them in excess of their share of the cost.

SEC. 10. That, except as provided in sections 9 and 11 hereof, all moneys received under the authority of this Act shall be deposited in the Treasury of the United States as miscellaneous receipts, but 25 per centum of all moneys received from each grazing district during any fiscal year is hereby made available, when appropriated by the Congress, for expenditure by the Secretary of the Interior for the construction, purchase, or maintenance of range improvements, and 50 per centum of the money received from each grazing district during any fiscal year shall be paid at the end thereof by the Secretary of the Treasury to the State in which said grazing district is situated, to be expended as the State legislature may prescribe for the benefit of the county or counties in which the grazing district is situated: *Provided,* That if any grazing district is in more than one State or county, the distributive share to each from the proceeds of said district shall be proportional to its area therein.

SEC. 11. That when appropriated by Congress, 25 per centum of all moneys received from each grazing district on Indian lands ceded to the United States for disposition under the public-land laws during any fiscal year is hereby made available for expenditure by the Secretary of the Interior for the construction, purchase, or maintenance of range improvements; and an additional 25 per centum of the money received from grazing during each fiscal year shall be paid at the end thereof by the Secretary of the Treasury to the State in which said lands are situated, to be expended as the State legislature may prescribe for the benefit of public schools and public roads of the county or counties in which such grazing lands are situated. And the remaining 50 per centum of all money received from such grazing lands shall be deposited to the credit of the Indians pending final disposition under applicable laws, treaties, or agreements. The applicable public land laws as to said Indian ceded lands within a district created under this Act shall continue in operation, except that each and every application for nonmineral title to said lands in a district created under this Act shall be allowed only if in the opinion of the Secretary of the Interior the land is of the character suited to disposal through the Act under which application is made and such entry and disposal will not affect adversely the best public interest, but no settlement or occupation of such lands shall be permitted until ninety days after allowance of an application.

SEC. 12. That the Secretary of the Interior is hereby authorized to cooperate with any department of the Government in carrying out the purposes of this Act, and in the coordination of range administration, particularly where the same stock grazes part time in a grazing district and part time in a national forest or other reservation.

SEC. 13. That the President of the United States is authorized to reserve by proclamation and place under national-forest administration in any State where national forests may be created or enlarged by Executive order any unappro-priated public lands lying within watersheds forming a part of the national forests which, in his opinion, can best be administered in connection with existing national-forest administration units, and to place under the Interior Department administration any lands within national forests, principally valuable for grazing which, in his opinion, can best be administered under the provisions of this Act: *Provided,* That such reservation or transfers shall not interfere with legal rights acquired under any public-land laws so long as such rights are legally maintained. Lands placed under the national-forest administration under the authority of this Act shall be subject to all the laws and regulations relating to national forests, and lands placed under the Interior Department adminis-tration shall be subject to all public-land laws and regulations applicable to grazing districts created under authority of this Act. Nothing in this section shall be construed so as to limit the powers of the President (relating to reorgan-izations in the executive departments) granted by title 4 of the Act entitled "An Act making appropriations for the Treasury and Post Office Departments for the fiscal year ending June 30, 1934, and for other purposes", approved March 3, 1933.

SEC. 14. That section 2455 of the Revised Statutes, as amended, is amended to read as follows:

"SEC. 2455. Notwithstanding the provisions of section 2357 of the Revised Statutes (U.S.C., title 43, sec. 678) and of the Act of August 30, 1890 (26 Stat. 391), it shall be lawful for the Secretary of the Interior to order into market and sell at public auction, at the land office of the district in which the land is situated, for not less than the appraised value, any isolated or disconnected tract or parcel of the public domain not exceeding seven hundred and sixty acres which, in his judgment, it would be proper to expose for sale after at least thirty days' notice by the land office of the district in which such land may be situated: *Provided,* That for a period of not less than thirty days after the highest bid has been received, any owner or owners of contiguous land shall have a preference right to buy the offered lands at such highest bid price, and where two or more persons apply to exercise such preference right the Secretary of the Interior is authorized to make an equitable division of the land among such applicants, but in no case shall the adjacent land owner or owners be required to pay more than three times the appraised price: *Provided further,* That any legal subdivisions of the public land, not exceeding one hundred and sixty acres, the greater part of which is mountainous or too rough for cultivation, may, in the discretion of the said Secretary, be ordered into the market and sold pursuant to this section upon the application of any person who owns land or holds a valid entry of lands adjoining such tract, regardless of the fact that such tract may not be isolated or disconnected within the meaning of this sec-tion: *Provided further,* That this section shall not defeat any valid right which has already attached under any pending entry or location. The word 'person' in this section shall be deemed to include corporations, partnerships, and associations."

SEC. 15. The Secretary of the Interior is further authorized in his discretion, where vacant, unappropriated, and unreserved lands of the public domain are situated in such isolated or disconnected tracts of six hundred and forty acres or more as not to justify their inclusion in any grazing district to be established pursuant to this Act, to lease any such lands to owners of lands contiguous thereto for grazing purposes, upon application therefor by any such owner, and upon such terms and conditions as the Secretary may prescribe.

SEC. 16. Nothing in this Act shall be construed as restricting the respective States from enforcing any and all statutes enacted for police regulation, nor shall the police power of the respective States be, by this Act, impaired or restricted, and all laws heretofore enacted by the respective States or any thereof, or that may hereafter be enacted as regards public health or public welfare, shall at all times be in full force and effect: *Provided, however,* That nothing in this section shall be construed as limiting or restricting the power and authority of the United States.

Approved, June 28, 1934.

ESTABLISHING FEDERAL POLICY
FOR WATER POWER

THE RIGHTS OF WAY ACT*
February 15, 1901

The obvious necessity to cross public lands brought about the first law establishing a system of permits for the use of rights of way. Before 1901, water power sites throughout the public domain had been lost when private companies managed to secure title before the sites had been preserved through Presidential reservation. This law was primarily intended as a means of facilitating reclamation and irrigation programs adjacent to public lands, but was broadened to cover many utility functions. An amendment in 1911 (36 Statutes at Large, 1253) broadened the power of both the Secretary of the Interior and the Secretary of Agriculture under the law.

An Act relating to rights of way through certain parks, reservations, and other public lands.

Be it enacted by the Senate and House of Representatives of the United States of America in Congress assembled, That the Secretary of the Interior be, and hereby is, authorized and empowered, under general regulations to be fixed by him, to permit the use of rights of way through the public lands, forest and other reservations of the United States, and the Yosemite, Sequoia, and General Grant national parks, California, for electrical plants, poles, and lines for the generation and distribution of electrical power, and for telephone and telegraph purposes, and for canals, ditches, pipes and pipe lines, flumes, tunnels, or other water conduits, and for water plants, dams, and reservoirs used to promote irrigation or mining or quarrying, or the manufacturing or cutting of timber or lumber, or the supplying of water for domestic, public, or any other beneficial uses to the extent of the ground occupied by such canals, ditches, flumes, tunnels, reservoirs, or other water conduits or water plants, or electrical or other works permitted hereunder, and not to exceed fifty feet on each side of the marginal limits thereof, or not to exceed fifty feet on each side of the center

*31 *Statutes at Large,* 790–91.

line of such pipes and pipe lines, electrical, telegraph, and telephone lines and poles, by any citizen, association, or corporation of the United States, where it is intended by such to exercise the use permitted hereunder or any one or more of the purposes herein named: *Provided,* That such permits shall be allowed within or through any of said parks or any forest, military, Indian, or other reservation only upon the approval of the chief officer of the Department under whose supervision such park or reservation falls and upon a finding by him that the same is not incompatible with the public interest: *Provided further,* That all permits given hereunder for telegraph and telephone purposes shall be subject to the provision of title sixty-five of the Revised Statutes of the United States, and amendments thereto, regulating rights of way for telegraph companies over the public domain: *And provided further,* That any permission given by the Secretary of the Interior under the provisions of this Act may be revoked by him or his successor in his discretion, and shall not be held to confer any right, or easement, or interest in, to, or over any public land, reservation, or park.

Approved, February 15, 1901.

PRESIDENT ROOSEVELT'S VETO OF PRIVATE
USE OF MUSCLE SHOALS*
March 3, 1903

Theodore Roosevelt's veto of a bill to allow a private power firm to build a dam on the Tennessee River at Muscle Shoals, Alabama, not only protected this site for later government development—which evolved into the Tennessee Valley Authority—but also helped establish the principle of national ownership of resources previously considered only of local value.

To the House of Representatives:

I return without approval House bill 14051, entitled "An Act granting the consent of Congress to N. F. Thompson and associates to erect a dam and construct a power station at Muscle Shoals, Alabama."

The recent development of the application of water power to the production of electricity available for use at considerable distances has revealed an element of substantial value in streams which the Government is or is liable to be called upon to improve for purposes of navigation, and this value, in my judgment, should be properly utilized to defray the cost of the improvement. Wherever the Government constructs a dam and lock for the purpose of navigation there is a waterfall of great value. It does not seem right or just that this element of local value should be given away to private individuals of the vicinage, and at the same time the people of the whole community should be taxed for the local improvement.

It seems clear that justice to the taxpayers of the country demands that when the Government is or may be called upon to improve a stream the improvement should be made to pay for itself, so far as practicable. I am advised that at another point on the same river to which this bill refers there is an authorized project for improvement by the Government at a cost of over $800,000 and that an offer has been made by a responsible citizen to do the entire work without expense to the Government provided he can be authorized to use the water power. I think it is desirable that the entire subject of granting privileges of the kind referred to in this bill should be considered in a comprehensive way and that a general policy appropriate to the new conditions caused by the advance in electrical science should be adopted under which these valuable rights will not be practically given away, but will be disposed of after full competition in such a way as shall best conserve the public interests.

Theodore Roosevelt

White House
March 3, 1903

Cong. Rec., Vol. 36, 57th Cong., 2nd sess., 3071.

THE GENERAL DAM ACT*
June 21, 1906

Roosevelt vetoed several bills to allow private power companies to build dams on navigable streams, but allowed others to become law when the grant of rights was not so broad. The widespread construction of hydroelectric dams after the turn of the century made it simpler to provide for general regulations for the approval of dams in a general law.

An Act to regulate the construction of dams across navigable waters.

Be it enacted by the Senate and House of Representatives of the United States of America in Congress assembled, That when, hereafter, authority is granted by Congress to any persons to construct and maintain a dam for water power or other purposes across any of the navigable waters of the United States, such dams shall not be built or commenced until the plans and specifications for its construction, together with such drawings of the proposed construction and such map of the proposed location as may be required for a full understanding of the subject, have been submitted to the Secretary of War and Chief of Engineers for their approval, or until they shall have approved such plans and specifications and the location of such dam and accessory works; and when the plans for any dam to be constructed under the provisions of this Act have been approved by the Chief of Engineers and by the Secretary of War it shall not be lawful to deviate from such plans either before or after completion of the structure unless the modification of such plans has previously been submitted to and received the approval of the Chief of Engineers and of the Secretary of War: *Provided,* That in approving said plans and location such conditions and stipulations may be imposed as the Chief of Engineers and the Secretary of War may deem necessary to protect the present and future interests of the United States, which may include the condition that such persons shall construct, maintain, and operate, without expense to the United States, in connection with said dam and appurtenant works, a lock or locks, booms, sluices, or any other structures which the Secretary of War and the Chief of Engineers at any time may deem necessary in the interest of navigation, in accordance with such plans as they may approve, and also that whenever Congress shall authorize the construction of a lock, or other structures for navigation purposes, in connection with such dam, the person owning such dam shall convey to the United States, free of cost, title to such land as may be required for such constructions and approaches and shall grant to the United States a free use of water power for building and operating such constructions.

*34 *Statutes at Large,* 386–87.

SEC. 2. That the right is hereby reserved to the United States to construct, maintain, and operate, in connection with any dam built under the provisions of this Act, a suitable lock or locks, or any other structures for navigation purposes, and at all times to control the said dam and the level of the pool caused by said dam to such an extent as may be necessary to provide proper facilities for navigation.

SEC. 3. That the person, company, or corporation building, maintaining, or operating any dam and appurtenant works, under the provisions of this Act, shall be liable for any damage that may be inflicted thereby upon private property, either by overflow or otherwise. The persons owning or operating any such dam shall maintain, at their own expense, such lights and other signals thereon and such fishways as the Secretary of Commerce and Labor shall prescribe.

SEC. 4. That all rights acquired under this Act shall cease and be determined if the person, company, or corporation acquiring such rights shall, at any time, fail to comply with any of the provisions and requirements of the Act, or with any of the stipulations and conditions that may be prescribed as aforesaid by the Chief of Engineers and the Secretary of War.

SEC. 5. That any persons who shall fail or refuse to comply with the lawful order of the Secretary of War and the Chief of Engineers, made in accordance with the provisions of this Act, shall be deemed guilty of a violation of this Act, and any persons who shall be guilty of a violation of this Act shall be deemed guilty of a misdemeanor and on conviction thereof shall be punished by a fine not exceeding five thousand dollars, and every month such persons shall remain in default shall be deemed a new offense and subject such persons to additional penalties therefor; and in addition to the penalties above described the Secretary of War and the Chief of Engineers may, upon refusal of the persons owning or controlling any such dam and accessory works to comply with any lawful order issued by the Secretary of War or Chief of Engineers in regard thereto, cause the removal of such dam and accessory works as an obstruction to navigation at the expense of the persons owning or controlling such dam, and suit for such expense may be brought in the name of the United States against such persons, and recovery had for such expense in any court of competent jurisdiction; and the removal of any structures erected or maintained in violation of the provisions of this Act or the order or direction of the Secretary of War or Chief of Engineers made in pursuance thereof may be enforced by injunction, mandamus, or other summary process, upon application to the circuit court in the district in which such structure may, in whole or in part, exist, and proper proceedings to this end may be instituted under the direction of the Attorney-General of the United States at the request of the Chief of Engineers or the Secretary of War; and in case of any litigation arising from any obstruction or alleged obstruction to navigation created by the construction of any dam under this Act, the cause or question arising may be tried before the circuit court of the

United States in any district in which any portion of said obstruction or dam touches.

SEC. 6. That whenever Congress shall hereafter by law authorize the construction of any dam across any of the navigable waters of the United States, and no time for the commencement and completion of such dam is named in said Act, the authority thereby granted shall cease and be null and void unless the actual construction of the dam authorized in such Act be commenced within one year and completed within three years from the date of the passage of such Act.

SEC. 7. That the right to alter, amend, or repeal this Act is hereby expressly reserved as to any and all dams which may be constructed in accordance with the provisions of this Act, and the United States shall incur no liability for the alteration, amendment, or repeal thereof to the owner or owners or any other persons interested in any dam which shall have been constructed in accordance with its provisions.

SEC. 8. That the word "persons" as used in this Act shall be construed to import both the singular and the plural, as the case demands, and shall include corporations, companies, and associations.

Approved, June 21, 1906.

PRESIDENT ROOSEVELT'S VETO OF PRIVATE POWER RIGHTS*
January 15, 1909

Toward the end of his term of office, Theodore Roosevelt vetoed a bill to give power rights on the James River in Missouri to a private company. His veto message includes quotations from his veto the previous year of the Rainy River bill, which also failed to meet his standards in respect to grant of rights on a navigable stream. The Rainy River veto is perhaps the best known of the Roosevelt vetoes, but the James River message presents his case in greater detail.

To the House of Representatives:

I return herewith without my approval House bill 17707 to authorize William H. Standish to construct a dam across James River, in Stone County, Mo., and divert a portion of its waters through a tunnel into the said river again to create electric power. My reasons for not signing the bill are:

The bill gives to the grantee a valuable privilege, which by its very nature is monopolistic, and does not contain the conditions essential to protect the public interest.

In pursuance of a policy declared in my message of February 26, 1908 (S. Doc. No. 325), transmitting the report of the Inland Waterways Commission to Congress, I wrote on March 13, 1908, the following letter to the Senate Committee on Commerce:

> Numerous bills granting water rights in conformity with the general act of June 21, 1906, have been introduced during the present session of Congress, and some of these have already passed. While the general act authorizes the limitation and restriction of water rights in the public interest and would seem to warrant making a reasonable charge for the benefits conferred, those bills which have come to my attention do not seem to guard the public interests adequately in these respects. The effect of granting privileges such as are conferred by these bills, as I said in a recent message, "taken together with rights already acquired under state laws, would be to give away properties of enormous value. Through lack of foresight we have formed the habit of granting without compensation extremely valuable rights, amounting to monopolies, on navigable streams and on the public domain. The repurchase at great expense of water rights thus carelessly given away without return has already begun in the East, and before long will be necessary in the West also. No rights involving water power should be granted to any corporation in perpetuity, but only for a length of time sufficient to allow them to conduct their business profitably. A reasonable charge should, of course, be made for valuable rights and privileges which they obtain from the National Government. The values for which this charge is made will ultimately, through the natural growth and orderly development of our population and industries, reach enormous amounts. A fair share of the increase should be safeguarded for the benefit of the people, from whose labor it springs. The proceeds thus secured, after the cost of administration and improvement has been met, should naturally be devoted to the development of our inland waterways." Accordingly I have decided to sign no bills hereafter which do not provide specifically for the right to fix and make a charge and for a definite limitation in time of the rights conferred.

Cong. Rec., Vol. 43, 60th Cong., 2nd sess., 978–80.

In my veto message of April 13, 1908, returning House bill 15444, to extend the time for the construction of a dam across Rainy River, I said:

> We are now at the beginning of great development in water power. Its use through electrical transmission is entering more and more largely into every element of the daily life of the people. Already the evils of monopoly are becoming manifest; already the experience of the past shows the necessity of caution in making unrestricted grants of this great power.
>
> The present policy pursued in making these grants is unwise in giving away the property of the people in the flowing waters to individuals or organizations practically unknown, and granting in perpetuity these valuable privileges in advance of the formulation of definite plans as to their use. In some cases the grantees apparently have little or no financial or other ability to utilize the gift, and have sought it merely because it could be had for the asking.

The Rainy River Company, by an agreement in writing, approved by the War Department, subsequently promised to submit to and abide by such conditions as may be imposed by the Secretary of War, including a time limit and a reasonable charge. Only because of its compliance in this way with these conditions did the bill extending the time limit for that project finally become a law.

An amendment to the present bill expressly authorizing the Government to fix a limitation of time and impose a charge was proposed by the War Department. The letter, veto message, and amendment above referred to were considered by the Senate Committee on Commerce, as appears by the committee's report on the present bill, and the proposed amendment was characterized by the committee as a "new departure from the policy heretofore pursued in respect to legislation authorizing the construction of such dams." Their report set forth an elaborate legal argument intended to show that the Federal Government has no power to impose any charge whatever for such a privilege.

The fact that the proposed policy is new is in itself no sufficient argument against its adoption. As we are met with new conditions of industry seriously affecting the public welfare, we should not hesitate to adopt measures for the protection of the public merely because those measures are new. When the public welfare is involved, Congress should resolve any reasonable doubt as to its legislative power in favor of the people and against the seekers for a special privilege.

My reason for believing that the Federal Government, in granting a license to dam a navigable river, has the power to impose any condition it finds necessary to protect the public, including a charge and a limitation of the time, is that its consent is legally essential to an enterprise of this character. It follows that Congress can impose conditions upon its consent. This principle was clearly stated in the House of Representatives on March 28, 1908, by Mr. WILLIAMS, of Mississippi, when he said:

> . . . There can be no doubt in the mind of any man seeking merely the public good and public right, independently of any desire for local legislation, of this general proposition, that whenever any sovereignty, state or federal, is required to issue a charter or a license or a consent, in order to confer powers upon individuals or corporations. It is the duty of that

sovereignty in the interests of the people so to condition the grant of that power as that it shall redound to the interest of all the people, and that utilities of vast value should not be gratuitously granted to individuals or corporations and perpetually alienated from the people or the state or the government.

. . . It is admitted that this power to erect dams in navigable streams can not be exercised by anybody except by an act of Congress. Now, then, if it require an act of Congress to permit any man to put a dam in a navigable stream, then two things follow: Congress should so exercise the power in making that grant as, first, to prevent any harm to the navigability of the stream itself, and, secondly, so as to prevent any individual or any private corporation from securing through the act of Congress any uncompensated advantage of private profit.

The authority of Congress in this matter was asserted by Secretary Taft on April 17, 1908, in his report on Senator Newland's Inland Waterways Commission bill (S. 500), where he said:

In the execution of any project and as incidental to and inseparably connected with the improvement of navigation, the power of Congress extends to the regulation of the use and development of the waters for purposes subsidiary to navigation.

And by the Solicitor-General in a memorandum prepared after a careful investigation of the subject.

Believing that the National Government has this power, I am convinced that its power ought to be exercised. The people of the country are threatened by a monopoly far more powerful, because in far closer touch with their domestic and industrial life, than anything known to our experience. A single generation will see the exhaustion of our natural resources of oil and gas and such a rise in the price of coal as will make the price of electrically transmitted water power a controlling factor in transportation, in manufacturing, and in household lighting and heating. Our water power alone, if fully developed and wisely used, is probably sufficient for our present transportation, industrial, municipal, and domestic needs. Most of it is undeveloped and is still in national or state control.

To give away, without conditions, this, one of the greatest of our resources, would be an act of folly. If we are guilty of it, our children will be forced to pay an annual return upon a capitalization based upon the highest prices which "the traffic will bear." They will find themselves face to face with powerful interests intrenched behind the doctrine of "vested rights" and strengthened by every defense which money can buy and the ingenuity of able corporation lawyers can devise. Long before that time they may and very probably will have become a consolidated interest, controlled from the great financial centers, dictating the terms upon which the citizen can conduct his business or earn his livelihood, and not amenable to the wholesome check of local opinion.

The total water power now in use by power plants in the United States is estimated by the Bureau of the Census and the Geological Survey as 5,300,000 horsepower. Information collected by the Bureau of Corporations shows that thirteen large concerns, of which the General Electric Company and the Westinghouse Electric and Manufacturing Company are most important, now hold water-power installations and advantageous power sites aggregating about 1,046,000 horsepower, where the control by these concerns is practically admitted. This is a quantity equal to over 19 per cent of the total now in use. Further evidence of a very strong nature as to additonal intercorporate relations, furnished by the Bureau, leads me to the conclusion that this total should be increased to 24 per cent; and still other evidence, though less conclusive, nevertheless affords reasonable ground for enlarging this estimate by 9 per cent additional. In other words, it is probable that these thirteen concerns directly or indirectly control developed water power and advantageous power sites equal to more than 33 per cent of the total water power now in use. This astonishing consolidation has taken place practically within the last five years. The movement is still in its infancy, and unless it is controlled the history of the oil industry will be repeated in the hydro-electric power industry, with results far more oppressive and disastrous for the people. It is true that the great bulk of our potential water power is as yet undeveloped, but the sites which are now controlled by combinations are those which offer the greatest advantages and therefore hold a strategic position. This is certain to be strengthened by the increasing demand for power and the extension of long-distance electrical transmission.

It is, in my opinion, relatively unimportant for us to know whether or not the promoters of this particular project are affiliated with any of these great corporations. If we make an unconditional grant to this grantee, our control over it ceases. He, or any purchaser from him, will be free to sell his rights to any one of them at pleasure. The time to attach conditions and prevent monopoly is when a grant is made.

The great corporations are acting with foresight, singleness of purpose, and vigor to control the water powers of the country. They pay no attention to state boundaries and are not interested in the constitutional law affecting navigable streams except as it affords what has been aptly called a "twilight zone," where they may find a convenient refuge from any regulation whatever by the public, whether through the national or the state governments. It is significant that they are opposing the control of water power on the Desplaines River by the State of Illinois with equal vigor and with like arguments to those with which they oppose the National Government pursuing the policy I advocate. Their attitude is the same with reference to their projects upon the mountain streams of the West, where the jurisdiction of the Federal Government as the owner of the public lands and national forests is not open to question. They are demanding legislation for unconditional grants in perpetuity of land for reservoirs, conduits, power houses, and transmission lines to replace the existing statute which authorizes the administrative officers of the Government to impose conditions to protect the public when any permit is issued. Several bills for that purpose are now pending in both Houses, among them the bill, S. 6626, to subject lands owned or held by the United States to condemnation in the state courts, and the bills, H. R. 11356 and S. 2661, respectively, to grant locations and rights of way for electric and other power purposes through the public lands and reservations of the United States. These bills were either drafted by representatives of the power companies, or are similar in effect to those thus drafted. On the other hand, the administration proposes that authority be given to issue power permits for a term not to exceed fifty years, irrevocable except for breach of condition. This provision to prevent revocation would remove the only valid ground of objection to the act of 1901, which expressly makes all permits revocable at discretion. The following amendment to authorize this in national forests was inserted in last year's argicultural appropriation bill:

> And hereafter permits for power plants within national forests may be made irrevocable, except for breach of condition, for such term, not exceeding fifty years, as the Secretary of Agriculture may by regulation prescribe, and land covered by such permits issued in pursuance of an application filed before entry, location, or application, subsequently approved under the act of June 11, 1906, shall in perpetuity remain subject to such permit and renewals thereof.

The representatives of the power companies present in Washington during the last session agreed upon the bill above mentioned as the most favorable to their interests. At their request frequent conferences were held between them and the representatives of the administration for the purpose of reaching an agreement if possible. The companies refused to accept anything less than a grant in perpetuity and insisted that the slight charge now imposed by the Forest Service was oppressive. But they made no response to the specific proposal that the reasonableness of the charge be determined through an investigation of their business by the Bureau of Corporations.

The amendment of the agricultural bill providing for irrevocable permits being new legislation was stricken out under the House rules upon a point of order made by friends of the House bill—that is, by friends of the power companies. Yet, in the face of this record, the power companies complain that they are forced to accept revocable permits by the policy of the administration.

The new legislation sought in their own interest by some companies in the West, and the opposition of other companies in the East to proposed legislation in the public interest, have a common source and a common purpose. Their source is the rapidly growing water-power combination. Their purpose is a centralized monopoly of hydro-electric power development free of all public control. It is obvious that a monopoly of power in any community calls for strict public supervision and regulation.

The suggestion of the Senate Committee on Commerce in their report on the present bill that many of the streams for the damming of which a federal license is sought are, in fact, unnavigable is sufficiently answered in this case by the

[172]

action of the House Committee on Interstate and Foreign Commerce upon this very measure. As stated in the House on March 18, 1908, by Mr. RUSSELL of Missouri, a bill to declare this river unnavigable was rejected by that committee.

I repeat the words with which I concluded my message vetoing the Rainy River bill:

> In place of the present haphazard policy of permanently alienating valuable public property we should substitute a definite policy along the following lines:
>
> First. There should be a limited or carefully guarded grant in the nature of an option or opportunity afforded within reasonable time for development of plans and for execution of the project.
>
> Second. Such a grant or concession should be accompanied in the act making the grant by a provision expressly making it the duty of a designated official to annul the grant if the work is not begun or plans are not carried out in accordance with the authority granted.
>
> Third. It should also be the duty of some designated official to see to it that in approving the plans the maximum development of the navigation and power is assured, or at least that in making the plans these may not be so developed as ultimately to interfere with the better utilization of the water or complete development of the power.
>
> Fourth. There should be a license fee or charge which, though small or nominal at the outset, can in the future be adjusted so as to secure a control in the interest of the public.
>
> Fifth. Provision should be made for the termination of the grant or privilege at a definite time, leaving to future generations the power or authority to renew or extend the concession in accordance with the conditions which may prevail at that time.

Further reflection suggests a sixth condition, viz:

The license should be forfeited upon proof that the licensee has joined in any conspiracy or unlawful combination in restraint of trade, as is provided for grants of coal lands in Alaska by the act of May 28, 1908.

I will sign no bill granting a privilege of this character which does not contain the substance of these conditions. I consider myself bound, as far as exercise of my executive power will allow, to do for the people, in prevention of monopoly of their resources, what I believe they would do for themselves if they were in a position to act. Accordingly I shall insist upon the conditions mentioned above not only in acts which I sign, but also in passing upon plans for use of water power presented to the executive departments for action. The imposition of conditions has received the sanction of Congress in the general act of 1906, regulating the construction of dams in navigable waters, which authorizes the imposing of "such conditions and stipulations as the Chief of Engineers and the Secretary of War may deem necessary to protect the present and future interests of the United States."

I inclose a letter from the Commissioner of Corporations, setting forth the results of his investigations and the evidence of the far-reaching plans and operations of the General Electric Company, the Westinghouse Electric and Manufacturing Company, and other large concerns, for consolidation of the water powers of the country under their control. I also inclose the memorandum of the Solicitor-General above referred to.

[173]

I esteem it my duty to use every endeavor to prevent this growing monopoly, the most threatening which has ever appeared, from being fastened upon the people of this nation.

Theodore Roosevelt

The White House
January 15, 1909

AN AMENDMENT TO THE 1906 DAM ACT*
June 23, 1910

This law amended the General Dam Act of June 21, 1906, by limiting the grant of rights to 50 years, by reserving the right to revoke the grant any time for public uses upon payment for the works constructed, and by directing that consideration be given to the bearing of any proposed plan on a comprehensive scheme of development for the river or the river system.

An Act to amend an Act entitled "An Act to regulate the construction of dams across navigable waters," approved June twenty-first, nineteen hundred and six.

Be it enacted by the Senate and House of Representatives of the United States of America in Congress assembled, That the Act entitled "An Act to regulate the construction of dams across navigable waters," approved June twenty-first, nineteen hundred and six, be, and the same is hereby, amended to read as follows:

"SECTION 1. That when authority has been or may hereafter be granted by Congress, either directly or indirectly or by any official or officials of the United States, to any persons, to construct and maintain a dam for water power or other purpose across or in any of the navigable waters of the United States, such dam shall not be built or commenced until the plans and specifications for such dam and all accessory works, together with such drawings of the proposed construction and such map of the proposed location as may be required for a full understanding of the subject, have been submitted to the Secretary of War and the Chief of Engineers for their approval, nor until they shall have approved such plans and specifications and the location of such dam and accessory works; and when the plans and specifications for any dam to be constructed under the provisions of this Act have been approved by the Chief of Engineers and by the Secretary of War it shall not be lawful to deviate from such plans or specifications either before or after completion of the structure unless the modification of such plans or specifications has previously been submitted to and received the approval of the Chief of Engineers and of the Secretary of War: *Provided,* That in approving the plans, specifications, and location for any dam, such conditions and stipulations may be imposed as the Chief of Engineers and the Secretary of War may deem necessary to protect the present and future interests of the United States, which may include the condition that the persons constructing or maintaining such dam shall construct, maintain, and operate, without expense to the United States, in connection with any dam and accessory or ap-

*36 *Statutes at Large,* 593–96.

purtenant works, a lock or locks, booms, sluices, or any other structure or structures which the Secretary of War and the Chief of Engineers or Congress at any time may deem necessary in the interests of navigation, in accordance with such plans as they may approve, and also that whenever Congress shall authorize the construction of a lock or other structures for navigation purposes in connection with such dam, the persons owning such dam shall convey to the United States, free of cost, title to such land as may be required for such constructions and approaches, and shall grant to the United States free water power or power generated from water power for building and operating such constructions: *Provided further,* That in acting upon said plans as aforesaid the Chief of Engineers and the Secretary of War shall consider the bearing of said structure upon a comprehensive plan for the improvement of the waterway over which it is to be constructed with a view to the promotion of its navigable quality and for the full development of water power; and, as a part of the conditions and stipulations imposed by them, shall provide for improving and developing navigation, and fix such charge or charges for the privilege granted as may be sufficient to restore conditions with respect to navigability as existing at the time such privilege be granted or reimburse the United States for doing the same, and for such additional or further expense as may be incurred by the United States with reference to such project, including the cost of any investigations necessary for approval of plans and of such supervision of construction as may be necessary in the interests of the United States: *Provided further,* That the Chief of Engineers and the Secretary of War are hereby authorized and directed to fix and collect just and proper charge or charges for the privilege granted to all dams authorized and constructed under the provisions of this Act which shall receive any direct benefit from the construction, operation, and maintenance by the United States of storage reservoirs at the headwaters of any navigable streams, or from the acquisition, holding, and maintenance of any forested watershed, or lands located by the United States at the headwaters of any navigable stream, wherever such shall be, for the development, improvement, or preservation of navigation in such streams in which such dams may be constructed.

"SEC. 2. That the right is hereby reserved to the United States to construct, maintain, and operate, in connection with any dam built in accordance with the provisions of this Act, a suitable lock or locks, booms, sluices, or any other structures for navigation purposes, and at all times to control the said dam and the level of the pool caused by said dam to such an extent as may be necessary to provide proper facilities for navigation.

"SEC. 3. That the persons constructing, maintaining, or operating any dam or appurtenant or accessory works, in accordance with the provisions of this Act, shall be liable for any damage that may be inflicted thereby upon private property, either by overflow or otherwise. The persons owning or operating any such dam, or accessory works, subject to the provisions of this Act, shall maintain, at their own expense, such lights and other signals thereon and such fishways as the Secretary of Commerce and Labor shall prescribe, and for failure so to do in any respect shall be deemed guilty of a misdemeanor and subject to a fine of not less than five hundred dollars, and each month of such failure shall constitute a separate offense and subject such persons to additional penalties therefor.

"Sec. 4. That all rights acquired under this Act shall cease and be determined if the person, company, or corporation acquiring such rights shall, at any time, fail, after receiving reasonable notice thereof, to comply with any of the provisions and requirements of the Act, or with any of the stipulations and conditions that may be prescribed as aforesaid by the Chief of Engineers and the Secretary of War, including the payment into the Treasury of the United States of the charges provided for by section one of this Act: *Provided,* That Congress may revoke any rights conferred in pursuance of this Act whenever it is necessary for public use, and, in the event of any such revocation by Congress, the United States shall pay the owners of any dam and appurtenant works built under authority of this Act, as full compensation, the reasonable value thereof, exclusive of the value of the authority or franchise granted, such reasonable value to be determined by mutual agreement between the Secretary of War and the said owners, and in case they can not agree, then by proceedings instituted in the United States circuit court for the condemnation of such properties: *And provided also,* That the authority granted under or in pursuance of the provisions of this Act shall terminate at the end of a period not to exceed fifty years from the date of the original approval of the project under this Act, unless sooner revoked as herein provided or Congress shall otherwise direct: *Provided, however,* That this limitation shall not apply to any corporation or individual heretofore authorized by the United States, or by any State, to construct a dam in or across a navigable waterway, upon which dam expenditures of money have heretofore been made in reliance upon such grant or grants.

"Sec. 5. That any persons who shall fail or refuse to comply with the lawful order of the Secretary of War and the Chief of Engineers, made in accordance with the provisions of this Act, shall be deemed guilty of a violation of this Act, and any persons who shall be guilty of a violation of this Act shall be deemed guilty of a misdemeanor and on conviction thereof shall be punished by a fine not exceeding five thousand dollars, and every month such persons shall remain in default shall be deemed a new offense and subject such persons to additional penalties therefor; and in addition to the penalties above described the Secretary of War and the Chief of Engineers may, upon refusal of the persons owning or controlling any such dam and accessory works to comply with any lawful order issued by the Secretary of War or Chief of Engineers in regard thereto, cause the removal of such dam and accessory works as an obstruction to navigation at the expense of the persons owning or controlling such dam, and suit for such expense may be brought in the name of the United States against such persons and recovery had for such expense in any court of competent jurisdiction. Said provision as to recovery of expense shall not apply wherever the United States has been previously reimbursed for such removal; and the removal or any structures erected or maintained in violation of the provisions of this Act or the order or direction of the Secretary of War or the Chief of Engineers made in pursuance thereof may be enforced by injunction, mandamus, or other summary process, upon application to the circuit court in the district in which such structure may, in whole or in part, exist, and proper proceedings to this end may be instituted under the direction of the Attorney-General of the United States at the request of the Chief of Engineers or the Secretary of War; and in case of any litigation arising from any obstruction or alleged obstruction to navigation created by the construction of any dam under this Act the cause or question arising may be tried before the circuit court of the United States in any district in which any portion of said obstruction or dam touches.

"SEC. 6. That whenever Congress shall hereafter by law authorize the construction of any dam across any of the navigable waters of the United States, and no time for the commencement and completion of such dam is named in said Act, the authority thereby granted shall cease and be null and void unless the actual construction of the dam authorized in such Act be commenced within one year and completed within three years from the date of the passage of such Act.

"SEC. 7. That the right to alter, amend, or repeal this Act is hereby expressly reserved as to any and all dams which may be constructed in accordance with the provisions of this Act, and the United States shall incur no liability for the alteration, amendment, or repeal thereof to the owner or owners or any other persons interested in any dam which shall have been constructed in accordance with its provisions.

"SEC. 8. That the word 'persons' as used in this Act shall be construed to import both the singular and the plural, as the case demands, and shall include corporations, companies, and associations. The word 'dam' as used in this Act shall be construed to import both the singular and the plural, as the case demands."

Approved, June 23, 1910.

WATER POWER AND NAVIGATION DEVELOPMENT*
June 25, 1910

Section 3 of the rivers and harbors appropriation bill for 1910 contains a provision providing for Corps of Engineers surveys of the feasibility of water power development "coordinated in a logical and proper manner with improvements for navigation" on various rivers. The language of the proviso makes clear that power would be an item secondary to navigation development.

SEC. 3. That for examinations, surveys, and contingencies for rivers and harbors for which there may be no special appropriation, the sum of five hundred thousand dollars is hereby appropriated: *Provided,* That no preliminary examination, survey, project, or estimate for new works other than those designated in this or some prior Act or joint resolution shall be made: *Provided further,* That after the regular or formal reports made as required by law on any examination, survey, project, or work under way or proposed are submitted no supplemental or additional report or estimate shall be made unless ordered by a concurrent resolution of Congress. The Government shall not be deemed to have entered upon any project for the improvement of any waterway or harbor mentioned in this Act until funds for the commencement of the proposed work shall have been actually appropriated by law.

The Secretary of War is hereby authorized and directed to cause preliminary examinations and surveys to be made at the localities named in this section, as hereinafter set forth, and a sufficient sum to pay the cost thereof may be allotted from the amount appropriated in this section. In all cases a preliminary examination of the river, harbor, or other proposed improvement mentioned shall first be made, and a report as to the advisability of its improvement shall be submitted, unless a survey or estimate is herein expressly directed. If upon such preliminary examination the proposed improvement is not deemed advisable, no further action shall be taken thereon without the further direction of Congress; but in case the report shall be favorable to such proposed improvement, or that a survey and estimate should be made to determine the advisability of improvement, the Secretary of War is hereby authorized, in his discretion, to cause surveys to be made, and the cost and advisability to be reported to Congress. And such reports containing plans and estimates shall also contain a statement as to the rate at which the work should be prosecuted. Such examinations and surveys shall be reviewed by the Board of Engineers for Rivers and Harbors, as provided in section three of the river and harbor Act of March second, nineteen hundred and seven: *Provided,* That every examination and

*36 *Statutes at Large,* 668–69.

survey report submitted to Congress, as provided for herein or as may be provided for hereafter, in addition to full information regarding the present and prospective commercial importance of the project covered by the report, and the benefit to commerce likely to result from any proposed plan of improvement, shall contain also such data as it may be practicable to secure regarding (first) the establishment of terminal and transfer facilities, (second) the development and utilization of water power for industrial and commercial purposes, and (third) such other subjects as may be properly connected with such project: *Provided further,* That in the investigation and study of these questions consideration shall be given only to their bearing upon the improvement of navigation and to the possibility and desirability of their being coordinated in a logical and proper manner with improvements for navigation to lessen the cost of such improvements and to compensate the Government for expenditures made in the interest of navigation: *And provided further,* That the investigation and study of these questions as provided herein may, upon review by the Board of Engineers for Rivers and Harbors when called for as now provided by law, be extended to any work of improvement now under way and to any locality the examination and survey of which has heretofore been, or may hereafter be, authorized by Congress.

The surveys of navigable streams herein or hereafter authorized shall include such stream-flow measurements and other investigations of the watersheds as may be necessary for preparation of plans of improvement and a proper consideration of all uses of the stream affecting navigation, and whenever necessary similar investigations may be made in connection with all navigable streams under improvement. Whenever permission for the construction of dams in navigable streams is granted, or is under consideration by Congress, such surveys and investigations of the sections of the streams affected may be made as are necessary to secure conformity with rational plans for the improvement of the streams for navigation.

All reports of preliminary examinations and surveys which may be prepared during the recess of Congress shall, in the discretion of the Secretary of War, be printed by the Public Printer as documents of the following session of Congress.

PRESIDENT TAFT'S VETO OF PRIVATE
DEVELOPMENT OF A DAM*
August 6, 1912

In 1912, President William Howard Taft still accepted enough of Roosevelt's philosophy in opposition to monopolistic development of waterways to veto a private development bill for a dam on the White River in Arkansas. The language is not as strong as Roosevelt's, but it refers to the same standards.

To the House of Representatives:

I return herewith, without my approval, H. R. 20347, being a bill to authorize the Dixie Power Co. to construct a dam across White River at or near Cotter, Ark.

The White River, on which this dam is proposed to be built, is a navigable stream. In March, 1899, Congress adopted a project for the improvement of the navigation of the river from Batesville, Ark., upstream to Buffalo Shoals, by a series of 10 locks and dams. Of these, three have already been constructed by the Federal Government, and the Government is also engaged in improving the river by channel work in other portions. This bill proposes to authorize the construction of a dam at or near Cotter, a short distance above the portion covered by the aforesaid project of 1899, and situated well below Forsyth, Mo., which is generally considered to be the head of high-water steamboat navigation. The dam will increase the navigable capacity of the stream above it, and could be constructed so as to form a part of an extension of the above-mentioned projected canalization scheme below it. While the Board of Engineers for Rivers and Harbors has, in a subsequent recommendation, advised against the present prosecution of this project on account of the lack of present commerce in the river, it is quite possible, according to the report of the Chief of Engineers of the United States Army, that conditions may so change in the future as to lead to an extension of the lock and dam system as far as the site of the dam proposed by this bill.

By a provision inserted into the bill since its introduction in Congress it is provided that upon the expiration of the Federal permit the dam shall become the property of the State of Arkansas at the option of said State. In my opinion, this provision is likely to introduce serious complications in the orderly development of navigation in the river. The lower river is being improved by a series of dams belonging to the Federal Government. This dam, situated in the upper reaches of the river, is, according to the report of the engineers, capable of becoming a part of this general Federal improvement of navigation. To intro-

*Cong. Rec., Vol. 48, 62nd Cong., 2nd sess., 10318.

duce a diversity of title into a series of dams which may all become eventually a part of a single improvement directed at the same end would, in my opinion, be highly objectionable. Furthermore, the policy of this provision would seem to be in conflict with the policy of the general dam act of June 23, 1910, by which, at the expiration of such a permit, the control and title of such a dam apparently vest in the Federal Government, as pointed out in the recent final report of the National Waterways Commission, page 57.

The bill also fails to reserve to the Federal Government any right to receive from the grantee of this privilege any compensation therefor to be used in the interest of furthering the navigation of said river. This is a subject to which the National Waterways Commission has given much study and made urgent recommendations, and in regard to which the Secretary of War has, with my approval, written a letter, under date of July 30, 1912, to the chairman of Committee on Interstate and Foreign Commerce of the House of Representatives. In view, however, of the serious objection to the bill, contained in the provision which I have already discussed, I do not deem it necessary to enter into a discussion of this feature of the bill.

Wm. H. Taft

The White House
August 6, 1912

THE FEDERAL POWER COMMISSION ACT*
June 10, 1920

The legislation establishing the Federal Power Commission grew out of the long fight to establish a system for federal leasing and control of hydroelectric-power dam sites. A bill establishing theoretical federal control of all sites on navigable streams, but containing so many waivers of control through a very limited definition of navigability, passed both Houses of Congress in 1917, but was barred from passage by a last minute filibuster of Senator Robert M. LaFollette of Wisconsin, who had the help of Senator Joseph France of Maryland.

World War I delayed new consideration of the issue, but Senator Wesley Jones of Washington sponsored a bill acceptable to the conservationists in 1920. Federal ownership and jurisdiction were established over all navigable waters from source to mouth, without regard to shoals or falls. A power commission was created, consisting of three cabinet members, with authority to make 50-year leases for power development. One of the most important provisions for the future was a requirement that public bodies receive preference in the case of conflicting applications and in the sale of the power generated.

Although Pinchot and most of the Roosevelt conservationists supported the bill, George Norris and other Progressives voted against it because it still made possible leases that made private monopolies of public waters. They also opposed the political nature of the commission.

The bill was also used as a vehicle to repeal the Newlands waterway commission law, which had never been put into effect after the death of the Senator (Section 29).

In 1930, the authority of the Federal Power Commission was somewhat broadened, and the President was given power to appoint a five-man commission rather than three Cabinet officers as under the 1920 act.

An Act to create a Federal Power Commission; to provide for the improvement of navigation; the development of water power; the use of the public lands in relation thereto, and to repeal section 18 of the River and Harbor Appropriation Act, approved August 8, 1917, and for other purposes.

Be it enacted by the Senate and House of Representatives of the United States of America in Congress assembled, That a commission is hereby created and established, to be known as the Federal Power Commission (hereinafter referred to as the commission), which shall be composed of the Secretary of

*41 *Statutes at Large,* 1063–77.

[183]

War, the Secretary of the Interior, and the Secretary of Agriculture. Two members of the commission shall constitute a quorum for the transaction of business, and the commission shall have an official seal, which shall be judicially noticed. The President shall designate the chairman of the commission.

SEC. 2. That the commission shall appoint an executive secretary, who shall receive a salary of $5,000 a year, and prescribe his duties, and the commission may request the President of the United States to detail an officer from the United States Engineer Corps to serve the commission as engineer officer, his duties to be prescribed by the commission.

The work of the commission shall be performed by and through the Departments of War, Interior, and Agriculture and their engineering, technical, clerical, and other personnel except as may be otherwise provided by law.

All the expenses of the commission, including rent in the District of Columbia, all necessary expenses for transportation and subsistence, including, in the discretion of the commission, a per diem of not exceeding $4 in lieu of subsistence incurred by its employees under its orders in making any investigation, or conducting field work, or upon official business outside of the District of Columbia and away from their designated points of duty, shall be allowed and paid on the presentation of itemized vouchers therefor approved by a member or officer of the commission duly authorized for that purpose; and in order to defray the expenses made necessary by the provisions of this Act there is hereby authorized to be appropriated such sums as Congress may hereafter determine, and the sum of $100,000 is hereby appropriated, out of any moneys in the Treasury not otherwise appropriated, available until expended, to be paid out upon warrants drawn on the Secretary of the Treasury upon order of the commission.

SEC. 3. That the words defined in this section shall have the following meanings for the purposes of this Act, to wit:

"Public lands" means such lands and interest in lands owned by the United States as are subject to private appropriation and disposal under public-land laws. It shall not include "reservations," as hereinafter defined.

"Reservations" means national monuments, national parks, national forests, tribal lands embraced within Indian reservations, military reservations, and other lands and interests in lands owned by the United States, and withdrawn, reserved, or withheld from private appropriation and disposal under the public-land laws; also lands and interests in lands acquired and held for any public purpose.

"Corporation" means a corporation organized under the laws of any State or of the United States empowered to develop, transmit, distribute, sell, lease, or utilize power in addition to such other powers as it may possess, and authorized to transact in the State or States in which its project is located all business necessary to effect the purposes of a license under this Act. It shall not include "municipalities" as hereinafter defined.

"State" means a State admitted to the Union, the District of Columbia, and any organized Territory of the United States.

"Municipality" means a city, county, irrigation district, drainage district, or other political subdivision or agency of a State competent under the laws thereof to carry on the business of developing, transmitting, utilizing, or distributing power.

"Navigable waters" means those parts of streams or other bodies of water over which Congress has jurisdiction under its authority to regulate commerce with foreign nations and among the several States, and which either in their natural or improved condition, notwithstanding interruptions between the navigable parts of such streams or waters by falls, shallows, or rapids compelling land carriage, are used or suitable for use for the transportation of persons or property in interstate or foreign commerce, including therein all such interrupting falls, shallows, or rapids; together with such other parts of streams as shall have been authorized by Congress for improvement by the United States or shall have been recommended to Congress for such improvement after investigation under its authority.

"Municipal purposes" means and includes all purposes within municipal powers as defined by the constitution or laws of the State or by the charter of the municipality.

"Government dam" means a dam or other work, constructed or owned by the United States for Government purposes, with or without contribution from others.

"Project" means complete unit of improvement or development, consisting of a power house, all water conduits, all dams and appurtenant works and structures (including navigation structures) which are a part of said unit, and all storage, diverting, or forebay reservoirs directly connected therewith, the primary line or lines transmitting power therefrom to the point of junction with the distribution system or with the interconnected primary transmission system, all miscellaneous structures used and useful in connection with said unit or any part thereof, and all water rights, rights of way, ditches, dams, reservoirs, lands, or interest in lands, the use and occupancy of which are necessary or appropriate in the maintenance and operation of such unit.

"Project works" means the physical structures of a project.

"New investment" in a project means the actual legitimate original cost thereof as defined and interpreted in the "classification of investment in road and equipment of steam roads, issue of 1914, Interstate Commerce Commission," plus similar costs of additions thereto and betterments thereof, minus the sum of the following items properly allocated thereto, if and to the extent that such items have been accumulated during the period of the license from earnings in excess of a fair return on such investment: (a) Unappropriated surplus, (b) aggregate credit balances of current depreciation accounts, and (c) aggregate appropriations of surplus or income held in amortization, sinking fund, or similar reserves, or expended for additions or betterments or used for the purposes for which such reserves were created. The term "cost" shall include, in so far as applicable, the elements thereof prescribed in said classification, but shall not include expenditures from funds obtained through donations by States, municipalities, individuals, or others, and said classification of investment of the Interstate Commerce Commission shall in so far as applicable be published and promulgated as a part of the rules and regulations of the commission.

Sec. 4. That the commission is hereby authorized and empowered—

(a) To make investigations and to collect and record data concerning the utilization of the water resources of any region to be developed, the water power industry and its relation to other industries and to interstate or foreign commerce, and concerning the location, capacity, development costs, and relation to markets of power sites, and whether the power from Government dams can be advantageously used by the United States for its public purposes, and what is a fair value of such power, to the extent the commission may deem necessary or useful for the purposes of this Act.

In order to aid the commission in determining the net investment of a licensee in any project, the licensee shall, upon oath, within a reasonable period of time, to be fixed by the commission, after the construction of the original project or any addition thereto or betterment thereof, file with the commission, in such detail as the commission may require, a statement in duplicate showing the actual legitimate cost of construction of such project, addition, or betterment, and the price paid for water rights, rights of way, lands, or interest in lands. The commission shall deposit one of said statements with the Secretary of the Treasury. The licensee shall grant to the commission or to its duly authorized agent or agents, at all reasonable times, free access to such project, addition, or betterment, and to all maps, profiles, contracts, reports of engineers, accounts, books, records, and all other papers and documents relating thereto.

(b) To cooperate with the executive departments and other agencies of State or National Governments in such investigations; and for such purpose the several departments and agencies of the National Government are authorized and directed upon the request of the commission, to furnish such records, papers, and information in their possession as may be requested by the commission, and temporarily to detail to the commission such officers or experts as may be necessary in such investigations.

(c) To make public from time to time the information secured hereunder, and to provide for the publication of its reports and investigations in such form and manner as may be best adapted for public information and use. The commission, on or before the first Monday in December of each year, shall submit to Congress for the fiscal year preceding a classified report showing the permits and licenses issued under this Act, and in each case the parties thereto, the terms prescribed, and the moneys received, if any, on account thereof.

(d) To issue licenses to citizens of the United States, or to any association of such citizens, or to any corporation organized under the laws of the United States or any State thereof, or to any State, or municipality for the purpose of constructing, operating, and maintaining dams, water conduits, reservoirs, power houses, transmission lines, or other project works necessary or convenient for the development and improvement of navigation, and for the development, transmission, and utilization of power across, along, from or in any of the navigable waters of the United States, or upon any part of the public lands and reservations of the United States (including the Territories), or for the purpose of utilizing the surplus water or water power from any Government dam, except as herein provided: *Provided,* That licenses shall be issued within any reservation only after a finding by the commission that the license will not interfere or be inconsistent with the purpose for which such reservation was created or acquired, and shall be subject to and contain such conditions as the Secretary of the department under whose supervision such reservation falls shall deem necessary for the adequate protection and utilization of such reservation: *Provided further,* That no license affecting the navigable capacity of any navigable waters of the United States shall be issued until the plans of the dam or other structures affecting navigation have been approved by the Chief of Engineers and the Secretary of War. Whenever the contemplated improvement is, in the judgment of the commission, desirable and justified in the public interest for the purpose of improving or developing a waterway or waterways for the use or benefit of interstate or foreign commerce, a finding to that effect shall be made by the commission and shall become a part of the records of the commission: *Provided further,* That in case the commission shall find that any Government dam may be advantageously used by the United States for public purposes in addition to navigation, no license therefor shall be issued until two years after it shall have reported to Congress the facts and conditions relating thereto, except that this provision shall not apply to any Government dam constructed prior to the passage of this Act: *And provided further,* That upon the filing of any application for a license which has not been preceded by a preliminary permit under subsection (c) of this section, notice shall be given and published as required by the proviso of said subsection.

(e) To issue preliminary permits for the purpose of enabling applicants for a license hereunder to secure the data and to perform the acts required by section 9 hereof: *Provided, however,* That upon the filing of any application for a preliminary permit by any person, association, or corporation the commission, before granting such application, shall at once give notice of such application in writing to any State or municipality likely to be interested in or affected by such application; and shall also publish notice of such application for eight weeks in a daily or weekly newspaper published in the county or counties in which the project or any part thereof or the lands affected thereby are situated.

(f) To prescribe rules and regulations for the establishment of a system of accounts and for the maintenance thereof by licensees hereunder; to examine all books and accounts of such licensees at any time; to require them to submit at such time or times as the commission may require statements and reports, including full information as to assets and liabilities, capitalization, net investment and reduction thereof, gross receipts, interest due and paid, depreciation and other reserves, cost of project, cost of maintenance and operation of the project, cost of renewals and replacements of the project works, and as to depreciation of the project works and as to production, transmission, use and sale of power; also to require any licensee to make adequate provision for currently determining said costs and other facts. All such statements and reports shall be made upon oath, unless otherwise specified, and in such form and on such blanks as the commission may require. Any person who, for the purpose of deceiving, makes or causes to be made any false entry in the books or the accounts of such licensee, and any person who, for the purpose of deceiving, makes or causes to be made any false statement or report in response to a request or order or direction from the commission for the statements and report herein referred to shall, upon conviction, be fined not more than $2,000 or imprisoned not more than five years, or both.

(g) To hold hearings and to order testimony to be taken by deposition at any designated place in connection with the application for any permit or license, or the regulation of rates, service, or securities, or the making of any investigation, as provided in this Act; and to require by subpoena, signed by any member of the commission, the attendance and testimony of witnesses and the production of documentary evidence from any place in the United States, and in case of disobedience to a subpoena the commission may invoke the aid of any court of the United States in requiring the attendance and testimony of witnesses and the production of documentary evidence. Any member, expert, or examiner of the commission may, when duly designated by the commission for such purposes, administer oaths and affirmations, examine witnesses and receive evidence. Depositions may be taken before any person designated by the commission or by its executive secretary and empowered to administer oaths, shall be reduced to writing by such person or under his direction, and subscribed by the deponent. Witnesses summoned before the commission shall be paid the same fees and mileage that are paid witnesses in the courts of the United States, and witnesses whose depositions are taken and persons taking the same shall severally be entitled to the same fees as are paid for like services in the courts of the United States.

(h) To perform any and all acts, to make such rules and regulations, and to issue such orders not inconsistent with this Act as may be necessary and proper for the purpose of carrying out the provisions of this Act.

Sec. 5. That each preliminary permit issued under this Act shall be for the sole purpose of maintaining priority of application for a license under the terms of this Act for such period or periods, not exceeding a total of three years, as in the discretion of the commission may be necessary for making examinations and surveys, for preparing maps, plans, specifications, and estimates, and for making financial arrangements. Each such permit shall set forth the conditions under which priority shall be maintained and a license issued. Such permits shall not be transferable, and may be canceled by order of the commission upon failure of permittees to comply with the conditions thereof.

Sec. 6. That licenses under this Act shall be issued for a period not exceeding fifty years. Each such license shall be conditioned upon acceptance by the licensee of all the terms and conditions of this Act and such further conditions, if any, as the commission shall prescribe in conformity with this Act, which said terms and conditions and the acceptance thereof shall be expressed in said license. Licenses may be revoked only for the reasons and in the manner prescribed under the provisions of this Act, and may be altered or surrendered only upon mutual agreement between the licensee and the commission after ninety days' public notice.

Sec. 7. That in issuing preliminary permits hereunder or licenses where no preliminary permit has been issued and in issuing licenses to new licensees under section 15 hereof the commission shall give preference to applications therefor by States and municipalities, provided the plans for the same are deemed by the commission equally well adapted, or shall within a reasonable time to be fixed by the commission be made equally well adapted, to conserve and utilize in the public interest the navigation and water resources of the region; and as between other applicants, the commission may give preference to the applicant the plans of which it finds and determines are best adapted to develop, conserve, and utilize in the public interest the navigation and water resources of the region, if it be satisfied as to the ability of the applicant to carry out such plans.

That whenever, in the judgment of the commission, the development of any project should be undertaken by the United States itself, the commission shall not approve any application for such project by any citizen, association, corporation, State, or municipality, but shall cause to be made such examinations, surveys, reports, plans, and estimates of the cost of the project as it may deem necessary, and shall submit its findings to Congress with such recommendations as it may deem appropriate concerning the construction of such project or completion of any project upon any Government dam by the United States.

The commission is hereby authorized and directed to investigate and, on or before the 1st day of January, 1921, report to Congress the cost and, in detail, the economic value of the power plant outlined in project numbered 3, House Document numbered 1400, Sixty-second Congress, third session, in view of existing conditions, utilizing such study as may heretofore have been made by any department of the Government; also in connection with such project to submit plans and estimates of cost necessary to secure an increased and adequate water supply for the District of Columbia. For this purpose the sum of $25,000, or so much thereof as may be necessary, is hereby appropriated.

SEC. 8. That no voluntary transfer of any license, or of the rights thereunder granted, shall be made without the written approval of the commission; and any successor or assign of the rights of such licensee, whether by voluntary transfer, judicial sale, foreclosure sale, or otherwise, shall be subject to all the conditions of the license under which such rights are held by such licensee and also subject to all the provisions and conditions of this Act to the same extent as though such successor or assign were the original licensee hereunder: *Provided,* That a mortgage or trust deed or judicial sales made thereunder or under tax sales shall not be deemed voluntary transfers within the meaning of this section.

SEC. 9. That each applicant for a license hereunder shall submit to the commission—

(a) Such maps, plans, specifications, and estimates of cost as may be required for a full understanding of the proposed project. Such maps, plans, and specifications when approved by the commission shall be made a part of the license; and thereafter no change shall be made in said maps, plans, or specifications until such changes shall have been approved and made a part of such license by the commission.

(b) Satisfactory evidence that the applicant has complied with the requirements of the laws of the State or States within which the proposed project is to be located with respect to bed and banks and to the appropriation, diversion, and use of water for power purposes and with respect to the right to engage in the business of developing, transmitting, and distributing power, and in any other business necessary to effect the purposes of a license under this Act.

(c) Such additional information as the commission may require.

SEC. 10. That all licenses issued under this Act shall be on the following conditions:

(a) That the project adopted, including the maps, plans, and specifications, shall be such as in the judgment of the commission will be best adapted to a comprehensive scheme of improvement and utilization for the purposes of navigation, of water-power development, and of other beneficial public uses; and if necessary in order to secure such scheme the commission shall have authority to require the modification of any project and of the plans and specifications of the project works before approval.

(b) That except when emergency shall require for the protection of navigation, life, health, or property, no substantial alteration or addition not in conformity with the approved plans shall be made to any dam or other project works constructed hereunder of a capacity in excess of one hundred horsepower without the prior approval of the commission; and any emergency alteration or addition so made shall thereafter be subject to such modification and change as the commission may direct.

(c) That the licensee shall maintain the project works in a condition of repair adequate for the purposes of navigation and for the efficient operation of said works in the development and transmission of power, shall make all necessary renewals and replacements, shall establish and maintain adequate depreciation reserves for such purposes, shall so maintain and operate said works as not to impair navigation, and shall conform to such rules and regulations as the commission may from time to time prescribe for the protection of life, health, and property. Each licensee hereunder shall be liable for all damages occasioned to the property of others by the construction, maintenance, or operation of the project works or of the works appurtenant or accessory thereto, constructed under the license, and in no event shall the United States be liable therefor.

(d) That after the first twenty years of operation out of surplus earned thereafter, if any, accumulated in excess of a specified reasonable rate of return upon the actual, legitimate investment of a licensee in any project or projects under license the licensee shall establish and maintain amortization reserves, which reserves shall, in the discretion of the commission, be held until the termination of the license or be applied from time to time in reduction of the net investment. Such specified rate of return and the proportion of such surplus earnings to be paid into and held in such reserves shall be set forth in the license.

(e) That the licensee shall pay to the United States reasonable annual charges in an amount to be fixed by the commission for the purpose of reimbursing the United States for the costs of the administration of this Act; for recompensing it for the use, occupancy, and enjoyment of its lands or other property; and for the expropriation to the Government of excessive profits until the respective States shall make provision for preventing excessive profits or for the expropriation thereof to themselves, or until the period of amortization as herein provided is reached, and in fixing such charges the commission shall seek to avoid increasing the price to the consumers of power by such charges, and charges for the expropriation of excessive profits may be adjusted from time to time by the commission as conditions may require: *Provided,* That when licenses are issued involving the use of Government dams or other structures owned by the United States or tribal lands embraced within Indian reservations the commis-

[191]

sion shall fix a reasonable annual charge for the use thereof, and such charges may be readjusted at the end of twenty years after the beginning of operations and at periods of not less than ten years thereafter in a manner to be described in each license: *Provided,* That licenses for the development, transmission, or distribution of power by States or municipalities shall be issued and enjoyed without charge to the extent such power is sold to the public without profit or is used by such State or municipality for State or municipal purposes, except that as to projects constructed or to be constructed by States or municipalities primarily designed to provide or improve navigation licenses therefor shall be issued without charge; and that licenses for the development, transmission, or distribution of power for domestic, mining, or other beneficial use in projects of not more than one hundred horsepower capacity may be issued without charge, except on tribal lands within Indian reservations; but in no case shall a license be issued free of charge for the development and utilization of power created by any Government dam and that the amount charged therefor in any license shall be such as determined by the commission.

(f) That whenever any licensee hereunder is directly benefited by the construction work of another licensee, a permittee, or of the United States of a storage reservoir or other headwater improvement, the commission shall require as a condition of the license that the licensee so benefited shall reimburse the owner of such reservoir or other improvements for such part of the annual charges for interest, maintenance, and depreciation thereon as the commission may deem equitable. The proportion of such charges to be paid by any licensee shall be determined by the commission.

Whenever such reservoir or other improvement is constructed by the United States the commission shall assess similar charges against any licensee directly benefited thereby, and any amount so assessed shall be paid into the Treasury of the United States, to be reserved and appropriated as a part of the special fund for headwater improvements as provided in section 17 hereof.

(g) Such further conditions not inconsistent with the provisions of this Act as the commission may require.

(h) That combinations, agreements, arrangements, or understandings, express or implied, to limit the output of electrical energy, to restrain trade, or to fix, maintain, or increase prices for electrical energy or service are hereby prohibited.

(i) In issuing licenses for a minor part only of a complete project, or for a complete project of not more than one hundred horsepower capacity, the commission may in its discretion waive such conditions, provisions, and requirements of this Act, except the license period of fifty years, as it may deem to be to the public interest to waive under the circumstances: *Provided,* That the provisions hereof shall not apply to lands within Indian reservations.

[192]

SEC. 11. That if the dam or other project works are to be constructed across, along, or in any of the navigable waters of the United States, the commission may, in so far as it deems the same reasonably necessary to promote the present and future needs of navigation and consistent with a reasonable investment cost to the licensee, include in the license any one or more of the following provisions or requirements:

(a) That such licensee shall, to the extent necessary to preserve and improve navigation facilities, construct, in whole or in part, without expense to the United States, in connection with such dam, a lock or locks, booms, sluices, or other structures for navigation purposes, in accordance with plans and specifications approved by the Chief of Engineers and the Secretary of War and made part of such license.

(b) That in case such structures for navigation purposes are not made a part of the original construction at the expense of the licensee, then whenever the United States shall desire to complete such navigation facilities the licensee shall convey to the United States, free of cost, such of its land and its rights of way and such right of passage through its dams or other structures, and permit such control of pools as may be required to complete such navigation facilities.

(c) That such licensee shall furnish free of cost to the United States power for the operation of such navigation facilities, whether constructed by the licensee or by the United States.

SEC. 12. That whenever application is filed for a project hereunder involving navigable waters of the United States, and the commission shall find upon investigation that the needs of navigation require the construction of a lock or locks or other navigation structures, and that such structures can not, consistent with a reasonable investment cost to the applicant, be provided in the manner specified in section 11, subsection (a) hereof, the commission may grant the application with the provision to be expressed in the license that the licensee will install the necessary navigation structures if the Government fails to make provision therefor within a time to be fixed in the license and cause a report upon such project to be prepared, with estimates of cost of the power development and of the navigation structures, and shall submit such report to Congress with such recommendations as it deems appropriate concerning the participation of the United States in the cost of construction of such navigation structures.

SEC. 13. That the licensee shall commence the construction of the project works within the time fixed in the license, which shall not be more than two years from the date thereof, shall thereafter in good faith and with due diligence prosecute such construction, and shall within the time fixed in the license complete and put into operation such part of the ultimate development as the commission shall deem necessary to supply the reasonable needs of the then available market, and shall from time to time thereafter construct such portion of the balance of such development as the commission may direct, so as to supply adequately the reasonable market demands until such development shall have been completed. The periods for the commencement of construction may be extended once but not longer than two additional years and the period for the completion of construction carried on in good faith and with reasonable diligence may be extended by the commission when not incompatible with the public interests. In case the licensee shall not commence actual construction of the project works, or of any specified part thereof, within the time prescribed in the license or as extended by the commission, then, after due notice given, the license shall, as to such project works or part thereof, be terminated upon written order of the commission. In case the construction of the project works, or of any specified part thereof, have been begun but not completed within the time prescribed in the license, or as extended by the commission, then the Attorney General, upon the request of the commission, shall institute proceedings in equity in the district court of the United States for the district in which any part of the project is situated for the revocation of said license, the sale of the works constructed, and such other equitable relief as the case may demand, as provided for in section 26 hereof.

SEC. 14. That upon not less than two years' notice in writing from the commission the United States shall have the right upon or after the expiration of any license to take over and thereafter to maintain and operate any project or projects as defined in section 3 hereof, and covered in whole or in part by the license, or the right to take over upon mutual agreement with the licensee all property owned and held by the licensee then valuable and serviceable in the development, transmission, or distribution of power and which is then dependent for its usefulness upon the continuance of the license, together with any lock or locks or other aids to navigation constructed at the expense of the licensee, upon the condition that before taking possession it shall pay the net investment of the licensee in the project or projects taken, not to exceed the fair value of the property taken, plus such reasonable damages, if any, to property of the licensee valuable, serviceable, and dependent as above set forth but not taken, as may be caused by the severance therefrom of property taken, and shall assume all contracts entered into by the licensee with the approval of the commission. The net investment of the licensee in the project or projects so taken and the amount of such severance damages, if any, shall be determined by agreement between the commission and the licensee, and in case they can not agree, by proceedings in equity instituted by the United States in the district court of the United States in the district within which any such property may be located: *Provided,* That such net investment shall not include or be affected by the value of any lands, rights of way, or other property of the United States licensed by the commission under this Act, by the license, or by good will, going value, or prospective revenues: *Provided further,* That the values allowed for water rights, rights of way, lands, or interest in lands shall not be in excess of the actual reasonable cost thereof at the time of acquisition by the licensee: *Provided,* That the right of the United States or any State or municipality to take over, maintain, and operate any project licensed under this Act at any time by condemnation proceedings upon payment of just compensation is hereby expressly reserved.

SEC. 15. That if the United States does not, at the expiration of the original license, exercise its right to take over, maintain, and operate any project or projects of the licensee, as provided in section 14 hereof, the commission is authorized to issue a new license to the original licensee upon such terms and conditions as may be authorized or required under the then existing laws and regulations, or to issue a new license under said terms and conditions to a new licensee, which license may cover any project or projects covered by the original license, and shall be issued on the condition that the new licensee shall, before taking possession of such project or projects, pay such amount, and assume such contracts as the United States is required to do, in the manner specified in section 14 hereof: *Provided,* That in the event the United States does not exercise the right to take over or does not issue a license to a new licensee, or issue a new license to the original licensee, upon reasonable terms, then the commission shall issue from year to year an annual license to the then licensee under the terms and conditions of the original license until the property is taken over or a new license is issued as aforesaid.

SEC. 16. That when in the opinion of the President of the United States, evidenced by a written order addressed to the holder of any license hereunder, the safety of the United States demands it, the United States shall have the right to enter upon and take possession of any project, or part thereof, constructed, maintained, or operated under said license, for the purpose of manufacturing nitrates, explosives, or munitions of war, or for any other purpose involving the safety of the United States, to retain possession, management, and control thereof for such length of time as may appear to the President to be necessary to accomplish said purposes, and then to restore possession and control to the party or parties entitled thereto; and in the event that the United States shall exercise such right it shall pay to the party or parties entitled thereto just and fair compensation for the use of said property as may be fixed by the commission upon the basis of a reasonable profit in time of peace, and the cost of restoring said property to as good condition as existed at the time of the taking over thereof, less the reasonable value of any improvements that may be made thereto by the United States and which are valuable and serviceable to the licensee.

SEC. 17. That all proceeds from any Indian reservation shall be placed to the credit of the Indians of such reservation. All other charges arising from licenses hereunder shall be paid into the Treasury of the United States, subject to the following distribution: Twelve and one-half per centum thereof is hereby appropriated to be paid into the Treasury of the United States and credited to "Miscellaneous receipts"; 50 per centum of the charges arising from licenses hereunder for the occupancy and use of public lands, national monuments, national forests, and national parks shall be paid into, reserved, and appropriated as a part of the reclamation fund created by the Act of Congress known as the Reclamation Act, approved June 17, 1902; and 37½ per centum of the charges arising from licenses hereunder for the occupancy and use of national forests, national parks, public lands, and national monuments, from development within the boundaries of any State shall be paid by the Secretary of the Treasury to such State; and 50 per centum of the charges arising from all other licenses hereunder is hereby reserved and appropriated as a special fund in the Treasury to be expended under the direction of the Secretary of War in the maintenance and operation of dams and other navigation structures owned by the United States or in the construction, maintenance, or operation of headwater or other improvements of navigable waters of the United States.

SEC. 18. That the operation of any navigation facilities which may be constructed as a part of or in connection with any dam or diversion structure built under the provisions of this Act, whether at the expense of a licensee hereunder or of the United States, shall at all times be controlled by such reasonable rules and regulations in the interest of navigation, including the control of the level of the pool caused by such dam or diversion structure as may be made from time to time by the Secretary of War. Such rules and regulations may include the maintenance and operation by such licensee at its own expense of such lights and signals as may be directed by the Secretary of War, and such fishways as may be prescribed by the Secretary of Commerce; and for willful failure to comply with any such rule or regulation such licensee shall be deemed guilty of a misdemeanor, and upon conviction thereof shall be punished as provided in section 25 hereof.

SEC. 19. That as a condition of the license, every licensee hereunder which is a public-service corporation, or a person, association, or corporation owning or operating any project and developing, transmitting, or distributing power for sale or use in public service, shall abide by such reasonable regulation of the services to be rendered to customers or consumers of power, and of rates and charges of payment therefor, as may from time to time be prescribed by any duly constituted agency of the State in which the service is rendered or the rate charged. That in case of the development, transmission, or distribution, or use in public service of power by any licensee hereunder or by its customer engaged in public service within a State which has not authorized and empowered a commission or other agency or agencies within said State to regulate and control the services to be rendered by such licensee or by its customer engaged in public service, or the rates and charges of payment therefor, or the amount or character of securities to be issued by any of said parties, it is agreed as a condition of such license that jurisdiction is hereby conferred upon the commission, upon complaint of any person aggrieved or upon its own initiative, to exercise such regulation and control until such time as the State shall have provided a commission or other authority for such regulation and control: *Provided,* That the jurisdiction of the commission shall cease and determine as to each specific matter of regulation and control prescribed in this section as soon as the State shall have provided a commission or other authority for the regulation and control of that specific matter.

Sec. 20. That when said power or any part thereof shall enter into interstate or foreign commerce the rates charged and the service rendered by any such licensee, or by any subsidiary corporation, the stock of which is owned or controlled directly or indirectly by such licensee, or by any person, corporation, or association purchasing power from such licensee for sale and distribution or use in public service shall be reasonable, nondiscriminatory, and just to the customer and all unreasonable discriminatory and unjust rates or services are hereby prohibited and declared to be unlawful; and whenever any of the States directly concerned has not provided a commission or other authority to enforce the requirements of this section within such State or to regulate and control the amount and character of securities to be issued by any of such parties or such States are unable to agree through their properly constituted authorities on the services to be rendered or on the rates or charges of payment therefor, or on the amount or character of securities to be issued by any of said parties, jurisdiction is hereby conferred upon the commission, upon complaint of any person aggrieved, upon the request of any State concerned, or upon its own initiative to enforce the provisions of this section, to regulate and control so much of the services rendered, and of the rates and charges of payment therefor as constitute interstate or foreign commerce and to regulate the issuance of securities by the parties included within this section, and securities issued by the licensee subject to such regulations shall be allowed only for the bona fide purpose of financing and conducting the business of such licensee.

The administration of the provisions of this section, so far as applicable, shall be according to the procedure and practice in fixing and regulating the rates, charges, and practices of railroad companies as provided in the Act to regulate commerce, approved February 4, 1887, as amended, and that the parties subject to such regulation shall have the same rights of hearing, defense, and review as said companies in such cases.

In any valuation of the property of any licensee hereunder for purposes of rate making, no value shall be claimed by the licensee or allowed by the commission for any project or projects under license in excess of the value or values prescribed in section 14 hereof for the purposes of purchase by the United States, but there shall be included the cost to such licensee of the construction of the lock or locks or other aids of navigation and all other capital expenditures required by the United States, and no value shall be claimed or allowed for the rights granted by the commission or by this Act.

SEC. 21. That when any licensee can not acquire by contract or pledges an unimproved dam site or the right to use or damage the lands or property of others necessary to the construction, maintenance, or operation of any dam, reservoir, diversion structure, or the works appurtenant or accessory thereto, in conjunction with an improvement which in the judgment of the commission is desirable and justified in the public interest for the purpose of improving or developing a waterway or waterways for the use or benefit of interstate or foreign commerce, it may acquire the same by the exercise of the right of eminent domain in the district court of the United States for the district in which such land or other property may be located, or in the State courts. The practice and procedure in any action or proceeding for that purpose in the district court of the United States shall conform as nearly as may be with the practice and procedure in similar action or proceeding in the courts of the State where the property is situated: *Provided,* That United States district courts shall only have jurisdiction of cases when the amount claimed by the owner of the property to be condemned exceeds $3,000.

SEC. 22. That whenever the public interest requires or justifies the execution by the licensee of contracts for the sale and delivery of power for periods extending beyond the date of termination of the license, such contracts may be entered into upon the joint approval of the commission and of the public-service commission or other similar authority in the State in which the sale or delivery of power is made, or if sold or delivered in a State which has no such public-service commission, then upon the approval of the commission, and thereafter, in the event of failure to issue a new license to the original licensee at the termination of the license, the United States or the new licensee, as the case may be, shall assume and fulfill all such contracts.

SEC. 23. That the provisions of this Act shall not be construed as affecting any permit or valid existing right of way heretofore granted, or as confirming or otherwise affecting any claim, or as affecting any authority heretofore given pursuant to law, but any person, association, corporation, State, or municipality, holding or possessing such permit, right of way, or authority may apply for a license hereunder, and upon such application the commission may issue to any such applicant a license in accordance with the provisions of this Act, and in such case the provisions of this Act shall apply to such applicant as a licensee hereunder: *Provided,* That when application is made for a license under this section for a project or projects already constructed, the fair value of said project or projects, determined as provided in this section, shall for the purposes of this Act and of said license be deemed to be the amount to be allowed as the net investment of the applicant in such project or projects as of the date of such license, or as of the date of such determination, if license has not been issued. Such fair value may, in the discretion of the commission, be determined by mutual agreement between the commission and the applicant or, in case they can not agree, jurisdiction is hereby conferred upon the district court of the United States in the district within which such project or projects may be located, upon the application of either party, to hear and determine the amount of such fair value.

That any person, association, corporation, State, or municipality intending to construct a dam or other project works across, along, over, or in any stream or part thereof, other than those defined herein as navigable waters, and over which Congress has jurisdiction under its authority to regulate commerce between foreign nations and among the several States, may in their discretion file declaration of such intention with the commission, whereupon the commission shall cause immediate investigation of such proposed construction to be made, and if upon investigation it shall find that the interests of interstate or foreign commerce would be affected by such proposed construction, such person, association, corporation, State, or municipality shall not proceed with such construction until it shall have applied for and shall have received a license under the provisions of this Act. If the commission shall not so find, and if no public lands or reservations are affected, permission is hereby granted to construct such dam or other project works in such stream upon compliance with State laws.

SEC. 24. That any lands of the United States included in any proposed project under the provisions of this Act shall from the date of filing of application therefor be reserved from entry, location, or other disposal under the laws of the United States until otherwise directed by the commission or by Congress. Notice that such application has been made, together with the date of filing thereof and a description of the lands of the United States affected thereby, shall be filed in the local land office for the district in which such lands are located. Whenever the commission shall determine that the value of any lands of the United States so applied for, or heretofore or hereafter reserved or classified as power sites, will not be injured or destroyed for the purposes of power development by location, entry, or selection under the public-land laws, the Secretary of the Interior, upon notice of such determination, shall declare such lands open to location, entry, or selection, subject to and with a reservation of the right of the United States or its permittees or licensees to enter upon, occupy, and use any part or all of said lands necessary, in the judgment of the commission, for the purposes of this Act, which right shall be expressly reserved in every patent issued for such lands; and no claim or right to compensation shall accrue from the occupation or use of any of said lands for said purposes. The United States or any licensee for any such lands hereunder may enter thereupon for the purposes of this Act, upon payment of any damages to crops, buildings, or other improvements caused thereby to the owner thereof, or upon giving a good and sufficient bond to the United States for the use and benefit of the owner to secure the payment of such damages as may be determined and fixed in an action brought upon the bond in a court of competent jurisdiction, said bond to be in the form prescribed by the commission: *Provided,* That locations, entries, selections, or filings heretofore made for lands reserved as water-power sites or in connection with water-power development or electrical transmission may proceed to approval or patent under and subject to the limitations and conditions in this section contained.

SEC. 25. That any licensee, or any person, who shall willfully fail or who shall refuse to comply with any of the provisions of this Act, or with any of the conditions made a part of any license issued hereunder, or with any subpoena of the commission, or with any regulation or lawful order of the commission, or of the Secretary of War, or of the Secretary of Commerce as to fishways, issued or made in accordance with the provisions of this Act, shall be deemed guilty of a misdemeanor, and on conviction thereof shall, in the discretion of the court, be punished by a fine of not exceeding $1,000, in addition to other penalties herein prescribed or provided by law; and every month any such licensee or any such person shall remain in default after written notice from the commission, or from the Secretary of War, or from the Secretary of Commerce, shall be deemed a new and separate offense punishable as aforesaid.

SEC. 26. That the Attorney General may, on request of the commission or of the Secretary of War, institute proceedings in equity in the district court of the United States in the district in which any project or part thereof is situated for the purpose of revoking for violation of its terms any permit or license issued hereunder, or for the purpose of remedying or correcting by injunction, mandamus, or other process any act of commission or omission in violation of the provisions of this Act or of any lawful regulation or order promulgated hereunder. The district courts shall have jurisdiction over all of the above-mentioned proceedings and shall have power to issue and execute all necessary process and to make and enforce all writs, orders, and decrees to compel compliance with the lawful orders and regulations of the commission and of the Secretary of War, and to compel the performance of any condition imposed under the provisions of this Act. In the event a decree revoking a license is entered, the court is empowered to sell the whole or any part of the project or projects under license, to wind up the business of such licensee conducted in connection with such project or projects, to distribute the proceeds to the parties entitled to the same, and to make and enforce such further orders and decrees as equity and justice may require. At such sale or sales the vendee shall take the rights and privileges belonging to the licensee and shall perform the duties of such licensee and assume all outstanding obligations and liabilities of the licensee which the court may deem equitable in the premises; and at such sale or sales the United

States may become a purchaser, but it shall not be required to pay a greater amount than it would be required to pay under the provisions of section 14 hereof at the termination of the license.

SEC. 27. That nothing herein contained shall be construed as affecting or intending to affect or in any way to interfere with the laws of the respective States relating to the control, appropriation, use, or distribution of water used in irrigation or for municipal or other uses, or any vested right acquired therein.

SEC. 28. That the right to alter, amend, or repeal this Act is hereby expressly reserved; but no such alteration, amendment, or repeal shall affect any license theretofore issued under the provisions of this Act, or the rights of any licensee thereunder.

SEC. 29. That all Acts or parts of Acts inconsistent with this Act are hereby repealed: *Provided,* That nothing herein contained shall be held or construed to modify or repeal any of the provisions of the Act of Congress approved December 19, 1913, granting certain rights of way to the city and county of San Francisco, in the State of California: *Provided further,* That section 18 of an Act making appropriations for the construction, repair, and preservation of certain public works on rivers and harbors, and for other purposes, approved August 8, 1917, is hereby repealed.

SEC. 30. That the short title of this Act shall be "The Federal Water Power Act."

Approved, June 10, 1920.

FEDERAL FORESTRY

THE FOREST PRODUCTS LABORATORY*
October 28, 1908

The establishment of the Forest Products Laboratory in 1908 as a joint venture of the Forest Service and the University of Wisconsin was a major breakthrough in cementing relationships between the Forest Service and the forest industry.

The final determination of the site of the laboratory was not made until later, after a decision against the University of Michigan, but this initial letter from Associate Forester Overton W. Price was perhaps the most important document in the process. The fact that Charles R. Van Hise, the first conservation historian, was president of the University of Wisconsin was an important factor in the decision to establish the laboratory at Madison.

Washington, October 28, 1908

Dear Professor Turneaure:

You are probably aware that for some time the Forest Service has been experimentally investigating certain problems intimately associated with the utilization of forest products. Up to the present time the work has been carried on at laboratories and field stations located in various parts of the country. To secure closer coordination, however, it has now been decided to centralize the work either in a well-equipped laboratory located at Washington, D.C., or at a high-grade technical school. Past experience with cooperating technical schools has been so satisfactory that several leading institutions east of the Mississippi River are being consulted. I take pleasure in putting this statement of the situation in your hands in the hope that it may have your consideration before the Forest Service decides finally upon a location for its larger laboratory.

The lines of work which will be represented at the laboratory are as follows:

1. Experiments in wood preservation to determine the best methods of impregnating different woods with preservative fluids, such as creosote, zinc chlorid, etc. The equipment already purchased for this work includes one treating cylinder, 10-½ feet long, designed to stand a pressure of 250 pounds per square inch,

*Historical Correspondence on Establishment of Forest Products Laboratory at Madison, Wisconsin (Madison, Wis.: Forest Products Laboratory, Jan., 1960).

and one smaller treating cylinder, 4 feet long, designed to stand a pressure of 500 pounds per square inch, together with a complete complement of pumps, air compressors, pressure and storage tanks, and other equipment essential to the operation of a wood preservation plant. The actual cost of the equipment at present provided for this work was $4,500.

2. Wood-pulp experiments to determine the fitness of various woods and other vegetable fibers for the manufacture of paper; also to experiment with other methods of utilizing such fiber. The apparatus for this laboratory constitutes a miniature pulp mill fully equipped for manufacturing pulp by the sulfite process. The equipment includes a lead-lined digester, a beating engine, a pulp screen, a knuckle-joint press, and other accessory apparatus, aggregating in value $2,500.

3. Experiments in wood distillation to determine the best methods of securing certain products, such as turpentine, rosin, etc., from wood waste. For this work a still for refining crude turpentines is nearing completion. The value of the still is approximately, $1,200.

4. Timber tests to determine the mechanical properties of different woods and the influence on these properties of various methods of treating and handling. The equipment for this work includes one 200,000-pound extension-base Riehle testing machine, one 100,000-pound extension-base Olsen testing machine, one torsion machine, one impact machine, a Dorry abrasion machine, and various wood-working machinery, with a total aggregate value of $8,850.

5. Chemical analyses of commercial products derived from wood and of products intimately associated with its use. For this work the Service operates a well-equipped chemical laboratory; the equipment at present on hand being valued at $3,000.

6. Wood technology, including a microscopic study of treated and untreated woods, to determine their structure and the effectiveness of different preservative processes, as well as experiments to determine the heat-conductivity of different woods, and the best methods of drying them. The equipment consists of microscopes, a small cylinder and boiler for experiments in drying wood, and other apparatus, having a total value of $400.

To man the laboratory completely 14 technical men with 6 assistants, drawing salaries amounting to about $28,000 per annum, will be necessary. The amount of floor space required to provide for the present equipment, and that which it is hoped to secure as soon as funds are available for its purchase, is as follows:

	Sq.ft.
Wood Preservation	1500 (Ground floor)
Wood Pulp	3000 (Ground floor)
Wood Distillation	400 (Ground floor)
Timber Tests	3500 (Ground floor)
Chemical Analyses	2400 (Ground floor)

Wood Technology	600 (Ground floor)
Administrative Offices	1600 (Ground floor)
Total	13000

It seems to me that an agreement somewhat as follows would be to the mutual advantage of the Service and the cooperating university:

The university to furnish:

1. The floor space necessary to provide satisfactorily for the laboratories and offices.

2. Heat, light, steam, and electric power required.

3. Foundations for the different machines requiring them.

The Forest Service to:

1. Ship and install all apparatus and completely furnish the offices; also provide the material used in the experiments.

2. Make all apparatus available for student work of an advanced nature, such as thesis work, provided that such use of apparatus did not interfere unduly in the routine work of the laboratory. It would be expected that work of this nature would be carried on under the joint direction of a representative of the faculty and a representative of the laboratory organization.

3. Publish results of experiments, in all cases giving the university full credit as a cooperator.

4. Provide, without cost to the university, any lectures dealing with the general problems of forestry and the utilization of forest products which might be desired.

If the attitude of Cornell University is favorable toward entering into a cooperative agreement of this nature, I would be very glad to have Mr. Cline, Chief of the Office of Wood Utilization, personally take up the matter with you when he goes into the field to investigate the facilities of the different institutions which are being considered. I am very anxious to settle this question as soon as possible, and your early consideration of it would, therefore, be greatly appreciated.

Very truly yours,

Overton W. Price
Associate Forester

HOUSE DEBATE ON FOREST RESERVES*
June 24, 1910

The Weeks Act, which became law in 1911, is one of the landmarks of national conservation history. It gave the Federal Government, for the first time, the right to buy and maintain forest reserves. Because many had doubts about the constitutionality of such a program, the bill gave improvement of navigation as the reason for establishing new reserves.

Actually, the pressure for new forests came from forestry and conservation groups who were anxious to see the government help establish forests in the eastern part of the country, to offer some balance to the national forest reserves in the West created from the public domain. They were also joined by those who supported afforestation as a means of checking floods and soil erosion. (Note the forceful remarks of Representative James Robert Mann of Illinois.)

The proposal was first limited to a plan to establish an Appalachian Forest Reserve in the White Mountains, but in the long debate the plan evolved into general authority for the purchase of national forests.

Because of the importance of the Weeks Act, extended portions of the debate are presented here. John W. Weeks of Massachusetts was the author of the bill. Asbury Francis Lever of South Carolina was in charge of the bill on the floor, and Charles F. Scott of Kansas led the opposition.

Mr. [JOHN] WEEKS [Massachusetts]. Mr. Chairman, I regret very much that there is not more time to discuss this extremely meritorious bill. If there were sufficient time, I am satisfied that the opposition in the House and elsewhere might be convinced that the bill ought to pass. In fact, the only serious opposition to this measure seems to be centered in Congress. After many years of consideration I do not recall seeing in a single periodical or newspaper any criticism of this legislation. On the contrary, there might be produced here a multitude of editorials and other comments favoring its adoption. It has been indorsed by three Presidents. Former President Roosevelt in several of his messages to Congress advocated it, and he was one of its most vigorous indorsers, not only in messages, but on other occasions. President Taft in his annual message to Congress last December gave the idea his unqualified indorsement in the following words:

It has been proposed, and a bill for the purpose passed the Lower House in the last Congress, that the National Government appropriate a certain amount each year out of the receipts from the forestry business of the Government to institute reforestation at the sources of certain navigable streams, to be selected by the Geological Survey, with a view to deter-

*Cong. Rec., Vol. 45, 61st Cong., 2nd sess., 8975–77, 8984–85, 9017.

mining the practicability of thus improving and protecting the streams for federal purposes. I think a moderate expenditure for each year for this purpose, for a period of five or ten years, would be of the utmost benefit in the development of our forestry system.

Boards of trade and chambers of commerce in all sections of the country have appointed committees to investigate the subject, and have invariably, as a result of the reports of these committees, adopted resolutions favoring this bill. As in the case of all new and somewhat unusual legislation, it has, however, run the whole gamut of technical criticisms. First, it was unconstitutional, and it became necessary to change the form of the bill in order to meet the approval of the Judiciary Committee. It has been claimed by a few engineers of the army that there is no substantial connection between forestry and stream flow. These criticisms have been, it seems to me, successfully answered by engineers connected with the Geological Survey and many engineers of high standing in civil life. In fact, I do not recall any instance of antagonism to this measure or criticism of it coming from other engineers than those connected with the United States Army, and I think, after carefully weighing the evidence which they have submitted, that any criticism made has been successfully answered.

The latest and only new form of criticism to this measure comes from Dr. Willis Moore, the Chief of the Weather Bureau. I am not among those who deny to Doctor Moore scientific accomplishments, or his useful career as a public officer—I have even found excuses for the last inaugural-day predictions of the Weather Bureau—but his solemn statement that forestry has no influence on stream flow created country-wide amusement. It gave those in opposition to this measure a new technical peg on which to hang their fight to prevent the passage of this bill. To all others it was the joke of the season, for it proclaimed as a scientific fact that which every person who was brought up in the country knows is not true. There are some things about which we do not need to be informed by scientific men. This is one of them. It would be as logical to say that a brick would hold water as well as a sponge as to proclaim that the hard surface of an open field would retain water as readily as the spongy surface of forested land, or that snow, in a snow country, melts as rapidly in a forest as in an open field. Every New England boy knows that in crossing from a pasture to wooded territory in the month of April, where other conditions than the forested one are exactly the same, the pasture will frequently be bare of snow while there will be in the woods a foot, and frequently more, of snow. Of course, under such conditions, if the whole had been unforested the snow would have melted more rapidly, causing a larger flow of water at one time, and, as a natural result a lesser flow later on. European scientists, however, have made careful investigations along these lines, and I want to submit one which, it seems to me, is a complete answer to Doctor Moore's theory. At the International Congress of Navigation held a few years ago in Europe Professor Engler, of the forest experimental service of Switzerland, made the following report:

These experiments were carried on between 1900 and 1906. The sites of the observations, one a forested the other an unforested region, are in the Napf district of central Switzerland. The forest district, Sperbelgraben, has an area of about 140 acres; the unforested area, Rappengraben, has an area of 175 acres. These areas were selected for the reason that all other conditions, except forest cover, are practically the same.

The report fully sets forth that there is no considerable difference in the altitude, in the geological formation, in the strata of the rocks, in the soil, nor in the relief of the two basins. The forest area contains 97.3 per cent forests and 2.7 per cent pasture. The unforested area, on the other hand, is not entirely denuded of forest, having 32.2 per cent of forest, almost one-third of the total area, while the remainder is pasture, meadow, and farm land. The report fully explains the care taken to measure the rain and snow fall and the runoff of each stream; it also explains how the resulting data are classified and computed.

In his description of the results of observations up to the present time the speaker discussed—

1. The influence of the forest on stream flow caused by heavy rainfall.
2. By snow thaws.
3. The influence of forests on the condition of flow of springs in dry periods.

Considering, first the influence caused by heavy rainfall, the writer, after presenting several examples, reaches the conclusion that from the forested area the run-off at the period of the highest flow, following a heavy rainfall, was only about 70 per cent of the run-off from the highest stage from the unforested area. Considering the fact that the unforested area is nearly one-third forest, and making allowances therefor, the writer concludes that in the forested district the amount of run-off would be 40 per cent less after heavy rains than from the denuded surface.

Under the second heading the writer presents the results of the influence of forests in retarding the melting of snow and reaches the conclusion, from the examples presented, that the run-off following snowfalls on the forested watersheds is considerably less and more gradual than it is from an unforested watershed; also that the maximum stage is less, just as it is in the case of rains. He further says: "In the mountains the precipitation is greater, but the air is quickly cooled, so that snow begins to fall and the evil of heavy precipitation is neutralized. The snow prevents inundations in the mountains."

Under the third heading—the influence of the forest on the flow of springs in dry periods—Professor Engler also presents numerous examples and concludes that the unforested area yielded less seepage and spring water than the forested area; and here, also, the conclusion is drawn that the forest exerts a favorable influence.

Opponents of the theory that forests exert a beneficial influence on stream flow have called for exact measurements and figures upon which the conclusions might be based. Although the subject is a difficult one upon which to obtain exact figures, here is an experiment planned and carried out under the most exact conditions possible and by the best-trained scientific observers of Europe, and the results of the experiments are favorable to the forests on every point.

I wish to insert here one further quotation from a message to Congress by President Roosevelt. In commenting on the criticisms made by the engineer force of the army on the value of this work, he said:

Prominent officers of the Engineer Corps have recently even gone so far as to assert in print that waterways were not dependent upon conservation of the forests about their headwaters. This position is opposed to all the recent work of the scientific bureaus of the Government and to the general experience of mankind. They have failed to grasp the great underlying fact that every stream is a unit, from its source to its mouth, and that all its uses are interdependent.

This bill is very similar to the bill which passed the House of Representatives March 2, 1909, but which, on account of lack of sufficient time, failed to be acted on in the Senate. Some minor changes have been made in it, but they are in no sense important. The first section of the bill provides that States may arrange compacts with one another to carry out the work provided for in the bill. The purpose of this is that it is believed there may possibly be cases in which several States might be interested in the same project—a project in which the country at large would have no direct interest—and that they might in this way form a compact which would enable the carrying out of their purposes. I believe this is necessary, because I do not understand that any State can purchase and hold land in an adjoining State. Now, under the provisions of this bill, New Hampshire is the only New England State which would be directly affected; in other words, in which money would be likely to be spent, because the great rivers of New England—the Connecticut, the Merrimac, the Saco, and the Androscoggin, the rivers on which are located industries representing more than a hundred million of dollars—all rise in the state of New Hampshire, but the regularity of the flow of those streams, the possibilities of the water powers which they develop, and such navigation as they furnish near their mouths is, we believe, dependent on the New Hampshire forests. It would seem to be unfair and unreasonable that there should be imposed on New Hampshire the necessity to protect the headwaters of these streams when the larger part of the benefit would be obtained in adjoining and richer States.

Section 2 is the section which provides for fire protection. Millions of acres of land in this country are burned over every year, and millions of dollars of value are destroyed every year by these fires. States are commencing to establish fire patrol to prevent this destruction, and in every case where such a patrol has been established there is a marked decrease in the damage done. This section is, in my judgment, framed along model lines for such an enterprise, for it provides that no part of this appropriation—$200,000—shall be expended in any State which has not established a fire patrol, and then only in cases where the State appropriates the same amount of money which it may obtain under the provisions of this bill. For instance, if the State of New Hampshire has a properly organized fire patrol and appropriates $10,000 for fire protection, it may obtain from this fund a similar amount of money.

Section 4 provides for the purchase of lands located around the headwaters of streams, appropriating $1,000,000 for the year ending June 30, 1911, and $2,000,000 for each of the following years until 1916—$11,000,000 in all. Nobody denies that this legislation is experimental in a way. Nobody is prepared to say how far it should go, how much it may cost, if continued indefinitely, or what changes should be made in the bill which is now pending, as a result of practical experience. Therefore, it seemed wise to the framers of this bill that, instead of having no limitation, it should terminate at some definite time, so that, so to speak, an account of stock may be taken, and the Congress in 1916, the date fixed for its termination, may then decide what further action shall be taken. I especially emphasize this point, because gentlemen have said in the past, and doubtless will say again on this floor, that it is going to involve the Government in hundreds of millions of dollars' expenditure, which, of course, is not possible as this bill is framed, unless some succeeding Congress advises that the work which has been done should be continued, and that Congress will have the definite results obtained in the intervening years, between 1910 and 1916, in determining its action for the future. If the experiment is useful, naturally they will continue it. If not, it will fall of its own weight. When gentlemen contend that this $11,000,000 will be wasted, I want to call their attention to the fact that it will be expended under the direction of a board provided for in this bill, consisting of the Secretary of War, the Secretary of the Interior, the Secretary of Agriculture, two members of the Senate, and two Members of the House. It is not presumed that this board will pay more for land than it is actually worth; so that, in any case, the Government will have $11,000,000 of property which quite likely will be worth more than $11,000,000 in 1916, even if it is not considered desirable to continue the project. Further, no land will be purchased without the certification of the Attorney-General that the title is clear, and the certification of the Geological Survey that the purchase of the land contemplated has some material effect on stream flow, and only then in cases where the land is located around the headwaters of navigable streams. If there is any question in the mind of any Member that ample provision has not been made to protect the Government, I think that the mere statement of these precautions will satisfy him; but I know that some criticism has been made of the connection which the Geological Survey will have with this project, and I simply want to say that, in my judgment, the survey represents the government department best fitted to furnish such information, and for the following reasons: The principal conditions that modify stream flow are topography, geology, and vegetation cover, and I want to submit here a statement of the qualifications of the Geological Survey as to these three conditions.

First, topography; second, geology; and third, vegetation cover. These three are absolute. Therefore, in determining the proper areas to be acquired for the purposes comprehended in this bill, the government agency that has given the greatest study to these three natural phenomena is the one that may be depended upon to determine wisely. This bill designates the Geological Survey as the determinative agent. I ask those who allege that the principal support of this measure comes from mere forestry enthusiasts and land speculators whether this provision is not a complete refutation of that idea? The survey's record is clean. No one can justly claim that in its reports and decisions it has ever been influenced by other than purely physical and scientific facts, as it saw and interpreted them.

It is proper to ask what are the special qualifications of the Geological Survey with respect to the three physiographic features that I have cited as modifiers of stream flow.

First, as to topography: The survey leads the world, both scientifically and practically in the study and interpretation of topographic features. The Members of this House are all too familiar with the topographic maps of the survey and value them too highly to dispute this assertion. The topographic methods of the survey have been studied and in large measure copied by many of the other world powers. In designating the lands to be acquired under this bill all this expert knowledge will be applied to the problem at hand.

Second, with respect to geology: We believe that there are certain areas that no amount of forestation will beneficially affect. The flood waters will run off quickly and the lands will contribute practically nothing in times of low water. Other areas are of a character that will markedly conserve water supply if properly cared for. The determination of such characteristics is a matter of geology, and the survey's qualifications in this respect are fully on a par with those in respect to topography.

Third. For more than twenty years the survey has been making studies of stream flow from lands of diverse character. So broad has been the scope of this work that all physical factors modifying river discharge have been comprehended. No other federal agency has gone into the hills to find out the why and wherefore of stream flow. When the survey attacks the problem assigned to it in this bill it will not have to go into a new field. It is not generally known that the problem of stream flow in the uplands presents markedly different features from those in the lowlands. All other government agencies that have studied the subject have given their principal attention to lowland conditions. The Geological Survey alone has specialized on upland conditions.

Therefore, in designating the survey as the determinative agency in this matter, the advocates of this bill have submitted the matter to a federal bureau that in the course of its professional work has necessarily become familiar with the critical conditions, and its members are personally cognizant with the facts that determine the standards by which this measure may be wisely begun.

As there has been some question about the manner of purchasing these lands, and the powers of the commission, I append a memorandum on this subject, prepared by G. S. Arnold, acting law officer of the Forest Service:

February 16, 1909

Appalachian and White Mountains—Memorandum

The act of August 1, 1888, chapter 728, section 1 (25 Stat., 357), provides:
"That in every case in which the Secretary of the Treasury or any other officer of the Government has been, or hereafter shall be, authorized to procure real estate for the erection of a public building or for other public uses, he shall be, and hereby is, authorized to acquire

the same for the United States by condemnation, under judicial process, whenever in his opinion it is necessary or advantageous to the Government to do so."

As Senate bill 4825 provides for the purchase of lands by the Secretary of Agriculture for the public uses set forth in said bill, namely, such as may be necessary for the regulation of the flow of navigable streams, the provision in said bill for such purchase falls clearly within the letter of the above-quoted statute, and the Secretary of Agriculture is therefore by the authority of said statute empowered to acquire the same for the United States by condemnation proceedings. (See Shoemaker v. United States, 147 U.S., 282; Secombe v. Railroad Co., 90 U.S., 108.)

At first sight there would seem to be a conflict between the theory of condemnation proceedings, where the price to be paid is fixed by the court and the judgment is a binding contract upon seller and purchaser, and the provision in the proposed act that the commission shall "fix the price or prices." The escape from this would be that in no case would condemnation proceedings be resorted to until the commission had in advance thereof "considered and passed upon the lands" as desirable and necessary, "approved of" them for purchase, and "fixed the price" thereof at such figure as the court should determine to be reasonable. All of which is plainly provided for in the proposed act—lines 13–18, section 5—where the commission is authorized to "consider and pass upon such lands as may be recommended for purchase, as provided in section 6 of this act, and to fix the price or prices at which such lands may be purchased, and no purchases shall be made of any lands until such lands have been duly approved for purchase by said commission."

Any possible difficulty in connection with the restrictions embodied in section 9 is met by the principle that the good faith of the Government is sufficient to do away with the necessity of paying in advance. (In re Manderson, 51 Fed. Rep., 501, 504.)

In adopting this policy the United States Government is simply carrying out methods which have proven successful in most European countries, and which have been adopted by several States. Minnesota, Wisconsin, Pennsylvania, and New York have notable forest reserves. Those States and others, including Massachusetts, are now purchasing land and planting forests in a systematic manner. In the case of New York, at least, the purchases made for this purpose have been very profitable, and it is inconceivable that judicious purchases of lands, suitable for forestry purposes, either forested or otherwise, can fail to be a good investment. It has been suggested that we have large forest reserves, perhaps ample reserves for our needs, but every investigator of this subject knows that they are rapidly decreasing, not only in area but in proportion to our population. When this country was originally settled about 50 per cent was wooded. The latest obtainable figures indicate that this percentage has decreased to 29 per cent, which is less than the percentage of wooded area in Europe, the latest figures for Europe being 31 per cent. Every year, as our population increases, the requirements for wood increase in proportion, and therefore it must follow that in time we will be in distress, unless some action is taken by the Nation and by the States to encourage and to practically develop forestry. If there is any one question to which the people of this country are, almost without exception, committed, it is to a reasonable conservation of natural products. This bill is a practical method of assisting in the development of this idea and putting it into practical execution. I believe it is carefully drawn, that the Government's interests are thoroughly protected, and that a vote against it indicates a lack of conception of the needs of practical conservation, or is an indication of opposition to, and condemnation of, that principle; and I have no doubt that those who support this legislation will, if it becomes a law, look back on it in future years as one of the most commendable of their legislative acts.

* * *

APPALACHIAN FOREST RESERVE

The Committee of the Whole House on the state of the Union resumed its session.

Mr. [CHARLES] SCOTT [Kansas]. Mr. Chairman, the author of the bill stated a few moments ago that the sentiment in favor of this measure throughout the country is practically unanimous. I think the statement is probably accurate. The sentiment is unanimous for the measure because it is uninformed. Nobody has greater regard or respect than I for the sentiment of the people of the United States when it has been formed upon information, after discussion, and upon understanding of the issues involved. But there is no Member on this floor who can say that the issues involved in this measure have ever been fairly presented to the people of this country. The gentleman from Massachusetts [Mr. LAW-RENCE] this afternoon stated that the bill had passed the Senate twice and that it had passed the House of Representatives once as a reason why it should now receive favorable action. Let me remind him that it passed the Senate twice by unanimous consent, with no opposition, without any debate, passed because gentlemen in that body knew it would not receive consideration during that session of Congress in this House. Therefore there was no necessity for them to make a contest against it. But let me remind gentlemen that at this hour, when there is a prospect that if it passes the Senate, it will also pass the House and become a law, gentlemen in that body are debating the question seriously, so seriously in fact that there is no probability of favorable action at this session of Congress.

And how has it been in this House? It is true the House passed the bill at the last session of Congress, but we passed it after an hour or less of debate. It has never been really debated in either body of Congress, and I venture to say that if this measure could be brought before this House as the railroad bill was brought here, with unlimited time for general discussion and for debate under the five-minute rule, it would not get the support of a quorum of the Committee of the Whole. I doubt if it would get the support of one-fifth of that quorum.

Now, let us understand what the bill purports to do. In the title it provides that the bill is to enable any State to cooperate with any other State or States for the protection of the watersheds of navigable streams, and to appoint a commission for the acquisition of lands for the purpose of conserving the navigability of navigable rivers. Let it be remembered that there is no justification whatever for this bill except upon the theory that the purchase of these lands is necessary for the protection of navigable streams. That theory arises from an opinion by the Committee on the Judiciary of the House of Representatives, which declared that the Federal Government has no power to purchase forest lands at the headwaters of navigable rivers for the purpose of preserving the forests; that it has no power to purchase such lands unless it can be clearly shown that there is a direct and substantial connection between such lands and the conservation and improvement of the navigability of a river actually navigable in whole or in part.

Now, can it be established that there is any direct and substantial connection between the condition of the watersheds on the navigable rivers as to forestation or deforestation and the maintenance of the navigability of those rivers? I insist that the evidence of those best qualified to pass judgment on that question is substantially unanimous to the effect that no such direct and substantial connection exists.

I quote first from the testimony of Col. William S. Bixby, given before the Committee on Agriculture of the House. At that time Colonel Bixby was president of the Mississippi River Commission, and for many years past had been in charge of the river and harbor improvements in the Mississippi Valley. Since then he has been made Chief of the Engineer Corps of the Army of the United States. I doubt if there is a better-qualified man in the world to pass upon this problem, because he has been studying it for thirty years. And this is what he said in answer to a question propounded by the chairman of the Committee on Agriculture whether, if he had unlimited means at his disposal and was personally responsible for maintaining the navigability of the rivers of the United States, with permission to use any amount of money and any method, whether he would spend any part of the money in maintaining the forests at the headwaters of the rivers. When the question was first asked, he smiled as if it were asked as a pleasantry, but when he was satisfied it was serious he said, "I might put in 1 per cent"—he said that with a smile—"just to see what would happen; but I would not do it with any feeling that I would get my money's worth back."

His attention was called to the allegation that recently the floods in the Connecticut Valley and other valleys of New England had increased in height and frequency, and to the further allegation that such increase was due to the deforestation of the watersheds. His opinion was asked, and he said:

> I should ascribe fully 95 per cent of it to the improved farms, and the improved drainage, and the ditches along the roadways, and the nice roadways that form great, big channels to lead the waters along, and the streets and the sewers in the cities.

Now, gentlemen who are supporting this measure will no doubt cite to you what purports to be a summary of a large number of papers read before the famous conservation and navigation convention that was held at Milan in 1905. That summary makes it appear that practically all the papers read by the eminent engineers who gathered there agreed in the proposition that the protection of the forests upon the watersheds of the navigable rivers was essential to the maintenance of their navigability. The summary was read to Colonel Bixby, and he was asked what he thought about it. He said:

> I have read the original papers, and I do not agree with the man who made the summary. The conclusions are not warranted by the paper from which they are presumed to be drawn.

I submit that such a declaration from such a man eliminates the famous summary of the convention of Milan from further consideration in this debate.

Summing up the matter, the gentleman from Massachusetts stated that there seemed to be a consensus of opinion among the engineers that it was of the greatest importance to protect the watersheds of the navigable rivers by means of forests. This is the evidence of Colonel Bixby:

> As the result of my reading for the past twenty years, I can say that the consensus of opinion among the engineers of the world is that forestation or deforestation is a negligible factor so far as navigation is concerned.

Colonel Bixby is not the only witness. Two or three years ago the Bureau of Forestry preferred a request to the army engineers that investigation be made of the various rivers of the country with a view of ascertaining to what extent, if any, the navigable streams were influenced by forestation of the watersheds.

As a result of that request a great many army engineers were put to work studying that problem. Have you seen any of their reports published in the publications of the Bureau of Forestry? Not one. Why? Because, without exception, they were against the proposition. The Bureau of Forestry was in favor of it, and so it did not get anything it wanted to publish.

Here is a report from Colonel Russell, who made a long and painstaking inquiry into the effect which deforestation had had on the run-off of the Ohio River, and among a number of findings I read this:

> 4. That the effect of deforestation in causing an increase in the frequency and intensity of floods has not been established, and as yet is indeterminate from the data at hand.
> 5. That if it be later established that deforestation increases flood frequency and intensity, the effect will be found to be small upon a waterway the size of the Ohio River.

Later Major Hart made an inquiry into the same problem as it relates to the Cumberland and Tennessee rivers, in the course of which, referring to carefully drawn charts showing progressive deforestation of the watershed, the precipitation, and the heights of floods in the rivers, he says:

> I have examined these charts with minuteness, but can find no trace of any effect on the quantities of precipitation or on the fluctuations of stream flow that may be regarded as resulting beyond question from cutting off our forests. If any such effect has actually been brought about, it is so slight as to escape careful observation. The indications point in an opposite direction.

Here is another report from Col. Edward Burr, who, under instructions from the Chief Engineer of the United States Army, made an exhaustive study of the influence of forestation and deforestation upon stream flow in the Merrimac River in New Hampshire and Massachusetts. Now, the Merrimac River would seem to afford a particularly good subject for a study of this character, for the reason that whatever its position, there has been, first, deforestation and then reforestation. The records have been complete and accurate for nearly seventy years, during the first half of which there was progressive deforestation and during the latter half of said period there has been reforestation. And yet after the long and painstaking inquiry Colonel Burr makes a report, in which this is one of his conclusions:

> There has been no decrease of precipitation or rainfall in the basin with deforestation nor any increase with the progress of reforestation, long-time records of precipitation in or near the basin showing tendencies or cycles that bear no ascertainable relation to forest changes.
>
> There is no relation apparent between variable forest conditions in the basin and the varying conditions of stream flow; that is, a material increase in forest area since 1870 does not show any beneficial effect upon the height, frequency, or duration of floods, nor upon the height, frequency, or duration of low-water stages.
>
> There are perhaps more indications of the ill effects of forests on stream flow than there are of beneficial effects.

Think of that, gentlemen. Here is a little river, the banks of which are of such material that they are not easily eroded. Whatever damage comes to this river must come in large degree from the headwaters which it is proposed by this bill to protect; and yet, basing his conclusions upon data extending over a period of seventy years, during which there was deforestation which cut off 30 per cent, or more than 30 per cent, of forests, followed by a period during which those forests were restored, this engineer declares the deforestation showed no harmful influence upon the flow and that the reforestation shows no beneficial effect upon the height, frequency, or duration of floods. It seems to me, gentlemen, we might rest our case right here with a declaration such as that from one of the most expert of our army engineers upon a stream where the conditions have been ideal for observation.

But I will proceed to one further declaration made by Colonel Burr as summing up the result of his observations. I should precede this extract by saying that I wrote Colonel Burr a letter, asking him the question which I asked Colonel Bixby, as to how much money he would spend for foresting the watershed of a navigable river if he had all reasonable resources at his command and carte blanche as to methods, both as to the White Mountains and the Appalachians. He says:

> I am unable to give a definite reply to this question in so far as it relates to other navigable rivers flowing out of the Appalachians, but if I were charged with the responsibility of maintaining the navigability of the Merrimac or of any other stream in which the conditions were essentially similar to those in the Merrimac River basin, with unlimited means at my disposal but available only for the improvement of navigable waters—

And remember, there is no warrant for the passage of this bill except as it may contribute to the importance of navigable water. He says further:

> I should not consider it necessary or advisable to invest any part of such funds in the re-forestation of watersheds for the purpose of assisting in improving or maintaining such streams as navigable rivers.

And yet the gentleman from Massachusetts declares that there is no evidence that contradicts the theory of this bill. I stand here to say that there is no evidence worth considering that does not contradict the theory of the bill. Let me point you to some of the evidence upon which this bill is built.

Prof. L. C. Glenn, of Vanderbilt University, came before the committee of Congress and testified before the committee that he had spent three or four years in making a personal study, especially as related to the Tennessee River, and he made this statement:

> At Knoxville, Tenn., I found a government fleet—not one or two boats, but a fleet—engaged in dredging the channel and keeping it navigable. They dredge on a bar this summer, and they go back next summer and dredge the same bar. It fills up as fast as it is dredged out, and it is practically an unending work. They are receiving the effects of the erosion of the steep mountain slopes.

Now, then, what is the truth in regard to that? Why, the truth is that the $8,000,000 spent since the work was begun on that river, during a period of more than a century—of the $8,000,000 Professor Glenn practically said had all been spent in digging out the silt which was washed from the mountain slopes—of that $8,000,000, less than $1,000,000 has been spent on dredging out the silt. The rest of it has been spent how? In blasting and cutting away the solid rock ledges in different places across the bed of the stream and in building dams and canals around rapids upon that stream.

Another witness testified before our committee that the Government had spent a vast sum of money on the Saco River; and, if he did not say so, he certainly left the impression upon the committee that the expenditures had been made necessary because of the denudation of the watershed of the stream. Well, when the army officer came before the committee with the official record, as the testimony showed, there were only 5 miles of navigable waters on the Saco River; that it was tide water; and all the money spent upon that stream had been spent in keeping the sand from the sea from washing into the river, in dredging out the sand which washed into the river, and not from the headwaters.

In the case of the Connecticut River, a witness testified as to the greater height and suddenness of floods in recent years. Asked his view, Colonel Bixby stated that in his opinion at least 95 per cent of the increased height and suddenness of the flood was due to the improved drainage of the country. A witness testified that the increase in the height and frequency of the floods on the Ohio River was wholly due to the deforestation of the watershed, whereas the reports of the army engineers show that the increase is apparent rather than real, and due to the fact that the river has been greatly narrowed in its upper portions by encroachment upon its banks; and I quoted from the report of Colonel Russell, who made a careful and painstaking investigation, which brings him to a conclusion directly contradicting the testimony of the forestry experts.

So I could go on with much other evidence submitted by many honest men and honorable men, patriotic men, men of good intentions, but men who are not expert in the control of waterways, and show their testimony has been overthrown by the evidence of men who were expert. Why, the gentleman from Massachusetts declared that it was a common practice in Europe to use forestation for the benefit of navigation. If he will read the testimony in our hearings he will see that it is not a part of the improvement scheme of any country in the world to have a forestation of the watershed. He will find that whenever they want to protect the watershed from erosion they do not plant trees, but grass. They make a sod, and all of us know that. All of us have seen the embankments of a fortification, where they rise almost perpendicular, just as high as the fortification, and the soil will stand and it will stay there without a particle of erosion, because it is sodded with grass, and that was what Colonel Bixby said. If you want to protect the watersheds in general, he said the thing to do is to put grass upon them and not trees.

But, further than that, all the evidence of the army engineers shows that it is not the washing from the headwaters of the stream—and it is only the headwaters which this bill intends to protect—it is not the washing from the headwaters of the stream that contributes to these difficulties; it is the caving of the banks along the navigable reaches of the stream. There are thousands of millions of tons of silt caught below Cairo, and what comes down from the headwaters is inconsiderable in comparison with that. I reserve the balance of my time.

* * *

Mr. [EDGAR] CRUMPACKER [Indiana]. Mr. Chairman, I move to strike out the last two words. Mr. Chairman, it seems to me that this is the most chimerical scheme to get money out of the Federal Treasury that has ever been seriously proposed in Congress during the whole history of this Government. I can not see any real justification for this bill from any standpoint. Now, the difficulty that the advocates of the measure have in furnishing valid reasons for it is the best illustration of the fact that the measure has no real merit from the standpoint of the Government.

The gentleman from Michigan [Mr. FORDNEY], who has just addressed the committee, based his argument exclusively upon the fact that the bill was intended for the conservation of forests, and he justified it upon that ground and upon the ground that the Federal Government has the right to go into the market and buy lands from private citizens for the purpose of planting and cultivating forests for the common good. Other gentlemen admit that the Federal Government has no authority to go into the market and buy private lands for the purpose of planting and cultivating forests, but they undertake to justify the measure on the ground that it is for the preservation and for the improvement of navigation. Let me ask Members of the House what business man of this country, charged with the duty of maintaining the condition of navigation of the Connecticut River and other streams that might incidentally be affected by this project, would buy all these ranges of mountains with a view of permitting the undergrowth to sprout and grow on their slopes to conserve the water, hoping thereby to maintain a better stage of water in those streams? Take the Connecticut River alone. I do not know much about it, but it strikes me, from a business standpoint, that two old-fashioned windmills at the head of that river would pump more water into it and do more for navigation on that river than will be done under this scheme in a quarter of a century [laughter], in which time we may spend $50,000,000. [Laughter.]

Another thing: The sand bars of the Connecticut River that impede navigation can be removed. It is a navigable river, and it will be an easy task and a proper one, I think, for the Federal Government to remove them; much better than to enter upon a project that is so flimsy, so gauzy as this, and that so remotely and incidentally affects navigation. It seems to me that it is utterly unjustifiable from any standpoint.

The CHAIRMAN. The time of the gentleman has expired.

Mr. CRUMPACKER. I ask permission to have my time extended for five minutes.

The CHAIRMAN. Is there objection? [After a pause.] The Chair hears none.

Mr. CRUMPACKER. Mr. Chairman, there is not a plain, a valley, a hillside in all this country outside of the arid regions of the United States that does not in some measure contribute some of its surplus flow of water to navigable streams; and if this project is eligible, if it is a fair one, if it shall be adopted as the policy of the Federal Government in the future, there is not a farm in the Mississippi Valley that the Federal Government could not purchase upon the same pretext. There is not a hill in New England or in the Middle States or the Southern States that could not be bought under an act of Congress and the purchase justified upon the same theory exactly.

Fifty years ago and more the great prairie States in the Mississippi Valley were covered with swamps and sloughs that were saturated with water the year round. They contributed much toward the rainfall in the valley during the hot days of July and the dog-day season. They gave to the atmosphere vapor that went up into the clouds and made rain.

Those swamps have all been drained. They are dry. They are farms and gardens now. The Government might as well enter upon an undertaking for the common good to reestablish those swamps and sloughs on those fertile lands in the prairie States, with a view to promoting rainfall in the Mississippi Valley.

It strikes me, Mr. Chairman, that the claim made for this bill that it is in any way to promote navigation is a mere pretext. It simply gives an opportunity to the owners of those barren, sterile mountains to unload them upon the Government, and it puts upon the Federal Government the duty and the responsibility of taking care of those lands, those mountains, at a cost of nobody knows how many millions of dollars to the Public Treasury. In the course of the years there will be an army of forest rangers and fire fighters and federal policemen guarding and protecting the hills and mountains of New Hampshire and Vermont, and all down the ranges almost to the Gulf of Mexico. It will furnish jobs for a whole lot of men. The government reservations, perhaps, in the future will be stocked with wild game and we will have crown hunting preserves in this country, where men who can afford it will have the opportunity of hunting bear, elk, deer, and many other queer things.

A Member. Elephants.

Mr. CRUMPACKER. Possibly elephants, but hardly, if we do not take the Everglades of Florida, and we have not gotten to that level yet. But I do not know how soon it will come.

Now, seriously, Mr. Chairman, I can not give this bill my support. I can not justify it from any standpoint. I do not believe the benefits that will come to navigation will justify the manifest cost that this project will be to the Government. The expense of the scheme will be enormously out of proportion to the benefits. It is altogether proper for the Government to create timber reservations on the public domain which it already owns. I believe in reserving coal, oil, and mineral deposits on public lands for the benefit of the people, but I do protest against authorizing the Government to buy the hills and barren mountains of the country now in private ownership upon the pretext of promoting navigation. Before this scheme can be put in operation, if the bill shall pass, the worthless lands upon which it will operate will largely be in the hands of speculators, who will hold the Government up and make immense profits on the lands.

Mr. [JAMES] MANN [Illinois]. Mr. Chairman, I want to submit a few feeble remarks on this proposition. We have been a Nation for a little more than a hundred years. During that time a very large portion, if not proportion, of our forest lands have disappeared. If we are wise legislators, we do not legislate merely for today or for to-morrow. We bear in mind that we have a duty, not only to our children and their children, but to their descendants as well. We legislate not for a year, not for a hundred years. We legislate for our country so long as our flag shall fly, and God forbid that it should be hauled down soon. [Applause.] I do not hide behind the claim that this bill should be passed in order to conserve navigation interests. I believe it is the duty of our Government to conserve the forests of the United States. [Applause.] As was well said by the gentleman from Michigan, no individual can afford to keep young forests in growth for succeeding generations. We ought not to ask the States to do it, because the States that raise the forests at their own expense would not enjoy the benefits of it.

I was born and raised on the prairies of Illinois where the forests did not grow, but we wanted the products of the forests from the States where they did grow. We needed the forest products in Illinois as well as the States where they grew. I am in favor of the Government putting in trees those lands which are worthless for other purposes, so that the soil that will not raise annual crops may raise crops which may in the course of a century or centuries become valuable to our people. [Applause.]

I do not care about the constitutional hairsplitting; I believe that under the general-welfare clause of the Constitution we have the same right to raise forests that we have to hunt grasshoppers. [Laughter.] Who has raised the constitutional question on our sending out seeds throughout the country? We should protect the forests. Only the General Government can do it; and I hope that not only will we purchase these lands in the White Mountains and the Appalachian Range, but that we in the course of time will devote a large share of the public domain, or the private domain, as you please, worthless for other purposes, to reforestation, so that the ground shall be used economically, not for our benefit, but for the benefit of the country which we love and which we must protect for those who come after us. [Applause.]

THE WEEKS ACT*
March 1, 1911

When the Weeks Act became law, it not only authorized the purchase of new national forest land, but established a program for cooperation between the states and the Forest Service to protect watersheds from forest fires. There was very little implementation of the authority to buy land until Franklin D. Roosevelt became President.

An Act to enable any State to cooperate with any other State or States, or with the United States, for the protection of the watersheds of navigable streams, and to appoint a commission for the acquisition of lands for the purpose of conserving the navigability of navigable rivers.

Be it enacted by the Senate and House of Representatives of the United States of America in Congress assembled, That the consent of the Congress of the United States is hereby given to each of the several States of the Union to enter into any agreement or compact, not in conflict with any law of the United States, with any other State or States for the purpose of conserving the forests and the water supply of the States entering into such agreement or compact.

SEC. 2. That the sum of two hundred thousand dollars is hereby appropriated and made available until expended, out of any moneys in the National Treasury not otherwise appropriated, to enable the Secretary of Agriculture to cooperate with any State or group of States, when requested to do so, in the protection from fire of the forested watersheds of navigable streams; and the Secretary of Agriculture is hereby authorized, and on such conditions as he deems wise, to stipulate and agree with any State or group of States to cooperate in the organization and maintenance of a system of fire protection on any private or state forest lands within such State or States and situated upon the watershed of a navigable river: *Provided,* That no such stipulation or agreement shall be made with any State which has not provided by law for a system of forest-fire protection: *Provided further,* That in no case shall the amount expended in any State exceed in any fiscal year the amount appropriated by that State for the same purpose during the same fiscal year.

SEC. 3. That there is hereby appropriated, for the fiscal year ending June thirtieth, nineteen hundred and ten, the sum of one million dollars, and for each fiscal year thereafter a sum not to exceed two million dollars for use in the examination, survey, and acquirement of lands located on the headwaters of navigable streams or those which are being or which may be developed for navigable

*36 *Statutes at Large,* 961–63.

[221]

purposes: *Provided,* That the provisions of this section shall expire by limitation on the thirtieth day of June, nineteen hundred and fifteen.

SEC. 4. That a commission, to be known as the National Forest Reservation Commission, consisting of the Secretary of War, the Secretary of the Interior, the Secretary of Agriculture, and two members of the Senate, to be selected by the President of the Senate, and two members of the House of Representatives, to be selected by the Speaker, is hereby created and authorized to consider and pass upon such lands as may be recommended for purchase as provided in section six of this Act, and to fix the price or prices at which such lands may be purchased, and no purchases shall be made of any lands until such lands have been duly approved for purchase by said commission: *Provided,* That the members of the commission herein created shall serve as such only during their incumbency in their respective official positions, and any vacancy on the commission shall be filled in the manner as the original appointment.

SEC. 5. That the commission hereby appointed shall, through its president, annually report to Congress, not later than the first Monday in December, the operations and expenditures of the commission, in detail, during the preceding fiscal year.

SEC. 6. That the Secretary of Agriculture is hereby authorized and directed to examine, locate, and recommend for purchase such lands as in his judgment may be necessary to the regulation of the flow of navigable streams, and to report to the National Forest Reservation Commission the results of such examinations: *Provided,* That before any lands are purchased by the National Forest Reservation Commission said lands shall be examined by the Geological Survey and a report made to the Secretary of Agriculture, showing that the control of such lands will promote or protect the navigation of streams on whose watersheds they lie.

SEC. 7. That the Secretary of Agriculture is hereby authorized to purchase, in the name of the United States, such lands as have been approved for purchase by the National Forest Reservation Commission at the price or prices fixed by said commission: *Provided,* That no deed or other instrument of conveyance shall be accepted or approved by the Secretary of Agriculture under this Act until the legislature of the State in which the land lies shall have consented to the acquisition of such land by the United States for the purpose of preserving the navigability of navigable streams.

SEC. 8. That the Secretary of Agriculture may do all things necessary to secure the safe title in the United States to the lands to be acquired under this Act, but no payment shall be made for any such lands until the title shall be satisfactory to the Attorney-General and shall be vested in the United States.

SEC. 9. That such acquisition may in any case be conditioned upon the exception and reservation to the owner from whom title passes to the United States of the minerals and of the merchantable timber, or either or any part of them, within or upon such lands at the date of the conveyance, but in every case such exception and reservation and the time within which such timber shall be removed and the rules and regulations under which the cutting and removal of such timber and the mining and removal of such minerals shall be done shall be expressed in the written instrument of conveyance, and thereafter the mining, cutting, and removal of the minerals and timber so excepted and reserved shall be done only under and in obedience to the rules and regulations so expressed.

SEC. 10. That inasmuch as small areas of land chiefly valuable for agriculture may of necessity or by inadvertence be included in tracts acquired under this Act, the Secretary of Agriculture may, in his discretion, and he is hereby authorized, upon application or otherwise, to examine and ascertain the location and extent of such areas as in his opinion may be occupied for agricultural purposes without injury to the forests or to stream flow and which are not needed for public purposes, and may list and describe the same by metes and bounds, or otherwise, and offer them for sale as homesteads at their true value, to be fixed by him, to actual settlers, in tracts not exceeding eighty acres in area, under such joint rules and regulations as the Secretary of Agriculture and the Secretary of the Interior may prescribe; and in case of such sale the jurisdiction over the lands sold shall, ipso facto, revert to the State in which the lands sold lie. And no right, title, interest, or claim in or to any lands acquired under this Act, or the waters thereon, or the products, resources, or use thereof after such lands shall have been so acquired, shall be initiated or perfected, except as in this section provided.

SEC. 11. That, subject to the provisions of the last preceding section, the lands acquired under this Act shall be permanently reserved, held, and administered as national forest lands under the provisions of section twenty-four of the Act approved March third, eighteen hundred and ninety-one (volume twenty-six, Statutes at Large, page eleven hundred and three), and Acts supplemental to and amendatory thereof. And the Secretary of Agriculture may from time to time divide the lands acquired under this Act into such specific national forests and so designate the same as he may deem best for administrative purposes.

SEC. 12. That the jurisdiction, both civil and criminal, over persons upon the lands acquired under this Act shall not be affected or changed by their permanent reservation and administration as national forest lands, except so far as the punishment of offenses against the United States is concerned, the intent and meaning of this section being that the State wherein such land is situated shall not, by reason of such reservation and administration, lose its jurisdiction nor the inhabitants thereof their rights and privileges as citizens or be absolved from their duties as citizens of the State.

SEC. 13. That five per centum of all moneys received during any fiscal year from each national forest into which the lands acquired under this Act may from time to time be divided shall be paid, at the end of such year, by the Secretary of the Treasury to the State in which such national forest is situated, to be expended as the state legislature may prescribe for the benefit of the public schools and public roads of the county or counties in which such national forest is situated: *Provided,* That when any national forest is in more than one State or county the distributive share to each from the proceeds of such forest shall be proportional to its area therein: *Provided further,* That there shall not be paid to any State for any county an amount equal to more than forty per centum of the total income of such county from all other sources.

SEC. 14. That a sum sufficient to pay the necessary expenses of the commission and its members, not to exceed an annual expenditure of twenty-five thousand dollars, is hereby appropriated out of any money in the Treasury not otherwise appropriated. Said appropriation shall be immediately available, and shall be paid out on the audit and order of the president of the said commission, which audit and order shall be conclusive and binding upon all departments as to the correctness of the accounts of said commission.

Approved, March 1, 1911.

THE CAPPER REPORT*
June 1, 1920

One of the reasons why the 1920's saw considerable progress in the federal forestry program, by contrast with marking time in most other conservation fields, was the Capper report of 1920. The report was submitted to the Congress in response to a resolution sponsored by Senator E. H. Capper of Kansas. Assistant Forester Earle H. Clapp, in the midst of a distinguished career as a U.S. Forestry official, is credited with preparing the report. The letter of transmittal from the Secretary of Agriculture, which digests the report, is presented here.

June 1, 1920

The President of the United States Senate

Sir:

I have the honor to submit herewith a report on forest depletion in the United States, prepared by the Forest Service in this department pursuant to Senate resolution 311.

This resolution requests information on:

1. The depletion of timber in the United States.
2. The effects of timber depletion upon the high cost of materials.
3. The effects of lumber exports upon domestic industries.
4. The effects of depletion upon the concentration of timber ownership and manufacture and the relation of such concentration to the public welfare.

The outstanding facts reported by the Forest Service are:

(1) That three-fifths of the original timber of the United States is gone and that we are using timber four times as fast as we are growing it. The forests remaining are so localized as greatly to reduce their national utility. The bulk of the population and manufacturing industries of the United States are dependent upon distant supplies of timber as the result of the depletion of the principal forest areas east of the Great Plains.

(2) That the depletion of timber is not the sole cause of the recent high prices of forest products, but is an important contributing cause whose effects will increase steadily as depletion continues.

(3) That the fundamental problem is to increase the production of timber by stopping forest devastation.

The virgin forests of the United States covered 822 million acres. They are now shrunk to one-sixth of that area. All classes of forest land, including culled,

*U.S. Dept. of Agriculture, Forest Service, *Timber Depletion, Lumber Prices, Lumber Exports, and Concentration of Timber Ownership,* Report on Sen. Res. 311, 2nd ed. (Washington, D.C.: Government Printing Office, 1920), 3–5.

[225]

burned, and cut-over areas, now aggregate 463 million acres, or a little more than one-half of our original forests. Of the forest land remaining and not utilized for farming or any other purpose, approximately 81 million acres have been so severely cut and burned as to become an unproductive waste. This area is equivalent to the combined forests of Germany, Denmark, Holland, Belgium, France, Switzerland, Spain, and Portugal. Upon an enormous additional area the growth of timber is so small in amount or of such inferior character that its economic value is negligible.

The merchantable new timber remaining in the United States is estimated roughly at 2,215 billion board feet, something less than three-fourths of which is virgin stumpage. The rest is second growth of relatively inferior quality. About one-half of the timber left is in the three Pacific Coast States, and over 61 per cent is west of the Great Plains. A little over one-fifth of the timber left in the country, or 460 billion board feet, is hardwoods.

There is now consumed or destroyed annually in the United States 56 billion board feet of material of saw timber size. The total yearly consumption of all classes of timber is about 26 billion cubic feet. Our depleted forests are growing less than one-fourth of this amount. The United States is not only cutting heavily into its remaining virgin forests every year, but is also using up the smaller material upon which our future supply of saw timber depends much more rapidly than it is being replaced.

The two striking effects of timber depletion already apparent are:

(1) The injury to large groups of wood users and to many communities resulting from the exhaustion of the nearby forest regions from which they were formerly supplied; and

(2) The shortage of timber products of high quality.

Less than 5 per cent of the virgin forests of New England remain, and the total stand of saw timber in these States is not more than one-eighth of the original stand. New York, once the leading State in lumber production, now manufactures only 30 board feet per capita yearly, although the requirements of its own population are close to 300 board feet per capita. The present cut of lumber in Pennsylvania is less than the amount consumed in the Pittsburgh district alone. The original pine forests of the Lake States, estimated at 350 billion feet, are now reduced to less than 8 billion feet, and their yearly cut of timber is less than one-eighth of what it used to be. These four densely populated regions, containing themselves very large areas of forest land, are now largely dependent upon timber grown and manufactured elsewhere and are becoming increasingly dependent upon timber which must be shipped the width of the continent.

The bulk of the building lumber and structural timbers used in the Eastern and Central States during the last 15 years was grown in the pine forests of the South. The virgin pine forests of the South Atlantic and Gulf States have been reduced from about 650 billion board feet to about 139 billion feet. The production of yellow-pine lumber is now falling off and within ten years will probably not exceed the requirements of the Southern States themselves.

The United States at one time contained the most extensive temperate zone hardwood forests in the world. One region after another has been cut out. The production of hardwood products on the past scale can not be long continued. The scarcity of high-grade oak, poplar, ash, hickory, walnut, and other standard woods is now placing many American industries in a critical condition.

The depletion of forest resources is not confined to saw timber. Since 1909, the country has ceased being self-supporting in newsprint paper and now imports two-thirds of the pulp, pulp wood, or newsprint which we require. This condition is due in part to timber depletion, in part to failure of the paper industry to expand in our western forest regions as the lumber industry has expanded. In 1919 the production of turpentine and rosin had fallen off 50 per cent. Within ten years the United States will lose its commanding position in the world's market for these products and may in time be unable to supply its domestic requirements.

The termination of the war found the lumber industry with depleted stocks. Production during the war had been much less than normal on account of shortages of labor and equipment and embargoes on transportation. A large part of the lumber produced had been taken by the Government for war purposes. During the same time, the normal construction of dwellings and industrial structures and the use of lumber in many manufacturing industries had been greatly curtailed. Following the war, these pent-up demands were released. They caught the lumber industry not only with its stocks short and broken from war conditions but unable, on account of labor difficulties, lack of freight cars, and bad weather in important producing regions, to respond rapidly with increased production. Aside from the general causes affecting prices of most commodities, the expansion of credit accompanied by currency inflation and the wave of speculation and extravagance, an "auction" lumber market would no doubt have resulted from the frenzied competition of buyers to obtain the limited stocks available, wholly inadequate to satisfy current demands.

Under the combined influence of the general conditions making for high prices and this situation in the lumber industry itself, prices rose to unprecedented limits. In March, 1920, average mill prices in the South and West had increased 300 per cent and more over the prices received in 1914, and average retail prices in the Middle West showed increases ranging from 150 to 200 per cent. In the case of high quality hardwoods and other specialized products, the average advance in eastern wholesale markets was from 200 to 250 per cent, and the demand at this advance was still unsatisfied.

The timber market has been more unstable than ever before in our history. Many indistries have been unable to secure their supplies of timber at any price.

The output of certain entire industries has been reduced as much as 50 per cent. Middlemen and manufacturers of wooden commodities have been able to pass on to the consumer and even augment any price they might pay. Necessities have fared worse than luxuries. The ramifications of lumber shortages and high prices are limitless and have affected seriously practically our entire population.

Obviously these lumber prices bear no relation to the cost of production and distribution. While the costs of production in the lumber industry have at least doubled as compared with 1916, lumber prices have much more than doubled and have become wholly disproportionate to operating costs. Excessive profits have been made by the industry. The division of these profits between manufacture and distribution has varied in accordance with circumstances and the ability of the various elements in the industry to dominate the situation. That prices have been too high is recognized by the best thought in the industry, and some manufacturers have sought to stabilize the market.

The depletion of timber in the United States has not been the only cause of these excessive prices on forest products, but has been an important contributing cause. It has led to the migration of both the softwood and hardwood lumber industries from region to region and each is now cutting heavily into its last reserves. The exhaustion of timber in near-by forest regions has compelled many large lumber consuming centers to import their supplies from greater and greater distances. The wholesale prices on upper grades of softwood lumber in New York were from $20 to $25 per thousand prior to 1865 when mills in the same State supplied this market, from $35 to $45 between 1865 and 1917 when most of the supply came from the Lake States and the South, and are now entering a general level of $130 a thousand feet with a large part of the material coming from the Pacific coast. In the Middle West, the building grades of white pine lumber cut in Michigan, Wisconsin, and Minnesota, retailed at $15 to $20 per thousand feet prior to 1900. As lumber from the Lake States became exhausted and southern pine took over this market, the retail prices rose to a level of $25 to $35 per thousand feet. The replacement of southern pine by West Coast timbers now in progress is initiating a new price level of about $80 to $85 per thousand feet. The increased cost of transportation is but one factor in these new price levels, but it is an important one. The freight bill on the average thousand feet of lumber used in the United States is steadily increasing as the sawmills get farther and farther away from the bulk of the lumber users.

Much information is available to show the disadvantages of the lumber consumer in regions whose near-by forests have been exhausted. Retail prices in the Ohio Valley, for example, on certain grades exceed retail prices on the identical grades in Oregon in some instances by as much as $50 per thousand board feet after allowing for all transportation costs. The curtailment of lumber output in the eastern regions not only has compelled the average consumer to pay more for freight but has enhanced the effects of congestion in transportation and of climatic and other factors limiting the production in regions which still support a large lumber industry. It has restricted opportunity for competition and thereby increased the opportunity of the lumber manufacturer or dealer to auction his stocks for higher prices. In other words, the effects of forest depletion can not be measured in terms of the total quantity of timber remaining. Its injury is felt particularly through the steady process of regional exhaustion. Our remaining timber is so localized that its availability to the average user of wood is greatly reduced. Particularly does such a restricted location of the timber supplies assume a serious national aspect in the face of transportation congestion and inadequate transportation facilities such as the United States is now experiencing. Had the forests and forest industries of the Eastern States still existed, the opportunities for regional competition in supplying the lumber markets and the wider distribution of lumber transport undoubtedly would have afforded a curb upon rising prices which did not exist in 1919.

The export trade in lumber does not have a serious bearing upon timber depletion from the standpoint of quantity, but does have an important bearing upon the duration of our limited supply of high-grade timber, particularly of hardwoods. The exports of high-grade oak, walnut, hickory, ash, and other woods essential to many industries in the United States which now seem probable will further enhance the shortage of such products for the domestic market and the tendencies already evident toward sustained high prices. On the other hand, the United States imports from Canada about two-thirds of its total consumption of newsprint or newsprint materials. The effects of our export trade in lumber should be considered from the standpoint of the specific timber grades or products whose depletion is most imminent and threatening to American industries.

The concentration of timber ownership has not changed materially since the exhaustive report made upon this subject by the Bureau of Corporations in 1910. One-half of the privately owned timber in the United States is held by approximately 250 large owners, the ownership of the remaining timber being very widely distributed. The tendency toward the acquisition and speculative holding of timber beyond operating requirements has been checked, and the present tendency is toward the manufacture of large timber holdings. At the same time the lumber industry, particularly in the Western States, is going through a partial reorganization into larger operating and marketing groups. In this there is a tendency for small mills to disappear and small timber holdings to be blocked into larger ones adapted to extensive lumber manufacture. While there is still a large number of individual timber owners and of sawmills operating as separate units, the larger interests are acquiring a more dominant place in lumber manufacture in the West. It is to be expected that these large interests or groups will maintain, as time goes on, a fairly constant supply of timber for their manufacturing plants by acquiring smaller holdings. No information is at hand which would justify a conclusion that monopolistic conditions on any general scale have grown out of this situation. There are many instances to the contrary. On the other hand, the degree of control of the timber remaining in the United

States exercised by a comparatively small number of large interests will steadily increase as timber depletion continues, approaching a natural monopoly in character, and this control will extend particularly to the diminishing supply of high-grade material.

In 1918 our per capita consumption of lumber was about 300 board feet. The homes and industries of the United States require at least 35 billion feet of lumber yearly, aside from enormous quantities of paper and other products of the forest. A reduction in the current supply of lumber below this figure would seriously curtail our economic development. Appreciable increases in lumber imports are not possible except at excessive prices. We can not afford to cut our per capita use of lumber to one-half or one-third the present amount—to the level of European countries where lumber is an imported luxury. We must produce the great bulk of the timber which we need ourselves and we have the resources for doing so.

The solution of the problem presented by forest depletion in the United States is a national policy of reforestation. Increased and widely distributed production of wood is the most effective attack upon excessive prices and monopolistic tendencies. Depletion has not resulted from the use of forests but from their devastation, from our failure, while drawing upon our reservoirs of virgin timber, to also use our timber-growing land. If our enormous areas of forest growing land, now idle or largely idle, which are not required for any other economic use, can be restored to timber growth, a future supply of forest products adequate in the main to the needs of the country will be assured.

I therefore most earnestly request your consideration of the practical measures proposed in the accompanying report for putting a stop to forest devastation and restoring our idle land to timber production. I would emphasize especially the immediate urgency of legislation (1) which will permit effective cooperation between the Federal Government and the several States in preventing forest fires and growing timber on cut-over lands, and (2) which will greatly extend the National Forests. Enlargement of the National Forests offers immediate relief. On these publicly administered areas high quality timber can be grown and utilized to the maximum advantage; regrowth will follow cutting; and, under the regulations of the Forest Service, the disposal of timber will foster competitive conditions in the lumber industry. These steps are the foundation of an effective national policy for insuring a permanent and adequate supply of timber.

Concurrently with these measures, a comprehensive survey of the forest resources of the United States should be made.

Respectfully yours,

E. T. Meredith
Secretary

JOHN ISE ON THE 1910 FORESTRY COALITION*
1920

John Ise's The United States Forest Policy *in itself is an important document of conservation. Here is a brief passage listing the varied interest groups which were lined up in support of the Weeks bill before its final passage.*

INFLUENCES FAVORING ITS PASSAGE

Various influences favored the passage of the bill. In the first place, many of the influential government officials favored it. President Taft approved of the proposal, just as McKinley and Roosevelt had approved of similar proposals before; and of course Secretary of Agriculture James Wilson and most of the officials in the Forest Service and in the Geological Survey were favorably disposed.

Many influential organizations throughout the country registered their approval of forest reserves in the Appalachian and White mountains. Among these organizations were the following: the Adirondack Murray Memorial Association, the American Civic League, the American Cotton Manufacturers' Association, the American Association for the Advancement of Science, the American Forestry Association, the American Institute of Electrical Engineers, the American Mutual Newspaper Association, the American Paper and Pulp Association, the American Society of Civil Engineers, the Appalachian National Forest Association, the American Association for the Preservation of the Adirondacks, the Daughters of the American Revolution, the Eastern States Retail Lumber Dealers' Association, the Irrigation Congresses of 1907, 1908, 1909, and 1910, the Massachusetts Forestry Association, the Merchants' Association of New York, the National Association of Carriage Builders, the National Association of Manufacturers, the National Association of Box Manufacturers, the National Association of State University Presidents, the National Association of Cotton Manufacturers, the National Board of Trade, the National Forest Association (organized at Atlanta, Georgia), the National Federation of Women's Clubs, the National Hardwood Lumber Association, the National Lumber Manufacturers' Association, the National Slack Cooperage Manufacturers' Association, the National Wholesale Lumber Dealers' Association, the Pennsylvania Lumbermen's Association, the Pennsylvania Water Supply Commission; and even the United States Hay Fever Association. Favorable resolutions were also adopted by the Chambers of Commerce of various cities; New York, Boston, Cleveland, Pittsburgh, and Los Angeles; and by the legislatures of several of the states; North and South Carolina, Virginia, Georgia, Tennessee, and Oregon.

*John Ise, *The United States Forest Policy* (New Haven: Yale University Press, 1920), 217–18.

THE CLARKE-McNARY ACT*
June 7, 1924

Senator Charles McNary of Oregon had a hand in most of the beneficial conservation legislation passed during the 1920's. As a Republican leader, he managed to secure passage of several important advances in the forestry program during a period when relatively little progress was made on conservation issues.

The Clarke-McNary Act authorized an expanded cooperative federal-state fire control program, without the old limitation to navigable watersheds. It also provided for a cooperative program with the states in the planting of seedlings.

An Act to provide for the protection of forest lands, for the reforestation of denuded areas, for the extension of national forests, and for other purposes, in order to promote the continuous production of timber on lands chiefly suitable therefor.

Be it enacted by the Senate and House of Representatives of the United States of America in Congress assembled, That the Secretary of Agriculture is hereby authorized and directed, in cooperation with appropriate officials of the various States or other suitable agencies, to recommend for each forest region of the United States such systems of forest fire prevention and suppression as will adequately protect the timbered and cut-over lands therein with a view to the protection of forest and water resources and the continuous production of timber on lands chiefly suitable therefor.

Sec. 2. That if the Secretary of Agriculture shall find that the system and practice of forest fire prevention and suppression provided by any State substantially promotes the objects described in the foregoing section, he is hereby authorized and directed, under such conditions as he may determine to be fair and equitable in each State, to cooperate with appropriate officials of each State, and through them with private and other agencies therein, in the protection of timbered and forest-producing lands from fire. In no case other than for preliminary investigations shall the amount expended by the Federal Government in any State during any fiscal year, under this section, exceed the amount expended by the State for the same purpose during the same fiscal year, including the expenditures of forest owners or operators which are required by State law or which are made in pursuance of the forest protection system of the State under State supervision and for which in all cases the State renders satisfactory accounting. In the cooperation extended to the several States due consideration shall be given to the protection of watersheds of navigable streams, but such

*43 *Statutes at Large,* 653–55.

cooperation may, in the discretion of the Secretary of Agriculture, be extended to any timbered or forest producing lands within the cooperating States.

Sec. 3. That the Secretary of Agriculture shall expend such portions of the appropriations authorized herein as he deems advisable to study the effects of tax laws, methods, and practices upon forest perpetuation, to cooperate with appropriate officials of the various States or other suitable agencies in such investigations and in devising tax laws designed to encourage the conservation and growing of timber, and to investigate and promote practical methods of insuring standing timber on growing forests from losses by fire and other causes. There is hereby authorized to be appropriated annually, out of any money in the Treasury not otherwise appropriated, not more than $2,500,000, to enable the Secretary of Agriculture to carry out the provisions of sections 1, 2, and 3 of this Act.

Sec. 4. That the Secretary of Agriculture is hereby authorized and directed to cooperate with the various States in the procurement, production, and distribution of forest-tree seeds and plants, for the purpose of establishing wind breaks, shelter belts, and farm wood lots upon denuded or nonforested lands within such cooperating States, under such conditions and requirements as he may prescribe to the end that forest-tree seeds or plants so procured, produced, or distributed shall be used effectively for planting denuded or nonforested lands in the cooperating States and growing timber thereon: *Provided,* That the amount expended by the Federal Government in cooperation with any State during any fiscal year for such purposes shall not exceed the amount expended by the State for the same purposes during the same fiscal year. There is hereby authorized to be appropriated annually, out of any money in the Treasury not otherwise appropriated, not more than $100,000, to enable the Secretary of Agriculture to carry out the provisions of this section.

Sec. 5. That the Secretary of Agriculture is hereby authorized and directed, in cooperation with appropriate officials of the various States or, in his discretion, with other suitable agencies, to assist the owners of farms in establishing, improving, and renewing woodlots, shelter belts, windbreaks, and other valuable forest growth, and in growing and renewing useful timber crops: *Provided,* That, except for preliminary investigations, the amount expended by the Federal Government under this section in cooperation with any State or other cooperating agency during any fiscal year shall not exceed the amount expended by the State or other cooperating agency for the same purpose during the same fiscal year. There is hereby authorized to be appropriated annually out of any money in the Treasury not otherwise appropriated, not more than $100,000 to enable the Secretary of Agriculture to carry out the provisions of this section.

Sec. 6. That section 6 of the Act of March 1, 1911 (Thirty-sixth Statutes at Large, page 961), is hereby amended to authorize and direct the Secretary of Agriculture to examine, locate and recommend for purchase such forested, cut-over or denuded lands within the watersheds of navigable streams as in his judgment may be necessary to the regulation of the flow of navigable streams or for the production of timber and to report to the National Forest Reservation Commission the results of such examination; but before any lands are purchased by the commission said lands shall be examined by the Secretary of Agriculture, in cooperation with the Director of the Geological Survey, and a report made by them to the commission showing that the control of such lands by the Federal Government will promote or protect the navigation of streams or by the Secretary of Agriculture showing that such control will promote the production of timber thereon.

SEC. 7. That to enable owners of lands chiefly valuable for the growing of timber crops to donate or devise such lands to the United States in order to assure future timber supplies for the agricultural and other industries of the State or for other national forest purposes, the Secretary of Agriculture is hereby authorized, in his discretion, to accept on behalf of the United States title to any such land so donated or devised, subject to such reservations by the donor of the present stand of merchantable timber or of mineral or other rights for a period not exceeding twenty years as the Secretary of Agriculture may find to be reasonable and not detrimental to the purposes of this section, and to pay out of any moneys appropriated for the general expenses of the Forest Service the cost of recording deeds or other expenses incident to the examination and acceptance of title. Any lands to which title is so accepted shall be in units of such size or so located as to be capable of economical administration as national forests either separately or jointly with other lands acquired under this section, or jointly with an existing national forest. All lands to which title is accepted under this section shall, upon acceptance of title, become national forest lands, subject to all laws applicable to lands acquired under the Act of March 1, 1911 (Thirty-sixth Statutes at Large, page 961), and amendments thereto. In the sale of timber from national forest lands acquired under this section preference shall be given to applicants who will furnish the products desired therefrom to meet the necessities of citizens of the United States engaged in agriculture in the States in which such national forest is situated: *Provided,* That all property, rights, easements, and benefits authorized by this section to be retained by or reserved to owners of lands donated or devised to the United States shall be subject to the tax laws of the States where such lands are located.

SEC. 8. That the Secretary of Agriculture is hereby authorized to ascertain and determine the location of public lands chiefly valuable for stream-flow protection or for timber production, which can be economically administered as parts of national forests, and to report his findings to the National Forest Reservation Commission established under the Act of March 1, 1911 (Thirty-sixth Statutes at Large, page 961), and if the commission shall determine that the administration of said lands by the Federal Government will protect the flow of streams used for navigation or for irrigation, or will promote a future timber supply, the President shall lay the findings of the commission before the Congress of the United States.

SEC. 9. That the President, in his discretion, is hereby authorized to establish as national forests, or parts thereof, any lands within the boundaries of Government reservations, other than national parks, reservations for phosphate and other mineral deposits or water-power purposes, national monuments, and Indian reservations, which in the opinion of the Secretary of the department now administering the area and the Secretary of Agriculture are suitable for the production of timber, to be administered by the Secretary of Agriculture under such rules and regulations and in accordance with such general plans as may be jointly approved by the Secretary of Agriculture and the Secretary formerly administering the area, for the use and occupation of such lands and for the sale of products therefrom. That where such national forest is established on land previously reserved for the Army or Navy for purposes of national defense the land shall remain subject to the unhampered use of the War or Navy Department for said purposes, and nothing in this section shall be construed to relinquish the authority over such lands for purposes of national defense now vested in the Department for which the lands were formerly reserved. Any moneys available for the maintenance, improvement, protection, construction of highways and general administration of the national forests shall be available for expenditure on the national forests created under this section. All receipts from the sale of products from or for the use of lands in such national forests shall be covered into the Treasury as miscellaneous receipts, forest reserve fund, and shall be disposed of in like manner as the receipts from other national forests as provided by existing law. Any person who shall violate any rule or regulation promulgated under this section shall be guilty of a misdemeanor, and upon conviction thereof shall be fined not more than $500 or imprisoned for not more than one year, or both.

Approved, June 7, 1924.

THE WOODRUFF-McNARY ACT*
April 30, 1928

This brief amendment to the Weeks Act expanded federal authority to buy timberlands and establish national forests. It prepared the way for significant new holdings when vast acreages were forfeited to the states for unpaid taxes and federal ownership was needed to prevent rapid deterioration.

An Act authorizing an appropriation to be expended under the provisions of section 7 of the Act of March 1, 1911, entitled "An Act to enable any State to cooperate with any other State or States, or with the United States, for the protection of the watersheds of navigable streams, and to appoint a commission for the acquisition of lands for the purpose of conserving the navigability of navigable rivers," as amended.

Be it enacted by the Senate and House of Representatives of the United States of America in Congress assembled, That there is hereby authorized to be appropriated, out of any money in the United States Treasury not otherwise appropriated, to be expended under the provisions of section 7 of the Act of March 1, 1911 (Thirty-sixth Statutes, page 961), as amended by the Acts of March 4, 1913 (Thirty-seventh Statutes, page 828), June 30, 1914 (Thirty-eighth Statutes, page 441), and the Act of June 7, 1924 (Public, 270), available July 1, 1928, $2,000,000; available July 1, 1929, $3,000,000; available July 1, 1930, $3,000,000; in all for this period, $8,000,000, to be available until expended: *Provided,* That, except for the protection of the headwaters of navigable streams or the control and reduction of floods therein, no lands shall be purchased under the appropriations herein authorized in excess of one million acres in any one State.

Approved, April 30, 1928.

*45 *Statutes at Large,* 468.

THE McSWEENEY-McNARY ACT*
May 22, 1928

This third important forestry law sponsored by Senator McNary authorized a major expansion in forest research, including forest economics, primarily through the experiment station system.

An Act to insure adequate supplies of timber and other forest products for the people of the United States, to promote the full use for timber growing and other purposes of forest lands in the United States, including farm wood lots and those abandoned areas not suitable for agricultural production, and to secure the correlation and the most economical conduct of forest research in the Department of Agriculture, through research in reforestation, timber growing, protection, utilization, forest economics, and related subjects, and for other purposes.

Be it enacted by the Senate and House of Representatives of the United States of America in Congress assembled, That the Secretary of Agriculture is hereby authorized and directed to conduct such investigations, experiments, and tests as he may deem necessary under sections 2 to 10, inclusive, in order to determine, demonstrate, and promulgate the best methods of reforestation and of growing, managing, and utilizing timber, forage, and other forest products, of maintaining favorable conditions of water flow and the prevention of erosion, of protecting timber and other forest growth from fire, insects, disease, or other harmful agencies, of obtaining the fullest and most effective use of forest lands, and to determine and promulgate the economic considerations which should underlie the establishment of sound policies for the management of forest land and the utilization of forest products: *Provided,* That in carrying out the provisions of this Act the Secretary of Agriculture may cooperate with individuals and public and private agencies, organizations, and institutions, and, in connection with the collection, investigation, and tests of foreign woods, he may also cooperate with individuals and public and private agencies, organizations, and institutions in other countries; and receive money contributions from cooperators under such conditions as he may impose, such contributions to be covered into the Treasury as a special fund which is hereby appropriated and made available until expended as the Secretary of Agriculture may direct, for use in conducting the activities authorized by this Act, and in making refunds to contributors: *Provided further,* That the cost of any building purchased, erected, or as improved in carrying out the purposes of this Act shall not exceed $2,500, exclusive in each instance of the cost of constructing a water supply or sanitary

*45 *Statutes at Large,* 699–702.

system and of connecting the same with any such building: *Provided further,* That the amounts specified in sections 2, 3, 4, 5, 6, 7, 8, and 10 of this Act are authorized to be appropriated up to and including the fiscal year 1938, and such annual appropriations as may thereafter be necessary to carry out the provisions of said sections are hereby authorized: *Provided further,* That during any fiscal year the amounts specified in sections 3, 4, and 5 of this Act making provision for investigations of forest tree and wood diseases, forest insects, and forest wild life, respectively, may be exceeded to provide adequate funds for special research required to meet any serious public emergency relating to epidemics: *And provided further,* That the provisions of this Act shall be construed as supplementing all other Acts relating to the Department of Agriculture, and except as specifically provided shall not limit or repeal any existing legislation or authority.

SEC. 2. That for conducting fire, silvicultural, and other forest investigations and experiments the Secretary of Agriculture is hereby authorized, in his discretion, to maintain the following forest experiment stations for the regions indicated, and in addition to establish and maintain one such station for the Intermountain region in Utah and adjoining States, one in Alaska, and one in the tropical possessions of the United States in the West Indies:

Northeastern forest experiment station, in New England, New York, and adjacent States;

Allegheny forest experiment station, in Pennsylvania, New Jersey, Delaware, Maryland, and in neighboring States;

Appalachian forest experiment station, in the southern Appalachian Mountains and adjacent forest regions;

Southern forest experiment station, in the Southern States;

Central States forest experiment station, in Ohio, Indiana, Illinois, Kentucky, Missouri, Iowa, and in adjacent States;

Lake States forest experiment station, in the Lake States and adjoining States;

California forest experiment station, in California and in adjoining States;

Northern Rocky Mountain forest experiment station, in Idaho, Montana, and adjoining States;

Northwestern forest experiment station, in Washington, Oregon, and adjoining States, and in Alaska;

Rocky Mountain forest experiment station, in Colorado, Wyoming, Nebraska, South Dakota, and in adjacent States; and

Southwestern forest experiment station, in Arizona, and New Mexico, and in adjacent States, and in addition to establish and maintain one such station for the intermountain region of Utah and adjoining States, one for Alaska, one in Hawaii, and one in the tropical possessions of the United States in the West Indies, and one additional station in the Southern States.

There is hereby authorized to be appropriated annually out of any money in the Treasury not otherwise appropriated, not more than $1,000,000 to carry out the provisions of this section.

SEC. 3. That for investigations of the diseases of forest trees and of diseases causing decay and deterioration of wood and other forest products, and for developing methods for their prevention and control at forest experiment stations, the Forest Products Laboratory, or elsewhere, there is hereby authorized to be appropriated annually, out of any money in the Treasury not otherwise appropriated, not more than $250,000.

SEC. 4. That for investigations of forests insects, including gypsy and brown-tail moths, injurious or beneficial to forest trees or to wood or other forest products, and for developing methods for preventing and controlling infestations, at forest experiment stations, the Forest Products Laboratory, or elsewhere, there is hereby authorized to be appropriated annually, out of any money in the Treasury not otherwise appropriated, not more than $350,000.

SEC. 5. That for such experiments and investigations as may be necessary in determining the life histories and habits of forest animals, birds, and wild life, whether injurious to forest growth or of value as supplemental resource, and in developing the best and most effective methods for their management and control at forest experiment stations, or elsewhere, there is hereby authorized to be appropriated annually, out of any money in the Treasury not otherwise appropriated, not more than $150,000.

SEC. 6. That for such investigations at forest experiment stations, or elsewhere, of the relationship of weather conditions to forest fires as may be necessary to make weather forecasts, there is hereby authorized to be appropriated annually, out of any money in the Treasury not otherwise appropriated, not more than $50,000.

SEC. 7. That for such experiments and investigations as may be necessary to develop improved methods of management, consistent with the growing of timber and the protection of watersheds, of forest ranges and of other ranges adjacent to the national forests, at forest or range experiment stations, or elsewhere, there is hereby authorized to be appropriated annually, out of any money in the Treasury not otherwise appropriated, not more than $275,000.

SEC. 8. That for experiments, investigations, and tests with respect to the physical and chemical properties and the utilization and preservation of wood and other forest products, including tests of wood and other fibrous material for pulp and paper making, and such other experiments, investigations, and tests as may be desirable, at the Forest Products Laboratory or elsewhere, there is hereby authorized to be appropriated annually, out of any money in the Treasury not otherwise appropriated, not more than $1,000,000, and an additional appropriation of not more than $50,000 annually for similar experiments, investigations, and tests of foreign woods and forest products important to the industries of the United States, including necessary field work in connection therewith.

SEC. 9. That the Secretary of Agriculture is hereby authorized and directed, under such plans as he may determine to be fair and equitable, to cooperate with appropriate officials of each State of the United States, and either through them or directly with private and other agencies, in making a comprehensive survey of the present and prospective requirements for timber and other forest products in the United States, and of timber supplies, including a determination of the present and potential productivity of forest land therein, and of such other facts as may be necessary in the determination of ways and means to balance the timber budget of the United States. There is hereby authorized to be appropriated annually, out of any money in the Treasury not otherwise appropriated, not more than $250,000: *Provided,* That the total appropriation of Federal funds under this section shall not exceed $3,000,000.

SEC. 10. That for such investigations of costs and returns and the possibility of profitable reforestation under different conditions in the different forest regions, of the proper function of timber growing in diversified agriculture and in insuring the profitable use of marginal land, in mining, transportation, and in other industries, of the most effective distribution of forest products in the interest of both consumer and timber grower, and for such other economic investigations of forest lands and forest products as may be necessary, there is hereby authorized to be appropriated annually, out of any money in the Treasury not otherwise appropriated, not more than $250,000.

Approved, May 22, 1928.

THE BALLINGER-PINCHOT CONTROVERSY

THE RECOMMENDATION OF BALLINGER
FOR LAND COMMISSIONER*
January 11, 1907

This note reveals how Judge Richard A. Ballinger was made Commissioner of Public Lands, upon the recommendation of Secretary of the Interior James Garfield.

TO GIFFORD PINCHOT

Washington, January 11, 1907

Dear Gifford:

After talking over the matter with Jim I feel we ought not to wait in the Land Office business. On Jim's recommendation, as he personally knows the man, who was in Williams and in the class ahead of him, I shall offer the Land Commissionership to Judge Ballinger of Seattle. I am not sure that we can get him. Keep your eyes open, however, so that we may be sure to have alternative choices.

Faithfully yours

*The Letters of Theodore Roosevelt, Vol. 5, Elting E. Morison, ed. (Cambridge: Harvard University Press, 1952), 549.

GLAVIS' ACCUSATION OF BALLINGER*
November 13, 1909

Louis R. Glavis, chief of the field division of the General Land Office, was a zealous believer in the Roosevelt conservation doctrine, and a stickler for form in land grant cases. In 1907, he started checking the validity of some Alaskan coal-land claims and came up with strong suspicion of fraud. This article from Collier's *recounts how the case developed.*

Glavis does not report here that after he became convinced that Secretary of the Interior Richard A. Ballinger was improperly blocking his investigation, he took his story to Ballinger's predecessor, James R. Garfield, and to Gifford Pinchot. When Garfield and Pinchot became convinced that publicizing the incident would improve Ballinger's conduct within the Interior Department, they arranged for publication of the article in Collier's.

From 1902 to 1909 I was in the field service of the General Land Office, for the last two and a half years as Chief of Field Division. In September, 1909, I was summarily removed from my position without a formal hearing by Richard A. Ballinger, Secretary of the Interior, by authorization of the President of the United States. That removal was accompanied by the publication of a letter of the President to Mr. Ballinger. I believe that my removal was unfair. I believe the President's letter was grievously unfair, because in it the President gives weight to a charge against me which I never had the opportunity to see or answer. The President states in his letter that I withheld from him information favorable to my superiors. I do not know of any such information withheld by me, nor am I conscious of doing my superiors injustice. Nevertheless, I should not now make any public statement of the matter were it not still possible to save for the Government many thousands of acres of coal lands which I believe the Land Office may in the near future grant to fraudulent claimants. The hope that my statement will help to arouse public sentiment, and that this danger to the national resources may be averted, is what actuates me. This statement will simply give facts and leave to the judgment of those who read whether or not the Land Office has been zealous in the public service.

THE FACTS ARE THESE

The coal lands of Alaska owned by the Government amount to over 100,000 acres. They are the future coal supply of the nation, of almost inestimable value. Possession of them by private individuals means great wealth—a monopoly of them would be a national menace.

*L. R. Glavis, "The Whitewashing of Ballinger," *Collier's* (Nov. 13, 1909), 15–17, 27.

[242]

On November 12, 1906, President Roosevelt withdrew all coal lands in Alaska from public entry; but previous to that time there were about 900 claims filed, covering about 100,000 acres (nearly the whole of the coal fields). The law attempts to prevent monopoly of such claims by limiting the amount of each claim and providing that each claimant must take up the land in his own interest and for his own use. This law has been interpreted by the Supreme Court of the United States to forbid speculating in coal lands before entry—either by dummy entrymen or by previous agreements to consolidate claims after entry. Of these 900 claims to Alaska coal lands—among them the so-called Cunningham group—the majority are fraudulent.

As to the action of the Land Office on these claims, I assert that the Land Office ordered the Cunningham claims to patent without due investigation when Commissioner Ballinger knew they were under suspicion; that while in office Commissioner Ballinger urged Congress to pass a law which would validate fraudulent Alaska claims; that shortly after resigning from office he became attorney for the Cunningham group and other Alaska claims; that soon after he became Secretary of the Interior his office rendered a decision which would have validated all fraudulent Alaska claims. A reversal of that decision on every point was obtained from Attorney-General Wickersham. Had it not been for Mr. Wickersham's decision, every fraudulent Alaska claim would have gone to patent. I assert that in the spring of 1909 the Land Office urged me to an early trial of these cases before the investigation was finished, and when Secretary Ballinger, as the President has stated; knew that the Cunningham claims were invalid. When I appealed to Secretary Ballinger for postponement, he referred me to his subordinates. The Department of Agriculture intervened. I was superseded in the charge of the cases, and the man who superseded me endorsed my recommendations, and the postponement was granted. Immediately thereafter I made my report on the Cunningham cases to President Taft, and was dismissed from the service for insubordination.

THE ALASKA FRAUDS

The President has seen fit to raise broader issues than those contained in my report. In view of this fact, I shall in this report use material not favorable to the people concerned which I did not use in my report to the President, because these facts did not immediately concern the Cunningham cases.

The first official communication to the Land Office which suggested that some or all of the Alaska coal claims were fraudulent was made by Special Agent H. K. Love in October, 1905. In June, 1907, Special Agent Horace T. Jones was detailed by Mr. Fred Dennett, First Assistant Commissioner of the General Land Office, to make a complete investigation. Subsequently Jones was instructed by Mr. Ballinger to make the report a preliminary one. Jones reported on

August 10, 1907, requesting further investigation "by an experienced and fearless agent." On August 2, 1907, Love made a report favorable to the issuance of patents to the Cunningham claims.

My first connection with these cases was when in the fall of 1907 I discovered in Seattle, while investigating other matters, that some or all of the coal claims were not bona fide. My report of this matter to Mr. Ballinger stated that one claimant had refused me an affidavit on the ground that Mr. Ballinger himself had told some of the claimants to make no statement until the charges were made, IN ORDER THAT THEY MIGHT KNOW WHAT THEY HAD TO MEET, but that I could not believe this statement. Mr. Ballinger never commented to me on this phase of my report. In December, 1907, I was called to Washington, and explained to Mr. Ballinger, then Land Commissioner, what I had found out about all the claims, including the Cunningham claims. I also stated that the Department of Justice would know these facts and would investigate them if the Land Office did not. Mr. Ballinger told me he was a friend of many of the claimants, but that I was authorized to go ahead and investigate all these claims, no matter what the result. He then wrote me a letter, putting me in charge of the investigation of all the Alaska coal claims. *It was agreed by Mr. Ballinger that inasmuch as Special Agent Love was a candidate for United States Marshal in Alaska, he was not in a position to make an impartial investigation.* At our conference in December, 1907, the good faith of the Alaska entries was discussed by Mr. Ballinger. *On January 7, 1908, ten days afterward, Mr. Dennett, Assistant Commissioner, notified me, as investigator of the whole field, that the Cunningham claims had been approved for patent on the Love report.* Three days before this a telegram, signed "R. A. Ballinger," was sent to Love in Alaska, directing him to forward the plats which the Land Office would require in issuing patents to the Cunningham claims. Again, on January 11, 1908, a telegram was sent, signed with Mr. Ballinger's name, to Love, asking him whether he had acted on the previous telegram. Love telegraphed that he had sent the plats. The envelope of this telegram in the Land Office was endorsed "Hand to Carr. O. K. Carr." Carr was then private secretary to Mr. Ballinger.

A LEAK IN THE LAND OFFICE

On January 15, 1908, Cunningham, agent for the claimants, wrote a letter to the Juneau Land Office, in which he said:

"The Commissioner [Mr. Ballinger] has furnished us with copies of all the correspondence and telegrams relating to our entries between the various special agents and also with your office. Up to date everything seems to have been approved by each department chief, so now our only delay will be occasioned through failure to receive plats according to Judge Ballinger's advice."

If the Cunningham claims had then gone to patent, 5,000 acres of coal land, containing, according to Mr. Cunningham's expert, 91,000,000 tons of coal, would have gone to the Cunningham group without adequate investigation of title. When the Cunningham claims were ordered to patent, Mr. Ballinger and his assistants must have known, from the reports of Special Agent Jones and myself, the suspicious character of these claims.

Here was my first dilemma. I did not wish to protest to Secretary of the Interior Garfield against the action of the Commissioner, and I did not like to see 5,000 acres of coal lands go to the Cunningham group when I believed the claims fraudulent. I did protest immediately, by telegram and letter, direct to Commissioner Ballinger, against the issuance of the patents. The order clearlisting the Cunningham claims to patent was almost immediately revoked, and, on March 1, 1908, I again took up the work on these claims. Special Agent Jones and I, at Wallace, Idaho, procured affidavits of Cunningham claimants showing their intention to consolidate their claims. Then we went to see Cunningham. *Cunningham stated that he had heard that some one complained that he was taking claims for the Guggenheims. (The Jones report to Ballinger contained the allegation that all indications pointed to the Guggenheims, but it does not appear how Cunningham got this confidential information.)* In order to refute this charge, Cunningham showed us his books. These books contained a memorandum of agreement, dated 1903, between the entrymen to consolidate the coal lands. This agreement was illegal for two reasons—because it attempted to consolidate more than the law allowed, and *because the agreement showed that the entrymen took up the land with the intention of deeding it to a company and giving Cunningham one-eighth of the stock.*

Afterward, and while Jones and I were taking Cunningham's affidavit, ex-Governor Miles C. Moore of Washington, one of the Cunningham claimants, came in and stated that he had had a recent interview with Mr. Ballinger in Washington, and that Mr. Ballinger would have patented the Cunningham claims but for my protest. This information given Moore, and announced by him in Cunningham's presence, came near preventing my obtaining the affidavit from Cunningham. In fact, the information obtained by this claimant, Miles C. Moore, from the Land Office in Washington, considerably hampered me in my effort to get evidence. The giving out of such information was contrary to express regulations of the Interior Department.

By order of Mr. Dennett, by telegram and letter, I was taken off the Alaska cases in May, 1908, and ordered on other work. The reason given for this action was lack of funds. I reported by telegram that delay of the investigation would greatly lessen the Government's chance to secure evidence.

In October, 1908, I was ordered back to the Alaska cases by a letter of Acting Assistant Commissioner Schwartz, stating that my work had been suspended pending legislation.

BALLINGER URGES CONGRESS TO HELP CLAIMS

Mr. Ballinger retired as Commissioner of the Land Office in March, 1908. *A few days before, while still an officer of the United States, Mr. Ballinger appeared before the House Committee on Public Lands in favor of the Cale bill, then pending.* In the course of his statement, he said:

"... *the last section of the bill provides for a consolidation of existing entries and does not call for the proof of good faith of the original entry or location.* There are a great many charges pending against some of the original entries in Alaska. At the time these fields were located, corporations were organized. The men had really no method of taking advantage of these coal measures. It resulted in their getting involved in conditions which, upon the records of the Land Office, are *a technical violation of the statute,* and it is a situation which should be cleared up. In my estimation it has not been the intention of the people in the field nor in Alaska to put them in hostility to the laws, but they have been in a position where they could not, by virtue of the circumstances, accommodate themselves to the laws, and with this last provision they could transmute their present entries into the form suggested by this bill, and those new entries would be treated as primary entries. In other words, it would be an abandonment of the old conditions which have made a great deal of difficulty in the matter of the disposition of the land in many instances."

When Mr. Ballinger made this statement (before the Committee on Public Lands) he was urging a change in the law by which fraudulent entries would be made valid—by which the Cunningham group and the other Alaska claims would have received patents to practically 100,000 acres of Alaska coal fields. Whether or not we agree that a fraudulent entry is a "technical violation" of a statute, there seems little doubt that Mr. Ballinger was then well informed as to the defects in the Alaska coal claims (which included the Cunningham group).

BALLINGER BECOMES ATTORNEY

It is with Mr. Ballinger's testimony before this Committee in mind that we come to the next step. Within a short time after he resigned, Mr. Ballinger became attorney for the Cunningham group of claims.

There was at that time, and now is, in force, a statute of the United States which says:

"It shall not be lawful for any person appointed after the first day of June, 1872, as an officer, clerk, or employee in any of the departments, to act as counsel, attorney, or agent for prosecuting any claim against the United States which was pending in either of said departments while he was such an officer, clerk, or employee, nor in any manner, nor by any means, to aid in the prosecution of any such claim, within two years next after he shall have ceased to be such officer, clerk, or employee."

This is the only statute that I know of regarding the impropriety of a Government officer taking claims against the Government after his resignation.

THE PRESIDENT WHITEWASHES BALLINGER

Of that employment, President Taft has said:

"In the interval, when you were not holding office, one of the Cunningham coal claimants consulted you in regard to the prospect of securing a patent upon the claims, and invited your attention to the character of certain evidence which was being used to impeach the validity of the claims by Special Agent Glavis. You accepted the employment; visited Secretary Garfield and Commissioner Dennett; presented the question to them in respect to which you had been consulted; found that there was no probability of securing a patent of the claims without presenting them under recent remedial legislation imposing conditions which the claimants were either unwilling or unable to meet. You so advised your clients. To pay your traveling expenses and for your services you received $250 and no more.

"The inference which Mr. Glavis seeks to have drawn to your discredit in this connection is that you, while Commissioner of the General Land Office, came into possession of facts concerning the so-called Cunningham group of coal land claims, which made it improper for you to use such facts after your resignation in the course of securing the patents. *I find the fact to be that, as Commissioner, you acquired no knowledge in respect to the claims except that of the most formal character, and nothing which was not properly known to your clients when they consulted you.*"

I do not quite understand the President's statement that Mr. Ballinger had only the most "formal knowledge" of the Cunningham cases. *Mr. Ballinger had all the knowledge anybody in the department had, because Special Agent Jones and I told him all we knew. Mr. Ballinger knew that he had revoked the order to patent Mr. Cunningham's claims on account of my protest that I believed they were not bona-fide entries.* He knew, or might have known, that I then had no conclusive proof against the claims. Mr. Ballinger had made a statement to the Congressional Committee as to these claims, the nature of the defenses, and the legislation which was needed to make them valid, and he had ordered them investigated by Love, Jones, and myself. Whether there was any impropriety in his later acting for the Cunningham group, the President is doubtless a better judge than I. One point, however, is interesting in the light of later events. The President in his letter states that Mr. Ballinger, as a private attorney, advised that the Cunningham group could not obtain patents—presumably because the entries were not, under the law, made in good faith for the benefit of each entryman. Nevertheless, *the affidavit of Mr. Cunningham, presented by Mr. Ballinger to Secretary Garfield after he became attorney for the Cunningham group and other Alaska coal claimants, and which attempts to explain away the fraudulent character of the claims, is now the chief obstacle to Government success in the Cunningham cases.*

Nor do I understand why the President puts so much stress on the fact that Mr. Ballinger received only $250 for ten or fifteen days' services and the expenses of a trip from Seattle to Ohio and Washington. Even if that be credible, *Mr. Ballinger was then attorney for other Alaska coal claimants, and according to sworn information made to me in the course of my investigation, for at least one Congressman interested in Alaska coal lands.*

From October, 1908, when I was directed to continue my investigations of the Alaska coal-land cases, until March, 1909, I was continuously engaged in that and other work in my department.

In March, 1909, Mr. Ballinger became Secretary of the Interior, succeeding Hon. James R. Garfield. *On March 10 (six days after Mr. Ballinger took office) I received a telegram from Mr. Dennett, then Commissioner of the General Land Office, directing me to submit at once complete reports upon the status of my investigation of the Alaska coal cases. On April 21, 1909, I received a telegram from the General Land Office, saying that the Alaska coal investigation must be completed within sixty days.*

The Chief of Field Service and I had agreed that a field examination of the Alaska coal lands in question was necessary to show whether the claims in the various groups were being developed separately or together. Thus, if a field examination should prove that all the claims of the Cunningham group were as a matter of fact being worked together, that fact would be highly indicative that the entries were made with that intent. Such a field investigation could take place only in summer. I therefore protested repeatedly to the Land Office that the cases should be postponed until fall.

In May, 1909, I came on to Washington, and consulted as to the Alaska coal cases with Secretary Ballinger, Land Commissioner Dennett, and the Chief of the Field Service. At the conference there came up a question of the effect of a statute of 1908, allowing consolidation of Alaska coal entries to the amount of 2,560 acres where the original entries were made by the *"entrymen in good faith" and in their own interest.* Mr. Schwartz and I contended that this act did not have the effect of validating fraudulent entries previously made, *and pointed out that if it did, the Government must lose all the Alaska coal cases. Mr. Dennett expressed the contrary view. Mr. Schwartz and I, by direction of Mr. Ballinger, drew up a letter submitting this question to the Attorney-General. This letter summarized the evidence I had secured in these cases of conspiracies to defraud the Government.*

[248]

On May 18 or 19 I was sent for by Assistant Secretary Pierce of the Interior Department. *Mr. Pierce informed me that Mr. Ballinger did not wish to have anything more to do with the cases on account of his employment as attorney for the Cunninghams; that the question of law was not to be submitted to the Attorney-General; that the opinion was going to be written by the Interior Department,* and he referred me to the legal department of the Interior Department. E. C. Finney, who had been made assistant to the Secretary by Mr. Ballinger, and F. W. Clements of the legal department of the Interior Department, were drawing up a decision conforming to Mr. Dennett's view that under the new law the former fraudulent entries could be made good and consolidated. My opinion was asked, *and I said that the law only allowed bona-fide entries to consolidate, and that I did not see how they could get around that.*

PIERCE'S DECISION ON THE FRAUDULENT CLAIMS

On the following day Mr. Dennett, in a conversation, told me to make my reports in conformity to his decision, and at my request a letter was sent to me on May 24, directing me so to report.

On the 26th I reported that, according to the decision rendered by the Interior Department, it was useless to proceed with any further investigation, and that under the decision I was obliged to report 782 claims, including the Cunningham group, for the consideration of the Commissioner under this decision. The decision rendered by Mr. Pierce was as follows:

Department of the Interior
The Commissioner of the General Land Office   Washington, May 19, 1909

Sir
    Referring to your recent request for instructions relative to unperfected coal-land entries within Alaska, made by qualified persons prior to the passage of the act of May 28, 1908 (35 Stat., 424), concerning which you report that under varying conditions arrangements had been entered into looking to the transfer and consolidation of the entries into groups, in order to secure such acerage as would warrant the economic development of the groups, and that application is now being made to perfect said entries under said act, I have to advise you that the act of May 28, 1908, was a curative act and should be liberally construed so as to further the object intended to be advanced by said legislation, namely, the consolidation of coal claims in Alaska, initiated prior to November 12, 1906, through means of associations or corporations, so as to permit of the acquirement of title to contiguous locations not exceeding 2,560 acres.
    "There are, of course, conditions respecting the qualifications of the persons constituting the association or corporation making the consolidated entry, its length, etc., with respect to which your inquiry has no relation. It is assumed that the difficulty with which your office is confronted in passing upon these applications is merely that technical objection might have been raised as to the good faith of the claimant or entryman because of the understanding, arrangement, or agreement contemplated or entered into with respect to the completion of such entries prior to the passage of the act of May 28, 1908. With respect thereto I am of the opinion that to so limit the scope and purpose of the act of 1908, as to refuse the privilege of

perfecting such claims under its liberal provisions, solely because of such previous arrangement or agreement, is unwarranted, and that in passing upon entries sought to be perfected under the act of 1908, where the only objection thereto is an arrangement or agreement of the character specifically described in your letter, the same might and should be accepted and passed to patent.

Very respectfully,

(Signed) *Frank Pierce*
First Assistant Secretary

I was then in a very difficult position. I knew what the law was, and my superiors were against me. *If I accepted their ruling, 100,000 acres of Alaska coal lands were slipping from the United States with no hope of recovery*—and were going to claimants many of whom were fraudulent. *The chance for the wise regulation of Alaska coal lands urged by President Roosevelt would be gone.*

WICKERSHAM OVERRULES BALLINGER

Without consulting with my superiors, I went to Attorney-General Wickersham and stated the matter to him. I understand that he asked Mr. Ballinger to refer the matter to him. *Mr. Ballinger requested me to withdraw my report, which showed that if the Pierce decision was correct, the Government had no ground to object to any of the Alaska claims.* I withdrew that report.

Ten days later the Attorney-General delivered an opinion on the question—it is long, and I shall not quote it. *Suffice it to say it overruled the Pierce decision on every point, upheld my contention, and saved the Alaska coal cases.*

BALLINGER AGAINST INVESTIGATION OF CONGRESSMAN

One other fact arose on my visit to Washington (and of this I have no documentary evidence).

In my conference with Mr. Ballinger, I stated to him that I was going to see one of the Congressmen, regarding whose participation in the Alaska coal cases I had sworn testimony; HE REPLIED THAT THERE HAD BEEN TOO MUCH OF THIS SORT OF THING, AND THAT THAT WAS A MATTER FOR CONGRESSIONAL INVESTIGATION. In consequence, after consultation with other Government officials, I decided not to see any Congressman; but I afterward found out—from sworn testimony obtained by me and now in the Land Office—THAT MR. BALLINGER HAD, ABOUT A YEAR BEFORE, REPRESENTED A CONGRESSMAN IN ALASKA COAL MATTERS.

At the expiration of the sixty days allotted for the completion of my reports, I telegraphed that I was getting new evidence, and that I could not consistently make final reports while further evidence was available, Cunningham cases included, and that the time should be extended at least sixty days longer.

BALLINGER PUSHES TRIAL
WHEN GOVERNMENT IS NOT READY

In answer to this telegram I received a despatch from the General Land Office *that the reports must be submitted at once and that an agent would be sent to Seattle to take charge of the investigation.* I urged by letter and telegrams to the Commissioner postponement for field examination. On July 7 I was informed by letter from the Land Office that the Cunningham cases would go to trial at once, and that the evidence would be submitted to Commissioner Dennett without having the Alaska Land Office pass on the claims first. *I believe that no precedent can be found in the entire history of the Land Office for such action.*

On the 16th I received a telegram from the Land Office saying Mr. Sheridan would report to assist me in the trial. Mr. Ballinger was then in Seattle, and I went to see him and called his attention to my written demand for a field examination. *Mr. Ballinger said he thought the Cunningham group would admit that the land was being developed as a whole.* I telegraphed to Commissioner Dennett that, at the suggestion of the Secretary of the Interior, I wanted to know whether my report (urging field examination) had been considered when the last telegram was sent. In reply, on the 17th, the Land Office wired that Mr. Sheridan would report to take full charge of the cases.

At that time I felt very despondent about the outcome of these cases. My conversation with Secretary Ballinger, the fact that Mr. Dennett was to be the judge in the case, and the difficulties I had had with the Land Office in my preparation of the cases, led me, without consulting my superiors, to appeal to the Department of Agriculture to intervene. This it did, and requested an adjournment until a field examination could be made.

On July 17, 1909, Mr. Sheridan superseded me in charge of the Alaska land cases, and within four days after reaching Seattle reported, concurring in my recommendations and suggesting that the cases be postponed to allow the field examination to be made. In this period Commissioner Dennett frequently communicated with Secretary Ballinger on the subject of the postponement. In one of his letters to the Chief of Field Service at this time, Commissioner Dennett said:

"Sheridan has gone over the cases thoroughly and thinks that the evidence which it is hoped to gain from Kennedy's visit to Alaska will be very material, and therefore it is the best to postpone until October 15. I have concurred, anticipating your acquiescence by the character of your telegram to me. *The Forestry can be blamed for the action in the matter. . . .*

"Sheridan has taken charge of the Cunningham case, and impresses me very favorably; I think he can handle it against any rival they may bring against him. The rest of the Alaska cases are in a bad mess. *Glavis is very much enthused on the proposition of canceling them all and getting the lands back in cold storage, and this is just what will happen unless Congress helps out.*"

THE LAND OFFICE TELLS THE TRUTH

In another letter to the Chief of the Field Service, Mr. Dennett wrote: *"Glavis has these coal cases on the brain and can not see anything but just one line. I have told him how it looks to us, and have reminded him of everything we have done for him, and it looks as if he were returning our favors by not standing by us as he ought."*

On July 22 Mr. Dennett telegraphed from Seattle to Secretary Ballinger: "Advise telegraphing Schwartz authorizing him to delay issuing notices in important cases subject our talk here until Sheridan can examine evidence collected."

On July 23 Mr. Ballinger telegraphed Mr. Dennett: "Considering my personal reluctance to direct proceedings in Alaska coal cases you should make necessary direction to Schwartz."

THE ALASKA COAL LANDS ARE IN DANGER IN BALLINGER'S HANDS

It was at this time that I laid the facts in my possession regarding the Cunningham cases before the President. The President has chosen to treat my report as a charge of criminality. I made no such charge, nor do I make it now. The President's letter is a defense of Mr. Ballinger and Mr. Dennett from charges not made in my report to him. I was not investigating either Mr. Ballinger or Mr. Dennett, but *the Alaska coal cases. Because I knew that these cases were to come before Mr. Dennett and that there was no appeal from his decision save to Secretary Ballinger, because Secretary Ballinger had stated he would not act in these cases and because the next ranking officer of the department was Assistant Secretary Pierce, who had signed the decision which Mr. Wickersham had overruled, I believed the Alaska coal cases were in danger.* The President has seen in this nothing but overzeal and insubordination on my part, and an opportunity to praise the Secretary of the Interior. I have not been informed what answer the Department of the Interior has made to my statement, *but the public will judge whether I am right in thinking the Alaska coal claims are still in danger.*

FINAL REPORT FROM THE REPUBLICAN MAJORITY
ON THE BALLINGER INVESTIGATION*
1911

President Taft upheld Ballinger against the charges made by Glavis and carried forward by journalists like Norman Hapgood, editor of Collier's, who likened the incident to an American Dreyfus case. Glavis was discharged. When Pinchot continued to press the case against Ballinger, Taft fired the Chief Forester.

The administration was unable to forestall a full-scale congressional investigation, but the Republican majority on the committee give Ballinger a clean bill of health. Taft did not keep him as Secretary in the face of a reelection fight, however.

Despite the majority report, the Pinchot-Ballinger controversy ballooned into a full-scale attack of the Pinchot supporters upon the Taft administration. The break with the conservationists helped inspire the effort of Theodore Roosevelt to oust Taft as the Republican nominee and Taft's subsequent campaign on the Progressive ticket, which insured the election of Woodrow Wilson.

The voluminous hearings and report of the special joint committee which made the Ballinger investigation are difficult to highlight. Reprinted here are the portions of the report giving the conclusions of the Republican majority of the joint committee.

The charges against Mr. Ballinger appear to have had their origin in a strong feeling of animosity created by a supposed difference in policy respecting the conservation of natural resources. The accusers evidently had this policy very deeply at heart and were evidently disposed to take a most unfavorable view of the character and motives of anyone whom they supposed to be opposed to their views. They thus came to regard Mr. Ballinger with suspicion and to regard the most natural and innocent acts occurring in the ordinary course of department administration as furnishing evidence of some sinister purpose. A great mass of evidence has been produced in the effort to support this view of Mr. Ballinger's conduct. That the whole field of evidence has been covered we can not doubt, since for weeks we listened to all the petty squabbles and jealousies of the subordinates in the Interior Department and the Forest Service, and were even furnished with the information secretly secured from Mr. Ballinger's confidential stenographer who had charge of his private papers and took down the dictation of his private correspondence. The evidence has wholly failed to make out a case. Neither any fact proved nor all the facts put together exhibit Mr.

*Sen. Doc. 719. 61st Cong., 3rd sess., 89–92.

Ballinger as being anything but a competent and honorable gentleman, honestly and faithfully performing the duties of his high office with an eye single to the public interest.

Aside from our conclusions upon the several matters hereinbefore referred to and stated in detail, our general conclusions upon the charges made against Secretary Ballinger are as follows:

First. That the charges and insinuations against him in regard to the Cunningham coal-land entries or other coal-land claims in Alaska are not justified and his conduct in respect thereto is not justly censurable.

Second. That he was, under the circumstances stated, fully justified in revoking the Indian cooperative agreement referred to.

Third. That the restoration of water-power sites by Secretary Ballinger was made in good faith and not in enmity to the Government and policy of conservation of natural resources but pursuant to an honest opinion as to the legality of the withdrawals in which many Members of the Senate and House, as well as many competent and disinterested authorities in private life, agree with him; that the question is a doubtful one and in the opinion of the committee the withdrawals could not be justified on the broad grounds of supervisory power which had been alleged in their support, and Secretary Ballinger is not censurable for having or acting on his honest opinion thereon. That the rewithdrawal of the portions of the lands in question necessary to enable Congress to act, and for that purpose only, was justifiable; and that no injury appears to have been done to the Government or the cause of conservation by either the restorations or rewithdrawals.

Fourth. That in view of the opinion of the Attorney-General he was justified in abandoning the use of the so-called water-users' cooperative certificates, in connection with the reclamation of arid lands.

Fifth. That the administration of the reclamation law presented features justly subject to criticism. More projects were undertaken than the money in hand would complete, some projects applied to little or no Government land and were wholly or chiefly for the benefit of private lands. In some cases the cost was greatly in excess of what settlers had been led to expect, and the scope of the work had been enlarged beyond the cash resources contemplated by the statute by the use of so-called cooperative certificates of doubtful legality. These things called for active investigation, criticism, and corrective measures so far as practicable on the part of the Secretary of the Interior. No unfair criticism or improper conduct on Secretary Ballinger's part has been shown nor any action by him not within the sound discretion of the head of the Interior Department in the faithful performance of his duty.

Sixth. That he is not an enemy of, nor hostile to, a reasonable and judicious policy of conservation; and that no ground whatever has been shown justifying the opinion that he is not a faithful and efficient public officer.

Seventh. A. The entire known coal fields of Alaska, covering more than 8,000,000 acres, is still in Government ownership. Not an acre has been patented to any corporation or person. Several hundred claims of 160 acres each were heretofore located, but most of the locators did not proceed to entry, and the time for doing so under the law having expired, their claims have lapsed. Substantially the only important exceptions are the so-called Cunningham claims, 33 in number, covering an aggregate of 5,280 acres, or about one-fifteenth of 1 per cent of the known coal field. All the coal land in Alaska has been withdrawn from entry since November 12, 1906. From that time to the present it has been and still is impossible for anyone to make a coal location or initiate a new claim to coal land there. Your committee, therefore, find that the interests of the people of the United States as owners of the Alaska coal field are not threatened or endangered under existing conditions.

B. The 33 Cunningham claimants, having made their locations before November 12, 1906, paid to the Government in 1907 sums aggregating $52,800, covering the Government price of $10 per acre under the law at the time their locations and entries were made. Patents to these claimants have been and are withheld, pending a decision as to alleged frauds or irregularities. While it is within the province of this committee to pass upon the conduct of public officials who have thus far dealt with these claims, it is not within our authority, and would, indeed, be improper for us to pass upon the merits of the claims, and thus prejudge them while they are pending. If they are regular, patents should be allowed. If they are fraudulent, the claims should be canceled. The claimants are entitled to an impartial judgment upon their rights in the premises. In ordinary course, this judgment would be rendered by the Commissioner of the General Land Office, with an appeal to the Secretary of the Interior, or the Assistant Secretary acting in his place. Your committee find no reason to doubt that those officers would decide these cases fairly and impartially; but the nature and wide publication of the charges and imputations referred to in this report would inevitably impair the confidence, both of the claimants and of the public, in the impartiality of such a decision. For that reason your committee recommend the enactment of a law for the transfer of these and any other cases involving claims to Alaska coal lands to an appropriate court of the United States for hearing and decision.

C. The conditions above stated, while adequately safeguarding the Government ownership of Alaska coal lands, are a serious hindrance to the proper and desirable development of the Territory and unjust to residents of Alaska and to such worthy citizens of the United States as may seek there a field for honest and legitimate enterprise. The resources of Alaska can not be made generally available for the benefit of mankind without the use of coal. Unable to buy or obtain coal from Government lands, the people there are now obtaining coal from distant States and foreign countries at prices ranging from $12 to $24 per ton. It is not sensible to require the importation of coal at such enormous expense while these vast coal fields are at hand. Such a course must end sometime if the coal of Alaska is ever to be of value to anyone. Your committee believe that it would be the height of unwisdom to permit these great coal fields to be monopolized, or gathered into the private ownership of a few for speculative purposes. As they increase in value, the increment should inure to the benefit of all the people. To bring about this result, and at the same time put an end to the unreasonable condition now existing, your committee recommend that the Government refuse to sell these lands, but that, retaining their ownership, it shall grant leases at fair royalties for periods limited, but long enough, and covering areas large enough, to justify the necessary investments upon sound business principals, and thus secure the opening and operation of sufficient mines to meet the necessities of Alaskan consumption; afford relief from the present outrageous prices paid by consumers, and at the same time afford some revenue to the Government. We recommend legislation to that end, and that, pending such legislation, the existing withdrawal from entry of the Alaska coal lands be continued.

Knute Nelson
Frank P. Flint
Geo. Sutherland
Elihu Root
Samuel W. McCall
Marlin E. Olmsted
Edwin Denby

"DID BALLINGER DECEIVE THE PRESIDENT?"*
1911

The Democratic minority of the special joint committee made it very clear that they believed Ballinger did deceive President Taft.

On November 4, 1909, Mr. Pinchot addressed a letter to the President charging that Mr. Ballinger was actually hostile to conservation policies. (Compl., 28.) On November 6, 1909, Mr. Garfield wrote the President on the same line. (Compl., 31.) Both these letters were forwarded to Mr. Ballinger.

In his letter to the President of November 15, 1909, in reply to the foregoing communications, Mr. Ballinger says, speaking of the officers of the Reclamation Service (Compl., 37):

> As none of said officers have ever intimated any such idea to me, and it is unfair to assume that they are so regardless of their obligations to their responsible head as to secretly indulge in criticism to an officer who has no legal right to interfere in their affairs, etc.

No doubt the language last above refers to Mr. Pinchot. But what of the facts stated herein? Is it true, as here stated, that Mr. Newell or Mr. Davis never intimated to the Secretary that the Reclamation Service had lost his support? We think it is not.

Mr. Newell contradicts it (1943, 1965, 1978) and Mr. Davis also contradicts it (1766). In conveying to him the very ideas which the Secretary says were not even intimated to him, Mr. Davis says:

> I told him then in as strong language as I felt politeness and the proper respect would permit that his whole course since he had been announced as Secretary of the Interior had been subversive of the interests of efficiency in the Reclamation Service, and tended to its disintegration.

In the matter of the restoration of lands withdrawn by Mr. Garfield the evidence is even clearer. The President, in his letter exonerating Mr. Ballinger, says with reference to these restorations,

> soon after you became Secretary of the Interior you brought this order to my attention, and said that it included a great deal of land that had no water-power sites on it; . . . that you had applied to the Reclamation Bureau to know whether it was desired for reclamation purposes and what their recommendation was in the premises, *and that they recommended* that it be returned to the public domain [italics ours]. (1189.)

In his direct testimony Mr. Ballinger reiterates this statement. (3688.)

Mr. Ballinger's attention is called to the testimony of Davis, to the effect that the Secretary directed him—Davis—to recommend restorations (3687), and he

---

*Sen. Doc. 719, 61st Cong., 3rd sess., 142–47.

says (3688): "I made no such order as that at any time," and further down the page he says: "I did not give them any direction at all." Again he says (4194): "The restoration movement began with the Reclamation Service." Now, mark you, on page 4198, he admits that the initiation of the movement is properly attributed to him, and he assumes all the responsibility for it, and that his direction to the reclamation officers as to what should be done in the premises was tantamount, possibly, to an order. Mr. Davis makes it very plain (1734) that the restorations up to and including April 16, except three small ones, were made on the initiative and by the order of Mr. Ballinger, including all these shown on page 86 of S. D., 248. (See also 1699, 1736–1737.)

Mr. Newell says (1964) that Mr. Ballinger's statement quoted above is not correct; that he (Newell) never recommended any restorations. So that Newell, Davis, and Ballinger himself directly and specifically contradict the Secretary's statement to the President, which statement the latter acted upon as true in deciding the controversy and ordering the discharge of Glavis.

Mr. Ballinger also shifts his ground as to his purpose concerning restorations. At first he did not have restorations in mind when making the withdrawals (1736–1737, 4799), but in his letter of November 15, to the President, he says he should have had the withdrawals and restorations made concurrently. (Compl., 33.)

The Ronald letter furnishes another instance of Mr. Ballinger's insincerity with the President. This letter was written by Mr. Ballinger's former law partner, Mr. Ronald, to Dr. Lyman Abbott, editor of the Outlook, for the purpose of inducing him to retract some editorial comment upon Mr. Ballinger's connection, while out of office, with the Cunningham claims. There were three propositions announced in the editorial: (1) Special Agent Jones *did* made an adverse report on the Cunningham claims before they were clear listed; (2) the clear-listing order was suspended through the intervention of Glavis; (3) Mr. Ballinger, with full knowledge of the alleged fraudulent character of these claims, urged legislation (the Cale bill) which would have benefited the claimants.

Mr. Ronald, in his letter to Doctor Abbott, denied the truth of all three propositions, and it appears his denials were based solely on marginal comments made by Mr. Ballinger in the marked copy of the Outlook sent Ronald by Mrs. Ballinger.

Opposite proposition 1 was the comment: "Not these claims."

Opposite proposition 2 was the comment: "No."

Opposite proposition 3 was the comment: "No."

Mr. Ronald admits that if these propositions were true the charge of "bad taste" made by the Outlook would be logical. We have dealt already with all three of these propositions and shown that the evidence shows each of them to be true, and hence Judge Ronald's letter loses all force as a defense.

The remarkable thing about it is how Mr. Ballinger could bring himself to send this letter to the President, resting as it does on statements which the evidence shows to be manifestly and palpably erroneous; nay, untrue. A decent regard for the President's judgment and sense of fairness compels the belief that he was deceived in these as well as in other statements made to him by the Secretary, statements which he innocently accepted and acted on as true.

In another part of this statement we have mentioned what we believe to be deceptions practiced by Mr. Ballinger on the President relative to matters coming within the scope of this inquiry, and have no desire to unnecessarily extend this statement by repetition. Our conclusion is that Mr. Ballinger did, in the matters referred to, supress facts and misstate facts in his official intercourse with the President, and that by such suppressions and misstatements he did deceive the President in material official matters.

Mr. Ballinger as a witness fell far short of what should be expected from a man in his high position. He was sadly lacking in frankness. His answers were often evasive and irresponsive. At times his manner was dictatorial, almost to the point of arrogance. Although at the outset he stated to the committee (Compl., 8) "the records, books, documents, and papers in the department or any of its bureaus, as well as my personal letters and files, are all freely at its service for the purpose of the investigation," yet, as a matter of fact, it was often only after repeated calls that material documents and correspondence was produced, and in some instances they would not have been produced at all but for accidental disclosures and knowledge obtained from other sources, as in the instance of the Ballinger-Perkins-Thomson correspondence and the so-called Lawler memorandum.

Mr. Ballinger professed to have but little knowledge of the details of affairs in his department work, claiming to deal with them only from the broad administrative point of view.

His testimony differed radically from that of many other witnesses on matters about which he should have knowledge, and there were frequent and irreconcilable differences in his own statements. We propose, by way of illustration, to point out a few of these differences or contradictions.

Mr. Ballinger's testimony concerning the so-called Lawler memorandum will be found, beginning on page 3685 (3865–3868). For instance (3865):

Q. What did Lawler take with him when he went to Beverly the latter part of the week?
A. A grip with some clothes in it. *I do not know what else he took.*
Q. You know that he did have something else.
Q. And some records. I know he had other things; yes.

Other answers on page 3866, figuratively speaking, dragged out of the Secretary, disclose that he knew very well what Mr. Lawler had with him on that occasion, but at first he denied knowledge of it, and then, bit by bit, step by step, as it became more and more apparent that his questioner had knowledge of the real facts, he admitted, rather than stated, what the fact was. His course of dealing with the Reclamation Service in the matter of restorations and withdrawals, and his statement to the President in connection therewith, which has been already noticed, is equally uncandid, wherein he specifically, and contrary to known facts, tells the President the withdrawals were recommended by the Reclamation Service.

There are numerous instances, too, where he contradicts, or is contradicted by, other witnesses under circumstances which forbid the acceptance of his version. For instance, Mr. Davis says that when Mr. Ballinger ordered Director Newell to submit lists for restoration, that Newell asked for instructions in writing (1700) and that the Secretary promised to give them. Newell corroborates Davis. (1948.)

Mr. Ballinger says this is a misstatement, that no such demand was made, and no such promise given. (3688.) The weight of probability must be added to the weight of numbers in this case. Mr. Davis and Mr. Ballinger differ squarely as to whether the latter instructed the former to direct Lind not to hurt Mr. Perkins's feelings. (1793, 3678.) But as the instructions to Lind—written by Davis —contained such a direction, it is highly probable, in view of all the antecedent and subsequent circumstances, that Mr. Davis is right. They also differ openly as to whether Davis mentioned the Huffer report on Perkins to the Secretary, and asked if he wanted to see it. Davis says (1793) he did so ask; Ballinger says (3679–3680) this is not true.

We have already pointed out sharp conflicts of statements between Mr. Ballinger and "this man Hoyt." Mr. Ballinger says (4120) Hoyt did not tell the truth. Later he modifies this language, but not the thought. We do not agree with him. Mr. Hoyt impressed us as a truthful and honorable man, entirely worthy of credit, who told the truth simply because it was the truth. We have also pointed out and discussed sharp conflicts of statements between Mr. Ballinger and Mr. Glavis, notably the Davis affidavit. Mr. Ballinger also contradicts Jones (3565), Kerby (4446), and Garfield (3582–3583) on points already noticed, when, in our judgment, the weight of the evidence is against him. We would place ourselves in a ridiculous, if not a contemptible position, if we did not conclude that these and other parallel instances seriously affect the weight to be given Mr. Ballinger's testimony.

We are aware that in the transaction of the departmental business there will necessarily be a vast amount of detail work which it would be impossible for the Secretary or the head of a great bureau to keep track of, and that he is, to a great extent, dependent on subordinates for the carrying out of these details, and that he must as a matter of course sign many communications without reading when they come to him properly initialed. But in our opinion this furnishes no explanation or excuse in the matter of the Cunningham coal claims. The course of the correspondence covered so long a period, the drift and meaning of it was so uniform and tended so steadily and consistently in one direction as to show that it was the result of a fixed and settled policy which originated in and was approved by those at the head of the department.

Mr. Ballinger, it is true, frankly avows his responsibility for the acts of his subordinates (3575), but even if he did not he would have to be held responsible for them. If the management of the Department of the Interior was such as to justify an inference of bad faith in handling the public domain or any part of it and the Secretary knew of it, he is unfit for the place; and if the department was managed in that way without his knowledge, he is unfit from a want of capacity.

After a careful, thorough, and, we believe, an impartial examination of the whole record, we feel constrained to make the following findings based on the evidence:

1. That the evidence does not show that Mr. Ballinger drew up an escrow agreement in the Watson Allen matter, and we exonerate him from that accusation.

2. That the evidence does not show any conspiracy against Mr. Ballinger, and that the alleged conspiracy had no existence in fact; that what has been referred to as a conspiracy was merely the efforts of certain persons to thwart and prevent the Secretary of the Interior and the officers of the General Land Office from accomplishing what these persons believed to be the fraudulent transfer of very valuable public property from the Government to certain private interests, and to prevent the making of radical and injurious changes in the management of the Reclamation Service, then in a high state of efficiency.

3. That Gifford Pinchot and L. R. Glavis were faithful and efficient agents of the Government and the people, devoted to their work and conscientious in the discharge of their onerous duties and in the rendition of their valuable services; that their protests and actions restrained the officers of the Interior Department and prevented the consummation of a great public wrong, and that their conduct throughout was wholly in the interest of the people.

4. That in his statement of September 13, 1909, to the President, and in other correspondence and communications with the President, Mr. Ballinger has been frequently uncandid, that he has on a number of occasions been guilty of duplicity, and that his conduct in the premises was intended to and did have the effect of deceiving the President.

5. That Mr. Ballinger, while Commissioner of the General Land Office, "clear listed" the so-called Cunningham claims on insufficient evidence, and under circumstances which convince us he was aware of the existence of other material evidence which he did not call for, or consider, and which if considered should surely have prevented the clear listing of the claims, and we find that

in so clear listing said claims Mr. Ballinger showed either a lamentable want of capacity and competence or such a disregard for the rights of the public as amounted to bad faith.

6. That as Commissioner of the General Land Office Mr. Ballinger prepared the Cale bill, that he appeared before a committee of the House of Representatives in advocacy of said bill, and that he then knew and intended that said bill, if it became a law, would have the effect of validating the said Cunningham coal claims and other coal claims in Alaska, which claims were in fact fraudulent because of noncompliance with the law.

7. That after resigning as Commissioner of the General Land Office Mr. Ballinger resumed the practice of the law in Seattle, Wash., that he became interested as an attorney in cases which were pending in the General Land Office while he was commissioner, that in at least one such case he received compensation for his services, and that such conduct was highly reprehensible.

8. While Secretary Ballinger claims that because of his professional connection with some of the claimants he turned the consideration and control of all Alaska coal-claim matters over to Mr. Frank Pierce, his assistant, we find from the evidence that he did not in fact do so, but, on the contrary, improperly continued his connection therewith, and from time to time was consulted by his subordinates, and gave directions with regard to said claims.

9. That he aided the movement to force the Cunningham claims to a hearing before the Government was ready to proceed and properly produce its evidence, and placed the management of the cases in the hands of an inexperienced young attorney with full knowledge of the importance of the cases, both as to the great value of the property and the fact that, being the first cases of their kind, and there being hundreds of other Alaska coal claim cases, they were, in a measure, test cases.

10. That he encouraged insubordination in the Reclamation Service by trying to discredit the director or head of that service in a general way, and by issuing orders direct to subordinates in said service without either consulting or communicating with the proper person or persons in charge of said service.

11. That he condoned highly improper official conduct on the part of Mr. Perkins, head of the Chicago office of the Reclamation Service, and, instead of reprimanding him, or of asking for his resignation, as recommended by the director and chief engineer, he retained him in the same office with increased power, directing him to report to Director Newell, whose authority he had already overridden.

Under these circumstances, and in view of these findings, which are forced upon us by a consideration of the evidence, we are under the stern necessity of making a further finding—

12. That Mr. Ballinger has not been true to the trust reposed in him as Secre-

tary of the Interior; that he is not deserving of public confidence, and that he should be requested by the proper authority to resign his office as Secretary of the Interior.

Respectfully submitted.

Duncan U. Fletcher
William E. Purcell
Ollie M. James
James M. Graham

"AN AMERICAN DREYFUS"?*
May 25, 1940

Secretary of the Interior Harold Ickes reopened the Ballinger case with this article in The Saturday Evening Post. *Ickes' introduction to the article is incomplete, in that it does not mention his breaks with Glavis and Pinchot, which preceded the writing of this article.*

After Ickes had hired Glavis as a special auditor of the Public Works Administration, the man Secretary Ballinger had fired, turned out to be too suspicious for Secretary Ickes, who said of Glavis and his staff, "These investigators have become persecutors, man hunters, and they are just as eager to hunt and drag down members of my staff as they are lobbyists and crooked contractors."

During this same period Pinchot was effectively leading the fight against Ickes' plan to transfer the Forest Service back to the Department of the Interior.

NOT GUILTY!

RICHARD A. BALLINGER—
AN AMERICAN DREYFUS

This article is by way of confession and penance. In writing it, I am hoping that a grave wrong may be righted. For thirty years I have clung to the commonly held opinion that one of my predecessors in the Department of the Interior, Richard A. Ballinger, was a dishonest and unworthy public official. For three decades I have believed Ballinger guilty; possibly because my friends were among those who broke Ballinger, and my political enemies were among those who supported him. My conviction of Ballinger's guilt was so deep that until a few months ago I continued to place particular trust in Gifford Pinchot, the chief offender against Ballinger, and one of my earliest acts upon becoming Secretary of the Interior was to give an important position to Louis R. Glavis, the agent whose investigations had led to the Ballinger conspiracy. Both Pinchot and Glavis had been dismissed from their jobs by the Taft Administration— unjustly, we were all convinced then.

It was not until recently, when I read Henry F. Pringle's scholarly Life and Times of William Howard Taft, that I was shocked into the awareness that during all of these years, in common with the American people, I had been doing a grave injustice to an innocent man. The facts of the Ballinger case, as outlined in the Pringle book, were such as to lead me to reopen the record. I had the

*Harold L. Ickes, "Not Guilty! Richard A. Ballinger—An American Dreyfus," *The Saturday Evening Post* (May 25, 1940), 9–11, 123–29.

departmental records—both printed and unprinted—brought down from the heavily laden shelves and thoroughly gone over by fresh minds that had no prejudices or preconceived notions. The result of this research is enough to show that in the Ballinger case, which was a principal factor in the destruction of the Taft Administration and broke Secretary Ballinger's life and career, we have a veritable American Dreyfus affair. President William Howard Taft called the conspiracy against Ballinger "the most cruel persecution that I am familiar with in modern times." Today, thirty years after these words were written, I am inclined to agree.

Of the chief characters in the Ballinger drama, only four are still living. Let me introduce them: Justice Louis D. Brandeis, the retired justice of the Supreme Court, even then a brilliant lawyer. Gifford Pinchot, a friend of Theodore Roosevelt and Chief Forester in the latter's Administration as well as that of Taft. H. H. Schwartz, who was chief of the Field Service of the Interior Department's Land Office, and today is United States senator from Wyoming. Finally, Louis R. Glavis, the young investigator in the Land Office whose work in connection with the Cunningham coal claims in Alaska formed the basis for Pinchot's conspiracy. Incidentally, all four of the men mentioned are living in the capital.

The story is so bewildering and so legally entangled that the record of the hearings covers 7600 printed pages, which add up to almost 4,000,000 words. The reader may get some notion as to the vastness of the subject if he will recall that an ordinary novel consists of about 75,000 words. The Ballinger tragedy, in short, covers the printed space of fifty novels.

The central figure of the amazing story, Richard Achilles Ballinger, was born in Iowa in 1858. His career was that of a hard-working and able professional man. At first he practiced law at Kankakee, Illinois, then he moved to the rising city of Seattle where, at the age of forty-six, he became the reform mayor. His record was excellent. He became a legal expert, especially in mining law.

In 1907, Ballinger's schoolmate at Williams College, James R. Garfield, who was Theodore Roosevelt's Secretary of the Interior, asked his friend in Seattle to take over the commissionership of the General Land Office. It required a personal appeal from President Theodore Roosevelt to make him give up his growing law practice and come to Washington. It is important to remember that Ballinger, who is indelibly associated in the public mind with the Taft Administration, was a personal appointee of Theodore Roosevelt's. It should also be kept in mind that the reason for Ballinger's appointment was that he believed in Roosevelt's conservation policies. "I pride myself," Ballinger wrote to the editor of The Outlook in May, 1909, "on being a follower of Theodore Roosevelt in the matter of conservation of public utilities in all parts of the country where the Government can regularly and legally interfere."

Later, Ballinger was to be destroyed politically by Pinchot on the trumped-up charge that he was an enemy of conservation.

As commissioner of the Land Office, Ballinger was immediately faced with a complicated situation in connection with pending claims to coal lands in Alaska. Ballinger could not know it, but these Alaskan lands were loaded with political dynamite, capable of being detonated with devastating effect. Over 900 of these claims had been filed and were awaiting final action. Of these, thirty-three had been filed on October 24, 1905, by one Clarence Cunningham, acting for himself and thirty-two others.

Let it be said once and for all that although Glavis and Pinchot put an astronomical value upon these Alaskan coal lands, they were then, as they are today, almost valueless; especially the Cunningham claims. The coal, if mined, could never have reached market by any development of transportation to date.

It has never even been alleged that Ballinger knew anything about these Clarence Cunningham claims before coming to Washington. Yet, within two or three years, they were to be the corpus delicti upon which Pinchot was to convict Ballinger in the court of public opinion and decree that his public life was to be hanged by the neck until dead.

THE CUNNINGHAM CLAIMS

Upon entering the Land Office, Ballinger received an inquiry about the Cunningham claims from ex-Governor Moore, of Washington, who represented the claimants. Having no personal knowledge of them, Commissioner Ballinger, following the usual practice, called on Chief of the Field Service H. H. Schwartz to advise him as to their status.

After examining the case, Schwartz advised Ballinger there was nothing in the file against these claims and that they had been favorably reported on by Special Agent Love. Schwartz recommended that the claims be clear-listed— *i.e.,* approved for patenting; Ballinger concurred and an appropriate order was made.

Unknown to Ballinger, Schwartz or anyone else in the Department of the Interior, there was a secret agreement between the Cunningham claimants whereby they acted as an association, although they purported to act separately and independently. In the aggregate their claims included 5280 acres of public coal lands. Under the law at that time an association of claimants could not acquire more than 640 acres. Therefore, since the Cunningham group filed their claims as the result of a clandestine joint enterprise, such claims were illegal.

Glavis—a young field investigator who was a good friend of Schwartz and who, at the latter's instance, had been sent by Ballinger to investigate Alaskan coal claims in general—developed a suspicion that the Cunningham claimants were not acting independently, as they pretended, and, as soon as he received word from the General Land Office that the claims had been clear-listed, he recommended that their approval be held up, and that he be given a chance to investigate them more fully. Ballinger, after a conference with Secretary Garfield, immediately suspended the order approving the claims and instructed Glavis to proceed with further investigation. Glavis wrote that he would submit a report within a few months. This was 1907.

Ballinger's action in suspending the order approving the Cunningham claims *ended his connection, as Land Commissioner, with these claims.*

Less than two months after suspending the clear-listing of the Cunningham claims, Ballinger resigned the commissionership in order to return to private practice in Seattle. He left Washington with the warm praise of Secretary Garfield and the regrets of President Roosevelt, who wrote him:

"I greatly regret that you feel obliged to leave the public service, but I thank you heartily for the admirable work you have done during your altogether too brief term of office. When I requested you to come here I realized the sacrifice I was asking you to make, and I appreciate the genuine patriotism which made you willing to suffer the discomfort and the pecuniary loss incident to your accepting the office."

There is nothing in the record to show that, when he resumed his private law practice in Seattle, Ballinger ever expected again to find himself in public office. He was not a rich man and he realized that he had reached the time of life when he ought to build up his law practice. He had already learned from experience the havoc that even a temporary occupation of public office can wreak upon a growing practice. As a private citizen engaged in the practice of the law, there was no reason why he should not take cases involving matters in the Department of the Interior. There was no prohibition against his practicing law before that department. [When the writer became Secretary of the Interior in 1933, for the first time he issued an order providing that no former member of the staff could practice before the department until the lapse of two years after his resignation or separation.]

THE SEEDS OF TROUBLE

In September, 1908, Clarence Cunningham applied to Lawyer Ballinger for advice in connection with his Alaskan coal-land claims. Glavis, it seems, had found a journal containing facts which, unless explained, might militate against these claims. This discovery was made by Glavis after Ballinger had resigned as Land Commissioner. Cunningham asked Ballinger to prepare an affidavit explaining the journal. Ballinger did this, and on his way east on other business, called on Secretary Garfield at his home at Mentor, Ohio, and presented the affidavit to him. The two discussed the matter in a perfunctory way. For his services in preparing and presenting the affidavit, he received from Cunningham a fee of $200 or $250. This included expenses.

This was the only connection that Ballinger had with the Cunningham claims during the interval between his resignation as commissioner of the General Land Office and his appointment as Secretary of the Interior.

The Cunningham claims were still in the files of the Land Office when, in

1909, President Taft succeeded Roosevelt, and Ballinger became Secretary of the Interior in place of Garfield. Thereby hangs a dramatic story and a significant one in connection with the Ballinger-Pinchot affair.

Theodore Roosevelt on one occasion told me the following (I do not pretend to quote the exact words, but to give the general effect): After Taft was elected President, he said to Roosevelt, "Theodore, I intend to keep all of your Cabinet who will stay." President Roosevelt replied, "You won't want to do that, Will. You ought to select for your Cabinet your own friends; men of whom you have knowledge and in whom you have confidence."

"Well, in any event," replied Taft, "I intend to keep Garfield."

Roosevelt was pleased at the prospect of his close friend, Garfield, carrying on as Secretary of the Interior. The President asked Taft if he might inform Garfield of his intentions, because he knew that the latter was somewhat anxious about his future. Taft authorized Roosevelt to tell Garfield; whereupon the Secretary of the Interior renewed the lease on his Washington home. This was the last that Garfield ever heard from Taft, directly or indirectly, on the subject of the Secretaryship of the Interior. Subsequently, Taft denied this story. I may say from my personal knowledge that both Garfield and his friend, Pinchot, believed that it was Taft's intention to retain Garfield. They had been told this by Theodore Roosevelt. The Rough Rider never forgave Taft for failing to carry out what he had regarded as a voluntary promise. Pinchot likewise never forgave Taft and undoubtedly carried over his feeling of disappointment and dislike to Taft's appointee, Ballinger.

As Secretary of the Interior, Ballinger, as an honorable man, realized that his previous connection with the Cunningham claims, even though both proper and unimportant, might be embarrassing now. Accordingly, on March 15, 1909, he issued an order assigning "all matters from the General Land Office" to First Assistant Secretary Pierce. To make doubly sure, Secretary Ballinger gave verbal directions to his private secretary, Carr, as well as to Pierce and to Schwartz, never to refer any question in connection with the Cunningham claims to himself personally. Once, when Schwartz submitted a letter dealing with the Cunningham claims to Ballinger, the latter refused to sign it and scolded his subordinate. "He," Schwartz later testified, "told me that he had told me once or twice before that he did not want any of these Cunningham letters to come to him for signature or action. He was a little bit crusty about it for a moment."

The evidence shows that First Assistant Secretary Pierce had full and exclusive charge of the Cunningham claims during the time that Ballinger was Secretary of the Interior.

A DELAYED REPORT

We must now go into the field with Glavis. Instructed to investigate the Alaskan coal claims in 1907, Glavis was still there in 1909, despite repeated orders from Schwartz, of the Land Office, that he bring in his report. On April 20, 1909, the month after Ballinger became Secretary of the Interior, Schwartz ordered Glavis to report in sixty days. Glavis replied that he would do better than this. As a matter of fact, Glavis had no intention of finishing the investigation. He wanted to continue to delay because he felt that Land Office Commissioner Dennett—the official authorized to pass on any evidence Glavis might submit and then make a decision as to the validity of the Cunningham claims was biased in favor of the Cunningham claimants. Therefore, when the time came for him to make his report he asked for still another extension. Then Schwartz became convinced that Glavis was jockeying, and wired him: "Reports must be submitted at once."

At that point Glavis appealed directly to Secretary Ballinger, who was then at his home in Seattle. Ballinger was sympathetic with Glavis' demand for more time and advised him to wire Schwartz for an extension. But Schwartz had had enough of Glavis' procrastinations. He wired Glavis sharply that "case already consumed more time and expense of men than any other case pending. Investigation cannot proceed indefinitely." Glavis was informed another agent was on his way to "bring case to a prompt . . . close."

At this point, the plot, as the novelists used to say, began to thicken. Upon the scene entered Chief Forester Gifford Pinchot and his merry men of the Forest Service.

For Glavis, thwarted in his efforts to keep Dennett from passing on the claims, now appealed to the Forest Service to procure more delay, and at the same time threw a carefully baited hook in the direction of Chief Forester Pinchot, who had built up a strong propaganda organization and had taken the stage as the exclusive and, necessarily, righteous crusader in the realm of conservation. Upon receipt of the wire from Schwartz, Glavis promptly got in touch with A. C. Shaw, legal aide of Gifford Pinchot. In asking the "cooperation" of the Forest Service, Glavis artfully appealed to Pinchot's consuming ambition. Glavis made the absurd claim that the Alaskan coal lands contained "practically the future coal supply of the United States," and suggested that it would be an easy matter to persuade Congress to turn these coal lands over to the Forest Service.

To a man of Pinchot's ambitions, the temptation was irresistible.

That Glavis was guilty of insubordination in appealing to an official outside his own department apparently did not concern Chief Forester Pinchot, whose own subsequent course was one of high disloyalty to his own superior, the President of the United States.

When Glavis asked for the intervention of an outside department, the investigation of the coal claims passed from the sphere of the objective and the factual to the realm of devious intrigue. Glavis received encouragement from the Pinchot group in the Department of Agriculture, for two weeks later he wrote a strange letter to his immediate superior, Schwartz:

"Keep out of the [Cunningham] cases; if possible let Dennett [commissioner of the Land Office] fight his own battles. It is my opinion that neither Dennett nor B. [Ballinger] will last long, and surely not Dennett—he cannot remain in. *Now, under such circumstances, why not you try for the place?* [Italics mine. H. L. I.] I am quite sure you can win out."

As Assistant Attorney General Oscar Lawler, in a memorandum to President Taft, later pointed out, when Glavis wrote this letter he knew full well that every step taken in connection with the Cunningham claims had been initiated by Schwartz. Now Glavis asked Schwartz to intrigue for the position of his immediate chief. Glavis himself might have been in line for Schwartz's place.

Two days after this letter to Schwartz, Glavis wired to Pinchot's aide, Shaw: "Have damaging and conclusive evidence showing official misconduct of parties." Ballinger and Dennett were the "parties" referred to.

Later, during the congressional investigation, Glavis was to admit that he had no "damaging" or "conclusive" evidence against his superiors, who were still unaware that a pit was being dug for their feet. Before the congressional committee, Vertrees, Ballinger's lawyer, asked Glavis: "So you wish to say to this committee that . . . you have observed nowhere a corrupt motive as to any of these officers?"

Glavis: "Well, yes, sir; there was no evidence of it."

Vertrees: "You saw no corrupt conduct on the part of any of them, but . . . what you did mean to say . . . in your array of facts . . . was simply that you did not think the affairs of the Government—that is, those conducted by the Interior Office—were in safe hands."

Glavis: "Yes, sir."

It was loudly publicized charges of official misconduct, to support which there was a total lack of evidence, that made the Pinchot intrigue one of the dirtiest in American history. And Pinchot's actions were all the more reprehensible because of his exceptional background of family, wealth, associations and education.

The question is: Why did Pinchot display such eagerness to persecute and discredit Secretary Ballinger? In my opinion, Pinchot was moved by a bitter, personal hostility. He actually referred to Ballinger as a "yellow dog." This animus had its beginnings in Ballinger having taken Garfield's place as Secretary of the Interior. All of Garfield's friends resented his loss of the office, and this feeling was aggravated when the new Secretary reversed many of Garfield's policies in the field of conservation. It is important to remember that Pinchot's influence with Garfield had been paramount during the latter's incumbency.

Pinchot met Glavis in Spokane and advised him to present his material to President Taft. It was Pinchot's aide, Shaw, who was responsible for the drafting of the charges to present to the President. Glavis signed them. The Chief Forester vouched for Glavis in a letter of introduction to the President, saying, "I have known him (Glavis) for several years."

Later, on the witness stand, Pinchot was forced to admit that he had seen Glavis but once, and did not believe that he would have recognized him had he seen him again.

Taking with him Pinchot's letter, Glavis went to the President and laid before him his charges against Secretary Ballinger, Assistant Secretary Pierce, Commissioner Dennett and Chief of the Field Service Schwartz, with respect to the Cunningham claims. Glavis, in short, was attacking the whole Department of the Interior.

BRANDEIS' BRIEF

Well, what were these charges, you ask? No one can say definitely, to this day. In the report and accompanying papers submitted to President Taft on August 18, 1909, Glavis made no specific accusation, but through innuendo and implication charged that Ballinger, Pierce, Dennett and Schwartz had taken steps to aid the Cunningham claimants to obtain patents based on claims which these officials knew or had reason to believe were fraudulent. As to Ballinger, the charges implicit in the report were: (1) That his action as an attorney in preparing the affidavit for Cunningham which he submitted to Secretary Garfield in 1908 was *improper* because it involved the use by Ballinger, to the detriment of the Government, of facts concerning the Cunningham claims which came into his possession while he was Land Commissioner; and (2) that although Ballinger, as Secretary, formally withdrew from any official connection with the Cunningham claims, yet actually he continued to exercise his influence with regard to them and to interfere with Glavis' efforts to defeat the claims.

If it had been possible to make the charges definite, surely a lawyer of Brandeis' talents would have done so in his brief at the close of the investigation, yet here is what appears in that brief:

> The paramount question for the committee to decide is this:
> 1. Is the Department of the Interior in safe hands? Or, to put the issue more specifically,
> 2. Have the conduct and associations of Mr. Ballinger been such, are his character and his conceptions such, that he may be safely continued as a trustee of our vast public domain and the manager of the reclamation and other services, the administration of which will so largely determine the welfare of the present and of future generations of Americans? Or, to put the issue in still other words,
> 3. Is Mr. Ballinger a man singleminded, able, enlightened, and courageous, so zealously devoted to the interests of the common people, so vigilant and resolute in resisting the insidious aggressions of the special interests, that to him may be safely intrusted the carrying forward of the broad policy of conservation of our national resources?

Probably in all our history no such flimsy accusations have ever been presented against high Government officials. Nevertheless, President Taft scrupulously examined the record. No one has ever accused Taft, whether as Chief Executive or as Chief Justice, of lack of thoroughness in considering a case at law: and in its very essence, this was a case at law.

[271]

President Taft not only went into the record thoroughly himself, he also consulted George W. Wickersham, the Attorney General, and asked Lawler, the Assistant Attorney General, to prepare a memorandum for his signature. The President, however, did not use Lawler's memorandum because he thought it too severely critical of Pinchot and Glavis. Attorney General Wickersham, who was one of the leading lawyers of his generation, went through the record and wrote a forthright letter to the President:

"The insinuations or charges of improper action on the part of Secretary Ballinger, Assistant Secretary Pierce, Commissioner Dennett, or Chief of the Field Division Schwartz are, in my opinion, entirely disproved. . . . The record clearly shows that Secretary Ballinger was scrupulously careful not in any respect to act upon these [Cunningham] claims. . . . Glavis' 'report' and summary abound in contradictions and misstatements. They omit to a degree that amounts to absolute suppression letters, telegrams, and other documents. . . . His action in appealing to the Forest Service of the Department of Agriculture to intervene in these cases . . . was a breach of all proper discipline. . . . Glavis' actions appear to have been founded upon a wholly exaggerated sense of his own importance, and a desire for personal advancement, rather than on any genuine desire to protect the interests of the Government."

FRONT-PAGE CONDEMNATION

Two days after this stinging appraisal of Glavis' charges, on September 13, 1909, President Taft sweepingly exonerated Ballinger and the other officials whom Glavis had maligned. The President directed Secretary Ballinger to dismiss Glavis for "filing a disingenuous statement, unjustly impeaching the official integrity of his superior officers."

Now hell really did break loose. In any ordinary case, the Glavis-Pinchot house of cards would have collapsed from the blasts of such honorable and distinguished lawyers as Taft and Wickersham. But this was not an ordinary case. Personal animus, devouring ambitions, conniving schemes to defeat Taft and renominate Roosevelt in 1912, all got tangled up in the Ballinger affair. Moreover, Taft, Ballinger and Wickersham were babes in the woods so far as public opinion was concerned. Pinchot, on the other hand, was skillful in the arts of propaganda, and he was assisted by such able propagandists as Norman Hapgood and Mark Sullivan. These men were aided and abetted by the United States Forest Service. With such forces against him, Ballinger never had a fighting chance; especially since he persisted in trying his case on the law and the facts.

After President Taft had exonerated Ballinger, Chief Forester Pinchot concluded that the President of the United States himself could not be trusted. Pinchot and his group, therefore, decided that they had "no alternative but to appeal to the people by giving further publicity to the material contained in the Glavis report." The Pinchotites fired a broadcast against Ballinger in an article in Collier's Weekly. [Collier's Weekly, it should be emphasized, is under different management today and should not be held responsible for the nefarious part it played thirty years ago in the anti-Ballinger conspiracy.] The hand that signed the article was that of Glavis.

The press of the country now took up the hue and cry. Front pages screamed scandal. In headlines, news articles, editorials and cartoons, the hapless Secretary of the Interior was pilloried as an unfaithful, dishonest public official. The press, be it said to its shame, condemned an innocent and upright man without giving him a chance to be heard. And having crucified him, brutally and unjustly, in order to cover its own shame, it was to see to it that incontrovertible evidence adduced before the later hearing of the joint congressional committee would not be permitted to vindicate him in public estimation. So effective was the campaign that Ballinger has remained condemned in public opinion to this very day. It is my earnest hope that this article will help to clear the fair name of an honest man.

There was only one course open to Ballinger, who suffered under this ferocious attack, and that course he took. In December, 1909, the Secretary of the Interior asked the United States Senate to make a full and open investigation of him and his department. Only thus could he hope to expose the Glavis prevarications and the Pinchot propaganda. Every document in the case was submitted to the joint committee that was subsequently set up. Among the papers were two which were to cause considerable trouble. One was the unused memorandum by Assistant Attorney General Lawler. Another was Attorney General Wickersham's opinion, which was dated September 11, 1909, two days before Taft's letter exonerating Ballinger. Actually the Wickersham opinion was prepared one month after Taft's letter was written. This technicality was to have unfortunate reverberations.

A RESOLUTION TO INVESTIGATE

Pinchot, however, could not wait for the findings of Congress. In his mind Ballinger was condemned, and necessarily this concluded the matter.

One must marvel at President Taft's patience with a subordinate who ran the gamut from impertinences to defiant insubordination. Taft knew that Theodore Roosevelt was right when he had characterized Pinchot as a "fanatic." The President also knew of his own knowledge that the Chief Forester was hoping to win the martyr's crown.

Nevertheless, even the capacious Taft could stomach Pinchot no longer. On January 7, 1910, Taft dismissed him for insubordination. Immediately a loud outcry went up from the well-organized ranks of the Pinchot zealots. "We are living in an age of supreme hypocrisy," Taft wrote bitterly to his brother, Horace, "when the man who can yell loudest . . . has the advantage."

In the midst of all the turmoil, on January 19, 1910, Congress passed a joint resolution "authorizing an investigation of the Department of the Interior . . . and of the Forest Service, in the Department of Agriculture." Here was recognition that Forestry was up to its neck in the intrigue against Ballinger and the Department of the Interior. However, no investigation of Forestry was made. It was too expert in its use of "stop thief."

LEGAL PALADINS

The congressional committee consisted of six members from each House. The caliber of the committee may be gathered from the fact that one of the members was Sen. Elihu Root, who had been Theodore Roosevelt's Secretary of State and was considered perhaps the greatest lawyer in the country. Another was Sen. George Sutherland, who later became an Associate Justice of the Supreme Court.

A rumor spread that if the congressional committee should exonerate Ballinger, the latter would file a libel suit against Collier's Weekly for damages in the amount of $1,000,000. Accordingly, the editors of Collier's called a conference in the office of Henry L. Stimson in New York to discuss the situation. Among those present, in addition to Stimson, were Pinchot, Garfield, Norman Hapgood and Glavis. The degree of their fear lest Ballinger be exonerated is measured by the talent of the lawyer they decided to engage. Louis D. Brandeis, one of the most brilliant members of the bar, was called in to represent Glavis. Collier's paid Brandeis a $25,000 fee.

George Wharton Pepper, a distinguished Philadelphia lawyer, was employed to represent Pinchot. Here were a formidable pair of lawyers to appear against Ballinger. On his part, Ballinger seemed rather listless about looking to his own defense. It was Taft who finally insisted that he engage counsel and, in fact, employed one for him—Vertrees, whom Taft had known and respected when he was a judge in Ohio. Unfortunately, Mr. Vertrees was no longer young, and he was quite without knowledge of or experience with the law as it related to public lands. Counsel fees were to cost Ballinger a total of $20,000—a staggering sum for a man who was necessarily living beyond his inadequate salary and who had no other resources.

Early in the investigation, members of the committee sought to learn exactly what were the charges against Ballinger. They never found out. The following colloquy is typical:

> Mr. DENBY: Mr. Brandeis, we are seeking to ascertain specifically what the charges were. Do I understand now that they are, first, that upon certain occasions Mr. Ballinger acted improperly, but not entirely corruptly, and upon other occasions he designed and intended to act corruptly, but was prevented from doing so by Mr. Glavis?

Mr. BRANDEIS: I have not used the word 'corrupt' in any case. I say without due regard to the interests of the people and the Government.

Mr. DENBY: That is, he acted improperly; that is, without propriety; secondly, he intended to act without due regard to the public interests—in other words, corruptly—and was prevented from doing so by Mr. Glavis.

Mr. BRANDEIS: I have not used the word 'corruptly.' I have desired to bring, and I desire now to bring, without characterization, the facts before the committee. It seems to me an extremely solemn matter, a matter in which no charge of corruption ought to be made, but that your committee should, with due regard to the seriousness of its situation, pass upon the details of this evidence and determine whether the great trust of holding this land for the people of the country, present and future generations, *is in safe hands. I carefully refrained from making any charges except* the charge of the facts, in order that you gentlemen may, upon the fullest consideration, determine what the safety and the honor of the country demand.

A member of the President's Cabinet was on trial for his public reputation. It is difficult to imagine any man more unfortunately situated. In the circumstances, one might have expected the press of the country at least to withhold judgment until all of the evidence was in. However, throughout the investigation a large number of newspapers and magazines continued to print inflammatory articles attacking Ballinger.

Out in front, as usual, was Collier's Weekly. It devoted a major part of its issue of March 24, 1910, to the case. Its cover carried a picture of a bill of indictment across which was written "The American People versus Richard A. Ballinger." One of the articles was entitled "Ballinger—Shyster." Thus, recklessly, irreparable damage was done to the reputation of an innocent man.

Apparently there was nothing to which the break-Ballinger cabal would not stoop. While the investigation was in progress there was a meeting one night at Pinchot's home in Washington, attended by Garfield, Brandeis and Frederick Kerby. The latter, a young man, was private stenographer to Secretary Ballinger, and was familiar with the circumstances surrounding the writing of the Lawler memorandum. How he came to associate himself with this group has never been disclosed.

THE LAWLER MEMORANDUM

The Lawler memorandum; its preparation; the degree to which President Taft had relied upon it in writing his letter exonerating Ballinger; and the mystery surrounding its whereabouts until it was finally produced by the Attorney General during the investigation, were built by the clever Brandeis into a major issue that almost exceeded in importance the question that the joint committee was supposed to be investigating—namely, whether Ballinger had acted improperly in connection with the Cunningham claims. As a matter of fact, no circumstance connected with the preparation of the Lawler memorandum was, of itself, important. The astute Brandeis made an enormous mountain out of this molehill.

But however much Brandeis built up from the circumstances surrounding the Lawler memorandum, it was as nothing compared with the havoc that he wrought in connection with the predated opinion of Attorney General Wickersham to President Taft. It was really to this innocent technicality that Ballinger owed his political crucifixion.

Brandeis discovered this discrepancy in dates. There is no criticism of him for making the most of it. After all, he was a lawyer representing a client, and he was having a tough enough time trying to convict Ballinger on Pinchot's and Glavis' "facts." Brandeis probably felt that he could rely implicitly upon the data presented to him for use against Ballinger by men whom he trusted. Possessing a keen interest in public affairs and being something of a crusader in the interest of good government, Brandeis naturally sympathized with those who attacked or pretended to attack corruption in high places. It may well be that Brandeis did believe that Wickersham's opinion was an afterthought and was prepared, ex post facto, to support the President's exoneration of Ballinger. But this constituted no crime; it was no evidence of negligent administration on the part of Ballinger. The Wickersham opinion, whether it was predated or postdated or dated contemporaneously, had nothing to do with the innocence or guilt of Ballinger.

Both Taft and Wickersham, in letters to the committee, explained the circumstances surrounding the dating of the Wickersham opinion. Taft said: "The conclusions which I reached were based upon my reading of the record and were fortified by the oral analysis of the evidence and the conclusions which the Attorney General gave me, using the notes which he had made during his reading of the record. I was very sorry not to be able to embody this analysis in my opinion, but time did not permit. I therefore directed him to embody in a written statement such analysis and conclusions as he had given me, file it with the record, and date it prior to the date of my opinion, so as to show that my decision was fortified by his summary of the evidence and his conclusions therefrom." Wickersham's explanation was to the same effect. He added that "There is no mystery about the matter and nothing which may not be freely stated." But these were too late to do Ballinger any good. Brandeis' assaults convinced the people that the President of the United States and his Attorney General were trying to cover up. From this they reasoned that there must be something to cover up, and so, in their minds, they convicted Ballinger. At the very least, as they saw it, there was "a conspiracy" to protect Ballinger, and the inevitable conclusion from this was "why go to so much trouble to protect him unless he is in desperate need of protection?"

That Norman Hapgood—and perhaps Louis D. Brandeis also—was not unaware of the basis upon which Ballinger stood convicted in public opinion is evidenced by the following quotation from Hapgood's The Changing Years [Farrar & Rinehart, Inc.] (page 189):

> By the time the . . . committee saw the document [the Lawler memorandum] produced, the whole country had decided that there was a conspiracy to shelter Ballinger at any cost. The rest was comparatively easy. As Mr. Brandeis said to me: "It was the lying that did it. If they had brazenly admitted everything, and justified it on the ground that Ballinger was at least doing what he thought best, we should not have had a chance. Refusal to speak the truth is the history of many a downfall."

Ballinger made matters worse for himself by being an inept witness. The most that can be said against him is that he failed to answer questions forthrightly, when full and frank answers could have done him no harm. If all of the facts in connection with these two documents had been fully disclosed, the committee still would have had no facts whatever reflecting upon Ballinger's official conduct. It was indeed tragic that a man whose official conduct was above reproach should have been adjudged guilty in the public mind because of unfortunate circumstances that occurred during the course of the investigation and which, *it cannot be too strongly urged,* had no connection with the charges under which Ballinger had been brought to trial.

PINCHOT ON THE STAND

Ironically, although press and public condemned Ballinger, there was no such righteous indignation, or even much interest, in the case of Pinchot, who, under cross-examination, was forced to confess that he had told what was not true about Ballinger. Before he started his testimony, he was permitted to read a brief prepared statement. In effect it charged Ballinger was an *enemy to conservation,* that the report made by Glavis to the President proved Ballinger to be an *unfaithful* public servant, and that Ballinger's explanation to the President of his action in reversing Garfield's policy as to water-power sites was *essentially false.* Squirming, Pinchot attempted to justify specific misstatements of fact by complaining that they had been told to him "by a man in whom he had had confidence." Unwillingly, he admitted that he knew nothing of his own knowledge that would reflect upon Secretary Ballinger in any way with respect to, first, Alaskan coal-land matters; or, secondly, Ballinger's representations to the President; or, thirdly, the charge that Ballinger was an enemy of conservation. But the press largely ignored these forced and public confessions.

On the witness stand Glavis did little better than Pinchot. Under cross-examination he also made a series of admissions which destroyed his whole fabric of imagined or trumped-up charges against Ballinger and the Interior Department. Glavis conceded that none of Secretary Ballinger's subordinates except one was guilty of intentional wrongdoing or bad faith. He would not include Land Commissioner Dennett. He also admitted that, in accusing Ballinger and other Interior officials of "official misconduct," he did not mean that they were guilty of corrupt conduct, but that they "were not properly protecting the Government's interests as Government officials should do." One might question Glavis' qualifications to be the final judge of what was "proper."

The testimony of Schwartz deserves special attention. As chief of the Field Service, he had more to do with the Cunningham claims than any other official. On the witness stand Schwartz completely absolved Ballinger of all the charges made against him in connection with these claims. Today, thirty years later, Senator Schwartz is still of the opinion that Ballinger was "an able, conscientious and efficient public official, rendering service in the public interest." [As he wrote me in a letter dated March 14, 1940.] So convincing was Schwartz's testimony that Brandeis declined to cross-examine him.

After the hearings, the majority of the congressional committee came to exactly the same conclusions as had President Taft and Attorney General Wickersham. It found that the evidence had wholly failed to make out a case. The committee exonerated Secretary Ballinger absolutely and unequivocally.

"Neither any fact proved," so read the committee's conclusion, "nor all the facts put together exhibit Mr. Ballinger as being anything but a competent and honorable gentleman, honestly and faithfully performing the duties of his high office with an eye single to the public interest."

The committee thus completely exonerated Ballinger, but refused to pass any opinion upon the validity of the Cunningham claims. Later, the Land Office investigation of the Cunningham claims was completed, and Dennett decided that the claims were invalid—an opinion concurred in by Ballinger's successor, Secretary Fisher.

But so effective had the Pinchot conspiracy been in its propaganda that public opinion turned a deaf ear to the findings of the committee. In the minds of the people Ballinger stood condemned.

Presently Taft became the victim. So inflamed was public opinion against the innocent Secretary of the Interior that great pressure was brought to bear to oust him from office. It is to President Taft's eternal credit that he stood stanchly by his crucified Secretary. Taft, in fact, was outraged to the depth of his soul by the campaign of slander against Ballinger. The President's letters show character of sterling integrity. "If I were to turn Ballinger out," Taft wrote to the Rev. Dr. P. A. Baker, "in view of his innocence and in view of the conspiracy against him, I should be a white-livered skunk. I don't care how it affects my Administration. . . . Mr. Ballinger has done nothing of any kind that should subject him to criticism. He has been made the object of a despicable conspiracy, in which unscrupulous methods have been used that ought to bring shame to the faces of everyone connected with it. . . . Life is not worth living and office is not worth having if, for the purpose of acquiring public support, we have to either do a cruel injustice or acquiesce in it."

TAFT'S INTEGRITY

In another letter, to Pres. Cyrus Northrop, of the University of Minnesota, Taft wrote with equal bluntness: "I cannot get rid of Ballinger and don't want to get rid of him, because there never was such an unjust conspiracy against a man as there has been against him. I am not in the habit of quitting and I don't propose to go back on a man just because somebody has done him an injury when he has done nothing to deserve the opprobrium that is heaped on him and the Administration. . . ."

This integrity and loyalty on the part of Taft helped to lose him the presidency in 1912. For not only did the anti-Ballinger Camorra turn on the President and discredit his Administration, as he fully expected that it would, but Pinchot also poisoned Theodore Roosevelt's mind against his former friend and protégé in the White House. It is not too much to say that the Ballinger scandal cost Taft and the Republicans the presidency in 1912.

But Pinchot and the foresters have not remained satisfied with their stupendous, but shameful, victory. For thirty years Pinchot has been relentlessly attacking the name and the memory of Ballinger. He will not even permit his victim to lie quietly in his grave. At the same time the former Chief Forester, now seventy-five years old, has never let up in his remorseless campaign of smearing the Department of the Interior.

As for Ballinger, his health broke under the strain. In March, 1911, he resigned. "My health and financial interests," Ballinger sadly wrote to President Taft, "have greatly suffered, to the extent that I can no longer sustain the burden." He left for Seattle, followed by the warmest wishes and admiration of President Taft, and resumed his law practice. Be it said to the credit of Seattle's citizens that they treated Ballinger as the honorable and upright citizen that his whole public life showed him to be. He died in 1922, respected by his community.

All who knew Ballinger testify to his honesty and his ability. Franklin K. Lane, Woodrow Wilson's Secretary of the Interior, wrote of his predecessor: "Like some others . . . I came here with somewhat of a prejudice against Secretary Ballinger. The results of my survey, however, have been a revelation to me. I find that Secretary Ballinger in his administration did the very things that I had hoped to do, and had established a highly efficient organization. . . . I can find nothing to improve. He exhibited rare judgment of men in selecting subordinate executives. . . . If, when I leave the department, there remains behind me that fine sense of loyalty, devotion and affection that exists throughout the department towards Judge Ballinger, I shall feel abundantly rewarded. . . . I have gone through this department with a fine-tooth comb and have analyzed with care every act of his when he was Secretary of the Interior and . . . I find every one of them meeting all tests of patriotism, service to the public, and the preservation of national interests."

VINDICATION

Alexander Vogelsang, First Assistant Secretary of the Interior in Wilson's Administration, gave Ballinger a similar testimonial. On March 15, 1921, Vogelsang wrote to Ballinger, confessing that, like Secretary Lane, he had started out with a prejudice against him. "Before my retirement," Vogelsang concluded, "I feel it due to myself to say that my experience here and the study and investigation I have made convince me that my impressions and my opinion were entirely wrong and unjust to you; that I now believe that you were an able administrator and as honest in impulse and action as any man who has ever held the office of Secretary of the Interior; and that in the history of the Republic the high-water mark of cruelty and injustice to a public officer was reached in the treatment accorded to you."

In the Taft collection of manuscripts in the Library of Congress may be found the President's letter of March 7, 1911, to Richard Ballinger: ". . . With the hypocritical pretense that they did not accuse you of corruption, in order to avoid the necessity . . . of a definitely formulated charge of some misconduct, they showered you with suspicion and by the most pettifogging methods exploited to the public matters which had no relevancy to an issue either of corruption or inefficiency in office, but which, paraded before an hysterical body of headline readers, served to blacken your character and to obscure the proper issue of your honesty and effectiveness as a public servant. . . ."

With all these words, I, another successor to Ballinger in the Department of the Interior, am in full accord. From the beginning, I was on the side of Pinchot in the Ballinger affair. I continued to believe that my predecessor had been a faithless, if not a crooked, public official, until I had reason to distrust the words and public actions and the intellectual integrity of a man who had been my close political and personal friend for more than a decade.

After I had read Henry F. Pringle's admirable work, things began to click in my mind. A study of the record now has convinced me that Ballinger was the victim of what President Taft justly called a "despicable conspiracy."

In all honor, the American people owe both contrition and atonement to the maligned memory of a fine and devoted public servant.

CONTROLLING THE MISSISSIPPI

THE FIRST FLOOD CONTROL ACT*
March 1, 1917

The Ransdell-Humphreys bill to provide a federal flood control program on the lower Mississippi River became law after a long and prolonged campaign by the citizens of the Mississippi Valley. Since the plans of the Mississippi River Commission referred to in the bill were limited to the construction of levees as a preventive measure for floods, the program authorized was far from comprehensive river development.

To help pass the bill the proponents agreed to passage of the Newlands Waterways Commission bill, and added to their bill a provision for flood control on the Sacramento River. The law is memorable as the first direct federal commitment to flood control.

An Act to provide for the control of the floods of the Mississippi River and of the Sacramento River, California, and for other purposes.

Be it enacted by the Senate and House of Representatives of the United States of America in Congress assembled, That for controlling the floods of the Mississippi River and continuing its improvement from the Head of the Passes to the mouth of the Ohio River the Secretary of War is hereby empowered, authorized, and directed to carry on continuously, by hired labor or otherwise, the plans of the Mississippi River Commission heretofore or hereafter adopted, to be paid for as appropriations may from time to time be made by law, not to exceed in the aggregate $45,000,000: *Provided,* That not more than $10,000,000 shall be expended therefor during any one fiscal year.

(a) All money appropriated under authority of this section shall be expended under the direction of the Secretary of War in accordance with the plans, specifications, and recommendations of the Mississippi River Commission as approved by the Chief of Engineers, for controlling the floods and for the general improvement of the Mississippi River, and for surveys, including the survey

*39 *Statutes at Large,* 948-51.

from the Head of the Passes to the headwaters of the river, and a survey of the Atchafalaya Outlet so far as may be necessary to determine the cost of protecting its basin from the flood waters of the Mississippi River either by its divorcement from the Mississippi River or by other means, and for salaries, clerical, office, traveling, and miscellaneous expenses of the Mississippi River Commission.

(b) That no money appropriated under authority of this section shall be expended in the construction or repair of any levee unless and until assurances have been given satisfactory to the commission that local interests protected thereby will contribute for such construction and repair a sum which the commission shall determine to be just and equitable but which shall not be less than one-half of such sum as may have been allotted by the commission for such work: *Provided,* That such contributions shall be expended under the direction of the commission, or in such manner as it may require or approve, but no contribution made by any State or levee district shall be expended in any other State or levee district except with the approval of the authorities of the State or district so contributing.

(c) Any funds which may hereafter be appropriated under authority of this Act for improving the Mississippi River between the Head of the Passes and the mouth of the Ohio River, and which may be allotted to levees, may be expended upon any part of said river between the Head of the Passes and Rock Island, Illinois.

(d) No money appropriated under authority of this Act shall be expended in payment for any right of way for any levee which may be constructed in cooperation with any State or levee district under authority of this Act, but all such rights of way shall be provided free of cost to the United States: *Provided,* That no money paid or expense incurred by any State or levee district in securing such rights of way, or in any temporary works of emergency during an impending flood, or for the maintenance of any levee line, shall be computed as a part of the contribution of such State or levee district toward the construction or repair of any levee within the meaning of paragraph (b) of this section.

That the watercourses connected with the Mississippi River to such extent as may be necessary to exclude the flood waters from the upper limits of any delta basin, together with the Ohio River from its mouth to the mouth of the Cache River, may, in the discretion of said commission, receive allotments for improvements now under way or hereafter to be undertaken.

Upon the completion of any levee constructed for flood control under authority of this Act, said levee shall be turned over to the levee district protected thereby for maintenance thereafter; but for all other purposes the United States shall retain such control over the same as it may have the right to exercise upon such completion.

SACRAMENTO RIVER, CALIFORNIA

Sec. 2. That for controlling the floods, removing the débris, and continuing the improvement of the Sacramento River, California, in accordance with the plans of the California Debris Commission, the Secretary of War is hereby authorized and directed to carry on continuously, by hired labor or otherwise, the plan of said commission contained in its report submitted August tenth, nineteen hundred and ten, and printed in House Document Numbered Eighty-one, Sixty-second Congress, first session, as modified by the report of said commission submitted February eighth, nineteen hundred and thirteen, approved by the Chief of Engineers of the United States Army and the Board of Engineers for Rivers and Harbors, and printed in Rivers and Harbors Committee Document Numbered Five, Sixty-third Congress, first session, in so far as said plan provides for the rectification and enlargement of river channels and the construction of weirs, to be paid for as appropriations may from time to time be made by law, not to exceed in the aggregate $5,600,000: *Provided,* that not more than $1,000,000 shall be expended therefor during any one fiscal year.

(a) All money appropriated under authority of this section shall be expended under the direction of the Secretary of War, in accordance with the plans, specifications, and recommendations of the California Débris Commission, as approved by the Chief of Engineers, for the control of floods, removal of débris, and the general improvement of the Sacramento River: *Provided,* That no money shall be expended under authority of this section until assurances have been given satisfactory to the Secretary of War (a) that the State of California will contribute annually for such work a sum equal to such sum as may be expended annually therefor by the United States under authority of this section; (b) that such equal contributions by the State of California will continue annually until the full equal share of the cost of such work shall have been contributed by said State; and (c) that the river levees contemplated in the report of the California Débris Commission, dated August tenth, nineteen hundred and ten, will be constructed to such grade and section and within such time as may be required by said commission: *Provided further,* That said State shall not be required to expend for such work, for any one year, a sum larger than that expended thereon by the United States during the same year: *And provided further,* That the total contributions so required of the State of California shall not exceed in the aggregate, $5,600,000.

(b) All money contributed by the State of California, as herein provided, shall be expended under the direction of the California Débris Commission and in such manner as it may require or approve, and no money appropriated under authority of this section shall be expended in the purchase of or payment for any right of way, easement, or land acquired for the purposes of this improvement, but all such rights of way, easements, and lands shall be provided free of cost to the United States: *Provided,* That no money paid or expense incurred therefor shall be computed as a part of the contribution of the State of California toward the work of improvement herein provided for within the meaning of paragraph (a) of this section.

(c) Upon the completion of all works for flood control herein authorized the said works shall be turned over to the State of California for maintenance thereafter; but for all other purposes the United States shall retain such control over the same as it may have the right to exercise upon such completion.

GENERAL PROVISIONS

Sec. 3. That all the provisions of existing law relating to examinations and surveys and to works of improvement of rivers and harbors shall apply, so far as applicable, to examinations and surveys and to works of improvement relating to flood control. And all expenditures of funds hereafter appropriated for works and projects relating to flood control shall be made in accordance with and subject to the law governing the disbursement and expenditure of funds appropriated for the improvement of rivers and harbors.

All examinations and surveys of projects relating to flood control shall include a comprehensive study of the watershed or watersheds, and the report thereon in addition to any other matter upon which a report is required shall give such data as it may be practicable to secure in regard to (a) the extent and character of the area to be affected by the proposed improvement; (b) the probable effect upon any navigable water or waterway; (c) the possible economical development and utilization of water power; and (d) such other uses as may be properly related to or coordinated with the project. And the heads of the several departments of the Government may, in their discretion, and shall upon the request of the Secretary of War, detail representatives from their respective departments to assist the Engineers of the Army in the study and examination of such watersheds, to the end that duplication of work may be avoided and the various services of the Government economically coordinated therein: *Provided,* That all reports on preliminary examinations hereafter authorized, together with the report of the Board of Engineers for Rivers and Harbors thereon and the separate report of the representative of any other department, shall be submitted to the Secretary of War by the Chief of Engineers, with his recommendations, and shall be transmitted by the Secretary of War to the House of Representatives, and are hereby ordered to be printed when so made.

In the consideration of all works and projects relating to flood control which may be submitted to the Board of Engineers for Rivers and Harbors for consideration and recommendation, said board shall, in addition to any other matters upon which it may be required to report, state its opinion as to (a) what Federal interest, if any, is involved in the proposed improvement; (b) what share of the expense, if any, should be borne by the United States; and (c) the advisability of adopting the project.

All examinations and reports which may now be made by the Board of Engineers for Rivers and Harbors upon request of the Committee on Rivers and Harbors relating to works or projects of navigation shall in like manner be made upon request of the Committee on Flood Control on all works and projects relating to flood control.

Sec. 4. That the salary of the civilian members of the Mississippi River Commission shall hereafter be $5,000 per annum.

Approved, March 1, 1917.

THE FLOOD CONTROL ACT OF 1928*
May 15, 1928

The lower Mississippi flood control bill that became law was far closer to the Jadwin plan than the Reid bill reported to the House. President Coolidge had made it clear that he would veto any bill which deviated far from the Jadwin bill cost. Public opinion in the country, seemingly unanimous for a federal flood control plan in the immediate aftermath of the flood the year before, had now begun to cool, and big city newspapers were calling every plan a "raid on the treasury."

The lower Mississippi flood control program has been based on the 1928 act, but, through the years, the law has been repeatedly modified, and the spending authorization increased. A system of reservoirs is now included on all of the major tributaries of the Mississippi. No major flood has occurred on the Mississippi since 1927.

An Act for the control of floods on the Mississippi River and its tributaries, and for other purposes.

Be it enacted by the Senate and House of Representatives of the United States of America in Congress assembled, That the project for the flood control of the Mississippi River in its alluvial valley and for its improvement from the Head of Passes to Cape Girardeau, Missouri, in accordance with the engineering plan set forth and recommended in the report submitted by the Chief of Engineers to the Secretary of War dated December 1, 1927, and printed in House Document Numbered 90, Seventieth Congress, first session, is hereby adopted and authorized to be prosecuted under the direction of the Secretary of War and the supervision of the Chief of Engineers: *Provided,* That a board to consist of the Chief of Engineers, the president of the Mississippi River Commission, and a civil engineer chosen from civil life to be appointed by the President, by and with the advice and consent of the Senate, whose compensation shall be fixed by the President and be paid out of the appropriations made to carry on this project, is hereby created; and such board is authorized and directed to consider the engineering differences between the adopted project and the plans recommended by the Mississippi River Commission in its special report dated November 28, 1927, and after such study and such further surveys as may be necessary, to recommend to the President such action as it may deem necessary to be taken in respect to such engineering differences and the decision of the President upon all recommendations or questions submitted to him by such board shall be followed in carrying out the project herein adopted. The board

*45 *Statutes at Large,* 534–39.

shall not have any power or authority in respect to such project except as herein-before provided. Such project and the changes therein, if any, shall be executed in accordance with the provisions of section 8 of this Act. Such surveys shall be made between Baton Rouge, Louisiana, and Cape Girardeau, Missouri, as the board may deem necessary to enable it to ascertain and determine the best method of securing flood relief in addition to levees, before any flood-control works other than levees and revetments are undertaken on that portion of the river: *Provided,* That all diversion works and outlets constructed under the provisions of this Act shall be built in a manner and of a character which will fully and amply protect the adjacent lands: *Provided further,* That pending completion of any floodway, spillway, or diversion channel, the areas within the same shall be given the same degree of protection as is afforded by levees on the west side of the river contiguous to the levee at the head of said floodway, but nothing herein shall prevent, postpone, delay, or in anywise interfere with the execution of that part of the project on the east side of the river, including rais-ing, strengthening, and enlarging the levees on the east side of the river. The sum of $325,000,000 is hereby authorized to be appropriated for this purpose.

All unexpended balances of appropriations heretofore made for prosecuting work of flood control on the Mississippi River in accordance with the provisions of the Flood Control Acts approved March 1, 1917, and March 4, 1923, are hereby made available for expenditure under the provisions of this Act, except section 13.

SEC. 2. That it is hereby declared to be the sense of Congress that the princi-ple of local contribution toward the cost of flood-control work, which has been incorporated in all previous national legislation on the subject, is sound, as recognizing the special interest of the local population in its own protection, and as a means of preventing inordinate requests for unjustified items of work having no material national interest. As a full compliance with this principle in view of the great expenditure estimated at approximately $292,000,000, hereto-fore made by the local interests in the alluvial valley of the Mississippi River for protection against the floods of that river; in view of the extent of national con-cern in the control of these floods in the interests of national prosperity, the flow of interstate commerce, and the movement of the United States mails; and, in view of the gigantic scale of the project, involving flood waters of a volume and flowing from a drainage area largely outside the States most affected, and far exceeding those of any other river in the United States, no local contribution to the project herein adopted is required.

SEC. 3. Except when authorized by the Secretary of War upon the recommen-dation of the Chief of Engineers, no money appropriated under authority of this Act shall be expended on the construction of any item of the project until the States or levee districts have given assurances satisfactory to the Secretary of War that they will (a) maintain all flood-control works after their completion, except controlling and regulating spillway structures, including special relief levees; maintenance includes normally such matters as cutting grass, removal of weeds, local drainage, and minor repairs of main river levees; (b) agree to accept land turned over to them under the provisions of section 4; (c) provide without cost to the United States, all rights of way for levee foundations and levees on the main stem of the Mississippi River between Cape Girardeau, Missouri, and the Head of Passes.

No liability of any kind shall attach to or rest upon the United States for any damage from or by floods or flood waters at any place: *Provided, however,* That if in carrying out the purposes of this Act it shall be found that upon any stretch of the banks of the Mississippi River it is impracticable to construct levees, either because such construction is not economically justified or because such construction would unreasonably restrict the flood channel, and lands in such stretch of the river are subjected to overflow and damage which are not now overflowed or damaged by reason of the construction of levees on the opposite banks of the river it shall be the duty of the Secretary of War and the Chief of Engineers to institute proceedings on behalf of the United States Government to acquire either the absolute ownership of the lands so subjected to overflow and damage or floodage rights over such lands.

SEC. 4. The United States shall provide flowage rights for additional destructive flood waters that will pass by reason of diversions from the main channel of the Mississippi River: *Provided,* That in all cases where the execution of the flood-control plan herein adopted results in benefits to property such benefits shall be taken into consideration by way of reducing the amount of compensation to be paid.

The Secretary of War may cause proceedings to be instituted for the acquirement by condemnation of any lands, easements, or rights of way which, in the opinion of the Secretary of War and the Chief of Engineers, are needed in carrying out this project, the said proceedings to be instituted in the United States district court for the district in which the land, easement, or right of way is located. In all such proceedings the court, for the purpose of ascertaining the value of the property and assessing the compensation to be paid, shall appoint three commissioners, whose award, when confirmed by the court, shall be final. When the owner of any land, easement, or right of way shall fix a price for the same which, in the opinion of the Secretary of War is reasonable, he may purchase the same at such price; and the Secretary of War is also authorized to accept donations of lands, easements, and rights of way required for this project. The provisions of sections 5 and 6 of the River and Harbor Act of July 18, 1918, are hereby made applicable to the acquisition of lands, easements, or rights of way needed for works of flood control: *Provided,* That any land acquired under the provisions of this section shall be turned over without cost to the ownership of States or local interests.

SEC. 5. Subject to the approval of the heads of the several executive departments concerned, the Secretary of War, on the recommendation of the Chief of Engineers, may engage the services and assistance of the Coast and Geodetic Survey, the Geological Survey, or other mapping agencies of the Government, in the preparation of maps required in furtherance of this project, and funds to pay for such services may be allotted from appropriations made under authority of this Act.

SEC. 6. Funds appropriated under authority of section 1 of this Act may be expended for the prosecution of such works for the control of the floods of the Mississippi River as have heretofore been authorized and are not included in the present project, including levee work on the Mississippi River between Rock Island, Illinois, and Cape Girardeau, Missouri, and on the outlets and tributaries of the Mississippi River between Rock Island and Head of Passes in so far as such outlets or tributaries are affected by the backwaters of the Mississippi: *Provided,* That for such work on the Mississippi River between Rock Island, Illinois, and Cape Girardeau, Missouri, and on such tributaries, the States or levee districts shall provide rights of way without cost to the United States, contribute 33⅓ per centum of the costs of the works, and maintain them after completion: *And provided further,* That not more than $10,000,000 of the sums authorized in section 1 of this Act, shall be expended under the provisions of this section.

In an emergency, funds appropriated under authority of section 1 of this Act may be expended for the maintenance of any levee when it is demonstrated to the satisfaction of the Secretary of War that the levee can not be adequately maintained by the State or levee district.

SEC. 7. That sum of $5,000,000 is authorized to be appropriated as an emergency fund to be allotted by the Secretary of War on the recommendation of the Chief of Engineers, in rescue work or in the repair or maintenance of any flood-control work on any tributaries of the Mississippi River threatened or destroyed by flood including the flood of 1927.

SEC. 8. The project herein authorized shall be prosecuted by the Mississippi River Commission under the direction of the Secretary of War and supervision of the Chief of Engineers and subject to the provisions of this Act. It shall perform such functions and through such agencies as they shall designate after consultation and discussion with the president of the commission. For all other purposes the existing laws governing the constitution and activities of the commission shall remain unchanged. The commission shall make inspection trips of such frequency and duration as will enable it to acquire first-hand information as to conditions and problems germane to the matter of flood control within the area of its jurisdiction; and on such trips of inspection ample opportunity for hearings and suggestions shall be afforded persons affected by or interested in such problems. The president of the commission shall be the executive officer thereof and shall have the qualifications now prescribed by law for the Assistant Chief of Engineers, shall have the title brigadier general, Corps of Engineers, and shall have the rank, pay, and allowances of a brigadier general while actually assigned to such duty: *Provided,* That the present incumbent of the office may be appointed a brigadier general of the Army, retired, and shall be eligible for the position of president of the commission if recalled to active service by the President under the provisions of existing law.

The salary of the president of the Mississippi River Commission shall hereafter be $10,000 per annum, and the salary of the other members of the commission shall hereafter be $7,500 per annum. The official salary of any officer of the United States Army or other branch of the Government appointed or employed under this Act shall be deducted from the amount of salary or compensation provided by, or which shall be fixed under, the terms of this Act.

SEC. 9. The provisions of sections 13, 14, 16, and 17 of the River and Harbor Act of March 3, 1899, are hereby made applicable to all lands, waters, easements, and other property and rights acquired or constructed under the provisions of this Act.

SEC. 10. That it is the sense of Congress that the surveys of the Mississippi River and its tributaries, authorized pursuant to the Act of January 21, 1927, and House Document Numbered 308, Sixty-ninth Congress, first session, be prosecuted as speedily as practicable, and the Secretary of War, through the Corps of Engineers, United States Army, is directed to prepare and submit to Congress at the earliest practicable date projects for flood control on all tributary streams of the Mississippi River system subject to destructive floods which projects shall include: The Red River and tributaries, the Yazoo River and tributaries, the White River and tributaries, the Saint Francis River and tributaries, the Arkansas River and tributaries, the Ohio River and tributaries, the Missouri River and tributaries, and the Illinois River and tributaries; and the reports thereon, in addition to the surveys provided by said House Document 308, Sixty-ninth Congress, first session, shall include the effect on the subject of further flood control of the lower Mississippi River to be attained through the control of the flood waters in the drainage basins of the tributaries by the establishment of a reservoir system; the benefits that will accrue to navigation and agriculture from the prevention of erosion and siltage entering the stream; a determination of the capacity of the soils of the district to receive and hold waters from such reservoirs; the prospective income from the disposal of reservoired waters; the extent to which reservoired waters may be made available for public and private uses; and inquiry as to the return flow of waters placed in the soils from reservoirs, and as to their stabilizing effect on stream flow as a means of preventing erosion, siltage, and improving navigation: *Provided,* That before transmitting such reports to Congress the same shall be presented to the Mississippi River

Commission, and its conclusions and recommendations thereon shall be transmitted to Congress by the Secretary of War with his report.

The sum of $5,000,000 is hereby authorized to be used out of the appropriation herein authorized in section 1 of this Act, in addition to amounts authorized in the River and Harbor Act of January 21, 1927, to be expended under the direction of the Secretary of War and the supervision of the Chief of Engineers for the preparation of the flood-control projects authorized to be submitted to Congress under this section: *Provided further,* That the flood surveys herein provided for shall be made simultaneously with the flood-control work on the Mississippi River provided for in this Act: *And provided further,* That the President shall proceed to ascertain through the Secretary of Agriculture and such other agencies as he may deem proper, the extent to and manner in which the floods in the Mississippi Valley may be controlled by proper forestry practice.

SEC. 11. That the Secretary of War shall cause the Mississippi River Commission to make an examination and survey of the Mississippi River below Cape Girardeau, Missouri, (a) at places where levees have heretofore been constructed on one side of the river and the lands on the opposite side have been thereby subjected to greater overflow, and where, without unreasonably restricting the flood channel, levees can be constructed to reduce the extent of this overflow, and where the construction of such levees is economically justified, and report thereon to the Congress as soon as practicable with such recommendations as the commission may deem advisable; (b) with a view to determining the estimated effects, if any, upon lands lying between the river and adjacent hills by reason of overflow of such lands caused by the construction of levees at other points along the Mississippi River, and determining the equities of the owners of such lands and the value of the same, and the commission shall report thereon to the Congress as soon as practicable with such recommendation as it may deem advisable: *Provided,* That inasmuch as the Mississippi River Commission made a report on the 26th day of October, 1912, recommending a levee to be built from Tiptonville, Tennessee, to the Obion River in Tennessee, the said Mississippi River Commission is authorized to make a resurvey of said proposed levee and a relocation of the same if necessary, and if such levee is found feasible, and is approved by the board created in section 1 of this Act, and by the President the same shall be built out of appropriations hereafter to be made.

SEC. 12. All laws or parts of laws inconsistent with the above are hereby repealed.

SEC. 13. That the project for the control of floods in the Sacramento River, California, adopted by section 2 of the Act approved March 1, 1917, entitled "An Act to provide for the control of the floods of the Mississippi River and of the Sacramento River, California, and for other purposes," is hereby modified in accordance with the report of the California Débris Commission submitted in Senate Document Numbered 23, Sixty-ninth Congress, first session: *Provided,* That the total amounts contributed by the Federal Government, including the amounts heretofore contributed by it, shall in no event exceed in the aggregate $17,600,000.

Sec. 14. In every contract or agreement to be made or entered into for the acquisition of land either by private sale or condemnation as in this Act provided the provisions contained in section 3741 of the Revised Statutes being section 22 of title 41 of the United States Code shall be applicable.

Approved, May 15, 1928.

REPORT FROM THE DEPARTMENT OF AGRICULTURE
ON FORESTS AND MISSISSIPPI FLOOD CONTROL*
February 11, 1929

After the 1927 flood, there was recalled the voice of Congressman Thomas McRae who, nearly forty years before, had sought reforestation programs to protect the lower Mississippi Valley from flooding. A report on forests and Mississippi flood control was prepared in the Department of Agriculture, but not submitted to the Congress until after action was completed on the 1928 flood control act. Reprinted here is a summary of the report.

The last paragraph of the "Conclusions" seems particularly moderate and reasonable in view of the conflicts which had developed over land treatment versus engineering works as the answer to flood prevention.

FINDINGS OF FACT[1]

The outstanding facts brought out by the study of the relation of the forest land in the Mississippi drainage basin to the general problem of floods appear to be the following:

The forests of the Mississippi Valley never covered more than 40 per cent of the total area of the drainage basin.

By necessary human use and by unnecessary abuse and neglect this proportion has been reduced until it is now about 20 per cent, or about 244,000 square miles.

A very small part of this total area of forest land is in a virgin condition, the remainder being largely cut-over, with 35,000 square miles so denuded of forest or other valuable growth as to be classified as "waste" or "idle" land.

About 115,000 square miles, of which 10,000 square miles are in the "idle" class, are in farm woodlands; and 129,000 square miles, of which 25,000 are "idle" or "waste," are within the commercial timberland class.

By reason of character of soil, topography, and precipitation the character and density of forest cover on certain of these lands have a direct relation to run-off or soil erosion or both, and on such areas forest destruction increases torrential run-off and causes serious erosion. Areas with such characteristics were therefore classified as "critical areas."

The regions classified as critical areas on the Mississippi drainage amount to 289,000 square miles, of which, upon the basis of the present tendency toward increase or decrease in the ability to help prevent floods, 64,000 square miles were found to be beneficial, 75,000 neutral, and 150,000 detrimental.

*H. Doc. 573, 70th Cong., 2nd sess., 48–51.
[1] Round numbers used generally.

The actual acreage of critical forest land within the regions outlined is about 150,000 square miles; and the approximate distribution by class is, beneficial, 35,000 square miles; neutral, 40,000 square miles; detrimental, 75,000 square miles.

With the exception of the lands within public forests and parks, amounting to 700 square miles in State ownership and 43,000 square miles gross in national ownership, the forests on critical areas are not contributing full service in the direction of flood control. This is due largely to injury by fires in commercial woodlands and to too heavy grazing in farm woodlands.

About 700 square miles of publicly owned forest land in the Mississippi Basin adjoin existing national forests and are similar to them in character and importance from the standpoint of preventing erosion and regulating stream flow.

The adequate protection of the forests in the Mississippi Basin, as recommended by the Senate Select Committee on Forestry and as authorized by section 2 of the Clarke-McNary law, would require an annual expenditure of $490,000 by the Federal Government and $1,470,000 by private owners and the States, making a total for the Mississippi drainage of $1,960,000 annually. The present (1928) expenditure by the Federal Government is $170,000 and by private owners and States $474,000.

The upper Mississippi wild life and fish refuge area, which is being purchased by the Federal Government, safeguards the narrowing of the river overflow channel as far south as Rock Island, Ill., and is therefore a favorable factor in future stream-flow regulation.

In addition to the critical forest lands 15,000 square miles of Bad Lands and 17,000 square miles of the Breaks (although treeless) should also be classified as critical areas because of their great contributions of silt to the Mississippi flood problem. The Bad Lands appear to be responsible for contributing an annual burden of silt aggregating 144,000,000 tons and the Breaks for contributing a somewhat smaller amount.

The loss of soil by erosion from cultivated fields is a serious menace not only to the channel of the Mississippi River but to the permanency of profitable agriculture in many parts of the valley which have thus far flourished through the virgin fertility of rapidly eroding soils.

RECOMMENDATIONS

The foregoing findings of fact lead inevitably to recommendations for remedial action by the Government of the United States. This action would not take the place of levees, reservoirs, by-passes, or spillways as flood preventive measures. The action recommended is not in any way intended to minimize the necessity of such works but is supplemental thereto. The effect of such action on floods either as to volume or frequency will be slow in manifesting itself. It will be largely unrecorded for the reason that its significance will be largely in what does not happen under changed conditions but would have happened had the old order continued.

It should, of course, be understood that appropriation or expenditures are suggested or recommended only upon condition that they be made at such times and in such amounts as may be in harmony with the fiscal policy of the Government.

First in order of importance is the extension of fire cooperation under section 2 of the Clarke-McNary law. The blanket of organized protection should be extended to all forests on the Mississippi watershed as rapidly as the States and private owners are willing to undertake the work. Ultimate cost per year for entire watershed [is] about $490,000. This includes all forest lands as well as "critical areas," for flood control, since it is impractical to attempt a definite separation into classes for protection purposes. This would be accomplished with the appropriations now authorized by the Clarke-McNary law.

Idle waste land on farms and submarginal land used agriculturally should be planted to forests under the Clarke-McNary Act as rapidly as the States and private land owners will expand such work and as cooperative expenditure will be in accord with the fiscal policy of the Government.

Instruction to owners of 115,000 square miles of forest land in farm ownership should keep pace with planting and need for advice in use and marketing forest products.

The purchase of about 2,642,000 acres of protection forest lands in national forest purchase units already approved and established by the National Forest Reservation Commission on the Mississippi watershed should be completed and in addition approximately 5,900,000 acres of protection forest lands adjoining two existing national forests in Arkansas and in 15 other units on the Mississippi drainage should be purchased. Inclusive of forest lands still to be acquired in completing units now approved under the Weeks law the total amount of land would be 8,542,000 acres. These purchases could be made under the provisions of the Weeks Act and Clarke-McNary Act during a period of from 5 to 10 years, subject to the appropriations authorized under the fiscal policy of the Government.

Protection and administration of present national forests, parks, and game refuges should be continued under present policies; and adjoining forested areas of unreserved public domain should be added to national forests.

Investigations of the Bad Lands and the Breaks should be authorized as a research project with a view to discovering some method of preventing serious erosion.

Plan of control of public grazing lands recommended by the Secretary of Agriculture and the Secretary of the Interior should be adopted. Expense, nominal appropriation to start; after starting, activity will be self-supporting from fees.

Provision should be made for securing a permanent record hereafter of stream-flow measurements and silt content of the Mississippi River at some point below Cairo and on each of the principal tributaries entering the river below that point and data essential to a long-time study of land use and erosion remedies thereby secured.

CONCLUSIONS

If these recommendations are carried out, a reasonable effort will have been made to take advantage of the power of good forest cover to hold water and soil and thus to play its part in restraining the violence of floods and erosion. Just how great or how small this influence would be in a vast watershed like the Mississippi no one can ever say, for the forces involved are too vast and complex for measurement. Yet such quantitative measurements as are available, combined with the cumulative force of common-sense observation and circumstantial evidence, point clearly to the conclusion that this influence is too important to neglect.

The benefits of good vigorous forest cover do not end with their ameliorating effect on stream flow and silting. Keeping our forest soils in place instead of letting them waste away to clog our river channels, making those soils fully and perpetually productive—these objects in themselves justify large investments in protecting and restoring our forests. Such investments are financially sound, because they will pay interest and dividends in timber products, and the resultant benefits in river protection will be a by-product without cost.

Forest rehabilitation is not urged as an alternative to engineering works for flood control. It is supplementary to the engineering program, but it is a supplement of such importance that no complete plan of flood control can omit it.

THE MISSISSIPPI VALLEY PLAN*
October 1, 1934

The Mississippi Valley Committee, a distinguished group of engineers and conservationists, submitted a tentative proposal for comprehensive development of the Mississippi Valley. Morris L. Cooke was chairman of the committee, which was financed by the Works Progress Administration, an agency under Secretary Ickes.

The committee had been established with little grass-roots support in the Mississippi Valley, or in Congress, and this was one reason the report never received serious consideration.

SUMMARY

I. LAND, WATER, AND PEOPLE

"Make no little plans. They have no magic to stir men's souls."
—Charles D. Norton

The time has passed when isolated or unrelated plans were adequate to American needs. When one strand in the interwoven web of our national fabric is touched every other strand vibrates. Land, water, and people go together. The people cannot reach the highest standard of well-being unless there is the wisest use of the land and water.

The divisions into which the Mississippi Valley Committee was forced, by the sheer logic of the situation, to analyze its problem will indicate the amazing diversity of the task of using and controlling water. Flood control, low-water control, navigation, power, water supply, sanitation, and erosion are integral parts of the picture. All of these elements are met with in the Great Valley. All of them may be encountered in the treatment of a single stream.

Merely to list them is to suggest that we cannot plan—that we can hardly hope to develop even a single sound project—unless we study also the uses of the land. So we have other factors we cannot overlook; agriculture and irrigation, industry and commerce, water storage, forestry, recreation, the conservation of wildlife.

Every plan and detail of a plan must be checked against as many of these factors as are pertinent to the particular case if we are to be certain of wholly beneficial results. From a consideration of projects we come to the consideration of a pattern on which are dependent the lives and happiness of millions now living and millions still to be born.

Report of the Mississippi Valley Committee of the Public Works Administration, Vol. 1 (Washington, D.C.: Government Printing Office, 1934), 7–19.

Engineering does not exist for its own sake. It is of little use to control rivers if we cannot thereby improve the quality of human living. Therefore, the final and most significant element which the committee has considered is neither land nor water, but the people who live on the land and are dependent on the water.

II. WATER IN MOTION

A drainage basin, big or little, is a region through which water moves. No act of man can permanently halt this flow of power, nor even diminish it to an appreciable degree. The water must come down—we could not stop it if we would. We can, however, figuratively as well as literally, canalize it so that it will do what we want it to do and not do what we do not want it to do.

The Problem of Control: The ideal river, which would have a uniform flow, does not exist in nature. Something usually has to be done, to equalize the flow or to take advantage of variations in flow, if the stream is to resemble even remotely an ideal river. But before this stage can be reached the question has to be answered, For what or for whom is the river to be ideal? The problem of control involves not only the physical nature of the stream, but the often conflicting claims of various uses and various users. Scientific planning requires a use pattern for each community, district, or region, as well as a geographical pattern which will reflect as fairly as possible the dominant needs of each locality.

The same principle must hold when we attempt to prevent a stream or a river system from doing damage. There is no one method of flood control which is applicable to the entire Mississippi system. The improvement of natural channels; the building of reservoirs—sometimes well adapted for purposes of irrigation and power; the construction of levees, such as now exist along the lower Mississippi; reforestation and a change in certain areas from tilled crops to grass crops, may all play a part in slowing down the rush of water to the sea, or in keeping it away from cities, towns, and valuable lands.

Floods pay no attention to political jurisdictions. Any coordinated system of control will demand the cooperation of neighboring States with each other as well as the cooperation of States with the Federal Government. Obviously the Federal Government should bear its share of the costs and the responsibility. Obviously, too, the States should do the same. To make this easily possible we need uniform State flood control laws, Federal legislation to expedite interstate compacts, and a permanent policy of Federal participation based on accurate estimates of the benefits to be derived. The integrity of State and local governments is certain to be impaired if the Federal Government is regarded as a kind of Santa Claus.

It is suggested that the Federal Government might pay 30 percent of the cost of labor and materials for projects of chief benefit only to local communities; a larger proportion as the measurable general benefits increased; and 100 percent of the construction cost when the benefits to be derived were, as they are now recognized to be on the lower Mississippi and its backwater areas, a national affair. In each instance there should be responsible and legally constituted local agencies with which the Government could deal.

The same principles that are applied to flood control may be applied to low-water control. Sometimes the multiple purposes of power development, irrigation, navigation, water supply, low-water control, and even flood control may be served by a single project. As in the case of flood control, low-water control may be paid for by the different agencies in proportion to the benefits received. Since pollution, by sewage or industrial waste, is a common accompaniment of low-stream stages in closely settled regions it is reasonable to ask that local authorities and industrial interests shall control this element as a preliminary to Federal participation.

The Federal Government manifestly should not be asked to police local streams.

Navigation: Inland waterways in the United States fixed the lines which the first westward migrations were to follow. As highways, canals and finally railroads were thrust westward from the Atlantic coast, waterways lost their supreme significance. Nevertheless they have continued to play a part in the national life, billions of dollars have been invested in them, and they have a romantic and traditional interest which cannot be disregarded.

Certain disadvantages attach to any river development: Rivers are crooked and often do not follow normal lines of traffic movement; reshipment is often necessary; variations in the water level make it difficult to establish proper docking and warehousing facilities; the northern waterways are closed by ice during many months of the year.

On the other hand some waterways have continued to prove economically justifiable; inland waterway transportation has sometimes had a chastening influence on railroad rates; and there is already a large Federal, State and local investment in waterways which would be lost if they were abandoned. Furthermore, navigation may well be part of a plan which provides also for irrigation, flood control, low-water control and power development. We must measure its costs and advantages in their relation to some or all of these other elements.

Down to the end of 1932 the United States Government had spent a little less than two billion dollars on river and harbor improvements, of which 94 percent was expended after 1882, 74 percent after 1906, and 46 percent after 1920. Of this amount about a billion and a half dollars were chargeable to navigation alone, and about $440,000,000 to navigation on the Mississippi river system. We have 27,406 miles of inland waterways which are legally defined as navigable, of which 12,798 miles—nearly half—are in the Mississippi system.

These legally navigable channels are in some cases no more than that. We need new estimating, accounting and cost-finding technique not only to weigh the advantages and disadvantages of river transportation, but to determine the proper place of inland waterways in a coordinated national transportation system. It may be desirable to introduce a new element by imposing charges where they are justified by special services and special facilities and where the traffic can bear them.

The movement toward ultimate unification might be hastened by the setting up of a commission to regulate water rates and to cooperate with the Interstate Commerce Commission in fixing joint rail and water rates. In time, with experience and with the accumulation of data which we now lack, the two agencies might be combined.

Power: The production and distribution of electricity, more than most other factors, demands Valley-wide coordination as part of a unified national system. The opportunities for power development are great, out of a potential of 16,000,000 kilowatts on the Mississippi and its tributaries only 2,000,000 have so far been utilized. In cases where potential power is not near an existing market a region-wide tie-up—an electrical "pool" to which all power sources would contribute—would often make it economically feasible to develop. In any such combination there would be a residue of continuous power, even when many individual plants were contributing only a part of the time.

If coordination is taken as the key we see the unfortunate effects of the present set-up in a power map which shows a "crazy patchwork of operating areas" and "a mass of independent unrelated generating units". Congested areas have more installed power than their inhabitants can utilize under present conditions; other areas, especially the rural ones, have little or no electric service, and there is a general underconsumption of power.

Coordination, under Government leadership, would not only benefit the consumer, but would aid the private producers by eliminating unnecessary duplications of plant and equipment, stabilizing service and making available new sources of energy.

The Federal Government should regulate transmission, regardless of the number of generating plants or transmission lines it may ultimately own. During the next 20 years it could profitably spend a billion dollars on river works in the Mississippi Valley, half of which would be for self-liquidating power installations. With this nucleus it could experiment as well as regulate.

Beyond lies the great task of rural electrification—the need for which is indicated by the fact that only one farm out of every seven in the United States is now electrified, even counting private power installations. Only 1 in 10 of the nation's farms, only 1 in 16 of those in the Mississippi Valley, actually buys electricity from power lines.

An allotment of $100,000,000 to build independent, self-liquidating rural electric projects would be a safe and socially justifiable experiment. Such an enterprise would not compete with private capital, since it would serve territory not now served or likely to be served in any other way. There is every reason to expect that the low rates which would be possible would result in a great expansion in the rural uses of electricity and a consequent increase in rural living standards.

Water Supply and Sanitation: The provision of an ample supply of pure water for domestic uses is a problem throughout the basin. Low water everywhere intensifies pollution. Planning obviously must look far ahead, providing for future supplies and for purification works; establishing water and sewerage districts, by which the needs and uses of neighboring communities can be reconciled; arranging for the better disposal of sewage and industrial waste; and in rural districts encouraging better sanitation.

Chemical, physical, and biological analyses of the water in the basin have been few, and are badly needed.

The situation calls for State legislation, where necessary, to give health departments supervision over water supplies, sewage and industrial waste in the interests of public health; for the creation of State agencies to inventory and allocate intrastate waters; for State laws, where needed, to establish water supply and sewer districts; for interstate compacts in some cases; and for the pooling and correlation, by State and Federal agencies, including the Public Health Service, of information now existing, as well as data to be secured by comprehensive surveys.

Erosion Control: It is only in comparatively recent years that the menace of soil erosion in the Mississippi Valley has been generally realized. Yet a large portion of the agricultural land in the basin has lost from 3 to 6 inches of top soil, and "no less than 25 percent of the tilled lands, have actually been stripped to the subsoil." About 5 percent has reached the gullying stage, and have been permanently ruined for agricultural use. Four hundred million dollars a year is a conservative estimate of the tangible loss in the United States.

Erosion is insidious: The first stage is sheet erosion, often so imperceptible that the effect can be detected only by changes in the color of the soil or by an otherwise inexplicable lowering of productivity. Next comes "shoestring erosion", and finally gully erosion, like the last stage in an incurable disease. In the arid regions, and in seasons of drought in the normally humid areas, the wind may be an eroding agent: Witness the clouds of dust which were carried last spring from the Mississippi Valley over eastern seaboard cities. The very land is dying. Measured by man's brief generations it is losing forever its ability to produce food.

Meanwhile living standards on the afflicted land have dropped, farm tenancy, tax delinquencies, bankruptcies and land abandonments have increased, and once smiling regions become a desolate testimonial to man's folly.

Progress in erosion control may be measured by the 18,000,000 acres of farm lands terraced between 1915 and 1932, and by the large number of farmers who have been induced to use such measures of soil protection as improved tillage, crop rotation, and strip-cropping. But it has become apparent that soil protection cannot be left solely to education and self-interest. A national policy and program is imperative.

Public agencies should not be expected to do all the work but unless they intervene it is apparent that the work will not be done, or will not be done in time. Because the emergency is national the National Government must take the lead.

The cost of protection against erosion is but a minute fraction of the cost of erosion. A twenty-year Federal program, calling for joint action with States, counties, land districts, and individual owners, would cost the National Government $20,000,000 a year—5 percent of the measurable annual loss from erosion at the present rate.

III. WATER ON THE LAND

If the water resources of a region are to be planned for effectively, there must also be coordinating planning for the land resources. Therefore it has seemed essential to the committee to consider as relevant to water uses problems of agriculture, including irrigation, of forestry, and, because man is not exclusively a working animal, of recreation and the conservation of wildlife. We come again on a maze of interrelated elements, no one completely independent of the others.

Land, Water, and the Farmer: American farm practice, as it relates to the continuing productivity of the land, is now not merely an individual concern—it is a national concern.

Given the existing markets, agriculture has been much overexpanded, even though not much more than one-third of the tillable soil which would be available under such extreme pressure of population as exists in China is now devoted to harvested crops. Fewer farmers and farm laborers are at work than was the case a generation ago, but this diminished number produce more than can be domestically consumed or exported. These generalizations, true of the whole country, are especially pertinent for the Mississippi Valley—the Nation's granary.

Improvements in farming technique have not protected the land itself, as the erosion situation shows. The diversified cropping system of the pioneers was easier on the land, if harder on the pioneer. We cannot return to pioneer conditions, but we probably should return to diversification, which in turn would mean a better balanced agriculture.

A successful national agricultural policy would require that all our soils (of which there are hundreds of types) be analyzed and grouped; that from these studies the best uses of each kind of land be determined; and that scientific cropping systems be developed for each type of land. Local, State, and Federal Governments should unite in this program, preferably through a national body which would obtain the active support of the other agencies.

Irrigation: Farming in regions of inadequate rainfall, such as that part of the Mississippi Valley lying west of the one hundredth meridian, demands a special technique on the part of the farmer. The dry farmer, taking his chances with the weather, is relatively independent. The irrigation farmer must usually resort to collective action to bring running water to his land. The semiarid regions, in which the rainfall hovers around the marginal line of 15 to 20 inches annually, furnish a special problem, since their crops may grow without irrigation in rainy years and fail disastrously in dry years.

Irrigation in the American West was practiced to some extent in prehistoric times. White settlers employed it in New Mexico toward the end of the seventeenth century and in California a hundred years later. In modern times it had its greatest expansion after the passage of the Federal Reclamation Act in 1902, empowering the Federal Government to build reservoirs and canals on public lands. At the time of the last census only 14 million out of 168 million crop-bearing acres in the 17 Western States were irrigated of which 5,000,000 acres were in the Mississippi Basin.

About one-third of the Western irrigated lands is controlled by individuals or informal partnerships; another third is supplied through cooperative or mutual enterprises; about one-sixth is served through irrigation districts; Federal irrigated lands account for about one-tenth, and the small remaining fraction is dependent on commercial irrigation systems.

The costs vary widely. The average for all irrigated lands in the United States is $68 an acre for capital investments, in the Mississippi Basin only $25 an acre. Whatever the auspices under which irrigation is undertaken some system of long-term payment usually has to be arranged. Irrigation, on public as well as private lands, has been the ruin of many a farmer who started out with insufficient capital or who could not keep up his cash income. Nearly every private irrigation enterprise has been in difficulties at one time or another, and on the Federal projects it has been necessary to extend the time allowed for repayment of capital charges from the original 10 years to 20 and finally to 40 years.

Neither the agricultural situation as a whole nor the situation on the irrigated lands justifies Federal action to extend the irrigated area. Where necessary, however, steps should be taken to protect investments in irrigation works and irrigation farms from deterioration. Irrigation should be studied in connection with the recommended national program of land uses. Particularly should there be more accurate estimates of costs and profits. These studies should include irrigation practice in the ordinarily humid regions of the East and South, where a supplementary water supply has been found useful for producing certain crops on individual farms. In Arkansas and Louisiana, for example, about 161,000 irrigated acres are devoted to rice culture.

Supplementary irrigation of this sort may be aided by the use of electric power for pumping during the off-peak night hours. Natural lakes, ponds, streams, and subsurface waters not available by natural flow may thus be economically utilized. In regions where natural ponds and perennial streams are scarce the wet-season flow might be conserved in artificial ponds or reservoirs. It is believed that detailed cost studies would justify this experiment.

Forestry: "The history of the American Forests has been one of exploitation, depletion, and, on large areas, actual devastation." Fires have supplemented shockingly wasteful methods of cutting as agents of destruction. In the Mississippi Basin about 40 percent of the land was originally forested. Only about 20 percent is now rated as forest land, and of this a large portion consists of cut-over land or second growth of little or no present commercial importance. Eighty percent of the forest areas of the entire United States is privately owned, and nearly 50 percent is held by commercial owners, who for various reasons have been slow to apply the principles of scientific forestry to their properties. About 25 percent is still without adequate fire protection. Private ownership, as a means of maintaining the forests in productive condition, has broken down.

The National Forests, about 25 percent of which lie within the Mississippi Basin, now include 165,000,000 acres. Forest lands acquired by 31 States and by a considerable number of counties and towns have reached a total of about 11,000,000 acres. As the result of a recent survey of the situation the Forest Service has recommended that about 225,000,000 additional acres of forest be brought under public ownership—about 60 percent by the Federal Government and about 40 percent by the States and local governmental units.

The mere acquisition of public forests is admittedly not enough. Cooperative protection from fires, insects and diseases; scientific planting programs; erosion control; more equitable systems of taxation; public credit for the improvement of private lands; continuing research; and a general economic survey of forests should be parts of a national forest program. A permanent policy of regulation for privately owned forests, embodying some of the provisions of the N.R.A. Lumber Code, should be adopted. In return for public assistance of the nature described private owners may justly be required to maintain their holdings with due regard to the public interest.

The cost of the procedure recommended by the Forest Service would be about $47,000,000 a year for 20 years for the acquisition and improvement of forest lands, and about $27,000,000 a year for 20 years for other purposes. This national plan would be well adapted to meet the regional needs of the Mississippi Valley.

Recreation: Year by year recreation is becoming a larger factor in any plan for land and water uses. Commercial recreation, in city and country alike, has become a major industry, but it does not meet all the needs of all the people. Public recreational opportunities are offered in the National Forests, in the 6,000,000 acres of the National Parks, in the 6,000,000 acres of State parks and forest preserves, in the many State and national wildlife preserves, and in numerous city parks and a few county parks. But these opportunities should be greatly enlarged. In particular, the possibilities of a recreational byproduct of any development of water uses should be studied. Recreation is a necessity, not a luxury. It should have parity with other necessities.

A national recreation policy, adapted to the Mississippi Valley but applicable everywhere, should include a comprehensive examination of all recreation problems and areas; a definite distribution of responsibility between the Federal and other governmental agencies on the one hand and private interests on the other; the coordination of such Federal activities as touch on recreation; the extension of "wilderness areas"; the recognition of recreation as a motive for acquiring new Federal lands not suitable for National Parks or National Forests; provision for new National Parks where the proper standards can be met, and for additions to existing Parks; and, in general, more liberal appropriations for recreation in the Parks and Forests.

Wildlife Conservation: Wildlife has been increasingly depleted with the increase and spread of population. Excessive killing and the destruction of natural habitats have been jointly responsible. In recent years, however, the cause of conservation has been advanced by private associations, by civic organizations, and by scientific and educational institutions. State and Federal legislation has been improved and an intelligent public opinion stimulated.

* * *

Wildlife is public rather than private property. A wildlife program for the Federal Government should include the acquisition of refuges and preserves, as recommended early in 1934 by the President's Committee on Wildlife Restoration; larger appropriations for conservation activities; common action of all water-use agencies with the Biological Survey to protect migratory waterfowl; an enlarged research program; education; leadership in suppressing diseases and other dangers to wildlife; and liberal financial support for the protection of the inland fisheries.

IV. THE GREAT BASINS

So far we have been considering the problems of water uses and related land uses insofar as they are applicable to the Valley as a whole. If we subdivide the Valley into five Basins or Regions we find that each has problems which make it desirable to treat it as a unit. These regional problems, however, should be looked at against the background of the general water problems of the Valley. Of these, erosion has already been treated.

The situation with regard to rainfall and run-off and ground water and the water table may be briefly indicated.

Rainfall and Run-off: Probably nowhere in the world within a comparable area is there more diversity in these respects than is encountered in the Mississippi Valley. West of the general line of the one hundredth meridian the climate is normally arid or semiarid; East of that line it is normally humid. Area for area the Ohio Valley has twice as much precipitation as the Valley of the Missouri. In drought years like 1934 the arid climate may temporarily sweep far Eastward into the very heart of the Valley. There is no reason to believe, however, that over long periods, the average precipitation either decreases or increases.

The amount of run-off varies with the rainfall, the amount and character of the vegetation, and the nature of the soil. For the Valley as a whole less than half the water precipitated as rain or snow is carried to the sea; in the Great Plains region the proportion may be 20 percent, or even less, while East of the Mississippi it averages between 35 and 45 percent. West of the Mississippi half the annual precipitation occurs during the four months from April through July; in the Eastern part of the Valley it is more evenly distributed. The flood season fortunately varies in different sections of the Valley, but melting snow and Spring rains make the months from December through April the most critical in this respect.

Ground Water and the Water Table: The "ground water table" is the name given to the level at which water normally lies beneath the surface. A fall in the water table is a serious matter for any population which depends, as probably 95 percent of the population of the Mississippi Valley outside the larger cities does, on subsurface water.

There is no conclusive evidence that a serious decline in ground water levels has taken place generally in the more humid parts of the basin. On the other hand a progressive decline has taken place in North Dakota, the Eastern part of South Dakota, Nebraska, Kansas, Western Minnesota, Western Iowa, and Western Missouri. The new evidence for this decline is based on a questionnaire to which 1,482 well drillers in the sections mentioned sent replies. The data indicated that during average periods ranging from 10 to 44 years there has been a ground level drop of more than 10 feet in Nebraska, Minnesota, Iowa, and the Dakotas, and of somewhat less than that average in Kansas and Missouri.

Averages, of course, tend to conceal the seriousness of some local situations. Large areas in the Western part of North Dakota show a drop of more than 20 feet; in Minnesota the decline ranges from 10 to 20 feet, in South Dakota from

[306]

10 to 35 feet, in Nebraska from 10 to more than 20 feet, on the Missouri-Mississippi divide in Iowa from 20 to 30 feet. The diminishing flow of artesian wells, due to wasteful methods of construction and maintenance, led the Legislature of North Dakota to pass an artesian water conservation law as far back as 1921. Some benefit has already resulted, but the artesian water head in North Dakota has fallen at the rate of a foot a year for the past 18 years. In South Dakota there has been a drop of at least 40 feet in 20 years.

The water level obviously depends on the amount of rainfall (although because of underground movements rainfall in one region may affect water levels in another), on changes in surface conditions allowing more or less water to sink into the ground, and on the amount of withdrawals. In most of the States mentioned the fall of the water table has been accompanied by the lowering or drying up of springs, ponds, lakes, and streams.

Since there is no known way of increasing the rainfall, ground water should be conserved by economical use and added to by methods of cultivation that will diminish the direct surface run-off. Conditions undoubtedly warrant an immediate and comprehensive investigation to determine the critical facts for those portions of the basin where subsurface water resources are of paramount importance.

THE UPPER MISSISSIPPI

The Upper Mississippi Basin is that part of the Mississippi Valley lying North of the mouths of the Ohio and Missouri. It includes about 15 percent of the land area of the Valley. Because their economic problems are similar the present study includes parts of the Hudson Bay and Great Lakes basins. This enlarged area has a population a little less than that of the Ohio Valley and a little less than one-third that of the entire Mississippi Valley. Its percentage of land in crops is nearly twice the average for the United States. It produces 80 percent of the nation's iron ore, 11 percent of the coal, 10 percent of the copper, and 16 percent of the manufactured goods. Obviously the latter figures would be greatly reduced if the Great Lakes drainage area were excluded. The economic culture of the region is high but, as the economic map in the body of the report shows, very unevenly distributed.

Water is an important but not a dramatic factor. The land is fairly level; parts of it, in Illinois particularly, form one of the most nearly level areas in the United States. The ice age left thousands of pockets in northwestern Wisconsin and northern Minnesota, accounting for 13,000 existing fresh-water lakes and numerous swamps and marshes. Almost the whole region lies in the humid belt, with a rainfall ranging from 18 inches in the northwest to 42 inches in the southeast. The drought of 1934 upset these averages and in some sections caused considerable losses. The northwestern section lies in an area in which the ground-water level has been seriously lowered. Navigation projects on the Upper Mississippi system have cost the Federal Government, to June 1934, a total of more than $126,000,000 for construction alone, to which the completion of existing projects will add another $91,000,000. At the present no strictly economic justification can be found for this expenditure; it is possible that the future will tell a different story. The water-power potential is not high. Listed projects indicate a total of about 800,000 kilowatts. Drainage is a serious problem in the flat lands of the valleys of the Red River and the Illinois River. Because of the sluggish flow of most of the streams water supply and sanitation present grave difficulties. As an outstanding example, the city of Chicago, drawing its domestic water from Lake Michigan, is hard put to it to dispose of its sewage and waste. The disposal of industrial waste is a knotty problem also for St. Paul, Minneapolis, and numerous lesser cities.

Erosion is at work throughout the region, with an especially serious situation in an area extending from southwestern Wisconsin to northeastern Iowa, and from southwestern Minnesota to northwestern Illinois; and in a second area in southeastern Iowa and northeastern Missouri. Floods are usually local in character, doing damage in the wet and poorly drained valleys. Heavy losses are sometimes caused when the Illinois River levee system breaks. These levees should be set back and strengthened and much of the now cultivated bottom land set aside for reforestation, bird refuges, and reservoirs.

The economic culture map indicates that prosperity in the region is decidedly spotty. Sometimes undrained marsh lands, drought, erosion, or a lowered water table may be responsible for a low economic status. The decline of the copper industry or the competition of cheap oil and gas with the local coal supply may cause an economic recession, as in two instances in this area. In some areas the draining of infertile lands has proven to be an economic blunder of the first magnitude.

The bright side of the picture is that constructive planning is already under way more or less effectively in all the states of the region, notably in Wisconsin and Minnesota. No new projects calling for Federal participation are recommended, but the Committee believes that a unique opportunity exists for Federal, State, and local participation in a general regional planning program which might serve as a model for other areas.

THE OHIO BASIN

The Ohio River contributes to the Mississippi a minimum flow of 25,000 cubic feet per second, a maximum flow which has gone as high as 1,500,000 second-feet, and a normal flow of between 250,000 and 300,000 second-feet. On the average its flow is more than one-half that of the Mississippi below Cairo. Rarely do its waters fall so low as to hinder navigation or other necessary uses. At long intervals, usually a generation or more apart, it sends down huge and destructive floods.

The area of the Basin is about one-sixth of that of the Mississippi Valley, its population more than one-third that of the Valley, the living standards of its people equal to or a little above the national average. Its annual agricultural product, amounting to about two billion dollars, supports a farm population of about five million people. Its manufacturing output is more than four times as great. In general the industrial centers are north of the Ohio River, and the highest living standards exist there. South of the Ohio the predominantly rural section has a considerably lower standard of living.

We have here the regional phases of many of the general problems of the Mississippi Valley—those having to do with arid conditions excepted. Complete flood control of the main river is difficult if not impossible. Effective control on some of the tributaries is perfectly feasible. In the body of the present report a program is suggested for thirteen new flood-control projects, in addition to the two already approved. The total cost of these fifteen projects would be $117,000,000, of which it is suggested that the Federal Government furnish about $61,000,000. Further surveys are needed, both for flood control and for low-water control.

The extensive use of the Ohio system for navigation is indicated by the fact that the Monongahela alone leads all the inland rivers of the United States in traffic, and that the Ohio itself carries more than the Mississippi. Coal, coke, sand and gravel, iron and steel, and petroleum are the principal commodities carried. With costs to the Federal Government for improving and maintaining channels ranging from one mill for each ton-mile on the Monongahela to 23.2 cents per ton-mile on the Big Sandy it is clear that some of the river improvements in the Basin have justified themselves and that others have passed their peak of usefulness. There is a middle group whose future status should be determined by further inquiry. It is suggested that a study be made to determine if it would be practicable to levy shipping charges for the special services and facilities now provided at government expense. New navigation projects may well wait such determination.

The Ohio Valley will probably double its demands for power within the next 20 years. That is to say, it will probably need in 1955 about twice the 17 billion kilowatt-hours consumed in the peak year of 1929. At present only 14.8 percent of its installed electric generators are waterdriven. Since the Basin contains large coal deposits water power must meet keen competition, and it seems better to wait further developments, including those now being made by the Tennessee Valley Authority, before making recommendations for specific power projects on the Ohio and its tributaries.

Erosion is at work in the Ohio Basin as it is elsewhere in the Great Valley. Four demonstration stations have been established by the Erosion Service within the Basin and work is being done by C.C.C. units in filling up gullies. Beyond these undertakings erosion control must await the carrying-out of the urgently needed national program.

Water supply has been a problem this year in parts of the Ohio Valley, but more urgent is the question of the disposal of sewage and industrial waste. Planning for the future should balance the demand for "quality water" for domestic use against quantity demand for flushing sewers and carrying away factory waste. The Federal Government should extend its surveys of streams and other sources and help in educating the public in the need of protecting water supplies and preventing pollution.

The Basin is lacking in natural lakes and ponds but otherwise offers many facilities for recreation—not without reason did the French call the Ohio the "Beautiful River". Here, as elsewhere, the recreational purpose can and should be combined with power, flood control and navigation projects. An example worth imitating is that of the Miami Conservancy District, where a total area of between 1,500 and 2,000 acres, in tracts adjoining four dams, has been designated for public use as camping and picnic grounds.

THE MISSOURI BASIN

Exceeding in size the combined areas of Germany, France, and Italy, the Missouri Basin has 43 percent of the land in the Mississippi drainage area but only a little more than 15 percent of the population. It contains parts of four of the major physical divisions of the United States: the Ozark Plateau, the Central Lowland, the Great Plains, and the Rocky Mountains.

In the Eastern third of the Basin are found most of the population and nearly all the large cities and manufacturing industries. Forty percent or more of this zone is normally cropped with winter wheat and corn dominant in the South and spring wheat in the North. With certain exceptions the soil is fertile and agriculture is relatively stable.

West of this section lies the great middle zone, a true "Land of Little Rain", in which cities are few and small, and where the agricultural front has been held at great hazard and often with heavy loss. The dry farming and irrigation farming problems of this region are many and the solutions still seem far ahead.

The third and westernmost zone includes the foothills and ridges of the Rocky Mountains and adjacent plains. Here, on the Eastern slopes of the Continental Divide, mining and irrigation agriculture have produced "islands" of growing population in the sea of sparsely settled mountainous areas and semiarid plains. The petroleum industry, probably now near its peak in this region, and the coal industry, with most of its probable development still ahead, are factors making for growth.

Water, whether as a flood menace or as the very lifeblood of the region, is a vital factor in all three zones. Flood control is a problem in the headwater areas and in the Kansas River-Lower Missouri area. The flood problem in and around the two Kansas Cities is the most serious in the Basin and one of the most serious in the United States. High water here may paralyze one of the nation's chief transportation centers. The feasibility of local levee protection seems doubtful.

The Kiro dam is considered impracticable. It is recommended that an immediate technical and economic survey be made cooperatively by Federal and local interests in order to determine the practicability of controlling floods on the Kansas (or Kaw) River, and that steps be taken to form an interstate conservatory district which may participate with the Federal Government in any flood-control measures undertaken.

It is estimated that about 950,000 acres of land, capable of supporting a farm population of about 75,000, might be reclaimed in the Missouri Basin through irrigation. Certain of these projects should be studied, with the Federal Government bearing half the cost of the surveys and participating in whatever enterprises may be found worth while. Other irrigated areas which are suffering from serious water shortages require supplemental works. In general, however, a further extension of irrigation cannot be expected to contribute in a large way to the general welfare of the Basin.

A regional regulation of streams to insure a dependable domestic water supply and guard against pollution is desirable. Denver and its neighboring communities are now facing a water shortage, and in the Dakotas, as has been pointed out, there has been a marked and disastrous drop in the water table. Although the project to divert flood waters of the Missouri into North Dakota is not feasible, it is recommended that the Federal Government bear part of the cost of surveying and constructing stream regulation works for groups of communities which will organize responsible conservancy districts. The Government should also encourage the drilling of deep wells which in the Dakotas should afford some relief in times of water scarcity.

Although large sums have been spent in improving channels along the Missouri system the commercial usefulness of the river has not been great as yet. Until the value of further improvements, costing about $250,000,000, is determined, no further projects are recommended. It is recommended that the Osage River project be abandoned.

The undeveloped water power in the Basin is estimated at 2,110,000 kilowatts. No water-power projects are recommended for present development, but it is urged that power sites on Federal lands shall not be allowed to come under private ownership. Attention is called, however, to an apparently exceptional opportunity for cooperatively planned social betterment in the Black Hills Region, through the medium, in part, of an abundant supply of low-priced power. A proposed "mouth of the mine" steam plant at Gillette, Wyoming, may be able to furnish the required power. A thorough technical and social investigation of this possibility is earnestly recommended.

Recreational facilities are abundant on the slopes of the Rocky Mountains but are relatively restricted on the Great Plains and Eastern Lowlands, and in the latter areas it is particularly desirable that they should be developed in harmony with the national policy already outlined.

In the body of the report six project areas in the Basin are discussed. In these, multiple-purpose planning should be considered, with attention to the social and economic needs of the people as the key to whatever is done.

THE SOUTHWEST BASINS

The valleys of the Red, Arkansas, White and Ouachita Rivers, containing more than one-fifth of the total area of the Mississippi Valley and having only about one-sixth of the population, are still underpopulated. They offer pioneering opportunities hard to find in any other part of the United States. Not only is there much good agricultural land, but the basins are rich in gold, silver, petroleum, and other underground resources. Almost every kind of crop can be produced somewhere in the region, with the Arkansas Valley marking the Northern boundary of the cotton belt as well as "the boundary of cultures where North and South meet."

Hydroelectric developments in the steep western reaches of the rivers will be of great importance in developing the whole territory. At the same time there is a need for flood protection in the form of levees, channel improvements, spillways or reservoirs further down. In the Western portions of all four rivers the water supply requires to be conserved; in the Eastern portions it must be regulated and controlled.

Flood control is a serious problem on the Red River below Denison; along a large part of the channel of the Arkansas; on the lower stretches of the White, which are subject to backwater flow from the Mississippi, and in the Ouachita Basin, which in flood time may receive backwater or overflow from the Mississippi, the Red, and the Arkansas.

Water-power developments in the region face competition from steam power produced cheaply from coal, oil, or gas. At the same time the fact that nearly half the population lives on farms and that only five percent of the farm homes use electricity indicates one large potential market for power. Six hundred thousand horsepower could be developed along the Red River system; the Arkansas is still wholly undeveloped along its main stem; the White River can produce about three-quarters of a million horsepower; and there are partly exploited possibilities on the Upper Ouachita.

Navigation is possible on all four streams for varying distances, and a considerable amount of Federal money has been spent on channel improvements, but the actual use made of these facilities is minor and no further improvements are recommended. Irrigation is important on the western stretches of the Red and Arkansas Rivers and in lower sections of the Red River devoted to rice culture. A thorough study of potential water supply and sanitation requirements is recommended in order to meet the needs of the growing population. Forestry is important chiefly in the Eastern section, and much of the best forest land has been cut over. Outdoor recreation has been inadequately provided for, and should be included in any comprehensive plan for the development of the Southwest Basins.

In the body of the report will be found a classified list of projects for power, navigation, irrigation, water supply, and recreation. From this list it will be possible with little delay to select projects which are consistent with the general plan of Mississippi Valley development as conceived by the present committee.

THE LOWER MISSISSIPPI

The Lower Mississippi Valley contains something more than one-twelfth of the population of the Mississippi Basin, and its area is somewhat over one-twentieth that of the entire Basin. Sixty percent of the population live in the Alluvial Valley or Delta, and 40 percent in the uplands. The lowlands are fertile and capable of supporting a far larger population than they actually do; the uplands are perhaps overpopulated in proportion to their resources.

In both sections about two-thirds of the population is rural and about half depends directly on agriculture. The key to the future of the area as a whole lies in the Alluvial Valley, and the key to the future of the Alluvial Valley is dependent on the solution of the flood problem. Further economic—and, it may be added, social—developments there must of necessity be restricted for the most part to be protected areas. Under the Adopted Plan for Lower Mississippi flood protection about half the Delta area is now safe from the waters of the main river. The Federal Government, which provides the protection, has a vital interest, as it has a vital influence, in the nature of the economic and social life that its work makes possible.

The protected lands of the Delta should be capable of supporting a highly prosperous rural society; actually cash incomes are strikingly low, living conditions are substandard, and farm tenancy has increased until about 80 percent of all farm operators now are tenants. If new Delta lands are to be developed and protected a program should be worked out, under Federal auspices, which will enable farm operators to acquire ownership and which will raise the general standard of living.

If we consider types of land areas in the region as related to water problems we find erosion in the uplands a critical factor, with conditions and proposed remedies similar to those described earlier in the present summary. In the protected Delta lands drainage involves serious difficulties—so serious, indeed, that a third of the land now protected from all floods still remains unoccupied. There is an abundant water supply, but pollution and the disposal of sewage are problems in many areas. Navigation on the tributary streams is of slight importance, despite costly channel improvements. Navigation on the Mississippi itself has been declining since 1926. In view of the fact that the Federal Government has spent or authorized the spending of about $190,000,000 for improving the channel between New Orleans and Cairo an inquiry as to whether or not shippers should bear a portion of the cost is highly desirable.

Flood control on the main river involves: the levee system, now more than two centuries old; recent experiments with floodways, into which flood waters not containable within any existing or conceivable levee system may be automatically diverted; attempts at channel stabilization; and an expenditure, since 1928, of more than $300,000,000. The system of "fuse plug" levees and projected spillways brings up questions of equities in the lands which would thus be flooded; these questions should be settled with as little delay as is consistent with fairness to all concerned and a definite floodway policy and program entered upon.

Three specific projects, in the Yazoo Basin, in the St. Francis Basin, and in the Black River Basin, are discussed in the body of the report. It is recommended that studies for the development of these areas be commenced at once. "The time is ripe to initiate a new, more comprehensive and enlightened system of land reclamation and community planning designed to secure ultimately to the settlers an improved standard of living."

The protection of land involves the protection of the people, and the protection of the people stops short of its proper objective if it does not lead toward what sociologists call the "good life."

INTERRELATION OF INTERESTS

As communities increase in population, extent and complexity, new and far-reaching agencies have to be called in or created to deal with their water problems. The family well gives way to a city water system, that in turn, perhaps, to a district or sectional water system. In time, as the present report suggests, a national program is required to reconcile the needs of the 49,000,000 people who live on the 1,235,000 square miles of the Mississippi River System. The multiple uses of water add to the intricacy of the problem.

There consequently should be a revaluation of controlling agencies, both local and general. Where the physical problem to be attacked transcends existing political boundaries, new types of regional organization, such as the New England Council or the Ohio River Board of Health Commissioners, have already appeared. Other types are the "Authority", or publicly owned corporation, of which the Port Authority of New York is an example; the intrastate conservancy district; agencies set up by two or more states under interstate compacts; and Regional Authorities set up by the Federal Government, for which the Tennessee Valley Authority may be regarded as a precedent.

Either on its own initiative or on request from the States, the Federal Government should stand ready to investigate projects or situations. In planning and carrying out actual operations the benefits and responsibilities should be as accurately assessed as possible as between the National, State and local governments. The Federal Government's responsibility should not be too narrowly interpreted, since it is in practice and by the terms of the Constitution account-able for the general welfare. Measurable benefits are not always the only criter-ia which can be set up. "The ideal allotment of costs will be that which will produce the best total economic effect within the limits of public support and of administrative practicality, with due regard to all equitable considerations."

The final criterion is that of public support. There should be, and invariably is, a constant flux and interplay between Federal guidance and spontaneous local activity. An emergency such as a flood or even the swift and deadly pro-cesses of erosion, may require instant action by whatever agencies are most effective. When quick action is not imperative, as in the acquisition of new lands for parks, the approach should be through an education of the popular will. Governments, national or local, should not attempt the impossible, nor can they safely go against the grain of public opinion—whose servants, in a democ-racy, they are. Sometimes situations will develop for which there is no govern-mental remedy; these situations should be recognized as such, however painful the realization. Policies making for industrial decentralization and local self-sufficiency should be outlined and encouraged wherever they do not act against the general welfare.

"Above all, the Federal Government will need to make clear to the people that its function is not to take over the direction and responsibility for individual enterprises, but to provide these physical and economic adjustments that will lead to a generally favorable environment in which local enterprises may oper-ate."

PLANNING

The words "plan" and "planning" have grown to have a precise meaning for engineers and industrialists, expressing definite objectives and definite ways of attaining those objectives. The only assumption with which they have been loaded in the present report is one which ought to be held as self-evident in a democratic society, that no social or economic technique is sound which does not make for the health and well-being of the people.

Industrial and engineering practice distinguishes three "planes" of planning; directive planning, which defines major purposes, ways and means; general administrative planning, which carries out in the individual plans or project the policies of directive planning; and operative planning, which determines detailed operations. Similarly the steps in planning include an original definition of pur-pose; the adoption of policies, which represents an adaptation to the human and material factors which must be dealt with; the formulation of a program or tenta-tive chart of operations; and a final design, in which precise qualitative, quan-titative, and functional relationships are established. This done, the final plan may be subdivided into projects.

That these proven principles of private planning may be adapted to governmental planning the Committee is convinced; that anything less than planning of this nature will suffice to meet the nation's needs is extremely doubtful.

The principles outlined permit both the long-range view and the early preparation of specifications for particular projects which may be entered upon at once, or which may be kept ready for some future time when a large amount of unemployment exists. Both the enactments of the Congress and current public opinion suggest that desirable public works should be so used as a means of balancing employment both in good times and bad.

Practically all varieties of public works involve design and require detailed specifications before construction can begin. Hence it is strongly urged, as good public policy, that on improvements that are reasonably sure of being ultimately built, detailed plans and even specifications be promptly carried as far as practicable. For instance, borings for dam sites should be undertaken as soon as it seems likely that a given dam will in time be built. After this policy has been in force for some time the need for emergency employment can be met much more expeditiously than is now possible.

It is hardly necessary to point out at this stage that the general planning of the use and control of water resources must rest with the Federal Government as being the nearest we can come to an expression and reconciliation of the various purposes and desires of all our people and all our governmental agencies. In adapting an industrial technique of planning to the needs of the nation we would not be violating the principles of democracy and local self-government; we would merely be giving them a new tool.

The present plan is neither complete nor final. It is necessarily selective and in many ways tentative. The Committee has sought to combine a broad and long-range view of the problems of the Mississippi Valley with definite proposals for doing certain things that ought to be done at once. The sooner certain projects arrive at the blue-print stage the better for the public welfare and safety. The plan as a whole is not a blue-print. It is rather an attempt to indicate desirable lines of growth. The plan will have best served its purpose if it, too, grows, changes, and improves as the years go by.

BROADER WATER PLANNING

REPORT FROM THE CHIEF HYDROGRAPHER
ON MULTIPURPOSE RESERVOIRS*
1912

The final report of Theodore Roosevelt's ill-fated National Waterways Commission consisted primarily of technical papers. This appendix to the report on the possibility of reservoirs designed for power, flood control, and navigation was prepared by M. O. Leighton of the United States Geological Survey, the engineer who first promoted the multipurpose concept. Leighton was later to become an active opponent of such development when he left government and became a spokesman for private power interests.

THE UTILITY OF STORAGE RESERVOIRS FOR FLOOD
PREVENTION, POWER, AND NAVIGATION

This report is submitted in compliance with a request of Hon. T. E. Burton, chairman, made March 10, 1911. It relates to the utility of flood-impounding reservoirs, either constructed or proposed, in the United States.

In November, 1907, I presented to the Inland Waterways Commission a report entitled "The Relation of Water Conservation to Flood Prevention and Navigation in Ohio River." This contribution has been included in the printed report of that commission, pages 451 to 490 (S. Doc. No. 325, 60th Cong., 1st sess.). The present report is in a sense supplementary to that of 1907, covering further studies, both in the Ohio basin and elsewhere in the United States.

The report of 1907 elicited much unfavorable comment. Had it no other virtue than that of provoking the discussion that ensued it would have amply served its purpose. During the four years that have intervened since the report was submitted the partisans on both sides have had an opportunity to give more mature consideration to reservoirs, and judgment concerning them is now less likely to be warped by feelings of loyalty to preconceived notions. As might have been expected, a common ground has been located toward which the various parties have converged. Reservoir advocates, including the present writer, have been led to modify certain radical views concerning relatively unimportant details, though the accuracy of the important contentions made in the

*Sen. Doc. 469, 62nd Cong., 2nd sess., 135–37.

report of 1907 has repeatedly been verified. On the other hand, those who earlier opposed the creation of reservoirs have shown a very marked tendency to adopt or at least to look more favorably on certain features of the scheme.

In order that the present report may be considered in the light of full information concerning past objections, it will be well to review briefly the principal objections that were made after the publication of the report of 1907.

The reservoir scheme was generally denounced because of its alleged inefficiency. Some of its opponents argued that storage would not materially change flood conditions; others held that suitable sites were lacking in places where reservoirs would be effective, though, strangely enough, those who so held showed that they were quite unfamiliar with the topography of the Ohio River Basin. Still others cited numerous unimportant local objections, such as the flooding of land and the interruption of travel along country roads. To many persons the submergence of large areas of comparatively worthless farm lands in the upland drainage basins of the Ohio tributaries seemed to be an insuperable objection. Notwithstanding the fact that these lands have never been very profitable as farms, certain good men drew tearful pictures of submerged homes and of banished, inconsolable families, forgetting, apparently, the compensating happiness in the rich valleys below. It ought to be apparent that the value of a few thousand acres of poor land in the highland region of any river system is not comparable with the value of a well-regulated river, whether the river be regarded as a source of power or an avenue of transportation. As a rule, the annual damage caused by floods far exceeds the value of the land whose submergence would partially or wholly prevent further floods.

Objections were also based on the supposed inefficiency of reservoirs in the double duty as preventers of floods and as aids to navigation. Many persons were inclined to contend that reservoirs would always be full when they were needed to store flood waters, or empty when water was needed to compensate low-water flow. The uses of the reservoirs were said to be antagonistic. To prevent floods the reservoirs must be emptied as soon as possible after a flood has abated, so as to be ready to receive the next flood; to serve the purposes of power and navigation the reservoirs must be full at the end of the wet season, so that the maximum use of their capacity can be made during the following dry season. Inasmuch as it is impossible to foretell the time of cessation of spring rains, no one would be able to decide when to empty the reservoir or when to close it to catch water for the dry season. To all these objections the simple answer is that such reservoir systems must be planned with a twofold capacity: First, planned to care for summer flow, providing permanent storage to be held as nearly uniform as possible; second, to provide excess capacity equivalent to maximum flood run-off; that is, sufficient to hold the largest floods. The water in this portion of the reservoir would be drawn down to the point of permanent storage as soon after a flood as possible, and the basin would be ready to catch another flood. At the same time the reservoir would store water for the low-water periods. Although this point has been repeatedly explained, these objections seem to stick in the minds of many critics.

Another objection was based on the danger of the breaking of a dam in such a system. The failure of dams with consequent loss of life has for many years been a favorite topic in song and story. It appears to give to an author just the environment and the train of circumstances necessary to produce a vivid effect and to secure an appreciative audience, but dam failures in fact are relatively few; each is traceable to some preventable error, and they will occur less frequently as engineering knowledge increases. The dam casualties of the past are not as numerous as those incident to ordinary foot traffic in the streets of a great city, especially since the day of the automobile. No one would advocate abolishing the automobile because its abuses result in damage to pedestrians. No one would propose giving up railroad trains because they are agents of death. The hazards are accepted because of manifold benefits conferred. So it is with the reservoir systems.

Another great objection to the reservoir scheme was the prospectively great cost. Little could be said in reply to this objection because no surveys or estimates had been made, and little more is known at the present time. It is probable that within a few months as the result of the investigations of the flood commission of Pittsburgh cost figures will be available for reservoir systems located on the Monongahela and Allegheny. Very few estimates are available for other places. It is known, however, that such investigations of flood reservoir benefits and costs as have thus far been completed—and some of these investigations will be discussed later on—show the benefits to far outweigh the costs, especially when flood benefits are united with benefits to water power, to navigation, and, in certain parts of the country, to irrigation.

Finally, the critics of the first report seem to forget that the report was largely, if not entirely, a plea for further investigation. Certain facts were given and deductions believed to be reasonable were made. It was contended that inasmuch as a showing of possibility if not of probability was made, it would be wise to fully investigate all of the premises. The present report goes a little further, discussing certain areas outside of the Ohio Basin in which reservoirs have been constructed or the effect of proposed reservoirs has been studied, and making certain statements concerning reservoir costs and efficiencies; but it is believed that this report will have fulfilled its best purpose if it emphasizes even more strongly than did that of 1907 the duty of the Government and of the Waterways Commission to look well into this reservoir matter and take no steps toward a permanent waterways policy until sufficient information is at hand concerning the practicability, efficiency, and cost of reservoirs.

THE RIVERS AND HARBORS ACT*
March 3, 1925

A paragraph in the Rivers and Harbors Act of 1925 directed the Corps of Engineers to survey all navigable streams in the United States where power development appeared feasible, as a step in formulation of general plans for navigation, flood control, and irrigation development. This was the basis of the "308" reports which the Engineers prepared extensively in the 1930's, and which are still used as a backlog of information about most of the streams in the country.

SEC. 3. The Secretary of War, through the Corps of Engineers of the United States Army, and the Federal Power Commission are jointly hereby authorized and directed to prepare and submit to Congress an estimate of the cost of making such examinations, surveys, or other investigations as, in their opinion, may be required of those navigable streams of the United States, and their tributaries, whereon power development appears feasible and practicable, with a view to the formulation of general plans for the most effective improvement of such streams for the purposes of navigation and the prosecution of such improvement in combination with the most efficient development of the potential water power, the control of floods, and the needs of irrigation: *Provided,* That no consideration of the Colorado River and its problems shall be included in the consideration or estimate provided herein.

*43 *Statutes at Large,* 1190.

PROPOSALS FROM PRESIDENT ROOSEVELT
FOR SEVEN LITTLE TVA'S*
June 3, 1937

The early recognition of the values of the Tennessee Valley Authority idea for unified development of a river valley attracted many proposals for similar developments in other river valleys. President Roosevelt modified and consolidated many of these ideas into a plan for seven regional authorities or agencies.

Even though the plan itself was only a planning program for four of the regions, it attracted heavy opposition, and never progressed beyond the stage of committee hearings. Roosevelt's message proposing the plan is given here.

To the Congress of the United States:

Nature has given recurrent and poignant warnings through dust storms, floods, and droughts that we must act while there is yet time if we would preserve for ourselves and our posterity the natural sources of a virile national life.

Experience has taught us that the prudent husbandry of our national estate requires far-sighted management. Floods, droughts, and dust storms are in a very real sense manifestations of nature's refusal to tolerate continued abuse of her bounties. Prudent management demands not merely works which will guard against these calamities but carefully formulated plans to prevent their occurrence. Such plans require coordination of many related activities.

For instance, our recent experiences of floods have made clear that the problem must be approached as one involving more than great works on main streams at the places where major disasters threaten to occur. There must also be measures of prevention and control among tributaries and throughout the entire headwaters areas. A comprehensive plan of flood control must embrace not only downstream levees and floodways and retarding dams and reservoirs on major tributaries but also smaller dams and reservoirs on the lesser tributaries, and measures of applied conservation throughout an entire drainage area, such as restoration of forests and grasses on inferior lands, and encouragement of farm practices which diminish run-off and prevent erosion on arable lands.

Taking care of our natural estate, together with the stopping of existing waste, and building it back to a higher productivity is a national problem. At last we have undertaken a national policy.

But it is not wise to direct everything from Washington. National planning

*Cong. Rec., Vol. 81, 75th Cong., 1st sess., 5926–27; H. Doc. 261, 75th Cong., 1st sess.

should start at the bottom, or, in other words, the problems of townships, counties, and States should be coordinated through large geographical regions and come to the Capital of the Nation for final coordination. Thus the Congress would receive a complete picture in which no local detail had been overlooked.

It is also well to remember that improvements of our national heritage frequently confer special benefits upon regions immediately affected, and a large measure of cooperation from State and local agencies in the undertaking and financing of important projects may fairly be asked for.

Any division of the United States into regions for the husbandry of its resources must possess some degree of flexibility. The area most suitable as a region for the carrying out of an integrated program designed to prevent floods is the basin, including the watersheds, of a pivotal river. But other problems dependent upon other combinations of natural economic and social factors may require a somewhat different area to permit the most effective functional program. For instance, the problem of the Great Plains area is a problem of deficient rainfall, relatively high winds, loose friable soils, and unsuitable agricultural practices. The natural area for solution of the Great Plains drought problem is different from that for the solution of dynamic water problems presented by the rivers which traverse that area. The rational area for administration of a Great Plains rehabilitation program crosses the drainage areas of a number of parallel major tributaries of the Mississippi River. It should, therefore, be kept in mind that in establishing a region for one type of comprehensive program, parts or all of the same area may be included in a different region for another type of comprehensive program, with the result of a Federal system, as it were, of programs and administrative areas for solution of basically different yet interrelated problems.

Neither the exact scope nor the most appropriate administrative mechanism for regional husbandry can at the start be projected upon any single blue print. But it is important that we set up without delay some regional machinery to acquaint us with our problem.

I think, however, that for the time being we might give consideration to the creation of seven regional authorities or agencies—one on the Atlantic seaboard; a second for the Great Lakes and Ohio Valley; a third for the drainage basin of the Tennessee and Cumberland Rivers; a fourth embracing the drainage basins of the Missouri River and the Red River of the North; a fifth embracing the drainage basins of the Arkansas, Red, and Rio Grande rivers; a sixth for the basins of the Colorado River and rivers flowing into the Pacific south of the California-Oregon line; and a seventh for the Columbia River Basin. And, in addition, I should leave undisturbed the Mississippi River Commission, which is well equipped to handle the problems immediately attending the channel of that great river.

Apart from the Tennessee Valley Authority, the Columbia Valley Authority, and the Mississippi River Commission, the work of these regional bodies, at least in their early years, would consist chiefly in developing integrated plans to conserve and safeguard the prudent use of waters, water power, soils, forests, and other resources of the areas entrusted to their charge.

Such regional bodies would also provide a useful mechanism through which consultation among the various governmental agencies working in the field could be effected for the development of integrated programs of related activities. Projected programs would be reported by the regional bodies annually to the Congress through the President after he has had the projects checked and revised in light of national budgetary considerations and of national planning policies. When the national planning board is established I should expect to use that agency to coordinate the development of regional planning to insure conformity to national policy, but not to give to the proposed national planning board any executive authority over the construction of public works or over management of completed works.

Projects authorized to be undertaken by the Congress could then be carried out in whole or in part by those departments of the Government best equipped for the purpose, or, if desirable in any particular case, by one of the regional bodies. There should be a close coordination of the work done by the various agencies of government to prevent friction, overlapping, and unnecessary administrative expense and to insure the integrated development of related activities. There should be the closest cooperation also with the developing State and local agencies in this field, particularly the State, regional, and local planning boards and the commissions on interstate cooperation which work through interstate compacts ratified by the Congress and through interstate administrative arrangements. And provision should be made for the effective administration of hydroelectric projects which have been or may be undertaken as a part of a multiple-purpose watershed development. The water-power resources of the Nation must be protected from private monopoly and used for the benefit of the people.

This proposal is in the interest of economy and the prevention of overlapping or one-sided developments. It leaves the Congress wholly free to determine what shall be undertaken and provides the Congress with a complete picture not only of the needs of each one of the regions but of the relationship of each of the regions to the whole of the Nation.

If, for example, the Congress could have had before it at this session a complete picture of immediate and long-term needs, I think its task in providing for flood prevention and drought emergencies would have been an easier one.

For nearly a year I have studied this great subject intensively and have discussed it with many of the Members of the Senate and House of Representatives.

[323]

My recommendations in this message fall into the same category as my former recommendation relating to the reorganization of the executive branch of the Government. I hope, therefore, that both of these important matters may have your attention at this session.

Franklin D. Roosevelt

The White House
June 3, 1937

LEGISLATION DISSOLVING THE NATIONAL RESOURCES PLANNING BOARD*
June 26, 1943

This legislative rider on the Independent Offices Appropriations Bill for 1943 was the death sentence for the National Resources Planning Board, a frail agency which F. D. R. had used for nearly ten years in an attempt to provide planning and coordination for conservation activities within the government.

The agency had been known as the National Resources Board, financed by a grant from Secretary Ickes' Public Works Administration. Although it was headed by Frederick A. Delano, an uncle of the President, it was identified in the congressional mind as an arm of Ickes. Efforts to give it permanent status were successfully resisted by most of the groups who were opposing Ickes' idea of a Conservation Department handling all government water programs.

The Planning Board was killed partly under the guise of wartime economy, and partly in opposition to any type of coordinated planning. The Bureau of the Budget took over the function of coordination.

NATIONAL RESOURCES PLANNING BOARD

Salaries and expenses: For all expenses incident to the discontinuance of the work of the Board, including personal services in the District of Columbia and elsewhere, printing and binding, traveling expenses, and the payment of accumulated and accrued annual leave of employees of the Board due them after June 30, 1943, $50,000: *Provided,* That the National Resources Planning Board is abolished effective August 31, 1943, and the functions exercised by such Board shall not be transferred to any other agency and shall not be performed after such date except as hereafter provided by law or as authorized in the ensuing proviso of this paragraph with respect to winding up the Board's affairs: *Provided further,* That the Director of the Board is authorized after August 31, 1943, and until January 1, 1944, to perform such duties and to exercise such administrative authority as may be incident to the effectuation of the discontinuance of the Board: *Provided further,* That the records and files of the Board shall be transferred to the National Archives.

The appropriation herein made for the National Resources Planning Board shall constitute the total amount to be available for obligation by such agency during the fiscal year 1944 and shall not be supplemented by funds from any source.

*57 *Statutes at Large,* 170.

PRESIDENT ROOSEVELT'S PROPOSAL FOR A MISSOURI VALLEY AUTHORITY*
September 21, 1944

In this brief message President Roosevelt proposed for the Missouri River Valley an agency similar to the Tennessee Valley Authority.

DEVELOPMENT OF THE MISSOURI RIVER BASIN

The PRESIDING OFFICER (Mr. MCCLELLAN in the chair) laid before the Senate the following message from the President of the United States, which was read by the Chief Clerk:

To the Congress of the United States:

I enclose a copy of a resolution adopted by all but one of the Missouri River States, represented in a recent meeting of their governors and the members of the Missouri River States Committee. In general, the resolution asks for executive and legislative action toward procuring a single, coordinated plan for the development of the Missouri River Basin "for the greatest benefit of its citizens both present and future, and for the greatest benefit to the United States."

As the Congress knows, I have for many years advocated the establishment of separate authorities to deal with the development of certain river basins where several States were involved. The general functions and purposes of the Tennessee Valley Authority might well serve as a pattern for similar developments of other river basins. The Tennessee Valley Authority was charged by the Congress with the development of practically all of the factors which are important in establishing better living standards and a better life for the people throughout that great watershed.

The benefits which have resulted in the Tennessee River Valley include flood prevention, irrigation, increased electric power for farms and shops and homes and industries, better transportation on land and water, reforestation and conservation of natural resources, the encouragement of small businesses, and the growth and expansion of new businesses, development and widespread use of fertilizers and improved agricultural methods, better educational and recreational facilities—and many kindred improvements which go to make for increased security and greater human happiness.

The Congress has at all times retained the final authority over the Tennessee Valley Authority, for the Authority comes before the Congress each year to obtain appropriations to continue its work and carry out its plans.

Cong. Rec., 78th Cong., 2nd sess., 8056.

[326]

I have heretofore suggested the creation of a similar authority for the development of the Arkansas River watershed from the Mississippi all the way west to its source in Colorado.

I have also suggested the creation of an authority to render a similar service in the Columbia River watershed, including the States of Washington, Oregon, Idaho, and Montana.

I now make a similar recommendation for the Missouri River Basin.

The resolution very properly asks that the legislation dealing with matters relating to the waters of the Missouri River Basin recognize that it is dealing with one river and one problem; and points out the necessity of a comprehensive development of the Missouri River, indicating that there can be no piecemeal legislative program. The resolution asks that "the Congress should recognize now the problem in its entirety as it affects the people of the Missouri Basin, and their economic destiny and that of the United States."

I am in hearty accord with these principles. I hope that the Congress will give careful and early consideration to the creation of this Federal authority to consider the problem in its entirety, remembering always that any appropriations to carry out any plan are and will be within the complete control of the Congress, and that the interest of each of the States in the basin will, of course, be given full consideration. I am sure that none of the States in the Tennessee River Basin have lost any of their rights because of the creation of the Authority in that valley.

May I also ask that renewed consideration be given to a study of the Arkansas and Columbia River Basins? The fact has been established that such legislation can do much to promote the welfare of the great mass of citizens who live there — as well as their fellow citizens throughout the United States.

I need hardly point out to the Congress, in addition, how helpful this legislation will be in the creation of employment and in the stimulation of industry, business, and agriculture throughout the areas involved, in the days which will follow the end of the war.

Franklin D. Roosevelt

The White House
September 21, 1944

ADMINISTRATIVE AGREEMENT ON THE PICK-SLOAN PLAN*
November 27, 1944

After the Congress had adopted the Pick-Sloan plan in preference to the Missouri Valley Authority, Roosevelt chose to interpret the action as a beginning of a solution which could still become a valley authority. Here is his message to the Congress on this point, with several accompanying papers.

MISSOURI VALLEY AUTHORITY

The PRESIDING OFFICER (Mr. DOWNEY in the chair). The Chair lays before the Senate a communication dated November 27, 1944, from the President of the United States relating to the creation of a Missouri Valley Authority, with accompanying papers, which will be read.

The communication was read by the legislative clerk.

Mr. O'MAHONEY. Mr. President, I ask unanimous consent that the communication from the President, together with the enclosure, be printed at length in the RECORD. The enclosure, as I understand, was the integrated report of the Army engineers and the Bureau of Reclamation which has heretofore been printed as Senate Document No. 274.

The PRESIDING OFFICER. Is there objection?

There being no objection; the communication and report were ordered to be printed in the RECORD as follows:

The White House
Washington, November 27, 1944

The President of the Senate:

Sir:

On September 21, 1944, I sent a message to the Congress recommending the creation of a Missouri Valley Authority that would be charged with the duty of preparing and carrying out a single coordinated plan for the development of the Missouri River Basin for the greatest benefit of its citizens, both present and future, and for the greatest benefit to the United States. At that time there was under consideration by the Congress two reports, the one presented by the Corps of Engineers, the other by the Bureau of Reclamation, which, while presenting comprehensive plans for the development of the Missouri River, were in

*Cong. Rec., 78th Cong., 2nd sess., 8479–80.

conflict in many details. The two bureaus have reconciled the technical differences in these two reports and have prepared a joint recommendation which, in conjunction with the two reports, constitutes a basic plan for the development and control of the waters of the Missouri River.

This joint plan represents a beginning in the solution of the problems of the Missouri Valley. But it is only a beginning, for other important matters not within the scope of this joint report bear very materially upon the entire region. As a practical matter, most of these cannot be dealt with by conference and agreement among the 10 States directly involved working with separate Federal agencies, for the delay in getting action would be too great to bring about the objectives important to the economy of the entire region. A single authority, such as the Tennessee Valley Authority, over the entire region would provide an adequate mechanism for the adjustment of the interests of the States and for the planning and development of the entire valley.

I am transmitting herewith a copy of that report of reconciliation together with accompanying papers. I now recommend that the plans of the two bureaus, published in House Document 475, Seventy-eighth Congress, and Senate Document 191, Seventy-eighth Congress, as modified in accordance with the recommendations of this joint report, be authorized as a basic engineering plan to be developed and administered by a Missouri Valley Authority, such as I have already recommended in my message of September 21.

Sincerely yours,

Franklin D. Roosevelt

Executive Office of the President
Bureau of the Budget
Washington, D.C., November 16, 1944

The President
The White House

Sir:

There are transmitted herewith for your consideration letters from the Secretary of War and of the Interior to me, a joint report of the Chief of Engineers and the Commissioner of Reclamation to the Secretaries of War and of the Interior, and a joint report of representatives of the Bureau of Reclamation and Corps of Engineers on plans for development of the Missouri River basin. I recommend that these papers be transmitted to Congress for its consideration in connection with the reports of the two agencies, published as House Document 475, 78th Congress, and Senate Document 191, 78th Congress.

Very respectfully,

Harold D. Smith,
Director

War Department
Washington, November 4, 1944

Hon. Harold D. Smith
Director, Bureau of the Budget
Washington, D.C.

Dear Mr. Smith:

Reference is made to your letter of October 27, 1944, wherein you request, for consideration by the President, a copy of the reconciliation proposed by the Corps of Engineers and the Bureau of Reclamation of the engineering plans for development of the water resources of the Missouri River basin as presented to Congress by those agencies in House Document 475, Seventy-eighth Congress, and Senate Document 191, Seventy-eighth Congress, respectively.

Complying with your request I am pleased to inclose herewith a joint report from the Chief of Engineers and the Commissioner of Reclamation to the Secretaries of War and Interior with its attached joint report by two engineering representatives of each agency. The joint report of the Chief of Engineers and the Commissioner of Reclamation was prepared in close collaboration among themselves and members of their staffs and completely reconciles the plans of the two agencies.

It is my opinion that the plans of the Corps of Engineers and of the Bureau of Reclamation, coordinated as proposed in the inclosures and authorized as a unified plan, will secure the maximum benefits from the water resources of the basin. I recommend that the joint report be made available for consideration by the Congress in its further deliberations on the pending flood control and river and harbor bills and other proposed legislation pertaining to the Missouri River basin.

Sincerely yours,

Robert P. Patterson,
Acting Secretary of War

The Secretary of the Interior
Washington, November 4, 1944

Hon. Harold D. Smith,
Director, Bureau of the Budget

My Dear Mr. Smith:

I am pleased to be able to reply to your letter of October 27 by transmitting a copy of the report reconciling the engineering features of the plans of the Bureau of Reclamation and the Corps of Engineers, which brings together the report of this Department as printed in Senate Document 191, Seventy-eighth Congress, second session, and the report of the War Department as published in House Document 475, Seventy-eighth Congress, second session. I recommend that this single coordinated plan be authorized in a manner that would modify both the reclamation plan and the Army plan and would carry with it the initial phases of both those plans. The Department of the Interior stands ready to prosecute its share and phases of the Missouri River program.

This agreement marks a definite step in advance toward solving the conflict between irrigation and navigation interests. More storage capacity will be constructed under it than under previous plans of either the Bureau of Reclamation or the Corps of Engineers. This additional storage will be sufficient to provide adequate water for irrigation needs and for navigation, and very adequate flood control storage. General Reybold has informed Commissioner Bashore of his complete agreement with this statement of the advance made as a result of the agreement.

The problem met by the agreement was that of providing adequate non-overlapping storage sufficient to furnish irrigation, navigation, flood control needs, and for power development. The problems of allocation and return of costs have not been met in it, and there was no intention of meeting them in it. The additional storage to be constructed will serve various purposes, and it is my hope that it will be fairly allocated, and that no disproportionate burden will fall on power that would both limit the market for power and limit the advantages to the region from low-cost power. The Commissioner of Reclamation informs that a final determination of the costs and allocations of the reconciled construction program will depend upon further joint studies.

This agreement is intended to present a comprehensive engineering plan for the Missouri River, parts of which could be carried out by either of the existing agencies in accordance with their authority or by any new agency that might be set up for the purpose. It does not, therefore, run counter to the principles of the message that the President has sent to the Congress regarding a Missouri Valley Authority. It is also my understanding that there is nothing in the agreement that renders impossible full and continual consultation between the construction agencies and other interests concerned in the program, or prevents passage of legislation embodying the general principles of the O'Mahoney amendment.

Sincerely yours,

Harold L. Ickes,
Secretary of the Interior

THE WATERS OF THE COLORADO

THE COLORADO RIVER COMPACT*
November 24, 1922

This agreement between seven western states interested in the distribution of Colorado River water was the first major interstate water compact.

The States of Arizona, California, Colorado, Nevada, New Mexico, Utah, and Wyoming, having resolved to enter into a compact under the Act of the Congress of the United States of America approved August 19, 1921 (42 Statutes at Large, page 171), and the Acts of the Legislatures of the said States, have through their Governors appointed as their Commissioners:

W. S. Norviel for the State of Arizona,
W. F. McClure for the State of California,
Delph E. Carpenter for the State of Colorado,
J. G. Scrugham for the State of Nevada,
Stephen B. Davis, Jr., for the State of New Mexico,
R. E. Caldwell for the State of Utah,
Frank C. Emerson for the State of Wyoming,

who, after negotiations participated in by Herbert Hoover, appointed by the President as the representative of the United States of America, have agreed upon the following articles:

ARTICLE I

The major purposes of this compact are to provide for the equitable division and apportionment of the use of the waters of the Colorado River System; to establish the relative importance of different beneficial uses of water; to promote interstate comity; to remove causes of present and future controversies; and to secure the expeditious agricultural and industrial development of the Colorado River Basin, the storage of its waters, and the protection of life and property from floods. To these ends the Colorado River Basin is divided into two Basins, and an apportionment of the use of part of the water of the Colorado River System is made to each of them with the provision that further equitable apportionments may be made.

*Colorado River Compact, H. Doc. 605, 67th Cong., 4th sess., 8–12.

ARTICLE II

As used in this compact:

(a) The term "Colorado River System" means that portion of the Colorado River and its tributaries within the United States of America.

(b) The term "Colorado River Basin" means all of the drainage area of the Colorado River System and all other territory within the United States of America to which the waters of the Colorado River System shall be beneficially applied.

(c) The term "States of the Upper Division" means the States of Colorado, New Mexico, Utah, and Wyoming.

(d) The term "States of the Lower Division" means the States of Arizona, California, and Nevada.

(e) The term "Lee Ferry" means a point in the main stream of the Colorado River one mile below the mouth of the Paria River.

(f) The term "Upper Basin" means those parts of the States of Arizona, Colorado, New Mexico, Utah, and Wyoming within and from which waters naturally drain into the Colorado River System above Lee Ferry, and also all parts of said States located without the drainage area of the Colorado River System which are now or shall hereafter be beneficially served by waters diverted from the system above Lee Ferry.

(g) The term "Lower Basin" means those parts of the States of Arizona, California, Nevada, New Mexico, and Utah within and from which waters naturally drain into the Colorado River System below Lee Ferry, and also all parts of said States located without the drainage area of the Colorado River System which are now or shall hereafter be beneficially served by waters diverted from the system below Lee Ferry.

(h) The term "domestic use" shall include the use of water for household, stock, municipal, mining, milling, industrial, and other like purposes, but shall exclude the generation of electrical power.

ARTICLE III

(a) There is hereby apportioned from the Colorado River system in perpetuity to the Upper Basin and to the Lower Basin, respectively, the exclusive beneficial consumptive use of 7,500,000 acre-feet of water per annum, which shall include all water necessary for the supply of any rights which may now exist.

(b) In addition to the apportionment in paragraph (a), the Lower Basin is hereby given the right to increase its beneficial consumptive use of such waters by one million acre-feet per annum.

(c) If, as a matter of international comity, the United States of America shall hereafter recognize in the United States of Mexico any right to the use of any waters of the Colorado River System, such waters shall be supplied first from the waters which are surplus over and above the aggregate of the quantities specified in paragraphs (a) and (b); and if such surplus shall prove insufficient for this purpose, then the burden of such deficiency shall be equally borne by the Upper Basin and the Lower Basin, and whenever necessary the States of the Upper Division shall deliver at Lee Ferry water to supply one-half of the deficiency so recognized in addition to that provided in paragraph (d).

(d) The States of the Upper Division will not cause the flow of the river at Lee Ferry to be depleted below an aggregate of 75,000,000 acre-feet for any period of ten consecutive years reckoned in continuing progressive series beginning with the first day of October next succeeding the ratification of this compact.

(e) The States of the Upper Division shall not withhold water, and the States of the Lower Division shall not require the delivery of water which can not reasonably be applied to domestic and agricultural uses.

(f) Further equitable apportionment of the beneficial uses of the waters of the Colorado River System unapportioned by paragraphs (a), (b), and (c) may be made in the manner provided in paragraph (g) at any time after October first, 1963, if and when either Basin shall have reached its total beneficial consumptive use as set out in paragraphs (a) and (b).

(g) In the event of a desire for a further apportionment, as provided in paragraph (f), any two signatory States, acting through their Governors, may give joint notice of such desire to the Governors of the other signatory States and to the President of the United States of America, and it shall be the duty of the Governors of the signatory States and of the President of the United States of America forthwith to appoint representatives, whose duty it shall be to divide and apportion equitably between the Upper Basin and Lower Basin the beneficial use of the unapportioned water of the Colorado River System, as mentioned in paragraph (f), subject to the legislative ratification of the signatory States and the Congress of the United States of America.

ARTICLE IV

(a) Inasmuch as the Colorado River has ceased to be navigable for commerce and the reservation of its waters for navigation would seriously limit the development of its basin, the use of its waters for purposes of navigation shall be subservient to the uses of such waters for domestic, agricultural, and power purposes. If the Congress shall not consent to this paragraph, the other provisions of this compact shall nevertheless remain binding.

(b) Subject to the provisions of this compact, water of the Colorado River System may be impounded and used for the generation of electrical power, but such impounding and use shall be subservient to the use and consumption of such water for agricultural and domestic purposes and shall not interfere with or prevent use for such dominant purposes.

(c) The provisions of this article shall not apply to or interfere with the regulation and control by any State within its boundaries of the appropriation, use, and distribution of water.

ARTICLE V

The chief official of each signatory State charged with the administration of water rights, together with the Director of the United States Reclamation Service and the Director of the United States Geological Survey, shall cooperate, ex officio:

(a) To promote the systematic determination and coordination of the facts as to flow, appropriation, consumption and use of water in the Colorado River Basin, and the interchange of available information in such matters.

(b) To secure the ascertainment and publication of the annual flow of the Colorado River at Lee Ferry.

(c) To perform such other duties as may be assigned by mutual consent of the signatories from time to time.

ARTICLE VI

Should any claim or controversy arise between any two or more of the signatory States (a) with respect to the waters of the Colorado River System not covered by the terms of this compact; (b) over the meaning or performance of any of the terms of this compact; (c) as to the allocation of the burdens incident to the performance of any article of this compact or the delivery of waters as herein provided; (d) as to the construction or operation of works within the Colorado River Basin to be situated in two or more States, or to be constructed in one State for the benefit of another State; or (e) as to the diversion of water in one State for the benefit of another State; the Governors of the States affected, upon the request of one of them, shall forthwith appoint Commissioners with power to consider and adjust such claim or controversy, subject to ratification by the Legislatures of the States so affected.

Nothing herein contained shall prevent the adjustment of any such claim or controversy by any present method or by direct future legislative action of the interested States.

ARTICLE VII

Nothing in this compact shall be construed as affecting the obligations of the United States of Amercia to Indian tribes.

[335]

ARTICLE VIII

Present perfected rights to the beneficial use of waters of the Colorado River System are unimpaired by this compact. Whenever storage capacity of 5,000,000 acre-feet shall have been provided on the main Colorado River within or for the benefit of the Lower Basin, then claims of such rights, if any, by appropriators or users of water in the Lower Basin against appropriators or users of water in the Upper Basin shall attach to and be satisfied from water that may be stored not in conflict with Article III.

All other rights to beneficial use of waters of the Colorado River System shall be satisfied solely from the water apportioned to that basin in which they are situate.

ARTICLE IX

Nothing in this compact shall be construed to limit or prevent any State from instituting or maintaining any action or proceeding, legal or equitable, for the protection of any right under this compact or the enforcement of any of its provisions.

ARTICLE X

This compact may be terminated at any time by the unanimous agreement of the signatory States. In the event to such termination all rights established under it shall continue unimpaired.

ARTICLE XI

This compact shall become binding and obligatory when it shall have been approved by the Legislatures of each of the signatory States and by the Congress of the United States. Notice of approval by the Legislatures shall be given by the Governor of each signatory State to the Governors of the other signatory States and to the President of the United States, and the President of the United States is requested to give notice to the Governors of the signatory States of approval by the Congress of the United States.

In witness whereof the Commissioners have signed this compact in a single original, which shall be deposited in the archives of the Department of State of the United States of America and of which a duly certified copy shall be forwarded to the Governor of each of the signatory States.

[336]

Done at the City of Santa Fe, New Mexico, this twenty-fourth day of November, A. D. one thousand nine hundred and twenty-two.

(Signed) *W. S. Norviel*
(Signed) *W. F. McClure*
(Signed) *Delph E. Carpenter*
(Signed) *J. G. Scrugham*
(Signed) *Stephen B. Davis, Jr.*
(Signed) *R. E. Caldwell*
(Signed) *Frank C. Emerson*

Approved:
(Signed) *Herbert Hoover*

BOULDER DAM*
December 21, 1928

Boulder Dam, the first major multipurpose reservoir authorized for construc-tion by the United States Government, grew out of a plan in the Reclamation Service developed by A. P. Davis.

The original congressional sponsor of the dam was Senator Hiram Johnson of California, but Herbert Hoover was probably its most influential backer in 1928. Hoover became interested when he was the federal referee for the Colorado River Compact. He helped persuade President Coolidge to sign the bill after it had been modified to provide that private power companies would get a major share of the power generated at the dam.

It was appropriate for Boulder Dam to later be named Hoover Dam. The reservoir behind it is Lake Mead and it is now a national recreation area in the national park system.

An Act to provide for the construction of works for the protection and development of the Colorado River Basin, for the approval of the Colorado River compact, and for other purposes.

Be it enacted by the Senate and House of Representatives of the United States of America in Congress assembled, That for the purpose of controlling the floods, improving navigation and regulating the flow of the Colorado River, providing for storage and for the delivery of the stored waters thereof for recla-mation of public lands and other beneficial uses exclusively within the United States, and for the generation of electrical energy as a means of making the project herein authorized a self-supporting and financially solvent undertaking, the Secretary of the Interior, subject to the terms of the Colorado River com-pact hereinafter mentioned, is hereby authorized to construct, operate, and maintain a dam and incidental works in the main stream of the Colorado River at Black Canyon or Boulder Canyon adequate to create a storage reservoir of a capacity of not less than twenty million acre-feet of water and a main canal and appurtenant structures located entirely within the United States connecting the Laguna Dam, or other suitable diversion dam, which the Secretary of the Interior is hereby authorized to construct if deemed necessary or advisable by him upon engineering or economic considerations, with the Imperial and Coa-chella Valleys in California, the expenditures for said main canal and appur-tenant structures to be reimbursable, as provided in the reclamation law, and shall not be paid out of revenues derived from the sale or disposal of water power or electric energy at the dam authorized to be constructed at said Black Canyon or Boulder Canyon, or for water for potable purposes outside of the Imperial

*45 *Statutes at Large,* 1057–66.

and Coachella Valleys: *Provided, however,* That no charge shall be made for water or for the use, storage, or delivery of water for irrigation or water for potable purposes in the Imperial or Coachella Valleys; also to construct and equip, operate, and maintain at or near said dam, or cause to be constructed, a complete plant and incidental structures suitable for the fullest economic development of electrical energy from the water discharged from said reservoir; and to acquire by proceedings in eminent domain, or otherwise, all lands, rights of way, and other property necessary for said purposes.

SEC. 2. (a) There is hereby established a special fund, to be known as the "Colorado River Dam fund" (hereinafter referred to as the "fund"), and to be available, as hereafter provided, only for carrying out the provisions of this Act. All revenues received in carrying out the provisions of this Act shall be paid into and expenditures shall be made out of the fund, under the direction of the Secretary of the Interior.

(b) The Secretary of the Treasury is authorized to advance to the fund, from time to time and within the appropriations therefor, such amounts as the Secretary of the Interior deems necessary for carrying out the provisions of this Act, except that the aggregate amount of such advances shall not exceed the sum of $165,000,000. Of this amount the sum of $25,000,000 shall be allocated to flood control and shall be repaid to the United States out of $62\frac{1}{2}$ per centum of revenues, if any, in excess of the amount necessary to meet periodical payments during the period of amortization, as provided in section 4 of this Act. If said sum of $25,000,000 is not repaid in full during the period of amortization, then $62\frac{1}{2}$ per centum of all net revenues shall be applied to payment of the remainder. Interest at the rate of 4 per centum per annum accruing during the year upon the amounts so advanced and remaining unpaid shall be paid annually out of the fund, except as herein otherwise provided.

(c) Moneys in the fund advanced under subdivision (b) shall be available only for expenditures for construction and the payment of interest, during construction, upon the amounts so advanced. No expenditures out of the fund shall be made for operation and maintenance except from appropriations therefor.

(d) The Secretary of the Treasury shall charge the fund as of June 30 in each year with such amount as may be necessary for the payment of interest on advances made under subdivision (b) at the rate of 4 per centum per annum accrued during the year upon the amounts so advanced and remaining unpaid, except that if the fund is insufficient to meet the payment of interest the Secretary of the Treasury may, in his discretion, defer any part of such payment, and the amount so deferred shall bear interest at the rate of 4 per centum per annum until paid.

(e) The Secretary of the Interior shall certify to the Secretary of the Treasury, at the close of each fiscal year, the amount of money in the fund in excess of the amount necessary for construction, operation, and maintenance, and payment of interest. Upon receipt of each such certificate the Secretary of the Treasury is authorized and directed to charge the fund with the amount so certified as repayment of the advances made under subdivision (b), which amount shall be covered into the Treasury to the credit of miscellaneous receipts.

SEC. 3. There is hereby authorized to be appropriated from time to time, out of any money in the Treasury not otherwise appropriated, such sums of money as may be necessary to carry out the purposes of this Act, not exceeding in the aggregate $165,000,000.

SEC. 4. (a). This Act shall not take effect and no authority shall be exercised hereunder and no work shall be begun and no moneys expended on or in connection with the works or structures provided for in this Act, and no water rights shall be claimed or initiated hereunder, and no steps shall be taken by the United States or by others to initiate or perfect any claims to the use of water pertinent to such works or structures unless and until (1) the States of Arizona, California, Colorado, Nevada, New Mexico, Utah, and Wyoming shall have ratified the Colorado River compact, mentioned in section 13 hereof, and the President by public proclamation shall have so declared, or (2) if said States fail to ratify the said compact within six months from the date of the passage of this Act then, until six of said States, including the State of California, shall ratify said compact and shall consent to waive the provisions of the first paragraph of Article XI of said compact, which makes the same binding and obligatory only when approved by each of the seven States signatory thereto, and shall have approved said compact without conditions, save that of such six-State approval, and the President by public proclamation shall have so declared, and, further, until the State of California, by act of its legislature, shall agree irrevocably and unconditionally with the United States and for the benefit of the States of Arizona, Colorado, Nevada, New Mexico, Utah, and Wyoming, as an express covenant and in consideration of the passage of this Act, that the aggregate annual consumptive use (diversions less returns to the river) of water of and from the Colorado River for use in the State of California, including all uses under contracts made under the provisions of this Act and all water necessary for the supply of any rights which may now exist, shall not exceed four million four hundred thousand acre-feet of the waters apportioned to the lower basin States by paragraph (a) of Article III of the Colorado River compact, plus not more than one-half of any excess or surplus waters unapportioned by said compact, such uses always to be subject to the terms of said compact.

The States of Arizona, California, and Nevada are authorized to enter into an agreement which shall provide (1) that of the 7,500,000 acre-feet annually apportioned to the lower basin by paragraph (a) of Article III of the Colorado River compact, there shall be apportioned to the State of Nevada 300,000 acre-feet and to the State of Arizona 2,800,000 acre-feet for exclusive beneficial consumptive use in perpetuity, and (2) that the State of Arizona may annually use one-half of the excess or surplus waters unapportioned by the Colorado River compact, and (3) that the State of Arizona shall have the exclusive beneficial consumptive use of the Gila River and its tributaries within the boundaries of said State, and (4) that the waters of the Gila River and its tributaries, except return flow after the same enters the Colorado River, shall never be subject to any diminution whatever by any allowance of water which may be made by treaty or otherwise to the United States of Mexico but if, as provided in paragraph (c) of Article III of the Colorado River compact, it shall become necessary to supply water to the United States of Mexico from waters over and above the quantities which are surplus as defined by said compact, then the State of California shall and will mutually agree with the State of Arizona to supply, out of the main stream of the Colorado River, one-half of any deficiency which must be supplied to Mexico by the lower basin, and (5) that the State of California shall and will further mutually agree with the States of Arizona and Nevada that none of said three States shall withhold water and none shall require the delivery of water, which can not reasonably be applied to domestic and agricultural uses, and (6) that all of the provisions of said tri-State agreement shall be subject in all particulars to the provisions of the Colorado River compact, and (7) said agreement to take effect upon the ratification of the Colorado River compact by Arizona, California, and Nevada.

(b) Before any money is appropriated for the construction of said dam or power plant, or any construction work done or contracted for, the Secretary of the Interior shall make provision for revenues by contract, in accordance with the provisions of this Act, adequate in his judgment to insure payment of all expenses of operation and maintenance of said works incurred by the United States and the repayment, within fifty years from the date of the completion of said works, of all amounts advanced to the fund under subdivision (b) of section 2 for such works, together with interest thereon made reimbursable under this Act.

Before any money is appropriated for the construction of said main canal and appurtenant structures to connect the Laguna Dam with the Imperial and Coachella Valleys in California, or any construction work is done upon said canal or contracted for, the Secretary of the Interior shall make provision for revenues, by contract or otherwise, adequate in his judgment to insure payment of all expenses of construction, operation, and maintenance of said main canal and appurtenant structures in the manner provided in the reclamation law.

If during the period of amortization the Secretary of the Interior shall receive revenues in excess of the amount necessary to meet the periodical payments to the United States as provided in the contract, or contracts, executed under this

[341]

Act, then, immediately after the settlement of such periodical payments, he shall pay to the State of Arizona 18¾ per centum of such excess revenues and to the State of Nevada 18¾ per centum of such excess revenues.

SEC. 5. That the Secretary of the Interior is hereby authorized, under such general regulations as he may prescribe, to contract for the storage of water in said reservoir and for the delivery thereof at such points on the river and on said canal as may be agreed upon, for irrigation and domestic uses, and generation of electrical energy and delivery at the switchboard to States, municipal corporations, political subdivisions, and private corporations of electrical energy generated at said dam, upon charges that will provide revenue which, in addition to other revenue accruing under the reclamation law and under this Act, will in his judgment cover all expenses of operation and maintenance incurred by the United States on account of works constructed under this Act and the payments to the United States under subdivision (b) of section 4. Contracts respecting water for irrigation and domestic uses shall be for permanent service and shall conform to paragraph (a) of section 4 of this Act. No person shall have or be entitled to have the use for any purpose of the water stored as aforesaid except by contract made as herein stated.

After the repayments to the United States of all money advanced with interest, charges shall be on such basis and the revenues derived therefrom shall be kept in a separate fund to be expended within the Colorado River Basin as may hereafter be prescribed by the Congress.

General and uniform regulations shall be prescribed by the said Secretary for the awarding of contracts for the sale and delivery of electrical energy, and for renewals under subdivision (b) of this section, and in making such contracts the following shall govern:

(a) No contract for electrical energy or for generation of electrical energy shall be of longer duration than fifty years from the date at which such energy is ready for delivery.

Contracts made pursuant to subdivision (a) of this section shall be made with a view to obtaining reasonable returns and shall contain provisions whereby at the end of fifteen years from the date of their execution and every ten years thereafter, there shall be readjustment of the contract, upon the demand of either party thereto, either upward or downward as to price, as the Secretary of the Interior may find to be justified by competitive conditions at distributing points or competitive centers, and with provisions under which disputes or disagreements as to interpretation or performance of such contract shall be determined either by arbitration or court proceedings, the Secretary of the Interior being authorized to act for the United States in such readjustments or proceedings.

(b) The holder of any contract for electrical energy not in default thereunder shall be entitled to a renewal thereof upon such terms and conditions as may be authorized or required under the then existing laws and regulations, unless the property of such holder dependent for its usefulness on a continuation of the contract be purchased or acquired and such holder be compensated for damages to its property, used and useful in the transmission and distribution of such electrical energy and not taken, resulting from the termination of the supply.

(c) Contracts for the use of water and necessary privileges for the generation and distribution of hydroelectric energy or for the sale and delivery of electrical energy shall be made with responsible applicants therefor who will pay the price fixed by the said Secretary with a view to meeting the revenue requirements herein provided for. In case of conflicting applications, if any, such conflicts shall be resolved by the said Secretary, after hearing, with due regard to the public interest, and in conformity with the policy expressed in the Federal Water Power Act as to conflicting applications for permits and licenses, except that preference to applicants for the use of water and appurtenant works and privileges necessary for the generation and distribution of hydroelectric energy, or for delivery at the switchboard of a hydroelectric plant, shall be given, first, to a State for the generation or purchase of electric energy for use in the State, and the States of Arizona, California, and Nevada shall be given equal opportunity as such applicants.

The rights covered by such preference shall be contracted for by such State within six months after notice by the Secretary of the Interior and to be paid for on the same terms and conditions as may be provided in other similar contracts made by said Secretary: *Provided, however,* That no application of a State or a political subdivision for an allocation of water for power purposes or of electrical energy shall be denied or another application in conflict therewith be granted on the ground that the bond issue of such State or political subdivision, necessary to enable the applicant to utilize such water and appurtenant works and privileges necessary for the generation and distribution of hydroelectric energy or the electrical energy applied for, has not been authorized or marketed, until after a reasonable time, to be determined by the said Secretary, has been given to such applicant to have such bond issue authorized and marketed.

(d) Any agency receiving a contract for electrical energy equivalent to one hundred thousand firm horsepower, or more, may, when deemed feasible by the said Secretary, from engineering and economic considerations and under general regulations prescribed by him, be required to permit any other agency having contracts hereunder for less than the equivalent of twenty-five thousand firm horsepower, upon application to the Secretary of the Interior made within sixty days from the execution of the contract of the agency the use of whose transmission line is applied for, to participate in the benefits and use of any main transmission line constructed or to be constructed by the former for carrying such energy (not exceeding, however, one-fourth the capacity of such line), upon payment by such other agencies of a reasonable share of the cost of construction, operation, and maintenance thereof.

The use is hereby authorized of such public and reserved lands of the United States as may be necessary or convenient for the construction, operation, and maintenance of main transmission lines to transmit said electrical energy.

SEC. 6. That the dam and reservoir provided for by section 1 hereof shall be used: First, for river regulation, improvement of navigation, and flood control; second, for irrigation and domestic uses and satisfaction of present perfected rights in pursuance of Article VIII of said Colorado River compact; and third, for power. The title to said dam, reservoir, plant, and incidental works shall forever remain in the United States, and the United States shall, until otherwise provided by Congress, control, manage, and operate the same, except as herein otherwise provided: *Provided, however,* That the Secretary of the Interior may, in his discretion, enter into contracts of lease of a unit or units of any Government-built plant, with right to generate electrical energy, or, alternatively, to enter into contracts of lease for the use of water for the generation of electrical energy as herein provided, in either of which events the provisions of section 5 of this Act relating to revenue, term, renewals, determination of conflicting applications, and joint use of transmission lines under contracts for the sale of electrical energy, shall apply.

The Secretary of the Interior shall prescribe and enforce rules and regulations conforming with the requirements of the Federal Water Power Act, so far as applicable, respecting maintenance of works in condition of repair adequate for their efficient operation, maintenance of a system of accounting, control of rates and service in the absence of State regulation or interstate agreement, valuation for rate-making purposes, transfers of contracts, contracts extending beyond the lease period, expropriation of excessive profits, recapture and/or emergency use by the United States of property of lessees, and penalties for enforcing regulations made under this Act or penalizing failure to comply with such regulations or with the provisions of this Act. He shall also conform with other provisions of the Federal Water Power Act and of the rules and regulations of the Federal Power Commission, which have been devised or which may be hereafter devised, for the protection of the investor and consumer.

The Federal Power Commission is hereby directed not to issue or approve any permits or licenses under said Federal Water Power Act upon or affecting the Colorado River or any of its tributaries, except the Gila River, in the States of Colorado, Wyoming, Utah, New Mexico, Nevada, Arizona, and California until this Act shall become effective as provided in section 4 herein.

SEC. 7. That the Secretary of the Interior may, in his discretion, when repayments to the United States of all money advanced, with interest, reimbursable hereunder, shall have been made, transfer the title to said canal and appurtenant structures, except the Laguna Dam and the main canal and appurtenant structures down to and including Syphon Drop, to the districts or other agencies of the United States having a beneficial interest therein in proportion to their respective capital investments under such form of organization as may be acceptable to him. The said districts or other agencies shall have the privilege at any time of utilizing by contract or otherwise such power possibilities as may exist upon said canal, in proportion to their respective contributions or obligations toward the capital cost of said canal and appurtenant structures from and including the diversion works to the point where each respective power plant may be located. The net proceeds from any power development on said canal shall be paid into the fund and credited to said districts or other agencies on their said contracts, in proportion to their rights to develop power, until the districts or other agencies using said canal shall have paid thereby and under any contract or otherwise an amount of money equivalent to the operation and maintenance expense and cost of construction thereof.

SEC. 8. (a) The United States, its permittees, licensees, and contractees, and all users and appropriators of water stored, diverted, carried, and/or distributed by the reservoir, canals, and other works herein authorized, shall observe and be subject to and controlled by said Colorado River compact in the construction, management, and operation of said reservoir, canals, and other works and the storage, diversion, delivery, and use of water for the generation of power, irrigation, and other purposes, anything in this Act to the contrary notwithstanding, and all permits, licenses, and contracts shall so provide.

(b) Also the United States, in constructing, managing, and operating the dam, reservoir, canals, and other works herein authorized, including the appropriation, delivery, and use of water for the generation of power, irrigation, or other uses, and all users of water thus delivered and all users and appropriators of waters stored by said reservoir and/or carried by said canal, including all permittees and licensees of the United States or any of its agencies, shall observe and be subject to and controlled, anything to the contrary herein notwithstanding, by the terms of such compact, if any, between the States of Arizona, California, and Nevada, or any two thereof, for the equitable division of the benefits, including power, arising from the use of water accruing to said States, subsidiary to and consistent with said Colorado River compact, which may be negotiated and approved by said States and to which Congress shall give its consent and approval on or before January 1, 1929; and the terms of any such compact concluded between said States and approved and consented to by Congress after said date: *Provided,* That in the latter case such compact shall be subject to all contracts, if any, made by the Secretary of the Interior under section 5 hereof prior to the date of such approval and consent by Congress.

SEC. 9. That all lands of the United States found by the Secretary of the Interior to be practicable of irrigation and reclamation by the irrigation works authorized herein shall be withdrawn from public entry. Thereafter, at the direction of the Secretary of the Interior, such lands shall be opened for entry, in tracts varying in size but not exceeding one hundred and sixty acres, as may be determined by the Secretary of the Interior, in accordance with the provisions of the reclamation law, and any such entryman shall pay an equitable share in accordance with the benefits received, as determined by the said Secretary, of the construction cost of said canal and appurtenant structures; said payments to be made in such installments and at such times as may be specified by the Secretary of the Interior, in accordance with the provisions of the said reclamation law, and shall constitute revenue from said project and be covered into the fund herein provided for: *Provided,* That all persons who have served in the United States Army, Navy, or Marine Corps during the war with Germany, the war with Spain, or in the suppression of the insurrection in the Philippines, and who have been honorably separated or discharged therefrom or placed in the Regular Army or Navy Reserve, shall have the exclusive preference right for a period of three months to enter said lands, subject, however, to the provisions of subsection (c) of section 4, Act of December 5, 1924 (Forty-third Statutes at Large, page 702); and also, so far as practicable, preference shall be given to said persons in all construction work authorized by this Act: *Provided further,* That in the event such an entry shall be relinquished at any time prior to actual residence upon the land by the entryman for not less than one year, lands so relinquished shall not be subject to entry for a period of sixty days after the filing and notation of the relinquishment in the local land office, and after the expiration of said sixty-day period such lands shall be open to entry, subject to the preference in this section provided.

SEC. 10. That nothing in this Act shall be construed as modifying in any manner the existing contract, dated October 23, 1918, between the United States and the Imperial Irrigation District, providing for a connection with Laguna Dam; but the Secretary of the Interior is authorized to enter into contract or contracts with the said district or other districts, persons, or agencies for the construction, in accordance with this Act, of said canal and appurtenant structures, and also for the operation and maintenance thereof, with the consent of the other users.

SEC. 11. That the Secretary of the Interior is hereby authorized to make such studies, surveys, investigations, and do such engineering as may be necessary to determine the lands in the State of Arizona that should be embraced within the boundaries of a reclamation project, heretofore commonly known and hereafter to be known as the Parker-Gila Valley reclamation project, and to recommend the most practicable and feasible method of irrigating lands within said project, or units thereof, and the cost of the same; and the appropriation of such sums of money as may be necessary for the aforesaid purposes from time to time is hereby authorized. The Secretary shall report to Congress as soon as practicable, and not later than December 10, 1931, his findings, conclusions, and recommendations regarding such project.

SEC. 12. "Political subdivision" or "political subdivisions" as used in this Act shall be understood to include any State, irrigation or other district, municipality, or other governmental organization.

"Reclamation law" as used in this Act shall be understood to mean that certain Act of the Congress of the United States approved June 17, 1902, entitled "An Act appropriating the receipts from the sale and disposal of public land in certain States and Territories to the construction of irrigation works for the reclamation of arid lands," and the Acts amendatory thereof and supplemental thereto.

"Maintenance" as used herein shall be deemed to include in each instance provision for keeping the works in good operating condition.

"The Federal Water Power Act," as used in this Act, shall be understood to mean that certain Act of Congress of the United States approved June 10, 1920, entitled "An Act to create a Federal Power Commission; to provide for the improvement of navigation; the development of water power; the use of the public lands in relation thereto; and to repeal section 18 of the River and Harbor Appropriation Act, approved August 8, 1917, and for other purposes," and the Acts amendatory thereof and supplemental thereto.

"Domestic" whenever employed in this Act shall include water uses defined as "domestic" in said Colorado River compact.

SEC. 13. (a) The Colorado River compact signed at Santa Fe, New Mexico, November 24, 1922, pursuant to Act of Congress approved August 19, 1921, entitled "An Act to permit a compact or agreement between the States of Arizona, California, Colorado, Nevada, New Mexico, Utah, and Wyoming respecting the disposition and apportionment of the waters of the Colorado River, and for other purposes," is hereby approved by the Congress of the United States, and the provisions of the first paragraph of article 11 of the said Colorado River compact, making said compact binding and obligatory when it shall have been approved by the legislature of each of the signatory States, are hereby waived, and this approval shall become effective when the State of California and at least five of the other States mentioned, shall have approved or may hereafter approve said compact as aforesaid and shall consent to such waiver, as herein provided.

(b) The rights of the United States in or to waters of the Colorado River and its tributaries howsoever claimed or acquired, as well as the rights of those claiming under the United States, shall be subject to and controlled by said Colorado River compact.

(c) Also all patents, grants, contracts, concessions, leases, permits, licenses, rights of way, or other privileges from the United States or under its authority, necessary or convenient for the use of waters of the Colorado River or its tributaries, or for the generation or transmission of electrical energy generated by means of the waters of said river or its tributaries, whether under this Act, the Federal Water Power Act, or otherwise, shall be upon the express condition and

[347]

with the express convenant that the rights of the recipients or holders thereof to waters of the river or its tributaries, for the use of which the same are necessary, convenient, or incidental, and the use of the same shall likewise be subject to and controlled by said Colorado River compact.

(d) The conditions and convenants referred to herein shall be deemed to run with the land and the right, interest, or privilege therein and water right, and shall attach as a matter of law, whether set out or referred to in the instrument evidencing any such patent, grant, contract, concession, lease, permit, license, right of way, or other privilege from the United States or under its authority, or not, and shall be deemed to be for the benefit of and be available to the States of Arizona, California, Colorado, Nevada, New Mexico, Utah, and Wyoming, and the users of water therein or thereunder, by way of suit, defense, or otherwise, in any litigation respecting the waters of the Colorado River or its tributaries.

SEC. 14. This Act shall be deemed a supplement to the reclamation law, which said reclamation law shall govern the construction, operation, and management of the works herein authorized, except as otherwise herein provided.

SEC. 15. The Secretary of the Interior is authorized and directed to make investigation and public reports of the feasibility of projects for irrigation, generation of electric power, and other purposes in the States of Arizona, Nevada, Colorado, New Mexico, Utah, and Wyoming for the purpose of making such information available to said States and to the Congress, and of formulating a comprehensive scheme of control and the improvement and utilization of the water of the Colorado River and its tributaries. The sum of $250,000 is hereby authorized to be appropriated from said Colorado River Dam fund, created by section 2 of this Act, for such purposes.

SEC. 16. In furtherance of any comprehensive plan formulated hereafter for the control, improvement, and utilization of the resources of the Colorado River system and to the end that the project authorized by this Act may constitute and be administered as a unit in such control, improvement, and utilization, any commission or commissioner duly authorized under the laws of any ratifying State in that behalf shall have the right to act in an advisory capacity to and in cooperation with the Secretary of the Interior in the exercise of any authority under the provisions of sections 4, 5, and 14 of this Act, and shall have at all times access to records of all Federal agencies empowered to act under said sections, and shall be entitled to have copies of said records on request.

SEC. 17. Claims of the United States arising out of any contract authorized by this Act shall have priority over all others, secured or unsecured.

SEC. 18. Nothing herein shall be construed as interfering with such rights as the States now have either to the waters within their borders or to adopt such policies and enact such laws as they may deem necessary with respect to the appropriation, control, and use of waters within their borders, except as modified by the Colorado River compact or other interstate agreement.

SEC. 19. That the consent of Congress is hereby given to the States of Arizona, California, Colorado, Nevada, New Mexico, Utah, and Wyoming to negotiate and enter into compacts or agreements, supplemental to and in conformity with the Colorado River compact and consistent with this Act for a comprehensive plan for the development of the Colorado River and providing for the storage, diversion, and use of the waters of said river. Any such compact or agreement may provide for the construction of dams, headworks, and other diversion works or structures for flood control, reclamation, improvement of navigation, division of water, or other purposes and/or the construction of power houses or other structures for the purpose of the development of water power and the financing of the same; and for such purposes may authorize the creation of interstate commissions and/or the creation of corporations, authorities, or other instrumentalities.

(a) Such consent is given upon condition that a representative of the United States, to be appointed by the President, shall participate in the negotiations and shall make report to Congress of the proceedings and of any compact or agreement entered into.

(b) No such compact or agreement shall be binding or obligatory upon any of such States unless and until it has been approved by the legislature of each of such States and by the Congress of the United States.

SEC. 20. Nothing in this Act shall be construed as a denial or recognition of any rights, if any, in Mexico to the use of the waters of the Colorado River system.

SEC. 21. That the short title of this Act shall be "Boulder Canyon Project Act."
Approved, December 21, 1928.

"NO DAM AT DINOSAUR"*
December 22, 1953

The title of this editorial from The New York Times *was prophetic. Thanks largely to a campaign spearheaded by eastern conservationists, the provision for a dam at Echo Park in the Dinosaur National Monument was taken out of the bill which authorized the Upper Colorado project.*

The disconcerting news that Secretary McKay has approved plans to construct a giant dam that would destroy one of the West's great scenic preserves has produced prompt and adverse reaction that we hope will be effective in stopping an inexcusable blunder. The Sierra Club of California, devoted to protection of the Western mountain country, has denounced the Secretary's decision as "the gravest threat to the national park system since its creation in 1916." Other conservation groups will doubtless follow suit. The battle over Dinosaur National Monument, more or less dormant for the past year or so, is about to begin again.

It is a battle that goes beyond the advisability of building this particular dam at this particular spot. Construction of Echo Park Dam, which the Secretary has now recommended to the President for submission to Congress, would mean that the bars are down for the invasion of any national park or monument so long as there is a likely water storage or power site within its confines. The pressures from both private and public agencies—in the latter group the Bureau of Reclamation stands in the forefront—against the national scenic and wildlife preserves is heavy and unremitting. If it is yielded to, in the present instance, there is literally no telling where or if it can ever again be curbed.

Of course the West needs power and water, and of course the Western (and Eastern) conservationists who for three years have been fighting this project are not fighting power and water for the West. What they are fighting is the needless ruination of a stretch of canyon country along the Green and Yampa Rivers on the Utah-Colorado border that has been compared in grandeur, in beauty and in potential national enjoyment to the most notable of our better known parks. But even this argument might not be sufficient if there were not alternate sites outside the National Monument where dams could be constructed that would accomplish the purpose of Echo Park Dam without destroying forever one of the unique remnants of primeval America.

If the Administration and Congress are so ill-advised as to proceed with construction of Echo Park Dam in Dinosaur National Monument we might as well look ahead to another dam flooding out part of Glacier National Park, still another one wrecking a chunk of the Grand Canyon, and lumber companies moving in on Olympic National Park. We also will hear Theodore Roosevelt, Gifford Pinchot and the other great Republican conservationists of a half-century ago turning in their graves.

THE UPPER COLORADO STORAGE PROJECT*
April 11, 1956

The final compromise version of the Upper Colorado River project became law in this form. Note the provisions barring reservoirs in national parks or monuments, and limiting the delivery of water from participating projects to producers of basic agricultural commodities "on newly irrigated lands."

An Act to authorize the Secretary of the Interior to construct, operate, and maintain the Colorado River storage project and participating projects, and for other purposes.

Be it enacted by the Senate and House of Representatives of the United States of America in Congress assembled, That, in order to initiate the comprehensive development of the water resources of the Upper Colorado River Basin, for the purposes, among others, of regulating the flow of the Colorado River, storing water for beneficial consumptive use, making it possible for the States of the Upper Basin to utilize, consistently with the provisions of the Colorado River Compact, the apportionments made to and among them in the Colorado River Compact and the Upper Colorado River Basin Compact, respectively, providing for the reclamation of arid and semiarid land, for the control of floods, and for the generation of hydroelectric power, as an incident of the foregoing purposes, the Secretary of the Interior is hereby authorized (1) to construct, operate, and maintain the following initial units of the Colorado River storage project, consisting of dams, reservoirs, powerplants, transmission facilities and appurtenant works: Curecanti, Flaming Gorge, Navajo (dam and reservoir only), and Glen Canyon: *Provided,* That the Curecanti Dam shall be constructed to a height which will impound not less than nine hundred and forty thousand acre-feet of water or will create a reservoir of such greater capacity as can be obtained by a high waterline located at seven thousand five hundred and twenty feet above mean sea level, and that construction thereof shall not be undertaken until the Secretary has, on the basis of further engineering and economic investigations, reexamined the economic justification of such unit and, accompanied by appropriate documentation in the form of a supplemental report, has certified to the Congress and to the President that, in his judgment, the benefits of such unit will exceed its costs; and (2) to construct, operate, and maintain the following additional reclamation projects (including power-generating and transmission facilities related thereto), hereinafter referred to as participating projects: Central Utah (initial phase); Emery County, Florida, Hammond, La Barge, Lyman, Paonia (including the Minnesota unit, a dam and reservoir on Muddy Creek

*70 *Statutes at Large,* 105–11.

just above its confluence with the North Fork of the Gunnison River, and other necessary works), Pine River Extension, Seedskadee, Silt and Smith Fork: *Provided further,* That as part of the Glen Canyon Unit the Secretary of the Interior shall take adequate protective measures to preclude impairment of the Rainbow Bridge National Monument.

SEC. 2. In carrying out further investigations of projects under the Federal reclamation laws in the Upper Colorado River Basin, the Secretary shall give priority to completion of planning reports on the Gooseberry, San Juan-Chama, Navajo, Parshall, Troublesome, Rabbit Ear, Eagle Divide, San Miguel, West Divide, Bluestone, Battlement Mesa, Tomichi Creek, East River, Ohio Creek, Fruitland Mesa, Bostwick Park, Grand Mesa, Dallas Creek, Savery-Pot Hook, Dolores, Fruit Growers Extension, Animas-La Plata, Yellow Jacket, and Sublette participating projects. Said reports shall be completed as expeditiously as funds are made available therefor and shall be submitted promptly to the affected States, which in the case of the San Juan-Chama project shall include the State of Texas, and thereafter to the President and the Congress: *Provided,* That with reference to the plans and specifications for the San Juan-Chama project, the storage for control and regulation of water imported from the San Juan River shall (1) be limited to a single offstream dam and reservoir on a tributary of the Chama River, (2) be used solely for control and regulation and no power facilities shall be established, installed or operated thereat, and (3) be operated at all times by the Bureau of Reclamation of the Department of the Interior in strict compliance with the Rio Grande Compact as administered by the Rio Grande Compact Commission. The preparation of detailed designs and specifications for the works proposed to be constructed in connection with projects shall be carried as far forward as the investigations thereof indicate is reasonable in the circumstances.

The Secretary, concurrently with the investigations directed by the preceding paragraph, shall also give priority to completion of a planning report on the Juniper project.

SEC. 3. It is not the intention of Congress, in authorizing only those projects designated in section 1 of this Act, and in authorizing priority in planning only those additional projects designated in section 2 of this Act, to limit, restrict, or otherwise interfere with such comprehensive development as will provide for the consumptive use by States of the Upper Colorado River Basin of waters, the use of which is apportioned to the Upper Colorado River Basin by the Colorado River Compact and to each State thereof by the Upper Colorado River Basin Compact, nor to preclude consideration and authorization by the Congress of additional projects under the allocations in the compacts as additional needs are indicated. It is the intention of Congress that no dam or reservoir constructed under the authorization of this Act shall be within any national park or monument.

[353]

Sec. 4. Except as otherwise provided in this Act, in constructing, operating, and maintaining the units of the Colorado River storage project and the participating projects listed in section 1 of this Act, the Secretary shall be governed by the Federal reclamation laws (Act of June 17, 1902, 32 Stat. 388, and Acts amendatory thereof or supplementary thereto): *Provided,* That (a) irrigation repayment contracts shall be entered into which, except as otherwise provided for the Paonia and Eden projects, provide for repayment of the obligation assumed thereunder with respect to any project contract unit over a period of not more than fifty years exclusive of any development period authorized by law; (b) prior to construction of irrigation distribution facilities, repayment contracts shall be made with an "organization" as defined in paragraph 2 (g) of the Reclamation Project Act of 1939 (53 Stat. 1187) which has the capacity to levy assessments upon all taxable real property located within its boundaries to assist in making repayments, except where a substantial proportion of the lands to be served are owned by the United States; (c) contracts relating to municipal water supply may be made without regard to the limitations of the last sentence of section 9 (c) of the Reclamation Project Act of 1939; and (d), as to Indian lands within, under or served by any participating project, payment of construction costs within the capability of the land to repay shall be subject to the Act of July 1, 1932 (47 Stat. 564): *Provided further,* That for a period of ten years from the date of enactment of this Act, no water from any participating project authorized by this Act shall be delivered to any water user for the production on newly irrigated lands of any basic agricultural commodity, as defined in the Agricultural Act of 1949, or any amendment thereof, if the total supply of such commodity for the marketing year in which the bulk of the crop would normally be marketed is in excess of the normal supply as defined in section 301 (b) (10) of the Agricultural Adjustment Act of 1938, as amended, unless the Secretary of Agriculture calls for an increase in production of such commodity in the interest of national security. All units and participating projects shall be subject to the apportionments of the use of water between the Upper and Lower Basins of the Colorado River and among the States of the Upper Basin fixed in the Colorado River Compact and the Upper Colorado River Basin Compact, respectively, and to the terms of the treaty with the United Mexican States (Treaty Series 994).

Sec. 5. (a) There is hereby authorized a separate fund in the Treasury of the United States to be known as the Upper Colorado River Basin Fund (hereinafter referred to as the Basin Fund), which shall remain available until expended, as hereafter provided, for carrying out provisions of this Act other than section 8.

(b) All appropriations made for the purpose of carrying out the provisions of this Act, other than section 8, shall be credited to the Basin Fund as advances from the general fund of the Treasury.

(c) All revenues collected in connection with the operation of the Colorado

River storage project and participating projects shall be credited to the Basin Fund, and shall be available, without further appropriation, for (1) defraying the costs of operation, maintenance, and replacements of, and emergency expenditures for, all facilities of the Colorado River storage project and participating projects, within such separate limitations as may be included in annual appropriation acts: *Provided,* That with respect to each participating project, such costs shall be paid from revenues received from each such project; (2) payment as required by subsection (d) of this section; and (3) payment as required by subsection (e) of this section. Revenues credited to the Basin Fund shall not be available for appropriation for construction of the units and participating projects authorized by or pursuant to this Act.

(d) Revenues in the Basin Fund in excess of operating needs shall be paid annually to the general fund of the Treasury to return—

(1) the costs of each unit, participating project, or any separable feature thereof which are allocated to power pursuant to section 6 of this Act, within a period not exceeding fifty years from the date of completion of such unit, participating project, or separable feature thereof;

(2) the costs of each unit, participating project, or any separable feature thereof which are allocated to municipal water supply pursuant to section 6 of this Act, within a period not exceeding fifty years from the date of completion of such unit, participating project, or separable feature thereof;

(3) interest on the unamortized balance of the investment (including interest during construction) in the power and municipal water supply features of each unit, participating project, or any separable feature thereof, at a rate determined by the Secretary of the Treasury as provided in subsection (f), and interest due shall be a first charge; and

(4) the costs of each storage unit which are allocated to irrigation pursuant to section 6 of this Act within a period not exceeding fifty years.

(e) Revenues in the Basin Fund in excess of the amounts needed to meet the requirements of clause (1) of subsection (c) of this section, and to return to the general fund of the Treasury the costs set out in subsection (d) of this section, shall be apportioned among the States of the Upper Division in the following percentages: Colorado, 46 per centum; Utah, 21.5 per centum; Wyoming, 15.5 per centum; and New Mexico, 17 per centum: *Provided,* That prior to the application of such percentages, all revenues remaining in the Basin Fund from each participating project (or part thereof), herein or hereinafter authorized, after payments, where applicable, with respect to such projects, to the general fund of the Treasury under subparagraphs (1), (2), and (3) of subsection (d) of this section shall be apportioned to the State in which such participating project, or part thereof, is located.

Revenues so apportioned to each State shall be used only for the repayment of construction costs of participating projects or parts of such projects in the State to which such revenues are apportioned and shall not be used for such purpose in any other State without the consent, as expressed through its legally constituted authority, of the State to which such revenues are apportioned. Subject to such requirement, there shall be paid annually into the general fund of the Treasury from the revenues apportioned to each State (1) the costs of each participating project herein authorized (except Paonia) or any separable feature thereof, which are allocated to irrigation pursuant to section 6 of this Act, within a period not exceeding fifty years, in addition to any development period authorized by law, from the date of completion of such participating project or separable feature thereof, or, in the case of Indian lands, payment in accordance with section 4 of this Act; (2) costs of the Paonia project, which are beyond the ability of the water users to repay, within a period prescribed in the Act of June 25, 1947 (61 Stat. 181); and (3) costs in connection with the irrigation features of the Eden project as specified in the Act of June 28, 1949 (63 Stat. 277).

(f) The interest rate applicable to each unit of the storage project and each participating project shall be determined by the Secretary of the Treasury as of the time the first advance is made for initiating construction of said unit or project. Such interest rate shall be determined by calculating the average yield to maturity on the basis of daily closing market bid quotations during the month of June next preceding the fiscal year in which said advance is made, on all interest-bearing marketable public debt obligations of the United States having a maturity date of fifteen or more years from the first day of said month, and by adjusting such average annual yield to the nearest one-eighth of 1 per centum.

(g) Business-type budgets shall be submitted to the Congress annually for all operations financed by the Basin Fund.

SEC. 6. Upon completion of each unit, participating project or separable feature thereof, the Secretary shall allocate the total costs (excluding any expenditures authorized by section 8 of this Act) of constructing said unit, project or feature to power, irrigation, municipal water supply, flood control, navigation, or any other purposes authorized under reclamation law. Allocations of construction, operation and maintenance costs to authorized nonreimbursable purposes shall be nonreturnable under the provisions of this Act. In the event that the Navajo participating project is authorized, the costs allocated to irrigation of Indian-owned tribal or restricted lands within, under, or served by such project, and beyond the capability of such lands to repay, shall be determined, and, in recognition of the fact that assistance to the Navajo Indians is the responsibility of the entire nation, such costs shall be nonreimbursable. On January 1 of each year the Secretary shall report to the Congress for the previous fiscal year, beginning with the fiscal year 1957, upon the status of the revenues from, and the cost of, constructing, operating, and maintaining the Colorado

River storage project and the participating projects. The Secretary's report shall be prepared to reflect accurately the Federal investment allocated at that time to power, to irrigation, and to other purposes, the progress of return and repayment thereon, and the estimated rate of progress, year by year, in accomplishing full repayment.

SEC. 7. The hydroelectric powerplants and transmission lines authorized by this Act to be constructed, operated, and maintained by the Secretary shall be operated in conjunction with other Federal powerplants, present and potential, so as to produce the greatest practicable amount of power and energy that can be sold at firm power and energy rates, but in the exercise of the authority hereby granted he shall not affect or interfere with the operation of the provisions of the Colorado River Compact, the Upper Colorado River Basin Compact, the Boulder Canyon Project Act, the Boulder Canyon Project Adjustment Act and any contract lawfully entered unto under said Compacts and Acts. Subject to the provisions of the Colorado River Compact, neither the impounding nor the use of water for the generation of power and energy at the plants of the Colorado River storage project shall preclude or impair the appropriation of water for domestic or agricultural purposes pursuant to applicable State law.

SEC. 8. In connection with the development of the Colorado River storage project and of the participating projects, the Secretary is authorized and directed to investigate, plan, construct, operate, and maintain (1) public recreational facilities on lands withdrawn or acquired for the development of said project or of said participating projects, to conserve the scenery, the natural, historic, and archeologic objects, and the wildlife on said lands, and to provide for public use and enjoyment of the same and of the water areas created by these projects by such means as are consistent with the primary purposes of said projects; and (2) facilities to mitigate losses of, and improve conditions for, the propagation of fish and wildlife. The Secretary is authorized to acquire lands and to withdraw public lands from entry or other disposition under the public land laws necessary for the construction, operation, and maintenance of the facilities herein provided, and to dispose of them to Federal, State, and local governmental agencies by lease, transfer, exchange, or conveyance upon such terms and conditions as will best promote their development and operation in the public interest. All costs incurred pursuant to this section shall be nonreimbursable and nonreturnable.

SEC. 9. Nothing contained in this Act shall be construed to alter, amend, repeal, construe, interpret, modify, or be in conflict with the provisions of the Boulder Canyon Project Act (45 Stat. 1057), the Boulder Canyon Project Adjustment Act (54 Stat. 774), the Colorado River Compact, the Upper Colorado River Basin Compact, the Rio Grande Compact of 1938, or the Treaty with the United Mexican States (Treaty Series 994).

SEC. 10. Expenditures for the Flaming Gorge, Glen Canyon, Curecanti, and

Navajo initial units of the Colorado River storage project may be made without regard to the soil survey and land classification requirements of the Interior Department Appropriation Act, 1954.

SEC. 11. The Final Judgment, Final Decree and stipulations incorporated therein in the consolidated cases of United States of America v. Northern Colorado Water Conservancy District, et al., Civil Nos. 2782, 5016 and 5017, in the United States District Court for the District of Colorado, are approved, shall become effective immediately, and the proper agencies of the United States shall act in accordance therewith.

SEC. 12. There are hereby authorized to be appropriated, out of any moneys in the Treasury not otherwise appropriated, such sums as may be required to carry out the purposes of this Act, but not to exceed $760,000,000.

SEC. 13. In planning the use of, and in using credits from, net power revenues available for the purpose of assisting in the pay-out of costs of participating projects herein and hereafter authorized in the States of Colorado, New Mexico, Utah, and Wyoming, the Secretary shall have regard for the achievement within each of said States of the fullest practicable use of the waters of the Upper Colorado River system, consistent with the apportionment thereof among such States.

SEC. 14. In the operation and maintenance of all facilities, authorized by Federal law and under the jurisdiction and supervision of the Secretary of the Interior, in the basin of the Colorado River, the Secretary of the Interior is directed to comply with the applicable provisions of the Colorado River Compact, the Upper Colorado River Basin Compact, the Boulder Canyon Project Act, the Boulder Canyon Project Adjustment Act, and the Treaty with the United Mexican States, in the storage and release of water from reservoirs in the Colorado River Basin. In the event of the failure of the Secretary of the Interior to so comply, any State of the Colorado River Basin may maintain an action in the Supreme Court of the United States to enforce the provisions of this section, and consent is given to the joinder of the United States as a party in such suit or suits, as a defendant or otherwise.

SEC. 15. The Secretary of the Interior is directed to continue studies and to make a report to the Congress and to the States of the Colorado River Basin on the quality of water of the Colorado River.

SEC. 16. As used in this Act—

The terms "Colorado River Basin", "Colorado River Compact", "Colorado River System", "Lee Ferry", "States of the Upper Division", "Upper Basin", and "domestic use" shall have the meaning ascribed to them in article II of the Upper Colorado River Basin Compact;

The term "States of the Upper Colorado River Basin" shall mean the States of Arizona, Colorado, New Mexico, Utah, and Wyoming;

[358]

The term "Upper Colorado River Basin" shall have the same meaning as the term "Upper Basin";

The term "Upper Colorado River Basin Compact" shall mean that certain compact executed on October 11, 1948 by commissioners representing the States of Arizona, Colorado, New Mexico, Utah, and Wyoming, and consented to by the Congress of the United States of America by Act of April 6, 1949 (63 Stat. 31);

The term "Rio Grande Compact" shall mean that certain compact executed on March 18, 1938, by commissioners representing the States of Colorado, New Mexico, and Texas and consented to by the Congress of the United States of America by Act of May 31, 1939 (53 Stat. 785);

The term "Treaty with the United Mexican States" shall mean that certain treaty between the United States of America and the United Mexican States, signed at Washington, District of Columbia, February 3, 1944, relating to the utilization of the waters of the Colorado River and other rivers, as amended and supplemented by the protocol dated November 14, 1944, and the understandings recited in the Senate resolution of April 18, 1945, advising and consenting to ratification thereof.

Approved April 11, 1956.

FRANKLIN D. ROOSEVELT

ANOTHER CONSERVATIONIST NAMED ROOSEVELT*
March 3, 1912

This speech, filled with good conservation doctrine, was made by young State Senator Franklin D. Roosevelt before the Troy, New York, People's Forum. Senator Roosevelt served as chairman of the Senate Forest, Fish and Game Committee, but he had already developed an interest in timber management and conservation as the squire of his Hyde Park estate. Note the dropping of the name Gifford Pinchot.

[*Excerpt*][1] To put it another way competition has been shown to be useful up to a certain point and no further. Co-operation must begin where competition leaves off and co-operation is as good a word for the new theory as any other. The founders of the republic were groping for the idea when they tried to form a government aimed to secure the greatest good for the greatest number and it is precisely that idea which is being developed to-day along every possible walk of life.

Let us take some examples of this, in what we call to-day, Conservation. We are taking merely a theory which began to be developed in other countries many years ago. It was recognized in Germany for instance one hundred years ago that the trees on the land were necessary for the preservation of the water power and indeed for the health of the people. As a result practically all of Germany is to-day working out the theory of the liberty of the Community rather than of the liberty of the individual.

One hundred and fifty years ago in Germany the individual was not restricted from denuding his lands of the growing trees. To-day he must cut only in a manner scientifically worked out, which is calculated to serve the ends of the community and not his ends.

They passed beyond the liberty of the individual to do as he pleased with his

---

Franklin D. Roosevelt and Conservation— 1911–1945, Vol. 1, Edgar B. Nixon, ed. (Hyde Park, N.Y.: General Services Administration, National Archives and Records Service, Franklin D. Roosevelt Library, 1957), 17–19.

[1]In the preceding paragraphs Roosevelt had developed the idea that the long struggle for the liberty of the individual had been largely successful but that it was now necessary to establish the "liberty of the community," the right of the community to require certain responsibilities of its members.

own property and found it was necessary to check this liberty for the benefit of the freedom of the whole people.

So in New York State we are beginning to do the same thing. As a whole we are beginning to realize that it is necessary to the health and happiness of the whole people of the State that individuals and lumber companies should not go into our wooded areas like the Adirondacks and the Catskills and cut them off root and branch for the benefit of their own pocket.

There are many persons left to-day that can see no reason why if a man owns land he should not be permitted to do as he likes with it. The most striking example of what happens in such a case, that I know of, was a picture shown me by Mr. Gifford Pinchot last week. It was a photograph of a walled city in northern China. Four or five hundred years ago this city had been the center of the populous and prosperous district. A district whose mountains and ridges were covered with magnificent trees. Its streams flowing without interruption and its crops in the valleys prospering. It was known as one of the most prosperous provinces in China, both as a lumber exporting center and as an agricultural community.

To-day the picture shows the walled town, almost as it stood 500 years ago. There is not a human being within the walls. There are but few human beings in the whole region. Rows upon rows of bare ridges and mountains stretch back from the city without a vestige of tree life, without a vestige of flowing streams and with the bare rocks reflecting the glare of the sun. Below in the plains the little soil which remains is parched and unable to yield more than a tiny fraction of its former crops. This is the best example I know of the liberty of the individual without anything further.

Every man 500 years ago did as he pleased with his own property. He cut the trees without affording a chance for reproduction and he thereby parched the ground, dried up the streams and ruined the valley and the sad part of it is that there are to-day men of the State who for the sake of lining their pockets during their own lifetime are willing to cause the same thing that happened in China. With them the motto is "After us the deluge."

They care not what happens after they are gone and I will go even further and say that they care not what happens even to their neighbors, to the community as a whole, during their own lifetime. The opponents of Conservation who, after all, are merely opponents of the liberty of the community, will argue that even though they do exhaust all the natural resources, the inventiveness of man and the progress of civilization will supply a substitute when the crisis comes. When the crisis came on that prosperous province of China the progress of civilization and the inventiveness of man did not find a substitute. Why will we assume that we can do it when the Chinese failed.

It is the same way with all of our other natural resources in addition to forests. Why, let me ask, are so many of the farms in the State of New York abandoned.

The answer is easy. Their owners 50 or 100 years ago took from the soil without returning any equivalent to the soil. In other words they got something for nothing. Their land was rich and the work was easy. They prospered for a while until the deluge came and when it came they discovered that their lands would not produce. They had taken the richness away and did not pay for it with fertilizers and other methods of soil regeneration.

To-day the people in the cities and the people on the farms are suffering because these early farmers gave no thought to the liberty of the Community. To have suggested to a New York State farmer one hundred years ago that the government would compel him to put so much lime or so much fertilizer on every acre he cultivated would have been an impossibility. He would have stared and muttered something about taking care of his own land in his own way.

Yet there are many thinking people in the State to-day who believe that the time is not far distant when the government of the State will rightly and of necessity compel every cultivator of land to pay back to that land some quid pro quo.

I have taken the conservation of our natural resources as the first lesson that points to the necessity for seeking community freedom, because I believe it to be the most important of all our lessons. Five hundred years ago the peasants of Europe, our ancestors, were not giving much thought to us who are here to-day. But I think a good many people in the audience have often considered what kind of a country we to-day are fashioning to hand down to our descendants.

ROOSEVELT'S ACCEPTANCE SPEECH*
July 2, 1932

This brief excerpt from Roosevelt's acceptance speech to the Democratic National Convention at Chicago makes it clear he was thinking of conservation programs as a tool in attacking unemployment.

[*Excerpt*] Let us use common sense and business sense. And just as one example, we know that a very hopeful and immediate means of relief, both for the unemployed and for agriculture will come from a wide plan of the converting of many millions of acres of marginal and unused land into timberland through reforestation. There are tens of millions of acres east of the Mississippi River alone in abandoned farms, in cut-over land, now growing up in worthless brush. Why, every European nation has a definite land policy and has had one for generations. We have none. Having none, we face a future of soil erosion and timber famine. It is clear that economic foresight and immediate employment march hand in hand in the call for the reforestation of these vast areas.

In so doing, employment can be given to a million men. That is the kind of public work that is self-sustaining, and therefore capable of being financed by the issuance of bonds which are made secure by the fact that the growth of tremendous crops will provide adequate security for the investment.

Yes, I have a very definite program for providing employment by that means. I have done it, and I am doing it today in the state of New York. I know that the Democratic party can do it successfully in the nation. That will put men to work and that is an example of the action that we are going to have.

Franklin D. Roosevelt and Conservation—1911–1945, Vol. 1, Edgar B. Nixon, ed. (Hyde Park, N.Y.: General Services Administration, National Archives and Records Service, Franklin D. Roosevelt Library, 1957), 112–13.

THE EMERGENCY CONSERVATION WORK ACT*
March 31, 1933

This bill was the basis for the establishment of the Civilian Conservation Corps (CCC), one of the now highly regarded successes of the New Deal. Congress passed the bill a week after it had been requested by F. D. R., despite a protest from William Green, president of the American Federation of Labor, that it was "fascism, Hitlerism and Sovietism," and a cry from the Communist Party that it would "establish and legalize a system of forced labor."

Six weeks after the bill passed, more than 1,300 camps had been designated and were in the process of being built by the first recruits. In less than ten years, more than two and one-half million unemployed youths had passed through the CCC. They planted more than two million acres of trees and thinned out the overgrowth in another four million acres. A half-million miles of fire trails, breaks, and forest roads were built in the national forests. Dozens of state and county parks blossomed from land the CCC boys prepared.

An Act for the relief of unemployment through the performance of useful public work, and for other purposes.

Be it enacted by the Senate and House of Representatives of the United States of America in Congress assembled, That for the purpose of relieving the acute condition of widespread distress and unemployment now existing in the United States, and in order to provide for the restoration of the country's depleted natural resources and the advancement of an orderly program of useful public works, the President is authorized, under such rules and regulations as he may prescribe and by utilizing such existing departments or agencies as he may designate, to provide for employing citizens of the United States who are unemployed, in the construction, maintenance and carrying on of works of a public nature in connection with the forestation of lands belonging to the United States or to the several States which are suitable for timber production, the prevention of forest fires, floods and soil erosion, plant pest and disease control, the construction, maintenance or repair of paths, trails and fire-lanes in the national parks and national forests, and such other work on the public domain, national and State, and Government reservations incidental to or necessary in connection with any projects of the character enumerated, as the President may determine to be desirable: *Provided,* That the President may in his discretion extend the provisions of this Act to lands owned by counties and municipalities and lands in private ownership, but only for the purpose of doing thereon such kinds of

*48 *Statutes at Large,* 22–23.

cooperative work as are now provided for by Acts of Congress in preventing and controlling forest fires and the attacks of forest tree pests and diseases and such work as is necessary in the public interest to control floods. The President is further authorized, by regulation, to provide for housing the persons so employed and for furnishing them with such subsistence, clothing, medical attendance and hospitalization, and cash allowance, as may be necessary, during the period they are so employed, and, in his discretion, to provide for the transportation of such persons to and from the places of employment. That in employing citizens for the purposes of this Act no discrimination shall be made on account of race, color, or creed; and no person under conviction for crime and serving sentence therefor shall be employed under the provisions of this Act. The President is further authorized to allocate funds available for the purposes of this Act, for forest research, including forest products investigations, by the Forest Products Laboratory.

Sec. 2. For the purpose of carrying out the provisions of this Act the President is authorized to enter into such contracts or agreements with States as may be necessary, including provisions for utilization of existing State administrative agencies, and the President, or the head of any department or agency authorized by him to construct any project or to carry on any such public works, shall be authorized to acquire real property by purchase, donation, condemnation, or otherwise, but the provisions of section 355 of the Revised Statutes shall not apply to any property so acquired.

Sec. 3. Insofar as applicable, the benefits of the Act entitled "An Act to provide compensation for employees of the United States suffering injuries while in the performance of their duties, and for other purposes", approved September 7, 1916, as amended, shall extend to persons given employment under the provisions of this Act.

Sec. 4. For the purpose of carrying out the provisions of this Act, there is hereby authorized to be expended, under the direction of the President, out of any unobligated moneys heretofore appropriated for public works (except for projects on which actual construction has been commenced or may be commenced within ninety days, and except maintenance funds for river and harbor improvements already allocated), such sums as may be necessary; and an amount equal to the amount so expended is hereby authorized to be appropriated for the same purposes for which such moneys were originally appropriated.

Sec. 5. That the unexpended and unallotted balance of the sum of $300,000,-000 made available under the terms and conditions of the Act approved July 21, 1932, entitled "An Act to relieve destitution", and so forth, may be made available, or any portion thereof, to any State or Territory or States or Territories without regard to the limitation of 15 per centum or other limitations as to per centum.

SEC. 6. The authority of the President under this Act shall continue for the period of two years next after the date of the passage hereof and no longer.
Approved, March 31, 1933.

THE CIVILIAN CONSERVATION CORPS ACT*
June 28, 1937

Although the life of this law was specifically limited to three years, it was an attempt to provide clarification for the Emergency Conservation Work Act, under which the CCC had been established. The Corps was not actually discontinued until after World War II was under way.

An Act to establish a Civilian Conservation Corps, and for other purposes.

Be it enacted by the Senate and House of Representatives of the United States of America in Congress assembled, That there is hereby established the Civilian Conservation Corps, hereinafter called the Corps, for the purpose of providing employment, as well as vocational training, for youthful citizens of the United States who are unemployed and in need of employment, and to a limited extent as hereinafter set out, for war veterans and Indians, through the performance of useful public work in connection with the conservation and development of the natural resources of the United States, its Territories, and insular possessions: *Provided,* That at least ten hours each week may be devoted to general educational and vocational training: *Provided,* That the provisions of this Act shall continue for the period of three years after July 1, 1937, and no longer.

SEC. 2. The President, by and with the advice and consent of the Senate, is authorized to appoint a Director at a salary of $10,000 per annum. The Director shall have complete and final authority in the functioning of the Corps, including the allotment of funds to cooperating Federal departments and agencies, subject to such rules and regulations as may be prescribed by the President in accordance with the provisions of this Act.

SEC. 3. In order to carry out the purpose of this Act, the Director is authorized to provide for the employment of the Corps and its facilities on works of public interest or utility for the protection, restoration, regeneration, improvement, development, utilization, maintenance, or enjoyment of the natural resources of lands and waters, and the products thereof, including forests, fish and wildlife on lands or interest in lands (including historical or archeological sites), belonging to, or under the jurisdiction or control of, the United States, its Territories, and insular possessions, and the several States: *Provided,* That the President may, in his discretion, authorize the Director to undertake projects on lands belonging to or under the jurisdiction or control of counties, and municipalities, and on lands in private ownership, but only for the purpose of doing thereon

*50 *Statutes at Large,* 319–22.

such kinds of cooperative work as are or may be provided for by Acts of Congress, including the prevention and control of forest fires, forest tree pests and diseases, soil erosion, and floods: *Provided further,* That no projects shall be undertaken on lands or interests in lands, other than those belonging to or under the jurisdiction or control of the United States, unless adequate provisions are made by the cooperating agencies for the maintenance, operation, and utilization of such projects after completion.

SEC. 4. There are hereby transferred to the Corps all enrolled personnel, records, papers, property, funds, and obligations of the Emergency Conservation Work established under the Act of March 31, 1933 (48 Stat. 22), as amended; and the Corps shall take over the institution of the camp exchange heretofore established and maintained, under supervision of the War Department, in connection with and aiding in administration of Civilian Conservation Corps work-camps conducted under the authority of said Act as amended: *Provided,* That such camp exchange shall not sell to persons not connected with the operation of the Civilian Conservation Corps.

SEC. 5. The Director and, under his supervision, the heads of other Federal departments or agencies cooperating in the work of the Corps, are authorized within the limit of the allotments of funds therefor, to appoint such civilian personnel as may be deemed necessary for the efficient and economical discharge of the functions of the Corps without regard to the civil-service laws and regulations.

SEC. 6. The President may order Reserve officers of the Army and officers of the Naval and Marine Reserves and warrant officers of the Coast Guard to active duty with the Corps under the provisions of section 37a of the National Defense Act and the Act of February 28, 1925, respectively.

SEC. 7. The Director is authorized to have enrolled not to exceed three hundred thousand men at any one time, of which not more than thirty thousand may be war veterans: *Provided,* That in addition thereto camps or facilities may be established for not to exceed ten thousand additional Indian enrollees and five thousand additional territorial and insular possession enrollees.

SEC. 8. The enrollees in the Corps (other than war veterans, enrollees in the Territories and insular possessions, Indians, not to exceed one mess steward, three cooks, and one leader per each company) shall be unmarried male citizens of the United States between the ages of seventeen and twenty-three years, both inclusive, and shall at the time of enrollment be unemployed and in need of employment: *Provided,* That the Director may exclude from enrollment such classes of persons as he may consider detrimental to the well-being or welfare of the Corps, except that no person shall be excluded on account of race, color, or creed: *Provided further,* That enrollments shall be for a period of not less than six months, and reenrollments (except in the case of one mess steward, three cooks, and one leader, in each company, and War Veterans) shall not exceed a total term of two years: *Provided further,* That in the discretion of the Director continuous service by the enrollee during his period of enrollment shall not be required in any case where the enrollee attends an educational institution of his choice during his leave of absence: *Provided further,* That the Director shall be authorized to issue certificates of proficiency and merit to enrollees under such rules and regulations as he may provide.

SEC. 9. The compensation of enrollees shall be in accordance with schedules approved by the President, and enrollees with dependent member or members of their families shall be required, under such regulations as may be prescribed by the Director, to make allotments of pay to such dependents. Other enrollees may make deposits of pay in amounts specified by the Director with the Chief of Finance, War Department, to be repaid in case of an emergency or upon completion of or release from enrollment and to receive the balance of their pay in cash monthly: *Provided,* That Indians may be excluded from these regulations: *Provided further,* That the pay of enrollees shall not exceed $30 per month, except for not more than ten per centum who may be designated as assistant leaders and who shall receive not more than $36 per month: *Provided further,* That not to exceed an additional 6 per centum of such enrollees who may be designated as leaders and may receive not more than $45 per month as such leaders.

SEC. 10. Enrollees shall be provided, in addition to the monthly rates of pay, with such quarters, subsistence, and clothing, or commutation in lieu thereof, medical attention, hospitalization, and transportation as the Director may deem necessary: *Provided,* That burial, embalming, and transportation expenses of deceased enrolled members of the Corps, regardless of the cause and place of death, shall be paid in accordance with regulations of the Employees' Compensation Commission: *Provided further,* That the provisions of the Act of February 15, 1934 (U. S. C., 1934 ed., title 5, sec. 796), relating to disability or death compensation and benefits shall apply to the enrolled personnel of the Corps.

SEC. 11. The Chief of Finance, War Department, is hereby designated, empowered, and directed, until otherwise ordered by the President, to act as the fiscal agent of the Director in carrying out the provisions of this Act: *Provided,* That funds allocated to Government agencies for obligation under this Act may be expended in accordance with the laws, rules, and regulations governing the usual work of such agency, except as otherwise stipulated in this Act: *Provided further,* That in incurring expenditures, the provisions of section 3709, Revised Statutes (U. S. C., 1934 ed., title 41, sec. 5), shall not apply to any purchase or service when the aggregate amount involved does not exceed the sum of $300.

SEC. 12. The President is hereby authorized to utilize the services and facilities of such departments or agencies of the Government as he may deem necessary for carrying out the purposes of this Act.

SEC. 13. The Director and, under his supervision, the cooperating departments and agencies of the Federal Government are authorized to enter into such cooperative agreements with States and civil divisions as may be necessary for the purpose of utilizing the services and facilities thereof.

SEC. 14. The Director may authorize the expenditure of such amounts as he may deem necessary for supplies, materials, and equipment for enrollees to be used in connection with their work, instruction, recreation, health, and welfare, and may also authorize expenditures for the transportation and subsistence of selected applicants for enrollment and of discharged enrollees while en route upon discharge to their homes.

SEC. 15. That personal property as defined in the Act of May 29, 1935 (49 Stat. 311), belonging to the Corps and declared surplus by the Director, shall be disposed of by the Procurement Division, Treasury Department, in accordance with the provisions of said Act: *Provided,* That unserviceable property in the custody of any department shall be disposed of under the regulations of that Department.

SEC. 16. The Director and, under his supervision, the heads of cooperating departments and agencies are authorized to consider, ascertain, adjust, determine, and pay from the funds appropriated by Congress to carry out the provisions of this Act any claim arising out of operations authorized by the Act accruing after the effective date thereof on account of damage to or loss of property or on account of personal injury to persons not provided for by section 10 of this Act, caused by the negligence of any enrollee or employee of the Corps while acting within the scope of his employment: *Provided,* That the amount allowed on account of personal injury shall be limited to necessary medical and hospital expenses: *Provided further,* That this section shall not apply to any claim on account of personal injury for which a remedy is provided by section 10 of this Act: *Provided further,* That no claim shall be considered hereunder which is in excess of $500, or which is not presented in writing within one year from the date of accrual thereof: *Provided further,* That acceptance by any claimant of the amount allowed on account of his claim shall be deemed to be in full settlement thereof, and the action of the Director or the head of a cooperating department or agency upon such claim so accepted by the claimant shall be conclusive.

SEC. 17. There is hereby authorized to be appropriated, out of any money in the Treasury not otherwise appropriated, such sums as may be necessary for the purpose of carrying out the purposes of this Act: *Provided,* That no part of any such appropriation shall be used in any way to pay any expense in connection with the conduct, operation, or management of any camp exchange, save and except such camp exchanges as are established and operated, in accordance with regulations to be prescribed by the Director, at such camps as may be designated by him, for real assistance and convenience to enrollees in supplying them and their supervising personnel on duty at any such camp with articles of ordinary use and consumption not furnished by the Government: *Provided further,* That the person in charge of any such camp exchange shall certify, monthly, that during the preceding calendar month such exchange was operated in compliance therewith.

SEC. 18. This Act, except as otherwise provided, shall take effect July 1, 1937. Approved, June 28, 1937.

ROOSEVELT AND PINCHOT*
January 15, 1940

Gifford Pinchot and Franklin Roosevelt exchanged correspondence on the subject of reorganization in federal resource management and administrative agencies, particularly with respect to a proposal to transfer the Forest Service from the Department of Agriculture to the Department of the Interior (the reverse of the Pinchot-T. R. transfer).

ROOSEVELT TO GIFFORD PINCHOT

[Washington] January 15, 1940

Dear Gifford:

I have received the form letters and my general reaction to them is unfavorable because this sort of organized drive is just as much a special group effort as drives on the Congress or the President by separate Protestant denominations or individuals like Coughlin or the United States Chamber of Commerce or the Cattlemen's Associations or, for that matter, horrid things like the K. K. K. itself.[1]

I do not believe in group drives anyway because I think they have hurt the improvement of the general processes of administrative government and Congressional decisions.

Furthermore, to suggest that we should have two recreation departments doing practically identical work, one in the Department of Agriculture and the other in the Department of the Interior is wasteful and inefficient.

There are two schools of thought in regard to the two Departments concerned—one is that everything that grows should be in the Department of Agriculture and only inanimate things, like minerals and oils, should be in the Department of the Interior. If this were done the Department of Agriculture would be bigger than all the other Departments of the Government put together, both in personnel and in money spending, and the Department of the Interior would have two or three minor Bureaus in it only. One of the essentials of Government is to prevent any one Department from becoming a tail that runs the Federal dog!

Franklin D. Roosevelt and Conservation—1911–1945, Vol. 2, Edgar B. Nixon, ed. (Hyde Park, N.Y.: General Services Administration, National Archives and Records Service, Franklin D. Roosevelt Library, 1957), 413–15.

[1] Pinchot had drafted a letter to Roosevelt opposing transfer of the Forest Service to the Interior Department and had sent mimeographed copies to faculty members of American forestry schools for signature. One hundred and thirty-nine signed letters and fourteen unsigned letters were returned to Pinchot; these were sent by him to Roosevelt with his covering letter of Jan. 13, 1940.

A more logical division goes back to the origin of both Departments. The Department of the Interior was organized primarily to take charge of Government owned land, and the Department of Agriculture was organized primarily to look over the needs of the private landowners of the United States.

Frankly, I am getting to the point of believing that logic favors the latter view. And, incidentally, the days have passed when any human being can say that the Department of Agriculture is wholly pure and honest and the Department of the Interior is utterly black and crooked.

Very sincerely yours,

[Franklin D. Roosevelt]

GIFFORD PINCHOT TO ROOSEVELT

Washington, D.C., January 17, 1940

Dear Franklin:

Many thanks for your letter of January 15.

Here are some of the reasons why, as a matter of sound government organization, the Forest Service should not be transferred.

The Service was born, grew up, and for a long generation has done admirable work in the Department of Agriculture. There is no tenable claim that it could do better elsewhere, and no reason to expect that it could do as well.

The Forest Service is a research as well as an executive organization. This union of research and administration underlies the progress of forestry and the morale and efficiency of the Service. To separate the two would ruin the Service. This union is also the distinguishing characteristic of the Department of Agriculture.

The Service is in constant necessary cooperation with more than half of the twenty-odd other organizations in the Department, such as the Soil Conservation Service, the Bureaus of Agricultural Economics, Entomology, Plant Industry, etc., etc. That cooperation would be badly dislocated if the transfer were made.

The sentiment of the people most concerned is overwhelmingly opposed to the transfer. Users of the National Forests; experts in forestry in and out of the government service; the great national agricultural organizations and many others; the people of the Rocky Mountain and Pacific coast states and their representatives in Senate and House, of both parties—all these are, in immense majority, vigorously opposed to the transfer and in favor of keeping the Service where it is.

Silcox did not believe that the Forest Service could continue to succeed if transferred to the Interior Department. I understand that he gave you his reasons.

[373]

The transfer is not a question of personalities, but of good permanent organization. Secretaries pass; the natural relations between lines of work do not. If Harold Ickes were in Agriculture and Henry Wallace in Interior, I would still be emphatically opposed to the proposed transfer.

To uproot the Service from its lifelong surroundings would do great injury to its morale, to its essential cooperation with other agricultural bureaus, to its relations with the users of the National Forests, and to public support. Only the strongest constructive reasons could justify it. So far as I know, such reasons do not exist.

It strikes me as particularly unfortunate that conservation should become a controversial issue just at this time when I believe it can be made the foundation of enduring peace between nations. This is what I have wanted to see you about. I enclose a memorandum on the subject.[1]

Faithfully yours,

Gifford Pinchot

And I still want to see you about it.

[1] "A Plan for Permanent Peace Through International Cooperation in the Conservation and Distribution of Natural Resources," a nine-page typescript, signed by Pinchot and dated Jan. 17, 1940.

FORESTER ROOSEVELT*
April 11, 1941

F. D. R. was proud of his practical knowledge of timber from the management of his Hyde Park estate. This memorandum to Harold D. Smith, Director of the Budget, gives some of his ideas on private timber operations.

[Washington] April 11, 1941

Memorandum for the Director of the Budget:

Here is "the law and the profits" in regard to privately owned timber:

1. Everybody should draw a line between the man and the corporation which owns land and uses it primarily for farming, and the man or corporation which owns land and uses it primarily for growing or raising or cutting trees. It is essential to accentuate the word "use." In effect, and as a matter of Government assistance, this can be attained by acreage limitation. For example, not one-tenth of one per cent of the farmers of the nation own more than one hundred acres of forest land—and most of them own, I suppose, an average of twenty or twenty-five acres.

2. The reason that what is known as woodlot forestry has never worked is that the farmer does not know how to dispose of his timber. Nobody has ever told him how. That is the duty of the federal and state governments—even to some method of agreeing to take his timber at the current market price. This would involve taking the lumber in the log because the woodlot forestry farmer, who has a small acreage, cannot afford and has no facilities for cutting his logs into boards or square lumber, nor does he know how to dispose of his smaller stuff.

3. Another wholly different class is the commercial, private lumber company or the company which buys stumpage on fairly large tracts and lumbers this stumpage.

4. Those individuals or companies are not farmers. They are lumbermen. They should not get any Government subsidy because they are primarily in the lumber business. They should receive all kinds of advice on fire-prevention, re-seeding, re-planting, etc., and they might be given a drawback or benefit up to a small amount if they can conform to our reforestation methods as laid down by the Government.

In regard to H. R. 969, there is no such thing as a mixture of woodlot management and commercial forestry.

If you want further instruction on growing trees and selling them, come and talk with me!

F. D. R.

Franklin D. Roosevelt and Conservation—1911–1945, Vol. 2, Edgar B. Nixon, ed. (Hyde Park, N.Y.: General Services Administration, National Archives and Records Service, Franklin D. Roosevelt Library, 1957), 501.

CONSERVATION FOR PEACE*
November 10, 1944
April 10, 1945

One of the last official acts of President Franklin Roosevelt was to hold a North American Conservation Conference in Washington, which he envisioned both as a tool of conservation and an instrument for peaceful relations.

The conference idea originated with Gifford Pinchot, who was one of those who pressed Franklin Roosevelt to accept the idea of an International Conference on Conservation and Natural Resources. These letters and memoranda right up to the time of F. D. R.'s death show that it was one of the last ideas he considered.

EDWARD R. STETTINIUS, JR., ACTING
SECRETARY OF STATE, TO ROOSEVELT

Washington, November 10, 1944

Memorandum for the President:
Proposed Conference on Conservation and Natural Resources: Further reference is made to your letter of October 24, 1944, suggesting the possibility of calling a conference of the United and Associated Nations on the conservation and use of natural resources. There can be little doubt that, as you suggest, the development of effective international cooperation in stimulating the adoption of sound national conservation policy on a world-wide basis, in promoting joint measures of attack upon common problems, and in enlarging our knowledge of the natural resource basis from which the peoples of the earth derive their living, might make a significant contribution to the solution of the problem of maintaining world peace.

There are, however, a number of considerations which I should like to bring to your attention that appear to me to make less urgent the need for a special international conference on conservation at this time. These considerations are set forth in the attached enclosure. Beginning with the projected Food and Agriculture Organization of the United Nations which grew out of the Hot Springs Conference, and extending through to the Economic and Social Council of the general international organization, our post-war economic policy planning has given and will continue to give a place of high importance to questions of conservation of natural resources.

I have considerable doubt as to the desirability of a separate international conference in the near future centering its attention exclusively on conservation.

Franklin D. Roosevelt and Conservation—1911-1945, Vol. 2, Edgar B. Nixon, ed. (Hyde Park, N.Y.: General Services Administration, National Archives and Records Service, Franklin D. Roosevelt Library, 1957), 606-8, 612-13, 636-37, 644-46.

It seems to me unlikely that most of the governments of the world will find themselves able to reach any firm views on the important problems of conservation in the absence of a clearer view than they now have on the prospects for production and trade and of the nature and extent of international collaboration therein.

I shall of course be glad to discuss this with you further if you should so desire.

E. R. Stettinius, Jr.

[*Enclosure*] PROPOSED CONFERENCE ON CONSERVATION AND NATURAL RESOURCES

1. In the years to come we shall be faced with a wide variety of situations pertaining to particular natural resources. In some of them, we shall be faced, for a few years at least, with continuing shortages in comparison with war and reconstruction needs. In others, we shall soon be faced with troublesome problems of surplus production and surplus capacity. I should be much inclined to doubt whether we should be able to reach significant international agreement on conservation programs without simultaneously considering the prospects for the orderly development and marketing of these resources. If this view is correct, it sets conservation as one part, and a very important part, of the total problem of international collaboration in the wisest use of the world's productive resources. This is the pattern which we have been attempting to follow to date.

2. The conservation and development of agricultural resources was one of the subjects discussed at the United Nations Conference on Food and Agriculture at Hot Springs, and Article I of the draft Constitution of the Food and Agriculture Organization of the United Nations specifically provides that the Organization "shall promote and, where appropriate, shall recommend national and international action with regard to . . . the conservation of natural resources and the adoption of improved methods of agricultural production." Under the terms of the proposed Constitution of the Food and Agriculture Organization, the scope of its activities covers fisheries and forestry, as well as agriculture proper. Arrangements are therefore well under way whereby provision will be made for the handling on an international basis of conservation problems in the fields of agriculture, fisheries and forestry.

3. The orderly development of world petroleum resources for the needs of international trade is a basic objective of the Anglo-American Petroleum Agreement now pending before the Congress and is similarly contemplated as an objective of the broader international agreement which is envisaged by the Anglo-American Agreement.

4. The preparation of the American program on other aspects of international post-war economic policy is, as you know, already far advanced. Part of this

program is a proposal for an appropriate international organization to facilitate study and discussion of international commodity programs and to aid in the negotiation and operation of particular international commodity arrangements. In this preparatory work, for example, it has been recognized that conservation is an important element to be considered in connection with international commodity arrangements. For the reasons which I have set forth in paragraph number one above, I believe that it would be preferable to introduce the problems of conservation as a part of the coming international discussions in the field of commercial policy and commodity problems, rather than to treat it separately from, and in advance of these negotiations.

5. To the extent that the foregoing steps would still leave need for special international machinery to deal with problems of conservation, the Economic and Social Council of the proposed general international organization might well be assigned this as one of its first and urgent tasks. This would safeguard against the possibility of creating too much international machinery with possibly overlapping fields of jurisdiction. The powers of the Economic and Social Council and its liaison with the Security Council will put this body in an excellent position to see the economic, social, and political ramifications of the entire problems of resource utilization in proper perspective. It can be expected to stimulate and supplement the activities of international agencies with specified responsibilities in its field.

ROOSEVELT TO EDWARD R. STETTINIUS, JR., UNDER SECRETARY OF STATE

Washington, November 22, 1944

Memorandum for the Under Secretary of State:

I am not satisfied with the Department's attitude on a Conservation Conference. Whoever wrote the memorandum for you has just failed to grasp the real need of finding out more about the world's resources and what we can do to improve them.

Just for example, take the case of Persia (Iran). The greater part of it, i.e., the North, used to be a forested country. Today it is utterly bare with a few cattle and a few very poor crops in the small valleys. The people are destitute. Anyone who knows forestry would say that an immediate program of tree planting is the only hope for the Persia of the future. The population is abject—poverty stricken—filthy. Very little water means that something drastic must be done and it will take several hundred years to accomplish it.

But it is a big country and there is plenty of labor. Persia has no resources to buy our products.

Very little is actually known about it, but I am sure there are enormous possibilities.

Lots of countries are like this.

My thought is that we should call a Conference to which each of the United and Affiliated Nations would send one representative. Most of them are poor. One man from each country is enough. The countries that wanted to send somebody could have them meet here in a more or less secluded spot and we would get world information which is now lacking, and in a short period of time we could begin a program to build up non-buying nations into good customers.

When I say a short space of time, I mean a hundred years but that is short in these times.

Will you let me have this memorandum back and also the letter from Governor Pinchot?

F. D. R.

GRACE G. TULLY, PERSONAL SECRETARY TO THE PRESIDENT, TO ROOSEVELT

Washington, March 23, 1945

Memorandum for the President:

Anna tells me you wish to be reminded about the world conservation plan in which Governor Pinchot is interested. Anna also said you were not very pleased with the memorandum on the suggestion from the State Department and that you mentioned you would like Gov. Pinchot and Mr. Hugh H. Bennett, Chief of Soil Conservation Service, to get together and work out something pretty concrete. After this has been done, you said you wanted it taken up with someone in the State Department who understands and is sympathetic to the idea.

Do you wish one of us to get in touch with Gov. Pinchot, explain to him that you are extremely busy but suggest that he get in touch with Bennett and even tell him that you were not satisfied with the State Department's working out of this matter?

G. G. T.

GIFFORD PINCHOT TO ROOSEVELT

Washington 6, D.C., March 28, 1945

Dear Mr. President:

Before your brilliantly successful visit to Yalta, you were good enough to agree that a rough plan for a World Conference on Conservation as a Basis of Permanent Peace should be worked out during your absence. Here it is.

T. R. introduced conservation to America. Nothing could be more fitting than that you, who have already done so much for conservation on this continent, should crown your good work by rendering the same great service to the rest of mankind.

If you decide to call such a Conference, you will guide all Nations toward the intelligent use of the earth for the general good of men, and you will make to the movement for permanent peace the most enduring contribution of all.

The proposed meeting would assist powerfully in attaining the objectives of the Bretton Woods and Dumbarton Oaks Conferences. It is intended to fit easily into the pattern of the coming international organization.

At your direction, I saw Secretary Wickard. He expressed agreement. Without exception, the Government experts I consulted approved holding the conference.

There will be objections, of course, but the thing can be done.

Every good wish to you,

Faithfully yours,

Gifford Pinchot

GIFFORD PINCHOT TO ROOSEVELT

Washington 6, D.C., April 10, 1945

Dear Mr. President:

You will be glad to know, I am sure, that the possibility of a conflict between the World Conference on Conservation and the Food and Agriculture Commission, concerning which Wickard sent for me, seems to have vanished. I had a talk with Pearson, head of the latter, who assured me that he could see no reason for such a conflict.

May I say how much I hope that you will have time to glance at the plan I sent you (on March 28th) before San Francisco, where perhaps some action should be taken.

Every good wish to you.

Faithfully yours,

Gifford Pinchot

WILLIAM L. CLAYTON, ASSISTANT SECRETARY OF STATE FOR ECONOMIC AFFAIRS, TO EDWARD R. STETTINIUS, JR., SECRETARY OF STATE

[Washington] April 17, 1945

Governor Pinchot's Proposal for a Conservation Conference:

I understand that you are soon to meet with Governor Pinchot to discuss his proposal for a world conference on "Conservation as a Basis of Permanent

Peace." This is a matter in which President Roosevelt took a personal interest and on which there is a background of correspondence between the Department and the White House. The chronology is as follows:

(1) On three previous occasions we commented at President Roosevelt's request on Governor Pinchot's proposal. Departmental memoranda, dated November 10, 1944, December 16, 1944, and March 19, 1945 (copies attached), were prepared and submitted to the White House.

(2) The memorandum of November 10 was adverse to the Pinchot proposal as we understood it. It was received unfavorably by President Roosevelt.

(3) The December 16 memorandum suggested a mild and partial acceptance of Governor Pinchot's proposals in the form of informal regional conferences on questions of conservation. It was received by the White House without comment.

(4) The March 19 memorandum was prepared upon the basis of your conversation with President Roosevelt and Secretary Wickard on March 16, and incorporated remarks along the lines of Secretary Wickard's comments which, when made orally, had apparently been well received by President Roosevelt. Our memorandum, however, was returned with the notation that he did not want to forward it to Governor Pinchot. It is not clear whether he disapproved the substance or merely wanted to handle the matter orally.

(5) All three of these previous memoranda were prepared without benefit of any detailed statement by Governor Pinchot of what his proposal specifically contemplated. We now have in hand a copy of what Governor Pinchot calls his "rough outline" for the kind of conference under discussion. It confirms our early misgivings. The suggested agenda and "possible recommendations" and "possible conclusions" all indicate a coverage of discussion that would overlap at almost every turn with the functions of the Food and Agriculture Organization, with the subject matter of the World Trade Conference which you announced in your Chicago speech, with the responsibilities of whatever organization may be established under the Economic and Social Council to deal with international commodity arrangements and related matters, and with such Article VII conversations with individual governments as may be held in the next year or so.

(6) Governor Pinchot and President Roosevelt apparently had the impression that other government agencies were unanimous in support of the Pinchot proposal and that only the State Department was reluctant to give its approval. This impression is not borne out by information received from contacts at working levels. I recommend that before you see Governor Pinchot you discuss the conservation conference proposal with Secretary Wickard and with Mr. Howard Tolley, United States representative on the United Nations Interim Commission on Food and Agriculture.

(7) An attached memorandum contains in summary form the principal points which have been developed in the Department previously on this subject, and

some further comments relating specifically to Governor Pinchot's outline proposal.

I recommend that in discussing this matter with Governor Pinchot the Department go no further in the way of encouraging the Governor than a promise to bring his proposal before the Executive Committee on Economic Foreign Policy for its consideration.

W. L. C.

[*Enclosure*] PROPOSED CONSERVATION CONFERENCE

April 17, 1945

It is recognized that the principles and practice of sound conservation of natural resources are of primary importance to nations and that a considerable measure of international collaboration with respect to conservation can be fruitful. There are, however, several considerations militating against the advisability of an early convocation of a separate conference to deal specifically with the question of conservation.

(1) Such a conference would necessarily be designed either (a) to facilitate the collection of information about natural resources and their utilization, or (b) to propose measures for a collaborative approach to problems of conservation.

(2) It is unnecessary to convoke a world conference in order to facilitate the collection of information. Indeed this can better be done by technicians in the various countries of the world communicating with one another when necessary through normal channels. It would be obviously undesirable to convoke any conference in the near future which is not absolutely necessary for the purpose intended.

(3) It is unlikely that nations could agree at the present time on measures of collaborative action with respect to conservation problems until some area of agreement has been blocked out with respect to larger problems of trade and commodity arrangements. To convoke at the present time a conservation conference which could not agree upon useful and constructive decisions would prejudice the benefits that might be anticipated from the convocation of a conservation conference at some later date when the general international economic and commodity situation might be clearer.

HAROLD ICKES

ICKES' CONSERVATION PHILOSOPHY*
December 23, 1933

This article in The Saturday Evening Post, *written by Marquis James for Harold Ickes, Roosevelt's Secretary of the Interior, is a brief review of conservation concepts during the first days of the New Deal.*

Here is a small piece of paper containing a few lines hastily written with a lead pencil. It is unsigned, but perhaps you might recognize the angular handwriting of the President of the United States. Let me read to you what he has written:

Total Dams & Ditches	[$]13,500,000
(Hydro Elec	6,000,000
1st year	$ 4,500,000
Acres to be irrigated	60,000
Elimination sub margin	300,000
subtract 60,000	
Total Elim	240,000

I intend to preserve this paper. It is interesting now. To my grandchildren it will be more so, as one of the acorns from which great oaks have grown.

The foregoing sets forth, in its shirt sleeves, the latest and most authoritative advices I have at hand on a pertinent phase of the spacious subject of our national domain and its conservation. The President jotted it down as we talked a few days ago. As everyone knows, reclamation of farming lands by irrigation is one arm of the diverse policy of conservation. That means bringing in more acres of tillable soil, and, quite naturally, the question arises: Why should we add to the sum of farming lands on the edge of the desert when, to get rid of the surplus of farm produce, we are having farmers in the old-established agricultural belts plow under standing crops? If that were all there is to irrigation, there would be no excuse for it; and such, indeed, has been the old irrigation policy.

But under the new set-up the case takes on a different color. By this policy, for every acre brought in by reclamation there will be withdrawn from cultivation, or attempted cultivation, submarginal lands of equal producing capacity, the ratio being about five acres withdrawn for every acre brought in.

*"The National Domain and the New Deal," an interview by Marquis James with Harold L. Ickes, *The Saturday Evening Post* (Dec. 23, 1933), 10–11, 55.

The President's memorandum portrays a hypothetical example. We engage to spend on irrigation dams and ditches $13,500,000, say, and for hydro-electric equipment $6,000,000 more; the first year's expenditure being $4,500,000. Assume that ultimately this will transform 60,000 desert acres into crop-bearing soil, every acre of which, productively, will be worth five acres of submarginal land. Thus 300,000 acres of poor land will be retired, and we shall have 240,000 fewer acres in production than before.

WHAT THE NEW LAND POLICY WILL DO

This exemplifies a good land policy, a good conservation policy, a good social policy. Think what it will mean to the poor devils now eking out a squalid existence on soil which, in this country, one has no business trying to farm, to put them on land where, with the same or less effort, they can enjoy their share of the desirable things of life. In 1929, which was a pretty good farm year, 28 per cent of all the farms in the United States produced less than $600 apiece; and this production comprised only 3.38 per cent of all farm products sold in the United States. Forty-nine per cent of our farms produced less than $1000 apiece, and this production was less than 11 per cent of the national cash farm income. This shows where approximately half of our farm population stands today. As for their influence on production and on the surplus—why, it amounts to only slightly more than the effect of a couple of good seasonable rains in the Corn Belt.

We are ascertaining for the first time the amount of poor land that should be retired from cultivation, and in round figures it seems to foot up to something in the neighborhood of 25,000,000 acres.

We have learned to take the bird's-eye view and to zone our cities, directing that in this area we shall have residences, in this retail stores, in this manufacturing. We now undertake to achieve a grand vision of the whole country, saying that this land shall be cropped, this shall be range, this shall be forest, this shall be worked for minerals. In this way, and no other, can we properly conserve—that is to say, use wisely—our natural resources and provide for a more equable distribution of their bounties.

We have reached the end of the pioneering period of go ahead and take. We are in an age of planning for the best use of everything for all. We must ultimately pull out from low-scale agricultural production, with its attendant evils of low-standard living, some millions of acres of submarginal lands. One-fifth as many good acres will take care of the people now scratching them for an existence and will open for these people the gates of a happier life. The abandoned acres should pass back to the control of the Federal Government to be administered for the benefit of the nation as a whole. In the East this land largely should be added to our national forests. In the West, generally speaking, it should revert to the public domain as an addition to our grazing ranges. The

Indians, who are badly in need, should also get their share. By such redistribution, this soil will be of vastly more service to society than as crop land whereon a sizable proportion of our farming population struggles in vain to make a decent livelihood.

As to water power, the alternative is to turn it over to private interests for exploitation or to retain it as a public trust for public use. I believe in developing public resources for the benefit of the public, and do not see why we should hand them over to someone and tell them to make a profit. Almost all reclamation projects are susceptible of water-power development.

BIG WRITER TO BE BIG RIGHTER

And one more parenthetical word about the Indians. They bring up a conservation problem of a special sort—a matter of human and spiritual values rather than material values entirely.

Creek Indians of the old generation in Oklahoma have a word for the Secretary of the Interior that contains a certain amount of irony. Translated, it means Big Writer. A century and a half of wrongs perseveringly visited upon the Indians have done much that is beyond repair. But as long as I am Big Writer, there will be no more thievery of Indian water rights and a dipping into tribal funds for the construction of fancy roads and bridges for white tourists to ride over.

Since 1904, our unreserved and unappropriated public lands have shrunk from 473,000,000 acres to 173,000,000. Much of this vast domain was taken up as farm and cattle-raising homesteads. That a considerable part of it was unsuited for those purposes, the present state of the agricultural proprietor and of the small stock raiser who has tried to make out on a homestead of 640 acres bears conclusive testimony. With all good intentions, the Government has been a party to an unsound business allurement from the effects of which a great many of our citizens have suffered and are suffering. This wrong we propose to correct, making the Government a party to the retirement of poor lands from cultivation and to the voluntary relocation of the people who are trying to cultivate them on better properties.

Moreover, I propose to exert my influence to retain our 173,000,000 acres of public domain, and whatever may be added to it, under the control of the Federal Government, rather than to grant it to the states in which it lies. One school of conservationists favors this latter course. I oppose it because I feel certain that the selfish and shortsighted influences which have done so much to plunder our public domain and bring upon our heads the problems that now vex us would find it much simpler to have their way with state governments than with the National Government. Especially will this be true when the arm of the Federal Government is strengthened by the contemplated reforms which I hope within a few months will have the sanction of law.

The public domain, exclusive of mineral properties, performs an important function in our social and economic scheme. These 173,000,000 acres are situated largely in the eleven Western States of Arizona, California, Colorado, Idaho, Montana, Nevada, New Mexico, Oregon, Utah, Washington and Wyoming, and these states produce about half of the sheep and one-sixth of the cattle that are raised in our country. By a decision of the United States Supreme Court, the public lands are a grazing common for the use of the public.

THE IMPORTANCE OF A BLADE OF GRASS

The Department of the Interior is charged with the administration of these lands, but has very limited authority to control their use. The result has been tragic. Many years ago, a member of the Geological Survey contemplated the bleak prospect of a grazing range upon which the very roots had been eaten, and recommended that there be some authority to regulate grazing. He pointed out that without such regulation overgrazing destroyed the cover. Next season one found the grass depleted, and the stock ate out the roots. Then erosion set in, the headwaters of the streams silted up and there were floods below—all traceable back to overgrazing.

As matters stand now, there is no authority to prevent overgrazing. I can go out with a thousand cattle and pick a range bare of everything that a cow or a steer will eat. You can follow with a herd of sheep. Sheep browse more closely than cattle and they can subsist on a range where cattle will starve. Sheep will eat and tread out the roots of the grass. This situation was the genesis of the great sheep and cattle wars in the early days of the powder-stained West. Animosity between sheepmen and cattlemen is not uncommon today, but instead of shooting it out, as they did in the olden days, they have recourse to the local courts. These courts can determine who shall use the range as between rivals, but they cannot restrict the extent of its use. Thus the fundamental evil of the destruction of the range continues.

The cattlemen, like the oilmen, the coal men, the timber men, and every one of us who has had anything to do with the utilization of our resources of nature, have played a shortsighted game. We are all tarred with the same stick, and in no quarter of the country have we learned our lesson except when those natural resources have been exhausted or seriously depleted. Why are so many of the leading conservationists Easterners? Take President Roosevelt, Gifford Pinchot, T. R., Rexford Tugwell, Henry Morgenthau, Jr.—all are from east of the Appalachians, where the people are now paying so dearly for the acts of their lusty pioneer forbears. Our cattlemen have merely carried on a great American tradition.

It is illegal to fence the national grazing range, but during the war, when it was necessary to overlook a number of precedents and ignore a good many laws, permission was granted to erect fences on parts of the public domain in

Arizona and in New Mexico. When the emergency passed, the fences were ordered down. Pressure was brought to bear and the fences stayed where they were, making, in effect, private preserves of the public range. Order has succeeded order, but the fences remain. I have directed that they shall be removed, and intend that this order shall be obeyed, even if it means some activity on the part of the United States marshals. I do not anticipate, however, that this will be the case. I feel that we shall soon have a new deal for the public domain that will mean so much for the cattle industry and so much for the country that this small, if vital, issue of the fences will solve itself in the right way.

TRUE CONSERVATION

In 1928 my predecessor in charge of the Department of the Interior obtained authority from Congress to undertake an experiment. Some of the poorest grazing land in Montana lay in the Mizpah River-Pumpkin Creek area in the southeastern part of the state. It had been abused until it hardly was fit for anything. The department obtained permission to segregate 108,000 acres, part of it public domain and part privately owned, but of little use to the owners. This land was withdrawn from grazing and given a rest. Then it was leased to a privately organized association for twenty dollars a section—a section being a square mile, or 640 acres. The association undertook to lease it to cattlemen at $1.25 a head. It put up fences, made water holes, dipping sheds and other improvements; and it regulated grazing. The result after three years is that there is twice as much grass in the Mizpah as before, although the carrying capacity has been increased from 3000 to 5000 head. Moreover, I have been told that the calves last year weighed on an average twelve pounds more than in any previous year before grazing was regulated on that range.

This is true conservation, which, I repeat, does not mean holding a public resource in idleness, but using it wisely.

The success of the Mizpah River-Pumpkin Creek experiment has brought numerous requests from different parts of the West for permission to form similar associations and work out the grazing problem under Federal supervision on other segments of the public domain. I feel, however, that rather than deal with the matter piecemeal, it would be wiser to deal at one swoop with the whole public domain by giving this department authority to regulate grazing on it, which, as a matter of fact, should have been done many years ago. Accordingly, last March there was presented in the House of Representatives, by Mr. Taylor, of Colorado, a bill whose objects were defined in this language: "To stop injury to the public grazing lands by preventing overgrazing and soil deterioration; to provide for their orderly use, improvement and development; to stabilize the livestock industry upon the public range, and for other purposes."

This bill was prepared in collaboration with the Department of Agriculture and had the benefit of its long experience with this problem. In the national forests, which are under the jurisdiction of the Department of Agriculture, grazing is regulated and there has been no such deterioration of the range as has occurred on the public domain. This bill was passed by the House, but the Senate did not have time to act on it before adjournment. When Congress convenes again in January, this bill will be punctually reintroduced.

The proposed legislation gives the Government an authority over its grazing lands that it should have possessed long ago, and will do for this great domain all and more than has been done in Montana by means of the Mizpah experiment. As drawn, however, the bill contains one serious defect. This is a provision that the act shall be ineffective in any state without the approval of the legislature of that state, and further provides that state lands may be lumped with Federal lands in a jointly administered project. I am opposed to this for the same reasons that I am opposed to transfer of our public domain to state control. The local political pressure for a return to the old evils would be a thing not easily resisted. But with this one section amended, I hope, and expect, that this great piece of legislation will be enacted at the coming session of Congress, and I cannot neglect this opportunity to urge my fellow citizens to support it.

To the lay mind, the word "conservation" usually connotes the work that has been done to preserve our forests and to create and maintain our national parks; and this, indeed, is an important aspect of the problem. A forest is the most highly developed of the natural social organizations of the vegetable kingdom, and the most useful. A forest is a community of trees, as a city is a community of human beings, and had there been no forests in this country there would be fewer cities.

JEFFERSON MISSED HIS RECKONING

In a forest there is a struggle for existence, it is true, with each tree fighting to obtain its share of the good things of the universe, but, on the other hand, a forest is a coöperative community in which each tree helps its neighbor and contributes its part to the common protection of the young. A forest perpetuates the richness of its own soil. Its influence on streams averts floods and droughts. It sustains a population of animals and has made large sections of this continent habitable for man, aside from the contributions to man in the form of fuel and building materials. The disappearance of forests has rendered millions of acres of our country so inhospitable to man that wisdom suggests that the residents move out and give this land an opportunity to recruit its life-sustaining powers as a part of the public domain.

Seven-eighths of the eight-hundred-odd millions of acres of virgin forest within the bounds of the United States already have been destroyed, and though abuses continue in what remains, the lumbering interests have awakened to the grave nature of affairs. Originally, lumbering was centered in the Eastern States. These forests denuded, it moved into the hardwood belt in the Middle States and into the Lake region. Then it went South. Now it is on the Sierra slopes and the Pacific Northwest, which is the last stand. Wasteful lumbering and fires have destroyed these forests, which, with the buoyance of youth, pioneer American enterprise deemed inexhaustible. As thoughtful a man as Thomas Jefferson reckoned that it would take civilization one hundred generations to march from the Appalachians to the Pacific. He missed it by ninety-five generations.

About half of the timber available for lumbering is in private hands and half lies within the Federally owned and protected national forests. That in private hands supplies 97 per cent of the current lumber production. Of late years, lumber companies have undertaken reforestation on a large scale.

NATIONAL FOREST ADDITIONS

I am unwilling, however, to intrust the entire problem to private owners. If it had not been for the farseeing and competent administration of our national forests by the Department of Agriculture, the situation would be much worse than it is. There should be large additions to our national forests, which now cover barely one-fifth of our possible timber-growing areas. The young men of the Civilian Conservation Corps have in six months accomplished as much that will enhance the happiness of coming generations as has been accomplished by all other agencies dealing with reforestation in the past fifteen years. They have planted trees on national land, state land, county land and private land. Nature and time will do the rest. And most people thought that this work was simply an excuse for taking a quarter of a million idle youngsters off the streets.

Moreover, $20,000,000 from the CCC funds have been set aside for the purchase of new lands to be added to the national forests. The National Forest Reservation Commission has in mind the acquisition of approximately forty-two tracts aggregating 7,280,000 acres. This will exhaust the fund. These units are located in fourteen states, the westernmost of which is Minnesota. Four of these states—Missouri, Illinois, Kentucky and Mississippi—now contain no national forests.

In the Far West, territory is being added to the national forests under the General Exchange Act by swapping land for land and land for stumpage. No money payments are involved.

The conservation of scenic values is one of the most interesting and worthwhile of our efforts, and it is a thing that cannot be done by the Federal Government alone. It must reach down to every village and community in the land. Grand Canyon, Yosemite, Glacier Park, Acadia, the Great Smokies—the very names expand the heart. But what would they have meant to us if the Government had not taken them in hand? Private interests will exploit anything. They would put a sign on the Washington Monument if you would let them. How often have you gone through the country and seen a beautiful, majestic bowlder turned into an advertisement?

We are approaching a time when we shall have more leisure. What better use can be made of it than just wandering about, looking at the scenery? Take the range: north in the summer, south in the winter, California at all times. But we must educate our people to a sane use of leisure. For one thing, I hope to see the system of national parks greatly enlarged. There are inspiring, beautiful places in nearly every state in the Union which could be set aside as national parks with profit to all.

They should be joined by great roads. The other day I listened to Senator Byrd, of Virginia, as he sketched his vision of a road a hundred feet wide from the Shenandoah to the Great Smoky National Park. The President amplified the picture. He said he would like to see the road begin at the Canadian border in Vermont and sweep down through the Green Mountains, through the Berkshires and to the Blue Ridge, joining the senator's project. This would be a great thing, a great thing for the interior life of our people. There shouldn't be a billboard in sight. The right of way should be landscaped and planted like the Bronx River Parkway and contiguous systems leading north from New York City. It costs little to set out trees when a road is built. Then, in twenty-five years, see what you have.

Suppose that you owned five acres. Would you go out and cut down every tree and burn it in the fireplace? We have five acres at our place in Winnetka, north of Chicago. When the house was built in 1916, a few trees had to be removed. These filled the cellar with firewood. Since then I have cut down only dead trees and worked up the windfalls, and the cellar is still filled. And I do not have a billboard on the front lawn.

We must get a sense of personal responsibility toward the national resources as a whole. That is all there is to conservation. If we do not, we waste; and if we waste, we find ourselves in the hands of the sheriff, as the coal industry has done.

BUYING BACK A GIFT

Conservation is economy. Consider Chicago. The early fathers were open-handed go-getters. They pressed miles of the beautiful lake front upon a railroad. Our generation is taxing itself hundreds of millions of dollars to get back that lake front. When we cut down a tree that has been a hundred years growing and make a house of it, we think we are being progressive. But, unless steps are taken to replace that tree, another generation will pay a heavy cost for our lack of imagination and of regard for the rights of the other fellow.

One afternoon I got to my home in Winnetka earlier than usual, and while walking about the grounds I found a woman inside the fence, filling a market basket with flowers.

I asked her if she was aware that she was on private property.

The inquiry did not disturb her. "Oh," she said, "I thought it would be all right."

That's the trouble. We've always thought it would be all right. We are not woods broke. We see something lovely or useful—and we reach and take. A century of this, and behold the evils that have followed in its train: depleted timber and mineral resources, depleted ranges, erosion and floods, millions of acres rendered unfit to support human life decently. Now, what are we going to do—go out and correct these conditions, complex as they have grown, and painful and expensive as readjustment at this late date may be in some of its details, or shall we fold our arms and say that these things are the way of the world and no help can be found for them?

ICKES COMPLAINS TO WALLACE*
August 19, 1936

Secretary Ickes guarded the prerogatives of the Interior Department just as zealously as he attempted to increase them. This letter to Secretary of Agriculture Henry A. Wallace protests an Agriculture Department presentation to Congress which he regarded as a threat to Interior's responsibility for the public domain.

HAROLD L. ICKES TO HENRY A. WALLACE, SECRETARY OF AGRICULTURE

Washington [Aug. 19, 1936]

My Dear Mr. Secretary:

Under date of April 29, 1936, the Senate Committee on Agriculture and Forestry ordered printed as Senate Document No. 199, a report entitled *The Western Range.* This report was submitted to you by the Chief of the Forest Service, ostensibly in compliance with Senate Resolution 289, 74th Congress, 2nd Session. This resolution requested the Secretary of Agriculture to transmit to the Senate a report incorporating certain information accumulated as a result of many years of research and administration of the national forests, and in addition to transmit recommendations as to constructive measures.

The report contains more than 600 pages of printed material, tables, maps, and other illustrations. It was forwarded to the Senate four days after approval of the resolution requesting the information purported to be contained therein. Obviously the report was prepared prior to the resolution and I feel some justification in assuming that the resolution was introduced at the request of some member of your department.

The report sets forth recognized principles of conservation and reasonably well established facts, but intermingled therewith are expressions of ill-considered opinions and discussions concerning matters within the jurisdiction of the Interior Department. All of the report is given the dignity of an authoritative pronouncement by a statement in a letter of transmittal from the Chief of the Forest Service that the report contains all pertinent information that could be obtained from any Federal Agency. The Interior Department, however, a Federal agency more definitely concerned with the western range than is the Forest Service, was not called upon for information to be used in the report, was not consulted as to its issue and had no part in its preparation.

Franklin D. Roosevelt and Conservation—1911–1945, Vol. 1, Edgar B. Nixon, ed. (Hyde Park, N.Y.: General Services Administration, National Archives and Records Service, Franklin D. Roosevelt Library, 1957), 550–55.

The report covers an area of 728 million acres, about 39 per cent of which is under Federal jurisdiction. A total of 12 per cent of the land is said to be under control of the Forest Service. The remaining 27 per cent comprises land in which regulation of the range is, for the most part, an Interior Department function. For this land, as well as for the public land within national forests, the General Land Office, the Geological Survey, Office of Indian Affairs, the Bureau of Reclamation, the National Park Service, and the Division of Grazing, in connection with their regularly assigned duties, have assembled a volume of factual material that should be incorporated in any comprehensive report on the western range region.

Failure to consult the Interior Department in the preparation of the Western Range report has resulted in an incomplete and inaccurate discussion, especially in outlining national land policies adopted in the administration of the public domain. The administration of these policies is a major Interior Department function and the report implies throughout that outstanding leadership for the proper performance of this function has been lacking. The report then offers as constructive suggestions conservation measures for the public domain that comprise part of a program not only advocated by this department for more than a half century but now rounded out by the enactment of the Taylor Grazing Act of June 26, 1934, as amended June 26, 1936.

The report also insists that management of the public domain should be centered in one department, and that, the Department of Agriculture. Such activities as relate to power reserves, reservoir site reserves, irrigation projects, recreation and scenic withdrawals, stock water reserves, stock driveway withdrawals, mineral reservations, public range reserves, grazing districts, leasing or other disposal of isolated tracts of public lands, and various miscellaneous purpose reservations on the public domain are now largely centered in the Interior Department. They contemplate conservation of every natural resource on the Federal domain except timber in national forests and wild life in Federal game reservations. These excepted activities are under the jurisdiction of your department but in the administration of the public domain not included in forest and game refuges, conservation of timber and game is a function of the Interior Department.

The Taylor Grazing Act under which range conservation on the public domain is established as a function of the Interior Department is made a topic of extensive discussion. Delay in enacting this legislation is given special emphasis in the report. It is strange that attention should be invited to this delay by that agency in your department which exerted every effort to secure the veto of the legislation. This same agency for many years has interposed intangible but real obstructions to such legislation mainly by attempting to incorporate in legislative proposals for the public domain, inapplicable rules and regulations adopted by your department for forest reservations. Apparently the assumption that

[393]

administration of grazing lands should be identical with the administration of the national forests is now abandoned by a statement in the report that the Forest Service and Grazing Service should be maintained as separate entities.

In a chapter headed "Unsuitable Land Policy" the report discloses either a reckless disregard for accuracy, or lack of proper consideration of opinions heretofore propounded by the best minds in the nation including experts of your department. In discussing enlarged homesteads the chapter states:

> In spite of the growing appreciation that crop agriculture was unsuited to most of the west and that economic range use must be substituted as the basis for land disposal, laws continued to pass which encouraged passage of title to private ownership with little regard to the area required, under proper use, to support a family.

The enlarged homestead act of 1909, sometimes known as the dry farm homestead law, is then described as among the "less wisely conceived" enactments establishing a national land policy. The influence exerted by your department in the formulation of that national land policy however is not mentioned, although the public records contain abundant evidence of the exercise of that influence.

Early in this century the Department of Agriculture began a systematic study and promotion of dry-land farming and the annual report of the department for 1908 states that a vast region formerly considered as of little use for cultivation is rapidly becoming of considerable agricultural importance under guidance of the department. Even in 1916 your department reported that it had introduced improved methods of dry farming that had opened up "vast areas of semiarid country which before were given over to sagebrush and cactus, the rattlesnake and the prairie dog." Should not your department therefore accept basic responsibility for the subsequent economic distress of settlers on dry farm homesteads in this area which contains most of the "abandoned shacks," "worn-out tractors" and "fallen-down barns," cited by the Forest Service as witnesses of improper national land policies?

The stock raising homestead law is described in the report as the most unfortunate of the land disposal laws and in a quoted statement by the Assistant Chief of the Forest Service as an outstanding example of a reasonably good law unwisely and improvidently administered. Apparently the reader is supposed to select which of these two inconsistent positions the report presumes to establish. Actual factual basis to support neither theory is submitted. Tables are copies from Interior Department reports in support of the alleged unwise administration but the discussion of these tables and their interpretation is erroneous. Whether the stock raising homestead act was in fact mainly beneficial, or mainly detrimental, to the West, is unknown and can be determined only by exhaustive research studies.

The discussion also states that a procedure for making waterhole withdrawals was not developed, while as a matter of fact since March 29, 1912, every application to appropriate land under the public land laws has been examined to determine whether valuable public watering places or key areas were involved. Where appropriate the involved land has been included in a public water reserve and the application rejected. In addition, since April 17, 1926, every applicant for public lands has been required to submit an affidavit certifying that no springs or waterholes needed for public purposes were involved therein.

The operation of the Mizpah-Pumpkin Creek grazing district, which has been under Interior jurisdiction since its organization under the act of March 29, 1928 (45 *Stat.* 380),[1] is discussed in one chapter and it is indicated that this district has been successful because of the counsel and advice of the Forest Service. The plan followed in that area, however, contains the essential elements of a grazing plan proposed by the Interior Department long prior to the creation of the Forest Service and is consistent with plans now being developed by this Department in organizing grazing districts under the Taylor Grazing Act.

The report repeatedly urges transfer of administration of the Taylor Grazing Act to the Department of Agriculture. Underlying this proposal is the calm assumption that all competence in the administration of grazing resides in the Department of Agriculture, and that the Interior Department is entirely innocent of competence in this field. I shall not comment further on such an assumption by one department of government about another, or upon the propriety of thus seeking to create a prejudice against this department.

The report is critical of several provisions of the Taylor Grazing law based upon a legal construction of the act. Some of these criticisms are a reiteration of objections that were urged upon the President in an effort to secure a veto of the original law at the time of its passage by the Congress. Others have been cured by the amendatory legislation enacted June 26, 1936. The President referred the objections offered in favor of a veto to the Attorney General who reported that in his opinion they were without substance. Therefore, on June 26, 1934, the President approved the Taylor Grazing Act and issued a statement from which the following passage is quoted:

> The passase of this act marks the culmination of years of effort to obtain from Congress express authority for Federal regulation of grazing on the Federal domain in the interests of conservation and the livestock industry. . . . The Federal Government by enacting this law has taken a great forward step in the interest of conservation which will prove of benefit not only to those engaged in the livestock industry but also to the nation as a whole.

Repetition in this report of criticisms heretofore held inadequate to justify a veto of the Taylor Act is a criticism of the President. Furthermore, under the guise of an objective technical document the report not only contains propaganda by one department of the Federal Government against another, but also attacks the private owners of western range lands. The report gives the Forest

---

[1] This authorized the Secretary of the Interior to lease certain public lands in Montana for grazing.

Service alone a creditable record. I am truly amazed that an organization composed of technically trained experts who have selected as a career the protection of the public interest in a most valuable natural resource should sponsor a report of this character. I am even more amazed at such sponsorship in the light of the valuable help in organizing the administration of the Taylor Grazing Act that has been afforded by many members of the Forest Service other than those who contributed to the writing of this report. The most astonishing thing of all is that one department, at public expense and without presidental sanction, should issue what is a thinly veiled attack upon a sister department. Such a report tends to create public prejudice against the good faith of all Federal agencies and in my opinion is injurious to the public service and to the administration.

Sincerely yours,

[Harold L. Ickes]

HENRY WALLACE'S OPPOSITION TO A
DEPARTMENT OF CONSERVATION*
November 27, 1937

When Secretary Ickes began to mobilize forces to secure a Department of Conservation, Agriculture Secretary Wallace counterattacked.

HENRY A. WALLACE, SECRETARY OF AGRICULTURE,
TO ROOSEVELT

Washington [November 27, 1937]

Dear Mr. President:

Both directly and indirectly I have been informed that the leading farm and conservation organizations are greatly concerned about one phase of your proposal to reorganize the government. These organizations approve about 99 per cent of your reorganization proposal. They have appreciated enormously your unprecedented interest in agriculture and conservation. Nevertheless, their opposition to one phase of your reorganization plan furnishes an opening which may seriously split your forces and even endanger other phases of your program. They are against the proposal to change the name of the Department of the Interior to the Department of Conservation.

The following organizations are among those against the proposal: American Farm Bureau Federation, National Grange, National Cooperative Council, National Farmers' Union, Farmers' National Grain Corporation, American Agricultural Editors Association, Association of Land Grant Colleges, Izaak Walton League (and other wildlife organizations), American Forestry Association (and other forestry and conservation organizations.)

(And may I add that I know of no agricultural, or forestry, or conservation organization of any strength or standing that is in favor of the Conservation Department proposal.) To be honest, I must admit that I am in sympathy with the point of view of these organizations toward the Conservation Department proposal. I do not see how agriculture and conservation can be divorced, nor why they should be. Nevertheless, I have refrained from stating my views publicly. I have asked all officials of the Department of Agriculture to adopt the same course. This course, however, is rendered increasingly difficult by two facts:

1. The Department of the Interior has carried on a concerted campaign of propaganda which clearly urges the transfer of many land use functions of the

*Franklin D. Roosevelt and Conservation—1911-1945, Vol. 2, Edgar B. Nixon, ed. (Hyde Park, N.Y.: General Services Administration, National Archives and Records Service, Franklin D. Roosevelt Library, 1957), 144-47.

Department of Agriculture to another government department. This campaign has grown bolder under the guise of upholding your endorsement of the Brownlow Committee report which calls for the establishment of a Department of Conservation. The campaign has culminated in a radio speech by the Secretary of the Interior, who has again attacked all opponents of the idea as agents of special interests and enemies of conservation. Whatever Secretary Ickes' intentions, the result of his campaign has been to stir the farm and conservation organizations to deep resentment and united action.

2. The farm and conservation organizations have construed my silence to mean consent. They are asking where I stand. The letter from H. H. Chapman, President of the Society of American Foresters, which I handed you several days ago illustrates the situation. I attach hereto another copy of this letter and my proposed reply. In ordinary circumstances they might subscribe to my feeling that differences of opinion between administration officials should be settled inside the administration, but they protest that Secretary Ickes has gone too far for that attitude to govern the present situation.

Let me say at once that I have given and will give the warmest possible support to your effort to reorganize the government. The need is pressing. I agree that we must have more efficiency and greater harmony in government. I feel keenly that you are harassed, day in and day out, by jurisdictional disputes which ought never to arise.

The long-standing conflicts between the Departments of Agriculture and the Interior usually have involved the land use functions of government. Somehow we shall have to solve the problem of properly locating these major land use functions within the government if we are to end the conflict.

I wish therefore to propose for most serious consideration a plan which in my judgment would finally bring harmony into the relations of at least the Departments of Agriculture and the Interior.

The premises of the plan are these:

Our government is engaged in a vast land use program looking toward the wise husbandry of our land resources, both public and private. In such a program some land must be in trees, some in grass, some in farm crops. Whether the land be in public or private ownership the problems are the same, the solutions demand scientific and economic information, and the programs must be manned by persons trained in the agricultural and related sciences.

Erosion must be controlled on grass land, forest land and crop land. No matter who owns the land, the scientific techniques are the same. Grazing must be controlled on both grass land and forest land, public and private. Fertility must be conserved on all. Human needs must be considered. Most of the people who live on and use the land are farmers. The Federal government cannot do the job alone. It must have the cooperation of state governments and millions of farmers and stockmen. That cooperation in solving our land use problems cannot be obtained if the federal part of the effort lacks unity and harmony.

I can see but one solution: the transfer to the Department of Agriculture of the Grazing Administration, the agricultural phases of the Reclamation Service, the General Land Office, and the National Parks. That would at once bring harmony and unity in land use programs. On the other hand, harmony in land use cannot be achieved by transferring three or four bureaus from the Department of Agriculture to a Department of Conservation. Such transfer would only increase the disunity, frictions and duplication of effort now extant. The Department of Conservation would have to have its own plant experts, its own animal experts, its own soil experts, its own agricultural economists, its own research organizations. If it used the resources of the Bureau of Plant Industry, of Animal Industry, of Soils, etc., the present frictions still would exist but in an intensified form. As it now stands, the Department of the Interior, in order to administer grazing, national parks and railroad lands, has added plant experts, livestock experts, foresters, agronomists, etc., all of whom perform functions better done in the Department of Agriculture.

To accomplish these transfers to the Department of Agriculture two small modifications in the bill now before Congress would be required:

1. Deletion of the section which provides for renaming the Department of the Interior the Department of Conservation.

2. A change in the definition of agriculture as expressed in the bill.

I am not urging an increase in the size of the Department of Agriculture. I am perfectly willing to surrender such parts of it as do not contribute to what I conceive to be the functions of a department of agriculture—to administer those branches of government which have to do with land use, the welfare of people on the land, and with growing things and living things that depend for life upon the soil and what grows from it. The budgets of certain bureaus in this department which could reasonably be transferred greatly exceed those of the bureaus which I suggest be transferred from Interior to Agriculture.

I believe that the majority of farm and conservation groups would heartily support reorganization if their concern respecting agriculture and conservation were eliminated. But if the bill remains as it is, my own silence and the silence of officials of my department will not restrain the active opposition of these groups. They feel that agriculture will be split wide open, that conservation will be endangered, that a wise land use program will be impossible. They do not see how private and public lands can provide a basis for divided jurisdiction when the two are so inextricably interwoven physically, economically, and socially. They fear that such a basis for division would in effect result in two departments of agriculture—one for public lands, to be known as "Conservation," the other for private lands, to be known as "Agriculture,"—with eastern farmers looking to one and western farmers looking to the other, with interminable conflicts and overlapping of functions. They are certain that changing the name of the Department of the Interior to the Department of Conservation will make it certain that in future administrations Secretaries of that Department will have a legal sanction for continuing efforts to gain control of many of the myriad functions which the Department of Agriculture properly should exercise.

You, Mr. President, are at present recognized as the real conservation leader in this Nation. I do not wish to see any change in public sentiment in this regard, particularly on the part of the farm and conservation organizations which long have fought for conservation principles and which on many counts are among your most earnest supporters.

The opposition so rapidly developing against this one phase of your reorganization plan may result in deep-seated resentments. The conservation organizations wield considerable power and their opposition may easily be a rallying point in Congress against you and the possible defeat of the whole reorganization plan. That opposition can be turned to support by the two modifications of the pending bill suggested on the preceding page.

May I have your permission to approach congressional leaders on the two changes above proposed?

In this way I believe you can attain the most harmony and efficiency in government and the widest support from farm and conservation groups in carrying out your reorganization and other programs.

Respectfully yours,

H. A. Wallace

SOIL CONSERVATION

SOIL EROSION: A NATIONAL MENACE*
April 1928

Few Department of Agriculture circulars have had greater influence than this one. Hugh H. Bennett, a soil scientist with the Bureau of Chemistry and Soils, produced this bulletin with the help of W. R. Chapline, who worked in grazing research with the Forest Service. The attention to soil erosion brought about by this bulletin, with the continued efforts of Bennett to publicize the problem, was primarily responsible for the establishment of the Soil Conservation Service as a New Deal innovation a few years later. Only Bennett's introduction and the conclusion of the pamphlet are reprinted here.

PART 1. SOME ASPECTS OF THE WASTAGE CAUSED BY SOIL EROSION[1]

This circular is concerned chiefly with that part of erosion which exceeds the normal erosion taking place in varying degrees, usually at a slow rate, as the result of artificial disturbance of the vegetative cover and ground equilibrium chiefly through the instrumentality of man and his domestic animals. Removal of forest growth, grass and shrubs and breaking the ground surface by cultivation, the trampling of livestock, etc., accentuate erosion to a degree far beyond that taking place under average natural conditions, especially on those soils that are peculiarly susceptible to rainwash. This speeding up of the washing varies greatly from place to place, according to soil character, climatic conditions, vegetative cover, degree of slope, disturbance of the ground surface, and depletion of the absorptive organic matter in the soil under continuous clean cultivation. Under normal conditions rock decay keeps pace with soil removal in many places; under the artificial conditions referred to, soil removal by the

---

*H. H. Bennett and W. R. Chapline, "Soil Erosion a National Menace," U.S. Department of Agriculture Circular No. 33, 1–8, 31–35.

[1] This part discusses only the evils of erosion by rainwash. Much damage is also done by wind erosion, but this phase of the problem is not treated here. The details of checking and preventing erosion and restoring to use the recoverable areas are not included, since that important side of the problem deserves a full paper in itself.

rains exceeds the rate of natural soil formation over a vast area of cultivated lands and grazing lands, often working down to bedrock.

GENERAL STATEMENT

Not less than 126,000,000,000 pounds of plant-food material is removed from the fields and pastures of the United States every year. Most of this loss is from cultivated and abandoned fields and overgrazed pastures and ranges. The value of the plant-food elements (considering only phosphorus, potash, and nitrogen) in this waste, as estimated on the basis of the chemical analyses of 389 samples of surface soil, collected throughout the United States, and the recent selling prices of the cheapest forms of fertilizer materials containing these plant nutrients, exceeds $2,000,000,000 annually. Of this amount there is evidence to indicate that at least $200,000,000 can be charged up as a tangible yearly loss to the farmers of the Nation. These calculations do not take into account the losses of lime, magnesia, and sulphur.

In this connection it must be considered that rainwash removes not only the plant-food elements but also the soil itself. The plant-food elements removed by crops (the crops do not take away the soil, but extract nutrients from it) can be restored in the form of fertilizers, manures, and soil-improving crops turned under; but the soil that is washed out of fields can not be restored, except by those exceedingly slow natural processes of soil building that require, in many instances, centuries to develop a comparatively thin layer. It would be entirely impracticable to replace even a small part of the eroded matter, which might be recoverable from stranded material not yet swept into the rivers.

A very considerable part of the wastage of erosion is obviously an immediate loss to the farmer, who in countless instances is in no economic position to stand the loss. Much of the wastage that perhaps might not be classed as an immediate farm loss is nevertheless a loss to posterity, and there are indications that our increasing population may feel acutely the evil effects of this scourge of the land, now largely unrestrained. A considerable part of the erosional débris goes to clog stream channels, to cover fertile alluvium with comparatively infertile sand and other coarse materials assorted from flood water, and to cause productive stream bottoms to become swampy and much less valuable. When the mellow topsoil is gone with its valuable humus and nitrogen, less productive, less permeable, less absorptive, and more intractable material is exposed in its place. As a rule this exposed material is the "raw" subsoil, which must be loosened, aerated, and supplied with the needed humus to put it into the condition best suited to plant growth. This rebuilding of the surface soil requires time, work, and money. In most places, this exposed material is heavier than the original soil, is stiffer, more difficult to plow, less penetrable to plant roots, less absorptive of rainfall and less retentive of that which is absorbed, and apparently its plant-food elements frequently have not been converted into available plant nutrients to anything like the degree that obtains in the displaced surface soil. This comparative inertness of the freshly exposed material is comparable to the lessened productivity brought about in some soils by suddenly plowing large quantities of the subsoil material to the surface. Such raw material must be given more intensive tillage in order to unlock its contained plant food, and on much of it lime and organic manures will be needed in order to reduce its stiffness sufficiently to make it amenable to efficient cultivation, to the establishment of a desirable seed-bed tilth. It bakes easier and, as a consequence, crops growing on it are less resistant to dry seasons, because of rapid evaporation from the hardened surface, and the many cracks that form deep into the subsoil to enlarge the area exposed to direct evaporation. Crops also suffer more in wet seasons because the material becomes more soggy or water-logged than did the original soil. On much of it both fertilizer and lime will be required for satisfactory yields.

Certain piedmont areas whose records are known have, within a period of 30 years, lost their topsoil entirely, 10 inches or more of loam and clay loam having been washed off down to the clay subsoil; and on this clay subsoil, substituted for the departed soil, from 400 to 600 pounds of fertilizer are required to produce as much cotton per acre as formerly was grown with 200 to 250 pounds of fertilizer of no better quality.

While these difficulties of tillage and the lowered productivity are being attended to by the farmer in those fields not yet abandoned, the unprotected fields continue to wash. Unfortunately the farmers in many localities are doing little or nothing to stop the wastage and much to accentuate it. In many instances the farmer does not know just what to do to slow down erosion. In many other cases he does not even suspect that the waning productivity of his fields results from any cause other than a natural reduction of the plant-food supply by the crops removed. He does not recognize the fact that gradual erosion, working unceasingly and more or less equally at all points, is the principal thief of the fertility of his soil until spots of subsoil clay or rock begin to appear over the sloping areas.

SOME WASTING AREAS

The southern part of the great Appalachian Valley is an admirable place to see the evil effects of that gradual land washing known as sheet erosion. Here in thousands of areas of formerly rich limestone soil of loam, silt loam, and clay loam texture, the topsoil has been removed. The numerous galls or clay exposures that now splotch the slopes lose their moisture quickly in dry weather. The damaging effects of drought upon crops are felt much quicker than formerly, according to those who have witnessed these changes in the soil. A much lighter rain than formerly now turns the Tennessee River red with wash from the red lands of its drainage basin. Added to the severe impoverishment of a tremendous area of land throughout this great valley, and its extensions southward into Georgia and Alabama and northward into Virginia, are the gullied areas, which are severely impaired or completely ruined by erosional ravines that finger out through numerous hill slopes and even many undulating valley areas. Field after field has been abandoned to brush, and the destruction continues.

Much erosion of the same type has taken place over the smoother uplands of south-central Kentucky; that is, in the rolling parts of the highland rim country; over much of the Piedmont region, and through many parts of the Appalachian Plateau. Land destruction of even worse types is to be seen in the great region of loessial soils that cover the uplands bordering the Mississippi and Missouri Rivers and many of their tributaries, from Baton Rouge, La., northward. Numerous areas, small and large, have been severely impoverished and even ruined in the famous black lands of Texas. Even the drier lands of the West and the comparatively smooth prairies and plains of the North-Central States have not escaped damage. Erosion is wasting the fertility of the soil and even the whole body of the soil in many places where the slope is sufficient for rain water to run downhill. There are some exceptions to this, or rather some partial exceptions, such as the nearly level lands, the loose, deep sandy lands, the highly absorptive gravelly areas, the loose glacial till and morainic deposits in parts of the northern border of the country, the peculiar red lands of the northern Pacific coastal region, and a few others. Although the total area of these more or less erosion-resistant soils is large, the area of those lands which are susceptible to washing and which are being washed in a wasteful way, more disastrously in some places than in others, is very much larger. Save when the fields are frozen or are covered with a blanket of hardened snow, erosion goes on upon these vulnerable lands during every rain that is sufficiently heavy to cause water to run downhill. Even the gentle spring rains cause some erosion, and the surface water flows away from sloping fields muddied red, yellow, or dun, according to the color of the soils of the neighborhood. This color is caused by soil materials started en route to the sea. Most of this material comes from the surface layer, the richest part of the soil.

FIGURES ON SOIL WASTAGE

The estimate of the quantity of plant-food elements annually lost by erosion, as given above, is a minimum estimate based upon a yearly discharge of 500,000,-000 tons of suspended material into the sea by rivers,[2] plus twice this amount stranded upon lower slopes and deposited over flood plains, in the channels of streams, and even in the basins of reservoirs, where it is not needed and not

[2]Dole and Stabler have estimated that 513,000,000 tons of suspended matter and 270,000,000 tons of dissolved matter are transported to tidewater every year by the streams of the United States. T. C. Chamberlin estimates that 1,000,000,000 or more tons of "richest soil matter" are washed into the oceans from the lands of this country every year.

wanted. Often this overwash does much more damage than good to the lands affected. It gradually reduces reservoir storage capacity and makes water-power plants dependent more and more upon the flow of the stream rather than upon the impounded water.

It is obvious to all who are familiar with field conditions that the amount of erosional débris in transit to the sea, but temporarily stranded on the way, each year very greatly exceeds twice the amount that actually passes out the mouths of rivers into tidewater. Some soil scientists believe the amount thus annually washed out of the fields and pastures and lodged on the way to the oceans is more than a hundred times greater than that actually entering the sea. The figure used above has been used merely because no satisfactory data upon which to base conclusively accurate estimates are available.

The estimates given do not include the dissolved matter which is annually discharged to the sea, a very considerable part of which obviously comes from erosional products. Furthermore, it is not known how much erosional detritus enters the ocean as drag material swept along the bottoms of streams. This material is exceedingly difficult to measure. The debris thus swept along the bottoms of many streams travels rather after the manner of waves or of sand dunes drifting before the wind. This characteristic of many river beds was brought out before a commissioner appointed by the Supreme Court of the United States in the expert testimony relating to the recent Red River boundary dispute between Texas and Oklahoma. Gilbert makes the following interesting observations regarding the process:

> Some particles of the bed load slide; many roll; the multitude make short skips or leaps, the process being called saltation. Saltation grades into suspension.
>
> When the conditions are such that the bed load is small, the bed is molded into hills, called dunes, which travel downstream. Their mode of advance is like that of eolian dunes, the current eroding their upstream faces and depositing the eroded material on the downstream faces. With any progressive change of conditions tending to increase the load, the dunes eventually disappear and the débris surface becomes smooth. The smooth phase is in turn succeeded by a second rhythmic phase, in which a system of hills travel upstream. These are called antidunes, and their movement is accomplished by erosion on the downstream face and deposition on the upstream face. Both rhythms of débris movement are initiated by rhythms of water movement.

The amount of plant food in this minimum estimate of soil wastage by erosion (1,500,000,000 tons of solid matter annually) amounts to about 126,000,000,000 pounds, on the basis of the average compositions of the soils of the country as computed from chemical analyses of 389 samples of surface soil collected by the Bureau of Soils (1.55 per cent potash, 0.15 per cent phosphoric acid, 0.10 per cent nitrogen, 1.56 per cent lime, and 0.84 per cent magnesia). This is more than twenty-one times the annual net loss due to crops removed (5,900,000,000 pounds, according to the National Industrial Conference Board). The amount of phosphoric acid, nitrogen, and potash alone in this annually removed soil material equals 54,000,000,000 pounds. Not all of this wasted plant food is immediately available, of course; but it comes principally from the soil layer, the main feeding reservoir of plants, and for this and for other reasons it is justifiable, doubtless, to consider the bulk of it as essentially representing lost plant food, without any quibbling about part of it having potential value only.

By catching and measuring the run-off and wash-off from a 3.68 per cent slope at the Missouri Agricultural Experiment Station, on the watershed of the Missouri River, it was found that for an average of six years 41.2 tons of soil material were annually washed from 1 acre of land plowed 4 inches deep, and that 68.73 per cent of the rainfall, the total precipitation amounting to 35.87 inches a year, was held back; that is, 24.65 inches of the 35.87 inches of precipitation were temporarily absorbed as an average for the six-year period. From a grass-covered area of the same slope and soil type less than 0.3 ton of solid matter was removed each year (or a total of 1.7 tons in six years), while 88.45 per cent of the rainfall was retained.

In 24 years this rate of erosion would result in the removal of a 7-inch layer of soil from the area tilled 4 inches deep; but for the removal of the same thickness of soil from the grassed area 3,547 years would be required.

At the Spur substation of the Texas Agricultural Experiment Station,[3] in the subhumid part of west Texas, 40.7 tons per acre of soil material were removed from a 2 per cent slope of fallow land by approximately 27 inches of rainfall. Of this precipitation only 55 per cent was retained (at least temporarily) on cultivated bare land of the same soil and slope without terracing, whereas 84 per cent was retained on an area covered with Buffalo grass.

The erosion station[4] in the piedmont region of North Carolina measured from an uncultivated plot a loss of 24.9 tons of solid matter to the acre each year, when the rainfall was only 35.6 inches, as against a normal of 43.9 inches. On the same slope and soil the erosion from grassland that year amounted to only 0.06 ton to the acre. In other words, the grass held back four hundred and fifteen times as much surface soil as was retained on untilled bare ground. It held back two hundred and fifteen times as much soil as was retained in the cotton plots on the same soil, having the same degree of slope. The uncultivated plot retained 64.5 per cent of the rainfall, the cotton plot 74.4 per cent, and grassland 98.5 per cent.

The agricultural scientists at the Missouri Agricultural Experiment Station have this to say of erosion:

> Most of the worn-out lands of the world are in their present condition because much of the surface soil has washed away, and not because they have been worn out by cropping. Productive soils can be maintained through centuries of farming if serious erosion is prevented. The

[3]Preliminary figures furnished by officials of the Texas Agricultural Experiment Station.
[4]Bartel, F. O. Second Progress Report, Soil-erosion Experiments, Experiment Station Farm, Raleigh, N.C. (A project of the Div. Agr. Engin., Bur. Public Roads, in cooperation with the N.C. Dept. Agr.)

soils of Missouri have become gradually less fertile during the last one hundred years due in large measure to the excessive cultivation of rolling lands. Many of the most fertile soils in the rolling prairies and timber lands of this state have been kept in corn until the "clay spots" are evident on nearly every hillside. So much soil has been lost from even the more gently rolling parts of the fields that the yields are far below those obtained by our grandfathers who brought the land into cultivation. The erosion of cultivated fields is taking place at such a rate that it is calling for a decided change in our system of soil management. If we are to maintain our acre-yields at a point where crops can be produced at a profit we must make every reasonable effort to reduce the amount of soil fertility that is carried away during heavy rains.

Approximately three-fourths of the area of Missouri is subject to more or less serious erosion. The map . . . shows where these soils are to be found. It will be seen from this map that erosion is serious on many of the most fertile soils of the state. This is particularly true in the rich rolling prairie regions of central and northwest Missouri, where owing to the fertility of these soils much of the land is kept in corn a large part of the time. It must be remembered that not all the soils . . . erode at the same rate . . . in the Ozark region, they [the soils] are largely covered with timber so that erosion cannot be considered a serious problem.

A single county in the southern part of the piedmont region was found by actual survey to contain 90,000 acres of land, largely cultivated at one time, which has been permanently ruined by erosion. The whole area has been dissected by gullies, and bedrock is exposed in thousands of places. Here and there islands and peninsulas of arable land have been left between hideous gullies, but most of these remnants are too small to cultivate. The land has been so devastated that it can not be reclaimed to cultivation until centuries of rock decay have restored the soil. It has some value, however, for growing shortleaf pine and for pasture. The extent of this devastated region unfortunately is yearly growing larger.

Another county in the Atlantic Coastal Plain has 70,000 acres of former good farm soil, which, since clearing and cultivation, has been gullied beyond repair. In one place where a schoolhouse stood 40 years ago gullies having a depth of 100 feet or more are now found, and these finger through hundreds of acres of land, whose reclamation would baffle human ingenuity.

The most severely eroded parts of this county are described as follows:

> The Rough gullied land includes areas which, as the result of erosion, are so steep and broken as to be unfit for agriculture. Much of the land classified under this head supports forest. Some areas are available for pasture, but a considerable total area is not even suitable for this use, as there are many deep gullies with steep or perpendicular sides on which no vegetation can find a footing. Providence and Trotman "Caves" . . . are examples of such areas. . . .
>
> In the southwestern part of the county in the Patterson Hills and in another large area . . . southwest of Spring Hill Church, a somewhat different condition is encountered. Here the Rough gullied land consists of narrow-topped ridges with precipitous slopes, covered with ferruginous sandstone fragments. No level land is found here and the slopes are generally too steep even to afford good pasture. . . . One of the largest [caves] within the county has developed in the memory of the present generation, having started with the formation of a small gully from the run-off of a barn. The caves, some of which are about 100 feet in depth and from 200 to 500 feet in width, ramify over large areas. There is little possibility of this gullied land being restored to a condition favorable to cultivation.

In the "brown loam" belt skirting the Mississippi bottoms on the east side, county after county includes 10,000, 20,000, or 30,000 acres of land which have been ruined by erosion. Agriculture has been driven out of a very large part of the upland of several counties in northwestern Mississippi by the gullied condition of the upland. Hundreds of farms in these and many other counties of the region have been abandoned to timber and brush. Unfortunately, the kind of timber that has established itself over much of these dissected areas is largely worthless blackjack oak, simply because pine seed have not been distributed to start valuable pine forests or because black locusts have not been planted.[5]

Not only have the uplands been widely and disastrously dissected, but large areas of former good alluvial land have been buried beneath infertile sands washed out of those upland gullies which have cut down through the soil strata into Tertiary deposits beneath. Stream channels have been choked with erosional débris, and overflows have become so common that large tracts of highly productive soil formerly tilled are now nothing more than swamp land.

The stream bottoms throughout the piedmont region from Virginia southward into east-central Alabama have been impaired by this process of overwash to an even greater extent. Here, probably, considerably more than 50 per cent of the bottom land has been converted into a nonarable swampy waste, entirely as the result of deposition of eroded material. In spite of the terracing that has long been practiced on many farms in the southern piedmont region, wastage of good agricultural uplands has gone on at a distressing rate, because many fields were not terraced and many terraces were not maintained. Thus, unleashed erosional waters, performing in the dual rôle of cutting away the topsoil of the uplands and depositing the less fertile assorted constituents of the eroded matter over the stream bottoms, have brought about an enormous amount of land impairment and destruction.

Some streams formerly navigable have been so choked with sand and mud, purely as a result of erosion, that they have not been plied by boats for a generation or more. E. N. Lowe, of the Mississippi Geological Survey, speaking of soil erosion and flood control in the Yazoo drainage basin, said five years ago:

> In many of our northern uplands [Mississippi] washing of the soil is progressing so rapidly without let or hindrance over large areas, that some necessary measures must be adopted soon to arrest the process, otherwise vast areas of formerly agricultural land will become hopeless

---

[5] In this connection W. R. Mattoon, of the United States Forest Service, says: "The State of Tennessee through its Division of Forestry has aided several hundred farmers and public organizations, particularly in west Tennessee, in checking gully erosion by the planting of black locust. This work has been done on a gradually increasing scale since its inception, about 1913. Practical methods have been developed of planting one-year-old locust seedlings, spaced about six feet apart each way, over the entire wash or gullied area. Preparatory to planting, the gully banks are plowed off and brush dams built across the channels at strategic points to catch the soil. The black locust produces a heavy surface root system adapted to holding the soil, it is a legume and enriches the soil, it is a vigorous grower and endures thin soils, and it ranks as the second most lasting fence-post timber in this country. Black walnut, yellow poplar, pines, and other trees have also been planted. In addition to checking erosion the land is put to profitable use by growing valuable fence posts and other timber crops and the blue grass that invariably comes in supports limited grazing. A large number of farmers by this method have realized excellent money returns from old gullied lands."

wastes. Large areas in at least a dozen upland counties of north-central Mississippi have already reached such a condition of soil depletion that they are now hardly suitable for any kind of agriculture, and their taxable values are reduced accordingly.

The erosion of these uplands has resulted not only in enormous losses of valuable agricultural soils, but also in concomitant stream-filling throughout those areas. Volumes of silt and sand after every heavy shower are poured into the streams from every furrow, gully and rill that trenches the hillsides, resulting in filling of their channels. The obliteration of their channels causes overflow of the streams after any considerable rain, with deposition of sand over valuable bottom lands, often doing irreparable damage.

For years rapid and destructive filling has affected the Coldwater. Forty years ago boats of large size came up the river to Coldwater to load cotton. Now no kind of a boat can come up Coldwater River, so choked is it with sand bars.

The Tallahatchie was formerly a navigable stream. Even as late of 1900 a small steamer drawing four feet of water plied on the Tallahatchie from Batesville downstream. Now the stream is choked with sand bars, and can be easily waded at almost any place.

In the great cotton-producing section of central Texas, known as the black waxy belt, white spots representing exposures of the basal chalk and marl beds that gave rise to the immensely productive black soil of this region, dot the landscape of the rolling areas. The same thing is to be seen in many parts of the Alabama-Mississippi prairie belt. These exposures represent the products of erosion—nonarable land that has been substituted for some of the most productive cotton soil of the world. In one county of this region 13.5 per cent of the total area was recently mapped as an eroded phase of the valuable Houston clay soil. It was found that much of this had been too severely washed to allow cultivation, whereas the remaining better parts become highly desiccated in dry seasons, giving lighter and lighter yields as the wearing off of the soil progresses.

* * *

WHAT NEEDS TO BE DONE

REESTABLISH THE VEGETATIVE COVER

This enormous wastage must be stopped. The problem is to determine and apply ways and means of checking the present extensive erosion, restoring the watersheds, preventing abnormal erosion, and obtaining permanent economic use of range land in the West.

Of first importance is the effort to reestablish and conserve the optimum vegetative cover. Plants not only lessen the force of rainfall but intercept part of it. Vegetation improves soil structure, allowing greater moisture penetration; it increases the water-holding capacity of the soil by increasing organic matter; it breaks the effect of wind; it binds the soil and lessens sheet erosion; it obstructs run-off and reduces the velocity of flow and the carrying power of the water; and by catching soil particles it tends to form miniature terraces on slopes and dams and fills in small gullies. The more complete the plant cover, the more adequate is the protection against erosion.

If erosion is checked on a depleted area the vegetation present will gradually spread, slowly increasing the vegetable matter and plant foods in the soil. Short-lived species will be replaced by perennials and better soil-binding plants and, as the fertility of the soil is further improved, the more permanent type of perennial forage plants will become established.

The value of this in controlling erosion is indicated by the experiments on high mountain watersheds at the Great Basin Experiment Station in Utah. After herbaceous vegetation had improved until it covered 40 per cent of the soil surface, the run-off from summer rains was 55 per cent less, and sediment eroded 56 per cent less than when the vegetation covered but 16 per cent of the surface. Run-off and erosion from melting snow appeared to be affected much less by the change in herbaceous vegetation. Though approximately 95 per cent of the annual run-off was from melting snow, it carried only 12 per cent of the sediment removed; the 5 per cent of run-off from summer rains carried 88 per cent of the sediment eroded annually. Thus, under the conditions prevailing in the experiment, the greatest need is for vegetation on the range to prevent the great erosion damage from summer rains.

Sometimes the range improvement is extremely slow, but every bit of progress helps not only in reducing erosion but in increasing the grazing value of the land. At the 1927 field day of the Great Basin Experiment Station it was shown that on an area on which the vegetation had been all but destroyed in 1903, the soil was so badly eroded and depleted that it had not yet built up to where it would support a stand of valuable forage species. Even so there had been a notable increase in carrying capacity. In 1927, 7.4 acres were required to support a cow for a month. On another area on which the stand of vegetation had been badly depleted but on which the soil was not so wasted, and adjoining a hillside where grass plants still remained under the protection of brush so that seed was available, a rather dense cover of valuable plants had become reestablished by 1927, and only 2.4 acres were required to support a cow a month. The greater part of this improvement has come in the last five years. The rate of improvement depends largely on the quantity of plants on the range which reseed or otherwise revegetate readily and on the methods of range management applied to aid recovery. In the Southwest rather badly depleted ranges can, with proper grazing, be reestablished, with three or four times as much forage as they are now supporting, in about five years.

The value of trees, shrubs, and grass for bank protection along small stream courses should be better appreciated, so that efforts will be made to protect them or to reestablish the stand if it has been destroyed.

REGULATE GRAZING

Stockmen are recognizing that conservative grazing keeps their animals in a good, thrifty condition throughout the year, increases the number of young produced, reduces death losses, and increases the weight and finish of salable animals, thus affording top prices and profitable production. Conservative grazing implies placing no more livestock on the range than the feed will support, and allowing the palatable plants to get enough of a start in the spring so that grazing will not impair their vigor. It also implies removing the livestock in the fall before the soil becomes so wet that trampling would injure it, unless the range and soil are of a character that allows yearlong use. A certain reserve of feed as an insurance against the ever-recurring drought is essential to assure sustained livestock production and watershed protection. Also, distribution of livestock over the range so as to obtain as even a use as practicable without undue concentration or trampling is important.

There are areas on which erosion injury is now occurring that could be greatly improved if grazed by a different class of livestock. This is true of certain rough mountain ranges where attempts to get full utilization of the feed on the range as a whole by cattle grazing is causing undue concentration in valleys and consequent erosion damage. Sheep would use the slopes to better advantage and could be more easily held off the damaged valley areas. Certain brush areas could be grazed more profitably by Angora goats than by the cattle and sheep now grazing there, bringing about improvement in the watershed and erosion conditions. Likewise, on some areas a change from sheep to cattle would prove desirable.

Deferred grazing or deferred and rotation grazing, which provides for reserving grazing from part or all of areas of range land until after seed maturity, although now widely applied, deserves more extensive use throughout the West. Other similar improved systems adapted to specific soil and forage types need to be devised or further developed so as to improve range lands without loss of use of the range forage. Experiments at the Great Basin station and on the Jornada and Santa Rita Range Reserves in the Southwest indicate that, except where the vegetative stand has been practically eliminated and the exposed soil is seriously eroded, the native cover can ordinarily be restored under properly regulated livestock grazing almost as well and as quickly as under total protection from grazing. Furthermore, the range can more easily be maintained at its best with grazing than without.

Some form of control of the unappropriated public domain is essential if it is to be restored. Most stockmen will agree that it should probably take the form of Federal regulation.

PROTECT THE COVER AGAINST FIRE

In recent years there has been a great awakening of the public to the need for fire prevention and quick suppression, especially in timber and brush lands. Most Western States have stringent laws regarding carelessness with fire, but, as brought out above, 336,000 acres of brush and grassland are burned yearly in California alone. The possible erosion danger should be carefully considered before fire is set with a view to improving the range. Under regulation, excessive grazing is sometimes practiced as a fire-prevention measure; but this in turn causes erosion, reduced feed values, and usually uneconomic livestock production. With depleted vegetative stands the fire danger is not great, but as the vegetation on range lands is improved for watershed protection it will be necessary to give more attention to fire protection.

AID EROSION CONTROL BY ARTIFICIAL MEANS

Artificial reseeding of range lands to known cultivated forage plants has not proved practicable except on areas with unusually favorable soil and moisture conditions. Tests are being made, however, of a number of species that show some promise. These tests deserve considerable expansion. In the meantime, management of the native vegetation so that it may serve to best advantage will be the main means of revegetating depleted areas. Of course, on important watersheds where the value of the stand is not alone determined by its grazing value it may pay to seed for erosion control.

Sampson and Weyl found terracing and planting of steep, barren, eroded, high-mountain hillsides to native plants possible but costly. They urge such methods on areas that have eroded to such a point that natural revegetation is extremely slow and the vegetation present noneffective in binding the soil and in preventing erratic run-off.

Engineering works for the control of erosion have been used extensively in the mountain regions of Europe. Large dams for holding back flood crests or even for the catching of excessive silt have been established in a few places in the West. Check dams, small structures of rocks, logs, brush, or other materials, have also been constructed in the smaller stream channels, largely for the purpose of reducing the velocity of the water and thereby its carrying and cutting power. Such works are usually costly and unless they are supplemented with the maintenance of the highest type of vegetation the land is capable of supporting are apt to prove ineffective. As the importance of erosion control is recognized, however, engineering works, especially check dams, will doubtless come into greater use.

CONCLUSION

With erosion losses on western grazing lands so great, corrective action must be taken soon if far greater damage and more difficult control are to be obviated. Owners of range land should consider the use of their land not alone for immediate gain, but still more in the light of the future productivity of the range, the protection of water supply, and stream-flow regulation. Overgrazing should be stopped at once; control or regulation of the badly abused unappropriated and unreserved public domain should not be longer delayed by the Federal Government. Arroyo cutting must be checked by engineering works and the establishment of vegetation in the bed and on the sides of the arroyos. Range landowners, irrigationists, and the State and Federal Governments should band together to use every available means for checking erosion, floods, and inadequate water supply at their source, on the slopes, in gullies, and on small drainages of the watersheds. The Federal Government has a direct responsibility since Federal lands occupy such a large part of the West.

The main obstacle to action and one that has greatly delayed remedial measures has been lack of information as to the seriousness of the situation and as to concrete things which should be done under specific conditions. Without this information it is possible to work only in a broad way, rather than to attain a permanent control of erosion on range lands in a really constructive and economical manner. In view of the important part that herbaceous and shrubby vegetation play in controlling erosion of such lands it is essential that research determine just what is the optimum stand of vegetation that can be made to grow on the widely varying soil types and under the extreme climatic conditions of the West and the influence of this vegetation on water supply. It is equally important to know more concretely just what grazing use can be allowed under each of the main range and watershed conditions to assure profitable livestock production and a maximum of protection to the soil. Along these lines research is already doing its best to help the stockman and range landowner, but hardly more than a start has as yet been made. Faced with so big a problem, research needs the most earnest encouragement and support.

THE BUCHANAN AMENDMENT*
February 16, 1929

After the publication of Bennett's paper on soil erosion, Representative James P. Buchanan of Texas secured the adoption of the following amendment to the Department of Agriculture appropriation bill for 1929. Under Buchanan's wing, Bennett carried on his soil conservation studies and demonstrations for the next four years.

Soil-erosion investigations: To enable the Secretary of Agriculture to make investigation not otherwise provided for, of the causes of soil erosion and the possibility of increasing the absorption of rainfall by the soil in the United States, and to devise means to be employed in the preservation of soil, the prevention or control of destructive erosion and the conservation of rainfall by terracing or other means, independently or in cooperation with other branches of the Government, State agencies, counties, farm organizations, associations of business men, or individuals, $160,000, of which amount $40,000 shall be immediately available.

---

*45 *Statutes at Large,* 1207–08.

GETTING READY FOR THE SOIL CONSERVATION SERVICE*
March 2, 1935

These letters, with the attached memoranda, show part of the White House activity to secure establishment of the Soil Conservation Service in the Department of Agriculture.

ROOSEVELT TO MARVIN H. McINTYRE, ASSISTANT SECRETARY TO THE PRESIDENT

Washington, March 2, 1935

Memo for Mac:
Will you arrange a conference for me with Secretary Ickes, Secretary Wallace, Bennett of Soil Erosion, and I want Richberg there too?
Will you give me the attached memoranda when they come?

F. D. R.

[*Enclosure 1*] HUGH H. BENNETT, DIRECTOR, SOIL EROSION SERVICE, TO HAROLD L. ICKES, SECRETARY OF THE INTERIOR

Washington, February 23, 1935

Memorandum to the Secretary:
. . . As you will recall, the Department of the Interior representative made application for a total of 943 of the new camps, including 533 camps for the Soil Erosion Service. It was our understanding that the Department of the Interior's request would be treated as a unit, but the breakdown of camps for Park Service prompts us to renew our application with the request that the President be asked to approve the allocation to the Soil Erosion Service of an adequate number of CCC camps to strengthen and supply the needs of the Soil Erosion Service program on agricultural lands. The Forest Service now has 1096 camps, of which 151 are erosion camps working on agricultural lands. The Soil Erosion Service now has 51 camps which are spread over 23 of our projects. At the present time we have 39 approved projects, leaving 16 projects without the supplementary labor resources of the CCC camps. The enlarged program of the Soil Erosion Service includes 50 additional demonstration projects which will in

---

*Franklin D. Roosevelt and Conservation—1911–1945, Vol. 1, Edgar B. Nixon, ed. (Hyde Park, N.Y.: General Services Administration, National Archives and Records Service, Franklin D. Roosevelt Library, 1957), 357–59, 361–64.

time grow to about 100 projects, each of which could be advantageously served by an average of 5 CCC camps.

It is our conviction that the time has arrived when the function of the Soil Erosion Service as a major agency to be responsible for erosion control on agricultural lands should be recognized. With such recognition it is expected that the CCC camps now under the jurisdiction of the Forest Service on agricultural lands duplicating in a less effective way the work of the Soil Erosion Service should be assigned to the Soil Erosion Service for administration. This recommendation in no way is intended to restrict or reduce the work of erosion control carried out by the Forest Service on the National Forest or range lands, or the National Park Service or other agencies on lands under their jurisdiction. The duplication and overlapping of erosion control work by CCC camps under the Forest Service often conflicts with the more complete program of the Soil Erosion Service. In the interest of greater efficiency and a more general approval of the Administration's attack upon the problem of soil and water conservation, it is urgently recommended that steps be taken to remove the duplication and conflicts, and that the work of erosion be adequately coordinated between the Soil Erosion Service, and the Forest Service and other government agencies.

We, therefore, earnestly recommend that the President be requested to allot to the Soil Erosion Service 533 camps as proposed in your letter of February 6, 1935, to Mr. Robert Fechner, Director of Emergency Conservation Work; and that a coordination of erosion control work be effected as above outlined. The attached letter making such request has been prepared for your signature.

H. H. Bennett

[*Enclosure 2*] DONALD R. RICHBERG, EXECUTIVE DIRECTOR, NATIONAL EMERGENCY COUNCIL, TO ROOSEVELT

Washington, February 28, 1935

Memorandum

. . . Consolidation of Soil Erosion Service in Department of Agriculture: Following your directions, I have taken up the question of how to consolidate soil erosion work in the Department of Agriculture.

After discussion with Secretary Wallace and an extensive investigation by the Solicitor of his department, I can summarize the following conclusions:

1. The soil erosion work now being carried on in the Department of the In-

terior can be transferred to the Department of Agriculture by an Executive Order, since that work has been established in the Department of the Interior by the Public Works Administrator, acting under Title II of the National Industrial Recovery Act.

2. A comprehensive program, such as outlined in the bill proposed by the Secretary of the Interior, including a consolidation of the work of all agencies now engaged in this field, cannot be put in effect without legislation. The President's legislative authority under the Act of June 30, 1932, as amended, expired June 30, 1934.

3. Soil erosion work outside of the Soil Erosion Service in the Department of the Interior is of a minor character, including the following: Office of Indian Affairs and Division of Grazing Control, both in the Department of the Interior; Tennessee Valley Authority, Emergency Conservation Work, Mississippi Valley Committee, California Debris Commission. These activities have such relative unimportance that a practical consolidation of soil erosion work can be effected by a transfer of the Soil Erosion Service in the Department of the Interior to the Department of Agriculture.

4. Under the terms of Title II of the National Industrial Recovery Act new expenditures cannot be made after June 16, 1935 and only the "remaining functions" of agencies established under the Act are to be transferred to such departments of the government as the President shall designate. Therefore, unless the new work relief appropriation provides for the continuance of this work, it would cease June 16th.

5. Apparently the Soil Erosion Service in the Department of the Interior anticipates the continuance of Soil Erosion Service, since agreements are now being entered into with agricultural colleges and State Representatives of the Soil Erosion Service are being directed to prepare plans for carrying on Soil Erosion Service with relief workers.

If this work is to be consolidated in the Department of Agriculture, it would seem important to have the Service transferred immediately to the Department of Agriculture, which will eventually have the responsibility for carrying on the work. If this is your desire, the Solicitor for the Department of Agriculture should be directed to prepare an Executive Order providing for this transfer. After this is done, if the Department of Agriculture thinks further legislation advisable to authorize a comprehensive program, they will naturally prepare such a bill for your consideration.

I have not taken this matter up with the Secretary of the Interior, having simply acted on your instructions to determine what was necessary to transfer this service to the Department of Agriculture.

[*Donald R. Richberg*]

HENRY A. WALLACE, SECRETARY OF AGRICULTURE, TO ROOSEVELT

Washington, D.C., March 7, 1935

Dear Mr. President:

Congressman Marvin Jones called me up early this week saying that he had a bill providing for setting up the Soil Erosion Service in a permanent way in the Department of Agriculture. He indicated that he didn't want to get his wires crossed and understood that action was in prospect from this end and that you were perhaps contemplating handling the Soil Erosion Service for a while longer on a temporary basis. He said if action was not contemplated on this end, that he would like to push his bill. I told him over the telephone that you had talked to me about it and I thought it would be wise if he would delay matters for the time being.

Enclosed I am sending you a clipping from the New York *Times* of February 25. On examination of the publication of the Department of Interior referred to in this New York *Times* article, I find that the Soil Erosion Service is apparently engaging in a great variety of agricultural work. There are articles in this bulletin on "Sweet Clover Planting," "Limestone," "Planting Oats," "Methods of Strip Cropping," etc. The work of the Soil Erosion Service is excellent but it is largely agricultural work and done in cooperation with the Agricultural Experiment Stations and Extension Services on individual farms.

I have the feeling that Secretary Ickes has no illusions whatever as to the character of the functions of the Soil Erosion Service and where it belongs but he is holding on to it because he thinks it is good trading stock. I know you don't want any fights within your family and I am sure that I don't want any disagreement within the progressive segment of the family; nevertheless, I am certain that inasfar as the Department of Interior deals with agricultural matters and with farmers, there is likely to be eventual serious trouble.

Respectfully yours,

H. A. Wallace

ROOSEVELT TO HAROLD L. ICKES, SECRETARY OF THE INTERIOR

Washington, March 20, 1935

Memorandum for the Secretary of the Interior:

I have had a very satisfactory talk with Mr. Bennett of the Soil Erosion Service. Mr. Bennett is most appreciative of the splendid cooperation which he has had from the Department of the Interior, and I want to make it perfectly clear to you that he has not in any shape, manner or form, advocated a transfer of the Soil Erosion Service to the Department of Agriculture.

Nevertheless, after full consideration of the functions involved, and leaving out all other considerations—which is after all the only way in which I have any right to look at the problem—I have definitely concluded that as a matter of function, the Soil Erosion Service should be transferred to the jurisdiction of the Department of Agriculture.

The functional work involved is concerned more with agriculture than with any other broad subject.

In view of this will you be good enough to ask the Public Works' administrative body to pass the necessary Resolution making the transfer? I think no Executive Order is necessary because the Soil Erosion Service was originally set up in the Department of Interior by Resolution of the Public Works Administration.

F. D. R.

ROOSEVELT TO HAROLD L. ICKES, SECRETARY OF THE INTERIOR

[Washington] March 22, 1935

Dear Harold:

I would certainly have waited in the matter of the Soil Erosion Bureau except for the fact that a very difficult situation started to come to a head on the Hill. I had already talked with Bennett, who, I think, preferred personally to stay in Interior because of the splendid treatment you have given them. Nevertheless, I had to decide the matter from the point of view of common sense administrative layout and charting and there is no question that Soil Erosion has more to do with Agriculture activities. I know you will understand.

As ever yours,

[*Franklin D. Roosevelt*]

THE SOIL CONSERVATION SERVICE*
April 27, 1935

This law gave permanent status to the Soil Conservation Service, after its first life as one of Secretary Ickes' emergency programs, the Soil Erosion Service. The law placed the new agency in the Department of Agriculture. Hugh Hammond Bennett continued as its chief.

Bennett was testifying before the Senate Public Lands Committee in behalf of the bill when the Capitol building itself was almost blacked out by a dust storm which had originated 2,000 miles to the west. The storm was Bennett luck, but also Bennett strategy, for he had helped time the hearing for a period when the winds were supposed to be bringing the dust east.

An Act to provide for the protection of land resources against soil erosion, and for other purposes.

Be it enacted by the Senate and House of Representatives of the United States of America in Congress assembled, That it is hereby recognized that the wastage of soil and moisture resources on farm, grazing, and forest lands of the Nation, resulting from soil erosion, is a menace to the national welfare and that it is hereby declared to be the policy of Congress to provide permanently for the control and prevention of soil erosion and thereby to preserve natural resources, control floods, prevent impairment of reservoirs, and maintain the navigability of rivers and harbors, protect public health, public lands and relieve unemployment, and the Secretary of Agriculture, from now on, shall coordinate and direct all activities with relation to soil erosion and in order to effectuate this policy is hereby authorized, from time to time—

(1) To conduct surveys, investigations, and research relating to the character of soil erosion and the preventive measures needed, to publish the results of any such surveys, investigations, or research, to disseminate information concerning such methods, and to conduct demonstrational projects in areas subject to erosion by wind or water;

(2) To carry out preventive measures, including, but not limited to, engineering operations, methods of cultivation, the growing of vegetation, and changes in use of land;

(3) To cooperate or enter into agreements with, or to furnish financial or other aid to, any agency, governmental or otherwise, or any person, subject to such conditions as he may deem necessary, for the purposes of this Act; and

(4) To acquire lands, or rights or interests therein, by purchase, gift, condemnation, or otherwise, whenever necessary for the purposes of this Act.

*49 *Statutes at Large,* 163–64.

SEC. 2. The acts authorized in section 1 (1) and (2) may be performed—

(a) On lands owned or controlled by the United States or any of its agencies, with the cooperation of the agency having jurisdiction thereof; and

(b) On any other lands, upon obtaining proper consent or the necessary rights or interests in such lands.

SEC. 3. As a condition to the extending of any benefits under this Act to any lands not owned or controlled by the United States or any of its agencies, the Secretary of Agriculture may, insofar as he may deem necessary for the purposes of this Act, require—

(1) The enactment and reasonable safeguards for the enforcement of State and local laws imposing suitable permanent restrictions on the use of such lands and otherwise providing for the prevention of soil erosion;

(2) Agreements or covenants as to the permanent use of such lands; and

(3) Contributions in money, services, materials, or otherwise, to any operations conferring such benefits.

SEC. 4. For the purposes of this Act, the Secretary of Agriculture may—

(1) Secure the cooperation of any governmental agency;

(2) Subject to the provisions of the civil-service laws and the Classification Act of 1923, as amended, appoint and fix the compensation of such officers and employees as he may deem necessary, except for a period not to exceed eight months from the date of this enactment, the Secretary of Agriculture may make appointments and may continue employees of the organization heretofore established for the purpose of administering those provisions of the National Industrial Recovery Act which relate to the prevention of soil erosion, without regard to the civil-service laws or regulations and the Classification Act, as amended; and any persons with technical or practical knowledge may be employed and compensated under this Act on a basis to be determined by the Civil Service Commission; and

(3) Make expenditures for personal services and rent in the District of Columbia and elsewhere, for the purchase of law books and books of reference, for printing and binding, for the purchase, operation, and maintenance of passenger-carrying vehicles, and perform such acts, and prescribe such regulations, as he may deem proper to carry out the provisions of this Act.

SEC. 5. The Secretary of Agriculture shall establish an agency to be known as the "Soil Conservation Service", to exercise the powers conferred on him by this Act and may utilize the organization heretofore established for the purpose of administering those provisions of sections 202 and 203 of the National Industrial Recovery Act which relate to the prevention of soil erosion, together with such personnel thereof as the Secretary of Agriculture may determine, and all unexpended balances of funds heretofore allotted to said organization shall be available until June 30, 1937, and the Secretary of Agriculture shall assume all obligations incurred by said organization prior to transfer to the Department of

Agriculture. Funds provided in H. J. Res. 117, "An Act making appropriation for relief purposes" (for soil erosion) shall be available for expenditure under the provisions of this Act; and in order that there may be proper coordination of erosion-control activities the Secretary of Agriculture may transfer to the agency created under this Act such functions, funds, personnel, and property of other agencies in the Department of Agriculture as he may from time to time determine.

SEC. 6. There are hereby authorized to be appropriated for the purposes of this Act such sums as Congress may from time to time determine to be necessary.

Approved, April 27, 1935.

LITTLE WATERS*
November 1935

This pamphlet, sponsored jointly by three New Deal agencies, is another with historic influence on government policy and conservation doctrine. More than any other factor, it helped bring about the small watershed program in the Department of Agriculture.

"Little Waters" also influenced a pastoral concept of rural rehabilitation that has been demonstrated as very unrealistic in a day of automated agriculture. The idea that "little waters" alone could halt heavy flooding was another unrealistic concept which gained unwarranted support as a result of the popularity of this pamphlet. Only the foreword to the pamphlet is presented here.

The pamphlet was prepared for the Soil Conservation Service, the Resettlement Administration, and the Rural Electrification Administration by H. S. Person, consulting economist, with the cooperation of E. Johnston Coil, economist, and Robert T. Beall, associate economist.

FOREWORD: LAND AND MAN

IF THE LAND PERISH, HOW SHALL MAN SURVIVE?

> *Against the wooded hill it stands,*
> *Ghosts of a dead home staring through*
> *Its broken lights on wasted lands*
> *Where old-time harvests grew.*

John Greenleaf Whittier

The successors of Columbus beheld a continent of abundance beyond their fondest dreams—a continent rich in land, minerals, and water; in fertile soils, timber, game, fish, and furs. They believed these things to be inexhaustible, and generally their descendants still cling to that belief.

Yet today fur-bearing animals and fish are to be found in quantities only in the more remote localities; and mere fragments remain of the great pine and hardwood forests of the North Atlantic and Central States.

But, you say, there remain the rich soils and the waters! We can no longer afford to be so confident, for there is something wrong, ominously wrong, about these also.

The rains and the snows still come as of old, but often their waters are returned to the seas more quickly, and without our receiving more than a fraction of the benefits they have to offer.

*H. S. Person, *Little Waters: A Study of Headwater Streams and Other Little Waters, Their Use and Relations to the Land* (Washington, D.C.: Government Printing Office, Nov., 1935), 1–4.

And in many places these waters now flow off the land in such a manner that rich topsoils are being washed into the rivers and the oceans, or blown away for lack of moisture, out of reach and use by man.

Many believe that another century of present trends would leave the United States unable to maintain the agriculture on which her civilization rests; that the United States is not a "permanent country", and is on the way to join decadent parts of China and Asia Minor, once opulent and magnificent, but now stripped of their fertile soils and buried in the dust of destructive exploitation of resources; that if something effective is not done within a generation, it will be too late over numerous large areas, for this earth disease, like some human diseases, can never be cured if neglected during the early stages.

The soil-erosion specialists tell us that the dust storm of May 11, 1934, swept 300 million tons of fertile topsoil off the great wheat plains; that 400 million tons of soil material are washed annually into the Gulf of Mexico by the Mississippi River; that generally water and wind erosion together each year remove beyond use 3 billion tons of soil.

They find that 100 million once-fertile acres of farm land—equal to Illinois, Ohio, Maryland, and North Carolina combined—have been essentially destroyed for profitable farming; that another 125 million acres are seriously impaired; and that another 100 million acres are threatened—all belonging to the best farm lands of the United States.

And further; that the present annual money loss to land owners and to the Nation is not less than 400 million dollars each year; that the annual rate has been increasing; that the cumulative loss may be conservatively stated as already not less than 10 billion dollars; and that, if the wastage is not stopped, in another 50 years the cumulative loss will reach the staggering figures of 25 or 30 billion dollars, equivalent to a loss of $4,000 on each and every farm in the United States.

This is not a loss of income the flow of which can be resumed, but of assets that cannot be recovered, for it takes Nature centuries to make the equivalent of the top soil which has been swept away—at the rate in some places of 3 to 6 inches in a single season.

In his ruthless exploitation of land and water resources Man has violated basic arrangements in a manner which Nature will not tolerate.

Through countless centuries there has been built up a balanced, fruitful relationship among waters, soils, grasses, and forests. Each dependent on and helpful to the others, they have learned to work together, through physical, chemical, and biological processes, to create and maintain a continent of abundant, useful resources for the habitation and sustenance of Man.

Then came the settlers—vigorous, keen, and intelligent with respect to matters of the moment, but unforeseeing and destructive with respect to matters of

[424]

the future. Unwittingly, for present gains they sacrificed the birthright they believed they were actually increasing for their descendants.

Blindly and ruthlessly they shattered that balance of Nature's forces which created and maintained the land and water resources that they assumed would last forever.

Impoverishment of these resources, in part by unwise selection for use, in part by improper methods of use, has become a real danger.

This danger is a vital concern of everyone. It is as significant to merchant, manufacturer, and banker as to those who work immediately on the land. Nature's gifts are the basis of all economic life. All conversion and interchange of goods rest on the application of human activity to the earth's materials. This is the basic reality.

Progress or decadence of a people is determined by the manner in which it accepts and utilizes these gifts of Nature. Soils and waters may be so used as to remain permanent assets yielding a perpetual income. On the other hand they may be destroyed as sources of income; may even be so used as to make them essentially self-destructive. A people must choose.

It is with these things that this report is concerned: The balance of forces which through centuries has been patiently and painstakingly developed; the things that Man has done which impair it and diminish the abundance it has created; the things which must be done—now, before it is too late—to recreate the heritage that each generation receives in trust for its successor.

Many of the things that must be done are little things—things each citizen can do and small communities can do—things little in themselves but vital, urgent, and far-reaching in combined results.

Therefore, the matters here discussed are not to be dismissed lightly, as the concern only of engineers, financiers, and governments.

Every citizen must understand and play his part.

It is to all citizens, to help them understand and act, individually and together, that this report is made.

AGRICULTURAL CONSERVATION*
February 29, 1936

When the Agricultural Adjustment Act, the first New Deal farm commodity program, was declared unconstitutional by the Supreme Court, the substitute decided upon was the Agricultural Conservation Program. With the principal purpose of the law, as outlined in Section 7, built around a conservation purpose, it withstood the constitutionality test.

An Act to promote the conservation and profitable use of agricultural land resources by temporary Federal aid to farmers and by providing for a permanent policy of Federal aid to States for such purposes.

Be it enacted by the Senate and House of Representatives of the United States of America in Congress assembled, That the Act entitled "An Act to provide for the protection of land resources against soil erosion, and for other purposes", approved April 27, 1935, is amended by inserting at the end thereof the following:

"SEC. 7. (a) It is hereby declared to be the policy of this Act also to secure, and the purposes of this Act shall also include, (1) preservation and improvement of soil fertility; (2) promotion of the economic use and conservation of land; (3) diminution of exploitation and wasteful and unscientific use of national soil resources; (4) the protection of rivers and harbors against the results of soil erosion in aid of maintaining the navigability of waters and water courses and in aid of flood control; and (5) reestablishment, at as rapid a rate as the Secretary of Agriculture determines to be practicable and in the general public interest, of the ratio between the purchasing power of the net income per person on farms and that of the income per person not on farms that prevailed during the five-year period August 1909–July 1914, inclusive, as determined from statistics available in the United States Department of Agriculture, and the maintenance of such ratio. The powers conferred under sections 7 to 14, inclusive, of this Act shall be used to assist voluntary action calculated to effectuate the purposes specified in this section. Such powers shall not be used to discourage the production of supplies of foods and fibers sufficient to maintain normal domestic human consumption as determined by the Secretary from the records of domestic human consumption in the years 1920 to 1929, inclusive, taking into consideration increased population, quantities of any commodity that were forced into domestic consumption by decline in exports during such period, current trends in domestic consumption and exports of particular commodities, and the quantities of substitutes available for domestic consumption within any

*49 *Statutes at Large,* 1148–52.

general class of food commodities. In carrying out the purposes of this section due regard shall be given to the maintenance of a continuous and stable supply of agricultural commodities adequate to meet consumer demand at prices fair to both producers and consumers.

"(b) The Secretary of Agriculture shall cooperate with States, in the execution of State plans to effectuate the purposes of this section, by making grants under this section to enable them to carry out such plans.

"(c) Any State which submits to the Secretary, prior to such time and in such manner and form as the Secretary prescribes, a State plan to effectuate the purposes of this section shall be entitled to payments, as provided in this section, for the year to which such plan is applicable, if such plan is approved by the Secretary as provided in this section.

"(d) No such plan shall be approved unless by its terms:

"(1) It provides that the agency to administer the plan shall be such State agency as may be designated by the Secretary if such agency is authorized by the State, or such other State agency as is authorized by the State and approved by the Secretary;

"(2) It provides for such methods of administration, and such participation in the administration of the plan by county and community committees or associations of agricultural producers organized for such purpose, as the Secretary finds necessary for the effective administration of the plan; and

"(3) It provides for the submission to the Secretary of such reports as he finds necessary to ascertain whether the plan is being carried out according to its terms, and for compliance with such requirements as the Secretary may prescribe to assure the correctness of and make possible the verification of such reports.

"(e) Such plan shall be approved if the Secretary finds that there is a reasonable prospect that—

"(1) Substantial accomplishment in effectuating the purposes of this section will be brought about through the operation of such plan and the plans submitted by other States, and

"(2) The operation of such plan will result in as substantial a furtherance of such accomplishment as may reasonably be achieved through the action of such State.

"(f) Upon approval of any State plan for any year the Secretary shall allocate to such State such sum (not in excess of the maximum amount fixed in pursuance of subsection (g) for such State for such year) as he finds necessary to carry out such plan for such year, and thereupon shall certify to the Secretary of the Treasury for payment to such agency of the State as the Secretary of Agriculture certifies is designated in the plan, and the Secretary of the Treasury shall pay to such agency, one-fourth of the amount so allocated. The remainder of the amount so allocated shall be similarly certified and paid in such installments

[427]

(payable prior to the end of the calendar year) as may be provided in the plan. No such installment shall be certified for payment if the Secretary of Agriculture finds that, prior to the due date of such installment, there has been a substantial failure by the State to carry out the plan according to its terms, or that the further operation of the plan according to its terms will not tend to effectuate the purposes of this section. No amount shall be certified for payment under any such installment in excess of the amount the Secretary finds necessary for the effective carrying out of the plan during the period to which the installment relates.

"(g) On or before November 1 of each year, the Secretary shall apportion among the several States the funds which will be available for carrying out State plans during the next calendar year, and in determining the amount to be apportioned to each State, the Secretary shall take into consideration the acreage and value of the major soil depleting and major export crops produced in the respective States during a representative period and the acreage and productivity of land devoted to agricultural production (including dairy products) in the respective States during a representative period: *Provided, however,* That apportionments of funds available for carrying out the purposes specified in this section for the year 1936 may be made at any time during 1936, and apportionments for 1937 may be made at any time during 1937. Notwithstanding the making of an apportionment to any State for any calendar year, the funds apportioned to any State for which no plan has been approved for such year, and any amount apportioned to any State which is not required to carry out an approved plan for such State for such year, shall be available for carrying out the provisions of sections 7 to 14, inclusive, of this Act.

"SEC. 8. (a) In order to carry out the purposes specified in section 7 (a) during the period necessary to afford a reasonable opportunity for legislative action by a sufficient number of States to assure the effectuation of such purposes by State action and in order to promote the more effective accomplishment of such purposes by State action thereafter, the Secretary shall exercise the powers conferred in this section during the period prior to January 1, 1938, except with respect to farming operations commenced in any State after the effective date of a State plan for such State approved pursuant to section 7. No such powers shall be exercised after December 31, 1937, except with respect to payments or grants in connection with farming operations carried out prior to January 1, 1938.

"(b) Subject to the limitations provided in subsection (a) of this section, the Secretary shall have power to carry out the purposes specified in clauses (1), (2), (3), and (4) of section 7 (a) by making payments or grants of other aid to agricultural producers, including tenants and share-croppers, in amounts, determined by the Secretary to be fair and reasonable in connection with the effectuation of such purposes during the year with respect to which such payments or grants are made, and measured by, (1) their treatment or use of their land, or a part thereof, for soil restoration, soil conservation, or the prevention of erosion, (2) changes in the use of their land, (3) a percentage of their normal production of any one or more agricultural commodities designated by the Secretary which equals that percentage of the normal national production of such commodity or commodities required for domestic consumption, or (4) any combination of the above. In determining the amount of any payment or grant measured by (1) or (2) the Secretary shall take into consideration the productivity of the land affected by the farming practices adopted during the year with respect to which such payment is made. In carrying out the provisions of this section, the Secretary shall, as far as practicable, protect the interests of tenants and share-croppers. In carrying out the provisions of this section, the Secretary is authorized to utilize county and community committees of agricultural producers and the agricultural extension service, or other approved agencies. In carrying out the provisions of this section, the Secretary shall not have power to enter into any contract binding upon any producer or to acquire any land or any right or interest therein. In carrying out the provisions of this section, the Secretary shall, in every practicable manner, protect the interests of small producers. The Secretary in administering this section shall in every practical way encourage and provide for soil conserving and soil rebuilding practices rather than the growing of soil depleting commercial crops.

"(c) Any payment or grant of aid made under subsection (b) shall be conditioned upon the utilization of the land, with respect to which such payment is made, in conformity with farming practices which the Secretary finds tend to effectuate the purposes specified in clause (1), (2), (3), or (4) of section 7 (a).

"SEC. 9. The Secretary is authorized to conduct surveys, investigations, and research relating to the conditions and factors affecting, and methods of accomplishing most effectively, the policy and purposes of section 7 (a). Notwithstanding any provision of existing law, the Secretary is authorized to make public such information as he deems necessary to carry out the provisions of this Act.

"SEC. 10. The term 'agricultural commodity' as used in this Act means any such commodity and any regional or market classification, type, or grade thereof.

"SEC. 11. All funds available for carrying out this Act shall be available for allotment to the bureaus and offices of the Department of Agriculture and for transfer to such other agencies of the Federal or State Governments as the Secretary may request to cooperate or assist in carrying out this Act.

"SEC. 12. Whenever the Secretary finds that the exercise of the powers conferred in this section will tend to carry out the purpose specified in clause (5) of section 7 (a), or will tend to provide for and maintain a continuous and stable supply of agricultural commodities adequate to meet consumer demand at prices fair to both producers and consumers, or both, he shall use such part as he deems necessary of the sums appropriated to carry out this Act for the expansion of domestic and foreign markets or for seeking new or additional markets for agricultural commodities or the products thereof or for the removal or disposition of surpluses of such commodities or the products thereof.

"SEC. 13. Notwithstanding the foregoing provisions of this Act, the Secretary is authorized and directed to provide for the execution by the Agricultural Adjustment Administration of such powers conferred upon him under sections 7 to 14, inclusive, of this Act as he deems may be appropriately exercised by such Administration, and for such purposes the provisions of law applicable to the appointment and compensation of persons employed by the Agricultural Adjustment Administration shall apply.

"SEC. 14. The facts constituting the bases for any payment or grant or the amount thereof authorized to be made under section 7 or 8 hereof, when officially determined in conformity with rules or regulations prescribed by the Secretary of Agriculture, shall be reviewable only by the Secretary of Agriculture.

"SEC. 15. To enable the Secretary of Agriculture to carry out the purposes of sections 7 and 8 there is hereby authorized to be appropriated for any fiscal year not exceeding $500,000,000.

"SEC. 16. The obligations incurred for the purpose of carrying out, for any calendar year, the provisions of sections 7 to 14, inclusive, of this Act shall not exceed $500,000,000.

"SEC. 17. (a) This Act shall apply to the United States, the Territories of Alaska and Hawaii, and the possession of Puerto Rico, and as used in this Act, the term 'State' includes Alaska, Hawaii, and Puerto Rico.

"(b) This Act may be cited as the 'Soil Conservation and Domestic Allotment Act'."

SEC. 2. Section 32 of the Act to amend the Agricultural Adjustment Act, and for other purposes, approved August 24, 1935, is amended by striking out clause (3) and inserting in lieu thereof, "(3) reestablish farmers' purchasing power by making payments in connection with the normal production of any agricultural commodity for domestic consumption. Determinations by the Secretary as to what constitutes diversion and what constitutes normal channels of trade and commerce and what constitutes normal production for domestic consumption shall be final." and by striking out that part of the last sentence thereof which precedes the second proviso and inserting in lieu thereof: "The sums appropriated under this section shall be expended for such one or more of the above-specified purposes, and at such times, in such manner, and in such amounts as the Secretary of Agriculture finds will effectuate substantial accomplishment of any one or more of the purposes of this section:".

SEC. 3. The unexpended balance of the funds appropriated by the second paragraph of Public Resolution Numbered 27, Seventy-third Congress, approved May 25, 1934, to carry out section 2 and section 6 of the Act entitled "An Act to amend the Agricultural Adjustment Act so as to include cattle and other products as basic agricultural commodities, and for other purposes", approved April 7, 1934, and the unexpended balance of the funds appropriated or reappropriated by section 37 of Public Act Numbered 320, Seventy-fourth Congress, entitled "An Act to amend the Agricultural Adjustment Act, and for other purposes", is authorized to be made available for the purposes enumerated in said Acts until June 30, 1937. The authorization, which is limited to June 30, 1936, contained in section 37 of Public Act Numbered 320, Seventy-fourth Congress, is likewise extended so that the funds therein authorized are authorized to be made available until June 30, 1937.

SEC. 4. The sum of $2,000,000 of the unobligated balance of the appropriation for relief purposes contained in the Emergency Relief Appropriation Act of 1935, approved April 8, 1935, is hereby made available to the Secretary of Agriculture for allocation and payment to the States in the Southern Great Plains area, or to farmers therein, for wind erosion control, under plans to be approved by the Secretary of Agriculture.

SEC. 5. Section 22 of the Agricultural Adjustment Act, as amended, is amended by inserting after the words "this title" wherever they appear the following: "or the Soil Conservation and Domestic Allotment Act, as amended"; and by striking out the words "an adjustment" wherever they appear and inserting in lieu thereof the word "any".

Approved, February 29, 1936.

A DEFENSE OF SOIL CONSERVATION*
May 8, 1937

When the owner of some Florida citrus groves protested the payment he had received for plowing under a cover crop on his land, President Roosevelt replied with this letter prepared by the Department of Agriculture.

ROOSEVELT TO HENRY C. TURNER

Galveston, Texas, May 8, 1937

My Dear Mr. Turner:

This is in reply to your letter of April twenty-first, concerning your check for $9.70 received from the Government in payment for plowing under 9.7 acres of a cover crop in a citrus grove in Florida, which you own.

I am informed by the Department of Agriculture that the check was issued after application for grant under the Agricultural Conservation Program had been made in the regular way by the Lake Wales Citrus Growers Association, acting as your agent. The application followed the filling out of a work sheet covering operations on your farm. Before the check was issued proof of compliance was given by your agent to the local committee.

Apparently the association acting as your agent was not informed of your desire not to receive any Government assistance in carrying out good conservation practice on your farm. Had it been so informed, the waste of effort by the local committee and the Government, in connection with the application made in your name, could have been avoided.

The majority of payments made to farmers under the program are larger than the one you received. While a payment of $9.70 may seem trivial to you, nevertheless there are many small farmers to whom even a payment of that size makes the difference between being able to finance a conservation practice and being forced to continue exploiting their soil.

If all landowners, unaided, could and would carry out proper soil conservation practice on their land, there would be no need for a soil conservation program sponsored by the Government. However, experience has shown that the pressure of competition forces most farmers, in the absence of government assistance, to mine and exploit their soil, so as to increase their immediate cash return, even though it might be in their own long-time interest to avoid such

*Franklin D. Roosevelt and Conservation—1911–1945, Vol. 2, Edgar B. Nixon, ed. (Hyde Park, N.Y.: General Services Administration, National Archives and Records Service, Franklin D. Roosevelt Library, 1957), 56–57.

exploitation. The government grants are intended to help the farmer avoid the cash sacrifice he would otherwise have to make in order to carry out good conservation practice.

The problem of stopping soil waste is especially acute on absentee-owned land which is occupied by tenants. The tenant naturally has little interest in conserving the soil for the benefit of some future occupant of the farm. The same is true of owners who are holding the land primarily for resale at a speculative profit.

Since the soil is the ultimate source of a large part of the Nation's wealth, the Nation cannot afford to permit the soil over large areas to be irretrievably ruined through the unrestrained operation of the competitive system. The Government's Agricultural Conservation Program represents the first serious and comprehensive effort by this Nation to save the good soil that is left. Expenditures by the Government which assure the conservation of the soil are in the interest of national economy in the truest sense of that word.

Very sincerely yours,

[*Franklin D. Roosevelt*]

THE SMALL WATERSHED ACT*
August 4, 1954

Public Law 566, also called the Hope-Aiken Act, after its sponsors, Representative Clifford Hope of Kansas and Senator George D. Aiken of Vermont, gave the Soil Conservation Service authority to build small reservoirs for their flood control value. The small watershed program is now one of the major functions of the Soil Conservation Service.

An Act to authorize the Secretary of Agriculture to cooperate with States and local agencies in the planning and carrying out of works of improvement for soil conservation, and for other purposes.

Be it enacted by the Senate and House of Representatives of the United States of America in Congress assembled, That erosion, floodwater, and sediment damages in the watersheds of the rivers and streams of the United States, causing loss of life and damage to property, constitute a menace to the national welfare; and that it is the sense of Congress that the Federal Government should cooperate with States and their political subdivisions, soil or water conservation districts, flood prevention or control districts, and other local public agencies for the purpose of preventing such damages and of furthering the conservation, development, utilization, and disposal of water and thereby of preserving and protecting the Nation's land and water resources.

SEC. 2. For the purposes of this Act, the following terms shall mean:

The "Secretary"—the Secretary of Agriculture of the United States.

"Works of improvement"—any undertaking for—

    (1) flood prevention (including structural and land-treatment measures) or

    (2) agricultural phases of the conservation, development, utilization, and disposal of water

in watershed or subwatershed areas not exceeding two hundred and fifty thousand acres and not including any single structure which provides more than five thousand acre-feet of total capacity. No appropriation shall be made for any plan for works of improvement which includes any structure which provides more than twenty-five hundred acre feet of total capacity unless such plan has been approved by resolutions adopted by the Committee on Agriculture and Forestry of the Senate and the Committee on Agriculture of the House of Representatives, respectively. A number of such subwatersheds when they are component parts of a larger watershed may be planned together when the local sponsoring organizations so desire.

"Local organization"—any State, political subdivision thereof, soil or water

*68 *Statutes at Large,* 666–68.

conservation district, flood prevention or control district, or combinations thereof, or any other agency having authority under State law to carry out, maintain and operate the works of improvement.

SEC. 3. In order to assist local organizations in preparing and carrying out plans for works of improvement, the Secretary is authorized, upon application of local organizations if such application has been submitted to, and not disapproved within 45 days by, the State agency having supervisory responsibility over programs provided for in this Act, or by the Governor if there is no State agency having such responsibility—

(1) to conduct such investigations and surveys as may be necessary to prepare plans for works of improvement;

(2) to make such studies as may be necessary for determining the physical and economic soundesss of plans for works of improvement, including a determination as to whether benefits exceed costs;

(3) to cooperate and enter into agreements with and to furnish financial and other assistance to local organizations: *Provided,* That, for the land-treatment measures, the Federal assistance shall not exceed the rate of assistance for similar practices under existing national programs;

(4) to obtain the cooperation and assistance of other Federal agencies in carrying out the purposes of this section.

SEC. 4. The Secretary shall require as a condition to providing Federal assistance for the installation of works of improvement that local organizations shall—

(1) acquire without cost to the Federal Government such land, easements, or rights-of-way as will be needed in connection with works of improvement installed with Federal assistance;

(2) assume such proportionate share of the cost of installing any works of improvement involving Federal assistance as may be determined by the Secretary to be equitable in consideration of anticipated benefits from such improvements: *Provided,* That no part of the construction cost for providing any capacity in structures for purposes other than flood prevention and features related thereto shall be borne by the Federal Government under the provisions of this Act;

(3) make arrangements satisfactory to the Secretary for defraying costs of operating and maintaining such works of improvement, in accordance with regulations presented by the Secretary of Agriculture;

(4) acquire, or provide assurance that landowners have acquired, such water rights, pursuant to State law, as may be needed in the installation and operation of the work of improvement; and

(5) obtain agreements to carry out recommended soil conservation measures and proper farm plans from owners of not less than 50 per centum of the lands situated in the drainage area above each retention reservoir to be installed with Federal assistance.

SEC. 5. At such time as the Secretary and the interested local organization have agreed on a plan for works of improvement, and the Secretary has determined that the benefits exceed the costs, and the local organization has met the requirements for participation in carrying out the works of improvement as set forth in section 4, the Secretary is authorized to assist such local organizations in developing specifications, in preparing contracts for construction, and to participate in the installation of such works of improvement in accordance with the plan: *Provided,* That, except as to the installation of works of improvement on Federal lands, the Secretary shall not construct or enter into any contract for the construction of any structure unless there is no local organization authorized by State law to undertake such construction or to enter into such contract, and in no event after July 1, 1956: *Provided,* That in participating in the installation of such works of improvement the Secretary, as far as practicable and consistent with his responsibilities for administering the overall national agricultural program, shall utilize the authority conferred upon him by the provisions of this Act: *Provided further,* That, at least forty-five days (counting only days occurring during any regular or special sessions of the Congress) before such installation involving Federal assistance is commenced, the Secretary shall transmit a copy of the plan and the justification therefor to the Congress through the President: *Provided further,* That any such plan (a) which includes reclamation or irrigation works or which affects public or other lands under the jurisdiction of the Secretary of the Interior, or (b) which includes Federal assistance for floodwater detention structures, shall be submitted to the Secretary of the Interior or the Secretary of the Army, respectively, for his views and recommendations at least sixty days prior to transmission of the plan to the Congress through the President. The views and recommendations of the Secretary of the Interior, and the Secretary of the Army, if received by the Secretary of Agriculture prior to the expiration of the above sixty-day period, shall accompany the plan transmitted by the Secretary of Agriculture to the Congress through the President: *Provided further,* That, prior to any Federal participation in the works of improvement under this Act, the President shall issue such rules and regulations as he deems necessary or desirable to carry out the purposes of this Act, and to assure the coordination of the work authorized under this Act and related work of other agencies including the Department of the Interior and the Department of the Army.

SEC. 6. The Secretary is authorized in cooperation with other Federal and with States and local agencies to make investigations and surveys of the watersheds of rivers and other waterways as a basis for the development of coordinated programs. In areas where the programs of the Secretary of Agriculture may affect public or other lands under the jurisdiction of the Secretary of the Interior, the Secretary of the Interior is authorized to cooperate with the Secretary of Agriculture in the planning and development of works or programs for such lands.

SEC. 7. The provisions of the Act of June 22, 1936 (49 Stat. 1570), as amended and supplemented, conferring authority upon the Department of Agriculture under the direction of the Secretary of Agriculture to make preliminary examinations and surveys and to prosecute works of improvement for runoff and waterflow retardation and soil erosion prevention on the watersheds of rivers and other waterways are hereby repealed: *Provided,* That (a) the authority of that Department of Agriculture, under the direction of the Secretary, to prosecute the works of improvement for runoff and waterflow retardation and soil erosion prevention authorized to be carried out by the Department by the Act of December 22, 1944 (58 Stat. 887), as amended, and (b) the authority of the Secretary of Agriculture to undertake emergency measures for runoff retardation and soil erosion prevention authorized to be carried out by section 7 of the Act of June 28, 1938 (52 Stat. 1215), as amended by section 216 of the Act of May 17, 1950 (64 Stat. 163), shall not be affected by the provisions of this section.

SEC. 8. There are hereby authorized to be appropriated such sums as may be necessary to carry out the purposes of this Act, such sums to remain available until expended.

SEC. 9. This Act may be cited as the "Watershed Protection and Flood Prevention Act".

Approved August 4, 1954.

THE DUST BOWL

A FIRESIDE CHAT ON DROUGHT*
September 6, 1936

This is an excerpt from the first of Roosevelt's "fireside chats" during the campaign of 1936, after an inspection trip through the Great Plains area. It foreshadowed, among other developments, the Water Facilities Act and the Shelterbelt program.

My Friends:

I have been on a journey of husbandry. I went primarily to see at first hand conditions in the drought states; to see how effectively Federal and local authorities are taking care of pressing problems of relief and also how they are to work together to defend the people of this country against the effects of future droughts.

I saw drought devastation in nine states.

I talked with families who had lost their wheat crop, lost their corn crop, lost their livestock, lost the water in their well, lost their garden and come through to the end of the summer without one dollar of cash resources, facing a winter without feed or food—facing a planting season without seed to put in the ground.

That was the extreme case, but there are thousands and thousands of families on western farms who share the same difficulties.

I saw cattlemen who because of lack of grass or lack of winter feed have been compelled to sell all but their breeding stock and will need help to carry even these through the coming winter. I saw livestock kept alive only because water had been brought to them long distances in tank cars. I saw other farm families who have not lost everything but who, because they have made only partial crops, must have some form of help if they are to continue farming next spring.

I shall never forget the fields of wheat so blasted by heat that they cannot be harvested. I shall never forget field after field of corn, stunted, earless, stripped of leaves, for what the sun left the grasshoppers took. I saw brown pasture that would not keep a cow on fifty acres.

*Franklin D. Roosevelt and Conservation—1911–1945, Vol. 1, Edgar B. Nixon, ed. (Hyde Park, N.Y.: General Services Administration, National Archives and Records Service, Franklin D. Roosevelt Library, 1957), 568–71.

[438]

Yet I would not have you think for a single minute that there is permanent disaster in these drought regions, or that the picture I saw meant depopulating these areas. No cracked earth, no blistering sun, no burning wind, no grasshoppers, are a permanent match for the indomitable American farmers and stockmen and their wives and children who have carried on through desperate days, and inspire us with their self-reliance, their tenacity and their courage. It was their fathers' task to make homes; it is their task to keep these homes; and it is our task to help them win their fight.

First let me talk for a minute about this autumn and the coming winter. We have the option, in the case of families who need actual subsistence, of putting them on the dole or putting them to work. They do not want to go on the dole and they are one thousand percent right. We agree, therefore, that we must put them to work, work for a decent wage; and when we reach that decision we kill two birds with one stone, because these families will earn enough by working, not only to subsist themselves, but to buy food for their stock, and seed for next year's planting. And into this scheme of things there fit of course the government lending agencies which next year, as in the past, will help with production loans.

Every Governor with whom I have talked is in full accord with this program of providing work for these farm families, just as every Governor agrees that the individual states will take care of their unemployables but that the cost of employing those who are entirely able and willing to work must be borne by the Federal Government.

If then we know, as we do today, the approximate number of farm families who will require some form of work relief from now on through the winter, we face the question of what kind of work they ought to do. Let me make it clear that this is not a new question because it has already been answered to a greater or less extent in every one of the drought communities. Beginning in 1934, when we also had a serious drought condition, the state and Federal governments cooperated in planning a large number of projects—many of them directly aimed at the alleviation of future drought conditions. In accordance with that program, for example, literally thousands of ponds or small reservoirs have been built in order to supply water for stock and to lift the level of the underground water to protect wells from going dry. Thousands of wells have been drilled or deepened; community lakes have been created and irrigation projects are being pushed.

Water conservation by means such as these is being expanded as a result of this new drought all through the Great Plains area, the western corn belt and in the states that lie further south. In the Middle West water conservation is not so pressing a problem, and here the work projects run more to soil erosion control and the building of farm-to-market roads.

Spending like this is not waste. It would spell future waste if we did not spend for such things now. These emergency work projects provide money to buy food and clothing for the winter; they keep the livestock on the farm; they provide seed for a new crop, and, best of all, they will conserve soil and water in the future in those areas that are most frequently hit by drought.

If, for example, in some local place the water table continues to drop and the top soil to blow away, the land values will disappear with the water and the soil. People on the farms will drift into the nearby cities; the cities will have no farm trade and the workers in the city factories and stores will have no jobs. Property values in those cities will decline. If, on the other hand, the farms within that area remain as farms with better water supply and no erosion, the farm population will stay on the land and prosper and the nearby cities will prosper too. Property values will increase instead of disappearing. That is why it is worth our while as a nation to spend money in order to save money. . . . I want to make it clear that no simple panacea can be applied to the drought problem in the whole of the drought area. Plans have to depend on local conditions, for these vary with all kinds of things, like annual rainfall, soil characteristics, altitude and topography. Water and soil conservation methods may differ in one county from those in an adjoining county. Work to be done in the cattle and sheep country differs, of course, in type from work in the wheat country or work in the corn belt.

The Great Plains Drought Area Committee has given me its preliminary recommendations for a long-time program for the Great Plains region. Using that report as a basis we are cooperating successfully and in entire accord with the Governors and state planning boards. As we get this program into operation the people more and more will be able to maintain themselves securely on the land. That will mean a steady decline in the relief burdens that the Federal Government and the states have had to assume in time of drought; but, more important, it will mean a greater contribution to general national prosperity by these regions that have been hit by drought. It will conserve and improve not only property values, but human values. The people in the drought area do not want to be dependent on Federal, or state or any other kind of charity. They want for themselves and their families an opportunity to share fairly by their own efforts in the progress of America. . . .

In the drought area people are not afraid to use new methods to meet changes in Nature, and to correct mistakes of the past. If over-grazing has injured range lands, they are willing to reduce the grazing. If certain wheat lands should be returned to pasture they are willing to cooperate. If trees should be planted as wind-breaks or to stop erosion they will work with us. If terracing or summer fallowing or crop rotation is called for, they will carry them out. They stand ready to fit, and not to fight, the ways of Nature.

We are helping, and shall continue to help the farmer to do those things, through local soil conservation committees and other cooperative local, state and federal agencies of government.

[440]

I wish I had time tonight to deal with other and more comprehensive agricultural policies. But that must wait till a later time.

With this fine help we are tiding over the present emergency. We are going to conserve soil, conserve water and conserve life. We are going to have long-time defenses against both low prices and drought. We are going to have a farm policy that will serve the national welfare. That is our hope for the future.

THE WATER FACILITIES ACT*
August 28, 1937

This law involved the Department of Agriculture in programs for irrigation in the West. Secretary of the Interior Ickes privately protested that the new law put the Department "in the reclamation business."

An Act to promote conservation in the arid and semiarid areas of the United States by aiding in the development of facilities for water storage and utilization, and for other purposes.

Be it enacted by the Senate and House of Representatives of the United States of America in Congress assembled, That it is hereby recognized that the wastage and inadequate utilization of water resources on farm, grazing, and forest lands in the arid and semiarid areas of the United States resulting from inadequate facilities for water storage and utilization contribute to the destruction of natural resources, injuries to public health and public lands, droughts, periodic floods, crop failures, decline in standards of living, and excessive dependence upon public relief, and thereby menace the national welfare. It is therefore hereby declared to be the policy of Congress to assist in providing facilities for water storage and utilization in the arid and semiarid areas of the United States.

SEC. 2. In order to effectuate this policy and promote proper land use in the said areas, the Secretary of Agriculture is hereby authorized, from time to time—

(1) To formulate and keep current a program of projects for the construction and maintenance in the said areas of ponds, reservoirs, wells, check-dams, pumping installations, and other facilities for water storage or utilization, together with appurtenances to such facilities. The facilities to be included within such program shall be located where they will promote the proper utilization of lands and no such facilities shall be located where they will encourage the cultivation of lands which are submarginal and which should be devoted to other uses in the public interest;

(2) To construct and to sell or lease, with or without a money consideration, under such terms and conditions as will advance the purposes of this Act, the facilities mentioned in section 2 (1) and included within the program there provided for, including the lands upon which such facilities are located if they have been acquired or reserved for the purposes of this Act;

(3) To cooperate or enter into agreements with, or to furnish financial or other aid to, any agency, governmental or otherwise, or any person, subject to such conditions as he may deem necessary for the purposes of this Act; and

*50 *Statutes at Large,* 869–70.

(4) To obtain options upon and to acquire lands, or rights or interests therein, or rights to the use of water, by purchase, lease, gift, exchange, condemnation, or otherwise, only when necessary for the purposes of this Act.

SEC. 3. The facilities included in the program provided for in section 2 (1) may be located—

(a) On lands owned or controlled by the United States or any of its agencies, with the cooperation of the agency having jurisdiction thereof; and

(b) On any other lands upon obtaining proper consent or the necessary rights or interests in such lands.

SEC. 4. As a condition to extending benefits under this Act to any lands not owned or controlled by the United States or any of its agencies, the Secretary of Agriculture may, insofar as he may deem necessary for the purposes of this Act, require—

(1) The enactment of State and local laws providing for soil conserving land uses and practices, and the storage, conservation and equitable utilization of waters;

(2) Agreements or covenants in regard to the maintenance and permanent use of such water, facilities, or lands benefited by such facilities;

(3) Contributions in money, services, materials, or otherwise to any operations conferring such benefits.

SEC. 5. The Secretary of Agriculture, in administering the provisions of this Act, shall utilize the officers, employees, and facilities of agencies within the Department of Agriculture whose functions are related to the program provided for in this Act, and may allot to such agencies or transfer to such other agencies of the Federal Government as he may request to assist in carrying out any of the provisions of this Act, any funds available for the purposes of this Act.

SEC. 6. For the purposes of this Act, the Secretary of Agriculture may—

(1) Secure the cooperation of any governmental agency;

(2) Make expenditures for personal services and rent in the District of Columbia and elsewhere, for the purchase of law books and books of reference, for printing and binding, for the purchase, exchange, operation, and maintenance of passenger-carrying vehicles, for supplies and equipment, for traveling expenses and for other administrative expenses; and

(3) Perform such acts, and prescribe such rules and regulations as he may deem proper to carry out the provisions of this Act.

SEC. 7. There are hereby authorized to be appropriated for the purposes of this Act such sums as Congress may from time to time determine to be necessary.

Approved, August 28, 1937.

THE SHELTERBELT PROGRAM*
May 3, 1940

The idea of a shelterbelt of trees, one or more miles apart, running from Canada south into Texas, was an idea that F. D. R. favored as part of an answer to the dust bowl problem of the Great Plains states, which began to take on some of the overtones of a national disaster in the mid-1930's.

Under the plan for the shelterbelts, which were planned to run from east to west because the most destructive winds ranged north and south, the landowner furnished planting sites and promised to cultivate the trees. The government furnished and planted the trees, furnished fencing for protection from cattle, and provided general technical assistance.

Local support for the project varied, and it attracted no general support in Congress, which halted appropriations for the work during World War II. This memorandum from the Bureau of the Budget explains some of the problems of the Shelterbelt program.

HAROLD D. SMITH, DIRECTOR, BUREAU OF THE BUDGET, TO ROOSEVELT

Washington, D.C., May 3, 1940

Memorandum for the President:

Reference is made to the attached letter addressed to you by the Secretary of Agriculture under date of March 28, 1940, urging the inclusion in the Emergency Relief Appropriation Act for the coming fiscal year of special authorizing language and an appropriation item of $2,120,000 to provide for continuation of the Prairie States Forestry Project (the Shelterbelt).

Possible courses of action with respect to this project have been considered with the Department of Agriculture and the Work Projects Administration, as follows:

1. Special language and appropriation item in the new Relief Act. It is believed that this course would almost certainly lead to pressures in Congress in behalf of a large number of other projects by special interest groups who may be able to present the case for such projects as appealingly as that for the Shelterbelt can be presented. Either a large increase in the total Relief Act appropriation, or a legislative breakdown of the total into numerous and frozen project items with resultant handicap to W. P. A. in administering the program would be the probable consequence.

Franklin D. Roosevelt and Conservation—1911–1945, Vol. 2, Edgar B. Nixon, ed. (Hyde Park, N.Y.: General Services Administration, National Archives and Records Service, Franklin D. Roosevelt Library, 1957), 445–48.

The Congressional history of the Shelterbelt as a distinct budgetary item is unfavorable. The 1937 Department of Agriculture Appropriation Act provided $170,000 for this project with what amounted to a mandate for its liquidation. This $170,000 was not used. Instead of liquidating the project it was continued with W. P. A. financing. Again in the Budget for 1939 you approved the inclusion of an item of $1,000,000 for the Shelterbelt, under the authority of the newly enacted Norris-Doxey Cooperative Farm Forestry Act. The item was rejected by Congress, the House Committee stating that "the proposed expenditure is not in accord with the purpose and intent of Congress" under the above Act.

Although, as indicated by the Secretary, more favorable public and Congressional sentiment with respect to the project has since developed, another submission as a special project in the Relief Act would incur serious risk of a rejection which would force an abrupt abandonment of the project on June 30 of this year.

These factors lead to my recommendation that the proposed course of special treatment in the Relief Act submission should not be adopted.

2. An allocation from the funds which will be appropriated in the Relief Act for the Rural Rehabilitation program of the Farm Security Administration. The Solicitor of the Department of Agriculture has rendered an opinion that such funds could not legally be used to provide the "sponsor contribution" for continuation of the project with W. P. A. labor.

3. Continuation as a Soil Conservation Service project. The regular appropriations of the Soil Conservation Service are legally available for the purposes of the project. In the 1941 Budget the S. C. S. estimates were sharply reduced. The Senate restored $1,700,000 of the cut, but this restored amount, if finally approved, is rather definitely earmarked by the Senate "for cooperation with Soil Conservation Districts," which are rapidly growing in number and area. The Department holds that, even with the restoration above indicated, its funds for cooperation with these organized Districts will be extremely short, and that a revision of the program to provide a $250,000 to $350,000 sponsor contribution for the Shelterbelt would not only be disadvantageous to the Conservation District program, but would involve unfortunate Congressional reactions.

4. Can the Work Projects Administration legally authorize exemptions which would permit continuation of the work, strictly as a W. P. A. Federal Agency Project? As stated by the Secretary, the Shelterbelt project has been carried forward wholly with W. P. A. funds for the past four years. The Department feels that it cannot be continued on this basis without material relief from present restrictions as to non-labor expense, 90–10 employment ratio, freezing of allotments by States and other administrative features. I have presented the above question to the Work Projects Administration, and have been assured that essential exemptions can and will be allowed. Consequently, I recommend that the Work Projects Administration and the Department be requested to work

out arrangements which will permit the work to be carried on through the fiscal year 1941, from Agriculture's share of the Federal Agency Project fund which the new Relief Act is expected to provide.

5. Action subsequent to Fiscal Year 1941. You will recall that the Department's regular estimates for 1941 included an item of $500,000 to provide administrative and supervisory personnel and basic facilities which would enable the Forest Service to carry on the Shelterbelt as a special project on a scale adapted to the availability each year of relief labor financed by W. P. A.

In deciding against inclusion of this item in the 1941 Budget, you indicated that as the feasibility and value of the shelterbelt plantings become more fully demonstrated, it should be possible to reduce the Federal contribution to the ordinary degree of cooperative action by inducing the affected States, local agencies and individuals to assume the major part in the long-term program.

The Department states that orderly liquidation of the project as a Federal activity could not be accomplished in less than two years. It believes that due to the wide range of technical requirements for success, the States would not continue the work as State WPA projects were the Forest Service to liquidate its set-up. The Secretary expresses the conviction that it is not time to relinquish operation of the project as a Federal activity and that the work constitutes an important phase of the agricultural program in the plains States.

While a way has been found to continue through 1941 on the present basis, I suggest that definite steps be taken toward changing the pattern of Federal participation to that indicated by the decision last fall against setting up the Shelterbelt as a distinct and permanent regular Budget item. Each of the six States involved has enacted legislation authorizing Soil Conservation Districts. The Shelterbelt area is likely to be largely embraced within such Districts. The maintenance and operation of nurseries and the furnishing of technical advice and assistance in tree planting are clearly authorized by the act establishing the Soil Conservation Service and there is further cooperative authority under the Farm Forestry Act which also is largely administered by the Soil Conservation Service. Within the regular annual appropriations to that Service for soil conservation research and cooperative operations, it appears that the Department should find it possible to do its proper part in continuing desirable tree planting and maintenance in the plains States. In the attached proposed draft of your reply to the Secretary's letter of March 28, this course is suggested. The proposed reply also has been referred to WPA and initialed to indicate concurrence of that agency as to the 1941 handling of the project.

Harold D. Smith

THE TENNESSEE VALLEY AUTHORITY

REQUEST FOR TVA*
April 10, 1933

Roosevelt's brief message to the Congress requesting legislation to establish the Tennessee Valley Authority is one of the most eloquent among American conservation documents.

Message from the President of the United States transmitting a request for legislation to create a Tennessee Valley Authority— a corporation clothed with the power of government but possessed of the flexibility and initiative of a private enterprise.

To the Congress:

The continued idleness of a great national investment in the Tennessee Valley leads me to ask the Congress for legislation necessary to enlist this project in the service of the people.

It is clear that the Muscle Shoals development is but a small part of the potential public usefulness of the entire Tennessee River. Such use, if envisioned in its entirety, transcends mere power development: it enters the wide fields of flood control, soil erosion, afforestation, elimination from agricultural use of marginal lands, and distribution and diversification of industry. In short, this power development of war days leads logically to national planning for a complete river watershed involving many States and the future lives and welfare of millions. It touches and gives life to all forms of human concerns.

I, therefore, suggest to the Congress legislation to create a Tennessee Valley Authority—a corporation clothed with the power of government but possessed of the flexibility and initiative of a private enterprise. It should be charged with the broadest duty of planning for the proper use, conservation, and development of the natural resources of the Tennessee River drainage basin and its adjoining territory for the general social and economic welfare of the Nation. This authority should also be clothed with the necessary power to carry these plans into effect. Its duty should be the rehabilitation of the Muscle Shoals development and the coordination of it with the wider plan.

Many hard lessons have taught us the human waste that results from lack of

Muscle Shoals Development, H. Doc. 15, 73rd Cong., lst sess., 1–2.

planning. Here and there a few wise cities and counties have looked ahead and planned. But our Nation has "just grown." It is time to extend planning to a wider field, in this instance comprehending in one great project many States directly concerned with the basin of one of our greatest rivers.

This in a true sense is a return to the spirit and vision of the pioneer. If we are successful here we can march on, step by step, in a like development of other great natural territorial units within our borders.

Franklin D. Roosevelt

The White House
April 10, 1933

THE TENNESSEE VALLEY AUTHORITY ACT*
May 18, 1933

The act establishing TVA contained several features unique to government operations at that time, and one is still unique—paragraph (h), Section 2—"All members of the board shall be persons who profess a belief in the feasibility and wisdom of this Act."

An Act to improve the navigability and to provide for the flood control of the Tennessee River; to provide for reforestation and the proper use of marginal lands in the Tennessee Valley; to provide for the agricultural and industrial development of said valley; to provide for the national defense by the creation of a corporation for the operation of Government properties at and near Muscle Shoals in the State of Alabama, and for other purposes.

Be it enacted by the Senate and House of Representatives of the United States of America in Congress assembled, That for the purpose of maintaining and operating the properties now owned by the United States in the vicinity of Muscle Shoals, Alabama, in the interest of the national defense and for agricultural and industrial development, and to improve navigation in the Tennessee River and to control the destructive flood waters in the Tennessee River and Mississippi River Basins, there is hereby created a body corporate by the name of the "Tennessee Valley Authority" (hereinafter referred to as the "Corporation"). The board of directors first appointed shall be deemed the incorporators, and the incorporation shall be held to have been effected from the date of the first meeting of the board. This Act may be cited as the "Tennessee Valley Authority Act of 1933."

SEC. 2. (a) The board of directors of the Corporation (hereinafter referred to as the "board") shall be composed of three members, to be appointed by the President, by and with the advice and consent of the Senate. In appointing the members of the board, the President shall designate the chairman. All other officials, agents, and employees shall be designated and selected by the board.

(b) The terms of office of the members first taking office after the approval of this Act shall expire as designated by the President at the time of nomination, one at the end of the third year, one at the end of the sixth year, and one at the end of the ninth year, after the date of approval of this Act. A successor to a member of the board shall be appointed in the same manner as the original members and shall have a term of office expiring nine years from the date of the expiration of the term for which his predecessor was appointed.

(c) Any member appointed to fill a vacancy in the board occurring prior to the

*48 *Statutes at Large,* 58–72.

expiration of the term for which his predecessor was appointed shall be appointed for the remainder of such term.

(d) Vacancies in the board so long as there shall be two members in office shall not impair the powers of the board to execute the functions of the Corporation, and two of the members in office shall constitute a quorum for the transaction of the business of the board.

(e) Each of the members of the board shall be a citizen of the United States, and shall receive a salary at the rate of $10,000 a year, to be paid by the Corporation as current expenses. Each member of the board, in addition to his salary, shall be permitted to occupy as his residence one of the dwelling houses owned by the Government in the vicinity of Muscle Shoals, Alabama, the same to be designated by the President of the United States. Members of the board shall be reimbursed by the Corporation for actual expenses (including traveling and subsistence expenses) incurred by them in the performance of the duties vested in the board by this Act. No member of said board shall, during his continuance in office, be engaged in any other business, but each member shall devote himself to the work of the Corporation.

(f) No director shall have financial interest in any public-utility corporation engaged in the business of distributing and selling power to the public nor in any corporation engaged in the manufacture, selling, or distribution of fixed nitrogen or fertilizer, or any ingredients thereof, nor shall any member have any interest in any business that may be adversely affected by the success of the Corporation as a producer of concentrated fertilizers or as a producer of electric power.

(g) The board shall direct the exercise of all the powers of the Corporation.

(h) All members of the board shall be persons who profess a belief in the feasibility and wisdom of this Act.

SEC. 3. The board shall without regard to the provisions of Civil Service laws applicable to officers and employees of the United States, appoint such managers, assistant managers, officers, employees, attorneys, and agents, as are necessary for the transaction of its business, fix their compensation, define their duties, require bonds of such of them as the board may designate, and provide a system of organization to fix responsibility and promote efficiency. Any appointee of the board may be removed in the discretion of the board. No regular officer or employee of the Corporation shall receive a salary in excess of that received by the members of the board.

All contracts to which the Corporation is a party and which require the employment of laborers and mechanics in the construction, alteration, maintenance, or repair of buildings, dams, locks, or other projects shall contain a provision that not less than the prevailing rate of wages for work of a similar nature prevailing in the vicinity shall be paid to such laborers or mechanics.

In the event any dispute arises as to what are the prevailing rates of wages, the question shall be referred to the Secretary of Labor for determination, and his decision shall be final. In the determination of such prevailing rate or rates, due regard shall be given to those rates which have been secured through collective agreement by representatives of employers and employees.

Where such work as is described in the two preceeding paragraphs is done directly by the Corporation the prevailing rate of wages shall be paid in the same manner as though such work had been let by contract.

Insofar as applicable, the benefits of the Act entitled "An Act to provide compensation for employees of the United States suffering injuries while in the performance of their duties, and for other purposes," approved September 7, 1916, as amended, shall extend to persons given employment under the provisions of this Act.

Sec. 4. Except as otherwise specifically provided in this Act, the Corporation—

(a) Shall have succession in its corporate name.

(b) May sue and be sued in its corporate name.

(c) May adopt and use a corporate seal, which shall be judicially noticed.

(d) May make contracts, as herein authorized.

(e) May adopt, amend, and repeal bylaws.

(f) May purchase or lease and hold such real and personal property as it deems necessary or convenient in the transaction of its business, and may dispose of any such personal property held by it.

The board shall select a treasurer and as many assistant treasurers as it deems proper, which treasurer and assistant treasurers shall give such bonds for the safe-keeping of the securities and moneys of the said Corporation as the board may require: *Provided,* That any member of said board may be removed from office at any time by a concurrent resolution of the Senate and the House of Representatives.

(g) Shall have such powers as may be necessary or appropriate for the exercise of the powers herein specifically conferred upon the Corporation.

(h) Shall have power in the name of the United States of America to exercise the right of eminent domain, and in the purchase of any real estate or the acquisition of real estate by condemnation proceedings, the title to such real estate shall be taken in the name of the United States of America, and thereupon all such real estate shall be entrusted to the Corporation as the agent of the United States to accomplish the purposes of this Act.

(i) Shall have power to acquire real estate for the construction of dams, reservoirs, transmission lines, power houses, and other structures, and navigation projects at any point along the Tennessee River, or any of its tributaries, and in the event that the owner or owners of such property shall fail and refuse to sell to the Corporation at a price deemed fair and reasonable by the board, then the Corporation may proceed to exercise the right of eminent domain, and to condemn all property that it deems necessary for carrying out the purposes of this Act, and all such condemnation proceedings shall be had pursuant to the provisions and requirements hereinafter specified, with reference to any and all condemnation proceedings.

(j) Shall have power to construct dams, reservoirs, power houses, power structures, transmission lines, navigation projects, and incidental works in the Tennessee River and its tributaries, and to unite the various power installations into one or more systems by transmission lines.

SEC. 5. The board is hereby authorized—

(a) To contract with commercial producers for the production of such fertilizers or fertilizer materials as may be needed in the Government's program of development and introduction in excess of that produced by Government plants. Such contracts may provide either for outright purchase of materials by the board or only for the payment of carrying charges on special materials manufactured at the board's request for its program.

(b) To arrange with farmers and farm organizations for large-scale practical use of the new forms of fertilizers under conditions permitting an accurate measure of the economic return they produce.

(c) To cooperate with National, State, district, or county experimental stations or demonstration farms, for the use of new forms of fertilizer or fertilizer practices during the initial or experimental period of their introduction.

(d) The board in order to improve and cheapen the production of fertilizer is authorized to manufacture and sell fixed nitrogen, fertilizer, and fertilizer ingredients at Muscle Shoals by the employment of existing facilities, by modernizing existing plants, or by any other process or processes that in its judgment shall appear wise and profitable for the fixation of atmospheric nitrogen or the cheapening of the production of fertilizer.

(e) Under the authority of this Act the board may make donations or sales of the product of the plant or plants operated by it to be fairly and equitably distributed through the agency of county demonstration agents, agricultural colleges, or otherwise as the board may direct, for experimentation, education, and introduction of the use of such products in cooperation with practical farmers so as to obtain information as to the value, effect, and best methods of their use.

(f) The board is authorized to make alterations, modifications, or improvements in existing plants and facilities, and to construct new plants.

(g) In the event it is not used for the fixation of nitrogen for agricultural purposes or leased, then the board shall maintain in stand-by condition nitrate plant numbered 2, or its equivalent, for the fixation of atmospheric nitrogen, for the production of explosives in the event of war or a national emergency, until the Congress shall by joint resolution release the board from this obligation, and if any part thereof be used by the board for the manufacture of phosphoric acid or potash, the balance of nitrate plant numbered 2 shall be kept in stand-by condition.

(h) To establish, maintain, and operate laboratories and experimental plants, and to undertake experiments for the purpose of enabling the Corporation to furnish nitrogen products for military purposes, and nitrogen and other fertilizer products for agricultural purposes in the most economical manner and at the highest standard of efficiency.

(i) To request the assistance and advice of any officer, agent, or employee of any executive department or of any independent office of the United States, to enable the Corporation the better to carry out its powers successfully, and as far as practicable shall utilize the services of such officers, agents, and employees, and the President shall, if in his opinion, the public interest, service, or economy so require, direct that such assistance, advice, and service be rendered to the Corporation, and any individual that may be by the President directed to render such assistance, advice, and service shall be thereafter subject to the orders, rules, and regulations of the board: *Provided,* That any invention or discovery made by virtue of and incidental to such service by an employee of the Government of the United States serving under this section, or by any employee of the Corporation, together with any patents which may be granted thereon, shall be the sole and exclusive property of the Corporation, which is hereby authorized to grant such licenses thereunder as shall be authorized by the board: *Provided further,* That the board may pay to such inventor such sum from the income from sale of licenses as it may deem proper.

(j) Upon the requisition of the Secretary of War or the Secretary of the Navy to manufacture for and sell at cost to the United States explosives or their nitrogenous content.

(k) Upon the requisition of the Secretary of War the Corporation shall allot and deliver without charge to the War Department so much power as shall be necessary in the judgment of said Department for use in operation of all locks, lifts, or other facilities in aid of navigation.

(l) To produce, distribute, and sell electric power, as herein particularly specified.

(m) No products of the Corporation shall be sold for use outside of the United States, its Territories and possessions, except to the United States Government for the use of its Army and Navy, or to its allies in case of war.

(n) The President is authorized, within twelve months after the passage of this Act, to lease to any responsible farm organization or to any corporation organized by it nitrate plant numbered 2 and Waco Quarry, together with the railroad connecting said quarry with nitrate plant numbered 2, for a term not exceeding fifty years at a rental of not less than $1 per year, but such authority shall be subject to the express condition that the lessee shall use said property during the term of said lease exclusively for the manufacture of fertilizer and fertilizer ingredients to be used only in the manufacture of fertilizer by said lessee and sold for use as fertilizer. The said lessee shall convenant to keep said property in first-class condition, but the lessee shall be authorized to modernize said plant numbered 2 by the installation of such machinery as may be necessary, and is authorized to amortize the cost of said machinery and improvements over the term of said lease or any part thereof. Said lease shall also provide that the board shall sell to the lessee power for the operation of said plant at the same schedule of prices that it charges all other customers for power of the same class and quantity. Said lease shall also provide that, if the said lessee does not desire to buy power of the publicly owned plant, it shall have the right to purchase its power for the operation of said plant of the Alabama Power Company or any other publicly or privately owned corporation engaged in the generation and sale of electric power, and in such case the lease shall provide further that the said lessee shall have a free right of way to build a transmission line over Government property to said plant paying the actual expenses and damages, if any, incurred by the Corporation on account of such line. Said lease shall also provide that the said lessee shall covenant that during the term of said lease the said lessee shall not enter into any illegal monopoly, combination, or trust with any privately owned corporation engaged in the manufacture, production, and sale of fertilizer with the object or effect of increasing the price of fertilizer to the farmer.

SEC. 6. In the appointment of officials and the selection of employees for said Corporation, and in the promotion of any such employees or officials, no political test or qualification shall be permitted or given consideration, but all such appointments and promotions shall be given and made on the basis of merit and efficiency. Any member of said board who is found by the President of the United States to be guilty of a violation of this section shall be removed from office by the President of the United States, and any appointee of said board who is found by the board to be guilty of a violation of this section shall be removed from office by said board.

SEC. 7. In order to enable the Corporation to exercise the powers and duties vested in it by this Act—

(a) The exclusive use, possession, and control of the United States nitrate plants numbered 1 and 2, including steam plants, located, respectively, at Sheffield, Alabama, and Muscle Shoals, Alabama, together with all real estate and buildings connected therewith, all tools and machinery, equipment, accessories, and materials belonging thereto, and all laboratories and plants used as auxiliaries thereto; the fixed-nitrogen research laboratory, the Waco limestone quarry, in Alabama, and Dam Numbered 2, located at Muscle Shoals, its power house, and all hydroelectric and operating appurtenances (except the locks), and all machinery, lands, and buildings in connection therewith, and all appurtenances thereof, and all other property to be acquired by the Corporation in its own name or in the name of the United States of America, are hereby intrusted to the Corporation for the purposes of this Act.

(b) The President of the United States is authorized to provide for the transfer to the Corporation of the use, possession, and control of such other real or personal property of the United States as he may from time to time deem necessary and proper for the purposes of the Corporation as herein stated.

SEC. 8. (a) The Corporation shall maintain its principal office in the immediate vicinity of Muscle Shoals, Alabama. The Corporation shall be held to be an inhabitant and resident of the northern judicial district of Alabama within the meaning of the laws of the United States relating to the venue of civil suits.

(b) The Corporation shall at all times maintain complete and accurate books of accounts.

(c) Each member of the board, before entering upon the duties of his office, shall subscribe to an oath (or affirmation) to support the Constitution of the United States and to faithfully and impartially perform the duties imposed upon him by this Act.

SEC. 9. (a) The board shall file with the President and with the Congress, in December of each year, a financial statement and a complete report as to the business of the Corporation covering the preceding governmental fiscal year. This report shall include an itemized statement of the cost of power at each power station, the total number of employees and the names, salaries, and duties of those receiving compensation at the rate of more than $1,500 a year.

(b) The Comptroller General of the United States shall audit the transactions of the Corporation at such times as he shall determine, but not less frequently than once each governmental fiscal year, with personnel of his selection. In such connection he and his representatives shall have free and open access to all papers, books, records, files, accounts, plants, warehouses, offices, and all other things, property and places belonging to or under the control of or used or employed by the Corporation, and shall be afforded full facilities for counting all cash and verifying transactions with and balances in depositaries. He shall make report of each such audit in quadruplicate, one copy for the President of the United States, one for the chairman of the board, one for public inspection at the principal office of the Corporation, and the other to be retained by him for the uses of the Congress. The expenses for each such audit may be paid from moneys advanced therefor by the Corporation, or from any appropriation or appropriations for the General Accounting Office, and appropriations so used shall be reimbursed promptly by the Corporation as billed by the Comptroller General. All such audit expenses shall be charged to operating expenses of the Corporation. The Comptroller General shall make special report to the President of the United States and to the Congress of any transaction or condition found by him to be in conflict with the powers or duties intrusted to the Corporation by law.

SEC. 10. The board is hereby empowered and authorized to sell the surplus power not used in its operations, and for operation of locks and other works generated by it, to States, counties, municipalities, corporations, partnerships, or individuals, according to the policies hereinafter set forth; and to carry out said authority, the board is authorized to enter into contracts for such sale for a term not exceeding twenty years, and in the sale of such current by the board it shall give preference to States, counties, municipalities, and cooperative organizations of citizens or farmers, not organized or doing business for profit, but primarily for the purpose of supplying electricity to its own citizens or members: *Provided,* That all contracts made with private companies or individuals for the sale of power, which power is to be resold for a profit, shall contain a provision authorizing the board to cancel said contract upon five years' notice in writing, if the board needs said power to supply the demands of States, counties, or municipalities. In order to promote and encourage the fullest possible use of electric light and power on farms within reasonable distance of any of its transmission lines the board in its discretion shall have power to construct transmission lines to farms and small villages that are not otherwise supplied with electricity at reasonable rates, and to make such rules and regulations governing such sale and distribution of such electric power as in its judgment may be just and equitable: *Provided further,* That the board is hereby authorized and directed to make studies, experiments, and determinations to promote the wider and better use of electric power for agricultural and domestic use, or for small or local industries, and it may cooperate with State governments, or their subdivisions or agencies, with educational or research institutions, and with cooperatives or other organizations, in the application of electric power to the fuller and better balanced development of the resources of the region.

SEC. 11. It is hereby declared to be the policy of the Government so far as practical to distribute and sell the surplus power generated at Muscle Shoals equitably among the States, counties, and municipalities within transmission distance. This policy is further declared to be that the projects herein provided for shall be considered primarily as for the benefit of the people of the section as a whole and particularly the domestic and rural consumers to whom the power can economically be made available, and accordingly that sale to and use by industry shall be a secondary purpose, to be utilized principally to secure a sufficiently high load factor and revenue returns which will permit domestic and rural use at the lowest possible rates and in such manner as to encourage increased domestic and rural use of electricity. It is further hereby declared to be the policy of the Government to utilize the Muscle Shoals properties so far as may be necessary to improve, increase, and cheapen the production of fertilizer and fertilizer ingredients by carrying out the provisions of this Act.

SEC. 12. In order to place the board upon a fair basis for making such contracts and for receiving bids for the sale of such power, it is hereby expressly authorized, either from appropriations made by Congress or from funds secured from the sale of such power, or from funds secured by the sale of bonds hereafter provided for, to construct, lease, purchase, or authorize the construction of transmission lines within transmission distance from the place where generated, and to interconnect with other systems. The board is also authorized to lease to any person, persons, or corporation the use of any transmission line owned by the Government and operated by the board, but no such lease shall be made that in any way interferes with the use of such transmission line by the board: *Provided,* That if any State, county, municipality, or other public or cooperative organization of citizens or farmers, not organized or doing business for profit, but primarily for the purpose of supplying electricity to its own citizens or members, or any two or more of such municipalities or organizations, shall construct or agree to construct and maintain a properly designed and built transmission line to the Government reservation upon which is located a Government generating plant, or to a main transmission line owned by the Government or leased by the board and under the control of the board, the board is hereby authorized and directed to contract with such State, county, municipality, or other organization, or two or more of them, for the sale of electricity for a term not exceeding thirty years; and in any such case the board shall give to such State, county, municipality, or other organization ample time to fully comply with any local law now in existence or hereafter enacted providing for the necessary legal authority for such State, county, municipality, or other organization to contract with the board for such power: *Provided further,* That all contracts entered into between the Corporation and any municipality or other political subdivision or cooperative organization shall provide that the electric power shall be sold and distributed to the ultimate consumer without discrimination as between consumers of the same class, and such contract shall be voidable at the election of the board if a discriminatory rate, rebate, or other special concession is made or given to any consumer or user by the municipality or other political subdivision or cooperative organization: *And provided further,* That as to any surplus power not so sold as above provided to States, counties, municipalities, or other said organizations, before the board shall sell the same to any person or corporation engaged in the distribution and resale of electricity for profit, it shall require said person or corporation to agree that any resale of such electric power by said person or corporation shall be made to the ultimate consumer of such electric power at prices that shall not exceed a schedule fixed by the board from time to time as reasonable, just, and fair; and in case of any such sale, if an amount is charged the ultimate consumer which is in excess of the price so deemed to be just, reasonable, and fair by the board, the contract for such sale between the board and such distributor of electricity shall be voidable at the election of the board: *And provided further,* That the board is hereby authorized to enter into contracts with other power systems for the mutual exchange of unused excess power upon suitable terms, for the conservation of stored water, and as an emergency or break-down relief.

SEC. 13. Five per centum of the gross proceeds received by the board for the sale of power generated at Dam Numbered 2, or from any other hydropower plant hereafter constructed in the State of Alabama, shall be paid to the State of Alabama; and 5 per centum of the gross proceeds from the sale of power generated at Cove Creek Dam, hereinafter provided for, or any other dam located in the State of Tennessee, shall be paid to the State of Tennessee. Upon the completion of said Cove Creek Dam the board shall ascertain how much additional power is thereby generated at Dam Numbered 2 and at any other dam hereafter constructed by the Government of the United States on the Tennessee River, in the State of Alabama, or in the State of Tennessee, and from the gross proceeds of the sale of such additional power 2½ per centum shall be paid to the State of Alabama and 2½ per centum to the State of Tennessee. These percentages shall apply to any other dam that may hereafter be constructed and controlled and operated by the board on the Tennessee River or any of its tributaries, the main purpose of which is to control flood waters and where the development of electric power is incidental to the operation of such flood-control dam. In ascertaining the gross proceeds from the sale of such power upon which a percentage is paid to the States of Alabama and Tennessee, the board shall not take into consideration the proceeds of any power sold or delivered to the Government of the United States, or any department or agency of the Government of the United States, used in the operation of any locks on the Tennessee River or for any experimental purpose, or for the manufacture of fertilizer or any of the ingredients thereof, or for any other governmental purpose: *Provided,* That the percentages to be paid to the States of Alabama and Tennessee, as provided in this section, shall be subject to revision and change by the board, and any new percentages established by the board, when approved by the President, shall remain in effect until and unless again changed by the board with the approval of the President. No change of said percentages shall be made more often than once in five years, and no change shall be made without giving to the States of Alabama and Tennessee an opportunity to be heard.

SEC. 14. The board shall make a thorough investigation as to the present value of Dam Numbered 2, and the steam plants at nitrate plant numbered 1, and nitrate plant numbered 2, and as to the cost of Cove Creek Dam, for the purpose of ascertaining how much of the value or the cost of said properties shall be allocated and charged up to (1) flood control, (2) navigation, (3) fertilizer, (4) national defense, and (5) the development of power. The findings thus made by the board, when approved by the President of the United States, shall be final, and such findings shall thereafter be used in all allocation of value for the purpose of keeping the book value of said properties. In like manner, the cost and book value of any dams, steam plants, or other similar improvements hereafter constructed and turned over to said board for the purpose of control and management shall be ascertained and allocated.

[458]

SEC. 15. In the construction of any future dam, steam plant, or other facility, to be used in whole or in part for the generation or transmission of electric power the board is hereby authorized and empowered to issue on the credit of the United States and to sell serial bonds not exceeding $50,000,000 in amount, having a maturity not more than fifty years from the date of issue thereof, and bearing interest not exceeding 3½ per centum per annum. Said bonds shall be issued and sold in amounts and prices approved by the Secretary of the Treasury, but all such bonds as may be so issued and sold shall have equal rank. None of said bonds shall be sold below par, and no fee, commission, or compensation whatever shall be paid to any person, firm, or corporation for handling, negotiating the sale, or selling the said bonds. All of such bonds so issued and sold shall have all the rights and privileges accorded by law to Panama Canal bonds, authorized by section 8 of the Act of June 28, 1902, chapter 1302, as amended by the Act of December 21, 1905 (ch. 3, sec. 1, 34 Stat. 5), as now compiled in section 743 of title 31 of the United States Code. All funds derived from the sale of such bonds shall be paid over to the Corporation.

SEC. 16. The board, whenever the President deems it advisable, is hereby empowered and directed to complete Dam Numbered 2 at Muscle Shoals, Alabama, and the steam plant at nitrate plant numbered 2, in the vicinity of Muscle Shoals, by installing in Dam Numbered 2 the additional power units according to the plans and specifications of said dam, and the additional power unit in the steam plant at nitrate plant numbered 2.

SEC. 17. The Secretary of War, or the Secretary of the Interior, is hereby authorized to construct, either directly or by contract to the lowest responsible bidder, after due advertisement, a dam in and across Clinch River in the State of Tennessee, which has by long custom become known and designated as the Cove Creek Dam, together with a transmission line from Muscle Shoals, according to the latest and most approved designs, including power house and hydroelectric installations and equipment for the generation of power, in order that the waters of the said Clinch River may be impounded and stored above said dam for the purpose of increasing and regulating the flow of the Clinch River and the Tennessee River below, so that the maximum amount of primary power may be developed at Dam Numbered 2 and at any and all other dams below the said Cove Creek Dam: *Provided, however,* That the President is hereby authorized by appropriate order to direct the employment by the Secretary of War, or by the Secretary of the Interior, of such engineer or engineers as he may designate, to perform such duties and obligations as he may deem proper, either in the drawing of plans and specifications for said dam, or to perform any other work in the building or construction of the same. The President may, by such order, place the control of the construction of said dam in the hands of such engineer or engineers taken from private life as he may desire: *And provided further,* That the President is hereby expressly authorized, without regard to the restriction or limitation of any other statute, to select attorneys and assistants for the purpose of making any investigation he may deem proper to ascertain whether, in the control and management of Dam Numbered 2, or any other dam or property owned by the Government in the Tennessee River Basin, or in the authorization of any improvement therein, there has been any undue or unfair advantage given to private persons, partnerships, or corporations, by any officials or employees of the Government, or whether in any such matters the Government has been injured or unjustly deprived of any of its rights.

SEC. 18. In order to enable and empower the Secretary of War, the Secretary of the Interior, or the board to carry out the authority hereby conferred, in the most economical and efficient manner, he or it is hereby authorized and empowered in the exercise of the powers of national defense in aid of navigation, and in the control of the flood waters of the Tennessee and Mississippi Rivers, constituting channels of interstate commerce, to exercise the right of eminent domain for all purposes of this Act, and to condemn all lands, easements, rights of way, and other area necessary in order to obtain a site for said Cove Creek Dam, and the flowage rights for the reservoir of water above said dam, and to negotiate and conclude contracts with States, counties, municipalities, and all State agencies and with railroads, railroad corporations, common carriers, and all public utility commissions and any other person, firm, or corporation, for the relocation of railroad tracks, highways, highway bridges, mills, ferries, electric-light plants, and any and all other properties, enterprises, and projects whose removal may be necessary in order to carry out the provisions of this Act. When said Cove Creek Dam, transmission line, and power house shall have been completed, the possession, use, and control thereof shall be intrusted to the Corporation for use and operation in connection with the general Tennessee Valley project, and to promote flood control and navigation in the Tennessee River.

SEC. 19. The Corporation, as an instrumentality and agency of the Government of the United States for the purpose of executing its constitutional powers, shall have access to the Patent Office of the United States for the purpose of studying, ascertaining, and copying all methods, formulæ, and scientific information (not including access to pending applications for patents) necessary to enable the Corporation to use and employ the most efficacious and economical process for the production of fixed nitrogen, or any essential ingredient of fertilizer, or any method of improving and cheapening the production of hydroelectric power, and any owner of a patent whose patent rights may have been thus in any way copied, used, infringed, or employed by the exercise of this authority by the Corporation shall have as the exclusive remedy a cause of action against the Corporation to be instituted and prosecuted on the equity side of the appropriate district court of the United States, for the recovery of reasonable compensation for such infringement. The Commissioner of Patents shall furnish to the Corporation, at its request and without payment of fees, copies of documents on file in his office: *Provided,* That the benefits of this section shall not apply to any art, machine, method of manufacture, or composition of matter, discovered or invented by such employee during the time of his employment or service with the Corporation or with the Government of the United States.

SEC. 20. The Government of the United States hereby reserves the right, in case of war or national emergency declared by Congress, to take possession of all or any part of the property described or referred to in this Act for the purpose of manufacturing explosives or for other war purposes; but, if this right is exercised by the Government, it shall pay the reasonable and fair damages that may be suffered by any party whose contract for the purchase of electric power or fixed nitrogen or fertilizer ingredients is hereby violated, after the amount of the damages has been fixed by the United States Court of Claims in proceedings instituted and conducted for that purpose under rules prescribed by the court.

SEC. 21. (a) All general penal statutes relating to the larceny, embezzlement, conversion, or to the improper handling, retention, use, or disposal of public moneys or property of the United States, shall apply to the moneys and property of the Corporation and to moneys and properties of the United States intrusted to the Corporation.

(b) Any person who, with intent to defraud the Corporation, or to deceive any director, officer, or employee of the Corporation or any officer or employee of the United States (1) makes any false entry in any book of the Corporation, or (2) makes any false report or statement for the Corporation, shall, upon conviction thereof, be fined not more than $10,000 or imprisoned not more than five years, or both.

(c) Any person who shall receive any compensation, rebate, or reward, or shall enter into any conspiracy, collusion, or agreement, express or implied, with intent to defraud the Corporation or wrongfully and unlawfully to defeat its purposes, shall, on conviction thereof, be fined not more than $5,000 or imprisoned not more than five years, or both.

SEC. 22. To aid further the proper use, conservation, and development of the natural resources of the Tennessee River drainage basin and of such adjoining territory as may be related to or materially affected by the development consequent to this Act, and to provide for the general welfare of the citizens of said areas, the President is hereby authorized, by such means or methods as he may deem proper within the limits of appropriations made therefor by Congress, to make such surveys of and general plans for said Tennessee basin and adjoining territory as may be useful to the Congress and to the several States in guiding and controlling the extent, sequence, and nature of development that may be equitably and economically advanced through the expenditure of public funds, or through the guidance or control of public authority, all for the general purpose of fostering an orderly and proper physical, economic, and social development of said areas; and the President is further authorized in making said surveys and plans to cooperate with the States affected thereby, or subdivisions or agencies of such States, or with cooperative or other organizations, and to make such studies, experiments, or demonstrations as may be necessary and suitable to that end.

Sec. 23. The President shall, from time to time, as the work provided for in the preceding section progresses, recommend to Congress such legislation as he deems proper to carry out the general purposes stated in said section, and for the especial purpose of bringing about in said Tennessee drainage basin and adjoining territory in conformity with said general purposes (1) the maximum amount of flood control; (2) the maximum development of said Tennessee River for navigation purposes; (3) the maximum generation of electric power consistent with flood control and navigation; (4) the proper use of marginal lands; (5) the proper method of reforestation of all lands in said drainage basin suitable for reforestation; and (6) the economic and social well-being of the people living in said river basin.

Sec. 24. For the purpose of securing any rights of flowage, or obtaining title to or possession of any property, real or personal, that may be necessary or may become necessary, in the carrying out of any of the provisions of this Act, the President of the United States for a period of three years from the date of the enactment of this Act, is hereby authorized to acquire title in the name of the United States to such rights or such property, and to provide for the payment for same by directing the board to contract to deliver power generated at any of the plants now owned or hereafter owned or constructed by the Government or by said Corporation, such future delivery of power to continue for a period not exceeding thirty years. Likewise, for one year after the enactment of this Act, the President is further authorized to sell or lease any parcel or part of any vacant real estate now owned by the Government in said Tennessee River Basin, to persons, firms, or corporations who shall contract to erect thereon factories or manufacturing establishments, and who shall contract to purchase of said Corporation electric power for the operation of any such factory or manufacturing establishment. No contract shall be made by the President for the sale of any of such real estate as may be necessary for present or future use on the part of the Government for any of the purposes of this Act. Any such contract made by the President of the United States shall be carried out by the board: *Provided,* That no such contract shall be made that will in any way abridge or take away the preference right to purchase power given in this Act to States, counties, municipalities, or farm organizations: *Provided further,* That no lease shall be for a term to exceed fifty years: *Provided further,* That any sale shall be on condition that said land shall be used for industrial purposes only.

Sec. 25. The Corporation may cause proceedings to be instituted for the acquisition by condemnation of any lands, easements, or rights of way which, in the opinion of the Corporation, are necessary to carry out the provisions of this

Act. The proceedings shall be instituted in the United States district court for the district in which the land, easement, right of way, or other interest, or any part thereof, is located, and such court shall have full jurisdiction to divest the complete title to the property sought to be acquired out of all persons or claimants and vest the same in the United States in fee simple, and to enter a decree quieting the title thereto in the United States of America.

Upon the filing of a petition for condemnation and for the purpose of ascertaining the value of the property to be acquired, and assessing the compensation to be paid, the court shall appoint three commissioners who shall be disinterested persons and who shall take and subscribe an oath that they do not own any lands, or interest or easement in any lands, which it may be desirable for the United States to acquire in the furtherance of said project, and such commissioners shall not be selected from the locality wherein the land sought to be condemned lies. Such commissioners shall receive a per diem of not to exceed $15 for their services, together with an additional amount of $5 per day for subsistence for time actually spent in performing their duties as commissioners.

It shall be the duty of such commissioners to examine into the value of the lands sought to be condemned, to conduct hearings and receive evidence, and generally to take such appropriate steps as may be proper for the determination of the value of the said lands sought to be condemned, and for such purpose the commissioners are authorized to administer oaths and subpoena witnesses, which said witnesses shall receive the same fees as are provided for witnesses in the Federal courts. The said commissioners shall thereupon file a report setting forth their conclusions as to the value of the said property sought to be condemned, making a separate award and valuation in the premises with respect to each separate parcel involved. Upon the filing of such award in court the clerk of said court shall give notice of the filing of such award to the parties to said proceeding, in manner and form as directed by the judge of said court.

Either or both parties may file exceptions to the award of said commissioners within twenty days from the date of the filing of said award in court. Exceptions filed to such award shall be heard before three Federal district judges unless the parties, in writing, in person, or by their attorneys, stipulate that the exceptions may be heard before a lesser number of judges. On such hearing such judges shall pass de novo upon the proceedings had before the commissioners, may view the property, and may take additional evidence. Upon such hearings the said judges shall file their own award, fixing therein the value of the property sought to be condemned, regardless of the award previously made by the said commissioners.

At any time within thirty days from the filing of the decision of the district judges upon the hearing on exceptions to the award made by the commissioners, either party may appeal from such decision of the said judges to the circuit court of appeals, and the said circuit court of appeals shall upon the hearing on said appeal dispose of the same upon the record, without regard to the awards or findings theretofore made by the commissioners or the district judges, and such circuit court of appeals shall thereupon fix the value of the said property sought to be condemned.

Upon acceptance of an award by the owner of any property herein provided to be appropriated, and the payment of the money awarded or upon the failure of either party to file exceptions to the award of the commissioners within the time specified, or upon the award of the commissioners, and the payment of the money by the United States pursuant thereto, or the payment of the money awarded into the registry of the court by the Corporation, the title to said property and the right to the possession thereof shall pass to the United States, and the United States shall be entitled to a writ in the same proceeding to dispossess the former owner of said property, and all lessees, agents, and attorneys of such former owner, and to put the United States, by its corporate creature and agent, the Corporation, into possession of said property.

_: the event of any property owned in whole or in part by minors, or insane persons, or incompetent persons, or estates of deceased persons, then the legal representatives of such minors, insane persons, incompetent persons, or estates shall have power, by and with the consent and approval of the trial judge in whose court said matter is for determination, to consent to or reject the awards of the commissioners herein provided for, and in the event that there be no legal representatives, or that the legal representatives for such minors, insane persons, or incompetent persons shall fail or decline to act, then such trial judge may, upon motion, appoint a guardian ad litem to act for such minors, insane persons, or incompetent persons, and such guardian ad litem shall act to the full extent and to the same purpose and effect as his ward could act, if competent, and such guardian ad litem shall be deemed to have full power and authority to respond, to conduct, or to maintain any proceeding herein provided for affecting his said ward.

SEC. 26. The net proceeds derived by the board from the sale of power and any of the products manufactured by the Corporation, after deducting the cost of operation, maintenance, depreciation, amortization, and an amount deemed by the board as necessary to withhold as operating capital, or devoted by the board to new construction, shall be paid into the Treasury of the United States at the end of each calendar year.

SEC. 27. All appropriations necessary to carry out the provisions of this Act are hereby authorized.

SEC. 28. That all Acts or parts of Acts in conflict herewith are hereby repealed, so far as they affect the operations contemplated by this Act.

SEC. 29. The right to alter, amend, or repeal this Act is hereby expressly declared and reserved, but no such amendment or repeal shall operate to impair the obligation of any contract made by said Corporation under any power conferred by this Act.

SEC. 30. The sections of this Act are hereby declared to be separable, and in the event any one or more sections of this Act be held to be unconstitutional, the same shall not affect the validity of other sections of this Act.

Approved May 18th, 1933.

NORRIS' DEFENSE OF TVA*
September 9, 1939

Secretary Ickes hoped to achieve his goal of a Department of Conservation under the authority the President had received in the Reorganization Act. When the Ickes plan reached out to include the Tennessee Valley Authority, Senator Norris registered this protest.

Ickes' Conservation Department plan was a behind-the-scenes issue for several years, but it never received formal endorsement from Roosevelt.

SENATOR GEORGE W. NORRIS OF NEBRASKA TO ROOSEVELT

Waupaca, Wisconsin, September 9, 1939

My dear Mr. President:

For some time, even before I left Washington, there came to my attention rumors of an indefinite nature that the next order you issued under the Reorganization Act the TVA would be placed under some other department of government or at least some of its branches would be taken away from the TVA and placed under other bureaus or departments. I paid but little attention to these rumors because I took it for granted that the TVA Act, one of the marked operations of your Administration that had proved so successful, that had withstood the fire of criticism of the most malicious and unjust propaganda ever instituted against any part of your Administration and had come through unscathed, unblemished, purified, and fully justified, would not be changed or modified by you. The rumors, however, have persisted, and although I do not know of any I consider well founded, nevertheless they have caused me some worry, and while my fears may be groundless, yet I have thought it best to write you concerning them.

I would never have supported the Reorganization bill, if I had had any idea or belief that the TVA was going to be modified in any way. From its very birth, it has been fought by the most powerful organized monopoly of human greed that has ever been put together by human hands. It has withstood these onslaughts, and has been victorious in the courts. History will show that it is one of the greatest and noblest of all the undertakings of your Administration. The law intended that it should be independent of any department or any bureau of

Franklin D. Roosevelt and Conservation—1911–1945, Vol. 2, Edgar B. Nixon, ed. (Hyde Park, N.Y.: General Services Administration, National Archives and Records Service, Franklin D. Roosevelt Library, 1957), 378–82.

government. It was intended by this means to avoid the changes that might come about for partisan political reasons.

The board was to be appointed entirely upon merit, with an express stipulation that the members should profess a belief in the principles involved in the TVA Act, so that those who administered the law were to be selected entirely because of their ability to handle the subject matter covered by the law and therefore would not be handicapped or interfered with by Cabinet changes or by other officials who had been appointed for political reasons, other than the very merits of the Act itself.

Admittedly, it was a unique law. Politicians criticized it because it placed beyond their influence any possibility of interference which would disrupt or dismantle the organization set up under the law. Rumors of some agitation that have come to me indicate there is an attempt on the part of other departments to take over part of the work of the TVA. For instance, it is argued that some of the duties of TVA ought to be in the Department of Agriculture. That others ought to be in the Department of the Interior, while still others ought to be in the War Department, either directly under the heads of these departments, or under the heads of bureaus connected with the departments. It is argued, also, that the budget, as it applies to TVA, should go through one or more of the various departments. Any of these changes would injure, and if enough changes were made, would ruin the real objects of TVA.

The Act is based primarily upon the power of Congress to control navigation. Navigation is modified, increased, improved, and perfected by the control of flood waters. Flood water, if uncontrolled, would destroy navigation a great portion of the year. Part of the time, the water would be too high. At other times, the water would be too low. Therefore, the control of flood waters has a direct effect upon navigation. These floods, in turn, are modified and controlled by erosion of the sloping hillsides of river valleys. If nothing is done to prevent erosion, the fertile soil of the valleys will be washed into the lakes made by the dams, filling them up, and, in time, rendering them useless.

This in the end would not only ruin navigation, but would also despoil the entire country of that fertility of the soil upon which, in the last analysis, everything depends. Therefore, erosion is intimately connected with navigation and flood control. Reforestation of denuded lands is necessary to save and perpetuate the capacity of reservoirs to hold water. It would follow, if this is done, that the soil which would thus be preserved ultimately might become one of the greatest things to be accomplished and brought about through the carrying out of the TVA Act. The manufacture of fertilizer has a direct effect upon the preservation and reclamation of already denuded portions of the country. If, by fertilization, the necessary plants can be induced to grow, to impede the flow of water and hold it back long enough to prevent the filling up of the reservoirs, then fertilizer is directly connected with and under the jurisdiction of the Act. The fact that fertilizer accomplishes other things, also, does not detract from this, but only adds to it and makes it the more essential that it should not be interfered with.

The building of these dams makes it possible to generate large quantities of electric power. If this were not done, one of the valuable resources of Nature would be dissipated and wasted. It follows that this power generated at these dams, to prevent its monopolization by private monopoly, should be carried to a proper place of sale on transmission lines. The sale of this power is going to pay for more than one-half of the cost of constructing these dams. And because this electricity so developed goes into the homes of the people, bringing happiness and comfort where they were unknown before, this is another reason why the sale of this power should not be permitted to pass into the hands of monopolistic organizations based upon a desire only for human greed.

The money that must be appropriated by Congress must be based upon a combination of all these factors, as well as other factors which I have not mentioned. While the Act provides that the cost of these dams should be allocated to flood control, navigation, and power, yet it is an impossibility, mathematically, to draw a line where the division should be.

It would be ruinous if these different activities of the TVA were to be divided up among the various departments and bureaus of the government. Without any question, there would come a time when a quarrel would arise over the jurisdiction of these activities, as to who should control this particular activity, and who should control that. The Act places all of these powers and duties under the jurisdiction of a board whose members are appointed because of their ability to handle these intermingled powers and duties. If you undertake to separate them, to place them under other jurisdictions, you have taken the first step which will ultimately interfere with the success of the entire undertaking and, in time, bring the TVA to ruin. If any separation of these powers and duties is contemplated by friends of the undertaking, it will result in throwing into the lap of the enemies of TVA the very possibilities they have been trying to bring about.

In the recent congressional investigation, the minority, composed of the bitterest enemies the TVA has ever had, suggested some of these very things. They have given up the idea of fighting the TVA fairly upon reasons originally given. The courts at last have decided in favor of TVA in all these controverted issues. Now, the enemy is trying to "chisel"—to take away this power and that power, none of which can be taken away without injury to all. The object of the enemies of TVA now seems to be to try to divide up the duties of the TVA among various departments, bureaus, and offices, which will bring about conflicts and injurious quarrels and claims as to jurisdiction. The TVA has passed unscathed through the most tremendous opposition that has ever been presented against any activity of the government. It is successful in its work. It is working in perfect harmony with all the departments and bureaus of the government. It has won its cases in the Supreme Court of the United States. There is no jar or conflict anywhere in its organization. Its great problems are now coming to be realized and appreciated. The men in charge are selected for the particular duties of the office. The organization at the present time is one of the most harmonious, one of the most successful in the federal government.

Partisan politics has been excluded. It has been a hard, tedious, laborious fight, but it has succeeded, and it would be the height of folly now to curtail its activities in any particular. It could not be done without injury to the whole. It was established as an independent activity and it ought to remain so.

I hear claims made by enemies of TVA that the civil service laws applying to other departments ought to be extended to TVA. I have always been a believer in civil service, not because it is perfect, but because it is an improvement, a great improvement, over the old spoils' system. But it is not perfect, and the TVA Act undertook to set up a method of civil service superior to that of civil service law. In that respect, it has been successful. The TVA has a better civil service than any other department or bureau of the government today. It is the one civil service that comes more nearly being perfect, it seems to me, than any other that has ever been attempted or attained.

From the very beginning it seemed to me perfectly clear that if civil service laws applied fully to TVA, there would be grave danger of the enemies of that institution, paid by monopolistic private power companies, succeeding in getting into the civil service and, through it, into the organization, thus honeycombing TVA with its enemies. This has been attempted, but it has not succeeded. If the general Civil Service Act had applied to TVA, it would have succeeded in many particulars. But the TVA is acting in perfect harmony with the Civil Service Commission. Wherever the Civil Service Act can be applied, it is applied. It has been applied, and the most thorough investigation has vindicated TVA in its action. In respect to civil service, it stands out preeminently above anything ever put into force by the federal government.

The only thing to do now, it seems to me, is to let it alone. This organization, under your Administration, has reached the highest type of perfection ever attained. It should not be modified, and should not be changed.

Nothing in any investigation of any charges made against TVA has sustained any claim that there has been anything wrong in any particular. Politicians, friendly and unfriendly, have tried to have appointments made upon partisan political grounds. They have failed. Even those who have tried to get their friends into the organization have generally admitted that TVA is one place in the federal government where machine politics is absolutely excluded and kept out.

I dislike to burden you with this long letter, when you have so many official duties to which you must give attention, but I do beg of you that you take the time to read everything I have said. I do not want this shining light of your Administration to be blighted or dimmed. Let it stand, Mr. President. Let it go on. The fruits of its accomplishments will come, many of them, long after you and I have passed away. Already, it stands as a shining example of efficiency and of humanity. It has already brought its blessings to millions of our people, and, regardless of politics, those who have stood aloof, who are disinterested, when they have been fair and honest, have been moved to praise, and to congratulate you and the country upon the success of this great undertaking.

Sincerely yours,

G. W. Norris

DIXON-YATES REVIEWED*
August 10, 1956

The growing demands for power for the Atomic Energy Commission, coupled with rapid growth of normal consumer power demands in the Tennessee Valley, made it necessary for TVA generating and transmission facilities to be enlarged if the Authority was to serve all the power needs within its normal distribution area.

The Eisenhower administration attempted to solve the problem without allowing TVA to expand its facilities. The result was the Dixon-Yates affair, a major embarrassment to the administration, which was best summarized in this introduction to a staff report of the Subcommittee on Antitrust and Monopoly of the Senate Committee on the Judiciary.

INTRODUCTION

The phrase "Dixon-Yates" is the abbreviation of the names of two men: Edgar H. Dixon, president of Middle South Utilities, Inc., and Eugene A. Yates, chairman of the board of the Southern Co. Both are holding companies for utilities that operate in Arkansas, Georgia, Louisiana, Mississippi, and Alabama. In years gone by the Southern Co. was part of the Insull empire and Middle South Utilities, Inc., was part of the great utility empire of the Electric Bond & Share Corp. Electric Bond & Share Corp. has, thus far, escaped the death sentence of the Public Utilities Holding Company Act administered by the Securities and Exchange Commission before which its application for exemption is now pending. It exists today as a holding company and it has a wholly owned subsidiary called Ebasco Services, Inc. (the letters standing for Electric Bond & Share Co.). As a practical matter, today as before the Public Utility Holding Company Act, Electric Bond & Share Corp. in New York, through Ebasco, continues to provide management services to utilities throughout the country, including the operating subsidiaries of Middle South Utilities, Inc. Though divested by Electric Bond & Share, the stock ownership of the Middle South Utilities, Inc., is widely diffused. Dixon's testimony was that, of 28,000 stockholders, no one owned so much as 2 percent. The result seems to be that management runs the company.

The Dixon-Yates contract was made in 1954 by the Atomic Energy Commission, perhaps the principal consumer of power in the Tennessee Valley, under which Middle South & Southern Co., jointly agreed to build at West Memphis, Ark., across the river from the city of Memphis, Tenn., a powerplant capable of producing 650,000 kilowatts of electricity at a cost of approximately

*Power Policy: Dixon-Yates Contract, Sen. Committee Print, 84th Cong., 2nd sess., ix–xxx.

$120 million. To the extent of 600,000 kilowatts of electricity, this plant would supply electricity to the Tennessee Valley Authority, ostensibly to replace power used by the Atomic Energy Commission.

The extra 50,000 kilowatts were to be a bonus to Dixon-Yates in that the contract permitted them to buy these 50,000 kilowatts at the energy rate of approximately 1.863 mills per kilowatt. This meant that while Dixon-Yates would pay for the coal and other costs of manufacturing this 50,000 kilowatts, they were not to be charged for the cost of the plant. The 50,000 kilowatts were a gift, plain and simple. The $120 million for the plant was to be paid entirely by the United States Government. Since Dixon had long desired a plant in northern Arkansas, the contract permitted Middle South to have a plant in its Arkansas territory from which it would derive 50,000 kilowatts of electricity free from plant cost.

But this was not all. The contract further provided that to the extent that TVA did not use the 600,000 kilowatts Dixon-Yates would manufacture, they were free to buy such excess at this energy rate of 1.863 mills. On the basis of a 600,000-kilowatt plant, the known demand of TVA was to supply the city of Memphis, Tenn. Its load factor was 68 percent and it was said that at peak Memphis would use 450,000 kilowatts per day. The unused 150,000 kilowatts could be purchased at the energy rate by Dixon-Yates so that there was a reasonable expectation that the plant would provide Dixon-Yates a minimum of 200,000 kilowatts per day free from plant cost.

The extent of the concessions granted under this contract cannot, however, be appreciated from the fact that the plant was to have a capacity of 650,000 kilowatts. That was itself a minimum figure, as such a plant in operation actually produces many more kilowatts than 650,000. Since Memphis at peak would use 450,000 kilowatts a day at an annual load factor of 68 percent, this would mean an average daily consumption of about 306,000 kilowatts throughout the year. On this basis Dixon-Yates stood to buy at the energy rate a minimum of approximately 350,000 kilowatts per day on the average.

To build the plant and make a contract with the Government, Dixon-Yates created, under the laws of Arkansas, an operating subsidiary at West Memphis, Ark., named the Mississippi Valley Generating Co. The charter of this company was signed by three incorporators who gave the same address: 120 Broadway, New York City; and each one signed for 1 share of $100 par stock. The charter recited that "the amount of paid-in capital with which the corporation will begin business is $300."

Under article 6 of the charter, it was provided that the generating company planned to issue 55,000 shares of $100 par stock. Thus the total capital, if all the stock were sold, would amount to $5,500,000. The two holding companies, however, in their application to the Securities and Exchange Commission for permission to issue this stock, estimated the cost of the project to be $106,115,000, of which $2 million would be working capital. Then the applicants stated that the excess of cost above the proposed capital of $5,500,000 was "expected to be raised by the borrowing of an aggregate of up to $99,915,000 from institutional investors (against the issuance of bonds) and banks (against the issuance of notes)." This explains the interest of the First Boston Corp. in the transaction and raises the question of the position of Mr. Adolphe Wenzell, officer and director of the First Boston Corp., as a consultant of the United States Bureau of the Budget. Its stock was owned 80 percent by Middle South Utilities, Inc., and 20 percent by the Southern Co. The Southern Co.'s lines were at the nearest point 150 miles south of Memphis, Tenn., so that to use any of the power it would have to draw on Middle South.

One other point. The electricity manufactured by Dixon-Yates through Mississippi Valley Generating Co. at West Memphis, Ark., had to be delivered to TVA. Dixon was opposed to entering Tennessee where he would be subject to regulation by the Tennessee Public Utility Commission and the contract provided that the electricity be delivered to TVA on President's Island in the Mississippi River at the boundary of the two States. To reach this island and pick up the current to carry it to the city of Memphis, TVA would have to build a transmission line, costing approximately $6½ million. Apparently for the purpose of relieving the generating company and the two holding companies of any responsibility for paying this sum, an appropriation to provide these funds for TVA was introduced into the 84th Congress and was passed by the House of Representatives on June 16, 1955.

It is a matter of public record that a majority of the Atomic Energy Commissioners were opposed to this contract because there was no Atomic Energy Commission installation in the vicinity of West Memphis, Ark., and the power was intended for consumption by the city of Memphis, Tenn. On paper the contract referred to the power as replacement for 600,000 kilowatts that the Atomic Energy Commission was purchasing from TVA many miles north at Oak Ridge, Tenn., and its other plants in that area. But transportation of the power north would necessitate new transmission lines that would be prohibitive in cost and result in an energy loss. Former Director of the Budget Hughes testified that the Atomic Energy Commission agreed to the contract only after he wrote them a letter on June 16, 1954, which began as follows:

> The President has asked me to instruct the Atomic Energy Commission to proceed with negotiation with the sponsors of the proposal made by Messrs. Dixon and Yates with a view of signing a definite contract.

It should be said that Adm. Lewis L. Strauss of the AEC, with Joseph Dodge, when he was Director of the Budget, conceived the Dixon-Yates contract. He testified before the subcommittee on December 5, 1955, but refused to disclose his conversations about the Dixon-Yates contract with the President or Sherman

Adams, the Assistant to the President. At the same time, he asserted that "the contract was soundly conceived, and that it was in the public interest at the time it was executed."

The recent study of the Atomic Energy Commission conducted by the Phoenix Memorial project of the University of Michigan calls attention to the fact that Mr. Gordon Dean, when he was Chairman of the AEC, acted "as a spokesman for the group, having consulted with his four colleagues in advance." The authors say that "Admiral Strauss departed somewhat from the practice of his predecessor," Mr. Dean, "because, in his relations with the President, he enjoyed a position which was different and in some respects larger than the chairmanship had been before." Strauss is not only Chairman with housekeeping powers, but he is also a member of the President's personal staff.

The position of Admiral Strauss was described by the House Appropriations Committee as follows:

> This . . . means, that he wears "two hats"; wearing one hat he is Chairman of the Atomic Energy Commission; wearing the other hat, he has the ear of the President on all matters relating to atomic energy.

Both the Michigan study of the AEC and the House Appropriations Committee express regret that so much time of the Commission under Strauss has been devoted to Dixon-Yates. The Michigan study makes the point that the President's order to the AEC to make a contract that was really TVA's business set a bad precedent. The House Appropriations Committee says it is "chagrined to learn the extent to which the Atomic Energy Commission has become involved in politics," using the Dixon-Yates matter as an example.

The tragedy of it all so far as AEC is concerned is that every available hour at that Commission should be devoted to problems of atomic energy. Both the congressional Joint Atomic Energy Committee and the House Appropriations Committee, in approving the Gore bill authorizing $400 million for the construction of Federal powerplants on Commission property, laid the blame for our slow solution of these important problems in part upon time that the Commission has spent in matters that should not concern it.

The authors of the Michigan study say that Admiral Strauss told the press—

> That he wished that the TVA had negotiated the contract directly but that it was a Presidential order for the AEC to do so and hence he had had to proceed.

It seems unlikely, however, that President Eisenhower would have ordered the AEC to make this contract if Admiral Strauss, his special adviser, had advised against it. Nevertheless, the President must accept personal responsibility for the decision.

The Tennessee Valley Authority was opposed to the Dixon-Yates contract.

[474]

It had desired to build a steam plant at Fulton, Tenn., with a capacity of 500,000 kilowatts that would be ample to supply the Memphis demand and leave an excess to provide for industrial expansion in the Tennessee Valley. In fact, TVA needed a capacity of only 460,000 to supply Memphis. The peak load of Memphis was 450,000 kilowatts at a load factor of 68 percent.

Joseph M. Dodge, then Director of the Budget, was disturbed about the debt limit which, in 1953, the administration was asking the Congress to raise to 275 billion. His job in the fall of 1952 and early 1953 was to cut as much as he could out of the budget prepared by President Truman. The 90 million needed by TVA for its Fulton steam plant promptly felt his ax. When Gordon Clapp, former Chairman of the TVA, found that TVA could not have Fulton, he asked as a substitute that there be a reduction in the consumption by AEC of approximately 25 percent of TVA's capacity. Dodge, then, turned to AEC for ways and means for it to obtain private power.

Taking the Fulton steam plant's cost of about 90 million out of the Truman budget may have been a wise political move. But it is difficult to see how that was good business. If the Government has 2 billion invested in TVA, is not the property a national asset? For this reason Dodge's worry about exceeding the debt limit by leaving in the budget the Fulton steam plant seems more political than real. When Hughes substituted the Dixon-Yates contract that over its 25-year span was destined to cost between 120 and 150 million, at the end of which the Government would not own the plant, one can only say that from a business standpoint the elimination of the Fulton steam plant was bad judgment indeed.

The Truman administration had authorized a contract with a group of private utilities to supply electricity to the Atomic Energy Commission at Portsmouth, Ohio. The operating company is the Ohio Valley Electric Co. and is known by its initials as Ovec. Also under the Truman administration the Atomic Energy Commission had been authorized to contract with another group of private utilities at Paducah, Ky., for electrical energy. The operating company that supplies this is Electric Energy, Inc., of which J. W. McAfee is president. It is called EEI and Edgar H. Dixon is vice president and director of it, representing Middle South, one of the private utilities that own it.

There is this basic difference between the EEI and Ovec contracts and the Dixon-Yates contract. When it made the EEI contract at Paducah, Ky., AEC made it for power to be supplied to it there. Likewise, when AEC made its Ovec contract, it was for power it needed at Portsmouth, Ohio, where the plant was to be built. Both of those contracts were for AEC's own needs. There was no use of AEC to buy power for a different agency, elsewhere from an AEC installation, and in an amount that the agency needing the power did not require.

The EEI plant was built by Ebasco but its cost soared and Ebasco was dismissed from the job. The incident has become known as the Ebasco fiasco.

Nevertheless, Dixon-Yates hired Ebasco to build the Mississippi Valley generating plant under a management contract. Tony Seal, an Ebasco vice president, was to be in charge of the construction.

In connection with the EEI financing it should be pointed out that Adm. Lewis Strauss before coming into Government was a partner for many years in the well-known investment banking house of Kuhn, Loeb & Co. On November 12, 1946, the admiral became a member of the Atomic Energy Commission from which he resigned on April 15, 1950. In March of 1953, returning to Government service, he became President Eisenhower's special adviser on Atomic Energy. He became Chairman of the AEC to succeed Gordon Dean on July 3, 1953.

In point of fact the original financing of EEI was $100 million. In 1953, it was necessary to increase that loan to $195 million. The additional $95 million was financed by sale of bonds to the Metropolitan and Prudential Insurance Cos., under an indenture of which the St. Louis Union Trust Co. is corporate trustee. It is dated June 1, 1953, and the sale of the bonds was negotiated with the insurance companies privately by Kuhn, Loeb & Co. for which the records of AEC indicate they were paid a fee of $70,000 in December of 1953.

Dixon had long desired more plant capacity for Middle South in Arkansas, and he suggested that Middle South would build the plant in Arkansas for the Atomic Energy Commission and the power manufactured be given to TVA at Memphis to replace power used by AEC in the north.

When the Ovec plant was built, it had been financed by a public bond issue that was marketed by the well-known utility investment banking house of the First Boston Corp. The detail work on the bond issue at First Boston had been done principally by Duncan Linsley and his assistant, Paul L. Miller, and the business had been lucrative. First Boston earned a fee of $150,000.

Having handled the Ovec financing, it was natural that as a leading financier in the public-utility field, First Boston would be interested in the budget message of President Eisenhower which eliminated funds for TVA to build its Fulton steam plant. Mr. George Woods, chairman of First Boston's board of directors, testified that this influenced him to call on Joseph M. Dodge, then Director of the Budget, in May 1953. During the course of his talk with Dodge, Woods offered the services of Adolphe Wenzell, a First Boston vice president and director, an engineer and an expert in the cost of construction of public-utility plants. Dodge accepted and Wenzell worked part time at the Bureau of the Budget from May 20, 1953, to September 3, 1953 preparing a report on TVA power-plant costs. His report was shown by Dodge to President Eisenhower and former President Hoover.

In the Northwest Power hearings of the subcommittee conducted in September 1955 by Senator O'Mahoney, there was discovered in the files of Ebasco a statement prepared early in January 1953 by C. W. Phillips, its director of research. It called attention to a statement of Gordon R. Clapp, then Chairman of

TVA, to the effect that every year "next year, the year after that, and each year after that—as far ahead as we can foresee, the Tennessee Valley must add 750,-000 kilowatts of new powerplant capacity." And the significant remark is made:

> If the property were sold to the public, it would probably be done by the corporate method, whereby the public would buy bonds and stocks and thereafter manage the property and be responsible for and provide for the future power needs of the service area.

From the above information it would appear that George Woods of First Boston, and Ebasco, with the coming of the Eisenhower administration, had their eyes on public power projects such as TVA, and were thinking about how they could be privately financed and operated. This statement of Ebasco bears striking resemblance to the Wenzell report.

When Dixon suggested building a powerplant at West Memphis, Ark., Rowland R. Hughes, then Deputy Director of the Budget, who had come to know Wenzell when he made his TVA study in 1953, asked him to assist the Budget Bureau again. From January 14, 1954, to April 10, 1954, Wenzell actively participated in the negotiations with Dixon and Yates. Wenzell drew his First Boston salary regularly but received only travel and per diem expense allowance from the Government, dividing his days between First Boston and the Budget Bureau as he had in 1953.

It will be recalled that President Eisenhower in the 1952 campaign pledged that "there will be no disposition on my part to impair the effective working out of TVA." Robert Donovan, the Washington correspondent of the New York Herald Tribune, in his new book, Eisenhower, The Inside Story, says that, of course, in authorizing the Dixon-Yates contract the President did not intend to break up or "impair" TVA. But one can legitimately ask if the normal growth of TVA is to be cut off, does that "impair" it?

When we recall the Ebasco memorandum of January and George Woods' visit to Dodge in May of 1953, and their discussion about public power everywhere, the more one comes to the conclusion that whether it "impaired" TVA or not, the Eisenhower administration was determined not to finance TVA's normal growth. It was not to be "impaired" or "broken up" but the purpose of the Dixon-Yates contract was to take Memphis out of TVA territory and force it to buy electricity from Dixon-Yates. Nor has the cancellation of the Dixon-Yates contract changed this result. Memphis has had to build its own plant and this leaves the TVA system impaired by the loss of its Memphis territory.

One can only conclude that it was the policy of the sponsors of the Dixon-Yates program to stop the expansion of TVA into the Memphis area, and to substitute for TVA a new company, a subsidiary of two holding companies, by means of a contract which was later acknowledged by the Government to have been illegal.

When Hughes called for Wenzell in January 1954, to help him put the Dixon-

Yates contract through, the decision to have private power finance future TVA expansion had been made.

As Hughes testified:

> This came to me as a finished job by Messrs. Dodge and Strauss, to find the solution by providing a relief to the TVA . . . of the AEC power demands on TVA.

Two proposals were made by Dixon-Yates. The first on February 25, 1954, called for construction of a plant capable of producing 650,000 kilowatts at a cost of about $200 per kilowatt and the second, which was accepted, called for a reduced cost of about $149 per kilowatt. Except for this cost differential there was no other substantial change in the contract from the one first proposed on February 25, 1954.

Before Dixon-Yates made this basic first proposal of February 25, 1954, they had to be sure they would have the money with which to build the plant. To get the funds, Dixon-Yates turned to First Boston Corp., which had successfully financed the Ovec plant at Portsmouth, Ohio. Wenzell attended the first important conferences of January 19 and 20, 1954, at the Atomic Energy Commission and the Bureau of the Budget, accompanied by Paul Miller of First Boston who, as assistant to Linsley, had handled the Ovec financing. Miller frankly testified that he hoped that First Boston would get the Dixon-Yates financing. And Wenzell with First Boston's money specialists, Harter and Cannon, and Miller worked up figures as to the cost of the financing. Wenzell, as the "mouthpiece" for First Boston, drafted a letter to Dixon, dated February 24, 1954, which said that in First Boston's opinion under the then existing market conditions, debt securities could be sold by the proposed generating company at an interest cost not to exceed 3½ percent per annum.

In the first Dixon-Yates proposal of February 25, 1954, this is the concluding paragraph:

> We have received assurances from responsible financial specialists expressing the belief that financial arrangements can be consummated on the basis which we have used in making the proposal and under existing market conditions and our offer is conditioned upon such consummation.

This paragraph in Dixon's first proposal was written after Wenzell drafted First Boston's letter of February 24, 1954, and showed it to Dixon. This very draft letter Wenzell discussed on February 26, 1954, with John Raben, Esq., of Messrs. Sullivan & Cromwell, who in turn discussed it with Arthur Dean, Esq., the firm's senior partner. Raben told Wenzell before First Boston should act as an agent in any financing for Dixon-Yates, he "should make clear that he had severed his entire relations with the Bureau of the Budget." He also told him to discuss the matter with Hughes and Dodge and that First Boston should do nothing without their approval and "as a matter of policy, not as a matter of law" ought to decide if they wanted to act as agent or if they did, to take a fee.

In giving this advice Messrs. Sullivan & Cromwell did not consider section 434 of title 13 (the subject of the staff study printed as appendix II.) Nor so far as we know did Edgar H. Dixon and his counsel, Daniel James. Both testified they discussed the point with Hughes and Wenzell in February. Like Raben and Dean at Sullivan & Cromwell, James also viewed the matter as "not raising a legal issue" but "a policy question which deserved serious consideration."

In argument with Arthur Dean of Sullivan & Cromwell at the hearings, it was the position of Senator Kefauver that—

> there is not any question in anyone's mind . . . (that) as of the time Mr. Wenzell left the Bureau of the Budget, his company, First Boston, was going to be the underwriter of the Dixon-Yates Mississippi Valley Generating Co.

And the Senator contended that resigning from public employment, as Sullivan & Cromwell advised, "a short time before the contract is signed," ought not to be any defense under the statute.

The same identical paragraph as to the availability of 3½ percent money that appeared in the first proposal of February 25, that was rejected, appeared also as the last paragraph in the Dixon-Yates proposal of April 10, 1954, that was accepted. In an almost identical letter to the Wenzell draft of February 24, 1954, shown to Raben, Duncan R. Linsley by letter dated April 14, 1954 (4 days after Wenzell had severed his connections at the Bureau of the Budget, as advised by Sullivan & Cromwell) assured Dixon-Yates that First Boston believed that 3½ percent money was available. The only significant difference between Wenzell's draft of February 24 and Linsley's letter of April 14, besides the date, is the fact that Linsley's letter was delivered to Dixon.

As Wenzell so frankly testified, the cost of the money needed to build the powerplant was "an essential part of the plan." No one else at First Boston talked to Dixon or Yates about this in February and March but Wenzell. As he says, "I was the mouthpiece so far as I know." Dixon relied upon him and the April 14 letter is not significant as in making their April 10 proposal that was accepted, Dixon-Yates relied on the oral advice that Wenzell gave in his draft letter of February 24 with respect to the first proposal of February 25. Wenzell testified that this is correct.

Yates, on March 2, 1954, sent a memorandum to the directors of the Southern Co. and E. H. Dixon, in which he said:

> The First Boston has advised Mid-South and Southern that they can sell 114 million of 2½ percent bonds to insurance companies on present market conditions.

Attached to this memo of Yates was a copy of their first proposal of February 25. From this it is clear that, acting on behalf of First Boston, Wenzell had, in February, assured Dixon-Yates that their powerplant could be financed. The fate of the business depended on the acceptance of the February 25 proposal or a revised version thereof.

Wenzell, as consultant to the Bureau of the Budget, was in a key position to further it. His activity at the Budget Bureau in this respect came first to public attention in a speech delivered to the United States Senate on February 18, 1955, by Senator Lister Hill, of Alabama. Senator Hill said that Tony Seal, of the Ebasco Corp., and Adolphe Wenzell, of First Boston Corp., had given the officials of the Budget Bureau a briefing on March 2, 1954, before they met the following day with officials of TVA to discuss the Dixon-Yates contract offer of February 25, 1954.

In June 1955, the subcommittee chairman, the late Senator Harley M. Kilgore, appointed a panel consisting of Senator Estes Kefauver, as chairman, and Senators Joseph C. O'Mahoney and William Langer, to investigate the charge of Senator Hill.

On June 27, 1955, at the beginning of the subcommittee's hearings, the first witness called was Rowland R. Hughes, then Director of the Bureau of the Budget following the resignation of Mr. Dodge. Asked about Senator Hill's speech, Mr. Hughes said he "was told it was not true." Mr. Hughes had sent two letters to Senator Hill. The first dated February 11, 1954, stated Wenzell had been hired by Director Joseph M. Dodge "as a technical expert to advise the Director of the Budget regarding the accounting system of the Tennessee Authority" from May 20, 1953, to March 2, 1954, for a period of 34 days. In the second letter of March 16, 1955, written after the speech of Senator Hill of February 18, 1955, and after a phone call by James Coggeshall, the president of the First Boston Corp., to Hughes on March 9, 1953, asking him to correct his first letter to Senator Hill, Hughes wrote that, in addition to the time mentioned (May 20, 1953, to March 2, 1954), Wenzell had attended a few meetings between "March 2 and April 3, 1954" and that "these meetings were concerned with technical aspects of the proposal then being made by the Dixon-Yates group."

His first letter to Senator Hill gives the impression that Hughes scarcely knew Wenzell and that all Wenzell did was to study TVA accounting methods for Dodge. The second letter, written at the request of First Boston to correct the first, is even more misleading. It inaccurately states that Wenzell attended meetings with respect to Dixon-Yates "between March 2 and April 3, 1954." The truth is that Hughes himself sent for Wenzell on January 14, 1954, and, as Hughes has admitted, continued as his Dixon-Yates consultant down to April 10, 1954. Hughes must have known this when he wrote Senator Hill these two letters.

Asked by Senator Kefauver if he had told the President that, "in working up the rates and negotiations with Ebasco and Dixon-Yates," that the Budget Bureau had Wenzell as one of its employees, Hughes answered:

> He knows, of course, that we had an expert working on this thing, and *he knows his name and his connection and all about him.* In fact, he approved him before we got him down here. [Emphasis supplied.]

But at the same time Hughes himself did not recollect phoning Wenzell in January and asking him to come down and help on the Dixon-Yates matter; said Wenzell "never had anything to do" with the policy of Dixon-Yates; professed not to know that First National City Bank of New York (of whose predecessor, National City, he was once comptroller) was to be corporate trustee under the Dixon-Yates mortgage; and said that he didn't think that First Boston acted as fiscal agent in the Dixon-Yates contract. Nor did he recall meeting Paul Miller of First Boston in January 1954.

On his second appearance before the subcommitte, Hughes recalled that in February 1954, Wenzell came to him and asked whether his "activity" would—

> preclude the First Boston taking any part in any syndicate that might be worked out if a contract is worked out.

Hughes answered:

> You will have to go back right away and talk to your own people and then come back and talk to Mr. Dodge.

Dixon and his counsel, Daniel James, Esq., testified they too in February had raised with Hughes whether Wenzell was in such a conflict of interest position as to make it unwise for First Boston to do their financing. But Hughes, on December 5, 1955, after reading their testimony, could not recall any such conversation.

The testimony that Hughes gave before the subcommittee defies understanding. When three people—Wenzell, Dixon and James—say that in February 1954, they all raised with him the question of Wenzell's conflict of interest, even though Hughes only recollects that Wenzell spoke to him, surely one would think that after Senator Lister Hill's speech, he would know whether First Boston was doing the Dixon-Yates financing. Hughes, himself, sent for Wenzell, and Hughes, in his testimony, has admitted that he worked closely with him. Moreover, documents Hughes himself has produced show the important role that Wenzell played as his adviser. When we add to this the fact that it was on orders from Hughes that Wenzell's name was dropped from the chronologies published by both Budget and AEC, but one conclusion is possible. Hughes deliberately attempted to conceal Wenzell's name and activity from public view.

As suggested by Hughes (on March 1 or 2 as Wenzell said, or on March 9, according to Dodge) Wenzell spoke to Dodge. Wenzell said Dodge told him it was "unnecessary" for Wenzell to do anything about it as—

> what everybody was talking about then was a proposal on a project that had many "ifs" in it; that was far from resulting in a complete proposal or a definitive matter.

At that same meeting Wenzell suggested to Dodge that Francis L. Adams of the Federal Power Commission be appointed in his place in spite of the fact that, unlike Wenzell, Adams was not familiar with power financing.

Dodge, however, said he told Wenzell "if there was any likelihood" that First Boston "would be involved in the financing," he ought to "wind up his services with the Bureau."

But Dodge also pointed out that on March 9 there was no assurance that the February 25 proposal would be revised to make it acceptable. Whatever the conversation, to the knowledge and with the approval of Hughes and perhaps also Dodge, Wenzell remained at the Budget Bureau until April 10, 1954.

It would seem that Dodge, like Raben, Dean, and James, thought all that would be necessary for First Boston to do the financing would be for Wenzell to resign. But as Senator Kefauver pointed out in the hearings, and as the staff study in appendix III confirms, it would defeat the purposes of section 434 of title 18 if this were so.

On his first appearance before the subcommittee, Hughes had testified that President Eisenhower knew not only that the Budget Bureau had an "expert" at work but that he knew also "Wenzell's name and his connection and all about him." However, on his second appearance, Hughes refused to testify to anything said to or "by Sherman Adams or anyone in the White House" and he said that he had made a mistake on July 27, 1955, in testifying about anything he said to the President.

At the first hearing Hughes had been asked if counsel for the subcommittee might come to the Budget Bureau and examine "the detailed memorandums, interoffice memorandums, letters, and other documents which relate to the Dixon-Yates matter." Hughes said "the only question" was that "we are under certain instructions from the President with regard to interdepartmental communications."

Reminded that the President in his press conference of August 18, 1954, had asserted "that there was nothing to be concealed," Hughes indicated he personally had no objection to producing the requested documents, but he said: "I shall be guided by the President's instructions, sir, to the very best of my ability."

On June 28, 1955 staff counsel went to the Bureau of the Budget and asked Hughes to permit them to see and study the requested documents. Hughes refused to produce any documents, even Wenzell's September 1953 report, although he did offer to give the staff copies of Wenzell's pay vouchers which had already been obtained from the Comptroller.

Following this oral refusal, Hughes wrote a letter to Senator Kefauver in which he stated that he had checked with the President and his general instructions stood that "interoffice and intraoffice staff material . . . is not to be made public." The President, himself, at his press conference on June 30, 1955, amplified the refusal. He said the files are filled with personal notes and "nobody has a right to go in . . . wrecking the processes of Government by taking every single file" and "paralyzing the processes of Government while they are going through them." As for "the Wenzell report," he said, "Mr. Wenzell was never called in or asked a single thing about the Dixon-Yates contract."

This prompted Senator Kefauver on June 29, 1955, to write the President a letter detailing Wenzell's activity at Budget and AEC as we then knew it. This letter concluded:

> . . . Now, Mr. President, when our committee asked to see the Budget Bureau files, relying upon your statement at a press conference dated August 18, 1954, at which you stated that all material pertinent to this contract was available for inspection, I can assure you that the committee was only seeking information pertaining to the participation of these and other individuals in the Dixon-Yates deal in which we are interested—not unimportant memoranda concerning this or that matter which might incidentally be in the files.
>
> Since the published statements put out by the Budget Bureau and the Atomic Energy Commission are devoid of any mention of these important individuals, and since your own staff people have not even now informed you of their participation, we believe we would be doing you, as well as the Nation, a service by bringing out all the facts. It is clear, Mr. President, that even at this late date you have not been fully and accurately informed with respect to the serious matter which our committee is now inquiring into.
>
> Respectfully,
>
> Estes Kefauver
United States Senator

After it developed during the course of the hearings that Mr. George Woods, chairman of the board of directors of First Boston Corp., had been shown the Wenzell report, Senator John Marshall Butler obtained a copy from the White House for the subcommittee. But nothing was done about producing the other requested documents down to the hearing of December 5, 1955.

At the conclusion of that December 5 hearing, the Bureau of the Budget at long last gave to the subcommittee certain of the documents that had been requested of Rowland R. Hughes, its Director, at the first hearing on June 27, 1955. Their importance cannot be over-emphasized and the above background statement puts them in a perspective where their pertinency can be fully appreciated.

The first Dixon-Yates proposal, of February 25, 1954, relied upon assurances by Wenzell of 3½ percent money. After it was presented to the Bureau of the Budget, this proposal had to be studied and approved on its merits by both the Budget Bureau and the Atomic Energy Commission and thereafter discussed with TVA. What Senator Hill had charged on the floor of the Senate on February 18, 1954, was that both Tony Seal, the Ebasco vice president in charge of the Dixon-Yates plant construction, and Adolphe Wenzell, First Boston's vice president, had "briefed" the employees of the Budget Bureau on how to present this first Dixon-Yates proposal in a favorable light to TVA. Senator Hill also emphasized Wenzell's First Boston connection and that he was acting at Budget to review a proposal he had assisted Dixon-Yates to make. It was to verify this that the subcommittee on June 27, 1955, had requested the Budget Director Rowland L. Hughes to produce intraoffice memorandums and prior drafts of the Dixon-Yates contract.

The Budget Bureau continued to refuse the documents until Hughes finally on December 5, 1955, when recalled to the stand, delivered to the subcommittee some 30 different original documents from the Bureau of the Budget files. They will be found analyzed, item by item, line by line, in appendix III. The analysis underlines the accuracy of Senator Lister Hill's statement when, on February 18, 1955, he said to the Senate of the United States that Seal of Ebasco and Wenzell of First Boston "briefed" the Bureau of the Budget on how to present the first Dixon-Yates proposal to TVA in a favorable light. However, these documents go far beyond that. Summarized, they establish:

1. Wenzell had complete information about TVA powerplant costs from working as a confidential consultant to the Director of the Bureau of the Budget in 1953. Working secretly, he could and did send Budget Bureau employees to TVA for information that the files lacked on TVA power costs.

2. The staff memorandum prepared by the Resources and Civil Works Division of the Bureau of the Budget was revised by Wenzell who changed it to make chances for the acceptance of the Dixon-Yates proposal better.

3. Seal of Ebasco played a great part in the criticism of the staff memo and succeeded in getting changes in it favorable to Dixon-Yates. But some of his arguments for the proposal, particularly that the costs of a plant producing 650,000 kilowatts would run $200 per kilowatt are weak. It seems Seal used these TVA costs in his first proposal, assuming they would be the same for a larger plant. It was after the TVA conferences that these costs were revised to about $149 per kilowatt and this was the only significant change between the first and second Dixon-Yates proposal that was made. Of course, from his 1953 study, we know Wenzell must have realized what these TVA Fulton steam plant costs were since he had been in many conferences with Dixon-Yates and Seal of Ebasco before their first proposal was made.

4. Objections much more fundamental than construction costs made by career men at Budget never found their way into the final staff memorandum. These were serious and well-founded objections, namely:

(*a*) Six hundred and fifty thousand kilowatts of power at Memphis would be too much for TVA to use even in 1957 so that the Atomic Energy Commission would be paying for a demand charge on electricity that neither it nor TVA could use. Though asked, Seal would not agree to building a 500,000-kilowatt plant, and insisted their proposal related to the President's budget message which contemplated 500,000 to 600,000.

(*b*) Fifty thousand kilowatts and any unused power under the proposal would go to Dixon-Yates at the energy rate. It might exceed 350,000 kilowatts.

(*c*) The contractual arrangement was roundabout in that at a 98 percent load factor at Shawnee in northern Tennessee, AEC could use 600,000 kilowatts, whereas TVA at Memphis, Tenn., with a load factor of 68 percent, could use at most 450,000 kilowatts.

(*d*) The final staff memo said—

that adequate information is not available to make a refined comparative cost analysis and that active participation by TVA would be required to come up with such an analysis.

What it refrained from saying was that whereas Seal had estimated the excess in cost of the Dixon-Yates plant at about $1,700,000 over what AEC was paying TVA for power at the Shawnee plant, the career employees of the Bureau of the Budget and the Atomic Energy Commission estimated the excess cost between four and seven million. TVA estimated the excess at $8,300,000.

(e) The career men at the Budget Bureau and the Atomic Energy Commis-·sion objected to the cancellation provision of the contract as—

based on a 25-year contract and a less flexible arrangement with a private utility than AEC had with TVA.

(f) Whereas if TVA built the plant and AEC did not need the current, TVA could use the excess in its system or sell it, Dixon-Yates—

stated categorically that in the event of cancellation by AEC, they would not sell the power to TVA unless TVA came to them and asked for the power and agreed to pay a higher rate for it.

Dixon-Yates even—

agreed that it was quite possible that AEC would end up paying cancellation charges for capacity which was remaining idle—

merely because TVA could not agree with Dixon-Yates on a rate.

(g) The staff memo mentions the advantage to the Government in that the necessity for a Federal investment of $100 million for power facilities would be eliminated but it does not point out that at the end of the contract "the Government will have no equity in a plant."

(h) Strong disagreement was expressed by the career men at Budget with respect to the statement in the memo that the proposed construction costs for the plant "should either be justified to the satisfaction of AEC or consideration given to requesting a downward escalation clause." They said "it did not seem realistic to place the burden for negotiating this cost element upon AEC, in view of the fact that this kind of arrangement was not AEC's idea and that AEC would be in a poor position to bargain with the private utilities, inasmuch as everyone knows that the Executive Office is anxious, for policy reasons, to have a private utility contract consummated." These career employees "raised the question of whether AEC could use its own judgment in deciding whether or not to accept the proposal" and expressed the opinion that "it was obvious that they would not be entirely free to do so."

The purpose of this staff memo was to brief Hughes for a March 3, 1954, meeting with TVA and AEC, with respect to the Dixon-Yates proposal, so that, consistent with the budget message, private utilities could supply the power growth

[485]

in the Tennessee Valley without TVA's having to build additional plants. Wenzell as consultant to the director had been asked on March 2, 1954, "whether or not there were some aspects of the proposal which were not entirely reasonable" and he was permitted to revise the staff memo.

The documents make clear that the policy of the Dixon-Yates sponsors of substituting private power for any new installations needed by TVA was forcing the Dixon-Yates contract against the objections of the career men at both the Atomic Energy Commission and the Bureau of the Budget, not only as to cost of construction but also as to the terms of the contract under which, as we have seen, Dixon-Yates was to receive a bonus in the form of a right to buy some 350,000 kilowatts or more at the energy rate of 1.863 mills.

Remembering Wenzell's secret mission at the Bureau of the Budget in 1953, and his immediate recall in 1954 when the Dixon-Yates proposal developed, the more one studies these documents the more one surmises that Wenzell was sent to the Bureau of the Budget in 1953 to assist it with respect to private financing of private power companies that would build the Fulton steam plant or other plants that TVA would need in the future to meet normal power growth in its territory.

Recalling Hughes' testimony that the President not only knew Wenzell was "working on this thing" but he knew "his name and his connection and all about him" and "in fact, approved him before we got him down here," the fact that Dodge gave Wenzell's report to only one other person than the President, namely, former President Herbert Hoover, is very significant.

Consider also the pressure that the White House was putting on the Securities and Exchange Commission to force the contract through that Agency, and quickly. Sherman Adams, the assistant to the President, phoned SEC Chairman J. Sinclair Armstrong on June 11, 1955, and discussed with him that the House of Representatives was scheduled to debate on June 13, 1955, the bill to provide TVA with $6½ million with which to build transmission lines to an island in the Mississippi River so as to connect with Dixon's lines at the Arkansas border. Linsley and Wenzell were to testify before the SEC on June 13, 1955, and Adams asked and received from Armstrong and his fellow SEC Commissioners an order to the hearing examiner to postpone their scheduled appearance. Thus it was not until June 16, the day the House voted the funds, that the SEC resumed its hearing and heard Linsley and Wenzell testify. This was merely another in a series of contacts that the White House had made with the Securities and Exchange Commission.

As early as April 9, 1954, Dixon had consulted SEC as to how SEC approved of his financing could be obtained. By August SEC was so anxious to assist the Administration with respect to the Dixon-Yates contract that, without being asked, Ralph H. Demmler, then Chairman, and Robert A. McDowell, then Director of the Division of Corporate Regulation, went to see Joseph Campbell, then an Atomic Energy Commissioner, to outline to him the difficult problems that the SEC would face in approving the contract. And again, on Labor Day 1954, though not invited, Demmler and McDowell invited themselves on the train that carried Admiral Strauss and other officials to Shippingport, Pa., where the admiral was to dedicate the construction of the pressurized water reactor powerplant of AEC. On the trip Demmler gave Strauss a confidential memo that blocked out these problems:

1. Whether SEC could approve when the ratio of debt was 95 percent to 5 percent.

2. Whether Middle South and Southern, as holding companies, could have an operating subsidiary at West Memphis, Ark., in the territory of Middle South but built to supply TVA and Memphis and over 150 miles from the lines of the Southern Co.

3. Whether the debt securities could be exempted from competitive bidding and sold privately to insurance companies.

4. Whether the Joint Atomic Energy Committee would approve.

5. Whether the balance sheet of the Mississippi Valley Generating Co. with its 95 percent of debt could be excluded from the consolidated balance sheet of Middle South Utilities, Inc.

6. Whether the contract would be presented to SEC (a) signed; (b) before being 30 days before the Joint Atomic Energy Committee; and (c) before being approved by the Federal Power Commission.

In October 1954, McDowell, of SEC, met twice with Mr. Rankin, of the Department of Justice, once accompanied by Mr. Timbers, then SEC General Counsel, and thereafter on October 20, 1954, Attorney General Brownell approved the Atomic Energy Commission's contracting with Dixon-Yates. The meeting of October 18, for instance, was attended also by some 6 lawyers from the Department of Justice, 1 from Budget, 2 from AEC, 1 from Agriculture, 1 from Internal Revenue, and 2 from the Federal Power Commission.

The SEC opened its equity hearings on December 7, 1954, closed them December 21, 1954, and in an opinion dated February 9, 1955, approved the financing. To accommodate the Dixon-Yates interests and conserve the time, the SEC sat en banc and did not have the proceeding heard in the first instance by a hearing examiner. Neither Armstrong nor Demmler were able to name another instance in which the SEC adopted such a procedure.

When the State of Tennessee appealed the decision of SEC, Demmler then had another White House conference as to whether AEC would contest the appeal with SEC. Sherman Adams, Admiral Strauss, Percival Brundage of Budget, Warren Burger, then head of the Civil Division of the Department of Justice and his assistant, George Leonard, were among those present. The position of the Justice Department that SEC must only consider points under the Public Utility Act permitted Demmler and lawyers for the SEC to object to any evidence as to illegality other than under the public Utility Act. Neither McDowell nor Demmler had any explanation for this, and it provoked Senator Kefauver to say:

> It is quite apparent here, Mr. Demmler, that you felt that the burden was on you and the Commission to work with the other agencies of the Government in getting this contract carried out and the stock issued.
>
> I certainly cannot justify and I think there is no way of justifying your activity in presenting the hurdles and showing how others had gotten over the hurdles to an agency.
>
> I think that you participated in getting this thing arranged so that you could follow precedents in approving it. I can see no justification for your ruling on evidence that you made here.
>
> It looks to me like you had arrived at a decision that you were going to render, and you went far, far afield in my opinion in your actions and in your rulings in getting the matter around to where you could render that opinion.
>
> There appears to me to be further evidence of agencies working together to get this thing done regardless of public policy, regardless of the validity, regardless of the conflict of interest involved, and I hope that one thing that will come out of this hearing is that there will not be a repetition of this kind of thing again.

The contract had also to be approved by the Federal Power Commission. Lambert McAllister, Assistant Chief, Bureau of Law of the Federal Power Commission, in a memorandum for the Commission said of the August 11, 1954, draft of the Dixon-Yates contract:

> I have never reviewed a power contract wherein each and every provision is written in such a fashion that one party has an absolute veto right whenever any adjustment or change is indicated and no provision is made for the resolving of the dispute. The contract gives the impression that the generating company dictated the terms and conditions of the contract and either AEC was inept or without any right or opportunity to insist on relative provisions which would spell out the representative rights and circumstances under which an adjustment might be justified and provide for a resolution of any difference that might arise through an established form of negotiation or arbitration . . . the contract is all one-sided.

But despite Wahrenbrock's disapproval, Jerome K. Kuykendall, Chairman of the Federal Power Commission, and the Commission approved the contract.

Thus, we see that despite the opposition of TVA, career men at Budget, AEC, and FPC, and over objections of the State of Tennessee before the SEC, the administration forced the approval of the Dixon-Yates contract. Pressure of this magnitude must have been directed by the White House. There is persuasive evidence that this is so. We know this much:

1. Hughes testified at the first hearing as to Wenzell, as follows:

> Senator KEFAUVER. Mr. Hughes, did you tell the President or have you ever told the President that in working up the rates and negotiations with Ebasco and Dixon-Yates that you had one of your negotiators, your employees, working these things up when at the very same time he was employed by the First Boston Corp., and they became the financial agents in arranging the financing?
>
> Mr. HUGHES. He knows, of course, that we had an expert working on this thing, and he knows his name and his connection and all about him. In fact, he approved him before we got him down there.

At the December 5, 1955, hearing, Hughes testified:

Senator KEFAUVER. Will you tell us whether you talked with Mr. Sherman Adams or any-one in the White House about this matter when Mr. Wenzell mentioned it to you?

Mr. HUGHES. No; I will have to say that I am—respectfully I say that is considered privi-leged, and I cannot testify as to that without breaking down the proper requirements of Execu-tive operation.

Senator KEFAUVER. Even in the face of the President's apparent desire that all the cards be put on the table here face up?

Mr. HUGHES. We have put all the cards on the table, so far as we are concerned. I do not think we can put the cards on the table about *somebody else* unless either the President tells us to or tells them to or *they* do it themselves. [Emphasis supplied.]

2. In June of 1953, Hughes was planning to arrange a luncheon with Wenzell and Burns (presumably Arthur Burns, the President's economic adviser).

3. Sherman Adams phoned J. Sinclair Armstrong, Chairman of the SEC, ask-ing that the Commission direct its hearing examiner holding the debt proceed-ings to adjourn the hearings from June 13 to June 16, 1955. The pretext was that Attorney General Brownell and the President's own lawyer, Gerald Morgan, wanted to decide whether to intervene. This is an excuse that cannot be cred-ited. The real reason was that the House was debating the bill to give TVA some $6½ millions to build a transmission line to President's Island in the Mississippi River to pick up power from Dixon-Yates' proposed plant at West Memphis, Ark. Adams unquestionably wanted to delay the appearance of Wenzell and Linsley scheduled for June 13 until after the vote. He succeeded, as the SEC directed the adjournment and did not hear Linsley and Wenzell until June 16, 1955, the day of the House vote.

4. While Armstrong asserted an executive privilege for the SEC and refused many times to testify, ultimately he testified fully as to everything except any conversations he had with Sherman Adams "relevant to this investigation." The advice was given to him by Gerald Morgan, the President's special counsel.

5. Admiral Strauss, on behalf of AEC, has asserted an executive privilege with respect to relevant documents at AEC and he has personally refused to testify as to any conversations he has had at the White House with the President, Sherman Adams, or anyone else. The admiral has gone so far as to say that he has done this on his own volition without consultation with William Mitchell, the AEC General Counsel, or with Herbert Brownell, the Attorney General. At the request of Senator Kefauver, the admiral agreed he would ask Attorney General Brownell if he was properly invoking his privilege. On December 8, 1955, K. E. Fields, the General Manager of the AEC, informed the Senator by letter that the Attorney General had been advised of the request and as soon as "we hear we will advise you." Only July 20, 1956, the General Counsel, William Mitchell, advised the staff of this subcommittee that AEC was yet to hear from the Attorney General. However, Admiral Strauss testified:

If I am advised that I have no privilege by the Attorney General, I might still feel that my construction of the Constitution was the one by which I should abide [and] if I am wrong, I will have to pay the penalty.

Inasmuch as the Attorney General twice advised J. Sinclair Armstrong that as Chairman of the SEC he had to answer, one would think there would be at least equal reason for the Attorney General to advise Admiral Strauss as Chairman of AEC to testify with respect to the Dixon-Yates contract. Perhaps that is why the Attorney General has yet to answer the inquiry of AEC.

6. The Bureau of the Budget, after delaying from June 27 to December 5, 1955, eventually produced most of the requested documents and as we have seen they confirm the charges of Senator Lister Hill. But following the lead of Strauss on his second appearance before the subcommittee, Hughes sought to withdraw the meager but important testimony he gave at the first hearing about his conversations with the President. Hughes refused to testify to any talks with Sherman Adams or others at the White House. He also admitted that in producing the requested documents he was not producing any correspondence he had with the President.

7. Sherman Adams refused to appear to testify, despite vigorous urging by Senators Kefauver, O'Mahoney, and Langer. It was after his first refusal to testify that Senator Kefauver dispatched a letter in which he said, in part:

> Your letter this morning is the fifth instance of a claim of privilege by officials of the executive department with respect to testimony this subcommittee is seeking in carrying out its responsibilities. These claims of privilege pose a serious issue for the Congress of the United States and the American people. It is our view that where there is evidence of corruption, no official of the Government, no matter how high his position, can properly claim privilege when a committee of the Congress is seeking the facts with respect to such corruption. Moreover, the record of our hearings to date indicates substantial and persuasive evidence that the chronologies of the Bureau of the Budget and the Atomic Energy Commission which were released in August 1954, are false documents. It is pertinent that one of the documents this subcommittee was first denied and eventually obtained was found to have been made available to the First Boston Corp., a private investment-banking firm, months ago.
>
> In these circumstances a claim of privilege is tantamount to suppression of evidence of possible crime and corruption. Not even the privilege of attorney-client can be used for such a nefarious purpose. Certainly officials of the Government itself cannot and should not assert privilege where the result would be the suppression of evidence which would show corruption and deception in a matter involving millions of dollars of public funds. The position which you, Mr. Armstrong, Mr. Hughes, and Admiral Strauss have taken is a repudiation of the President's promise to the Amercian people, that all the facts surrounding the Dixon-Yates matter would be made public.
>
> We hope you will reconsider the position you have taken. We sincerely hope that you will see fit to appear before our subcommittee in response to this renewed invitation.

This raises an issue which has never been settled in the courts; namely, the extent to which subordinates in the executive branch of Government can exercise the Presidential claim to deny information to Congress on the ground that the public interest might be violated. This is not a negotiation in the domain of foreign negotiation. It does not involve in any way the right of any individual to be free from pressure by any branch of the Government. It involves solely the issue of the negotiation of a contract between a Government agency and the subsidiary of two holding companies which eventually requires appropriations by Congress.

The subcommittee has been completely blocked from getting to the bottom of this Dixon-Yates contract by the very men in the White House who were involved in the negotiations. And until we can explore the seven matters above listed, there is no way that we can ascertain the full facts.

Having pointed out the acknowledged evidence that Wenzell did participate in some of the negotiations about the Dixon-Yates contract while he was a consultant of the Bureau of the Budget and, at the same time, an officer of First Boston Corp., Senator O'Mahoney said to Admiral Strauss that the official witnesses who had acknowledged the activities of Wenzell could not possibly have correctly advised the President prior to his press conference of June 30, 1955, because if they had, the President could not have said that Wenzell was never called in or asked a single thing about the Dixon-Yates contract.

Senator O'Mahoney also made the point that the AEC was not part of the executive but a legislative agency, the head of which cannot throw about himself "the cloak of this old protective doctrine."

Senator Langer was so provoked by the claims of privilege that he proposed to the subcommittee that Sherman Adams be subpenaed and inquiry be made of him as to what funds were contributed by Dixon-Yates and any private utilities to him when he was a candidate for Governor of New Hampshire. Senator Langer also asked that inquiry be made as to how a registered lobbyist named Purcell Smith spent money in the fight for the Dixon-Yates contract, and of Arthur Summerfield, the Postmaster General, formerly chairman of the Republican National Committee, as to what campaign funds Dixon-Yates or their associates contributed. The Senator also requested that all officers of First Boston be subpenaed, that Stephen Mitchell, former chairman of the Democratic National Committee, be asked what funds Dixon-Yates or their associates contributed to the 1952 campaign and that the Senate Committee on Privileges and Elections be asked to give the subcommittee such information as it has of contributions by Dixon-Yates or their associates.

To the above statements of Senators O'Mahoney and Langer, Senator Kefauver added:

> It would seem to me, Admiral Strauss, that there was a declaration and, as a matter of fact, an order from the White House itself to make every conversation, all negotiations, everything to do with this matter to be put into a chronology and given to the public.

The evidence presented in these hearings, as Senator Kefauver pointed out, seems to be that the privilege of the President to refuse to supply information or documents was asserted by subordinates of the President, in this case—a privilege that he himself waived.

The Dixon-Yates contract provides a dramatic case study of the waste, disorder, and confusion which inevitably surround governmental action which is calculated to serve big business interests rather than the public generally. From its very inception, Dixon-Yates was destined to end in public disgrace and disrepute. Its purpose was unwholesome; the methods used devious, and in carrying out the scheme every concept of decent government and fair and impartial administration of applicable law was ignored. Even a partial listing of the wreckage left strewn in the path of Dixon-Yates will demonstrate the damage that has been done:

(*a*) The independent character of the Atomic Energy Commission and the Tennessee Valley Authority was brought into serious question.

(*b*) Officials of the Department of Justice and the Securities and Exchange Commission were placed in the position of having been persuaded to take legal positions which ran counter to precedent of many years standing.

(*c*) The administration of law by SEC was brought into disrepute because of SEC's flagrant departures from accepted interpretations of the Public Utility Holding Company Act and its succumbing to pressures from "higher authority" emanating from the White House.

(*d*) AEC was forced to execute and sponsor a contract which the Department of Justice has since asserted violated the Holding Company Act, the Atomic Energy Act, and the conflict of interest statutes.

TVA IN A NEW GENERATION*
June 30, 1967

This excerpt from the TVA annual report for 1967 is a summary of some of the new conservation concepts being carried forward by the Authority.

CONSERVATION IN THE "NEW GENERATION"

The decade of the 1960's may be marked in history as the period in which the people of the Tennessee Valley entered a new era of watchfulness with respect to the conservation and use of their natural resources.

TVA became an entity in the Valley in the midst of a great depression, in its economic nadir. The story is familiar: soils were eroding, forests were cut over, burned and neglected; a river capable of supplying multiple economic needs was flowing wastefully to the sea. The task, in the beginning, was to reverse these trends, and this has been done. Pastures now hold erosion to a minimum. Forests are protected and replenished. The river is in use, its floods regulated, its waters supplying the region with electrical energy, with low cost transportation, with improved water supplies for cities and industries, and with innumerable recreation opportunities. The people of the region have put these resources to work fashioning an economy that each year steps closer to the national norm.

But as the nature of the regional economy has changed, the nature of its conservation problems has also changed. The danger to natural resources is due less to neglect and underdevelopment, as in the past, than to the possibility that overuse or improvident use may, in the future, diminish their utility. Consequently, before damage is done, TVA and the people of the region must achieve a public consciousness that they have entered a "new generation" of potential resource management problems requiring not only vigilance but serious, deliberate counterattack to hold them in check.

These are instances: The impoundment of Tennessee waters created an abundant supply of good quality water which cities and industries have used extensively in their rapid growth. They have not been as diligent, however, in treating their effluent. While watchful action through the years by Federal, State, and local bodies has more than held the line on water quality and the waters of the Tennessee are generally better than they were 30 years ago, anticipated increases in manufacturing and urbanization will require more intensive programs to stem the potential tide of pollution. Indeed, the demand for good quality water will make it necessary to do more than hold the line in the future; we

*Annual Report of the Tennessee Valley Authority for the Fiscal Year Ended June 30, 1967 (Washington, D.C.: Government Printing Office), 5–20.

must eliminate present sources of pollution, some of them ante-dating TVA, so that clean water is in greater supply than at any time in this century.

Similarly, the impoundment of TVA reservoirs transformed muddy streams into clear lakes where fish production multiplied and recreation flourished. But the attraction of people has been so great that pollution from recreation craft has become a concern. An aquatic weed—Eurasian watermilfoil—has somehow been transplanted from other watercourses and has become a major nuisance.

The handwriting on the wall says, in substance, "In using his river man can, in turn, narrow its usefulness." TVA intends to make sure that this forecast does not come true.

On another front, electric energy brought not only work saving devices to homes and farms but also a clean, dependable, automatic heat. The air in hundreds of cities in the Tennessee Valley is free of the smoke and smudge that otherwise would have come from fuel-burning furnaces. But the vast usefulness of power created a demand that outstripped generating capability of the river system. Large thermal plants burning coal had to supply the additional requirements. Again there was a secondary reaction upon resources. Much of the coal came from strip mines which churned the landscape and created erosion and acid pollution of streams. And even though most TVA steam plants were built in rural areas, precautions had to be taken to prevent the pollution of the air from the gases of combustion.

TVA'S RESPONSE

In 1967 a number of activities were initiated or carried on in extension of programs of previous years, some of them of long standing. TVA has almost from the beginning been sensitive to the changes in environment resulting from its own activities or the activities of others which might adversely affect the development of the region.

One of TVA's earliest efforts in this direction was development of a program for controlling the breeding of malaria carrying mosquitoes to assure that its system of multiple-use reservoirs, changing a running stream into a series of slackwater lakes, did not result in an increase in malaria, then prevalent in a number of areas along the Tennessee River. A system of naturalistic control through water level fluctuations, supplemented by engineering measures, use of larvicides, and control of shoreline vegetation, was devised. It has been notably successful over the past 20 years, and not a single case of malaria of local origin has been found in the region.

In the mid-1930's, TVA started a stream sanitation program because of the need for data on pollution in the Tennessee River basin. Reports on these early studies, published in 1941 and 1945, provided information helpful to the Valley States in developing and administering stream pollution control legislation.

Watermilfoil, which has infested Chesapeake Bay and areas in the Northeastern States, and more recently in Southern States, California, and the Midwest, was identified positively in TVA lakes in the mid-1950's. Efforts since that time to control it have only checked it temporarily. A combination of lowering lake levels and applying the chemical 2,4-D has been the best control so far, but the weed reestablishes itself easily.

TVA biologists are in touch with others doing research on this troublesome problem and are also conducting research on their own in an effort to solve it.

The reclamation of lands strip-mined for coal engaged TVA's attention as early as 1945, years before it became a major purchaser of coal for its steam electric generating plants. Studies of air pollution control began with the construction of the Johnsonville Steam Plant in west Tennessee in 1949, the first of a number of large post-World War II generating stations. Measures were taken in accordance with acceptable practices of the times to reduce fly ash emissions and to disperse the stack discharges in the air. Most TVA steam plants are located away from densely populated metropolitan areas, but efforts have been made through study, research, and improvements to assure that ground level concentrations of stack emissions are kept within acceptable limits.

As problems continued to grow with increasing industrialization and urbanization, and as higher public standards were accepted, TVA has accelerated its activities in the field. Some of the activities in 1967 are summarized in the following pages.

STEAM PLANT IMPROVEMENTS

TVA's newer steam plant generating units are equipped with high-efficiency electrostatic precipitators to remove dust from stack discharges. This year, as a part of its actions to conform with the provisions of Executive Order 11282, TVA embarked upon a $12 to $15 million program developed in consultation with the U.S. Public Health Service to upgrade facilities for cleaning stack emissions at some of its older plants. Among them are Shawnee and Gallatin Steam Plants built early in the 1950's and units added at the Widows Creek and Colbert plants in the early 1960's. While the units at these plants were equipped originally with facilities which were acceptable at the time of construction, the new facilities are intended to bring them up to meet the higher standards existing today.

At Shawnee Steam Plant on the Ohio River near Paducah, Ky., for example, electrostatic precipitators are being installed in addition to the mechanical dust collectors initially provided for the 10 generating units. The program will bring the design efficiency of the ash collectors to approximately 97 percent, approaching the efficiency of the most modern equipment now in operation at Bull Run Steam Plant.

While precipitators can satisfactorily meet the need for removal of fly ash from the stack emissions, removal of sulfur dioxide is much more difficult. Reliance for control is placed primarily upon the use of high stacks for the dispersal of stack gases. Progressively higher stacks have been built as units increased in size, culminating in the 800-foot-high stacks at the Bull Run Steam Plant and at the 1,150,000-kilowatt unit under construction at Paradise Steam Plant.

In 1951, in connection with the Johnsonville plant, TVA initiated a broad scope air pollution study program, and it has been expanded and refined during the years. This year a study to provide additional air pollution operational control criteria for the steam plants was commenced at Paradise Steam Plant, with the most elaborate instrumentation installation used so far. This included instrumentation for measuring dust concentrations and some 15 instruments for the continuous measurement of sulfur dioxide. They automatically record data for processing and analysis by computer.

A major objective of the study is to determine the meteorological conditions which may hinder the dispersion of stack gases and to perfect methods of predicting them in advance. Advance predictions would make possible adjustments to meet the problem, such as burning coal with a lower sulfur content or, when possible, transferring loads to other generating plants.

On a longer-range basis, TVA continued cooperating with the U.S. Public Health Service in an extensive program of research to develop processes for the removal of sulfur from stack gases. TVA has agreed to the installation of large scale pilot plants at one of its steam plants. They will test processes selected by the Public Health Service for further comparative study. Other research is directed toward development of a sulfur removal process which could provide a double benefit; in addition to improving air quality, the recovery of sulfur could help alleviate a shortage in the supply which is needed in the manufacture of fertilizer and for many other uses. At the same time, the sale of the recovered sulfur could also help to underwrite the cost of recovery and the consequent improvement in air quality.

STRIP MINE RECLAMATION

Since 1965, TVA has included reclamation requirements in its surface mine coal contracts. Under contract provisions, coal operators control water as mining progresses to reduce possible washing and contamination of streams. After mining is completed the disturbed areas are planted to trees or grasses as soon as practicable to stabilize the soil and return the mine area to productive use. This year 1,000 acres were revegetated by TVA coal suppliers.

At the end of the year, TVA had under inspection 57 contracts, including 30 in Tennessee, 23 in Kentucky, two in Virginia, and two in Alabama. They involved an estimated 5,500 acres being mined by 24 companies.

The contract requirements were instituted by TVA as a partial answer to the strip mining control problem, particularly in States having no strip mine control legislation. Despite the position of TVA as one of the major coal purchasers in the region, more than 80 percent of strip-mined coal produced in the five-State procurement area went to other buyers.

This year Tennessee became the third Tennessee Valley State and the ninth State in the Nation to adopt strip mine legislation. TVA has urged and encouraged this action for many years.

With the adoption of strip mine legislation by Tennessee, all but one of the States from which TVA obtains coal have established controls. The exception is Alabama, where TVA's sole supplier of strip-mined coal, Farco Company, Inc., has cooperated closely on reclamation since operations began in 1964. These activities included both the planting of pine seedlings and the planting of pine seeds. The direct-seeding tests were so promising in 1966 that they were expanded this year, with the tests including use of fertilizer and legumes as pine growth promoters.

TVA, in cooperation with other agencies, continued to explore methods leading to more rapid and effective reclamation. Tests of hydroseeding, which has gained wide acceptance for turf establishment on road cuts, were made using several materials in addition to the usual mixture of seed, fertilizer, and water. Among materials used experimentally were wood fiber mulch and soil conditioning materials such as fly ash from steam plants and organic compost made from municipal garbage.

Cooperative research was continued with Indiana State University on the effects of certain soil fungi on highly acid strip mine spoils to see if they can be used to speed up revegetation of areas normally toxic to trees and grasses.

In another experiment, the value of annual and perennial herbaceous plants was being tested as indicators of where trees will grow on acid spoil banks. Of 14 plants tested, eight showed definite value as indicators, with good correlation between plant establishment and tree survival. The experiment carried on in west Kentucky was in cooperation with the Kentucky Department of Natural Resources, Kentucky Reclamation Association, Peabody Coal Company, and the U.S. Forest Service.

A study was made during the year of four reclamation demonstrations established by TVA in 1963 on abandoned mines in Tennessee and Virginia. The four demonstration areas were compared with adjacent unreclaimed areas in terms of wildlife habitat. The treated areas had 12 percent more plants, 61 percent more plant canopy, 78 percent more deer browse, and 120 percent more cover for small animals than the untreated areas of the same age.

TVA participated in the preparation of the national strip mining report authorized by the Appalachian Regional Development Act of 1965 which was completed and sent to the President this year. TVA was represented on the national survey working committee, collected data on some of the sample areas involved, and helped estimate strip mine area in Valley States.

According to the comprehensive report, 3.2 million acres had been disturbed by strip and surface mining in the 50 States through 1964, with coal accounting for 41 percent of the total. Sand and gravel accounted for 26 percent; stone, gold, clay, phosphate, and iron accounted for 28 percent; and unclassified mining for the rest. Each year an additional 150,000 acres are disturbed by mining.

The report said 2 million acres needed reclamation in some degree and urged a 20-year rehabilitation program by the Federal Government in cooperation with State and local governments, landowners, and the mining industry.

The report showed 511,000 acres disturbed by strip mining in the seven Tennessee Valley States, with reclamation needed on 322,000 acres, mostly in Alabama, Kentucky, and Tennessee.

FERTILIZER PLANT MODERNIZATION

For the past several years, TVA has been modernizing its facilities at the National Fertilizer Development Center at Muscle Shoals, Ala. One of the main purposes of modernizing was to reduce the amounts of materials discharged into the air and in the waste water.

The modernization has had effective results in reducing waste discharges. Within the past 2 years, discharges to the atmosphere have been halved and liquid wastes have been reduced more than 80 percent. This year a closed system for treating and re-using water contaminated by elemental phosphorus was installed solely as a pollution control measure. The system has proved highly effective as a waste control measure.

In other instances, plant modifications were made to reduce the amount of wastes. This was the case with the new granular fertilizer unit, which initially showed excessive losses at several points. Experimentation last year led to modifications which largely solved the problems. A new nitric acid unit to replace World War I vintage equipment and a stainless steel phosphoric acid unit installed in recent years also have reduced losses significantly. Additional improvements will take place as major facilities now being installed go into operation.

TVA was the first of the producers of phosphate ore from the middle Tennessee deposits to embark on a program of leveling off surface-mined phosphate lands and restoring them to usefulness by revegetation. This practice, which TVA began many years ago, was subsequently adopted by chemical companies engaged in phosphate mining operations.

This year, 20 acres of the reclaimed phosphate lands located at the edge of Franklin, Tenn., were leased to the city and Williamson County for development of a city-county park.

NEW INTER-GOVERNMENTAL RELATIONSHIPS

As in resource development, so in Federal-State-local cooperation—a new generation is at hand. TVA's method since its inception has been to merge itself and its efforts with the initiative and institutions of the region. In most instances, the local machinery necessary for strong action in resource fields a generation ago was weak or non-existent.

Today most of the Tennessee Valley States have strong, on-going programs. For example, their planning organizations rank among the best in the Nation. They have conservation agencies, park commissions, health departments and fish and game bodies which are alert and progressive. TVA's programs must, therefore, mesh with theirs, complementing and supplementing, demonstrating the new, testing the experimental. It coordinates these activities on a regional basis.

In addition, a new sense of urgency has permeated national programs affecting the region. Poverty is unacceptable, either in the rural Appalachians or in the city slums, and pollution is to be thwarted, by the city with its wastes or by the houseboater in his remote mountain cove. The proliferation of Federal agencies has brought to the local level new financial and professional tools to work with, but it has made very complex the task of local administrators wishing to use these tools and has made necessary greater watchfulness against wasteful overlapping of functions.

One of TVA's instruments for working with State and local agencies is the network of subregional citizen organizations collaborating within the Tributary Area Development program. This is dealt with fully in another section of this report. Other instances of cooperative development which follow illustrate TVA methodology in this new administrative environment.

In 1967, two major planning studies were nearing completion. In the Upper French Broad River Basin of western North Carolina, where a plan has been developed for a system of 14 dams and reservoirs for flood control and other water use purposes, TVA, the North Carolina State Planning Task Force, the Upper French Broad Economic Development Commission, and other agencies are working on a program designed to accelerate the growth of the five-county area.

The program will outline public and private investments required to promote the sound development of this important part of western North Carolina. This cooperative effort, which began in the early stages of project formulation, will identify the highways, park and recreation facilities, and other investments needed to complement the planned water resource system. When implemented, the program will assure that the system will make its maximum contribution to regional development.

Similar coordinated planning activities were initiated in the Duck River area in Middle Tennessee, where TVA consulted with the Governor of Tennessee and his staff on proposals for water development. Arrangements were made for the cooperation and participation of major State agencies in the planning of water control facilities in the area.

Joint discussions and field reviews by staff members of TVA, the State of Tennessee, The Upper Duck River Development Association and Agency, and the Upper Duck River Regional Planning Commission produced new ideas for resource development in the area, for expansion of business and industry, and for promotion of wildlife in the Duck River Basin. The studies were to be continued in the 1968 fiscal year to relate the proposed Columbia Dam and reservoir more closely with the development of the city of Columbia, and to State and local plans for the expansion of industrial, recreational, and wildlife opportunities in the four-county region.

A similar approach was taken in Alabama, where TVA this year commenced construction of a water control project in the Bear Creek watershed. Joint planning with the State agencies in both Alabama and Mississippi have brought about improved channel widening plans which will result in better fish habitat and provide for a better relationship between channel improvements and State park development. Other benefits of coordinated planning include improvement of the highway network in a now relatively isolated area as a result of State highway improvements coupled with TVA road relocations in connection with the Bear Creek project.

In another significant advance, TVA is seeking to combine local flood protection construction projects with area and community development. This was illustrated by experience in Coeburn, Va., in the heart of a coal mining section of Appalachia, and in Sevierville, Tenn.

At Coeburn, project construction became a part of plans to improve the business district and to enhance the economic development opportunities within the locality. In Sevierville, a flood protection project was combined with a program to improve the business district and to expand the amount of usable land in that part of the town.

CHANGING POPULATION AND ECONOMIC TRENDS

The decade of the 1960's also marks a turning point in one of the significant indicators of employment opportunity. Recent figures on population and migration show that the region now is gaining in population at about the same rate as the Nation, signifying that net out-migration has halted.

The improved resource base accomplished largely under the TVA program has enabled the region to make a revolutionary transition from a low-income agricultural economy in the early 1930's to the present economy in which manufacturing and commercial employment are dominant. Average incomes have been progressing steadily toward the national average.

While the region experienced unusual growth in number of nonfarm jobs, there was an accompanying decline in the number of persons employed in agriculture. From 1933 to 1960 the region gained about a million jobs in industry, trades and services, and other nonfarm employment, but at the same time agricultural employment declined by about half a million jobs as improved farming methods, farm mechanization, improved fertilizers, and other factors permitted increased farm production and income with much less manpower. Thousands of young people reared in rural areas were not able to find jobs either on the farm or in nearby cities.

In the 1960's, however, the Tennessee Valley region reached the first decade in modern history in which total employment, including that on farms, has grown faster than the national trend. It reached 2,114,000 in 1966, according to figures based on State data from the U.S. Bureau of Labor Statistics, representing an increase of 338,000 since 1961. While farm jobs declined by 79,600 in this period, nonfarm employment increased by 417,700. Manufacturing employment in 1966 was four times as great as in 1933, and in that period manufacturing jobs increased from 12 to 32 percent of total employment. Farm employment, on the other hand, declined from 62 percent of the total to only 12 percent by 1966.

Employment totals for 1961 and 1966 in the region are shown in the following table:

	1961	1966	Increase or Decrease
Trade and service	592,800	722,200	+129,000
Manufacturing	494,000	682,000	+188,000
Government	260,400	332,000	+71,600
Contract construction	70,300	101,000	+30,700
Mining	18,700	16,700	−2,000
Total	1,436,200	1,853,900	+417,700
Agriculture	339,700	260,100	−79,600
Total	1,775,900	2,114,000	+338,100

The third largest increase in employment, 71,600 jobs in Government, resulted mainly from improved and expanded State and local services, and particularly additional school teachers for growing school systems.

In the same period of employment gains, the population of the 201-county Tennessee Valley region, which was 6,181,500 in 1960, is estimated to have reached 6,670,000 by July 1965, an increase of 8 percent. This rate of increase was approximately equal to that of the United States, in contrast to the 1950 to 1960 decade in which the regional rate of growth lagged significantly behind the Nation.

OUT-MIGRATION HALTED

This increased growth reflected a changed migration pattern. Between 1950 and 1960 the region lost through net migration about 700,000 people, or 12 percent of the 1950 population. In contrast, between 1960 and 1965 there was a net in-migration of about 70,000 people, or 1 percent of the 1960 population. Extreme variations among counties were experienced in population growth and migration. The Huntsville, Ala., metropolitan area, with an increase of 45 percent from 1960 to 1965, ranked fourth among 219 metropolitan areas in the Nation. Net in-migration accounted for 50,000 of its 70,000 increase in population. In contrast to the previous decade the non-metropolitan areas of the region as a group did not experience a net out-migration during 1960–1965.

If growth in the region keeps pace with projected national trends, as it has in the past 5 years, the population could well exceed 8 million by 1980.

INCOME GAINS

The shift toward employment in manufacturing and trades and services has also affected the income patterns of the Tennessee Valley region. Per capita income in calendar year 1966 reached $2,075, passing the $2,000 mark for the first time. This represented a 72-percent increase in 10 years, compared with a 50-percent gain in national average per capita income.

This gain brought income in the 201-county area (counties in the Tennessee Valley or nonwatershed served with TVA electricity) to 70 percent of the national average per capita income. In 1933, at the bottom of the depression, the regional income was only 45 percent of the national average.

Had the region's income only kept pace with the national growth rate, remaining at 45 percent of the Nation's rising average, the region's per capita income in 1966 would have been only $1,333.

The most striking growth has been in manufacturing wages and salaries which reached $3.2 billion in 1966, 26 times as much as in 1933. In the Nation, manufacturing wages and salaries multiplied 16 times over the same period. Other major sources of 1966 income included wages and salaries from trade and services, $3.3 billion; wages and salaries from government, $2.0 billion; property income, $1.3 billion; the income of nonfarm proprietors, $1.1 billion; and farm wages and salaries and farm proprietors' income, $1.0 billion. The overall total was over $13.7 billion.

THE ROLE OF FEDERAL EXPENDITURES

Because of TVA's unique status as a Federal agency and the unusual attention it has received, it is sometimes assumed that an unusually large investment of Federal funds has been responsible for the economic progress in the region. An analysis of Federal Government spending reveals, on the contrary, that on a population basis, the region falls well below the national average. In the years 1934–1965 Federal expenditures for all purposes averaged $11,907 per person; in the region they amounted to $6,982 per person, or less than three-fifths the national average.

In construction and aid to State and local governments—relatively small items in the national total—the region was above average. But in the larger categories, spending in the Tennessee Valley region was much less. For example, on a population basis, Federal payrolls were less than two-thirds, purchases of goods less than one-third, and transfer payments (social security, veterans' benefits, et cetera) less than three-fourths of the national averages.

In 1965, the latest year covered by the study, Federal expenditures in the region were estimated at $2.8 billion while Federal appropriations to TVA amounted to less than $48 million. Other major Federal installations in the valley include the atomic energy complex at Oak Ridge, Tenn.; the George C. Marshall Space Flight Center at Huntsville, Ala.; and the Arnold Engineering Development Center, an Air Force facility, at Tullahoma, Tenn.

THE ROLE OF TVA PERSONNEL POLICIES

In the total Valley development picture, TVA's own personnel practices and policies have been an influential factor increasing both employment and incomes. In its early years, TVA adopted the policy of encouraging employees to join unions of their choice and to engage in collective bargaining. A relationship with trade unions was established which has resulted in an unusually stable labor climate, fruitful to both labor and management. The Tennessee Valley Trades and Labor Council, composed of 16 international unions and representing all TVA trades and labor employees, reached its 30th anniversary in February 1967.

Besides representing the trades and labor employees in negotiations with TVA, the Council has joined in cooperative programs such as apprentice training and the establishment and activities of union-management cooperative committees. Such activities have helped create a highly skilled work force in the Tennessee Valley region, not only for TVA but for other employers as well.

The union-management cooperative committees have established channels which over the years have resulted in many improvements and increased efficiency in TVA's widespread operations.

TVA this year stepped up efforts to increase minority group employment. Special recruitment efforts were carried on at historically Negro schools in the area in addition to normal recruitment. The efforts resulted in an increased proportion of minority group employees, particularly in white collar positions. Negroes were employed in increasing numbers in professional and supervisory positions.

At the end of the fiscal year 1967, TVA had 18,508 employees, an increase of 889 over the previous year. The increase was accounted for chiefly by increased construction activities at TVA steam plant and dam projects. Of the total employed, 11,050 were trades and labor employees.

In summary, after a generation of development, the resources of the Tennessee Valley are in order, providing a firm foundation for a long period of sound economic growth. Commercial activity, industrialization and agricultural improvement are moving steadily forward, providing better incomes to a larger share of the population. One of the important factors in the continuation of this rate of progress is the realization that the evolving use of resources brings changing patterns and new problems which must be identified, analyzed and rectified. TVA is determined that resource improvement must move forward step by step with economic improvement and is confident that this policy has the support of the people of the Tennessee Valley.

FLOOD CONTROL AND WATER DEVELOPMENT PROGRAMS

THE FLOOD CONTROL ACT OF 1936*
June 22, 1936

Under this bill, federal responsibility for flood control throughout the country was assumed for the first time. It provided legal recognition of the complementary relationship between the improvement of waterways and the prevention of erosion in the watersheds, a direct result of the influence of the pamphlet "Little Waters," and placed this work in the Department of Agriculture. Agriculture and the Corps of Engineers thus became jointly involved in flood control surveys and planning. Only the policy provisions of the law are reprinted here.

An Act authorizing the construction of certain public works on rivers and harbors for flood control, and for other purposes.

Be it enacted by the Senate and House of Representatives of the United States of America in Congress assembled,

DECLARATION OF POLICY

SECTION 1. It is hereby recognized that destructive floods upon the rivers of the United States, upsetting orderly processes and causing loss of life and property, including the erosion of lands, and impairing and obstructing navigation, highways, railroads, and other channels of commerce between the States, constitute a menace to national welfare; that it is the sense of Congress that flood control on navigable waters or their tributaries is a proper activity of the Federal Government in cooperation with States, their political subdivisions, and localities thereof; that investigations and improvements of rivers and other waterways, including watersheds thereof, for flood-control purposes are in the interest of the general welfare; that the Federal Government should improve or participate in the improvement of navigable waters or their tributaries, including watersheds thereof, for flood-control purposes if the benefits to whomsoever they may accrue are in excess of the estimated costs, and if the lives and social security of people are otherwise adversely affected.

*49 *Statutes at Large,* 1570–72.

SEC. 2. That, hereafter, Federal investigations and improvements of rivers and other waterways for flood control and allied purposes shall be under the jurisdiction of and shall be prosecuted by the War Department under the direction of the Secretary of War and supervision of the Chief of Engineers, and Federal investigations of watersheds and measures for run-off and waterflow retardation and soil erosion prevention on watersheds shall be under the jurisdiction of and shall be prosecuted by the Department of Agriculture under the direction of the Secretary of Agriculture, except as otherwise provided by Act of Congress; and that in their reports upon examinations and surveys, the Secretary of War and the Secretary of Agriculture shall be guided as to flood-control measures by the principles set forth in section 1 in the determination of the Federal interests involved: *Provided,* That the foregoing grants of authority shall not interfere with investigations and river improvements incident to reclamation projects that may now be in progress or may be hereafter undertaken by the Bureau of Reclamation of the Interior Department pursuant to any general or specific authorization of law.

SEC. 3. That hereafter no money appropriated under authority of this Act shall be expended on the construction of any project until States, political subdivisions thereof, or other responsible local agencies have given assurances satisfactory to the Secretary of War that they will (a) provide without cost to the United States all lands, easements, and rights-of-way necessary for the construction of the project, except as otherwise provided herein; (b) hold and save the United States free from damages due to the construction works; (c) maintain and operate all the works after completion in accordance with regulations prescribed by the Secretary of War: *Provided,* That the construction of any dam authorized herein may be undertaken without delay when the dam site has been acquired and the assurances prescribed herein have been furnished, without awaiting the acquisition of the easements and rights-of-way required for the reservoir area: *And provided further,* That whenever expenditures for lands, easements, and rights-of-way by States, political subdivisions thereof, or responsible local agencies for any individual project or useful part thereof shall have exceeded the present estimated construction cost therefor, the local agency concerned may be reimbursed one-half of its excess expenditures over said estimated construction cost: *And provided further,* That when benefits of any project or useful part thereof accrue to lands and property outside of the State in which said project or part thereof is located, the Secretary of War with the consent of the State wherein the same are located may acquire the necessary lands, easements, and rights-of-way for said project or part thereof after he has received from the States, political subdivisions thereof, or responsible local agencies benefited the present estimated cost of said lands, easements, and rights-of-way, less one-half the amount by which the estimated cost of these lands, easements, and rights-of-way exceeds the estimated construction cost corresponding thereto: *And provided further,* That the Secretary of War shall determine the proportion of the present estimated cost of said lands, easements, and rights-of-way that each State, political subdivision thereof, or responsible local agency should contribute in consideration for the benefits to be received by such agencies: *And provided further,* That whenever not less than 75 per centum of the benefits as estimated by the Secretary of War of any project or useful part thereof accrue to lands and property outside of the State in which said project or part thereof is located, provision (c) of this section shall not apply thereto; nothing herein shall impair or abridge the powers now existing in the Department of War with respect to navigable streams: *And provided further,* That nothing herein shall be construed to interfere with the completion of any reservoir or flood control work authorized by the Congress and now under way.

SEC. 4. The consent of Congress is hereby given to any two or more States to enter into compacts or agreements in connection with any project or operation authorized by this Act for flood control or the prevention of damage to life or property by reason of floods upon any stream or streams and their tributaries which lie in two or more such States, for the purpose of providing, in such manner and such proportion as may be agreed upon by such States and approved by the Secretary of War, funds for construction and maintenance, for the payment of damages, and for the purchase of rights-of-way, lands, and easements in connection with such project or operation. No such compact or agreement shall become effective without the further consent or ratification of Congress, except a compact or agreement which provides that all money to be expended pursuant thereto and all work to be performed thereunder shall be expended and performed by the Department of War, with the exception of such reasonable sums as may be reserved by the States entering into the compact or agreement for the purpose of collecting taxes and maintaining the necessary State organizations for carrying out the compact or agreement.

FLOOD CONTROL ACT OF 1936

SEC. 5. That pursuant to the policy outlined in sections 1 and 3, the following works of improvement, for the benefit of navigation and the control of destructive flood waters and other purposes, are hereby adopted and authorized to be prosecuted, in order of their emergency as may be designated by the President, under the direction of the Secretary of War and supervision of the Chief of Engineers in accordance with the plans in the respective reports and records hereinafter designated: *Provided,* That penstocks or other similar facilities, adapted to possible future use in the development of adequate electric power may be installed in any dam herein authorized when approved by the Secretary of War upon the recommendation of the Chief of Engineers.

PRESIDENTIAL DIRECTION OF THE CORPS*
April 3 & 8, 1937

This exchange of correspondence between President Roosevelt and his Secretary of War, Harry H. Woodring, provides documentary evidence of a President's establishing a degree of control over the Corps of Engineers that had never previously been established—despite attempts by Theodore Roosevelt and Woodrow Wilson. Note the sentence in Secretary Woodring's letter: "Under former procedure this report would be submitted direct to the Chairman of the Committee on Flood Control."

ROOSEVELT TO HARRY H. WOODRING, SECRETARY OF WAR

[Washington] Apr. 3, 1937

My Dear Mr. Secretary:

It is my understanding that following a resolution of the Flood Control Committee of the House of Representatives, the United States Engineer Corps was delegated to review the flood control programs of the Ohio River and the Lower Mississippi River.

It is my further understanding that General Markham is prepared in the immediate future to submit a report on that subject.

In view of the great importance of this enterprise and its probable relationships to other water resources problems in the same areas, I am requesting that the report of General Markham be submitted to me for review before it is finally submitted to Congress and that it be withheld from any public use or release until it has been submitted to me.

It is my intention to submit this preliminary document to the National Resources Committee for review and for careful clearance and discussions with other Federal agencies having major water interests in both of these basins.

It is my wish that this procedure be followed with respect to any future similar reports which you may be called upon to submit to the Congress or to any Committee or member thereof.

Sincerely yours,

[*Franklin D. Roosevelt*]

Franklin D. Roosevelt and Conservation—1911-1945, Vol. 2, Edgar B. Nixon, ed. (Hyde Park, N.Y.: General Services Administration, National Archives and Records Service, Franklin D. Roosevelt Library, 1957), 33, 39.

HARRY H. WOODRING, SECRETARY OF WAR, TO ROOSEVELT

Washington, April 8, 1937

Dear Mr. President:

I submit herewith, in compliance with the instructions contained in your letter of April 3, 1937, the report of the Chief of Engineers containing a comprehensive flood control plan for the Ohio and Lower Mississippi Valleys called for by Resolution of the Committee on Flood Control of the House of Representatives.

Under former procedure this report would be submitted direct to the Chairman of the Committee on Flood Control. The Department has been of the view that the scope of the project makes it of such significance in the national program as to warrant deviation from the established procedure. Accordingly, the report was prepared prior to the receipt of your letter of April 3, with a view to its transmission to Congress with an appropriate message from you. A draft of such a message is also submitted herewith.[1]

Respectfully yours,

Harry H. Woodring

[1]This draft was not used.

A TRY AT MORE COMPREHENSIVE PLANNING*
April 28, 1937

Roosevelt's letter to W. M. Whittington of Mississippi, Chairman of the House Committee on Flood Control, shows the effort he was making to achieve better coordination of resource development work by his administration. The additional letter to Secretary Woodring shows his exasperation with the existing lack of coordination.

Despite the high resolve, the comprehensive report he describes never did develop. But there were improvements along this line in each succeeding flood control bill.

ROOSEVELT TO REPRESENTATIVE WILLIAM M. WHITTINGTON OF MISSISSIPPI, CHAIRMAN, HOUSE COMMITTEE ON FLOOD CONTROL

En Route to New Orleans, April 28, 1937

My Dear Judge Whittington:

I enclose the report of the Chief of Engineers made in pursuance of Resolution of the Committee on Flood Control dated February 10, 1937.

Under the Resolution, this report covers a review of the reports submitted in House Documents Nos. 259 and 306, which relate to plans for a comprehensive reservoir system in the Ohio and Mississippi River basins. It also covers a review of Flood Control Committee Document No. 1, 74th Congress, relating to a revision and perfection of flood control for the alluvial valley of the Mississippi.

The present report relates especially to further flood control measures in the light of the Ohio River flood of January, 1937.

It will be noted, of course, that the present report, like the three previous reports, takes up only the subject of flood control works such as levees and reservoirs, all of these works being intended to keep out or to hold back waters after they have reached the main stem of the Mississippi or one of the principal tributaries thereof.

Forty-five new reservoirs in addition to those already authorized are recommended. The cost of the additional reservoirs would be $245,958,000.

The total cost of the works proposed for the protection of the Ohio River

Franklin D. Roosevelt and Conservation—1911–1945, Vol. 2, Edgar B. Nixon, ed. (Hyde Park, N.Y.: General Services Administration, National Archives and Records Service, Franklin D. Roosevelt Library, 1957), 47–49.

Basin would run, in round numbers, $440,000,000; in the Missouri River Basin to $132,000,000; in the Middle Mississippi Basin to $153,000,000, and on the Arkansas and White Rivers to $81,000,000.

Mention is made of securing fee simple title to floodways on the Mississippi River. It occurs to me that, in view of the history of previous legislation and its results, this is advisable in order that no questions may arise if it is found necessary to flood these lands. At the same time, it may be well to consider the possibility of renting these lands, once fee simple title is acquired, to neighboring farmers, with the definite understanding that tillage of these lands is solely at the risk of the individuals renting them.

Finally, the Chief of Engineers recommends, for additional flood control and fee simple purchases in the Mississippi Valley proper, an additional sum of $52,000,000.

To sum up the report, it proposes additional projects over and above those already authorized at an estimated cost of more than eight hundred million dollars, of which approximately one-third would be borne by local interests under existing authority.

Recognizing the fact that the report of the Chief of Engineers is limited by the Committee Resolution to large works such as levees and reservoirs, I have consulted with other agencies of the Government concerned with the control and use of water.

The report of the Chief of Engineers considers, of course, only one phase of the very large interlocking problem. For this reason it may be considered neither truly comprehensive nor effectively integrated. No opportunity has been possible, in this short space of time, to consider the report in relation to other Federal agencies, such as the Soil Conservation Service, the Forestry Service, the Tennessee Valley Authority, the United States Public Health Service, the Federal Power Commission and others.

For example, the report apparently does not consider the flood regulation work now under construction or planned by the Tennessee Valley Authority, which system is expected to reduce crest flood flows at Paducah and Cairo by 200,000 second feet.

No serious delay can come if the present Session of the Congress appropriates funds to undertake and continue some of the projects already authorized by previous Congresses for the Mississippi and Ohio Rivers. The amount of these appropriations should, of course, be viewed in the light of the budgetary necessities of the Government.

In the light of all the circumstances attaching to this report, I am requesting that a further and complete study be made by all of the Government agencies involved, sitting together as a group to make recommendations for a complete picture. This report should be available to the Congress by next January.

One other subject remains—the participation of state and local authorities in the cost of any of these projects. It is my belief that, for many reasons, the Federal Government should not be charged with the cost of the land necessary for levees, dams and reservoirs. This policy was adopted by the Congress last year in connection with the projects in the Connecticut River Valley. In that case, while no work has yet been started, it is my understanding that the states of Vermont, New Hampshire, Massachusetts and Connecticut are substantially in agreement in regard to the purchase of the necessary land. It should be made clear, however, that if any electric power results from the erection of dams and reservoirs, the Federal Government alone should have complete authority over the sale of this power.

I am returning about May 12th, at which time I shall be glad to discuss this whole subject with you and the members of your Committee in case you should care to do so.[1]

Very sincerely yours,

[*Franklin D. Roosevelt*]

ROOSEVELT TO HARRY H. WOODRING, SECRETARY OF WAR

En Route to New Orleans, April 28, 1937

Dear Harry:

I have transmitted Gen. Markham's Flood Control Report to Chairman Whittington with a letter, of which I enclose a copy.

Will you be good enough to have a meeting with Sec. Ickes and Sec. Wallace in order that the three Departments (including the Water Resources Committee, National Resources Committee) may work out a plan for the comprehensive report which I propose be made to the Congress next January.

It seems to me that in the future, instead of authorizing any new list of projects for some incredible sum, such as the eight hundred million dollars recommended herein, we should get Congress to approve, but not authorize, a five year or ten year plan, authorizing only those works which we are all agreed on should be commenced within the next two years and appropriating only for those works to be commenced within the next year.

---

[1]Whittington replied in a long letter of May 5, 1937, defending the Chief of Engineers' plan:
"The proposed plan appears to be comprehensive for flood control. It would not conflict with the design and initiation of other improvements for water and soil conservation. The authorized beneficial activities of the several departments of the Government with respect to water and land conservation up to the present time have scarcely come in contact. When they do approach I feel that the War Department will fully cooperate with other governmental departments."

Please explain this to General Markham. The present system is an impossible one and because of budgetary considerations would necessitate my disapproval of any huge authorization.

When I get back we can all talk this over.

Very sincerely yours,

[*Franklin D. Roosevelt*]

ROOSEVELT'S VETO OF A CONGRESSIONAL INITIATIVE*
August 13, 1937

A resolution first introduced by Representative John McClellan of Arkansas was a logical improvement in the record of congressional and Corps of Engineers indifference to national planning in the field of waterway planning. For the President, however, the resolution had two fatal flaws—it virtually ignored the President and the rest of the executive department, and it emphasized flood control above other water uses. This is Roosevelt's veto message.

The White House, August 13, 1937

To the Senate:

I return herewith without my approval, Senate Joint Resolution No. 57, entitled "Joint Resolution to authorize the submission to Congress of a comprehensive national plan for the prevention and control of floods of all the major rivers of the United States, development of hydroelectric power resources, water and soil conservation, and for other purposes."

In my message of June 3, 1937, I proposed for the consideration of Congress, a thoroughly democratic process of national planning of the conservation and utilization of the water, and related land, resources of our country. I expressed the belief that such a process of national planning should start at the bottom through the initiation of planning work in the State and local units, and that it should contemplate the formulation of programs on a regional basis, the integration of fiscal and conservation policies on a national basis, and the submission of a comprehensive development program to the Congress by the President.

The reverse of such a process of national planning is prescribed in Senate Joint Resolution No. 57. By this resolution the War Department would become the national planning agency, not alone for flood control, but for all the other multiple uses of water. Although the Department of Agriculture would prepare reports on runoff retardation and soil erosion prevention, and the Department of the Interior be consulted on reclamation projects, the War Department would report for these coordinate agencies directly to Congress instead of to the Chief Executive. The local and regional basis of planning would be ignored, and there would be no review of the whole program, prior to its presentation to Congress, from the standpoints of national budgetary considerations and national conservation policies.

The corps of Army Engineers has had wide experience in the building of flood

Franklin D. Roosevelt and Conservation—1911–1945, Vol. 2, Edgar B. Nixon, ed. (Hyde Park, N.Y.: General Services Administration, National Archives and Records Service, Franklin D. Roosevelt Library, 1957), 102–3.

control projects and has executed the projects entrusted to it with great skill and ability. Its experience and background is not alone sufficient, however, for the planning of a comprehensive program for the development of the vast water and related resources of the Nation.

The planning of the use and control of water and related resources is distributed by law among numerous governmental agencies, such as the Departments of Agriculture and Interior, the Federal Power Commission, the United States Public Health Service, the International Boundary Commission, and the Tennessee Valley Authority. The Joint Resolution encroaches upon the functions of these agencies, and ignores and duplicates the coordinated planning work already in progress under the general guidance of the National Resources Committee.

I find it impossible to subscribe, therefore, to the proposal that has been embodied in this Joint Resolution.

This does not mean, however, that the objective of this Joint Resolution cannot be attained without the need of any legislation whatsoever. I propose to present to the Congress in January a comprehensive national plan for flood control and prevention and the development of water and soil conservation, such plan to be prepared by all of the many Government agencies concerned.

I trust that this will meet all of the desires of the Congress.

Franklin D. Roosevelt

ROOSEVELT TO MARVIN H. McINTYRE, SECRETARY TO THE PRESIDENT

Washington, August 17, 1937

Memorandum for Mac:
Will you prepare a nice letter to Congressman McClellan explaining why I vetoed his Bill?

F. D. R.

THE PRESIDENT'S RELUCTANT APPROVAL OF THE 1938 FLOOD CONTROL ACT*
June 29, 1938

These two letters urging the President to veto the bill which became the Flood Control Act of 1938, and the President's statement on signing it, offer a good summary of the problems of progress in conservation. The National Resources Committee opposed the bill because it had violated many comprehensive planning precepts. The Bureau of the Budget agreed, and was also opposed to the cost obligations involved. In view of the impossibility of achieving most of the points stressed by the National Resources Board, the President elected to settle for the improvements which were made.

DANIEL W. BELL, ACTING DIRECTOR, BUREAU OF THE BUDGET, TO MARVIN H. McINTYRE, SECRETARY TO THE PRESIDENT

Washington, June 23, 1938

My Dear Mr. McIntyre:

By your memorandum of June 16, 1938, you referred to me, by direction of the President, for advice as to whether there is any objection to its approval, the following bill: H. R. 10618, Authorizing the construction of certain public works on rivers and harbors for flood control, and for other purposes.

I have referred this bill to the Secretary of War, the Secretary of Agriculture, the Secretary of the Interior, the Chairman of the Federal Power Commission, and the Chairman of the National Resources Committee. I am transmitting herewith their reports, as follows:

Secretary of War: Report dated June 21, 1938, giving a brief synopsis of the various sections of the bill and stating that "While the War Department has not favored each and every feature of this Act, nevertheless it considers that the Act as a whole is in the public interest and therefore recommends its approval."

Secretary of Agriculture: Report dated June 20, 1938, in which it is stated that "The principles of the provisions of H. R. 10618 in respect of the responsibilities of the Department of Agriculture, and specifically section 1, the first paragraph of section 2, and sections 5, 6, 7, 8, and 9, are considered in the public interest; it is therefore recommended that the bill be approved."

Secretary of the Interior: Report of the Acting Secretary, dated June 22, 1938, stating that his Department does not consider the bill to be wholly satisfactory legislation for the reason that it provides for assumption by the United States of

*Franklin D. Roosevelt and Conservation—1911–1945, Vol. 2, Edgar B. Nixon, ed. (Hyde Park, N.Y.: General Services Administration, National Archives and Records Service, Franklin D. Roosevelt Library, 1957), 235–39, 243.

the entire cost of lands, easements, and rights-of-way in connection with flood control dams and reservoirs, which would establish a precedent which might weaken the repayment policy of the Reclamation Law and tend to create a strong pressure for extension of Federal subsidization to reclamation projects; also, that flood control projects in any given drainage basin are an integral part of any sound program for such drainage basin and that the bill makes no provision for cooperation, except indirectly, and at the pleasure of the War Department, with agencies of the Department of the Interior which are concerned with the conservation of water.

Chairman, Federal Power Commission: Report of the Acting Chairman, dated June 21, 1938, recommending a favorable report to the President on the bill and stating that "In undertaking to pay 100% of the cost of dam and reservoir projects and in expressly reserving title to such projects in the United States the bill, in the Commission's opinion, offers a practical solution to the flood control problem of this country, and at the same time protects the Federal interest in the water power resources of the nation" and that "The additional expenditure of funds by the Federal Government made necessary by the assumption of the entire cost of certain of the flood control projects included in the bill, and the cost of additional investigations which will be undertaken by the Federal Power Commission will be offset many fold by the advantages to the entire nation which will flow from the prompt initiation of the projects thereby made possible."

Chairman, National Resources Committee: Report of the Vice Chairman, dated June 22, 1938, inclosing a memorandum on each section of the bill; stating that the bill is inimical to the public interest and should be vetoed for reasons stated; and inclosing a suggested draft of memorandum of disapproval.

COST OF THE BILL

Facially, the bill authorizes $375,000,000 for carrying out the improvements provided for therein over the five-year period ending June 30, 1944, plus $11,-500,000 for examinations and surveys, total $386,500,000. However, the Secretary of War states that this amount will be insufficient to cover all the costs of lands and damages for previously authorized projects and that therefore the number of new projects instituted will have to be limited so that these costs can be met.

While the bill authorizes, facially, $386,500,000, it should be noted that with respect to certain of the authorizations going to make up that amount the bill provides that such authorizations are for the initiation and partial accomplishment of the plan. For example: The bill authorizes for the Ohio River Basin a total of $125,300,000 and states that such sum is for the initiation and partial accomplishment of the plan; same for Missouri River Basin, $9,000,000; same for White River Basin, $25,000,000; same for Arkansas River Basin, $21,000,000;

and same for Willamette River Basin, $11,300,000. What the additional cost for completion of these plans may amount to is unknown at this time.

Potentially, the bill involves possible heavy future demands upon the Treasury in furtherance of other phases of water control and development and, by establishing the principle of reimbursing local agencies for expenditures made by them under previous laws in partial payment for flood protection, invites demands that this principle be extended to all previous flood control projects and to other projects and to other fields.

RECOMMENDATION

From a Budget standpoint, I am opposed to the bill for the following reasons:

1. It violates the principle of local responsibility in the cost of all flood control projects involving dams and reservoirs, which should be maintained in the interest of sound financial policy and of fundamental equity. This establishes a dangerous precedent and will inevitably lead to its application to other projects in other fields. Heretofore the President has steadfastly adhered to the principle of local cooperation.

2. It authorizes the appropriation from the general fund of the Treasury of the quite appreciable sum of $386,500,000 over a five-year period, 1939–1944, without providing any means for the raising of the additional revenue which will be required therefor, such expenditures not now being provided for in the present tax structure.

3. It superimposes upon existing unliquidated authorizations for flood control and protection, amounting to approximately $425,000,000, an additional $386,-500,000.

I concur in the opinion of the National Resources Committee that the bill should not receive the approval of the President.

I recommend that before the President acts upon the bill that he confer with the Chairman of the National Resources Committee and the Chairman of the Water Resources Committee of the National Resources Committee.

Very truly yours,

D. W. Bell

[*Enclosure*] FREDERIC A. DELANO, VICE CHAIRMAN, NATIONAL RESOURCES COMMITTEE, TO DANIEL W. BELL

Washington, June 22, 1938

My Dear Mr. Bell:

In accordance with the request from the Bureau of the Budget, addressed to Chairman Ickes under date of June 17, 1938, I am transmitting to you herewith comments on HR–10618, a bill authorizing the construction of certain public works on rivers and harbors for flood control and other purposes. Owing to the absence of Chairman Ickes and the necessity for immediate reply, I am taking the liberty of forwarding these comments without the opportunity of having them reviewed by the members of the National Resources Committee.

HR–10618 is inimical to the public interest and should be vetoed.

(1) It approves plans for flood control which are in many instances inadequately studied, and in so doing provides that these plans may be modified at will by the Corps of Engineers and thereupon may be put into action without review by the Congress.

(2) It largely ignores the responsibility of local agencies to provide in equitable degree for their own protection from flood damage. In so doing, it not only assigns to the Federal Government a heavy burden which the latter should not be called upon to bear, but through establishment of a precedent, it also invites raids upon the Treasury in furtherance of other phases of water control and development for which the Congress has wisely not assumed responsibility in the past.

(3) It establishes the principle of reimbursing local agencies for expenditures made by them under earlier laws in partial payment for flood protection. Insistent demands that this pernicious principle be extended to other projects and to other fields would inevitably follow approval of the Bill.

(4) It largely ignores important corollary problems, and would not be likely to promote the unified control and development of the water resources of the river basins to which it relates.

(5) A flood control act should be drawn in consonance with a national water policy, and the present act includes certain advances toward this objective. None the less, it is seriously defective in various particulars.

(6) The Bill redefines national policy, embracing so many important fields, with such haste, that it should not become law. The Bill abandons principles and procedures which have reduced to some degree the raids on the Treasury and substitutes for them no restraints on unlimited pressures from local groups. These controls are eliminated under the claim that their existence has prevented the construction of flood control works. The facts point to the contrary. Sufficient undertakings, adequately explored, are available for construction for three or four years in the future. They may tax the financial and technical resources of the Federal Government, without throwing the gates wide open for the inclusion of projects now inadequately studied and in some instances actually ill-advised.

(7) The Bill explicitly reenacts the resolution vetoed by the President on August 13, 1937. The principles which the earlier resolution embodies were pernicious in 1937 and are no less so today.

(8) A memorandum on each section of the Bill is attached herewith.

Sincerely yours,

Frederic A. Delano

STATEMENT BY ROOSEVELT ON APPROVING THE FLOOD CONTROL ACT OF 1938

[Hyde Park, June 29, 1938]

I have approved this bill with some reluctance. It authorizes but does not appropriate the money for a large number of public works on rivers and harbors, these authorizations being in addition to many other very large authorizations already on the statute books but for which money has not yet been appropriated.

It is unnecessary for me to emphasize the importance of carrying on a large and continuing program to eliminate floods, lessen soil erosion, continue reclamation, encourage reforestation and improve navigation.

Insofar as this bill provides for an improvement in jurisdictional control over the properties involved, and a more adequate control over consequential power developments, it is a definite step in the right direction.

It is not a step in the right direction in the set-up provided for general government planning.

I am in doubt as to the value of some of the projects provided for and it is unwise to place recommendations to the Congress solely in the hands of the Engineer Corps of the Army in some cases and of the Department of Agriculture in other cases.

Coordination of all such public works involves a wider survey and the examination of more national problems than any one bureau or department is qualified for.

In these respects future legislation will be vitally important, in order to give to the Congress and to the country a complete picture which takes all factors into consideration.

For the coming year, however, I shall try to obtain this coordination by asking for complete consultation between all groups and government agencies affected. In this way the whole of the problem can be made more clear. I have, however, approved the bill because it accomplishes a number of good things, with, however, the reservation that its deficiencies should be corrected as early as possible.

[New York *Times,* June 30, 1938]

THE FLOOD CONTROL ACT OF 1944*
December 22, 1944

*Provisions of this act fully established the principle of multipurpose develop-
ment for federal reservoirs by specific inclusion of a provision for hydroelectric
power and for irrigation where feasible on Corps of Engineers projects. For the
first time consideration was given to the recreation potential of the reservoirs.
Section 9 is the formal approval of the Pick-Sloan Plan, the compromise solution
to proposals for a Missouri Valley Authority.*

An Act authorizing the construction of certain public works on
rivers and harbors for flood control, and for other purposes.

*Be it enacted by the Senate and House of Representatives of the United States
of America in Congress assembled,* In connection with the exercise of jurisdiction over the rivers of the Nation through the construction of works of improvement, for navigation or flood control, as herein authorized, it is hereby declared
to be the policy of the Congress to recognize the interests and rights of the States
in determining the development of the watersheds within their borders and likewise their interests and rights in water utilization and control, as herein authorized to preserve and protect to the fullest possible extent established and
potential uses, for all purposes, of the waters of the Nation's rivers; to facilitate
the consideration of projects on a basis of comprehensive and coordinated development; and to limit the authorization and construction of navigation works
to those in which a substantial benefit to navigation will be realized therefrom
and which can be operated consistently with appropriate and economic use of
the waters of such rivers by other users.

In conformity with this policy:

(a) Plans, proposals, or reports of the Chief of Engineers, War Department,
for any works of improvement for navigation or flood control not heretofore or
herein authorized, shall be submitted to the Congress only upon compliance
with the provisions of this paragraph (a). Investigations which form the basis
of any such plans, proposals, or reports shall be conducted in such a manner as
to give to the affected State or States, during the course of the investigations,
information developed by the investigations and also opportunity for consultation regarding plans and proposals, and, to the extent deemed practicable by the
Chief of Engineers, opportunity to cooperate in the investigations. If such investigations in whole or part are concerned with the use or control of waters arising
west of the ninety-seventh meridian, the Chief of Engineers shall give to the
Secretary of the Interior, during the course of the investigations, information

*58 *Statutes at Large,* 887–92.

developed by the investigations and also opportunity for consultation regarding plans and proposals, and to the extent deemed practicable by the Chief of Engineers, opportunity to cooperate in the investigations. The relations of the Chief of Engineers with any State under this paragraph (a) shall be with the Governor of the State or such official or agency of the State as the Governor may designate. The term "affected State or States" shall include those in which the works or any part thereof are proposed to be located; those which in whole or part are both within the drainage basin involved and situated in a State lying wholly or in part west of the ninety-eighth meridian; and such of those which are east of the ninety-eighth meridian as, in the judgment of the Chief of Engineers, will be substantially affected. Such plans, proposals, or reports and related investigations shall be made to the end, among other things, of facilitating the coordination of plans for the construction and operation of the proposed works with other plans involving the waters which would be used or controlled by such proposed works. Each report submitting any such plans or proposals to the Congress shall set out therein, among other things, the relationship between the plans for construction and operation of the proposed works and the plans, if any, submitted by the affected States and by the Secretary of the Interior. The Chief of Engineers shall transmit a copy of his proposed report to each affected State, and, in case the plans or proposals covered by the report are concerned with the use or control of waters which rise in whole or in part west of the ninety-seventh meridian, to the Secretary of the Interior. Within ninety days from the date of receipt of said proposed report, the written views and recommendations of each affected State and of the Secretary of the Interior may be submitted to the Chief of Engineers. The Secretary of War shall transmit to the Congress, with such comments and recommendations as he deems appropriate, the proposed report together with the submitted views and recommendations of affected States and of the Secretary of the Interior. The Secretary of War may prepare and make said transmittal any time following said ninety-day period. The letter of transmittal and its attachments shall be printed as a House or Senate document.

(b) The use for navigation, in connection with the operation and maintenance of such works herein authorized for construction, of waters arising in States lying wholly or partly west of the ninety-eighth meridian shall be only such use as does not conflict with any beneficial consumptive use, present or future, in States lying wholly or partly west of the ninety-eighth meridian, of such waters for domestic, municipal, stock water, irrigation, mining, or industrial purposes.

(c) The Secretary of the Interior, in making investigations of and reports on works for irrigation and purposes incidental thereto shall, in relation to an affected State or States (as defined in paragraph (a) of this section), and to the Secretary of War, be subject to the same provisions regarding investigations, plans, proposals, and reports as prescribed in paragraph (a) of this section for the Chief of Engineers and the Secretary of War. In the event a submission of views and recommendations, made by an affected State or by the Secretary of War pursuant to said provisions, sets forth objections to the plans or proposals covered by the report of the Secretary of the Interior, the proposed works shall not be deemed authorized except upon approval by an Act of Congress; and subsection 9 (a) of the Reclamation Project Act of 1939 (53 Stat. 1187) and subsection 3 (a) of the Act of August 11, 1939, (53 Stat. 1418), as amended, are hereby amended accordingly.

SEC. 2. That the words "flood control" as used in section 1 of the Act of June 22, 1936, shall be construed to include channel and major drainage improvements, and that hereafter Federal investigations and improvements of rivers and other waterways for flood control and allied purposes shall be under the jurisdiction of and shall be prosecuted by the War Department under the direction of the Secretary of War and supervision of the Chief of Engineers, and Federal investigations of watersheds and measures for run-off and water-flow retardation and soil-erosion prevention on watersheds shall be under the jurisdiction of and shall be prosecuted by the Department of Agriculture under the direction of the Secretary of Agriculture, except as otherwise provided by Act of Congress.

SEC. 3. That section 3 of the Act approved June 22, 1936 (Public, Numbered 738, Seventy-fourth Congress), as amended by section 2 of the Act approved June 28, 1938 (Public, Numbered 761, Seventy-fifth Congress), shall apply to all works authorized in this Act, except that for any channel improvement or channel rectification project provisions (a), (b), and (c) of section 3 of said Act of June 22, 1936, shall apply thereto, and except as otherwise provided by law: *Provided,* That the authorization for any flood-control project herein adopted requiring local cooperation shall expire five years from the date on which local interests are notified in writing by the War Department of the requirements of local cooperation, unless said interests shall within said time furnish assurances satisfactory to the Secretary of War that the required cooperation will be furnished.

SEC. 4. The Chief of Engineers, under the supervision of the Secretary of War, is authorized to construct, maintain, and operate public park and recreational facilities in reservoir areas under the control of the War Department, and to permit the construction, maintenance, and operation of such facilities. The Secretary of War is authorized to grant leases of lands, including structure or facilities thereon, in reservoir areas for such periods and upon such terms as he may deem reasonable: *Provided,* That preference shall be given to Federal, State, or local governmental agencies, and licenses may be granted without monetary consideration, to such agencies for the use of areas suitable for public park and recreational purposes, when the Secretary of War determines such action to be in the public interest. The water areas of all such reservoirs shall be open to public use generally, without charge, for boating, swimming, bathing, fishing, and other recreational purposes, and ready access to and exit from such water areas along the shores of such reservoirs shall be maintained for general public use, when such use is determined by the Secretary of War not to be contrary to the public interest, all under such rules and regulations as the Secretary of War may deem necessary. No use of any area to which this section applies shall be permitted which is inconsistent with the laws for the protection of fish and game of the State in which such area is situated. All moneys received for leases or privileges shall be deposited in the Treasury of the United States as miscellaneous receipts.

SEC. 5. Electric power and energy generated at reservoir projects under the control of the War Department and in the opinion of the Secretary of War not required in the operation of such projects shall be delivered to the Secretary of the Interior, who shall transmit and dispose of such power and energy in such manner as to encourage the most widespread use thereof at the lowest possible rates to consumers consistent with sound business principles, the rate schedules to become effective upon confirmation and approval by the Federal Power Commission. Rate schedules shall be drawn having regard to the recovery (upon the basis of the application of such rate schedules to the capacity of the electric facilities of the projects) of the cost of producing and transmitting such electric energy, including the amortization of the capital investment allocated to power over a reasonable period of years. Preference in the sale of such power and energy shall be given to public bodies and cooperatives. The Secretary of the Interior is authorized, from funds to be appropriated by the Congress, to construct or acquire, by purchase or other agreement, only such transmission lines and related facilities as may be necessary in order to make the power and energy generated at said projects available in wholesale quantities for sale on fair and reasonable terms and conditions to facilities owned by the Federal Government, public bodies, cooperatives, and privately owned companies. All moneys received from such sales shall be deposited in the Treasury of the United States as miscellaneous receipts.

SEC. 6. That the Secretary of War is authorized to make contracts with States, municipalities, private concerns, or individuals, at such prices and on such terms as he may deem reasonable, for domestic and industrial uses for surplus water that may be available at any reservoir under the control of the War Department: *Provided,* That no contracts for such water shall adversely affect then existing lawful uses of such water. All moneys received from such contracts shall be deposited in the Treasury of the United States as miscellaneous receipts.

SEC. 7. Hereafter, it shall be the duty of the Secretary of War to prescribe regulations for the use of storage allocated for flood control or navigation at all reservoirs constructed wholly or in part with Federal funds provided on the basis of such purposes, and the operation of any such project shall be in accordance with such regulations: *Provided,* That this section shall not apply to the Tennessee Valley Authority, except that in case of danger from floods on the Lower Ohio and Mississippi Rivers the Tennessee Valley Authority is directed to regulate the release of water from the Tennessee River into the Ohio River in accordance with such instructions as may be issued by the War Department.

SEC. 8. Hereafter, whenever the Secretary of War determines, upon recommendation by the Secretary of the Interior that any dam and reservoir project operated under the direction of the Secretary of War may be utilized for irrigation purposes, the Secretary of the Interior is authorized to construct, operate, and maintain, under the provisions of the Federal reclamation laws (Act of June 17, 1902, 32 Stat. 388, and Acts amendatory thereof or supplementary thereto), such additional works in connection therewith as he may deem necessary for irrigation purposes. Such irrigation works may be undertaken only after a report and findings thereon have been made by the Secretary of the Interior as provided in said Federal reclamation laws and after subsequent specific authorization of the Congress by an authorization Act; and, within the limits of the water users' repayment ability such report may be predicted on the allocation to irrigation of an appropriate portion of the cost of structures and facilities used for irrigation and other purposes. Dams and reservoirs operated under the direction of the Secretary of War may be utilized hereafter for irrigation purposes only in conformity with the provisions of this section, but the foregoing requirement shall not prejudice lawful uses now existing: *Provided,* That this section shall not apply to any dam or reservoir heretofore constructed in whole or in part by the Army engineers, which provides conservation storage of water for irrigation purposes.

SEC. 9. (a) The general comprehensive plans set forth in House Document 475 and Senate Document 191, Seventy-eighth Congress, second session, as revised and coordinated by Senate Document 247, Seventy-eighth Congress, second session, are hereby approved and the initial stages recommended are hereby authorized and shall be prosecuted by the War Department and the Department of the Interior as speedily as may be consistent with budgetary requirements.

(b) The general comprehensive plan for flood control and other purposes in the Missouri River Basin approved by the Act of June 28, 1938, as modified by subsequent Acts, is hereby expanded to include the works referred to in paragraph (a) to be undertaken by the War Department; and said expanded plan shall be prosecuted under the direction of the Secretary of War and supervision of the Chief of Engineers.

(c) Subject to the basin-wide findings and recommendations regarding the benefits, the allocations of costs and the repayments by water users, made in said House and Senate documents, the reclamation and power developments to be undertaken by the Secretary of the Interior under said plans shall be governed by the Federal Reclamation Laws (Act of June 17, 1902, 32 Stat. 388, and

Acts amendatory thereof or supplementary thereto), except that irrigation of Indian trust and tribal lands, and repayment therefor, shall be in accordance with the laws relating to Indian lands.

(d) In addition to previous authorizations there is hereby authorized to be appropriated the sum of $200,000,000 for the partial accomplishment of the works to be undertaken under said expanded plans by the Corps of Engineers.

(e) The sum of $200,000,000 is hereby authorized to be appropriated for the partial accomplishment of the works to be undertaken under said plans by the Secretary of the Interior.

SEC. 10. That the following works of improvement for the benefit of navigation and the control of destructive flood waters and other purposes are hereby adopted and authorized in the interest of the national security and with a view toward providing an adequate reservoir of useful and worthy public works for the post-war construction program, to be prosecuted under the direction of the Secretary of War and supervision of the Chief of Engineers in accordance with the plans in the respective reports hereinafter designated and subject to the conditions set forth therein: *Provided,* That the necessary plans, specifications, and preliminary work may be prosecuted on any project authorized in this Act to be constructed by the War Department during the war, with funds from appropriations heretofore or hereafter made for flood control, so as to be ready for rapid inauguration of a post-war program of construction: *Provided further,* That when the existing critical situation with respect to materials, equipment, and manpower no longer exists, and in any event not later than immediately following the cessation of hostilities in the present war, the projects herein shall be initiated as expeditiously and prosecuted as vigorously as may be consistent with budgetary requirements: *And provided further,* That penstocks and other similar facilities adapted to possible future use in the development of hydroelectric power shall be installed in any dam authorized in this Act for construction by the War Department when approved by the Secretary of War on the recommendation of the Chief of Engineers and the Federal Power Commission.

GOVERNOR ROOSEVELT'S ST. LAWRENCE PROJECT*
March 4, 1931

As Governor of New York, Franklin D. Roosevelt promoted development by New York State of power from both the Niagara and St. Lawrence Rivers by the New York State Power Authority, in cooperation with the Canadian Province of Ontario. This is a statement made in 1931 at the time of the introduction of his plan for a state authority to develop St. Lawrence power. Roosevelt was at this time an active candidate for the Democratic presidential nomination the next year.

I believe that the submission of this bill should be hailed by proponents of public, governmental water-power development as a remarkable step toward the attainment of their ultimate goal. If you had told the most ardent and enthusiastic three years ago that such a bill would be possible today, they would have laughed at you. And yet, here we are with a definite, concrete proposal, submitted after a careful survey by a commission authorized by the Legislature and equipped with expert legal and engineering assistance, which embodies every sound principle and policy which reasonable progressive opinion advocates.

The bill is in principle acceptable to me. There are a number of amendments which I should like to see made, and on which I propose to invite the legislative leaders into conference. I sincerely hope that this bill will pass, with the amendments I have in mind.

The bill conforms with the principles which I laid down in my messages of March 12, 1929 and January 19, 1931 to the Legislature on this subject, in practically all of its fundamentals:

1. It definitely establishes the policy and principle of constant, inalienable public ownership and control for all time to come.
2. It sets up a public agency, to be appointed by the Governor with the advice and consent of the Senate, to build the necessary dam and power houses by the issuance of bonds.
3. It declares that the primary purpose for the development of this electricity is the benefit of the people of the State as a whole, and particularly the domestic and rural consumers of the State so that the homes and farms of the State may receive cheap electricity; and that only the secondary purpose is the furnishing of cheaper electricity to factories and industrial establishments.

*"The Genesis of the New Deal, 1928–1932," *The Public Papers and Addresses of Franklin D. Roosevelt,* Vol. 1, Samuel I. Rosenman, ed. (New York: Random House, 1938), 193–97.

4. The people of the State can be fully and adequately protected from every angle in the sale of this power, right down to and including the time when it actually comes into their homes and farms, for the following reasons:

A. The rates to be charged for electricity shall be definitely fixed by a contract or contracts. In this way, all of the troubles which now exist in fixing rates of utilities will be avoided, in that all the judge-made law concerning good will, reproduction cost, going value, franchise value, etc., etc., will be avoided. Rates will be based only on actual costs, under accounting methods which will avoid all of the present ingenious methods of devious financing used by some of our utility companies. The Public Service Commission will not be able to grant any increase in rates under any circumstances.

B. The Power Authority is given power to enter into one or more contracts with any corporation or corporations, whether now existing or to be formed in the future, for the transmission of this electricity from the power house to the various localities in the State, and with any corporation, old or new, for its distribution into the individual homes and farms. Under the very terms of the bill, the details of these contracts are so laid out that the rates to be paid by the people, as before stated, will be fixed on an actual cost basis at the lowest possible figure. There is absolutely no limit as to which company or how many companies the Power Authority can contract with. Under the provisions of the bill, it can contract with one existing utility company or with several; if it wishes it can contract with any other kind of corporation, one or more; if it wishes it can contract with a new corporation or corporations to be organized for the purpose; and if it wishes it can be instrumental in forming a new corporation for the purpose of making a contract or contracts.

C. Any contract or contracts which it desires to enter into shall be subjected to public inspection and public hearings beforehand, after due public notice. The contract or contracts will be subject to the approval of the Governor, who will be given sufficient time and a sufficient appropriation to enable him to enter into an extended investigation of the contract and all that it means for the people of the State, and to permit him to entertain any objections made by various municipalities or groups of consumers, and so protect in every way the interests of the people.

D. In the event that the Power Authority decides that it cannot make a contract or contracts which are advantageous to the people of the State, or in the event that the Governor disapproves of the proposed contracts on the ground that they are not advantageous to the State, the Power Authority is then directed to get up a plan whereby the State can build its own transmission lines and distributing systems so as to do the whole job itself. Before, however, actually building the lines, the plan will have to be approved by the Legislature and the Governor.

E. Every municipality or municipal lighting district that has its own distribution system, or every municipality or municipal lighting district which establishes one, is to have a preference in the purchase of this electricity from the Power Authority for distribution among its citizens.

Therefore, the bill provides the two bargaining clubs which I have always insisted were necessary for the full protection of the people. The fact that these bargaining clubs clearly appear in this bill, proposed by the majority of the commission, shows plainly that the commission at all times, as I set forth in my message of January 19, 1931 to the Legislature, had in mind the necessity of these alternate methods in dealing with any existing utility company or companies which might refuse to enter into a contract which the Governor ultimately would deem advisable for the best interest of the people of the State. These alternatives are, of course, as above set forth: (1) The power to disregard any existing utility company or companies in making contracts for the transmission or distribution of the power; and (2) the definitely stated proposal for the State to enter into a plan of transmission by itself through its own transmission lines and distributing systems, built and maintained by itself.

I hope that I may be pardoned the expression of considerable pride and gratification that the Legislature and I have been able, during my short tenure in the Executive Chamber at Albany, to arrive thus far toward fulfilling what I know to be the universal desire in this State to develop the tremendous electrical energy in the St. Lawrence River by a State agency with the sole consideration in mind of providing cheap electricity to the people of the State. I hope that the principle enunciated in this bill will be the forerunner of similar legislation for the development of other water power in this State, as well as in other States. I consider it an outstanding triumph in the battle of the people for the retention for themselves of the benefits of their natural water power resources instead of turning them over to private corporations for selfish exploitation. The safeguards in this bill, whereby every proposed contract is wholly open not only to public inspection but also to approval by the Governor after careful investigation could only be circumvented in the future by a combination of complete lack of public interest plus a set of faithless public officials. There is no doubt in my mind that if contracts that are honestly in the public interest and that provide really reasonable rates for electricity cannot be made, then the Legislature and the Governor will take the next economically sound step for publicly owned transmission lines and some new form of public or quasi-public distribution.

THE SEAWAY AT LAST*
May 13, 1954

President Truman had energetically pushed for approval of the St. Lawrence project throughout his administration, but without success in the face of the combined opposition of railroad, coal mining, and private power interests, in addition to traditional geographic opposition from Atlantic seaboard areas.

President Eisenhower managed to change some of the traditional opposition by a plea for support for a Republican President. Secretary of the Treasury George M. Humphrey, on most issues the most conservative influence in Eisenhower's cabinet, was the chief supporter of the seaway. Before entering government, as head of the M. A. Hanna Company, Humphrey had campaigned for the seaway because of the connection it would give the Great Lakes to ore deposits in Labrador.

The bill to establish the St. Lawrence Seaway Development Corporation, patterned in some respects after the Tennessee Valley Authority, was one of the first major legislative enactments of the Eisenhower administration. The waterway was completed in time for President Eisenhower to join Queen Elizabeth II in dedicating the international venture.

As the law was finally passed, the St. Lawrence Corporation was surrounded with many restrictions, designed in the hope that the project would be self-liquidating.

An Act providing for creation of the Saint Lawrence Seaway Development Corporation to construct part of the Saint Lawrence Seaway in United States territory in the interest of national security; authorizing the Corporation to consummate certain arrangements with the Saint Lawrence Seaway Authority of Canada relative to construction and operation of the seaway; empowering the Corporation to finance the United States share of the seaway cost on a self-liquidating basis; to establish cooperation with Canada in the control and operation of the Saint Lawrence Seaway; to authorize negotiations with Canada of an agreement on tolls; and for other purposes.

Be it enacted by the Senate and House of Representatives of the United States of America in Congress assembled,

CREATION OF CORPORATION

SECTION 1. There is hereby created, subject to the direction and supervision of the President, or the head of such agency as he may designate, a body corpor-

*68 *Statutes at Large,* 92–97.

[530]

ate to be known as the Saint Lawrence Seaway Development Corporation (hereinafter referred to as the "Corporation").

MANAGEMENT OF CORPORATION

SEC. 2. (a) The management of the Corporation shall be vested in an Administrator who shall be appointed by the President, by and with the advice and consent of the Senate, and who shall receive compensation at the rate of $17,500 per annum.

(b) To assist the Administrator in the execution of the functions vested in the Corporation there shall be a Deputy Administrator who shall be appointed by the President, by and with the advice and consent of the Senate, and who shall receive compensation at the rate of $16,000 per annum. The Deputy Administrator shall perform such duties as the Administrator may from time to time designate, and shall be acting Administrator and perform the functions of the Administrator during the absence or disability of the Administrator or in the event of a vacancy in the Office of the Administrator.

(c) There is hereby established the Advisory Board of the Saint Lawrence Seaway Development Corporation, which shall be composed of five members appointed by the President, by and with the advice and consent of the Senate, not more than three of whom shall belong to the same political party. The Advisory Board shall meet at the call of the Administrator, who shall require it to meet not less often than once each ninety days; shall review the general policies of the Corporation, including its policies in connection with design and construction of facilities and the establishment of rules of measurement for vessels and cargo and rates of charges or tolls; and shall advise the Administrator with respect thereto. Members of the Advisory Board shall receive for their services as members compensation of not to exceed $50 per diem when actually engaged in the performance of their duties, together with their necessary traveling expenses while going to and coming from meetings.

FUNCTIONS OF CORPORATION

SEC. 3. (a) The Corporation is authorized and directed to construct, in United States territory, deep-water navigation works substantially in accordance with the "Controlled single stage project, 238–242" (with a controlling depth of twenty-seven feet in channels and canals and locks at least eight hundred feet long, eighty feet wide, and thirty feet over the sills), designated as "works solely for navigation" in the joint report dated January 3, 1941, of the Canadian Temporary Great Lakes-Saint Lawrence Basin Committee and the United States Saint Lawrence Advisory Committee, in the International Rapids section of the Saint Lawrence River together with necessary dredging in the Thousand Islands section; and to operate and maintain such works in coordination with the Saint

[531]

Lawrence Seaway Authority of Canada, created by chapter 24 of the acts of the fifth session of the Twenty-first Parliament of Canada 15–16, George VI (assented to December 21, 1951): *Provided,* That the Corporation shall not proceed with the aforesaid construction unless and until—

(1) the Saint Lawrence Seaway Authority of Canada provides assurances satisfactory to the Corporation that it will complete the Canadian portions of the navigation works authorized by section 10, chapter 24 of the acts of the fifth session of the Twenty-first Parliament of Canada 15–16, George VI, 1951, as nearly as possible concurrently with the completion of the works authorized by this section;

(2) the Corporation has received assurances satisfactory to it that the State of New York, or an entity duly designated by it, or other licensee of the Federal Power Commission, in conjunction with an appropriate agency in Canada, as nearly as possible concurrently with the navigation works herein authorized, will construct and complete the dams and power works approved by the International Joint Commission in its order of October 29, 1952 (docket 68) or any amendment or modification thereof.

(b) The Corporation shall make necessary arrangements to assure the coordination of its activities with those of the Saint Lawrence Seaway Authority of Canada and the entity designated by the State of New York, or other licensee of the Federal Power Commission, authorized to construct and operate the dams and power works authorized by the International Joint Commission in its order of October 29, 1952 (docket 68) or any amendment or modification thereof.

CORPORATE POWER

SEC. 4. (a) For the purpose of carrying out its functions under this joint resolution the Corporation—

(1) shall have succession in its corporate name;

(2) may adopt and use a corporate seal, which shall be judicially noticed;

(3) may sue and be sued in its corporate name;

(4) may adopt, amend, and repeal bylaws, rules, and regulations governing the manner in which its business may be conducted and the powers vested in it may be exercised;

(5) may make and carry out such contracts or agreements as are necessary or advisable in the conduct of its business;

(6) shall be held to be an inhabitant and resident of the northern judicial district of New York within the meaning of the laws of the United States relating to venue of civil suits;

(7) may appoint and fix the compensation, in accordance with the provisions of the Classification Act of 1949, of such officers, attorneys, and employees as

may be necessary for the conduct of its business, define their authority and duties, delegate to them such of the powers vested in the Corporation as the Administrator may determine, require bonds of such of them as the Administrator may designate, and fix the penalties and pay the premiums on such bonds;

(8) may acquire, by purchase, lease, condemnation, or donation such real and personal property and any interest therein, and may sell, lease, or otherwise dispose of such real and personal property, as the Administrator deems necessary for the conduct of its business; and

(9) shall determine the character of and the necessity for its obligations and expenditures, and the manner in which they shall be incurred, allowed and paid, subject to provisions of law specifically applicable to Government corporations.

FINANCING

SEC. 5. In order to finance its activities, the Corporation is authorized and empowered to issue to the Secretary of the Treasury, from time to time and to have outstanding at any one time in an amount not exceeding $105,000,000, its revenue bonds which shall be payable from corporate revenues: *Provided,* That not to exceed 10 per centum of the revenue bonds herein authorized shall be issued during the first year after the effective date of this Act and not to exceed 40 per centum during any year thereafter. Such obligations shall have maturities agreed upon by the Corporation and the Secretary of the Treasury, not in excess of fifty years. Such obligations may be redeemable at the option of the Corporation before maturity in such manner as may be stipulated in such obligations, but the obligations thus redeemed shall not be refinanced by the Corporation. Each such obligation shall bear interest at a rate determined by the Secretary of the Treasury, taking into consideration the current average rate on current marketable obligations of the United States of comparable maturities as of the last day of the month preceding the issuance of the obligation of the Corporation. The Secretary of the Treasury is authorized and directed to purchase any obligations of the Corporation to be issued hereunder and for such purpose the Secretary of the Treasury is authorized to use as a public debt transaction the proceeds from the sale of any securities issued under the Second Liberty Bond Act, as amended, and the purposes for which securities may be issued under the Second Liberty Bond Act, as amended, are extended to include any purchases of the Corporation's obligations hereunder.

GOVERNMENT CORPORATION CONTROL ACT

SEC. 6. Section 101 of the Government Corporation Control Act is hereby amended by inserting after the words "Federal Housing Administration" the words "Saint Lawrence Seaway Development Corporation".

[533]

PAYMENTS IN LIEU OF TAXES

SEC. 7. The Corporation is authorized to make payments to State and local governments in lieu of property taxes upon property which was subject to State and local taxation before acquisition by the Corporation. Such payments may be in the amounts, at the times, and upon the terms the Corporation deems appropriate, but the Corporation shall be guided by the policy of making payments not in excess of the taxes which would have been payable for such property in the condition in which it was acquired, except in cases where special burdens are placed upon the State or local government by the activities of the Corporation or its agents. The Corporation, its property, franchises, and income are hereby expressly exempted from taxation in any manner or form by any State, county, municipality, or any subdivision thereof, but such exemption shall not extend to contractors for the Corporation.

SERVICES AND FACILITIES OF OTHER AGENCIES

SEC. 8. (a) The Corporation may, with the consent of the agency concerned, accept and utilize, on a reimbursable basis, the officers, employees, services, facilities, and information of any agency of the Federal Government, except that any such agency having custody of any data relating to any of the matters within the jurisdiction of the Corporation shall, upon request of the Administrator, make such data available to the Corporation without reimbursement.

(b) The Corporation shall contribute to the civil-service retirement and disability fund, on the basis of annual billings as determined by the Civil Service Commission, for the Government's share of the cost of the civil-service retirement system applicable to the Corporation's employees and their beneficiaries. The Corporation shall also contribute to the employee's compensation fund, on the basis of annual billings as determined by the Secretary of Labor, for the benefit payments made from such fund on account of the Corporation's employees. The annual billings shall also include a statement of the fair portion of the cost of the administration of the respective funds, which shall be paid by the Corporation into the Treasury as miscellaneous receipts.

MISAPPROPRIATION OF FUNDS

SEC. 9. (a) All general penal statutes relating to the larceny, embezzlement, or conversion, of public moneys or property of the United States shall apply to the moneys and property of the Corporation.

(b) Any person who, with intent to defraud the Corporation, or to deceive any director, officer, or employee of the Corporation or any officer or employee of the United States, (1) makes any false entry in any book of the Corporation, or (2) makes any false report or statement for the Corporation, shall, upon conviction thereof, be fined not more than $10,000 or imprisoned not more than five years, or both.

(c) Any person who shall receive any compensation, rebate, or reward, or shall enter into any conspiracy, collusion, or agreement, express or implied, with intent to defraud the Corporation or wrongfully and unlawfully to defeat its purposes, shall, on conviction thereof, be fined not more than $5,000 or imprisoned not more than five years, or both.

REPORTS TO CONGRESS

SEC. 10. The Corporation shall submit to the President for transmission to the Congress at the beginning of each regular session an annual report of its operations under this Act.

SEPARABILITY OF PROVISIONS

SEC. 11. If any provision of this Act or the application of such provision to any person or circumstances shall be held invalid, the remainder of the Act and the application of such provision to persons or circumstances other than those to which it is held invalid shall not be affected thereby.

RATES OF CHARGES OR TOLLS

SEC. 12. (a) The Corporation is further authorized and directed to negotiate with the Saint Lawrence Seaway Authority of Canada, or such other agency as may be designated by the Government of Canada, an agreement as to the rules for the measurement of vessels and cargoes and the rates of charges or tolls to be levied for the use of the Saint Lawrence Seaway, and for an equitable division of the revenues of the seaway between the Corporation and the Saint Lawrence Seaway Authority of Canada. Such rules for the measurement of vessels and cargoes and rates of charges or tolls shall, to the extent practicable, be established or changed only after giving due notice and holding a public hearing. In the event that such negotiations shall not result in agreement, the Corporation is authorized and directed to establish unilaterally such rules of measurement and rates of charges or tolls for the use of the works under its administration: *Provided, however,* That the Corporation shall give three months' notice, by publication in the Federal Register, of any proposals to establish or change unilaterally the basic rules of measurement and of any proposals to establish or change unilaterally the rates of charges or tolls, during which period a public hearing shall be conducted. Any such establishment of or changes in basic rules of measurement or rates of charges or tolls shall be subject to and shall take effect thirty days following the date of approval thereof by the President, and shall be final and conclusive, subject to review as hereinafter provided. Any person aggrieved by an order of the Corporation establishing or changing such

[535]

rules or rates may, within such thirty-day period, apply to the Corporation for a rehearing of the matter upon the basis of which the order was entered. The Corporation shall have power to grant or deny the application for rehearing and upon such rehearing or without further hearing to abrogate or modify its order. The action of the Corporation in denying an application for rehearing or in abrogating or modifying its order shall be final and conclusive thirty days after its approval by the President unless within such thirty-day period a petition for review is filed by a person aggrieved by such action in the United States Court of Appeals for the circuit in which the works to which the order applies are located or in the United States Court of Appeals for the District of Columbia. The court in which such petition is filed shall have the same jurisdiction and powers as in the case of petitions to review orders of the Federal Power Commission filed under section 313 (b) of the Federal Power Act (16 U.S.C. 8251). The judgment of the court shall be final subject to review by the Supreme Court upon certiorari or certification as provided in sections 1254 (1) and 1254 (3) of title 28 of the United States Code. The filing of an application for rehearing shall not, unless specifically ordered by the Corporation, operate as a stay of the Corporation's order. The filing of a petition for review shall not, unless specifically ordered by the court, operate as a stay of the Corporation's order.

(b) In the course of its negotiations, or in the establishment, unilaterally, of the rates of charges or tolls as provided in subsection (a), the Corporation shall be guided by the following principles:

(1) That the rates shall be fair and equitable and shall give due consideration to encouragement of increased utilization of the navigation facilities, and to the special character of bulk agricultural, mineral, and other raw materials.

(2) That rates shall vary according to the character of cargo with the view that each classification of cargo shall so far as practicable derive relative benefits from the use of these facilities.

(3) That the rates on vessels in ballast without passengers or cargo may be less than the rates for vessels with passengers or cargo.

(4) That the rates prescribed shall be calculated to cover, as nearly as practicable, all costs of operating and maintaining the works under the administration of the Corporation, including depreciation, payment of interest on the obligations of the Corporation, and payments in lieu of taxes.

(5) That the rates shall provide, in addition, for the Corporation revenues sufficient to amortize the principal of the debts and obligations of the Corporation over a period not to exceed fifty years.

Approved May 13, 1954.

THE HOOVER COMMISSION*
February 5, 1949

Of the many proposals for reorganization, as well as policy change, in government water program activities, that of the Commission on Organization of the Executive Branch of the Government, better known as the Hoover Commission, has received the most attention.

The Hoover Commission proposals for reorganization of the Interior Department are presented here. Like most of the other recommendations of the commission, these were not adopted.

CHAPTER ONE

ROLE OF DEPARTMENT OF THE INTERIOR

We propose that the Department of the Interior be given more clearly the mission of development of subsoil and water resources. As these activities require large public works, we recommend that other major public works also be managed by this Department.

The organization of a department somewhat along the lines we recommend, and in which would be concentrated the major construction activities of the Federal Government, was proposed by the Joint Congressional and Presidential Committee on Reorganization of 1924, again in a Presidential message during 1932, and again by the President's Committee on Administrative Management of 1937. A partial accomplishment was represented in the Federal Works Agency, established in 1939 and embracing a number of these activities. Had such a department been created 25 years ago, hundreds of millions of dollars would have been saved to the public over these years. Today it is a complete necessity.

The magnitude of the problem is indicated by the fact that 1949 appropriations, for the agencies which we propose to bring together, exceed $1.3 billion. To complete the works now in construction will call for over $5.5 billion, and projects authorized by the Congress but not yet started will call for $7.3 billion more. In addition to these totals of over $15 billion, there are projects contemplated which exceed $30 billion. Approximately 100,000 persons are now employed in these agencies, plus other thousands by the contractors.

Phases of this problem have been investigated for this Commission by our task forces on Public Works, Natural Resources, and Agricultural Activities.

The Commission has the duty of assessing the weight of the recommendations

---

*U.S. Commission on Organization of the Executive Branch of the Government, *The Hoover Commission Report on Organization of the Executive Branch of the Government* (New York: McGraw-Hill, 1949), 263–90.

of these able men, reconciling their differences and working out a pattern of action.

BOARD OF IMPARTIAL ANALYSIS

There is no adequate check in the Government upon the validity or timing of development projects and their relation to the economy of the country.

RECOMMENDATION NO. 1

We therefore recommend the creation of a Board of Impartial Analysis for Engineering and Architectural Projects which shall review and report to the President and the Congress on the public and economic value of project proposals by the Department. The Board should also periodically review authorized projects and advise as to progress or discontinuance. The Board should comprise five members of outstanding abilities in this field and should be appointed by the President and included in the President's office.

This board should review projects not only from a technical point of view but also in their relation to the economy of the country.

Some effort has been made by the Office of the Budget to review projects but it has been without adequate staff and support. Forty-two projects objected to by the Office were nonetheless presented to Congress by the sponsoring agencies and 36 were authorized. The need for more exhaustive investigation and report than that provided by the Office of the Budget is indicated by the statement of our task force on Natural Resources, quoted below:

. . . this clearance procedure has not been as effective as it ought to be . . . project reports are submitted for review only after they are completed and long after plans have been publicized. It is then too late for effective coordination, and generally even too late to prevent authorization by Congress of projects found not feasible or not fully reconciled. The Corps of Engineers generally makes no effort to change a completed report when informed by the Budget Bureau that the report is not in accord with the President's program. The Corps submits the report to Congress with its favorable recommendation, but accompanied by a statement as to the advice received from the Budget Bureau. Furthermore, the Budget Bureau does not have the staff to make a thorough review of all projects. . . . Finally, the task of review is vastly complicated by the presentation of conflicting plans or views by the Corps of Engineers and the Bureau of Reclamation. Confronted with the completed, conflicting plans of two development agencies, working from the vaguest sort of statutory and administrative standards of feasibility and of benefit-cost evaluation, and operating with two professional staff members, the Budget Bureau as now staffed obviously cannot provide a fully adequate review. . . .

To the end that only economically feasible projects shall be instituted by the resource agencies and especially by the Water Development Service, the establishment . . . of a Board of Coordination and Review with responsibility for reviewing and coordinating plans for each major project from the time it is first proposed; for making certain that only projects which are economically and socially justifiable are recommended for approval; and for assuring effective participation by all Federal and State agencies concerned during the formative stage. . . .

In the past, projects have been carried through which should never have been undertaken at all. Others have been wastefully constructed, and without regard to important potential uses. Still others have been premature. Bad accounting methods have consistently underestimated costs. Inadequate basic data, interagency competition, and local political pressures bear the primary responsibility for this extravagance and waste. . . .

Corrections are relatively easy when plans are gestating, but when they have been perfected by an agency . . . it is often impossible to obtain the revisions which joint investigation or early review could achieve. . . .

One result of inadequate evaluation of projects is illustrated by underestimation of cost when presented to the Congress. Some part of underestimation is no doubt due to subsequent increase of costs of labor and materials. But some underestimates by the Bureau of Reclamation—such as, for example, the Colorado-Big Thompson Project which increased from $44 million to $131.8 million; the Hungry Horse Project in Montana from $6.3 million to $93.5 million; the Central Valley of California from $170 million to probably over several hundred million—hardly can be explained by increases in labor and material costs.

Our task force on Public Works strongly supports these views:

. . . It would be worth a great deal to the country to have a thorough, factual, unbiased report by the seagreen incorruptibles of the engineering profession on all major construction projects, especially if such a report were couched in plain, ordinary Anglo-Saxon English, understandable by the average layman. We have therefore recommended, as a most important feature of the . . . new Department, a board of three experts to be known as the Board of Impartial Analysis.

CHAPTER TWO

BASIC STRUCTURE OF THE DEPARTMENT

It has been recommended by some of our task forces that the Department of the Interior be abolished and replaced by a new department. The Interior Department is a century old in national life and has served in many of these fields. Aside from sentiment, the cost of merely changing its name would be considerable. The laws and authorizations under which it acts would require much disentanglement. And there is conflict as to what a new name should be, i.e., "Natural Resources," "Works and Resources," or "Public Works." Altogether it seems to the Commission that a reorganization of the present Department would be preferable.

RECOMMENDATION NO. 2

We recommend that the Department of the Interior should be thoroughly reorganized along more functional and major purpose lines.

This involves the transfer of certain agencies from the Department and the incorporation of certain agencies within it.

RECOMMENDATION NO. 3

We recommend that the agencies listed below should be transferred to other offices or Departments, to which they are functionally more closely related:

a. The Bureau of Indian Affairs to a new department for social security, education, and Indian affairs.
b. The Bureau of Land Management (except minerals) to the Department of Agriculture.
c. The Commercial Fisheries from the Fish and Wildlife Service to the Department of Commerce.

RECOMMENDATION NO. 4

We recommend that the following agencies related to the major purposes of the Department be transferred to it:

a. Flood Control and Rivers and Harbors Improvement from the Department of the Army.
b. Public Building Construction from the Federal Works Agency.
c. Community Services from the Federal Works Agency.
d. Certain major construction to be assigned on behalf of other agencies of the Government, except where carried on by grants-in-aid programs.

OVER-ALL DEPARTMENTAL MANAGEMENT

We have urged in our first report that the foundation of good departmental administration is that the Secretary shall have authority from the Congress to organize and control his organization, and that Congressional grants of independent authority to subordinates be eliminated.

Under our recommendations made elsewhere, we propose a new form of "performance" budget for all departments. We also propose that the Department keep its own administrative accounts as prescribed by an Accountant General in the Treasury and subject to an approval of such system by the Comptroller General and audit by him. The Commission also recommends that all personnel recruitment should be decentralized in the Department (except possibly in some lower grade positions common to all departments and agencies), subject to standards and methods of merit selection to be proposed by the Department, but with the approval and enforcement of the Civil Service Commission. The Commission likewise recommends elsewhere that the procurement of supplies peculiar to the Department should be decentralized into the Department under standards and methods established by the proposed Office of General Services. Items of common use will of course be handled by the latter office. Further, we propose that the Department should strengthen its management research unit, working in cooperation with a comparable staff unit under the Office of the Budget.

DEPARTMENTAL STAFF

In making the following recommendations as to the assignment of officials and the service grouping of agencies, we are proposing no inflexible rules. The responsibility for these assignments should lie with the Secretary. Parts of such organization are already in force.

RECOMMENDATION NO. 5

We recommend that the top officials of the Department in addition to the Secretary and his personal assistants should be:

a. **Under Secretary** and his personal assistants

b. **Two Assistant Secretaries,** as at present

c. **Additional Assistant Secretary**

d. **Administrative Assistant Secretary**

e. **Solicitor**

The purpose of creating an Administrative Assistant Secretary is to provide more effective direction of the following departmental staff services:

a. **Financial Office** (accounting and budgeting)

b. **Personnel**

c. **Supply**

d. **Management Research**

e. **Publications**

f. **Liaison with Congress**

[541]

The officials in charge of these services should not have operational duties. Those duties 'must lie with the Divisional or Bureau Administrators. These staff officers must needs be linked in their work with the similar officials upon the President's staff. In the case, however, of the Financial Officer, he must coordinate his work with that of the Accountant General in the Treasury and with the Office of the Budget.

APPOINTMENTS

RECOMMENDATION NO. 6

We recommend that all officials of the rank of Assistant Secretary and above be appointed by the President and confirmed by the Senate.

We recommend, however, that the Administrative Assistant Secretary preferably be appointed from the career service.

It is essential in building up capable administrative staff in all departments that opportunities for promotion of capable administrative career employees be made as wide as possible.

RECOMMENDATION NO. 7

The Commission therefore recommends that all officials below the rank of Assistant Secretary be appointed by the Secretary, preferably from the career service.

MAJOR-PURPOSE GROUPING OF AGENCIES PROPOSED FOR DEPARTMENT

RECOMMENDATION NO. 8

We recommend as logical and practical the following major-purpose assignments of the reorganized department functions:

WATER DEVELOPMENT AND USE SERVICES

Reclamation

Rivers and Harbors Improvement

Flood Control

Bonneville Power Administration

Southwestern Power Administration

Division of Power

A study should be made as to separation of certain general survey activities from the Federal Power Commission and their inclusion in this department.

BUILDING CONSTRUCTION SERVICES

Public Building Construction

Community Services

Major Land Construction Work on behalf of Coast Guard in the Department of Commerce

Hospital Construction on behalf of other departments, except in cases where carried on by grants-in-aid programs

Civilian Airport Construction on behalf of the proposed Bureau of Civil Aviation of the Department of Commerce, except in cases where carried on by grants-in-aid programs

In none of these fields would the Department operate after construction is completed. Moreover, it is not proposed to absorb all construction into the Department solely because it is technical work. Many other agencies will need routine engineering and architectural staffs. We propose for the Department of the Interior only the preparation of plans, awarding of contracts, and supervision and inspection of major construction.

MINERAL RESOURCES SERVICES

Geological Survey

Bureau of Mines

Division of Oil and Gas

Administration of Mineral Leases, Title Records, and Reservations

Leasing of Mineral Lands (those functions now in the Department of Agriculture)

Investigations Into Natural Gas Resources, from the Federal Power Commission

Government Tin Smelter at Texas City, Texas, from the Reconstruction Finance Corporation

An Advisory Function to a score of Federal agencies dealing with minerals, to be established, for better information and elimination of duplicate staffs

RECREATION SERVICES

Public Parks and Monuments

Wildlife and Game Fishing

TERRITORIES AND POSSESSIONS

It is proposed that the Division of Territories and Island Possessions remain in the Department until some policy is determined by the Congress on the ques-

[543]

tion of our administration of overseas areas. This problem will be treated in our report on the Administration of Overseas Affairs.

CHAPTER THREE

OUR REASONS FOR THESE PROPOSALS

The over-all reasons for these recommendations are:

a. The grouping of those agencies related to the development of natural resources and construction, according to their major purposes, to secure coordinated policies in these fields.

b. Elimination of disastrous conflicts and overlaps which cost the taxpayers enormous sums annually.

c. Provision of a center for more energetic development in water and mineral resources.

d. Establishment of a center for collection of fundamental data upon which water conservation works should be based.

e. Provision of a center for coordination of State and Federal action in these fields.

f. Provision for a center in the Government where engineering advice can be obtained by other agencies of Government.

g. Provision for the Congress of an over-all view of the major construction activities of the Government.

h. Elimination of competition for construction labor and materials.

i. Provision of a center for planning and action of Federal construction to be coordinated with the ebb and flow of employment.

Amplification of these major proposals is given in the following sections of this report.

PLANNING AND ADMINISTERING CONSTRUCTION TO AID IN PREVENTING UNEMPLOYMENT

A further reason for these proposals lies in the need for long-view planning to meet the ebb and flow of employment.

In times of great employment in private construction, the Government should reduce its work (except for emergency needs) so as not to inflate costs and should save its construction for times of unemployment. Our task force on Public Works states:

. . . The advance planning and promotion of public works for such periods of slack employment should be recognized as a continued responsibility of the Federal Government, working in cooperation with States and municipalities.

It is senseless to proceed on the theory that every major slump in business and employment is an unexpected Divine visitation not to be anticipated and to be dealt with only on the basis of ineffective, wasteful, and hastily improvised emergency measures. . . .

Public works admittedly can take care of only a fraction of the depression employment problem, but it is an exceedingly important fraction; it is the marginal area in which men out of work will stew around helplessly unless the Government is ready to meet their problem. . . .

At the present time there is a short supply of construction labor and materials. They are urgently needed for national defense, for housing, and for current construction in private industry. In these circumstances the agencies enumerated here should carry on the minimum nonpostponable work, should undertake no new projects, but should have blueprints ready for use when unemployment creates a need.

BETTER ORGANIZATION IN WATER DEVELOPMENT AND USE

The Federal Government's interest in the development of our water resources has been constant since the foundation of the Republic.

At its beginnings, practically all transport was by water. River and canal improvement loomed large in Government interest. With the growth of the railways, the shallow draft channels on canals and rivers became less important.

The development, in modern terms, of our water resources begins with the present century. The systematic deepening of river and lake channels, and the expansion of intercoastal canals, show an increase in annual traffic carried over them to some 22 billion ton miles at the present time. Destructive floods have been lessened by great levee systems, alternate channels, and headwater storage.

The systematic development of irrigation and reclamation began with the Reclamation Act of 1902. Up to 1930 these works were primarily comprised of the easier or less complex types of projects, furnishing water to some 2,790,000 acres of land. Up to that time, some 17 small hydroelectric plants had been built by the Government as an adjunct to irrigation dams with a total installed electrical generating capacity of about 226,000 kilowatts. All of these electrical byproduct enterprises were operated by irrigation districts or under lease.

CHANGED PATTERN OF DEVELOPMENT

With the Hoover Dam in 1930, there began an enlargement of the water development concept. This new concept entailed the storage of water by large dams which would serve the multiple purposes of navigation, flood control, irrigation, and byproduct hydroelectric power.

In setting up the financial organization of these multiple-purpose projects, the Federal Government has established certain policies. Because flood control and navigation do not produce revenues, the portion of the capital cost attributable to them has been set aside as irrecoverable. Because other features, including irrigation, power, and domestic water, do produce revenue, a portion of the outlay is allocated in various amounts as recoverable by the Government.

The following are the active agencies engaged in this field:

Bureau of Reclamation
The Army Corps of Engineers
The Bonneville Power Administration
The Southwestern Power Administration

SCOPE OF ELECTRIC OPERATIONS

These operations by the Government, including those also of the Tennessee Valley Authority, have attained great magnitude.

By June 30, 1947, there had been constructed or purchased 46 hydroelectric and 10 steam power plants of an installed generating capacity of 4,909,582 kilowatts. There were 37 additional plants in construction with a capacity of 8,481,-400 kilowatts.

Construction authorized by the Congress contemplates 79 more plants of a capacity of about 6,842,655 kilowatts. Thus, in, say, 1960 when these 172 plants are in full operation, they will have a capacity of about 20,233,637 kilowatts.

The transmission lines now exceed 14,000 miles.

The total installed electrical generating capacity in the Nation in June 1947, owned by private enterprise, municipalities, and the Federal Government, was about 52,000,000 kilowatts. Allowing for increased installation of private and municipal plants during the next 5 years, plants of the Federal Government will be producing probably 15 or 20 percent of the power supply of the whole country by that time.

The total expenditure of the Federal Government on these multiple-purpose projects is roughly estimated at $3.7 billion as of June 30, 1948. Probably $4 billion will be required for completion of those in construction and authorized. Beyond the above-mentioned plants already authorized, there are several hundred other possible plants listed as feasible. They may or may not be constructed. The further plants thus listed, if constructed, would involve an expenditure of over $35 billion and would have an installed generating capacity about equal to the whole of the actual capacity of the country in June 1947.

The multiple-purpose dams constructed or planned are situated in many States. Those of the Corps of Engineers are in 37 States, in every part of the country—New England, the Middle West, the South, and the Mountain and Western States. The Bureau of Reclamation projects lie in 17 States, in the Western, Mountain, and Southwestern areas. These services have projects in

14 of the same States. Other Government agencies, such as the Tennessee Valley Authority or Bonneville Power Administration, have projects which will produce or distribute hydroelectric power in many of the same States in which either the Bureau of Reclamation or the Corps of Engineers, or both, operate.

THE BUREAU OF RECLAMATION

The Bureau of Reclamation has constructed, or now has under construction, and operates or manages multiple-purpose projects directed mainly to electric power and irrigation purposes. These projects have supplementary effects upon flood control and navigation.

The installed capacity of electric power in these projects is at present about 1,465,400 kilowatts and projects in construction or authorized, 4,181,837 kilowatts.

The Bureau of Reclamation, which employs about 17,000 persons, was created in June 1902. Its original financial support was derived from the disposal of public lands in 16 Western States and Territories (and, after 1906, Texas), and was to be used for irrigation and reclamation of arid lands in those States. In 1920, Congress added the royalties and other income received by the Government from certain minerals, including oil, on the public domain. In the same year Congress provided that 65 percent of the Government receipts from water-power licenses for use of public lands should be added to the Reclamation Fund.

Our task forces estimate that, from the inception of the fund until June 30, 1949, the Fund will have received from the United States Treasury a total of over $1,234,000,000, and from sales of public lands and its hydroelectric power, irrigation, and other revenues, a total of over $546,000,000, or an aggregate sum of over $1,777,000,000. The financial statements of the fund do not permit full analysis, but it appears that, by June 30, 1949, the Reclamation Fund will have expended on construction of projects up to date over $1,530,000,000; and further great sums are required to complete works already under construction.

IRRIGATION

As we have said, at the time the great multiple-purpose projects were inaugurated the easier projects of irrigation had been largely completed and were furnishing water to about 2,790,000 acres. In the 18 years since that time, about 1,500,000 acres of additional soil have been brought under irrigation with perhaps 550,000 acres more benefiting indirectly from the water supplied by the multiple-purpose projects.

The Congress, in setting up the irrigation system, provided that the farmers should repay the costs of the system without interest added to the cost during construction, or subsequent interest on the cost. Experience has shown, however, that even with this indirect subsidy of interest, these projects, on the average, do not pay off, as the capital cost is too great (with a few exceptions) for the farmers to bear. It is simply accepted that the national advantage of more farm homes and more national productivity are advantages which will offset Government losses.

U.S. ARMY CORPS OF ENGINEERS

This agency engages in flood control and river and harbor improvements. Since 1902, the Government has appropriated over $6 billion and actually expended over $5 billion on these projects. The recommended appropriation for fiscal year 1950 is $754,423,700. The estimated cost of completion of authorized projects is about $3.2 billion. The staff for civilian functions consists of some 200 Regular Army engineers, about 9,000 civilian engineers, and some 41,000 other employees.

In improvement of flood control and navigation the Corps of Engineers has constructed, and is engaged in constructing, numbers of multiple-purpose dams of which electrical power is one important by-product. These installations thus become Government business enterprises of importance. The business of marketing the power from Engineer Corps installations in certain instances is managed by the Department of the Interior, as in the cases of Bonneville Power Administration and Southwestern Power Administration. Generally this is the case in the Western and Southwestern States.

Outside these areas, the Engineers have under construction or authorized about 20 hydroelectric power plants of a total installed capacity of over 1,400,-000 kilowatts and a total cost of over $500 million, a portion of which costs will be assigned to power.

DEFECTS IN ORGANIZATION OF WATER DEVELOPMENT AND USE

There are glaring defects in the organization of these services in the Government.

a. There is no effective agency for the screening and review of proposed projects to determine their economic and social worth. There is no effective review of the timing of the undertaking of these projects in relation to the economic need or financial ability of the Nation to build them. We have dealt with this subject earlier.

b. There is duplication and overlap of effort, and policy conflicts exist between the Army Engineers and the Bureau of Reclamation in construction of, and jurisdiction over, projects.

c. There is an inherent conflict between the most efficient operation of storage dams for the purpose of flood control and of dams used for the generation of hydroelectric power. Flood control requires empty storage space prior to the high-water season, the storage of water during the flood season, and the emptying of the dams during dry spells. The generation of hydroelectric power needs as nearly an even flow of water as is possible the year around. And the irrigation cycle, which requires storage of water in the winter months and its release in the summer, conflicts with the continuous flow of water required for electrical operation. As flood-control concepts are in the hands of one agency of the Government and power concepts in another, there is inevitable conflict of the highest importance in design and operation, which can be solved only by a consolidated administration.

d. There is considerable doubt as to the proper assignment of capital costs as between irrecoverable costs attributable to flood control and navigation, on the one hand; and recoverable capital to be reimbursed from reclamation and sale of water and power, on the other.

e. The Federal laws in respect to the Bureau of Reclamation, embracing some 803 pages, are indefinite, complex, and contradictory.

f. There is no uniformity of principles guiding Congressional authorization of these projects. Some are authorized under the Reclamation Acts, some under the Flood Control Acts, and some projects have been created by individual legislation.

g. In their hydroelectric power and irrigation aspects, these agencies are essentially Government business enterprises. They are subject to many deficiencies and they lack flexibility of management, budgeting, accounting, and audit which successful business enterprises require.

ELIMINATION OF DISASTROUS CONFLICTS AND OVERLAPS

One of the major reasons for grouping these agencies into the Department of the Interior is the elimination of disastrously wasteful conflict. Our task force on Natural Resources discusses the conflicts on water development and use as follows:

. . . The function of river development is a multiple-purpose one, cutting across many of the unifunctional agencies. Experience has shown that parceling out river-development responsibilities among these functional agencies produces endless confusion and conflict. A plan for the development of a river basin cannot be devised by adding together the special studies and the separate recommendations of unifunctional agencies concerned respectively with navigation, flood control, irrigation, land drainage, pollution abatement, power development, domestic and industrial water supply, fishing, and recreation. These varied

[549]

and sometimes conflicting purposes must be put together and integrated in a single plan of development. . . .

Under conflicting laws, rival Federal agencies compete for taxpayer money in what often appear to be premature and unsound river development projects, duplicating each other's surveys and bidding against each other for local support at national expense. . . .

The Corps of Engineers and the Federal Power Commission have broad and overlapping survey authority, on a Nation-wide basis, while a third agency, the Bureau of Reclamation, was having its survey authority extended in scope in the Western States where the public domain was concentrated. . . .

Enactment of the Flood Control Act of 1936 marked the beginning of a new era of administrative confusion. In that act primary responsibility for flood protection on the main streams was assigned to the Corps of Engineers, and in the upper watersheds to the Department of Agriculture. The most serious consequence from the standpoint of organization was not the division of flood-control responsibility between the Corps of Engineers and the Department of Agriculture, but the effect on relations between the Corps and the Bureau of Reclamation. As the Corps' original responsibility for navigational improvements was expanded to cover flood control and other purposes incidental or related to flood protective works, and the Bureau's original responsibility for irrigation was expanded to include other potential byproducts of irrigation structure, the one agency working upstream met the other coming down. Now we are witnessing the spectacle of both agencies contending for the authorization, construction, and operation of projects in the same river basins, for example, in the Central Valley, Columbia, and Missouri Basins. . . .

Division of responsibility means duplication of surveys and investigations. Elaborate basin-wide surveys and plans have been made in several instances by the Corps of Engineers and the Bureau of Reclamation, in addition to the comprehensive basin surveys made by the Federal Power Commission and the watershed surveys of the Department of Agriculture. . . .

Jurisdictional jealousy is inevitable, and costly as well, so long as such organization separation is practiced. Friction therefrom operates as a perpetual drag on efficiency and as a stimulator of group and sectional competition for favor and undue influence. Without more inclusive operating units, plans are made which see only parts of the whole situation, and wasteful expenditure of funds results, while the total objective which might have been attained is only partly realized. . . .

Attempts have been made to secure coordination through interdepartmental committees, but the Natural Resources task force states:

. . . no effective method has been found for reconciling conflicting opinions and programs. . . .

The [interagency] committees have failed to solve any important aspects of the problem . . . because the dominant members, the Corps and the Bureau, have been unwilling to permit interagency committees to settle their differences. The result has been neglect or avoidance by the committees of virtually all major areas of interagency conflict, and concentration instead on technical studies and publicity. . . .

The development agencies sometimes compromise their differences. After sharp clashes over plans for the development of the Missouri Basin, the Corps and the Bureau announced complete agreement on the Pick-Sloan plan. Analysis of that plan reveals the fact that it contains many projects which previously had been subjected to devastating criticism by one or the other agency. The "compromise" consisted for the most part in a division of projects, each agency agreeing to forego the privilege of criticizing projects assigned by the agreement to the other. The result is in no sense an integrated development plan for the Basin, and there is serious question in this case whether agreement between the two agencies is not more costly to the public than disagreement. . . .

Each of the two major development agencies, the Corps and the Bureau, not unnaturally tries to stake out claims in advance of the other. Each completes its basin surveys as quickly as possible, and proposes its development plans for authorization. The Executive and the Congress are presented with conflicting proposals prepared by agencies with different water-use philosophies. The plans of the Corps of Engineers are built around navigation and flood-protection features, those of the Bureau of Reclamation around irrigation, with power development and other allied purposes given some consideration by both. Desirable though it would be, it is difficult to forestall authorization until thorough analysis has been made . . . once project plans are announced and publicized such powerful local pressures are usually generated that development cannot be postponed. Occasionally, however, interagency disputes have the opposite effect of retarding worthwhile developments for many years, as in the case of the Kings River project in the Central Valley of California. . . .

The existence of a number of survey and development agencies has encouraged the perpetuation of special-purpose policies and has accentuated statutory inconsistencies. Varying administrative standards of feasibility, benefit-cost evaluation, and cost allocation have added to the confusion in these areas. Interagency rivalry has fostered a sort of Gresham's law with respect to Federal financial policies, the tendency being for higher standards of repayment by State, local, and private beneficiaries to be replaced by lower. . . .

This particular overlap of authority exists not only in the 17 Western States, but the situation for the Nation as a whole is also highly confused. The Corps of Engineers is the principal survey and development agency, but has only minor authority in the Tennessee River Basin, where the Tennessee Valley Authority experiment was set up. Elsewhere the Corps must share its authority (1) on installation of power-generating equipment with the Federal Power Commission; (2) on disposal of all surplus power generated at its projects, with the Secretary of the Interior; (3) on fish and wildlife conservation, with the Fish and Wildlife Service; (4) on pollution abatement, with the Public Health Service. . . .

In addition to creating inequities among beneficiaries and a drain on the Federal Treasury, inconsistencies regarding repayment policies also are a source of friction between the Corps of Engineers and the Bureau of Reclamation. The Corps, emphasizing its primary responsibility for navigation and flood control, can offer more "free" improvements than the Bureau, whose projects are primarily for the purpose of irrigation. This difference is intensified by antispeculation provisions and acreage limitations that are established features of projects built under reclamation laws and that have no counterpart in projects built by the Corps of Engineers under flood control and navigation laws. . . .

There is simply no escaping the fact that so long as the present overlapping of functions exists with respect to the Corps of Engineers, the Bureau of Reclamation, and the Federal Power Commission, costly duplication, confusion, and competition are bound to result. It has been demonstrated time and again that neither by voluntary cooperation nor by executive coordination can the major conflicts be ironed out. . . .

An example of duplication and conflict may be found in the plans for a project at Hell's Canyon, Idaho. These were duplicated at a cost very roughly estimated at about $250,000 each by the Corps of Engineers and the Bureau of Reclamation.

They differed in essential particulars of construction and by over $75 million in cost of erection.

We have pointed out the inherent conflict in use of reservoirs for flood control and their use for power or irrigation. The greatest power development requires the most even flow of water possible. The greatest flood prevention use is to empty reservoirs prior to the flood season and soon thereafter. With the Reclamation Service in control of one function of some reservoirs and the Army Corps of Engineers in charge of others, there can be only continued friction. The consolidation of these agencies is the only remedy. An inquiry into the disastrous flood at Portland, Oreg., in 1948, might show the nature of this conflict in the use of reservoirs.

THE QUESTION OF EMPLOYMENT OF MILITARY ENGINEERS

It is contended that the conduct of Rivers, Harbors, and Flood Control by the Army Engineers has a value in their military training or an economy in Government. Upon this subject our task force on Public Works, which weighed it carefully, says:

The argument that river and harbor work can be directed only by the Army Engineers becomes even more absurd when it is realized that less than 200 Army Engineers are involved and that the remainder of the personnel under their control . . . are civilians who supply most of the detailed knowledge and continuing direction. If the Army Engineers supply unusual ability and obtain invaluable training by contact with this responsibility, there is no reason why the same and even better results cannot be obtained by assigning them and corresponding officers of the Navy and Air Forces, on a proper, dignified, and respected basis, to a central consolidated Works Department.

The Secretary of Defense temporarily should assign to the Secretary of the Interior engineer officers of the Army, Navy, and Air Force who would direct and be engaged in public works tasks commensurate with their rank and experience. In this way, particularly, junior officers would obtain varied training and experience. The Secretary of Defense would continue, as he does now, to prescribe regulations relating to service, rotation of duties, and promotion of these engineer officers, with full power to withdraw them from the Department of the Interior during times of emergency. The Corps of Engineers of the Army would continue in close contact with the best civilian engineering brains in the country to perform functions of a military engineering nature under the Secretary of Defense. Only the civil functions of the Corps would be transferred to the Works Department under the proposed plan.

This subject is far too important to be approached from the point of view of old school-tie tradition. A detached and scientific spirit is required.

Our task force on Natural Resources supports these views:

. . . Painful as the operation may be, the case for a unification of functions of the Corps of Engineers and the Bureau of Reclamation is so overwhelming that it ought to be effected without further delay. The training provided in peacetime for . . . Army engineers at present utilized on this civilian program can surely be secured in some far less costly fashion—perhaps by arrangement with the new Water Development Service or in various installations of the Armed Services themselves. There is a real question in any event as to how far these water resource activities are useful in training for wartime problems.

LACK OF HYDROLOGIC DATA

This division of agencies in the area of water development between different departments has resulted in no adequate provision of hydrologic data. There are great deficiencies in the fundamental data which have resulted, and are resulting, in great losses to the country. The consolidation of water services is essential to remedy this grievous situation.

Our task force on Natural Resources states:

The really disturbing thing is that so little progress has been made in obtaining reliable hydrologic data in advance of project planning and construction. Though the necessity for more adequate data has long been recognized, we find ourselves embarking on the most gigantic water projects ever devised with alarming gaps in our knowledge of the probable behavior of the waters we are trying to control and utilize. So serious are these deficiencies that it is estimated on the basis of experience that the limit of error or ignorance in present water developments is rarely less than 25 percent, and is frequently greater than that.

Present knowledge of the relationships among precipitation, run-off, evaporation, ground-water movement, soil condition, vegetal cover, transpiration, etc., is far from complete, but our greatest shortcoming has been the failure to provide sufficient funds for the utilization of rain gauges, snow surveys, stream-flow measurements, evaporation stations, run-off and erosion studies, ground-water observation wells, water-quality analyses, and other established methods of obtaining data essential to the planning and construction of river development projects. Continuous application of these techniques over a period of years is required to furnish reliable data, yet not infrequently the first intensive efforts to apply them are coincident with the commencement of a project study. Few areas are even adequately mapped for water development purposes. In the Columbia Basin, for example, less than half of the watershed has been topographically mapped or has had ground control lines established. Stream survey and stream gauging programs have lagged far behind project planning, notwithstanding the fact that development agencies have transferred considerable funds to data collecting agencies and have frequently undertaken surveys themselves. Conditions in the Missouri Basin are equally unsatisfactory.

Losses due to lack of adequate hydrologic data have always been heavy and may reach staggering figures during the next few years. The most spectacular form which such losses take is the failure of dams as a result of overtopping by floods. In a large proportion of the important dam failures of this kind structures were built too weak or too small because of lack of sufficient information as to precipitation, run-off, stream flow, etc. Made cautious by the number of such catastrophes in the past, engineers now tend to overbuild where adequate data are lacking, and as a result we have an increasing number of overelaborate spillways, power plants, and water-supply systems. Losses from overbuilding of structures are less spectacular than those that occur from underbuilding but may turn out to be even more costly.

Siltation of reservoirs due to absence of sufficient data concerning sedimentation is another common form of loss. Many river development works have failed to function as expected or are doomed to early failure due to loss of storage capacity for power production and other purposes. In some cases siltation has necessitated the raising of dams at considerable expense. . . .

Overextension of irrigation systems, arising from lack of dependable data as to amounts of available water, has resulted in many costly failures. . . .

RECOMMENDATION NO. 9

For the many reasons above, we recommend that the Rivers and Harbors and Flood Control activities of the Corps of Engineers be transferred to the Department of the Interior and that any Army engineers who can be spared from military duties be detailed to the Department in positions similar to those which they now hold in the Corps of Engineers.

BUSINESS ASPECTS OF MULTIPLE-PURPOSE PROJECTS

There are many reforms in finance, budgeting, accounting, and business management which are urgently needed in the conduct of the electrical and irrigation aspects of Water Development. The responsible officials cannot effect these reforms under the present laws.

The subjects are dealt with in reports of the Commission on Budgeting and Accounting, and on Government Business Enterprises, where we make specific recommendations.

There is great confusion in the laws governing the Bureau of Reclamation generally.

RECOMMENDATION NO. 10

We recommend a clarification and codification of the laws pertaining to the Bureau of Reclamation.

ORGANIZATION AND PLANNING UPON A DRAINAGE BASIN BASIS

A further reason for unified organization of water development agencies is to permit the determination of policies upon a watershed basis.

Our task force on Natural Resources says:

In the management of our great rivers, the coordinated development of whole river basins with their watershed tributaries is peculiarly essential. . . .

The (Water Development) Service would have a clear responsibility to devise for each river basin a plan of development designed to achieve the maximum benefits, after weighing all uses and interests. It would be charged with the responsibility for the Federal part in planning, constructing, and operating river development projects. . . .

There should be regional decentralization of the Water Development Service and the Forest and Range Service, by river basins where practicable, to facilitate "grass roots" decisions, interservice cooperation, and local participation in planning. . . .

In addition to unification of Federal Water Development agencies, the relation to, and participation of, the States in water development needs enlargement. As said, the unit of water development is the drainage area. Within it are the multiple purposes of navigation, flood control, irrigation, hydroelectric power, municipal and industrial water supply, and the problems of pollution. The governments of the States involved not only are interested, but also, for some purposes, should be called upon for contribution to expenditure. Nor can too much emphasis be laid upon any one of these multiple uses of water to the prejudice of other States. Moreover, State laws govern water rights.

Prior to 1936 the States were required to contribute to flood control, but the removal of this condition in 1938 in respect to reservoir projects has, in effect, imposed the whole burden on the Federal Government and at the same time removed effective restraints on projects of doubtful feasibility.

In order to bring about coordination of State interest and the different Federal agencies as well, the following recommendation is made:

RECOMMENDATION NO. 11

The Commission recommends that a Drainage Area Advisory Commission be created for each major drainage area, comprising representatives of the proposed Water Development and Use Service of the Department of the Interior, the proposed Agricultural Resources Conservation Service in the Department of Agriculture, and that each State concerned should be asked to appoint a representative. The purpose of these Drainage Boards should be coordinating and advisory, not administrative.

INTERNATIONAL BOUNDARY STREAMS

With respect to international boundary streams, our task force on Natural Resources states:

. . . There may be instances in which it will be desirable to have joint action by the Water Development Service and the State Department in view of the latter's responsibility for negotiating agreements. Insofar as the State Department is necessarily involved in planning and operation, it should utilize the facilities of the Water Development Service wherever practicable and should effect careful coordination with the Service so that the plans for the development of the national sections of streams are not in conflict. The Water Development Service, in turn, should clear all construction and operation plans for international streams with the State Department for conformity with international agreements.

RECOMMENDATION NO. 12

The Commission shares these views and recommends that the responsibility for negotiating international agreements continue with the State Department, but that all construction be made a function of the Water Development and Use Service.

REVIEW OF IRRIGATION PROJECTS BY THE DEPARTMENT OF AGRICULTURE

Our task force on Natural Resources recommends:

Serious friction can be avoided, it is believed, if the following general principles are adopted: (*a*) the Water Development Service should not engage in basic agricultural research; (*b*) the Water Development Service should not provide irrigation farmers with the type of services ordinarily furnished by the Department of Agriculture; (*c*) the Water Development Service should be required by statute to obtain and consider the views of the Department of Agriculture with respect to the agricultural feasibility of water projects before making its own determination. . . .

The Commission is convinced that the Department of Agriculture should play a more significant role with respect to irrigation than has been the case in the past.

RECOMMENDATION NO. 13

Therefore, we recommend that no irrigation or reclamation project be undertaken without a report to the Board of Impartial Analysis by the Department of Agriculture.

CONGRESSIONAL PROCEDURE ON WATER PROJECTS*
December 5, 1952

The cumbersome procedure under which Congress authorized surveys and reports, planning, and construction of water projects has been the subject of many reviews. A special subcommittee of the House Public Works Committee, headed by Representative Robert E. Jones of Alabama, made these recommendations with little effect.

THE CIVIL FUNCTIONS PROGRAM OF THE CORPS OF ENGINEERS, UNITED STATES ARMY

WORK OF SUBCOMMITTEE

On August 20, 1951, the Committee on Public Works adopted the following resolution:

> *Resolved,* That the chairman of the Committee on Public Works is hereby authorized to appoint a special subcommittee to study the policies, practices, and procedures in connection with the authorization and construction of river-and-harbor and flood-control projects and report back to the committee with the utmost dispatch its findings and recommendations thereon.

In accordance with this authority the chairman named a subcommittee which in due course was allotted funds and started work on its assignment with an especially recruited staff on October 1, 1951. The subcommittee has inspected work in the field and has conferred both in Washington and in the field with representatives of various departments and agencies of the executive branch, representatives of State and local governments, members of nongovernmental organizations, and with private citizens. Between March 27 and May 16, 1952, it held 20 public hearings at which Federal Government witnesses were heard from the Corps of Engineers, United States Army, the Department of Agriculture, the Department of the Interior, the Federal Power Commission, and the Tennessee Valley Authority. The transcripts of these hearings have been published in three volumes.

Work on the subcommittee assignment has served to emphasize the widespread distribution of responsibility within the Federal establishment for the development and utilization of the water resources of the Nation's rivers and harbors. The subcommittee studies have disclosed that there are 38 principal agencies of the executive branch directly responsible in. varying degrees for

*The Civil Functions Program of the Corps of Engineers, United States Army, H. Committee Print 21, 82nd Cong., 2nd sess., 1–4.

[558]

water-resource development and utilization. Another 13 agencies are intermittently and collaterally concerned with the subject matter. There are seven committees of the House of Representatives which are assigned definite responsibilities in the field and at least another four committees have responsibilities which bring them into the consideration of water resource development.

The hearings disclosed considerable information of interest to other committees of Congress. It has been the effort of the subcommittee to restrict the entire content of its report in general and its recommendations in particular to matters of direct concern to the Committee on Public Works. It believes, however, that these reports will be of interest to several of the other standing committees of the House of Representatives in connection with their assigned responsibilities.

The subcommittee knows that it has not arrived at a single complete solution to the many problems concerning the Federal water-resource development program. It believes, however, that its recommendations if adopted will mark substantial progress in the development, execution, and control of these programs. Further, your subcommittee is of the opinion that a permanent subcommittee of the Committee on Public Works should be specifically assigned responsibility for oversight and review of the water resource development programs coming under the jurisdiction of the committee and for study of the interrelationship unavoidably existing with programs and activities assigned as responsibilities of other committees of the Congress.

The subcommittee has not attempted specifically to prove or disprove any of the many charges which have been made about the civil works program executed by the Corps of Engineers on the basis of authorizations recommended by the Public Works Committees. Rather, it has examined the policies, procedures, and practices involved in the authorization and construction of the improvement of rivers and harbors for navigation, flood control, and other purposes. The findings of the subcommittee concerning the Corps of Engineers, its civil functions operations, and its relationships with Congress are sufficiently important to be the exclusive subject of a report to the Committee on Public Works. This document constitutes that report. Subsequent reports will consider other aspects of the water-resource development program germane to the responsibilities of the Committee on Public Works.

SUMMARY

The subcommittee finds that there is authorized a very large volume of river and harbor and flood-control work for prosecution by the Corps of Engineers. The probable cost is only generally estimated and the time to complete the work can be only guessed at. Some of the authorized work will never be undertaken. Costs have advanced since the projects were authorized and they can be expected to change further. While the projects were considered economically justified at the time of their authorization, their present worthiness and economic merit has not been reviewed by the committee. Notwithstanding the large backlog of authorized projects, it appears that works may be more urgently needed in other localities. Some of the authorizations are based on rather detailed surveys of individual projects whereas others are based on only general basin-wide programs.

There is a large backlog of surveys which have not been completed but which have been on the books for a number of years, and on the other hand additional surveys are needed in current problem areas.

The subcommittee believes that there is a necessity of revising the program so that it is current and of then keeping it current. This means that existing procedures must be changed.

The subcommittee believes that such control of the program as is exercised today lies largely with the Corps of Engineers and the Bureau of the Budget, and to some extent with the Appropriations Committees. It believes that the Public Works Committee must participate more actively in exercising adequate control.

It is the view of your subcommittee that the Committee on Public Works should exercise a sufficiently close supervision over the administration and execution of river and harbor and flood-control laws so that it is assured that when funds are sought for the initiation of authorized projects, it approves the scope, cost, economic justification, and priority. It believes that the Committee on Public Works cannot be satisfied merely with acceptance of proposals at the time of their authorization. Rather, the programs it has authorized for prosecution by the Corps of Engineers, the Bureau of Reclamation, the power administrations of the Interior Department, and other agencies must be kept under surveillance at all times.

The need for orderly prosecution of the water resource development program becomes more apparent each year. It is a significant part of our whole national program. It must be properly related to the balance of the program and must within itself be scheduled to provide economic accomplishment. There is a need therefore for the annual review by the committee not only of current progress and the proposed next year's project program but also of the schedule of work for the next several years ahead. Six-year programs should be prepared and kept current to reflect new authorizations, the annual budget and annual appropriations.

In light of the situation summarized above and discussed in more detail in this report, the subcommittee makes the recommendations set forth below generally directed at the program under charge of the Corps of Engineers, United States Army.

RECOMMENDATIONS

Your subcommittee recommends:

(1) That further authorizations for construction of river and harbor and flood-control projects without provision for subsequent review as hereinafter described not be made.

(2) That prior to requesting appropriations for the initiation of projects, integral units thereof, or other works of construction heretofore or hereafter authorized by flood-control acts or river and harbor acts, the responsible agency report to the Committee on Public Works on the proposed work in light of current considerations, if—

(a) More than 5 years shall have elapsed between the time the work was authorized and the time construction is proposed to be initiated.

(b) Authorization was based on the general approval of a basin program.

(c) Present plans contemplate changes in scope or purpose.

(d) Changes of design or engineering features, resulting in cost increases of 10 percent or more are proposed.

(e) Price fluctuations have changed the relationship of local contribution to Federal cost by 10 percent or more.

(f) Land acquisition costs have advanced by 10 percent or more.

(g) Changes due to unforeseen conditions or inadequacy result in cost estimate increases of 10 percent or more.

(3) That such reports be presented to the Committee on Public Works no later than May 1 of the year in which presentation of estimates for appropriation for initiation of the works to the Bureau of the Budget is proposed.

(4) That such reports include as a minimum a complete description of the project indicating any changes from the project as described in the survey reports; up-to-date estimates of construction cost; a statement of the most economical construction schedule and estimated money requirements; up-to-date economic analysis; a statement of relocation and land acquisition requirements; and the status of local cooperation.

(5) That requests for appropriations to the Bureau of the Budget and to the Appropriations Committee be submitted only for such of those projects or works as are positively approved for initiation by resolution of the House Committee on Public Works subsequent to receipt by the latter committee of the reports described in the paragraphs Nos. (2), (3), and (4) of these recommendations.

(6) That annually, at the time of presentation of the budget of the United States to the Congress by the President, the agencies responsible for works of the nature set forth in paragraph 2 above submit to the Committee on Public Works, in such number as it may request, a report, with necessary maps and charts, on the current status and proposed progress on construction works provided for in that budget and its current 6-year program.

(7) That upon completion of a project a report of completion with full cost and benefit data in comparison with the originally approved project be submitted to the Committee on Public Works.

(8) That an annual appropriation be made to the agencies concerned to permit them to prepare the materials necessary to comply with recommendations Nos. (1) to (7) inclusive.

(9) That the conclusions of the subcommittee as to preliminary examinations and surveys as set forth on pages 10–11 of this report be included in these recommendations.

"A RIVER IS A TREASURE"*
May 4, 1931

In New Jersey v. New York, *the State of New Jersey sought to prevent New York City from diverting water from the Delaware River and its tributaries. The case is best known for Justice Oliver Wendell Holmes' statement, "A river is more than an amenity, it is a treasure." It is also an example of the many court decisions involving the control of water and water rights.*

Mr. JUSTICE HOLMES delivered the opinion of the Court.

This is a bill in equity by which the State of New Jersey seeks to enjoin the State of New York and the City of New York from diverting any waters from the Delaware River or its tributaries, and particularly from the Neversink River, Willowemoc River, Beaver Kill, East Branch of the Delaware River and Little Delaware River, or from any part of any one of them. The other rivers named are among the headwaters of the Delaware and flow into it where it forms a boundary between New York and Pennsylvania. The Delaware continues its course as such boundary to Tristate Rock, near Port Jervis in New York, at which point Pennsylvania and New York are met by New Jersey. From there the River marks the boundary between Pennsylvania and New Jersey until Pennsylvania stops at the Delaware state line, and from then on the river divides Delaware from New Jersey until it reaches the Atlantic between Cape Henlopen and Cape May.

New York proposes to divert a large amount of water from the above-named tributaries of the Delaware and from the watershed of that river to the watershed of the Hudson River in order to increase the water supply of the City of New York. New Jersey insists on a strict application of the rules of the common law governing private riparian proprietors subject to the same sovereign power. Pennsylvania intervenes to protect its interests as against anything that might be done to prejudice its future needs.

We are met at the outset by the question what rule is to be applied. It is established that a more liberal answer may be given than in a controversy between neighbors members of a single State. *Connecticut* v. *Massachusetts,* 282 U.S. 660. Different considerations come in when we are dealing with independent sovereigns having to regard the welfare of the whole population and when the alternative to settlement is war. In a less degree, perhaps, the same is true of the quasi-sovereignties bound together in the Union. A river is more than an amenity, it is a treasure. It offers a necessity of life that must be rationed among those who have power over it. New York has the physical power to cut off all the water

*283 U.S. 341–48.

within its jurisdiction. But clearly the exercise of such a power to the destruction of the interest of lower States could not be tolerated. And on the other hand equally little could New Jersey be permitted to require New York to give up its power altogether in order that the River might come down to it undiminished. Both States have real and substantial interests in the River that must be reconciled as best they may be. The different traditions and practices in different parts of the country may lead to varying results, but the effort always is to secure an equitable apportionment without quibbling over formulas. See *Missouri* v. *Illinois,* 200 U.S. 496, 520. *Kansas* v. *Colorado,* 206 U.S. 46, 98, 117. *Georgia* v. *Tennessee Copper Co.,* 206 U.S. 230, 237. *Wyoming* v. *Colorado,* 259 U.S. 419, 465, 470. *Connecticut* v. *Massachusetts,* 282 U.S. 660, 670.

This case was referred to a Master and a great mass of evidence was taken. In a most competent and excellent report the Master adopted the principle of equitable division which clearly results from the decisions of the last quarter of a century. Where that principle is established there is not much left to discuss. The removal of water to a different watershed obviously must be allowed at times unless States are to be deprived of the most beneficial use on formal grounds. In fact it has been allowed repeatedly and has been practiced by the States concerned. *Missouri* v. *Illinois,* 200 U.S. 496, 526. *Wyoming* v. *Colorado,* 259 U.S. 419, 466. *Connecticut* v. *Massachusetts,* 282 U.S. 660, 671.

New Jersey alleges that the proposed diversion will transgress its rights in many respects. That it will interfere with the navigability of the Delaware without the authority of Congress or the Secretary of War. That it will deprive the State and its citizens who are riparian owners of the undiminished flow of the stream to which they are entitled by the common law as adopted by both States. That it will injuriously affect water power and the ability to develop it. That it will injuriously affect the sanitary conditions of the River. That it will do the same to the industrial use of it. That it will increase the salinity of the lower part of the River and of Delaware Bay to the injury of the oyster industry there. That it will injure the shad fisheries. That it will do the same to the municipal water supply of the New Jersey towns and cities on the River. That by lowering the level of the water it will injure the cultivation of adjoining lands; and finally, that it will injuriously affect the River for recreational purposes. The bill also complains of the change of watershed, already disposed of; denies the necessity of the diversion; charges extravagant use of present supplies, and alleges that the plan will violate the Federal Water Power Act, (but see U.S. Code, Tit. 16, § 821,) interfere with interstate commerce, prefer the ports of New York to those of New Jersey and will take the property of New Jersey and its citizens without due process of law.

The Master finds that the above-named tributaries of the Delaware are not navigable waters of the United States at and above the places where the City of New York proposes to erect dams. Assuming that relief by injunction still might be proper if a substantial diminution within the limits of navigability was threatened, *United States* v. *Rio Grande Dam & Irrigation Co.,* 174 U.S. 690, 709, he called as a witness General George B. Pillsbury, Assistant Chief of Engineers of the United States Army, who was well acquainted with the River and the plan, and who, although not speaking officially for the War Department, satisfied the Master's mind that the navigable capacity of the River would not be impaired. Of course in that particular as in some others New York takes the risk of the future. If the War Department should in future change its present disinclination to interfere, New York would have to yield to its decision, and the possible experiences of the future may make modifications of the plan as it now stands necessary in unforeseen particulars. This will be provided for in the decree. Subject to these considerations and to what remains to be said the New York plan as qualified here is reasonably necessary. Some plan must be formed and soon acted upon, and taking into account the superior quality of the water and the other advantages of the proposed site over others, it at least is not arbitrary or beyond the freedom of choice that must be left to New York.

With regard to water power the Master concludes that any future plan of New Jersey for constructing dams would need the consent of Congress and of the States of New York and Pennsylvania and, though possible as a matter of engineering, probably would not pay. He adds that there is no such showing of a present interest as to entitle New Jersey to relief. *New York* v. *Illinois,* 274 U.S. 488, 490. *New Jersey* v. *Sargent,* 269 U.S. 328. We have spoken at the outset of the more general qualifications of New Jersey's rights as against another State. The Master finds that the taking of 600 millions of gallons daily from the tributaries will not materially affect the River or its sanitary condition, or as a source of municipal water supply, or for industrial uses, or for agriculture, or for the fisheries for shad. The effect upon the use for recreation and upon its reputation in that regard will be somewhat more serious, as will be the effect of increased salinity of the River upon the oyster fisheries. The total is found to be greater than New Jersey ought to bear, but the damage can be removed by reducing the draft of New York to 440 million gallons daily; constructing an efficient plant for the treatment of sewage entering the Delaware or Neversink (the main source of present pollution,) thereby reducing the organic impurities 85%, and treating the effluent with a germicide so as to reduce the Bacillus Coli originally present in the sewage by 90%; and finally, subject to the qualifications in the decree, when the stage of the Delaware falls below .50 c. s. m. at Port Jervis, New York, or Trenton, New Jersey, by releasing water from the impounding reservoirs of New York, sufficient to restore the flow at those points to .50 c. s. m. We are of opinion that the Master's report should be confirmed and that a decree should be entered to the following effect, subject to such modifications as may be ordered by the Court hereafter.

1. The injunction prayed for by New Jersey so far as it would restrain the State

of New York or City of New York from diverting from the Delaware River or its tributaries to the New York City water supply the equivalent of 440 million gallons of water daily is denied, but is granted to restrain the said State and City from diverting water in excess of that amount. The denial of the injunction as above is subject to the following conditions.

(a) Before any diversion shall be made an efficient plant for the treatment of sewage at Port Jervis, New York, shall be constructed and the sewage of Port Jervis entering the Delaware or Neversink Rivers shall be treated to such an extent as to effect a reduction of 85% in the organic impurities. And the effluent from such plant shall be treated with a chemical germicide, or otherwise, so that the B. coli originally present in the sewage shall be reduced by 90%.

Untreated industrial waste from plants in said town of Port Jervis shall not be allowed to enter the Delaware or Neversink Rivers, and the treatment of such industrial wastes shall be such as to render the effluent practically free from suspended matter and non-putrescent; and said treatment of sewage and industrial waste shall be maintained so long as any diversion is made from the Delaware River or its tributaries.

(b) At any time the stage of the Delaware River falls below .50 c. s. m. at Port Jervis, New York, or Trenton, New Jersey, or both (.50 c. s. m. being equivalent to a flow of 1535 c. f. s. at Port Jervis and 3400 c. f. s. at Trenton), water shall be released from one or more of the impounding reservoirs of New York City in sufficient volume to restore the flow at Port Jervis and Trenton to .50 c. s. m., provided, however, that there is not required to be released at any time water in excess of 30% of the diversion area yield, and the diversion area yield having been ascertained to be 2.2 c. s. m., the maximum release required shall be 30% of that amount, or .66 cubic feet per second per square mile of the areas from which water is diverted.

In determining the quantity of water to be released so as to add to the flow of the Delaware River, the Neversink River shall be treated as if it flowed into the Delaware River above Port Jervis, and the number of second feet of water released from the impounding reservoir on the Neversink River shall be added to the number of second feet of water released from other reservoirs, so as to determine whether the quantity of water, required by this decree to be released, has been released.

(c) That the State of New Jersey and the Commonwealth of Pennsylvania, through accredited representatives, shall at all reasonable times have the right to inspect the dams, reservoirs and other works constructed by the City of New York and to inspect the diversion areas and the inflow, outflow and diverted flow of said areas, and to inspect the meters and other apparatus installed by the City of New York and to inspect all records pertaining to inflow, outflow and diverted flow.

2. The diversion herein allowed shall not constitute a prior appropriation and

shall not give the State of New York and City of New York any superiority of right over the State of New Jersey and Commonwealth of Pennsylvania in the enjoyment and use of the Delaware River and its tributaries.

3. The prayer of the intervener, Commonwealth of Pennsylvania, for the present allocation to it of the equivalent of 750 million gallons of water daily from the Delaware River or its Pennsylvania tributaries is denied without prejudice.

4. The prayer of the Commonwealth of Pennsylvania for the appointment of a river master is denied without prejudice.

5. This decree is without prejudice to the United States and particularly is subject to the paramount authority of Congress in respect to navigation and navigable waters of the United States, and subject to the powers of the Secretary of War and Chief of Engineers of the United States Army in respect to navigation and navigable waters of the United States.

6. Any of the parties hereto, complainant, defendants or intervenor, may apply at the foot of this decree for other or further action or relief and this Court retains jurisdiction of the suit for the purpose of any order or direction or modification of this decree, or any supplemental decree that it may deem at any time to be proper in relation to the subject matter in controversy.

7. The costs of the cause shall be divided and shall be paid by the parties in the following proportions: State of New Jersey 35 per cent., City of New York 35 per cent., State of New York 15 per cent., Commonwealth of Pennsylvania 15 per cent.

The CHIEF JUSTICE and Mr. JUSTICE ROBERTS took no part in the consideration or decision of this case.

THE DELAWARE RIVER BASIN COMPACT*
November 2, 1961

The Delaware River Basin Compact is the best known of the interstate agreements for handling regional water and conservation problems. The Delaware River Basin Commission, created under the compact, has rather wide powers.

This compact is especially significant because it is the first federal-interstate compact with the federal representation having equal voting power as a full partner to the agreement. Another federal-interstate compact for the Susquehanna River was attempted in 1968.

The non-administrative provisions of the compact are reproduced here.

United States: Public Law 87–328, Approved September 27, 1961.
75 Statutes at Large 688.

Delaware: 53 Delaware Laws, Chapter 71, Approved May 26, 1961.

New Jersey: Laws of 1961, Chapter 13, Approved May 1, 1961.

New York: Laws of 1961, Chapter 148, Approved March 17, 1961.

Pennsylvania: Acts of 1961, Act No. 268, Approved July 7, 1961.

PART I

COMPACT

Whereas the signatory parties recognize the water and related resources of the Delaware River Basin as regional assets vested with local, State, and National interests, for which they have a joint responsibility; and

Whereas the conservation, utilization, development, management, and control of the water and related resources of the Delaware River Basin under a comprehensive multipurpose plan will bring the greatest benefits and produce the most efficient service in the public welfare; and

Whereas such a comprehensive plan administered by a basinwide agency will provide effective flood damage reduction; conservation and development of ground and surface water supply for municipal, industrial, and agricultural uses; development of recreational facilities in relation to reservoirs, lakes, and streams; propagation of fish and game; promotion of related forestry, soil conservation, and watershed projects; protection and aid to fisheries dependent upon water resources; development of hydroelectric power potentialities; improved navigation; control of the movement of salt water; abate-

*Delaware River Basin Compact (Philadelphia: Delaware River Basin Advisory Committee, 1961), 3–30.

ment and control of stream pollution; and regulation of stream flows toward the attainment of these goals; and

Whereas decisions of the United States Supreme Court relating to the waters of the basin have confirmed the interstate regional character of the water resources of the Delaware River Basin, and the United States Corps of Engineers has in a prior report on the Delaware River Basin (House Document 179, Seventy-third Congress, second session) officially recognized the need for an interstate agency and the economies that can result from unified development and control of the water resources of the basin; and

Whereas the water resources of the basin are presently subject to the duplicating, overlapping, and uncoordinated administration of some forty-three State agencies, fourteen interstate agencies, and nineteen Federal agencies which exercise a multiplicity of powers and duties resulting in a splintering of authority and responsibilities; and

Whereas the joint advisory body known as the Interstate Commission on the Delaware River Basin (INCODEL), created by the respective commissions or Committee on Interstate Cooperation of the States of Delaware, New Jersey, New York, and Pennsylvania, has on the basis of its extensive investigations, surveys, and studies concluded that regional development of the Delaware River Basin is feasible, advisable, and urgently needed; and has recommended that an interstate compact with Federal participation be consummated to this end; and

Whereas the Congress of the United States and the executive branch of the Government have recognized the national interest in the Delaware River Basin by authorizing and directing the Corps of Engineers, Department of the Army, to make a comprehensive survey and report on the water and related resources of the Delaware River Basin, enlisting the technical aid and planning participation of many Federal, State, and municipal agencies dealing with the waters of the basin, and in particular the Federal Departments of Agriculture, Commerce, Health, Education, and Welfare, and Interior, and the Federal Power Commission; and

Whereas some twenty-two million people of the United States at present live and work in the region of the Delaware River Basin and its environs, and the government, employment, industry, and economic development of the entire region and the health, safety, and general welfare of its population are and will continue to be vitally affected by the use, conservation, management, and control of the water and related resources of the Delaware River Basin; and

[569]

Whereas demands upon the waters and related resources of the basin are expected to mount rapidly because of the anticipated increase in the population of the region projected to reach thirty million by 1980 and forty million by 2010, and because of the anticipated increase in industrial growth projected to double by 1980; and

Whereas water resources planning and development is technical, complex, and expensive, and has often required fifteen to twenty years from the conception to the completion of a large dam and reservoir; and

Whereas the public interest requires that facilities must be ready and operative when needed, to avoid the catastrophe of unexpected floods or prolonged drought, and for other purposes; and

Whereas the Delaware River Basin Advisory Committee, a temporary body constituted by the Governors of the four basin States and the mayors of the cities of New York and Philadelphia, has prepared a draft of an interstate-Federal compact for the creation of a basin agency, and the signatory parties desire to effectuate the purposes thereof: Now therefore

The states of Delaware, New Jersey and New York and the Commonwealth of Pennsylvania, and the United States of America hereby solemnly covenant and agree with each other, upon the enactment of concurrent legislation by the Congress of the United States and by the respective state legislatures, having the same effect as this Part, to the following Compact:

ARTICLE 1

SHORT TITLE, DEFINITIONS, PURPOSE AND LIMITATIONS

SECTION 1.1 SHORT TITLE. This Act shall be known and may be cited as the Delaware River Basin Compact.

1.2 DEFINITIONS. For the purposes of this compact, and of any supplemental or concurring legislation enacted pursuant thereto, except as may be otherwise required by the context:

(a) "Basin" shall mean the area of drainage into the Delaware River and its tributaries, including Delaware Bay;

(b) "Commission" shall mean the Delaware River Basin Commission created and constituted by this compact;

(c) "Compact" shall mean Part I of this act;

(d) "Cost" shall mean direct and indirect expenditures, commitment, and net induced adverse effects, whether or not compensated for, used or incurred in connection with the establishment, acquisition, construction, maintenance and operation of a project;

(e) "Facility" shall mean any real or personal property, within or without the basin, and improvements thereof or thereon, and any and all rights of way, water, water rights, plants, structures, machinery and equipment, acquired, constructed, operated or maintained for the beneficial use of water resources or related land uses including, without limiting the generality of the foregoing, any and all things and appurtenances necessary, useful or convenient for the control, collection, storage, withdrawal, diversion, release, treatment, transmission, sale or exchange of water; or for navigation thereon, or the development and use of hydroelectric energy and power, and public recreational facilities; or the propagation of fish and wildlife; or to conserve and protect the water resources of the basin or any existing or future water supply source, or to facilitate any other uses of any of them;

(f) "Federal government" shall mean the government of the United States of America, and any appropriate branch, department, bureau or division thereof, as the case may be;

(g) "Project" shall mean any work, service or activity which is separately planned, financed, or identified by the commission, or any separate facility undertaken or to be undertaken within a specified area, for the conservation, utilization, control, development or management of water resources which can be established and utilized independently or as an addition to an existing facility, and can be considered as a separate entity for purposes of evaluation;

(h) "Signatory party" shall mean a state or commonwealth party to this compact, and the federal government;

(i) "Water resources" shall include water and related natural resources in, on, under, or above the ground, including related uses of land, which are subject to beneficial use, ownership or control.

1.3 PURPOSE AND FINDINGS. The legislative bodies of the respective signatory parties hereby find and declare:

(a) The water resources of the basin are affected with a local, state, regional and national interest and their planning, conservation, utilization, development, management and control, under appropriate arrangements for intergovernmental cooperation, are public purposes of the respective signatory parties.

(b) The water resources of the basin are subject to the sovereign right and responsibility of the signatory parties, and it is the purpose of this compact to provide for a joint exercise of such powers of sovereignty in the common interests of the people of the region.

(c) The water resources of the basin are functionally interrelated, and the uses of these resources are interdependent. A single administrative agency is therefore essential for effective and economical direction, supervision and coordination of efforts and programs of federal, state and local governments and of private enterprise.

[571]

(d) The water resources of the Delaware River Basin, if properly planned and utilized, are ample to meet all presently projected demands, including existing and added diversions in future years and ever increasing economies and efficiencies in the use and reuse of water resources can be brought about by comprehensive planning, programming and management.

(e) In general, the purposes of this compact are to promote interstate comity; to remove causes of present and future controversy; to make secure and protect present developments within the states; to encourage and provide for the planning, conservation, utilization, development, management and control of the water resources of the basin; to provide for cooperative planning and action by the signatory parties with respect to such water resources; and to apply the principal of equal and uniform treatment to all water users who are similarly situated and to all users of related facilities, without regard to established political boundaries.

1.4 POWERS OF CONGRESS; WITHDRAWAL. Nothing in this compact shall be construed to relinquish the functions, powers or duties of the Congress of the United States with respect to the control of any navigable waters within the basin, nor shall any provision hereof be construed in derogation of any of the constitutional powers of the Congress to regulate commerce among the states and with foreign nations. The power and right of the Congress to withdraw the federal government as a party to this compact or to revise or modify the terms, conditions and provisions under which it may remain a party by amendment, repeal or modification of any federal statute applicable thereto is recognized by the signatory parties.

1.5 EXISTING AGENCIES; CONSTRUCTION. It is the purpose of the signatory parties to preserve and utilize the functions, powers and duties of existing offices and agencies of government to the extent not inconsistent with the compact, and the commission is authorized and directed to utilize and employ such offices and agencies for the purpose of this compact to the fullest extent it finds feasible and advantageous.

1.6 DURATION OF COMPACT.

(a) The duration of this compact shall be for an initial period of 100 years from its effective date, and it shall be continued for additional periods of 100 years if not later than 20 years nor sooner than 25 years prior to the determination of the initial period or any succeeding period none of the signatory states, by authority of an act of its legislature, notifies the commission of intention to terminate the compact at the end of the then current 100 year period.

(b) In the event that this compact should be terminated by operation of paragraph (a) above, the commission shall be dissolved, its assets and liabilities transferred, and its corporate affairs wound up, in such manner as may be provided by act of the Congress.

ARTICLE 2

ORGANIZATION AND AREA

SECTION 2.1 COMMISSION CREATED. The Delaware River Basin Commission is hereby created as a body politic and corporate, with succession for the duration of this compact, as an agency and instrumentality of the governments of the respective signatory parties.

2.2 COMMISSION MEMBERSHIP. The commission shall consist of the Governors of the signatory states, ex officio, and one commissioner to be appointed by the President of the United States to serve during the term of office of the President. MAKE A LINE

2.3 ALTERNATES. Each member of the commission shall appoint an alternate to act in his place and stead, with authority to attend all meetings of the commission, and with power to vote in the absence of the member. Unless otherwise provided by law of the signatory party for which he is appointed, each alternate shall serve during the term of the member appointing him, subject to removal at the pleasure of the member. In the event of a vacancy in the office of alternate, it shall be filled in the same manner as an original appointment for the unexpired term only.

2.4 COMPENSATION. Members of the commission and alternates shall serve without compensation but may be reimbursed for necessary expenses incurred in and incident to the performance of their duties.

2.5 VOTING POWER. Each member shall be entitled to one vote on all matters which may come before the commission. No action of the commission shall be taken at any meeting unless a majority of the membership shall vote in favor thereof.

2.6 ORGANIZATION AND PROCEDURE. The commission shall provide for its own organization and procedure, and shall adopt rules and regulations governing its meetings and transactions. It shall organize annually by the election of a chairman and vice-chairman from among its members. It shall provide by its rules for the appointment by each member in his discretion of an advisor to serve without compensation, who may attend all meetings of the commission and its committees.

2.7 JURISDICTION OF THE COMMISSION. The commission shall have, exercise and discharge its functions, powers and duties within the limits of the basin, except that it may in its discretion act outside the basin whenever such action may be necessary or convenient to effectuate its powers or duties within the basin, or to sell or dispose of water, hydroelectric power or other water resources within or without the basin. The commission shall exercise such power outside the basin only upon the consent of the state in which it proposes to act.

[573]

ARTICLE 3

POWERS AND DUTIES OF THE COMMISSION

SECTION 3.1 PURPOSE AND POLICY. The commission shall develop and effectuate plans, policies and projects relating to the water resources of the basin. It shall adopt and promote uniform and coordinated policies for water conservation, control, use and management in the basin. It shall encourage the planning, development and financing of water resources projects according to such plans and policies.

3.2 COMPREHENSIVE PLAN, PROGRAM AND BUDGETS. The commission shall, in accordance with Article 13 of this compact, formulate and adopt:

(a) A comprehensive plan, after consultation with water users and interested public bodies, for the immediate and long range development and uses of the water resources of the basin;

(b) A water resources program, based upon the comprehensive plan, which shall include a systematic presentation of the quantity and quality of water resources needs of the area to be served for such reasonably foreseeable period as the commission may determine, balanced by existing and proposed projects required to satisfy such needs, including all public and private projects affecting the basin, together with a separate statement of the projects proposed to be undertaken by the commission during such period; and

(c) An annual current expense budget, and an annual capital budget consistent with the water resources program covering the commission's projects and facilities for the budget period.

3.3 ALLOCATIONS, DIVERSIONS AND RELEASES. The commission shall have the power from time to time as need appears, in accordance with the doctrine of equitable apportionment, to allocate the waters of the basin to and among the states signatory to this compact and to and among their respective political subdivisions, and to impose conditions, obligations and release requirements related thereto, subject to the following limitations:

(a) The commission, without the unanimous consent of the parties to the United States Supreme Court decree in New Jersey v. New York, 347 U.S. 995 (1954), shall not impair, diminish or otherwise adversely affect the diversions, compensating releases, rights, conditions, obligations, and provisions for the administration thereof as provided in said decree; provided, however, that after consultation with the river master under said decree the commission may find and declare a state of emergency resulting from a drought or catastrophe and it may thereupon by unanimous consent of its members authorize and direct an increase or decrease in any allocation or diversion permitted or releases required by the decree, in such manner and for such limited time as may be necessary to meet such an emergency condition.

[574]

(b) No allocation of waters hereafter made pursuant to this section shall constitute a prior appropriation of the waters of the basin or confer any superiority of right in respect to the use of those waters, nor shall any such action be deemed to constitute an apportionment of the waters of the basin among the parties hereto: *Provided,* That this paragraph shall not be deemed to limit or restrict the power of the commission to enter into convenants with respect to water supply, with a duration not exceeding the life of this compact, as it may deem necessary for a benefit or development of the water resources of the basin.

(c) Any proper party deeming itself aggrieved by action of the commission with respect to an out-of-basin diversion or compensating releases in connection therewith, notwithstanding the powers delegated to the commission by this compact may invoke the original jurisdiction of the United States Supreme Court within one year after such action for an adjudication and determination thereof de novo. Any other action of the commission pursuant to this section shall be subject to judicial review in any court of competent jurisdiction.

3.4 SUPREME COURT DECREE; WAIVERS. Each of the signatory states and their respective political subdivisions, in consideration of like action by the others, and in recognition of reciprocal benefits, hereby waives and relinquishes for the duration of this compact any right, privilege or power it may have to apply for any modification of the terms of the decree of the United States Supreme Court in New Jersey v. New York, 347 U.S. 995 (1954) which would increase or decrease the diversions authorized or increase or decrease the releases required thereunder, except that a proceeding to modify such decree to increase diversions or compensating releases in connection with such increased diversions may be prosecuted by a proper party to effectuate rights, powers, duties and obligations under Section 3.3 of this compact, and except as may be required to effectuate the provisions of paragraphs IIIB3 and VB of said decree.

3.5 SUPREME COURT DECREE; SPECIFIC LIMITATIONS ON COMMISSION. Except as specifically provided in Sections 3.3 and 3.4 of this article, nothing in this compact shall be construed in any way to impair, diminish or otherwise adversely affect the rights, powers, privileges, conditions and obligations contained in the decree of the United States Supreme Court in New Jersey v. New York, 347 U.S. 995 (1954). To this end, and without limitation thereto, the commission shall not:

(a) Acquire, construct or operate any project or facility or make any order or take any action which would impede or interfere with the rights, powers, privileges, conditions or obligations contained in said decree;

(b) Impose or collect any fee, charge or assessment with respect to diversions of waters of the basin permitted by said decree;

(c) Exercise any jurisdiction, except upon consent of all the parties to said decree, over the planning, design, construction, operation or control of any projects, structures or facilities constructed or used in connection with withdrawals, diversions and releases of waters of the basin authorized by said decree or of the withdrawals, diversions or releases to be made thereunder; or

(d) Serve as river master under said decree, except upon consent of all the parties thereto.

3.6 GENERAL POWERS. The commission may:

(a) Plan, design, acquire, construct, reconstruct, complete, own, improve, extend, develop, operate and maintain any and all projects, facilities, properties, activities and services, determined by the commission to be necessary, convenient or useful for the purposes of this compact;

(b) Establish standards of planning, design and operation of all projects and facilities in the basin which affect its water resources, including without limitation thereto water and waste treatment plants, stream and lake recreational facilities, trunk mains for water distribution, local flood protection works, small watershed management programs, and ground water recharging operations;

(c) Conduct and sponsor research on water resources, their planning, use, conservation, management, development, control and protection, and the capacity, adaptability and best utility of each facility thereof, and collect, compile, correlate, analyze, report and interpret data on water resources and uses in the basin, including without limitation thereto the relation of water to other resources, industrial water technology, ground water movement, relation between water price and water demand, and general hydrological conditions;

(d) Compile and coordinate systematic stream stage and ground water level forecasting data, and publicize such information when and as needed for water uses, flood warning, quality maintenance or other purposes;

(e) Conduct such special ground water investigations tests, and operations and compile such data relating thereto as may be required to formulate and administer the comprehensive plan;

(f) Prepare, publish and disseminate information and reports with respect to the water problems of the basin and for the presentation of the needs, resources and policies of the basin to executive and legislative branches of the signatory parties;

(g) Negotiate for such loans, grants, services or other aids as may be lawfully available from public or private sources to finance or assist in effectuating any of the purposes of this compact; and to receive and accept such aid upon such terms and conditions, and subject to such provisions for repayment as may be required by federal or state law or as the commission may deem necessary or desirable;

(h) Exercise such other and different powers as may be delegated to it by this compact or otherwise pursuant to law, and have and exercise all powers necessary or convenient to carry out its express powers or which may be reasonably implied therefrom.

3.7 RATES AND CHARGES. The commission may from time to time after public notice and hearing fix, alter and revise rates, rentals, charges and tolls and classifications thereof, for the use of facilities which it may own or operate and for products and services rendered thereby, without regulation or control by any department, office or agency of any signatory party.

3.8 REFERRAL AND REVIEW. No project having a substantial effect on the water resources of the basin shall hereafter be undertaken by any person, corporation or governmental authority unless it shall have been first submitted to and approved by the commission, subject to the provisions of Sections 3.3 and 3.5. The commission shall approve a project whenever it finds and determines that such project would not substantially impair or conflict with the comprehensive plan and may modify and approve as modified, or may disapprove any such project whenever it finds and determines that the project would substantially impair or conflict with such plan. The commission shall provide by regulation for the procedure of submission, review and consideration of projects, and for its determinations pursuant to this section. Any determination of the commission hereunder shall be subject to judicial review in any court of competent jurisdiction.

3.9 COORDINATION AND COOPERATION. The commission shall promote and aid the coordination of the activities and programs of federal, state, municipal and private agencies concerned with water resources administration in the basin. To this end, but without limitation thereto, the commission may:

(a) Advise, consult, contract, financially assist, or otherwise cooperate with any and all such agencies;

(b) Employ any other agency or instrumentality of any of the signatory parties or of any political subdivision thereof, in the design, construction, operation and maintenance of structures, and the installation and management of river control systems, or for any other purpose;

(c) Develop and adopt plans and specifications for particular water resources projects and facilities which so far as consistent with the comprehensive plan incorporate any separate plans of other public and private organizations operating in the basin, and permit the decentralized administration thereof;

(d) Qualify as a sponsoring agency under any federal legislation heretofore or hereafter enacted to provide financial or other assistance for the planning, conservation, utilization, development, management or control of water resources.

3.10 ADVISORY COMMITTEES. The commission may constitute and empower advisory committees, which may be comprised of representatives of the public and of federal, state, county and municipal governments, water resources agencies, water-using industries, water-interest groups, labor and agriculture.

ARTICLE 4

WATER SUPPLY

SECTION 4.1 GENERALLY. The commission shall have power to develop, implement and effectuate plans and projects for the use of the water of the basin for domestic, municipal, agricultural and industrial water supply. To this end, without limitation thereto, it may provide for, construct, acquire, operate and maintain dams, reservoirs and other facilities for utilization of surface and ground water resources, and all related structures, appurtenances and equipment on the river and its tributaries and at such off-river sites as it may find appropriate, and may regulate and control the use thereof.

4.2 STORAGE AND RELEASE OF WATERS.

(a) The commission shall have power to acquire, operate and control projects and facilities for the storage and release of waters, for the regulation of flows and supplies of surface and ground waters of the basin, for the protection of public health, stream quality control, economic development, improvement of fisheries, recreation, dilution and abatement of pollution, the prevention of undue salinity and other purposes.

(b) No signatory party shall permit any augmentation of flow to be diminished by the diversion of any water of the basin during any period in which waters are being released from storage under the direction of the commission for the purpose of augmenting such flow, except in cases where such diversion is duly authorized by this compact, or by the commission pursuant thereto, or by the judgment, order or decree of a court of competent jurisdiction.

4.3 ASSESSABLE IMPROVEMENTS. The commission may undertake to provide stream regulation in the main stream or any tributary in the basin and may assess on an annual basis or otherwise the cost thereof upon water users or any classification of them specially benefited thereby to a measurable extent, provided that no such assessment shall exceed the actual benefit to any water user. Any such assessment shall follow the procedure prescribed by law for local improvement assessments and shall be subject to judicial review in any court of competent jurisdiction.

4.4 COORDINATION. Prior to entering upon the execution of any project authorized by this article, the commission shall review and consider all existing rights, plans, and programs of the signatory parties, their political subdivisions, private parties, and water users which are pertinent to such project, and shall hold a public hearing on each proposed project.

4.5 ADDITIONAL POWERS. In connection with any project authorized by this article, the commission shall have power to provide storage, treatment, pumping and transmission facilities, but nothing herein shall be construed to authorize the commission to engage in the business of distributing water.

[578]

ARTICLE 5

POLLUTION CONTROL

SECTION 5.1 GENERAL POWERS. The commission may undertake investigations and surveys, and acquire, construct, operate and maintain projects and facilities to control potential pollution and abate or dilute existing pollution of the water resources of the basin. It may invoke as complainant the power and jurisdiction of water pollution abatement agencies of the signatory parties.

5.2 POLICY AND STANDARDS. The commission may assume jurisdiction to control future pollution and abate existing pollution in the waters of the basin, whenever it determines after investigation and public hearing upon due notice that the effectuation of the comprehensive plan so requires. The standard of such control shall be that pollution by sewage or industrial or other waste originating within a signatory state shall not injuriously affect waters of the basin as contemplated by the comprehensive plan. The commission, after such public hearing may classify the waters of the basin and establish standards of treatment of sewage, industrial or other waste, according to such classes including allowance for the variable factors of surface and ground waters, such as size of the stream, flow, movement, location, character, self-purification, and usage of the waters affected. After such investigation, notice and hearing the commission may adopt and from time to time amend and repeal rules, regulations and standards to control such future pollution and abate existing pollution, and to require such treatment of sewage, industrial or other waste within a time reasonable for the construction of the necessary works, as may be required to protect the public health or to preserve the waters of the basin for uses in accordance with the comprehensive plan.

5.3 COOPERATIVE LEGISLATION AND ADMINISTRATION. Each of the signatory parties covenants and agrees to prohibit and control pollution of the waters of the basin according to the requirements of this compact and to cooperate faithfully in the control of future pollution in and abatement of existing pollution from the rivers, streams, and waters in the basin which flow through, under, into or border upon any of such signatory states, and in order to effect such object, agrees to enact any necessary legislation to enable each such party to place and maintain the waters of said basin in a satisfactory condition, available for safe and satisfactory use as public and industrial water supplies after reasonable treatment, suitable for recreational usage, capable of maintaining fish and other aquatic life, free from unsightly or malodorous nuisances due to floating solids or sludge deposits and adaptable to such other uses as may be provided by the comprehensive plan.

5.4 ENFORCEMENT. The commission may, after investigation and hearing, issue an order or orders upon any person or public or private corporation, or other entity, to cease the discharge of sewage, industrial or other waste into waters of the basin which it determines to be in violation of such rules and regulations as it shall have adopted for the prevention and abatement of pollution. Any such order or orders may prescribe the date, including a reasonable time for the construction of any necessary works, on or before which such discharge shall be wholly or partially discontinued, modified or treated, or otherwise conformed to the requirements of such rules and regulations. Such order shall be reviewable in any court of competent jurisdiction. The courts of the signatory parties shall have jurisdiction to enforce against any person, public or private corporation, or other entity, any and all provisions of this article or of any such order. The commission may bring an action in its own name in any such court of competent jurisdiction to compel compliance with any provision of this article, or any rule or regulation issued pursuant thereto or of any such order, according to the practice and procedure of the court.

5.5 FURTHER JURISDICTION. Nothing in this compact shall be construed to repeal, modify or qualify the authority of any signatory party to enact any legislation or enforce any additional conditions and restrictions to lessen or prevent the pollution of waters within its jurisdiction.

ARTICLE 6

FLOOD PROTECTION

SECTION 6.1 GENERAL POWERS. The commission may plan, design, construct and operate and maintain projects and facilities, as it may deem necessary or desirable for flood damage reduction. It shall have power to operate such facilities and to store and release waters on the Delaware River and its tributaries and elsewhere within the basin, in such manner, at such times, and under such regulations as the commission may deem appropriate to meet flood conditions as they may arise.

6.2 FLOOD PLAIN ZONING.

(a) The commission shall have power to adopt, amend and repeal recommended standards, in the manner provided by this section, relating to the nature and extent of the uses of land in areas subject to flooding by waters of the Delaware River and its tributaries. Such standards shall not be deemed to impair or restrict the power of the signatory parties or their political subdivisions to adopt zoning and other land use regulations not inconsistent therewith.

(b) The commission may study and determine the nature and extent of the flood plains of the Delaware River and its tributaries. Upon the basis of such studies, it may establish encroachment lines and delineate the areas subject to flood, including a classification of lands with reference to relative risk of flood and the establishment of standards for flood plain use which will safeguard the public health, safety and property. Prior to the adoption of any standards delineating such area or defining such use, the commission shall hold public hearings, in the manner provided by Article 14, with respect to the substance of such standards. At or before such public hearings the proposed standards shall be available, and all interested persons shall be given an opportunity to be heard thereon at the hearing. Upon the adoption and promulgation of such standards, the commission may enter into agreements to provide technical and financial aid to any municipal corporation for the administration and enforcement of any local land use ordinances or regulations giving effect to such standards.

6.3 FLOOD LANDS ACQUISITION. The commission shall have power to acquire the fee or any lesser interest in lands and improvements thereon within the area of a flood plain for the purpose of restricting the use of such property so as to minimize the flood hazard, converting property to uses appropriate to flood plain conditions, or preventing unwarranted constrictions that reduce the ability of the river channel to carry flood water. Any such action shall be in accord with the standards adopted and promulgated pursuant to Section 6.2.

6.4 FLOOD AND STREAM STAGE WARNINGS AND POSTING. The commission may cause lands particularly subject to flood to be posted with flood hazard warnings, and may from time to time cause flood advisory notices to be published and circulated as conditions may warrant.

ARTICLE 7

WATERSHED MANAGEMENT

SECTION 7.1 WATERSHEDS GENERALLY. The commission shall promote sound practices of watershed management in the basin, including projects and facilities to retard runoff and waterflow and prevent soil erosion.

7.2 SOIL CONSERVATION AND FORESTRY. The commission may acquire, sponsor or operate facilities and projects to encourage soil conservation, prevent and control erosion, and to promote land reclamation and sound forestry practices.

7.3 FISH AND WILDLIFE. The commission may acquire, sponsor or operate projects and facilities for the maintenance and improvement of fish and wildlife habitats related to the water resources of the basin.

7.4 COOPERATIVE PLANNING AND OPERATION.

(a) The commission shall cooperate with the appropriate agencies of the signatory parties and with other public and private agencies in the planning and effectuation of a coordinated program of facilities and projects authorized by this article.

(b) The commission shall not operate any such project or facility unless it has first found and determined that no other suitable unit or agency of government is available to operate the same upon reasonable conditions, in accordance with the intent and purpose expressed in Section 1.5 of this compact.

[581]

ARTICLE 8

RECREATION

SECTION 8.1 DEVELOPMENT. The commission shall provide for the development of water related public sports and recreational facilities. The commission on its own account or in cooperation with a signatory party, political subdivision or any agency thereof, may provide for the construction, maintenance and administration of such facilities, subject to the provisions of Section 8.2 hereof.

8.2 COOPERATIVE PLANNING AND OPERATION.

(a) The commission shall cooperate with the appropriate agencies of the signatory parties and with other public and private agencies in the planning and effectuation of a coordinated program of facilities and projects authorized by this article.

(b) The commission shall not operate any such project or facility unless it has first found and determined that no other suitable unit or agency of government is available to operate the same upon reasonable conditions, in accordance with the intent and purpose expressed in Section 1.5 of this compact.

8.3 OPERATION AND MAINTENANCE. The commission, within limits prescribed by this article, shall:

(a) Encourage activities of other public agencies having water related recreational interests and assist in the coordination thereof;

(b) Recommend standards for the development and administration of water related recreational facilities;

(c) Provide for the administration, operation and maintenance of recreational facilities owned or controlled by the commission and for the letting and supervision of private concessions in accordance with this article.

8.4 CONCESSIONS. The commission shall after notice and public hearing provide by regulation for the award of contracts for private concessions in connection with recreational facilities, including any renewal or extension thereof, upon sealed competitive bids after public advertisement therefor.

ARTICLE 9

HYDROELECTRIC POWER

SECTION 9.1 DEVELOPMENT. The waters of the Delaware River and its tributaries may be impounded and used by or under authority of the commission for the generation of hydroelectric power and hydroelectric energy, in accordance with the comprehensive plan.

9.2 POWER GENERATION. The commission may develop and operate, or authorize to be developed and operated, dams and related facilities and appurtenances for the purpose of generating hydroelectric power and hydroelectric energy.

9.3 TRANSMISSION. The commission may provide facilities for the transmission of hydroelectric power and hydroelectric energy produced by it where such facilities are not otherwise available upon reasonable terms, for the purpose of wholesale marketing of power and nothing herein shall be construed to authorize the commission to engage in the business of direct sale to consumers.

9.4 DEVELOPMENT CONTRACTS. The commission may after public notice and hearing enter into contracts on reasonable terms, consideration and duration under which public utilities or public agencies may develop hydroelectric power and hydroelectric energy through the use of dams, related facilities and appurtenances.

9.5 RATES AND CHARGES. Rates and charges fixed by the commission for power which is produced by its facilities shall be reasonable, nondiscriminatory, and just.

ARTICLE 10

REGULATION OF WITHDRAWALS AND DIVERSIONS

SECTION 10.1 POWER OF REGULATION. The commission may regulate and control withdrawals and diversions from surface waters and ground waters of the basin, as provided by this article. The commission may enter into agreements with the signatory parties relating to the exercise of such power or regulation or control and may delegate to any of them such powers of the commission as it may deem necessary or desirable.

10.2 DETERMINATION OF PROTECTED AREAS. The commission may from time to time after public hearing upon due notice determine and delineate such areas within the basin wherein the demands upon supply made by water users have developed or threaten to develop to such a degree as to create a water shortage or to impair or conflict with the requirements or effectuation of the comprehensive plan, and any such areas may be designated as "protected areas." The commission, whenever it determines that such shortage no longer exists, shall terminate the protected status of such area and shall give public notice of such termination.

10.3 WITHDRAWAL PERMITS. In any protected areas so determined and delineated, no person, firm, corporation or other entity shall divert or withdraw water for domestic, municipal, agricultural or industrial uses in excess of such quantities as the commission may prescribe by general regulation, except (i) pursuant to a permit granted under this article, or (ii) pursuant to a permit or approval heretofore granted under the laws of any of the signatory states.

10.4 EMERGENCY. In the event of a drought or other condition which may cause an actual and immediate shortage of available water supply within the basin, or within any part thereof, the commission may, after public hearing, determine and delineate the area of such shortage and declare a water supply emergency therein. For the duration of such emergency as determined by the commission no person, firm, corporation or other public or private entity shall divert or withdraw water for any purpose, in excess of such quantities as the commission may prescribe by general regulation or authorize by special permit granted hereunder.

10.5 STANDARDS. Permits shall be granted, modified or denied as the case may be so as to avoid such depletion of the natural stream flows and ground waters in the protected area or in an emergency area as will adversely affect the comprehensive plan or the just and equitable interests and rights of other lawful users of the same source, giving due regard to the need to balance and reconcile alternative and conflicting uses in the event of an actual or threatened shortage of water of the quality required.

10.6 JUDICIAL REVIEW. The determinations and delineations of the commission pursuant to Section 10.2 and the granting, modification or denial of permits pursuant to Section 10.3 through 10.5 shall be subject to judicial review in any court of competent jurisdiction.

10.7 MAINTENANCE OF RECORDS. Each state shall provide for the maintenance and preservation of such records of authorized diversions and withdrawals and the annual volume thereof as the commission shall prescribe. Such records and supplementary reports shall be furnished to the commission at its request.

10.8 EXISTING STATE SYSTEMS. Whenever the commission finds it necessary or desirable to exercise the powers conferred by this article any diversion or withdrawal permits authorized or issued under the laws of any of the signatory states shall be superseded to the extent of any conflict with the control and regulation exercised by the commission.

ARTICLE 11

INTERGOVERNMENTAL RELATIONS

SECTION 11.1 FEDERAL AGENCIES AND PROJECTS. For the purposes of avoiding conflicts of jurisdiction and of giving full effect to the commission as a regional agency of the signatory parties, the following rules shall govern federal projects affecting the water resources of the basin, subject in each case to the provisions of Section 1.4 of this compact:

(a) The planning of all projects related to powers delegated to the commission by this compact shall be undertaken in consultation with the commission;

(b) No expenditure or commitment shall be made for or on account of the construction, acquisition or operation of any project or facility nor shall it be deemed authorized, unless it shall have first been included by the commission in the comprehensive plan;

(c) Each federal agency otherwise authorized by law to plan, design, construct, operate or maintain any project or facility in or for the basin shall continue to have, exercise and discharge such authority except as specifically provided by this section.

11.2 STATE AND LOCAL AGENCIES AND PROJECTS. For the purposes of avoiding conflicts of jurisdiction and of giving full effect to the commission as a regional agency of the signatory parties, the following rules shall govern projects of the signatory states, their political subdivisions and public corporations affecting water resources of the basin:

(a) The planning of all projects related to powers delegated to the commission by this compact shall be undertaken in consultation with the commission;

(b) No expenditure or commitment shall be made for or on account of the construction, acquisition or operation of any project or facility unless it shall have first been included by the commission in the comprehensive plan;

(c) Each state and local agency otherwise authorized by law to plan, design, construct, operate or maintain any project or facility in or for the basin shall continue to have, exercise and discharge such authority, except as specifically provided by this section.

11.3 RESERVED TAXING POWERS OF STATES. Each of the signatory parties reserves the right to levy, assess and collect fees, charges and taxes on or measured by the withdrawal or diversion of waters of the basin for use within the jurisdictions of the respective signatory parties.

11.4 PROJECT COSTS AND EVALUATION STANDARDS. The commission shall establish uniform standards and procedures for the evaluation, determination of benefits, and cost allocations of projects affecting the basin, and for the determination of project priorities, pursuant to the requirements of the comprehensive plan and its water resources program. The commission shall develop equitable cost sharing and reimbursement formulas for the signatory parties including:

(a) Uniform and consistent procedures for the allocation of project costs among purposes included in multiple-purpose programs;

(b) Contracts and arrangements for sharing financial responsibility among and with signatory parties, public bodies, groups and private enterprise, and for the supervision of their performance;

(c) Establishment and supervision of a system of accounts for reimbursable purposes and directing the payments and charges to be made from such accounts;

(d) Determining the basis and apportioning amounts (i) of reimbursable revenues to be paid signatory parties or their political subdivisions, and (ii) of payments in lieu of taxes to any of them.

11.5 COOPERATIVE SERVICES. The commission shall furnish technical services, advice and consultation to authorized agencies of the signatory parties with respect to the water resources of the basin, and each of the signatory parties pledges itself to provide technical and administrative services to the commission upon request, within the limits of available appropriations and to cooperate generally with the commission for the purposes of this compact, and the cost of such services may be reimbursable whenever the parties deem appropriate.

ARTICLE 12

CAPITAL FINANCING

SECTION 12.1 BORROWING POWER. The commission may borrow money for any of the purposes of this compact, and may issue its negotiable bonds and other evidences of indebtedness in respect thereto.

All such bonds and evidences of indebtedness shall be payable solely out of the properties and revenues of the commission without recourse to taxation. The bonds and other obligations of the commission, except as may be otherwise provided in the indenture under which they were issued, shall be direct and general obligations of the commission and the full faith and credit of the commission are hereby pledged for the prompt payment of the debt service thereon and for the fulfillment of all other undertakings of the commission assumed by it to or for the benefit of the holders thereof.

12.2 FUNDS AND EXPENSES. The purposes of this compact shall include without limitation thereto all costs of any project or facility or any part thereof, including interest during a period of construction and a reasonable time thereafter and any incidental expenses (legal, engineering, fiscal, financial consultant and other expenses) connected with issuing and disposing of the bonds; all amounts required for the creation of an operating fund, construction fund, reserve fund, sinking fund, or other special fund; all other expenses connected with the planning, design, acquisition, construction, completion, improvement or reconstruction of any facility or any part thereof; and reimbursement of advances by the commission or by others for such purposes and for working capital.

12.3 CREDIT EXCLUDED; OFFICERS, STATE AND MUNICIPAL. The commission shall have no power to pledge the credit of any signatory party, or of any county or municipality, or to impose any obligation for payment of the bonds upon any signatory party or any county or municipality. Neither the commissioners nor any person executing the bonds shall be liable personally on the bonds of the commission or be subject to any personal liability or accountability by reason of the issuance thereof.

12.4 FUNDING AND REFUNDING. Whenever the commission deems it expedient, it may fund and refund its bonds and other obligations whether or not such bonds and obligations have matured. It may provide for the issuance, sale or exchange of refunding bonds for the purpose of redeeming or retiring any bonds (including the payment of any premium, duplicate interest or cash adjustment required in connection therewith) issued by the commission or issued by any other issuing body, the proceeds of the sale of which have been applied to any facility acquired by the commission or which are payable out of the revenues of any facility acquired by the commission. Bonds may be issued partly to refund bonds and other obligations then outstanding, and partly for any other purpose of the commission. All provisions of this compact applicable to the issuance of bonds are applicable to refunding bonds and to the issuance, sale or exchange thereof.

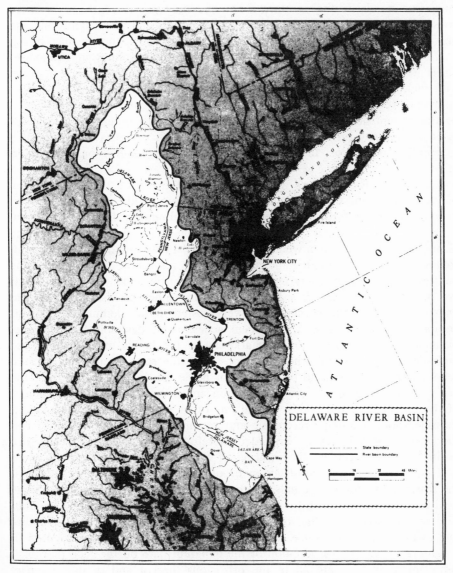

DELAWARE RIVER BASIN

12.5 BONDS; AUTHORIZATION GENERALLY. Bonds and other indebtedness of the commission shall be authorized by resolution of the commission. The validity of the authorization and issuance of any bonds by the commission shall not be dependent upon nor affected in any way by: (i) the disposition of bond proceeds by the commission or by contract, commitment or action taken with respect to such proceeds; or (ii) the failure to complete any part of the project for which bonds are authorized to be issued. The commission may issue bonds in one or more series and may provide for one or more consolidated bond issues, in such principal amounts and with such terms and provisions as the commission may deem necessary. The bonds may be secured by a pledge of all or any part of the property, revenues and franchises under its control. Bonds may be issued by the commission in such amount, with such maturities and in such denominations and form or forms, whether coupon or registered, as to both principal and interest, as may be determined by the commission. The commission may provide for redemption of bonds prior to maturity on such notice and at such time or times and with such redemption provisions, including premiums, as the commission may determine.

12.6 BONDS; RESOLUTIONS AND INDENTURES GENERALLY. The commission may determine and enter into indentures providing for the principal amount, date or dates, maturities, interest rate, denominations, form, registration, transfer, interchange and other provisions of the bonds and coupons and the terms and conditions upon which the same shall be executed, issued, secured, sold, paid, redeemed, funded and refunded. The resolution of the commission authorizing any bond or any indenture so authorized under which the bonds are issued may include all such covenants and other provisions other than any restriction on the regulatory powers vested in the commission by this compact as the commission may deem necessary or desirable for the issue, payment, security, protection or marketing of the bonds, including without limitation covenants and other provisions as to the rates or amounts of fees, rents and other charges to be charged or made for use of the facilities; the use, pledge, custody, securing, application and disposition of such revenues, of the proceeds of the bonds, and of any other moneys of the commission; the operation, maintenance, repair and reconstruction of the facilities and the amounts which may be expended therefor; the sale, lease or other disposition of the facilities; the insuring of the facilities and of the revenues derived therefrom; the construction or other acquisition of other facilities; the issuance of additional bonds or other indebtedness; the rights of the bondholders and of any trustee for the bondholders upon default by the commission or otherwise; and the modification of the provisions of the indenture and of the bonds. Reference on the face of the bonds to such resolution or indenture by its date of adoption or the apparent date on the face thereof is sufficient to incorporate all of the provisions thereof and of this compact into the body of the bonds and their appurtenant coupons. Each taker and subsequent holder of the bonds or coupons, whether the coupons are attached to or detached from the bonds, has recourse to all of the provisions of the indenture and of this compact and is bound thereby.

12.7 MAXIMUM MATURITY. No bond or its terms shall mature in more than fifty years from its own date and in the event any authorized issue is divided into two or more series or divisions, the maximum maturity date herein authorized shall be calculated from the date on the face of each bond separately, irrespective of the fact that different dates may be prescribed for the bonds of each separate series or division of any authorized issue.

12.8 TAX EXEMPTION. All bonds issued by the commission under the provisions of this compact and the interest thereof shall at all times be free and exempt from all taxation by or under authority of any of the signatory parties, except for transfer, inheritance and estate taxes.

12.9 INTEREST. Bonds shall bear interest at a rate of not to exceed six percent per annum, payable annually or semi-annually.

12.10 PLACE OF PAYMENT. The commission may provide for the payment of the principal and interest of bonds at any place or places within or without the signatory states, and in any specified lawful coin or currency of the United States of America.

12.11 EXECUTION. The commission may provide for the execution and authentication of bonds by the manual, lithographed or printed facsimile signature of officers of the commission, and by additional authentication by a trustee or fiscal agent appointed by the commission. If any of the officers whose signatures or counter signatures appear upon the bonds or coupons cease to be officers before the delivery of the bonds or coupons, their signatures or counter signatures are nevertheless valid and of the same force and effect as if the officers had remained in office until the delivery of the bonds and coupons.

12.12 HOLDING OWN BONDS. The commission shall have power out of any funds available therefor to purchase its bonds and may hold, cancel or resell such bonds.

12.13 SALE. The commission may fix terms and conditions for the sale or other disposition of any authorized issue of bonds. The commission may sell bonds at less than their par or face value but no issue of bonds may be sold at an aggregate price below the par or face value thereof if such sale would result in a net interest cost to the commission calculated upon the entire issue so sold of more than six percent per annum payable semi-annually, according to standard tables of bond values. All bonds issued and sold for cash pursuant to this act shall be sold on sealed proposals to the highest bidder. Prior to such sale, the commission shall advertise for bids by publication of a notice of sale not less than ten days prior to the date of sale, at least once in a newspaper of general circulation printed and published in New

York City carrying municipal bond notices and devoted primarily to financial news. The commission may reject any and all bids submitted and may thereafter sell the bonds so advertised for sale at private sale to any financially responsible bidder under such terms and conditions as it deems most advantageous to the public interest, but the bonds shall not be sold at a net interest cost calculated upon the entire issue so advertised, greater than the lowest bid which was rejected. In the event the commission desires to issue its bonds in exchange for an existing facility or portion thereof, or in exchange for bonds secured by the revenues of an existing facility, it may exchange such bonds for the existing facility or portion thereof or for the bonds so secured, plus an additional amount of cash, without advertising such bonds for sale.

12.14 NEGOTIABILITY. All bonds issued under the provisions of this compact are negotiable instruments, except when registered in the name of a registered owner.

12.15 LEGAL INVESTMENTS. Bonds of the commission shall be legal investments for savings banks, fiduciaries and public funds in each of the signatory states.

12.16 VALIDATION PROCEEDINGS. Prior to the issuance of any bonds, the commission may institute a special proceeding to determine the legality of proceedings to issue the bonds and their validity under the laws of any of the signatory parties. Such proceeding shall be instituted and prosecuted in rem and the judgment rendered therein shall be conclusive against all persons whomsoever and against each of the signatory parties.

12.17 RECORDING. No indenture need be recorded or filed in any public office, other than the office of the commission. The pledge of revenues provided in any indenture shall take effect forthwith as provided therein and irrespective of the date of receipts of such revenues by the commission or the indenture trustee. Such pledge shall be effective as provided in the indenture without physical delivery of the revenues to the commission or to the indenture trustee.

12.18 PLEDGED REVENUES. Bond redemption and interest payments shall, to the extent provided in the resolution or indenture, constitute a first, direct and exclusive charge and lien on all such rates, rents, tolls, fees and charges and other revenues and interest thereon received from the use and operation of the facility, and on any sinking or other funds created therefrom. All such rates, rents, tolls, fees, charges and other revenues, together with interest thereon, shall constitute a trust fund for the security and payment of such bonds and except as and to the extent provided in the indenture with respect to the payment therefrom of expenses for other purposes including administration, operation, maintenance, improvements or extensions of the facilities or other purposes shall not be used or pledged for any other purpose so long as such bonds, or any of them, are outstanding and unpaid.

12.19 REMEDIES. The holder of any bond may for the equal benefit and protection of all holders of bonds similarly situated: (a) by mandamus or other appropriate proceedings require and compel the performance of any of the duties imposed upon the commission or assumed by it, its officers, agents or employees under the provisions of any indenture, in connection with the acquisition, construction, operation, maintenance, repair, reconstruction or insurance of the facilities, or in connection with the collection, deposit, investment, application and disbursement of the rates, rents, tolls, fees, charges and other revenues derived from the operation and use of the facilities, or in connection with the deposit, investment and disbursement of the proceeds received from the sale of bonds; or (b) by action or suit in a court of competent jurisdiction of any signatory party require the commission to account as if it were the trustee of an express trust, or enjoin any acts or things which may be unlawful or in violation of the rights of the holders of the bonds. The enumeration of such rights and remedies does not, however, exclude the exercise or prosecution of any other rights or remedies available to the holders of bonds.

12.20 CAPITAL FINANCING BY SIGNATORY PARTIES; GUARANTEES.

(a) The signatory parties will provide such capital funds required for projects of the commission as may be authorized by their respective statutes in accordance with a cost sharing plan prepared pursuant to Article 11 of this compact; but nothing in this section shall be deemed to impose any mandatory obligation on any of the signatory parties other than such obligations as may be assumed by a signatory party in connection with a specific project or facility.

(b) Bonds of the commission, notwithstanding any other provision of this compact, may be executed and delivered to any duly authorized agency of any of the signatory parties without public offering and may be sold and resold with or without the guaranty of such signatory party, subject to and in accordance with the constitutions of the respective signatory parties.

(c) The commission may receive and accept, and the signatory parties may make, loans, grants, appropriations, advances and payments of reimbursable or non-reimbursable funds or property in any form for the capital or operating purposes of the commission.

ARTICLE 13

PLAN, PROGRAM AND BUDGETS

SECTION 13.1 COMPREHENSIVE PLAN. The commission shall develop and adopt, and may from time to time review and revise, a comprehensive plan for the immediate and long range development and use of the water resources of the basin. The plan shall include all public and private projects and facilities which are required, in the judgment of the commission, for the optimum planning, development, conservation, utilization, management and control of the water resources of the basin to meet present and future needs; provided that the plan shall include any projects required to conform with any present or future decree or judgment of any court of competent jurisdiction. The commission may adopt a comprehensive plan or any revision thereof in such part or parts as it may deem appropriate, provided that before the adoption of the plan or any part or revision thereof the commission shall consult with water users and interested public bodies and public utilities and shall consider and give due regard to the findings and recommendations of the various agencies of the signatory parties and their political subdivisions. The commission shall conduct public hearings with respect to the comprehensive plan prior to the adoption of the plan or any part of the revision thereof.

13.2 WATER RESOURCES PROGRAM. The commission shall annually adopt a water resources program, based upon the comprehensive plan, consisting of the projects and facilities which the commission proposes to be undertaken by the commission and by other authorized governmental and private agencies, organizations and persons during the ensuing six years or such other reasonably foreseeable period as the commission may determine. The water resources program shall include a systematic presentation of:

1) the quantity and quality of water resources needs for such period;

2) the existing and proposed projects and facilities required to satisfy such needs, including all public and private projects to be anticipated;

3) a separate statement of the projects proposed to be undertaken by the commission during such period.

13.3 ANNUAL CURRENT EXPENSE AND CAPITAL BUDGETS.

(a) The commission shall annually adopt a capital budget including all capital projects it proposes to undertake or continue during the budget period containing a statement of the estimated cost of each project and the method of financing thereof.

(b) The commission shall annually adopt a current expense budget for each fiscal year. Such budget shall include the commission's estimated expenses for administration, operation, maintenance and repairs, including a separate statement thereof for each project, together with its cost allocation. The total of such expenses shall be balanced by the commission's estimated revenues from all sources, including the cost allocations undertaken by any of the signatory parties in connection with any project. Following the adoption of the annual current expense budget by the commission, the executive director of the commission shall:

1) certify to the respective signatory parties the amounts due in accordance with existing cost sharing established for each project; and

2) transmit certified copies of such budget to the principal budget officer of the respective signatory parties at such time and in such manner as may be required under their respective budgetary procedures. The amount required to balance the current expense budget in addition to the aggregate amount of item (1) above and all other revenues available to the commission shall be apportioned equitably among the signatory parties by unanimous vote of the commission, and the amount of such apportionment to each signatory party shall be certified together with the budget.

(c) The respective signatory parties covenant and agree to include the amounts so apportioned for the support of the current expense budget in their respective budgets next to be adopted, subject to such review and approval as may be required by their respective budgetary processes. Such amounts shall be due and payable to the commission in quarterly installments during its fiscal year, provided that the commission may draw upon its working capital to finance its current expense budget pending remittances by the signatory parties.

THE RURAL ELECTRIFICATION ACT*
May 20, 1936

The Rural Electrification Administration (REA) was given the force of law one year after it had been established by Executive order. Representative Sam Rayburn of Texas joined Senator George Norris in sponsoring the legislation.

Few governmental programs have done so much to change literally the way of life of rural America. Under the law, farmers organized cooperative associations to distribute electricity to members, using capital supplied by the REA at low interest loans. The REA cooperatives have been universally successful. At their beginning only a small portion of the farms in the country were served by electricity, but today some 99 percent are served.

The cooperative electric associations qualified for preference in buying power generated at federal dams, but, from the beginning, most REA power has been furnished by private power companies.

An Act to provide for rural electrification, and for other purposes.

Be it enacted by the Senate and House of Representatives of the United States of America in Congress assembled, That there is hereby created and established an agency of the United States to be known as the "Rural Electrification Administration", all of the powers of which shall be exercised by an Administrator, who shall be appointed by the President, by and with the advice and consent of the Senate, for a term of ten years, and who shall receive a salary of $10,000 per year. This Act may be cited as the "Rural Electrification Act of 1936".

SEC. 2. The Administrator is authorized and empowered to make loans in the several States and Territories of the United States for rural electrification and the furnishing of electric energy to persons in rural areas who are not receiving central station service, as hereinafter provided; to make, or cause to be made, studies, investigations, and reports concerning the condition and progress of the electrification of rural areas in the several States and Territories; and to publish and disseminate information with respect thereto.

SEC. 3. (a) The Reconstruction Finance Corporation is hereby authorized and directed to make loans to the Administrator, upon his request approved by the President, not exceeding in aggregate amount $50,000,000 for the

*49 *Statutes at Large,* 1363–67.

fiscal year ending June 30, 1937, with interest at 3 per centum per annum upon the security of the obligations of borrowers from the Administrator appointed pursuant to the provisions of this Act or from the Administrator of the Rural Electrification Administration established by Executive Order Numbered 7037: *Provided,* That no such loan shall be in an amount exceeding 85 per centum of the principal amount outstanding of the obligations constituting the security therefor: *And provided further,* That such obligations incurred for the purpose of financing the construction and operation of generating plants, electric transmission and distribution lines, or systems shall be fully amortized over a period not to exceed twenty-five years, and that the maturity of such obligations incurred for the purpose of financing the wiring of premises and the acquisition and installation of electrical and plumbing appliances and equipment shall not exceed two-thirds of the assured life thereof and not more than five years. The Administrator is hereby authorized to make all such endorsements, to execute all such instruments, and to do all such acts and things as shall be necessary to effect the valid transfer and assignment to the Reconstruction Finance Corporation of all such obligations.

(b) There is hereby authorized to be appropriated, out of any money in the Treasury not otherwise appropriated, for the fiscal year ending June 30, 1938, and for each of the eight years thereafter, the sum of $40,000,000 for the purposes of this Act as hereinafter provided.

(c) Fifty per centum of the annual sums herein made available or appropriated for the purposes of this Act shall be allotted yearly by the Administrator for loans in the several States in the proportion which the number of their farms not then receiving central station electric service bears to the total number of farms of the United States not then receiving such service. The Administrator shall, within ninety days after the beginning of each fiscal year, determine for each State and for the United States the number of farms not then receiving such service.

(d) The remaining 50 per centum of such annual sums shall be available for loans in the several States and in the Territories, without allotment as hereinabove provided, in such amounts for each State and Territory as, in the opinion of the Administrator, may be effectively employed for the purposes of this Act, and to carry out the provisions of section 7: *Provided, however,* That not more than 10 per centum of said unallotted annual sums may be employed in any one State, or in all of the Territories.

(e) If any part of the annual sums made available for the purposes of this Act shall not be loaned or obligated during the fiscal year for which such sums are made available, such unexpended or unobligated sums shall be available for loans by the Administrator in the following year or years without allotment: *Provided, however,* That not more than 10 per centum of said sums may be employed in any one State or in all of the Territories: *And provided further,* That no loans shall be made by the Reconstruction Finance Corporation to the Administrator after June 30, 1937.

(f) All moneys representing payments of principal and interest on loans made by the Administrator under this Act shall be covered into the Treasury as miscellaneous receipts, except that any such moneys representing payments of principal and interest on obligations constituting the security for loans made by the Reconstruction Finance Corporation to the Administrator shall be paid to the Reconstruction Finance Corporation in payment of such loans.

SEC. 4. The Administrator is authorized and empowered, from the sums hereinbefore authorized, to make loans to persons, corporations, States, Territories, and subdivisions and agencies thereof, municipalities, peoples utility districts and cooperative nonprofit, or limited-dividend associations organized under the laws of any State or Territory of the United States, for the purpose of financing the construction and operation of generating plants, electric transmission and distribution lines or systems for the furnishing of electric energy to persons in rural areas who are not receiving central station service: *Provided, however,* That the Administrator, in making such loans, shall give preference to States, Territories, and subdivisions and agencies thereof, municipalities, peoples utility districts, and cooperative, nonprofit, or limited dividend associations, the projects of which comply with the requirements of this Act. Such loans shall be on such terms and conditions relating to the expenditure of the moneys loaned and the security therefor as the Administrator shall determine and may be made payable in whole or in part out of income: *Provided, however,* That all such loans shall be self-liquidating within a period of not to exceed twenty-five years, and shall bear interest at a rate equal to the average rate of interest payable by the United States of America on its obligations, having a maturity of ten or more years after the dates thereof, issued during the last preceding fiscal year in which any such obligations were issued: *Provided further,* That no loan for the construction, operation, or enlargement of any generating plant shall be made unless the consent of the State authority having jurisdiction in the premises is first obtained. Loans under this section and section 5 shall not be made unless the Administrator finds and certifies that in his judgment the security therefor is reasonably adequate and such loan will be repaid within the time agreed.

SEC. 5. The Administrator is authorized and empowered, from the sums hereinbefore authorized, to make loans for the purpose of financing the wiring of the premises of persons in rural areas and the acquisition and installation of electrical and plumbing appliances and equipment. Such loans may be made to any of the borrowers of funds loaned under the provisions of section 4, or to any person, firm, or corporation supplying or installing the said wiring, appliances, or equipment. Such loans shall be for such terms, subject to such conditions, and so secured as reasonably to assure repayment thereof, and shall be at a rate of interest equal to the average rate of interest payable by the United States of America on its obligations, having a maturity of ten or more years after the dates thereof, issued during the last preceding fiscal year in which any such obligations were issued.

SEC. 6. For the purpose of administering this Act and for the purpose of making the studies, investigations, publications, and reports herein provided for, there is hereby authorized to be appropriated, out of any money in the Treasury not otherwise appropriated, such sums as shall be necessary.

SEC. 7. The Administrator is authorized and empowered to bid for and purchase at any foreclosure or other sale, or otherwise to acquire, property pledged or mortgaged to secure any loan made pursuant to this Act; to pay the purchase price and any costs and expenses incurred in connection therewith from the sums authorized in section 3 of this Act; to accept title to any property so purchased or acquired in the name of the United States of America; to operate or lease such property for such period as may be deemed necessary or advisable to protect the investment therein, but not to exceed five years after the acquisition thereof; and to sell such property so purchased or acquired, upon such terms and for such consideration as the Administrator shall determine to be reasonable.

No borrower of funds under section 4 shall, without the approval of the Administrator, sell or dispose of its property, rights, or franchises, acquired under the provisions of this Act, until any loan obtained from the Rural Electrification Administration, including all interest and charges, shall have been repaid.

SEC. 8. The administration of loans and contracts entered into by the Rural Electrification Administration established by Executive Order Numbered 7037, dated May 11, 1935, may be vested by the President in the Administrator authorized to be appointed by this Act; and in such event the provisions of this Act shall apply to said loans and contracts to the extent that said provisions are not inconsistent therewith. The President may transfer to the Rural Electrification Administration created by this Act the jurisdiction and control of the records, property (including office equipment), and personnel used or employed in the exercise and performance of the functions of the Rural Electrification Administration established by such Executive order.

SEC. 9. This Act shall be administered entirely on a nonpartisan basis, and in the appointment of officials, the selection of employees, and in the promotion of any such officials or employees, no political test or qualification shall be permitted or given consideration, but all such appointments and promotions shall be given and made on the basis of merit and efficiency. If the Administrator herein provided for is found by the President of the United

States to be guilty of a violation of this section, he shall be removed from office by the President, and any appointee or selection of officials or employees made by the Administrator who is found guilty of a violation of this Act shall be removed by the Administrator.

SEC. 10. The Administrator shall present annually to the Congress not later than the 20th day of January in each year a full report of his activities under this Act.

SEC. 11. In order to carry out the provisions of this Act the Administrator may accept and utilize such voluntary and uncompensated services of Federal, State, and local officers and employees as are available, and he may without regard to the provisions of civil-service laws applicable to officers and employees of the United States appoint and fix the compensation of attorneys, engineers, and experts, and he may, subject to the civil-service laws, appoint such other officers and employees as he may find necessary and prescribe their duties. The Administrator is authorized, from sums appropriated pursuant to section 6, to make such expenditures (including expenditures for personal services; supplies and equipment; lawbooks and books of reference; directories and periodicals; travel expenses; rental at the seat of government and elsewhere; the purchase, operation, or maintenance of passenger-carrying vehicles; and printing and binding) as are appropriate and necessary to carry out the provisions of this Act.

SEC. 12. The Administrator is authorized and empowered to extend the time of payment of interest or principal of any loans made by the Administrator pursuant to this Act: *Provided, however,* That with respect to any loan made under section 4, the payment of interest or principal shall not be extended more than five years after such payment shall have become due, and with respect to any loan made under section 5, the payment of principal or interest shall not be extended more than two years after such payment shall have become due: *And provided further,* That the provisions of this section shall not apply to any obligations or the security therefor which may be held by the Reconstruction Finance Corporation under the provisions of section 3.

SEC. 13. As used in this Act the term "rural area" shall be deemed to mean any area of the United States not included within the boundaries of any city, village, or borough having a population in excess of fifteen hundred inhabitants, and such term shall be deemed to include both the farm and nonfarm population thereof; the term "farm" shall be deemed to mean a farm as defined in the publications of the Bureau of the Census; the term "person" shall be deemed to mean any natural person, firm, corporation, or association; the term "Territory" shall be deemed to include any insular possession of the United States.

SEC. 14. If any provision of this Act, or the application thereof to any person or circumstances, is held invalid, the remainder of the Act and the application of such provision to other persons or circumstances shall not be affected thereby.

Approved, May 20, 1936.

FEDERAL POWER POLICY*
January 3, 1946

This memorandum coordinated power policy in the Department of the Interior under Secretary Harold L. Ickes and President Harry S. Truman.

MEMORANDUM ON POWER POLICY

To all Staffs of the Department of the Interior

The Congress over a 40-year period has enacted a large number of laws relating to electrical power activities. Most, but not all, of these acts relate specifically to the Department of the Interior. The others serve equally to fix the general policy that must guide all Interior Department staffs and officials in their administration of power programs. In recent years the Congress has greatly increased the responsibilities of the Department for the development and disposition of electrical energy. It is, therefore, appropriate to recapitulate the guiding principles which emerge from the individual acts of Congress, and which must govern the administrative actions of this Department in discharging its responsibilities relating to electrical power.

The primary objectives of the acts of Congress (excerpted in the attachment) may be summarized as follows:

1. Federal dams shall where feasible include facilities for generating electrical energy.

Reclamation Act of April 16, 1906; Act of July 25, 1912; the Tennessee Valley Authority Act of 1933; the Flood Control Acts of 1938, 1944 and 1945.

2. Preference in power sales shall be given to public agencies and cooperatives.

Reclamation Act of April 16, 1906; the "Raker Act" of December 19, 1913; Federal Water Power Act of 1920; Boulder Canyon Act of 1928; Tennessee Valley Authority Act of 1933; Rural Electrification Act of 1936; Bonneville Act of 1937; Fort Peck Act of 1938; Reclamation Project Act of 1939; Flood Control Act of 1944.

3. Power disposal shall be for the particular benefit of domestic and rural consumers.

---

*Memorandum on Power Policy to All Staffs of the Department of the Interior from Harold L. Ickes, Secretary of the Interior, Jan. 3, 1946.

Tennessee Valley Authority Act of 1933; Rural Electrification Act of 1936; Bonneville Act of 1937; Fort Peck Act of 1938.

4. Power shall be sold at the lowest possible rates consistent with sound business principles.

Tennessee Valley Authority Act of 1933; Bonneville Act of 1937; Fort Peck Act of 1938; Flood Control Act of 1944.

5. Power disposal shall be such as to encourage widespread use and to prevent monopolization.

Tennessee Valley Authority Act of 1933; Rural Electrification Act of 1936; Bonneville Act of 1937; Fort Peck Act of 1938; Flood Control Act of 1944.

These basic policies are prescribed by Congress. It is the job of the Department of the Interior to carry them out, and to see that the administration of its power programs will in fact secure these objectives. The following principles are designed to implement the congressional policy. They will guide all staffs and officials of the Department who deal with power.

I. Planning and Construction.

a. Hydroelectric generating facilities shall be designed and installed in all projects where feasible. The project shall have its own steam standby and reserve facilities where necessary to independent operation on an economical and efficient basis.

b. Facilities shall be designed and installed to provide the type of power and service required by public agencies and cooperatives.

c. Construction shall be economical and efficient.

d. Government hydroelectric plants within a region shall be integrated by transmission ties.

e. Transmission outlets to existing and potential wholesale markets shall be adequate to deliver power to every preferred customer within the region upon fair and reasonable terms. They must be owned and controlled by the Government unless privately-owned facilities should be made available upon terms which assure full accomplishment of the basic objectives of the congressional power policy and which do not reward the private company simply because of its strategic location or monopolistic position.

f. Allocations of costs on multiple-purpose projects shall not result in power consumers paying for facilities not fairly to be attributed to the operation of the power system, except as may be necessary to make the project feasible as required by law.

II. *Operation and Sales.*

a. Active assistance, from the very beginning of the planning and authorization of a project, shall be given to the organization of public agencies and cooperatives for the distribution of power in each project area. The statutory objectives are not attained by merely waiting for a preferred customer to come forward and offer to purchase the power.

b. Operations shall be economical and efficient.

c. Wholesale rate schedules shall be nondiscriminatory and shall be designed to bring power at the lowest possible rates to distributors that are principally serving domestic and rural consumers.

d. Resale rate and other provisions shall be included in wholesale contracts with distributors to insure that power is furnished to the ultimate consumer at the lowest possible rates, which shall reflect as nearly as may be the cost of the service.

e. Public agencies and cooperatives shall be encouraged to build diversified loads and markets and neither the operations nor the markets of these agencies or of the Government facilities shall be restricted by contracts or operating agreements which might serve to limit the widespread use of the power from the Federal project.

f. No contracts shall be made that operate to foreclose public agencies and cooperatives from obtaining power from the Government project. Contracts with these organizations shall recognize their preferential character and assure them full opportunity to secure the benefits of Federal power. Contracts with privately owned companies shall be limited in time and shall contain provisions for the cancellation or modification by the Government as necessary to ensure preference to public agencies and cooperatives.

g. Rates, contracts and financial data shall be made public.

h. A diversified development of the industries and resources of the region shall be given active encouragement in order to benefit the load factor and to promote the economic stability of the project as well as to aid in regional development.

i. Public agencies and cooperatives which are existing or potential customers of the Federal project shall be given every assistance in promoting sound programs and operations.

This list of guiding principles is not intended to be exhaustive but is designed to serve as the primary operating basis for attaining the objectives which Congress has prescribed for Federal power programs. These principles will guide all staffs and reviewing officials of the Department of the Interior who are administering power activities. The administration and review of these activities will be continued by the agencies and officials heretofore designated.

Harold L. Ickes
Secretary of the Interior

Attachment.

ACTS OF CONGRESS PROVIDING THE BASIS OF THE FEDERAL POWER POLICY

The Reclamation Act of April 16, 1906 (34 Stat. 117; 43 U.S.C. sec. 522): The Secretary of the Interior may lease surplus power from irrigation projects, "giving preference to municipal purposes." (Sec. 5).

Act of July 25, 1912 (37 Stat. 201; 33 U.S.C. sec. 609): Works desirable for development of water power authorized to be provided in all navigation dams "in order to make possible the economical future development of water power." (Sec. 12).

The "Raker Act" of December 19, 1913 (38 Stat. 242): Use of National park land granted to the City of San Francisco for the purpose of storing water for domestic use and developing power. (Sec. 1). City "prohibited from ever selling or letting to any corporation or individual, except a municipality or a municipal water district or irrigation district, the right to sell or sublet the water or the electric energy sold or given to it or him" by the City. (Sec. 6; see *U.S. v. San Francisco,* 310 U.S. 16 (1940)).

The Federal Water Power Act of June 10, 1920 (41 Stat. 1063; 16 U.S.C. sec. 800): Federal Power Commission "shall give preference to applications . . . by States and municipalities" for permits and licenses to build and operate works upon navigable waters. (Sec. 7).

Boulder Canyon Project Act of December 21, 1928 (45 Stat. 1057; 43 U.S. C. sec. 617d(c)): Contracts for use of hydroelectric energy to be let "in conformity with the policy expressed in the Federal Water Power Act as to conflicting applications." (Sec. 5(c)).

Tennessee Valley Authority Act of May 18, 1933 (48 Stat. 58, as amended; 16 U.S.C. sec. 831 *et seq.*): Surplus power "shall be considered primarily as for the benefit of the people of the section as a whole and particularly the domestic and rural consumers to whom the power can economically be made available, and accordingly that sale to and use by industry shall be a secondary purpose, to be utilized principally to secure a sufficiently high load factor and revenue returns which will permit domestic and rural use at the lowest

[603]

possible rates and in such manner as to encourage increased domestic and rural use of electricity." (Sec. 11).

Rural Electrification Act of May 20, 1936 (49 Stat. 1363; 7 U.S.C. sec. 901 *et seq.*): Preference to be accorded public and cooperative bodies seeking loans under terms of Act. (Sec. 4).

Bonneville Act of August 20, 1937 (50 Stat. 731; 16 U.S.C. sec. 832 *et seq.*): To prevent monopolization of electric energy generated at Bonneville project, transmission facilities to be constructed and operated. (Sec. 2 (b)). Preference and priority to be accorded to public bodies and cooperatives to insure operation of project "for the benefit of the general public, and particularly of domestic and rural consumers." (Sec. 4 (a)). Policy of Congress declared to preserve preferential status of public bodies and cooperatives and to give people within economic transmission range reasonable time and opportunity to organize such bodies for purchase of electric energy. (Sec. 4 (d)). Contracts with privately owned utilities to contain cancellation clauses to permit power to be diverted to preferred customers. (Sec. 5 (a) (2)).

Fort Peck Act of May 18, 1938 (52 Stat. 403; 16 U.S.C. sec. 833 *et seq.*): To encourage widest possible use of electric energy and prevent monopolization thereof by limited groups, transmission lines and appurtenant facilities to be provided at Fort Peck project. (Sec. 2 (b)). Preference to be accorded public bodies and cooperatives to insure operation of project "for the benefit of the general public, and particularly of domestic and rural consumers." (Sec. 4).

Flood Control Act of June 28, 1938 (52 Stat. 1215; 33 U.S.C. sec. 701j): Penstocks to be installed in any dam "adapted to possible future use in the development of hydroelectric power." (Sec. 4).

Reclamation Project Act of August 4, 1939 (53 Stat. 1187; 43 U.S.C. sec. 485h(c)): Preference in sales of power to be given public bodies and to cooperatives and other nonprofit organizations financed in whole or part by the Rural Electrification Administration. (Sec. 9(c)).

Flood Control Act of December 22, 1944 (58 Stat. 887): Surplus electric energy developed at reservoir projects to be disposed of "in such a manner as to encourage the most widespread use thereof at the lowest possible rates to consumers consistent with sound business principles;" preference to be given in sale of such energy to "public bodies and cooperatives;" and, where necessary, transmission lines and related facilities to be constructed or acquired to make such energy available, in wholesale quantities, "on fair and reasonable terms and conditions to facilities owned by the Federal Government, public bodies, cooperatives and privately owned companies." (Sec. 5). Penstocks to be installed in any dam adapted to possible future use in the development of hydroelectric power. (Sec. 10).

Flood Control Act of March 2, 1945 (P.L. 14, 79th Cong.): Penstocks adapted to possible future use in the development of hydroelectric power to be installed in any dam when approved by the Secretary of War upon recommendation of Chief of Engineers and of Federal Power Commission; such recommendations to be based upon consideration of the proper utilization and conservation in the public interest of the resources of the region. (Sec. 2).

ROANOKE RAPIDS FOR PRIVATE POWER*
March 16, 1953

This decision in a case in which Oscar Chapman, President Truman's last Secretary of the Interior, sought to set aside a Federal Power Commission ruling, was a major setback for public power development. The Power Commission had granted a license to a private power company to develop a site on the Roanoke River. Secretary Chapman unsuccessfully sought to set the order aside on the grounds that the Congress had authorized development by the Federal Government of two sites on the Roanoke River, and consequently envisioned full federal development of all power sites on the river.

CHAPMAN v. FEDERAL POWER COMMISSION

SYLLABUS

United States ex rel. Chapman, Secretary of the Interior, *v.* Federal Power Commission et al. No. 28. Certiorari to the United States Court of Appeals for the Fourth Circuit.

Argued October 22, 1952.—Decided March 16, 1953.

The Corps of Engineers recommended to Congress a comprehensive plan for the development of the Roanoke River Basin for flood-control, power, and other purposes; but it did not clearly recommend that all projects be constructed by the United States. The Federal Power Commission concurred in this recommendation. In the Flood Control Act of 1944, Congress approved the plan and specifically authorized two projects not at Roanoke Rapids. Subsequently, the Commission ordered issuance of a license to a private power company to construct a hydroelectric generating plant at Roanoke Rapids, N.C. *Held:*

1. Petitioners, the Secretary of the Interior and an association of nonprofit rural electric cooperatives, had standing to institute this proceeding under § 313 (b) of the Federal Power Act to set aside the Commission's order. . . .
2. Congress has not withdrawn, as to the Roanoke Rapids site, the jurisdiction of the Federal Power Commission to issue such a license. . . .
3. Under § 7 (b) of the Federal Power Act, the Commission's concurrence in the recommendation of the Corps of Engineers did not preclude the Commission from issuing such a license. . . .

191 F. 2d 796, affirmed.

The Federal Power Commission ordered issuance of a license to a private power company to construct a hydroelectric generating plant at Roanoke Rapids, N.C. 87 P. U. R. (N. S.) 469. The Court of Appeals denied a petition to set aside this order. 191 F. 2d 796. This Court granted certiorari. 343 U.S. 941. *Affirmed. . . .*

U.S. Reports, Vol. 345, 153–82.

OPINION OF THE COURT

Gregory Hankin argued the cause and filed a brief for petitioner in No. 28.

Robert Whitehead argued the cause and filed a brief for the Virginia REA Association et al., petitioners in No. 29.

Bradford Ross argued the cause for the Federal Power Commission, respondent. With him on the brief were *Willard W. Gatchell, John Mason* and *Howard E. Wahrenbrock.*

T. Justin Moore argued the cause for the Virginia Electric & Power Co., respondent. With him on the brief were *George D. Gibson* and *Patrick A. Gibson.*

Charles F. Rouse and *David W. Robinson* submitted on brief for the Carolina Power & Light Co., respondent.

Herbert B. Cohn submitted on brief for the Appalachian Electric Power Co., respondent.

Mr. JUSTICE FRANKFURTER delivered the opinion of the Court.

In these two cases, the Secretary of the Interior and an association of non-profit rural electric cooperatives have challenged the authority of the Federal Power Commission to grant to the respondent power company, VEPCO, a license to construct a hydroelectric generating station at Roanoke Rapids, North Carolina. They claim that Congress, by approving a comprehensive plan set out in the Flood Control Act of 1944 for improvement of the Roanoke River Basin, has withdrawn all eleven sites proposed for development in the plan, including Roanoke Rapids, from the licensing jurisdiction of the Commission and has reserved them for public construction. The underlying premise, that the plan approved by Congress presupposed federal development of all sites included in the plan, also underlies petitioners' other main contention here, that the Commission's concurrence in the plan constituted a determination by the Commission that the development of these water resources should be undertaken by the United States itself. Such a determination, they say, requires the Commission under § 7 (b) of the Federal Power Act, 41 Stat. 1067, as amended, 49 Stat. 842, 16 U. S. C. § 800 (b), to make investigations and submit its findings together with appropriate recommendations to Congress and in any event bars the Commission from approving applications for private construction of the project. Petitioners unsuccessfully raised these contentions, along with attacks on the Commission's findings not pressed here, before the Court of Appeals for the Fourth Circuit, which denied their petitions to set aside the Commission's order granting a license to VEPCO. *United States* v. *Federal Power Comm'n,* 191 F. 2d 796. We granted certiorari, 343 U.S. 941. The cases present questions of importance in that they involve a conflict of view between two agencies of the Government having duties in relation to the development of national water resources. Determination of the issues may affect a substantial number of important potential sites for the development of hydroelectric power. Cf. Rules Sup. Ct. 38 (5) (b).

Both here and in the court below, petitioners' standing to raise these issues has been questioned. The Secretary of the Interior points to his statutory duty to act as sole marketing agent of power developed at public hydroelectric projects and not required for the operation of the project; § 5 of the Flood Control Act of 1944 directs him to transmit and dispose of such power in a manner calculated to "encourage the most widespread use thereof at the lowest possible rates to consumers consistent with sound business principles." 58 Stat. 890, 16 U. S. C. § 825s. This provision, it is said, announces a congressional policy for the guidance of the Secretary that would be disturbed by the respondent company's plan; thus a specific interest of the Secretary, in addition to his more general duties relating to the conservation and utilization of the Nation's water resources, is said to be adversely affected by the Commission's order. The REA Association, an association of cooperatives, asserts that, as an organization of consumers entitled, along with "public bodies," to a preference in sales by the Secretary under § 5, it has a substantial interest in the development of low-cost power at the Roanoke Rapids site and consequently in the kind of instrumentality, public or private, to which power development at this site is committed. Respondents say, however, that decisions of policy in the construction of power projects have been entrusted to the Commission, or at most also to the Secretary of the Army, under whom the Corps of Engineers performs its statutory functions of making surveys and constructing public works, and that the interests of petitioners arise only after a public project has been constructed and the Secretary of the Army has determined that there is excess power to be distributed and sold.

We hold that petitioners have standing. Differences of view, however, preclude a single opinion of the Court as to both petitioners. It would not further clarification of this complicated specialty of federal jurisdiction, the solution of whose problems is in any event more or less determined by the specific circumstances of individual situations to set out the divergent grounds in support of standing in these cases.

Petitioners' main contention, that Congress has, by a series of enactments to be construed as part of an evolving assumption by the Federal Government of comprehensive authority over navigable waters, reserved the Roanoke Rapids site for public development and so has placed it beyond the licensing power of the Federal Power Commission, requires us to consider with some particularity the steps by which plans for the Roanoke Rapids project have unfolded. Petitioners' contention reduces itself to the claim that the authority of the agency to which Congress has delegated the responsibility for safeguarding the public interest in the private development of power resources has been revoked *pro tanto* by congressional action as to this particular site.

In 1927, the Army Engineers were authorized to make a specific survey of the Roanoke River by § 1 of the Rivers and Harbors Act, 44 Stat. 1010, 1015, which "adopted and authorized" enumerated "works of improvement" including "surveys in accordance with" H. R. Doc. No. 308, 69th Cong., 1st Sess. (1926). That document, a milestone in the development of integrated federal planning for the use of the Nation's water resources, had recommended surveys of a large number of streams throughout the country, including the Roanoke River, "either for the preparation of plans for improvement to be undertaken by the Federal Government alone or in connection with private enterprise, or to secure adequate data to insure that waterway developments by private enterprise would fit into a general plan for the full utilization of the water resources of a stream." H. R. Doc. No. 308, 69th Cong., 1st Sess 4. The detailed survey of the Roanoke River was transmitted to Congress in 1934; in it the Chief of Engineers stated that a comprehensive plan for navigation and power, flood control or irrigation "is not economically justifiable at the present time," H. R. Doc. No. 65, 74th Cong., 1st Sess. 2 (1935), and concurred in the judgment of the investigating engineer that "[t]here is no justification for any Federal expenditures for either flood control or power." *Id.*, at 53; cf. *id.*, at 14–15.

In 1936, Congress enacted the Flood Control Act of 1936, 49 Stat. 1570, defining the public interest in flood control as follows: "It is hereby recognized that destructive floods upon the rivers of the United States . . . constitute a menace to national welfare; that it is the sense of Congress that flood control on navigable waters or their tributaries is a proper activity of the Federal Government . . . ; that the Federal Government should improve or participate in the improvement of navigable waters or their tributaries, including watersheds thereof, for flood-control purposes if the benefits to whomsoever they may accrue are in excess of the estimated costs, and if the lives and social security of people are otherwise adversely affected." 49 Stat. 1570, 33 U. S. C. § 701a. In the same Act, the Secretary of War was authorized to continue surveys at a number of localities, including "Reservoirs in Roanoke and Tar Rivers, North Carolina."[1] § 7, Act of 1936, 49 Stat. 1596. In § 6 of the Act, Congress provided that "the Government shall not be deemed to have entered upon any project for the improvement of any waterway mentioned in this Act until the project for the proposed work shall have been adopted by law." 49 Stat. 1592.

Following a destructive flood on the Roanoke River in 1940, the House Committee on Flood Control adopted a resolution requesting reappraisal of the

---

[1] Section 6 of the Flood Control Act of 1938 authorized the Secretary of War to make surveys "for flood control" of the Smith River, a tributary of the Roanoke on which two of the eleven projects in the comprehensive Roanoke Basin plan are located. 52 Stat. 1223.

previous reports on the Roanoke River to determine "whether any improvements in the interests of flood control and allied purposes are advisable at this time." See H. R. Doc. No. 650, 78th Cong., 2d Sess. 12 (1944). A similar resolution was adopted later by the House Committee on Rivers and Harbors, see *ibid.,* and as a result, the Corps of Engineers submitted its recommendations in a report which became H. R. Doc. No. 650, 78th Cong., 2d Sess. (1944). This report recommended the comprehensive Roanoke Basin plan here in issue. The report proposed a system of eleven dams and reservoirs, eight of them on the Roanoke River, and recommended authorization of two of those projects, designated Buggs Island and Philpott, "as the initial step." *Id.,* at 2.

Petitioners rely most strongly on two features of this report for their claim that Congress has, by approving the plan outlined in the report, withdrawn all sites in the plan from the licensing jurisdiction of the Federal Power Commission. As the report moved up through the hierarchy of the Corps of Engineers, comments upon the plan were made by the different responsible officers. The detailed report of the investigating engineer estimated costs, including interest, on bases obviously contemplating federal financing. These figures were accepted in the comments of each forwarding officer. Further, the Chief of Engineers, in submitting the report, stated, "To safeguard the interests of navigation and flood control, the dams and power facilities should be constructed, operated, and maintained under the direction of the Secretary of War and the supervision of the Chief of Engineers." *Ibid.* Neither the reports nor the comments of subordinates had contained any such suggestion or any engineering or other reasons why such a recommendation might be made, and the Chief of Engineers gave no reasons for his suggestion. Further, it is not clear from the context that the statement referred to all the projects and not simply to the two dams to be authorized, that is, the ones with flood-control features, or even that the words "under the direction . . . and the supervision" precluded construction by a private applicant; indeed, the order here granting the license specifically requires the licensee to "operate its project in such a manner as the Chief of Engineers, Corps of Engineers, Department of the Army, or his authorized representative, may prescribe." We do not think these disconnected statements would justify us in saying that the report as it went to Congress plainly proposed that the Government construct all the projects in the plan. There are contrary indications in the report itself; particularly pertinent in the light of congressional practice is the strong emphasis put on the flood-control aspects of the two projects recommended for authorization. In any event, we do not have a recommendation for public construction that is clearly an integral part of the plan, and the decisive question is not what this or that isolated statement in the report or the comments thereon imply but how Congress may fairly be said to have received and read the report in the light of the legislative practice in relation to such public works.

It deserves mention that the Roanoke Rapids site, although comprehended in the plan and found to be the most desirable power site of all eleven units, was to be developed simply for the production of power. The District Engineer pointed out that the two projects recommended for early authorization would provide practically all the flood-control benefits to be derived from the plan; installations at the two sites, Buggs Island and Philpott, would "eliminate over 90 percent of the flood losses to the two main flood-damage areas in the Roanoke River Basin." *Id.,* at 88. At those two sites were to be built multiple-purpose reservoirs for flood control, water power, and low-water regulation, while at the other nine sites, with one minor exception, there were simply to be power projects.

As is customary, the Federal Power Commission was asked to comment on the proposal; by letter to the Chief of Engineers dated May 3, 1944, the Commission suggested some technical changes but concurred substantially in the recommendations of the Engineers, "that the comprehensive development of the Roanoke River Basin, in general accordance with the plans prepared therefor by the district engineer consisting of 11 dam and reservoir projects with power, is desirable and that the Buggs Island and Philpott projects would constitute a desirable initial step in the development of the Roanoke River Basin." *Id.,* at 4.

The report was presented to Congress while the bill that became the Flood Control Act of 1944 was under consideration; although the House had already closed its hearings, the Senate Report proposed amending the bill to include provision for the Roanoke Basin, recommending "approval of the comprehensive plan and authorization for construction of the Buggs Island and Philpott Reservoirs in accordance with the recommendations of the Chief of Engineers." S. Rep. No. 1030, 78th Cong., 2d Sess. 8.

The proposal was accepted, and § 10 of the Act contains a corresponding provision. It provides that "the following works of improvement . . . are hereby adopted and authorized." Included in an omnibus listing of such "works of improvement" is the following: "The general plan for the comprehensive development" of the Roanoke Basin recommended in H. R. Doc. No. 650 "is approved" and construction of Buggs Island and Philpott is "hereby authorized substantially in accordance with the recommendations of the Chief of Engineers in that report at an estimated cost of $36,140,000."[2]

It is this statutory language that petitioners say withdrew the Roanoke Rapids site from the licensing jurisdiction of the Commission. They ask us to read the word "approved" as a reservation of the site for public construction and, by

[2] The full text of the provisions, so far as they are relevant, is as follows:
"Sec. 10. That the following works of improvement for the benefit of navigation and the control of destructive flood waters and other purposes are hereby adopted and authorized in the interest of the national security and with a view toward providing an adequate reservoir of useful and worthy public works for the post-war construction program, to be prosecuted under the direction of the

necessary implication, a withdrawal of the site from the Commission's licensing authority. A flat "approval" of a plan clearly recommending public construction as an indispensable constituent of the plan might indeed have that effect, but, as indicated above, we do not find that the plan made any such recommendation.

A separate argument of petitioners is based in part on the language of a proviso commonly inserted in authorizations for flood-control surveys,[3] that the Government shall not be deemed to have entered upon a project until the project is "adopted by law." From this language petitioners infer that the Government's entry upon a project so as to preclude private construction occurs when Congress adopts a project, and they ask us to say that such adoption occurred here when Congress "approved" the plan comprehending the Roanoke Rapids site. We do not think the word "approval" carries the implication of "adoption" or "authorization" by its own force. Read together with other legislative action concerning water resources and with the history of federal activity in that regard, congressional "approval" without more[4] cannot be taken, we think, to indicate in this case more than a legislative finding that the proposed projects, no matter by whom they may be built, are desirable and consistent with congressional standards for the ordered development of the Nation's water resources. Such a finding has meaning in conveying the congressional purpose and expressing a congressional attitude. Concretely it means that Congress has adopted a basic policy for the systematic development of a river basin. Decision is made

---

Secretary of War and supervision of the Chief of Engineers in accordance with the plans in the respective reports hereinafter designated and subject to the conditions set forth therein: [Provisos omitted].

* * *

"ROANOKE RIVER BASIN

"The general plan for the comprehensive development of the Roanoke River Basin for flood control and other purposes recommended by the Chief of Engineers in House Document Numbered 650, Seventy-eighth Congress, second session, is approved and the construction of the Buggs Island Reservoir on the Roanoke River in Virginia and North Carolina, and the Philpott Reservoir on the Smith River in Virginia, are hereby authorized substantially in accordance with the recommendations of the Chief of Engineers in that report at an estimated cost of $36,140,000." 58 Stat. 891–892, 894.

[3] See, e.g., § 6 of the Flood Control Act of 1936, quoted p. 158, supra.

[4] There is little force in the argument that the words "adopted and authorized" in § 10, see note 2, supra, apply to the Roanoke Rapids site. Not only is the specific provision as to the Roanoke Basin to control over the general, but that which is adopted and authorized is not "the following plans" but "the following works of improvement," which patently refers to such projects as Buggs Island and Philpott, rather than to all sites named in a comprehensive plan. This answers that part of petitioners' argument which relies on the language of § 10 speaking of prosecution of the projects "under the direction of the Secretary of War" when "budgetary requirements" permit. As a matter of language, apart from all other considerations, the "works of improvement" to which such language refers is better read as the projects authorized rather than as all projects named in plans that were approved.

on such questions as the locations of projects, the purposes they are to serve, their approximate size and the desirable order of construction; because of the necessary interrelationship of many technical engineering and economic features of the several dams in a single river basin, early choice among possible alternatives is imperative. The policy chosen by Congress when it approves a plan is, in the first place, directed to Congress itself in its appropriating function.[5] Approval also tells the Federal Power Commission—the executant of congressional policy—how to exercise its authority in relation to the authorization of sites in the Roanoke Basin. The findings had utility in this case in the guidance it gave the Commission in determining whether a private applicant would adequately develop all the benefits that should be derived from the proposed site.

In so interpreting the language Congress has used, we gain some light from the action Congress has taken to set projects in motion following enactment of statutes "approving" a comprehensive plan and "authorizing" certain projects set out in the plan. For the Roanoke River Basin itself, although Buggs Island and Philpott were specifically "authorized" in the Flood Control Act of 1944, separate steps were taken by Congress to complete the authorization; "planning money" was appropriated, a "Definite Project Report" was received for Buggs Island, and then funds for construction of Buggs Island were appropriated. Equally illuminating is the procedure by which Congress recently set in motion plans to build a project "approved" exactly as was the Roanoke Rapids project. At approximately the same time as the engineering reports on the Roanoke River were submitted, a comparable report was submitted concerning the Savannah River, Georgia, and recommending a comprehensive plan much like the Roanoke River Basin plan. Like Buggs Island and Philpott in the Roanoke plan, Clark Hill in the Savannah plan was recommended for immediate authorization, "as the initial step." See H. R. Doc. No. 657, 78th Cong., 2d Sess. 6. As the demand for power increased, other projects included in the plan were to

---

[5] The Rules of both the Senate and the House in 1944, as now, called for previous choice of policy through authorization by law before any item of appropriations might be included in a general appropriations bill. Rule XVI, Senate Manual, S. Doc. No. 239, 77th Cong., 2d Sess. 20; Rule XXI, Rules of the House of Representatives, H. R. Doc. No. 812, 77th Cong., 2d Sess. 384. The importance of this distinction in the context of authorization of power projects is brought out in the following colloquy between a representative of the Corps of Engineers and Chairman Whittington of the House Committee on Public Works:

"The CHAIRMAN. . . . Is not the word 'approved' an authorization for the plan but without appropriation, or without an authorization for the appropriation?

"What is the difference between approving and authorizing a plan?

"Colonel GEE. We have never construed the approval of the plan to carry with it the authorization to construct the elements of that plan.

"The CHAIRMAN. Nor do we." Hearings before the House Committee on Public Works on H. R. 5472 (Title II), 81st Cong., 1st Sess. 42.

follow, the first to be the Hartwell site. The Senate Report accepted this recommendation, S. Rep. No. 1030, 78th Cong., 2d Sess. 9–10, just as it had the Roanoke Basin recommendation, and called for "approval of the comprehensive plan and authorization for construction of the Clark Hill project." *Id.,* at 10. Section 10 of the Flood Control Act of 1944 contains a corresponding provision. 58 Stat. 894. Thus, the background as well as the precise terms of the provisions relating to projects in the Savannah River plan are closely parallel to those relating to the Roanoke projects. Recently, when further construction on the Savannah River was proposed and authorization of Hartwell, the site next in line, was recommended, neither Congress nor the Engineers treated the earlier "approval" of the comprehensive plan as a final step making unnecessary other than automatic appropriations for Hartwell. Rather, hearings were held, see Hearings before House Committee on Public Works on H. R. 5472 (Title II), 81st Cong., 1st Sess. 37–85 (May 16, 1949), and a separate authorization for construction was included in the Rivers and Harbors Act of 1950, 64 Stat. 171.[6]

Respondents further point out that at the same time hearings were held on the Hartwell project, there were also hearings on further construction in the Roanoke Basin, and the Corps of Engineers proposed the authorization of Smith Mountain, a project with minor flood-control benefits but not next in line under the plan as approved in the Flood Control Act of 1944. That plan had put the Roanoke Rapids site here involved and the Gaston site ahead of Smith Mountain. The reason given by the Engineers for changing the order of construction was that private applications, including the application here, had been made or contemplated for the Roanoke Rapids and Gaston sites. While we do not attach weight to subsequent statements by the Engineers that the Flood Control Act of 1944 did not preclude private construction of some projects in the plan, it is pertinent to note that a Committee of Congress responsible for water resources legislation was informed that an application was pending for private construction. Whether or not the Committee agreed that the Flood Control Act of 1944 allowed private construction of projects comprehended in plans there approved, in fact no action was taken by it to prevent the Commission from proceeding to hear the VEPCO application, although the Committee learned that the application was pending over a year and a half before the order was handed down by the Commission.

Whatever light these subsequent proceedings in Congress afford, both as to

---

[6] The general enacting provision, § 204, 64 Stat. 170, is substantially the same as § 10 of the Flood Control Act of 1944, *supra,* note 2. The specific provision as to the Savannah River is as follows:

"SAVANNAH RIVER BASIN

"There is hereby authorized to be appropriated the sum of $50,000,000 for the construction of the Hartwell project in the general plan for the comprehensive development of the Savannah River Basin, approved in the Act of December 22, 1944, in addition to the authorization for project construction in the Act of December 22, 1944." 64 Stat. 171.

the Roanoke Basin and as to the comparable Hartwell site in the Savannah River plan, we find no solid ground for concluding that Congress has taken over the entire river basin for public development with such definiteness and finality so as to warrant us in holding that Congress has withdrawn as to this whole river basin its general grant of continuing authority to the Federal Power Commission to act as the responsible agent in exercising the licensing power of Congress. Extensive review of the need for integration of federal activities affecting waterways, see, *e. g.,* Report of Secretary of War Stimson, H. R. Doc. No. 929, 62d Cong., 3d Sess. 32–35 (1912), and of the breadth of authority granted to the Commission by Congress in response to that need is hardly necessary to establish the role of the Commission in hydroelectric power development. See, *e. g., First Iowa Coop.* v. *Power Comm'n,* 328 U.S. 152, 180, 181, and cases cited. From the time that the importance of power sites was brought to public and congressional consciousness during the administration of President Theodore Roosevelt, the significant development has been the devising of a general power policy instead of *ad hoc* action by Congress, with all the difficulties and dangers of local pressures and logrolling to which such action gave rise. See the Veto Messages of Presidents Roosevelt and Taft, *e. g.,* 36 Cong. Rec. 3071 (Muscle Shoals, Ala., 1903); 42 Cong. Rec. 4698 (Rainy River, 1908); H. R. Doc. No. 1350, 60th Cong., 2d Sess. (James River, 1909); H. R. Doc. No. 899, 62d Cong., 2d sess. (White River, 1912); S. Doc. No. 949, 62d Cong., 2d Sess. (Coosa River, 1912). It soon became clear that indispensable to a wise national policy was the creation of a commission with functions and powers comparable to those of the Interstate Commerce Commission in the field of transportation. It took the usual time for such a commission to come into being, and the process was step-by-step. Originally Congress entrusted its policy to a commission composed of three Cabinet officers. 41 Stat. 1063. An agency so burdened with other duties was naturally found inadequate as the instrument of these important water-power policies. And so, in 1930, the Commission was reorganized as an expert body of five full-time commissioners. 46 Stat. 797, 16 U. S. C. § 792. These enactments expressed general policies and granted broad administrative and investigative power, making the Commission the permanent disinterested expert agency of Congress to carry out these policies. Cf. 41 Stat. 1065, as amended, 49 Stat. 839, 16 U. S. C. § 797; 3 Report of the President's Water Resources Policy Comm'n 501 (1950).

A principal responsibility of the Commission has always been that of determining whether private construction is consistent with the public interest. See, *e. g.,* S. Rep. No. 180, 66th Cong., 1st Sess. 3. Express provision is made to charge the Commission with the task of deciding whether construction ought to be undertaken by the United States itself. 41 Stat 1067, as amended, 49 Stat. 842, 16 U. S. C. § 800 (b). Further, even if private construction is to be allowed, approval of private applications requires a determination that the proposed project is "best adapted to a comprehensive plan" for water resources development. 41 Stat. 1068, as amended, 49 Stat. 842, 16 U. S. C. § 803 (a). Thus, congressional approval of a comprehensive plan can be read, as we think it should in this case, simply as saying that a plan such as that here, recommended by the Corps of Engineers for the fullest realization of the potential benefits in the river basin, should be accepted by the Commission as the comprehensive plan to be used in the application of these statutory provisions. That "approval" as such does not reserve all projects in the plan for public construction is perhaps further indicated by the fact that when Congress has wished to reserve particular sites for public construction, it has chosen to say so. See 41 Stat. 1353, 45 Stat. 1012, 45 Stat. 1062.

Of course it is not for us to intimate a preference between private or public construction at this site. Nor are we even asked to review the propriety of the Commission's determination in this case that private construction is "in harmony with" the comprehensive plan for the Roanoke Basin. *Re Virginia Electric & Power Co.,* 87 P. U. R. (N. S.) 469, 483. We are simply asked to decide whether Congress has withdrawn the power to decide this question from the Commission. To conclude that Congress has done so by approving a general plan for development that may be, and in this case was, a plan for long-term development, would be to contract, by a tenuous chain of inferences, the broad standing powers of the Commission. Particularly relevant in this regard is the estimate that public development at this site would not in the normal course be undertaken for many years. See Examiner's Decision of March 17, 1950, R., I, 109. Congress was of course aware that, by granting a license to private enterprise, the Federal Power Commission would not commit the site permanently to private development and preclude all further congressional action. The Commission would, as it did here, simply express its judgment that, at the time, private development of the site was consistent with the general conception of the way in which the Roanoke River Basin should be developed. For, at any time short of the fifty years in which a site automatically becomes available to the Government without compensation, the Government may determine that the public interest makes it more desirable that the project be operated publicly and has the right then, by appropriate steps, to take over the project. 41 Stat. 1071, as amended, 49 Stat. 844, 16 U. S. C. § 807. The purpose of Congress would have to be much more clearly manifested to justify us in inferring that Congress revoked the Commission's power to decide whether a private license consonant with the general scheme of development for this river basin ought now to be granted in the public interest.

Our conclusion is in accord with the implications of the manifest reluctance of Congress to enter upon power projects having no flood-control or navigational benefits. It cannot be said that as unclear a term as "approval" was to have settled, for this entire river basin, a major controversy that has arisen again and again in connection with legislation authorizing public construction of hydroelectric projects. The declaration of policy in the Flood Control Act of 1936, *supra,* pp. 157–158, puts strong emphasis on the flood-control aspects of plans for sites that would also produce power; no change in this policy can be read into § 10 of the Flood Control Act of 1944. Cf., *e. g.,* 90 Cong. Rec. 4126; *id.,* at 4127. And the sponsor in the House of the Flood Control Act of 1944 stated in answer to a question: ". . . we have repeatedly stated during the debate that no project, reservoir, or dam, or other improvement is embraced in this bill unless it is primarily for flood control. If power can be developed as an incident, or if reclamation can be provided, they are cared for in the bill." 90 Cong. Rec. 4199; cf. *id.,* at 4202. In the light of this history and these specific declarations, it strains belief that "approval" of the comprehensive plan for the Roanoke Basin reserves all projects named in the plan for federal construction when the two projects that provided the chief flood-control features of the plan were the only ones specifically authorized.

Subordinate arguments are made, bearing partly on the power of the Commission to issue any license for private development and partly on the Commission's exercise of its power in granting this license. The arguments involve technical engineering and economic details which it would serve no useful purpose to canvass here. Once recognizing, as we do, that the Commission was not deprived of its power to entertain this application for a license, we cannot say, within the limited scope of review open to us, that the Commission's findings were not warranted. Judgment upon these conflicting engineering and economic issues is precisely that which the Commission exists to determine, so long as it cannot be said, as it cannot, that the judgment which it exercised had no basis in evidence and so was devoid of reason.

At the heart of these arguments is the fact that the Roanoke Rapids site is, under present estimates, the most desirable site for power in the Roanoke Basin. For that reason, as petitioners argue, removal of the Roanoke Rapids site from a government-operated system would result in loss to the Federal Government of the potential benefits of that site and a decrease, but only by the amount of the Roanoke Rapids profits, in the potential profits of the system as a whole. But it has never been suggested that such is the criterion under which the Commission is to determine whether a project ought to be undertaken by the United States, let alone that such considerations could demonstrate that Congress withdrew the Roanoke Rapids site from the licensing jurisdiction of the Commission. If it could be shown that the plan could not be executed successfully without the Roanoke Rapids site, it would be arguable that congressional approval of the plan presupposed that all units of the plan be centrally administered. The findings are to the contrary. The Commission has found that the proposed private project is consistent with the plan contained in the Flood Control Act of 1944, *Re Virginia Electric*

& *Power Co., supra,* at 483; that there is no reason to believe that the "interest of the public at large will not be fully protected and promoted" by the issuance of this license, *id.,* at 472; and that there was no showing that the Roanoke Rapids site would "at any time" be developed by the United States. *Id.,* at 483. Further, there is express recognition of the possibility that the site may be benefited by government projects in operation and consequently of the fact that VEPCO may be required to compensate the Government for any such "headwater benefits" conferred.[7] *Id.,* at 477–478.

Finally, we do not find merit in the contention that the Commission was required by § 7 (b) of the Federal Power Act to recommend public construction of the project.[8] As the report of the Corps of Engineers does not clearly recommend that all projects be constructed by the United States, the Commission's concurrence in that report cannot provide a basis for invoking the provisions of § 7 (b). Section 7 (b) is a direction to the Commission not to approve a private application for a project "affecting" any development of water resources which, in the judgment of the Commission, should be undertaken by the United States itself. Petitioners in effect ask us to tell the Commission what it thought—to say to the Commission that it was its judgment that Roanoke Rapids, as well as all the other seven projects in the Roanoke plan not yet under consideration, should be built by the Government. It is not clear that the Commission's concurrence in the general plan would have been much more than simple approval of the location of the dams, the purposes they would serve, and the engineering characteristics of the projects, even if the report had clearly recommended public construction. Primary responsibility for the enforcement of the provisions of § 7 (b) must remain with the Commission; we cannot infer a judgment of the Commission that it never expressed and now specifically disavows.

---

[7] Thus, whatever benefits may be conferred by such government projects as Buggs Island on the Roanoke Rapids site will not be lost to the United States. The Commission is required by § 10 (f) of the Federal Power Act, 41 Stat. 1070, as amended, 49 Stat. 843, 16 U.S.C. § 803 (f), to determine the charges to be paid by the licensee. The parties are in dispute over the value of the benefits, but, as the Commission said, "[t]he amount of the payments for headwater benefits due under the Federal Power Act cannot be estimated with any degree of accuracy until after the project has been placed in operation for such time as necessary to demonstrate what actual benefits are being conferred." *Re Virginia Electric & Power Co., supra,* at 478. We do not consider the correct basis for ascertaining the amount due to the United States, because, as the Commission's statement indicates, the question is not before us in this case.

[8] Section 7 (b) of the Federal Power Act provides:

"Whenever, in the judgment of the Commission, the development of any water resources for public purposes should be undertaken by the United States itself, the Commission shall not approve any application for any project affecting such development, but shall cause to be made such examinations, surveys, reports, plans, and estimates of the cost of the proposed development as it may find necessary, and shall submit its findings to Congress with such recommendations as it may find appropriate concerning such development."

For these reasons, we agree with the Court of Appeals that the Commission's order must stand. In the bits and pieces of legislative history which we have set out, we find no justification for inferring that Congress withdrew the Commission's authority regarding the Roanoke River Basin from the general authority given the Commission to grant licenses for private construction of hydroelectric projects with appropriate safeguards of the public interest. Whatever the merits of the controversy as to which agency—the Government or a private party—should construct this project, that question is not within our province.

Affirmed.

Mr. JUSTICE CLARK, concurring.

I agree with the majority that the sole question before us is whether Congress has withdrawn the Roanoke Rapids site from the licensing jurisdiction of the Commission and that the answer is in the negative. But in reaching this result weight should be given the administrative interpretation of the 1944 Flood Control Act both by the Army Corps of Engineers and the Federal Power Commission. Taken together with the fact that Congress was fully advised of the Commission's action and the Corps' agreement with it as early as May 1949 and failed to express any disagreement during the period of more than two years when the application was under consideration, this administrative interpretation seems to me decisive.

We are cited to three cases in which the Commission, with the full approval of the Corps of Engineers, has licensed private developments despite prior congressional action adopting and authorizing public construction as part of river basin improvement plans.[9] While the plans included in those projects may not have been as comprehensive as The Roanoke River Basin Plan, each had been approved by Acts of Congress using language similar to that in § 10 of the Flood Control Act of 1944. With this as background, a colloquy between Colonel Gee of the Corps of Engineers and the House Flood Control Committee on May 16, 1949, gains significance. Colonel Gee mentioned VEPCO's then pending application and stated that the Corps had not re-

[9] License issued to County of Placer, California, August 8, 1951. Project No. 2021, for power plant at debris storage dam on North Fork, American River, constructed pursuant to authorization in River and Harbor Act of August 30, 1935 (49 Stat. 1028, 1038), as recommended in House Rivers and Harbors Committee Document No. 50, 74th Cong., 1st Sess. License issued to St. Anthony's Falls Water Power Co., August 31, 1951, Project No. 2056, to use water from United States navigation dam at St. Anthony's Falls, Minnesota, authorized in the River and Harbor Act of 1937 (50 Stat. 844, 848), as recommended in House Rivers and Harbors Committee Document No. 34, 75th Cong., 1st Sess. Two licenses issued in 1934 and 1936 to Kanawha Valley Power Co., Projects Nos. 1175 and 1290, for three power plants at navigation dams on Kanawha River, West Virginia, authorized in River and Harbor Act of 1930 (46 Stat. 918, 928) as recommended in H. R. Doc. No. 190, 70th Cong., 1st Sess.

garded the 1944 approval as precluding such private licensing.[10] I would affirm on the basis of this administrative interpretation by two agencies charged by Congress with direct flood control and power licensing responsibilities.

Mr. JUSTICE DOUGLAS, with whom The CHIEF JUSTICE and Mr. JUSTICE BLACK concur, dissenting.

Roanoke Rapids is a power site belonging to the Federal Government and now surrendered to private power interests under circumstances that demand a dissent.

Roanoke Rapids is a part of the *public domain.*

(1) The Roanoke is a navigable stream over which Congress has complete control for purposes of navigation, flood control, watershed development, and the generation of electric power. *United States* v. *Appalachian Power Co.,* 311 U.S. 377, 426; *Oklahoma* v. *Atkinson Co.,* 313 U.S. 508, 525.

(2) The water power inherent in the flow of a navigable stream belongs to the Federal Government. *United States* v. *Appalachian Power Co., supra,* at 424.

(3) The dam sites on this navigable stream are public property. The technical title to the bed of the stream may be in private hands. But those private interests have no compensable interest as against the control of the Federal Government. *United States* v. *Chicago, M., St. P. & P. R. Co.,* 312 U.S. 592, 596–597; *United States* v. *Commodore Park,* 324 U.S. 386, 390.

This is familiar law that emphasizes the *public* nature of the project which the Court now allows to be used for the aggrandizement of private power interests. This project is as much in the public domain as any of our national forests or national parks. It deals with assets belonging to all the people.

These facts must be kept in mind in reading § 10 of the Flood Control Act of 1944, 58 Stat. 887, 891.[11] From that starting point I think it only fair to conclude (1) that if Congress undertook to remove this project from the *public domain,* it would make its purpose plain; and (2) that when Congress approved the project it meant to reserve it for the public good, not to make it available to private interests to exploit for their own profit.

Section 10 "adopted and authorized" the development of the Roanoke River Basin "in the interest of the national security and with a view toward providing

[10]"Mr. ANGELL. Is the Federal Government at the present time planning to develop any of those dams on the lower part of the river which are devoted exclusively to power production?

"Colonel GEE. No, sir. They have the same status in this basin plan as the eight remaining projects. They are part of the approved plan. Their being in that plan certainly is no bar to a private utility company coming in and seeking to develop one of these projects.

"Mr. ANGELL. And that is what is being done now.

"Colonel GEE. That is being done now at Roanoke Rapids, sir." Hearings before the House Committee on Public Works on H. R. 5472 (Tit. II), 81st Cong., 1st Sess. 144.

[11] Section 10 of the Flood Control Act of 1944 reads in pertinent part as follows: "That the following works of improvement for the benefit of navigation and the control of destructive flood waters

an adequate reservoir of useful and worthy public works for the post-war construction program." The words "public works" certainly connote *public* not private construction.

Section 10 further provided that the projects which are "adopted and authorized" are "to be prosecuted under the direction of the Secretary of War and supervision of the Chief of Engineers." That language also suggests *public* projects, not private undertakings.

Section 10 also provided that these projects "shall be initiated as expeditiously and prosecuted as vigorously as may be consistent with budgetary requirements." Plainly Congress was concerned with the "budgetary requirements" of the Federal Government, not with the budgetary requirements of private power companies. Section 10, after approving the general plan for the comprehensive development of the Roanoke River Basin, authorizes the construction of the Buggs Island Reservoir on the Roanoke River and the Philpott Reservoir on the Smith River.

This Act, passed before the end of World War II, was designed to serve a post-war need. It was drawn so as to provide a backlog of public works projects which would take up the slack of unemployment expected at the war's end. Congressman Whittington, in charge of the bill in the House, made the following significant statement concerning this objective, 90 Cong. Rec. 4122:

---

and other purposes are hereby adopted and authorized in the interest of the national security and with a view toward providing an adequate reservoir of useful and worthy public works for the post-war construction program, to be prosecuted under the direction of the Secretary of War and supervision of the Chief of Engineers in accordance with the plans in the respective reports hereinafter designated and subject to the conditions set forth therein: *Provided,* That the necessary plans, specifications, and preliminary work may be prosecuted on any project authorized in this Act to be constructed by the War Department during the war, with funds from appropriations heretofore or hereafter made for flood control, so as to be ready for rapid inauguration of a post-war program of construction: *Provided further,* That when the existing critical situation with respect to materials, equipment, and manpower no longer exists, and in any event not later than immediately following the cessation of hostilities in the present war, the projects herein shall be initiated as expeditiously and prosecuted as vigorously as may be consistent with budgetary requirements: *And provided further,* That penstocks and other similar facilities adapted to possible future use in the development of hydroelectric power shall be installed in any dam authorized in this Act for construction by the War Department when approved by the Secretary of War on the recommendation of the Chief of Engineers and the Federal Power Commission.

* * *

"ROANOKE RIVER BASIN

"The general plan for the comprehensive development of the Roanoke River Basin for flood control and other purposes recommended by the Chief of Engineers in House Document Numbered 650, Seventy-eighth Congress, second session, is approved and the construction of the Buggs Island Reservoir on the Roanoke River in Virginia and North Carolina, and the Philpott Reservoir on the Smith River in Virginia, are hereby authorized substantially in accordance with the recommendations of the Chief of Engineers in that report at an estimated cost of $36,140,000."

We recall the depression following World War No. 1. We are apprehensive of another debacle following the present war. It is difficult to arm. It is more difficult to disarm. Post-war unemployment will be a major national problem. While we are defending our freedom and our way of life, we must not fail to take stock of the problem of unemployment which we must face when the war is over.

We must profit by the experience of 1920. We must profit by the experience of 1930. A reservoir of projects must be adopted. Backlogs should be provided and they should be real backlogs. Many wasteful and extravagant activities to provide employment were adopted in 1933. Haste and speed were imperative. There was hunger in the land. Unemployment was widespread. There must be no repetition of waste and extravagance. There are Federal activities and there are public works that will promote the general welfare.

This statement highlights the meaning of "public works" as used in § 10; it discloses an important reason for lodging the program with public officials; it emphasizes the occasion for referring to the budgetary requirements of the Federal Government and the importance of linking flood control with post-war unemployment problems.

The argument that when Congress by § 10 of the Act "adopted and authorized" the "following works of improvement," it "adopted and authorized" *only* the Buggs Island and Philpott reservoirs involves an invented distinction between "works of improvement" and "general plans for development"—a distinction without any rational basis. The "works of improvement" which are "adopted and authorized" by § 10 are 38 in number. Some of these are described in the sub-headings as "projects" that are "authorized," some as "plans of improvement" that are "approved" and "authorized," some as "general plans" for the comprehensive development of river basins that are "approved" together with the "construction" of specific projects that are "authorized." This makes plain that "works of improvement" which are "adopted and authorized" by § 10 include a variety of undertakings, not merely works of construction which are first steps in general comprehensive plans being adopted and authorized.

From this it seems almost too plain for argument that Congress, in approving the plan for the development of the Roanoke River Basin, was setting it aside for federal development, the several public works projects under the plan to be authorized as, if, and when conditions warranted them and budgetary requirements permitted.[12] In this setting "approval" by Congress meant a dedication of the projects for public development.[13]

[12] Congressman Curtis, one of the House conferees, explained the same language in §9 of the Act whereby Congress "approved" comprehensive plans for the development of the Missouri River Basin (90 Cong. Rec. 9284):

"It means that Congress has approved the general plans of the engineers, and it means that these plans are authorized by law and are, therefore, eligible for future appropriations. Without such an authorization, no appropriation can be had."

[13] The interpretations placed on the Act by the Army Corps of Engineers are entitled to no weight. The Corps of Engineers is not an administrative agency charged with the responsibility of deciding issues of policy. Its powers are limited to the making of investigations and the preparation and submission of recommendations and reports based on engineering considerations. See, for example,

If that view is not taken, then why did Congress call these projects "public works"? If these projects were destined for development by private power interests, why did Congress place their construction under the Secretary of War and the Chief of Engineers? If Congress left this part of the public domain for exploitation by private power groups, why did it gear them to the employment requirements of the post-war period and the budget requirements of the Federal Government? Approval of the projects by Congress under these various terms and conditions can only mean one thing—that Congress gave its sanction to their development as public projects.

To be sure, Congress in the Federal Power Act left part of the public domain to be exploited by private interests, if the Federal Power Commission so orders. But the action relative to the Roanoke River Basin was action by Congress without reference to the Federal Power Commission. Its action was not made dependent on the approval of the Federal Power Commission. The Act in no way links the Roanoke River Basin program to the Commission. To the contrary, the Congress undertook to authorize specific projects under the plan, plainly suggesting that these were *public* projects whose authorization was in no way dependent on Commission action.

The true character of this raid on the *public domain* is seen when Roanoke Rapids is viewed in relation to the other projects in the comprehensive plan. Roanoke Rapids is the farthest downstream of the 11 units in the plan. Upstream from Roanoke Rapids is Buggs Island (now under construction with federal funds) with an ultimate installed capacity of 204,000 kw. and a controlled reservoir capacity of over 2,500,000 acre-feet. Roanoke Rapids is indeed the powerhouse of the Buggs Island Reservoir. That reservoir increases the dependable capacity of Roanoke Rapids from 4 hours during the peak month of December to 288 hours in the same peak month. Buggs Island contributes 70,000,000 kw.-hr. to the Roanoke Rapids project. This is on-peak energy, firm energy made dependable by the storage in the Buggs Island Reservoir. There is evidence that this energy will have a value in excess of $700,000 a year.[14]

That $700,000 of value is created by the taxpayers of this country. Though it derives from the investment of federal funds, it will now be appropriated by private power groups for their own benefit. The master plan now becomes clear: the Federal Government will put up the auxiliary units—the unprofitable ones; and the private power interests will take the plums—the choice ones.

---

§ 1 (a) of the Act of December 22, 1944, 58 Stat. 887, adopting and authorizing the Roanoke River Basin plan; 33 U. S. C. § 701- (a). Congress alone makes policy decisions affecting the public domain.

[14] Even the evidence submitted by the private power company applicant belies the Commission's figure of $250,000 (see 87 P. U. R. (N. S.) 469, 477–478) and places the value in excess of $700,000. The Commission's figure of $250,000 is indubitably a plain error.

There is not a word in the Act which allows such an unconscionable appropriation of the *public domain* by private interests. To infer that Congress sanctioned such a scheme is to assume it was utterly reckless with the *public domain*. I would assume that Congress was a faithful trustee, that what it approved as "public works" projects it dedicated to the good of all the people.

MULTIPLE-USE FORESTRY

A COOPERATIVE PROGRAM FOR TREE PLANTING*
May 18, 1937

The Norris-Doxey Act, sponsored by Senator George Norris and Representative Wall Doxey of Mississippi, greatly expanded the system of federal grants to the states for forest seedlings and general reforestation and afforestation. It is still the basis for programs in this field.

An Act to authorize cooperation in the development of farm forestry in the States and Territories, and for other purposes.

Be it enacted by the Senate and House of Representatives of the United States of America in Congress assembled, That in order to aid agriculture, increase farm-forest income, conserve water resources, increase employment, and in other ways advance the general welfare and improve living conditions on farms through reforestation and afforestation in the various States and Territories, the Secretary of Agriculture is authorized in cooperation with the land-grant colleges and universities and State forestry agencies, each within its respective field of activities, according to the statutes, if any, of the respective States, wherever such agencies can and will cooperate, or in default of such cooperation to act directly, to produce or procure and distribute forest trees and shrub planting stock; to make necessary investigations; to advise farmers regarding the establishment, protection, and management of farm forests and forest and shrub plantations and the harvesting, utilization, and marketing of the products thereof; and to enter into cooperative agreements for the establishment, protection, and care of farm- or other forest-land tree and shrub plantings within such States and Territories; and, whenever suitable Government-owned lands are not available, to lease, purchase, or accept donations of land and develop nursery sites for the production of such forest planting stock as is needed to effectuate the purposes of this Act, but not including ornamental or other stock for landscape plantings commonly grown by established commercial nurserymen, and no stock grown in Government and cooperating nurseries shall be allowed to enter regular trade channels. No cooperative reforestation or affor-

*50 *Statutes at Large,* 188.

estation shall be undertaken pursuant to this Act unless the cooperator makes available without charge the land to be planted. There is hereby authorized to be appropriated annually not to exceed $2,500,000 for carrying out the purposes of this Act. This Act shall be known as the Cooperative Farm Forestry Act.

Approved, May 18, 1937.

REPORT OF THE JOINT COMMITTEE ON FORESTRY*
March 24, 1941

This report was never implemented by broad new law, partly because World War II intervened. The recommendations presented here were used to support many administrative improvements, however, and to justify funding other programs after the war.

RECOMMENDATION NO. 1

FOREST FIRE PROTECTION

Extension and intensification of cooperative protection against fire on private- and State-owned forest lands by increasing the authorization of the Clarke-McNary Act for this purpose from $2,500,000 to $10,000,000, increasing the present appropriation by $2,500,000 annually until the total authorization has been reached, provided the respective States pass legislation providing for proper State, county, and district fire protection and regulations governing minimum forestry practices to be administered as approved by the Secretary of Agriculture.

The principles on which to base such legislation might well include:

(1) That State legislation and standards of enforcement shall be satisfactory to the Federal Government, with mandatory provisions that Federal financial assistance, in fire control and regulation, be withdrawn if enforcement proves unsatisfactory.

(2) The Federal Government shall have discretionary authority to withhold other forest cooperative funds in whole or in part from any State which, after the formative period, does not satisfactorily administer or cooperate in regulation.

(3) That full opportunity shall be assured to forest-land owners directly concerned to (a) participate along with representatives of public, agricultural, labor, and other interested groups through advisory boards, in formulating special requirements which shall be subject to approval by designated and responsible governmental agencies, (b) appeal through nongovernmental boards or other channels for review and reconsideration of such requirements.

(4) The States shall have the opportunity to administer regulations with a reasonable, but definite, period of perhaps from 3 to 5 years within which to pass State legislation and apply same.

(5) The authority of and administrative action by the Federal Government shall be exercised by or through the Secretary of Agriculture.

*Forest Lands of the United States, Sen. Doc. 32, 77th Cong., 1st sess., 28–33.

RECOMMENDATION NO. 2

FOREST INSECTS AND DISEASES

Extension of the Clarke-McNary Act to provide for cooperative protection against forest insects and diseases on private and State-owned forest lands.

RECOMMENDATION NO. 3

REFORESTATION OF PRIVATE FOREST LANDS

Extension of the Clarke-McNary Act to authorize the furnishing of tree-seed and seedlings to all landowners, and authorization of such amounts as are necessary for this purpose.

RECOMMENDATION NO. 4

FOREST EXTENSION

We recommend that the provisions of the Cooperative Farm Forestry Act, approved May 18, 1937, be continued and expanded, and that sufficient annual appropriations be made to carry out the purposes of the Cooperative Farm Forestry Act.

RECOMMENDATION NO. 5

COOPERATIVE SUSTAINED-YIELD UNITS

Legislation authorizing the establishment of cooperative sustained units to enable sustained-yield management of intermingled public and private holdings conditional upon management and woods practices approved by the Secretary of Agriculture.

The purpose of this legislation is to authorize the Secretary of Agriculture:

(a) To declare joint private timber and national forest timber sustained-yield units.

(b) To make agreements with land owners for cooperative management which will give the Secretary control of the rate and methods of cutting on the private lands.

(c) Pursuant to such agreements, permit the Secretary to sell national forest timber to a cooperator at not less than its appraised value without competitive bids and under such practices as will maintain a fair price and otherwise safeguard the public interest.

RECOMMENDATION NO. 6

FOREST CREDITS

Provision for a forest credit system to make long-term, low interest rate loans to private forest and naval stores operators through facilities already available in such agencies as the Reconstruction Finance Corporation, the Farm Credit Administration, and the Federal Land bank. These loans should be conditional upon both sound forest practice and sound investment. A system of forest credits suited to the peculiar long-term nature of the forestry and naval stores business will be an aid to forest conservation.

Specifically, forest credits are needed to—

(a) Make forest investments more liquid without liquidating the forest resource itself.

(b) Pay carrying costs and prevent sacrifice of immature or economically unripe timber.

(c) Consolidate or round out holdings for efficient forest practice.

(d) Provide improvements and facilities needed for efficient administration, production, and utilization under sustained-yield management.

(e) Refund unduly burdensome loans.

(f) Assist forest cooperative associations or small owners in management, processing, and marketing.

RECOMMENDATION NO. 7

FARM FOREST COOPERATIVES

Legislation authorizing cooperation with the States in encouragement and development of farm forest cooperatives, including financial aid in building and operating forest industries and woodworking plants.

RECOMMENDATION NO. 8

LEASES AND COOPERATIVE AGREEMENTS

Legislation providing for leases and cooperative agreements with private forest land owners, communities, institutions, and States.

The purpose of this recommended measure is to (a) furnish technical experience in carrying out proper forestry practices, (b) overcome a serious financial handicap, (c) help this class of citizen to operate on a cooperative basis, (d) provide urgently needed employment, particularly in times of economic stress, and at the same time (e) afford an additional means of building up and managing deteriorated forests. Such a plan would provide sufficient flexibility for expanding the work program in times of unemployment and contracting it at other times.

The principles on which to base such a plan might well include:

(*a*) Entering into a lease or a cooperative agreement on a voluntary basis.

(*b*) Retention of title by the owner. Owners would pay the taxes, but in case of lease would receive a nominal annual rental not to exceed the average annual tax for the 5 years preceding the lease. In the case of cooperative agreement, the owner would have the privilege of handling the rehabilitation work himself with Federal financial cooperation.

(*c*) The Federal Government should be reimbursed for its costs from the use of the land and sale of its products on a 50–50 basis for properties of less than 500 acres, and on a 100 percent basis above 500 acres.

(*d*) The administration should be done under the States in cooperation with and the approval of the Secretary of Agriculture.

(*e*) The President should be authorized to allocate to the Secretary of Agriculture such sums from relief, public works, or similar appropriations as may be needed, in addition to regular appropriations to effectuate the plan.

RECOMMENDATION NO. 9

FOREST PRODUCTS AND FOREST MANAGEMENT RESEARCH

Extension and intensification of forest products research and forest management research at the United States forest products laboratory and the United States forest experiment stations, provided that provision be made by the Secretary of Agriculture to get the results of forestry research to the public at large. Existing State agencies, agriculture colleges, and the public schools should be used where possible to accomplish this recommendation.

RECOMMENDATION NO. 10

STATE FOREST ACQUISITION ACT OF 1935

Amend the State Forest Acquisition Act of 1935, making it applicable to institutions, communities, and subdivisions of the State. Increasing the authorization to $10,000,000 to be appropriated annually at an increased rate of $2,500,000.

Briefly, the importance of this legislation and the need for the increase in the authorization is:

(1) The States recognize that their forest systems should be extended through direct purchase and by placing State laws and procedures for transferring tax-delinquent forest lands to public ownership on a more efficient basis.

(2) It would tend to solve the problem of properly utilizing millions of acres of cut-over lands and tax-delinquent lands.

(3) It would increase employment, income, and would raise much additional revenue.

[630]

(4) It would promote educational and demonstration work in the various sections of the States where it is urgently needed.

(5) These lands are now being bought up by large operators at sacrifice prices or they are being forced into the ownership of the Federal Government.

RECOMMENDATION NO. 11

FEDERAL FOREST LAND ACQUISITION

Federal forest land acquisition in our national forests should continue at its present rate and when possible should be accelerated. In purchasing such land particular emphasis should be placed on blocking up present scattered areas of forest land in national forests before additional national forests are established. We recommend the appropriation of additional funds annually for acquisition purposes in national forests in order to carry out this recommendation.

RECOMMENDATION NO. 12

FINANCIAL TAX CONTRIBUTION TO LOCAL GOVERNMENTS

Legislation authorizing an equitable system of financial contribution to local government in lieu of taxes on forest land removed from the tax rolls through Federal acquisition.

There is a serious need for a general Government policy for cash contribution in lieu of taxes to counties containing Federally owned forest lands.

RECOMMENDATION NO. 13

NATIONAL FOREST PROTECTION

Provision for more adequate protection against fire, insects, and diseases on National forests.

RECOMMENDATION NO. 14

NATIONAL FOREST MANAGEMENT

More intensified management of timber, forage, wildlife, recreation, and watershed resources on National forests.

RECOMMENDATION NO. 15

FOREST SURVEY

Amendment to section 9 of the McSweeney-McNary forest research Act of 1928 to authorize an annual authorization of $750,000 for early completion of the forest survey of the United States.

RECOMMENDATION NO. 16

PULPWOOD INVESTIGATION

To investigate the apparent monopolistic purchasing of pulpwood by pulp and paper mills under a contract purchase system from farmers and other owners, price fixing of paper and other pulp products under trade practice rules and regulations, including cost of distribution.

The purpose of this legislation is to investigate:

(1) The apparent monopolistic purchasing procedure of pulpwood through contractors and prices being paid to these contractors and the price paid to subcontractors and buyers of pulpwood and the price paid to farmers and owners of pulpwood, including standards of wages paid in pulp and paper mills to wage earners, and including wages paid for cutting and hauling pulpwood;

(2) the current cost of producing and distributing wood pulp and paper;

(3) any related factors required in determining whether wage earners, farmers, and other forest owners or operators are receiving for their wages, stumpage, and pulpwood a fair and equitable share of the sale price of pulp and paper during the past year and a fair and equitable share of the 30 percent recent increase in the price of paper;

(4) the relationship of pulp and paper associations of which the manufacturers of pulp and paper are members;

(5) the ownership and control of domestic pulp and paper mills;

(6) the influence and control that these associations have over the operations of their members as to controlled production, distribution, and the actual fixing of prices under trade-practice rules and regulations formulated and agreed to by members of said associations; and

(7) the effect of prices of imports on domestic prices.

John H. Bankhead 2d
Chairman
H. P. Fulmer
Vice   Chairman
E. D. Smith
Chas. L. McNary
W. J. Bulow
D. Worth Clark
Daniel A. Reed
Harry L. Englebright
Wall Doxey
Walter M. Pierce

THE SUSTAINED-YIELD FOREST MANAGEMENT ACT*
March 29, 1944

This law formalized programs for management of federally-owned lands on a sustained-yield basis. The force of law made possible larger and more efficient logging and marketing procedures for selling the timber.

An Act to promote sustained-yield forest management in order thereby (a) to stabilize communities, forest industries, employment, and taxable forest wealth; (b) to assure a continuous and ample supply of forest products; and (c) to secure the benefits of forests in regulation of water supply and stream flow, prevention of soil erosion, amelioration of climate, and preservation of wildlife.

Be it enacted by the Senate and House of Representatives of the United States of America in Congress assembled, That in order to promote the stability of forest industries, of employment, of communities, and of taxable forest wealth, through continuous supplies of timber; in order to provide for a continuous and ample supply of forest products; and in order to secure the benefits of forests in maintenance of water supply, regulation of stream flow, prevention of soil erosion, amelioration of climate, and preservation of wildlife, the Secretary of Agriculture and the Secretary of the Interior are severally authorized to establish by formal declaration, when in their respective judgments such action would be in the public interest, cooperative sustained-yield units which shall consist of federally owned or administered forest land under the jurisdiction of the Secretary establishing the unit and, in addition thereto, land which reasonably may be expected to be made the subject of one or more of the cooperative agreements with private landowners authorized by section 2 of this Act.

SEC. 2. The Secretary of Agriculture, with respect to forest land under his jurisdiction, and the Secretary of the Interior, with respect to forest land under his jurisdiction, are severally authorized, for the purposes specified in section 1 of this Act, to enter into cooperative agreements with private owners of forest land within a cooperative sustained-yield unit, established pursuant to section 1 of this Act, providing for the coordinated management of such private forest land and of federally owned or administered forest lands within the sustained-yield unit involved.

Each cooperative agreement may give the cooperating private landowner the privilege of purchasing without competitive bidding at prices not less than their appraised value, subject to periodic readjustments of stumpage rates and to such other conditions and requirements as the Secretary may prescribe, timber and other forest products from federally owned or administered forest land

*58 *Statutes at Large,* 132–35.

within the unit, in accordance with the provisions of sustained-yield management plans formulated or approved by the Secretary for the unit; shall limit the time, rate, and method of cutting or otherwise harvesting timber and other forest products from the land of the cooperating private landowner, due consideration being given to the character and condition of the timber, to the relation of the proposed cutting to the sustained-yield plan for the unit, and to the productive capacity of the land; shall prescribe the terms and conditions, but not the price, upon which the cooperating private landowner may sell to any person timber and other forest products from his land, compliance by the purchaser with such conditions to be required by the contract of sale; shall contain such provisions as the Secretary deems necessary to protect the reasonable interest of other owners of forest land within the unit; and shall contain such other provisions as the Secretary believes necessary to carry out the purposes of this Act.

Each cooperative agreement shall be placed on record in the county or counties in which the lands of the cooperating private landowner covered thereby are located, and the costs incident to such recordation may be paid out of any funds available for the protection or management of federally owned or administered forest land within the unit. When thus recorded, the agreement shall be binding upon the heirs, successors, and assigns of the owner of such land, and upon purchasers of timber or other forest products from such land, throughout the life of such cooperative agreement.

SEC. 3. The Secretary of Agriculture and the Secretary of the Interior are further severally authorized, whenever in their respective judgments the maintenance of a stable community or communities is primarily dependent upon the sale of timber or other forest products from federally owned or administered forest land and such maintenance cannot effectively be secured by following the usual procedure in selling such timber or other forest products, to establish by formal declaration for the purpose of maintaining the stability of such community or communities a sustained-yield unit consisting of forest land under the jurisdiction of the Secretary establishing such unit, to determine and define the boundaries of the community or communities for whose benefit such unit is created, and to sell, subject to such conditions and requirements as the Secretary believes necessary, federally owned or administered timber and other forest products from such unit without competitive bidding at prices not less than their appraised values, to responsible purchasers within such community or communities.

SEC. 4. Each of the said Secretaries is further authorized in his discretion to enter into cooperative agreements with the other Secretary, or with any Federal agency having jurisdiction over federally owned or administered forest land, or with any State or local agency having jurisdiction over publicly owned or administered forest land, providing for the inclusion of such land in any coordi-

[634]

nated plan of management otherwise authorized by the provisions of this Act when by such a cooperative agreement he may be aided in accomplishing the purposes of this Act; but no federally or publicly owned or administered forest land not under the jurisdiction of the Secretary establishing the sustained-yield unit concerned shall be included in any such plan except in pursuance of a cooperative agreement made under this section.

SEC. 5. Before any sustained-yield unit authorized by section 1 or section 3 of this Act shall be established, and before any cooperative agreement authorized by section 2 or section 4 of this Act shall be entered into, advance notice thereof shall be given by registered mail to each landowner whose land is proposed to be included and by publication in one or more newspapers of general circulation in the vicinity of the place where the timber is located, and the costs incident to such publication may be paid out of any funds available for the protection or management of the federally owned or administered forest land involved. This notice shall state: (1) the location of the proposed unit; (2) the name of each proposed cooperator; (3) the duration of the proposed cooperative agreement or agreements; (4) the location and estimated quantity of timber on the land of each proposed cooperator and on the Federal land involved; (5) the expected rate of cutting of such timber; and (6) the time and place of a public hearing to be held not less than thirty days after the first publication of said notice for the presentation of the advantages and disadvantages of the proposed action to the community or communities affected.

Before any sale agreement made without competition and involving more than $500 in stumpage value of federally owned or administered timber shall be entered into under this Act, advance notice thereof shall be given by publication once weekly for four consecutive weeks in one or more newspapers of general circulation in the vicinity of the place where the timber is located, and the costs incident to such publication may be paid out of any funds available for the protection or management of federally owned or administered forest land within the unit concerned. This notice shall state: (1) the quantity and appraised value of the timber; (2) the time and place of a public hearing to be held not less than thirty days after the first publication of said notice if requested by the State or county where the timber is located or by any other person deemed to have a reasonable interest in the proposed sale or in its terms; and (3) the place where any request for a public hearing shall be made. Such requests need be considered only if received at the place designated in the notice not later than fifteen days after the first publication of such notice. If a request for a hearing is received within the time designated, notice of the holding of the hearing shall be given not less than ten days before the time set for such hearing, in the same manner as provided for the original notice.

The determination made by the Secretary having jurisdiction upon the proposals considered at any such hearing, which determination may include the modification of the terms of such proposals, together with the minutes or other record of the hearing, shall be available for public inspection during the life of any coordinated plan of management or agreement entered into in consequence of such determination.

SEC. 6. In addition to any other remedy available under existing law, upon failure of any private owner of forest land which is subject to a cooperative agreement entered into pursuant to this Act to comply with the terms of such agreement, or upon failure of any purchaser of timber or other forest products from such land to comply with the terms and conditions required by such agreement to be included in the contract of sale, the Attorney General, at the request of the Secretary concerned, is authorized to institute against such owner or such purchaser a proceeding in equity in the proper district court of the United States, to require compliance with the terms and conditions of said cooperative agreement; and jurisdiction is hereby conferred upon said district courts to hear and determine such proceedings, to order compliance with the terms and conditions of cooperative agreements entered into pursuant to this Act, and to make such temporary and final orders as shall be deemed just in the premises. As used in this section the term "owner" shall include the heirs, successors, and assigns of the landowner entering into the cooperative agreements.

SEC. 7. Whenever used in this Act, the term "federally owned or administered forest land" shall be construed to mean forest land in which, or in the natural resources of which, the United States has a legal or equitable interest of any character sufficient to entitle the United States to control the management or disposition of the timber or other forest products thereon, except land heretofore or hereafter reserved or withdrawn for purposes which are inconsistent with the exercise of the authority conferred by this Act; and shall include trust or restricted Indian land, whether tribal or allotted, except that such land shall not be included without the consent of the Indians concerned.

SEC. 8. The Secretary of Agriculture and the Secretary of the Interior may severally prescribe such rules and regulations as may be appropriate to carry out the purposes of this Act. Each Secretary may delegate any of his powers and duties under this Act to other officers or employees of his Department.

SEC. 9. Nothing contained in this Act shall be construed to abrogate or curtail any authority conferred upon the Secretary of Agriculture or the Secretary of the Interior by any Act relating to management of federally owned or administered forest lands, and nothing contained in any such Acts shall be construed to limit or restrict any authority conferred upon the Secretary of Agriculture or the Secretary of the Interior by this Act.

SEC. 10. Funds available for the protection or management of Federally owned or administered forest land within the unit concerned may also be expended in carrying out the purposes of this Act, and there are hereby authorized to be appropriated such additional sums for the purposes of this Act as the Congress may from time to time deem necessary, but such additional sums shall not exceed $150,000 for the Department of Agriculture and $50,000 for the Department of the Interior, for any fiscal year.

Approved March 29, 1944.

THE COOPERATIVE FOREST MANAGEMENT ACT*
August 25, 1950

This new authority for financial assistance to states in providing technical assistance to private landowners was in the tradition of the expanding forestry programs first initiated by Charles McNary.

An Act to authorize the Secretary of Agriculture to cooperate with the States to enable them to provide technical services to private forest landowners, and for other purposes.

Be it enacted by the Senate and House of Representatives of the United States of America in Congress assembled, That the Secretary of Agriculture is hereby authorized to cooperate with State foresters or equivalent officials of the several States, Territories, and possessions for the purpose of encouraging the States, Territories, and possessions to provide technical services to private forest landowners and operators, and processors of primary forest products with respect to the management of forest lands and the harvesting, marketing, and processing of forest products, and, where necessary to avoid uneconomic duplication of certain technical and training services, to make such services available to private agencies and persons. All such technical services shall be provided in each State, Territory, or possession in accordance with a plan agreed upon in advance between the Secretary and the State forester or equivalent official of the State, Territory, or possession. The provisions of this Act and the plan agreed upon for each State, Territory, or possession shall be carried out in such manner as to encourage the utilization of private agencies and individuals furnishing services of the type described in this section.

SEC. 2. There is hereby authorized to be appropriated annually, to enable the Secretary to carry out the provisions of this Act, the sum of $2,500,000. Apportionment among the participating States, administrative expenses in connection with cooperative action with such States, and the amount to be expended by the Secretary to make technical services available to private persons and agencies, shall be determined by the Secretary after consultation with a national advisory board of not less than five State foresters or equivalent officials selected by a majority of the State foresters or equivalent officials of all States, Territories, or possessions participating in the program. The amount paid by the Federal Government to any State, Territory, or possession for cooperative action in the State, Territory, or possession shall not exceed during any fiscal year the amount expended by the cooperating State, Territory, or possession for the same purpose during the same fiscal year, and the Secretary of Agriculture

*64 *Statutes at Large,* 473.

is authorized to make such expenditures on the certificate of the appropriate official of the State, Territory, or possession having charge of the cooperative work for the State, Territory, or possession that the expenditures as herein provided have been made: *Provided,* That it is the intent of Congress that the Secretary may continue to cooperate with persons and private agencies in furnishing technical forestry services under existing authority.

SEC. 3. The Act of May 18, 1937 (50 Stat. 188), known as the Cooperative Farm Forestry Act, is hereby repealed effective June 30, 1951.

SEC. 4. This Act shall be known as the Cooperative Forest Management Act. Approved August 25, 1950.

THE MULTIPLE-USE ACT OF 1960*
June 12, 1960

This law was the first major revision in the specific laws dealing with forest management since the Pettigrew amendment of 1897. It established multiple-use for "outdoor recreation, range, timber, watershed, and wildlife and fish purposes" in addition to the sustained-yield concept first introduced under Gifford Pinchot.

An Act to authorize and direct that the national forests be managed under principles of multiple use and to produce a sustained yield of products and services, and for other purposes.

Be it enacted by the Senate and House of Representatives of the United States of America in Congress assembled, That it is the policy of the Congress that the national forests are established and shall be administered for outdoor recreation, range, timber, watershed, and wildlife and fish purposes. The purposes of this Act are declared to be supplemental to, but not in derogation of, the purposes for which the national forests were established as set forth in the Act of June 4, 1897 (16 U.S.C. 475). Nothing herein shall be construed as affecting the jurisdiction or responsibilities of the several States with respect to wildlife and fish on the national forests. Nothing herein shall be construed so as to affect the use or administration of the mineral resources of national forest lands or to affect the use or administration of Federal lands not within national forests.

SEC. 2. The Secretary of Agriculture is authorized and directed to develop and administer the renewable surface resources of the national forests for multiple use and sustained yield of the several products and services obtained therefrom. In the administration of the national forests due consideration shall be given to the relative values of the various resources in particular areas. The establishment and maintenance of areas of wilderness are consistent with the purposes and provisions of this Act.

SEC. 3. In the effectuation of this Act the Secretary of Agriculture is authorized to cooperate with interested State and local governmental agencies and others in the development and management of the national forests.

SEC. 4. As used in this Act, the following terms shall have the following meanings:

(a) "Multiple use" means: The management of all the various renewable surface resources of the national forests so that they are utilized in the combination that will best meet the needs of the American people; making the most judicious use of the land for some or all of these resources or related services over areas

*74 *Statutes at Large,* 215.

large enough to provide sufficient latitude for periodic adjustments in use to conform to changing needs and conditions; that some land will be used for less than all of the resources; and harmonious and coordinated management of the various resources, each with the other, without impairment of the productivity of the land, with consideration being given to the relative values of the various resources, and not necessarily the combination of uses that will give the greatest dollar return or the greatest unit output.

(b) "Sustained yield of the several products and services" means the achievement and maintenance in perpetuity of a high-level annual or regular periodic output of the various renewable resources of the national forests without impairment of the productivity of the land.

Approved June 12, 1960.

HARRY S. TRUMAN

HOLDING THE 160-ACRE LIMITATION*
October 29, 1949

On the premise that reclamation programs were primarily for the benefit of family farms, water supply was traditionally limited to 160 acres of irrigable land. Under community property arrangements, this meant 320 acres per family.

The first major breakthrough on this limitation was attempted in relation to the San Luis Valley project in Colorado. But President Truman vetoed the bill, and vigorously reaffirmed support for the limitation.

I am withholding my approval from S. 1385, a bill providing that the excess-land provisions of the Federal reclamation laws shall not apply to lands that will receive a supplemental water supply from the San Luis Valley project, Colorado.

Under the excess-land provisions of the Federal reclamation laws, water from a Federal reclamation project may be supplied to any one landowner, on a permanent basis, for not to exceed 160 acres of irrigable land within the project. Where the land is held in community or joint ownership by a husband and wife, water may be furnished for as much as 320 acres. The enrolled bill would increase the basic limitation, insofar as lands within the San Luis Valley project are concerned, from 160 acres to 480 acres. This change would have the effect of increasing the husband-and-wife limitation, for lands within that project, from 320 acres to 960 acres.

One great objective of the Federal reclamation program is to foster the establishment and maintenance of farm homes throughout those portions of our country where agricultural operations cannot rely solely upon nature for a water supply. The excess-land provisions of the law provide the legal mechanism for assuring that the benefits of the irrigation systems will inure to family-size farming enterprises. This is true whether the purpose of the particular project is to open up new land for settlement by providing an original water supply, or to stabilize an existing irrigation economy as in the case of the San Luis Valley

Public Papers of the Presidents of the United States, Harry S. Truman, 1949 (Washington, D.C.: Government Printing Office, 1964), 539–41.

project. In the absence of requirements designed to channel the water to those who are striving to build or conserve farm homes for their families, the heavy investments of interest-free funds being made for the reclamation program would lose much of their justification.

The San Luis Valley project, when completed, will provide a supplemental supply of water for approximately 500,000 acres. The only unit of the San Luis Valley project planned for construction at the present time is the Conejos division. The great bulk of the 86,000 acres that would be served by this division is already held in farm units that comply with the excess-land provisions of the Federal reclamation laws. Most of these existing farm units will be fully capable of supporting a farm family at an acceptable standard of living, once a regulated water supply is made available. On the other hand, approximately 24,000 acres of land within the Conejos division are of such quality, considering the comparatively short growing season of the region, as to make questionable their capacity to provide satisfactory family livelihoods if the farming operations must be in units meeting the present limitations. The enrolled bill, however, is not restricted to these 24,000 acres, or to the Conejos division, but would apply to the San Luis Valley project as a whole. In striving to meet the problems of a small part of the area, it would relax the existing acreage limitations for a much larger block of lands where adequate family-size farms can be maintained within these limitations.

It does not seem to me to be desirable or necessary to enact a bill of this sweeping character in order to achieve whatever corrective action may be needed to adapt the principle of aiding family-size farms to the particular conditions of the San Luis Valley project. It will be at least two years before the construction work on the Conejos division is completed. In the meantime, I hope that the Congress will consider legislation amending the excess-land provisions of the reclamation laws so as to authorize appropriate adjustments in maximum acreages, where necessary, under carefully-worked out standards, which could be applied not only to the San Luis Valley project, but also to other projects in which some adjustment may be warranted. Such legislation would seem to me to provide the proper way to meet special and unique situations, such as those in the San Luis Valley, without doing violence to the basic and often re-affirmed principle of maintaining the family-size farm on reclamation projects.

Harry S. Truman

A WATER POLICY FOR THE AMERICAN PEOPLE*
1950

The report of President Truman's Water Resources Policy Commission pre-
sented detailed recommendations about national water policy. Although the
report itself resulted in no general legislation on the subject, a substantial num-
ber of the recommendations have been put into effect, either through law or
administrative regulation.

OUTLINE OF POLICY

On these principles the Commission has framed a water policy for the American people which is embodied in the following series of recommendations:

PROGRAM PLANNING

1. As a guide to national investment in natural resources development, all
Federal agencies should be directed to judge new river basin programs in terms
of a set of clearly defined national objectives established by Congress.

2. These objectives, as outlined in detail by this Commission, should reflect
the general purpose of water resources investment to achieve the maximum
sustained use of lakes, rivers, and their associated land and ground water resources, to support a continuing high level of prosperity throughout the country.
They should include the safeguarding of our resources against deterioration
from soil erosion, wasteful forest practices, and floods; the improvement and
higher utilization of these resources to support an expanding economy and
national security; assistance to regional development; expansion of all types of
recreational opportunity to meet increasing needs; protection of public health;
and opportunity for greater use of transportation and electric power.

3. Congress should direct the responsible Federal agencies to submit new
proposals for water resources development to Congress only in the form of
basin programs which deal with entire basins as units and which take into account all relevant purposes in water and land development. This multiple-
purpose basin approach should apply to the whole process by which water
resources projects move from the survey to the authorization and appropriation
stages. It would enable Congress and the people concerned to have a clear picture of the entire program for each basin and its relation to the economic and
social development of the region and the Nation.

4. To insure the preparation of sound basin programs, Congress should direct
the responsible Federal agencies to cooperate with each other and with the

*A Water Policy for the American People, The Report of the President's Water Resources Policy
Commission, Vol. 1 (Washington, D.C.: Government Printing Office, 1950), 10–17.

appropriate State agencies in the necessary surveys and plans. Such action requires some definite coordination of the efforts of Federal and State agencies. While administrative reorganization in the field of natural resources is outside the assignment of this Commission, the Commission believes that, lacking such agency reorganization as was recommended by the Commission on Organization of the Executive Branch of the Government (Hoover Commission), Congress should set up a separate river basin commission for each of the major basins. These commissions, set upon a representative basis, should be authorized to coordinate the surveys, construction activities, and operations of the Federal agencies in the several basins, under the guidance of independent chairmen appointed by the President and with the participation of State agencies in the planning process.

5. Congress should designate the Federal departments and independent agencies to participate in the river basin commissions. Such participation should provide for representation of all agencies with functions included in water resources programs. Congress should assure all such agencies adequate authority to participate in comprehensive planning on an equal basis, together with appropriations consistent with such participation.

EVALUATION

6. Procedure for evaluation of proposed water resources developments should be revised to apply to multiple-purpose basin programs, and to projects only as constituent parts of such programs.

7. To assure uniformity in the application of evaluation procedure, Congress should direct all Federal agencies to apply the same standards and methods to the evaluation of all river basin programs.

8. The orderly formulation of national water resources programs requires the establishment of a Federal Board of Review appointed by the President with the confirmation of the Senate. This Board should perform, among others, the functions of the review agencies recommended in the reports of the Hoover Commission.

9. The evaluation procedure should start with the measurement of direct benefits from and costs of programs, but should be supplemented with standard procedure for taking account of secondary costs and benefits. Similarly, values should be assigned to public benefits and costs which affect the general welfare. This could be accomplished in accordance with a standard form of investment appraisal statement for each program or project within that program.

10. The investment appraisal statement should be in a form which would present the benefits and costs simply and clearly for the guidance of Congress and of interested citizen groups.

11. The investment appraisal statement should include a complete estimate of the costs to the American people, both direct and indirect, of undertaking

any project. Direct costs should include the initial investment in preliminary investigation, survey, and plan; construction; land acquisition; rights-of-way; utility replacement; and administration and overhead. Indirect costs comprise those resulting from displacement of population, loss of land and minerals, loss of wildlife, and loss of scenic or historic values. The indirect costs may be stated in nonmonetary terms.

12. The investment appraisal statement should also include a complete estimate of primary and secondary benefits. Primary benefits should be evaluated in terms of a procedure which places a monetary value on those susceptible of such evaluation. Secondary benefits should be estimated by the interested agencies according to a uniform procedure jointly developed with the approval of the Board of Review. They should reflect the increase in national income resulting from the program.

13. The evaluation procedure should also provide that, where the sum of the benefits so estimated is not sufficient to balance the direct and indirect costs, the final decision by the basin commission on the merits of the project should include a judgment as to whether the balance of general welfare benefits and detriments contributes sufficient additional value to warrant construction of the project.

14. Congress should direct all Federal departments and agencies responsible for the development of water and land resources, in cooperation with interested States, to promptly review all existing plans and programs, and to cooperate in preparing coordinated plans for water resources development for the several river basins. Plans already authorized by Congress should remain undisturbed unless this review results in specific recommendations for change.

BASIC DATA

15. Congress should make ample provision, in the national water resources program, for compilation and analysis of the necessary basic information to assure sound, comprehensive multiple-purpose basin planning. This should include geologic, hydrologic, climatic, land and soil analysis, and economic data to meet the needs of the planning agencies.

16. Congress should require that all basin recommendations carry a precise statement as to the adequacy of the data upon which they are based. Congress should be prepared to withhold approval of recommendations in areas where the data are inadequate.

17. A survey program designed to supply the country with full geological and hydrological knowledge of its surface and ground water resources, including all their characteristics, should be initiated immediately, with ample funds for the early compilation of essential information. Thereafter it should be continued to meet all of the requirements of basin programs.

18. The appropriate agency should be directed to undertake the annual compilation of and report on all water uses and requirements in relation to available sources of supply. This should be comprehensive and should be reported for regions and localities on a basis permitting 10- and 20-year running forecasts of requirements and supply.

19. A survey should be undertaken promptly to evaluate the possibilities of and provide a program for developing the water now being consumed in the West by unneeded, water-loving plants whose roots tap the water table or the capillary fringe above it.

FINANCING PROGRAMS

20. The financing of the Nation's river basin programs should be set up on a long-range basis, with each annual budget request therefor subdivided by river basins. These budget requests, in turn, should be subdivided by projects, functions, and agencies. To obtain these results, Congress should direct all Federal agencies to submit their budget requests, insofar as they involve water resources, by river basins. The entire procedure should result in 6-year river basin capital investment programs and annual budgets, originating in the agencies, coordinated by the river basin commissions, and reviewed by the Board of Review for submission to the Bureau of the Budget. Congress should make an annual appropriation to each river basin commission for its activities.

21. The annual water resources investment program should be based on a thorough review of the Nation's resources and of its resources development requirements. The budget should show the expenditures required to maintain the Nation's heritage of land and water resources, to increase the national and regional productivity, and to provide for health and recreation.

REIMBURSEMENT

22. Congress, in drafting new legislation or amending existing legislation, should provide for a uniform national reimbursement policy and specify the principles to be applied.

23. Reimbursement procedure should aim, as far as possible, to recover a reasonable portion of the benefits accruing from public expenditures for water resources development. This should provide for charges for benefits where they can be collected, and agreements with interested States under which they would utilize their powers of taxation or assessment to assure reimbursement to the Federal Government for primary and secondary benefits not susceptible of direct collection.

24. Reimbursement policy for given functions such as reclamation by irrigation or drainage should be uniform for all Federal agencies.

25. Reimbursement for various types of benefits from water resources programs should be determined in accordance with the following principles: (*a*) For domestic and industrial water supply and hydroelectric power it should provide for full repayment of water supply or power costs including operation and maintenance, repayment with interest of an appropriate allocation of the program investment, and payment in lieu of local and State taxes which would have been paid on acquired properties; (*b*) for drainage, irrigation, and watershed management it should be based on ability to pay, without interest, measured by the resulting increase in the land operator's net earnings; (*c*) for navigation it should be determined in connection with a general program for putting charges for all forms of transportation on a cost basis, including interest; (*d*) for all other benefits, the responsibility for securing repayment of the cost of primary and secondary benefits should be shared by the States on an agreed basis, while general welfare benefits should be the responsibility of the Federal Government.

26. The Federal contribution to the cost of a river basin program or project should be considered as balancing the contributions to the general welfare estimated to result from the undertaking.

27. Congress, in appropriating for basin programs, should distinguish between the portions of the total investment allocable to the different benefits on the basis of proposals by the basin commissions, passed upon by the Board of Review. Multipurpose program accounts should be established for each basin and for the national water resources program as a whole to assure clear identification of all costs, benefits, and repayments.

28. Irrigation projects should be placed on the same basis as other water resources projects for which full reimbursement is not required as a test of feasibility.

WATER RESOURCES MANAGEMENT

29. Ground water resources should be included in comprehensive basin programs, with clear recognition of their interrelationship with surface waters, and with due regard to the rights and interests of the States. The Federal Government should encourage enactment of State laws and negotiation of interstate compacts that foster water management for optimum yield and use, especially with respect to surface and ground water storage opportunities.

30. Watershed management should be included as a principal objective in the planning and development of basin programs, with large enough allotments of funds to enable soil conservation, range management, and forest agencies to undertake activities which will bring economically controllable deterioration of the land under control within a reasonable period of time.

31. All related Federal policies and activities, including the price support, agricultural conservation, irrigation, credit programs, and administration of

Federal mining laws should be adjusted to strengthen the effectiveness of watershed management.

32. Flood control should be considered as an important part of water resources management. Conservation storage of floodwaters in the soil, underground, and in surface reservoirs on tributaries and upper reaches of rivers should be a principal factor in the planning and development of river basin programs.

33. Consistent with other aspects of the basin program, flood storage should be located and designed to assure the greatest possible use and reuse of floodwaters in the course of their journey to the sea.

34. Congress should authorize the responsible Federal agencies, in reviewing river basin programs, to consider all of the possibilities of flood protection, flood storage, and utilization of floodwaters. They should consider such measures as local flood protection works, flood plain zoning, flood forecasting, design of levees and related works to release sediment-laden water on the land where this would contribute to fertility of the soil. They should also consider all types and combinations of reservoirs designed to meet the Nation's requirements in all fields of water utilization.

LAND RECLAMATION

35. An over-all program should be prepared for the employment of all methods for orderly expansion of agricultural production to meet the Nation's expanding needs. This program should coordinate irrigation, drainage, flood control, clearing, and the sound farm practices which are an essential part of watershed management.

36. The first objective of this program should be adequate provision of farm products from soil so managed that its productivity is enhanced. Irrigation and drainage projects should be authorized only after review by the Department of Agriculture indicating that they are in harmony with sound use of land.

37. The weight to be given reclamation of land (including irrigation, drainage, clearing, and other measures) in determining the relative priority of programs and order of construction of specific multiple-purpose projects should be based on regional as well as national considerations. National considerations should include Federal responsibility for continuing adequacy of dependable farm production, taking cognizance of the time required to bring new lands into the Nation's agricultural economy. The expansion of local production to meet the requirements of growing regional economies should also be considered.

38. In determining the desirable schedule for adding to the Nation's agricultural acreage through reclamation, full consideration should be given to the probable rate of increase in the productivity of existing agricultural lands through improved agricultural practices, including supplemental irrigation in

humid areas. To the extent that such increased productivity is associated with sound land management, it should be recognized as of primary importance. But, beyond this, improved agricultural practices should be left to private business endeavors with the cooperation of the United States Department of Agriculture and the land-grant colleges until such time as the economically sound possibilities of expanding farm acreage through irrigation or drainage have been fully realized. The justification for public investment in irrigation is that there are public ends to be attained which the commercial price system cannot reflect.

39. Decisions as to the relative priority of projects involving various types of reclamation as a means of expanding the country's agricultural acreage should be made in terms of both national and regional economic considerations. They should recognize the extent to which individual projects are integral parts of comprehensive river basin programs serving other important purposes. Important weight should be given to the comparative costs of meeting agricultural production objectives by alternative undertakings, but consideration should also be given to the special usefulness of certain irrigation opportunities in stabilizing agriculture, meeting expanding regional requirements, or contributing to regional expansion. The weight to be given these separate considerations should be determined by the Board of Review upon recommendation of the basin commissions.

40. To protect its interest in securing the maximum reasonable reimbursement from direct beneficiaries of reclamation projects, the Federal Government should make more effective provision for the adequate planning, sound financing, and scientific farming of agricultural development and land settlement on reclamation projects. This should include extension of Federal credit at reasonable interest rates for the farmer's investment in structures, equipment, fertilizer, stock and seed, and the technical training and guidance of settlers.

41. Special consideration should be given to rehabilitation of existing irrigation projects, both Federal and private, as well as to small new irrigation projects offering the possibility of stabilizing the agriculture of an area.

42. The principle embodied in the reclamation law that the benefits of Federal financial assistance through irrigation projects should go only to family-sized farms, together with other antispeculation and antimonopoly provisions, should be maintained and enforced. It should be extended to apply without discrimination to all new projects involving Federal investment in the reclaiming of land, whether by irrigation, drainage, or other methods.

43. The present 160-acre limitation provision should be considered as a maximum, with flexibility for adjustment downward after hearings, to adapt it to types of farming characteristic of different areas. It should apply only to the reclaimed portion of a farm.

[650]

44. In regions where it is proposed to deliver supplemental water to areas already under irrigation, provision should be made for the supplying of an equitable share of such water to existing farms exceeding the acreage limitation under utility-type contracts. In these contracts the charges for the water should be based on the full cost of supplying water to such lands, including amortization with interest of the full investment allocable to this purpose.

45. Before new Federal reclamation projects, or projects providing supplemental water or drainage for existing projects, are undertaken, every effort should be made to secure agreements or contracts with the State or States involved or the local interests to be benefited under which surface and ground water benefits will be considered together. All beneficiaries should be subject to the standard reimbursement obligations, whether securing the benefits from augmented surface or ground waters.

46. The same conditions as to authorization, repayment, technical and financial assistance, and acreage limitation should apply to all projects or project beneficiaries, where Federal investment in reclamation of land is concerned. This principle should be applied irrespective of the method of reclamation or the Federal agency responsible for the project.

WATER SUPPLY

47. Municipal water supply should continue to be primarily a local responsibility, including intercommunity cooperation through the formation of metropolitan water districts to make possible area-wide coordination of water supply sources to meet the needs of an increasing population. The growing needs of communities for water supply should, however, be considered in connection with the planning of all comprehensive basin programs. Their use of water from multiple-purpose reservoirs and improved stream flow should constitute a fully reimbursable service under such programs.

48. Possible future water requirements of large water-using industries should be considered as an important regional and national factor in connection with the planning of comprehensive basin programs. This should be particularly the case in regions where deposits of oil shales or other special resources point to industrial developments of significance to the Nation's economic and military security.

49. The possibilities of contributing to municipal and industrial water supply and irrigation through recharging of ground water reservoirs and flows should be given full consideration in connection with all comprehensive basin planning. More complete knowledge of the country's ground water resources may open the way to ground water storage of surplus floodwaters as an important supplement to surface storage.

POLLUTION CONTROL

50. Pollution control should be considered in the planning and development of river basin programs. It should be recognized as a major contribution to the Nation's objectives in the fields of water supply, recreation, fish and wildlife.

51. A 10-year period should be set within which to accomplish a reasonable program for cleaning up the Nation's polluted waters. Cooperative efforts of private industries, organizations, municipalities, States, and the Federal Government should be mobilized to that end.

52. Sufficient funds should be appropriated for the administrative and regulatory activities of the Public Health Service, Division of Water Pollution Control to make sure that present congressional policy is adequately tested. Ample funds for Federal loans to municipalities should be made available at not more than 2 percent interest covering the entire cost of constructing the necessary sewage treatment works.

53. Multiple-purpose reservoirs should, as far as consonant with other major purposes, be planned and operated so as not to aggravate but to contribute to the control of pollution. This should include regulation of releases of water to make fullest use of the stream's potential self-purification capacity, with advance determination of the schedule of releases to permit proper classification of the stream by the Public Health Service for pollution control purposes.

WATERWAY TRANSPORTATION

54. The Nation should continue the improvement of its inland and intracoastal waterways to standard depth as an important objective of comprehensive basin programs. This part of water resources development should be integrated into a broader program designed to provide the Nation with an economical and efficient coordinated transportation system including railroads, motor transport, waterways, and airways. In such a coordinated system all forms of transportation should be considered as complementary rather than competitive with each other.

55. Waterway charges should not be considered as yardsticks for railroad rates, but rather as rates for traffic which, in the coordinated transportation system, can move more economically by water than by rail. In order to assure the greatest over-all contribution of the transportation system to the Nation's well-being, railroads should not be permitted to establish discriminatory rates paralleling waterway rates.

56. Decisions as to user charges, or tolls, for waterway commerce should be worked out as part of the whole problem of reconciling and making workable a coordinated transportation system. But, with rates for all forms of transportation based on full costs, an interconnected system of modern waterways, coordinated

with land transportation, should be able to sustain itself with tolls based on full costs and yield returns on the public investment while contributing to most economic use of the Nation's resources.

HYDROELECTRIC POWER

57. Full development of the Nation's undeveloped water power resources, as an integral part of comprehensive basin programs, should be considered a major Federal responsibility, to be exercised in such a way as to assure ample supplies of hydroelectric energy well in advance of expanding regional and national needs.

58. Federal hydroelectric plants should be designed to produce ultimate capacity and energy which will best fit into the requirements of potential markets on the assumption of complete regional integration of power supply.

59. Future licenses for new non-Federal water power developments should be issued only with the joint consent of the Federal agencies responsible for power in basin programs. In exercising this responsibility, the Federal agencies should continue to recognize the preferential position accorded State and municipal applicants under the Federal Power Act.

60. The Federal power marketing policy heretofore adopted by Congress, authorizing Federal agencies to build transmission facilities, giving preferences in power sales to public and cooperative bodies and fostering low rates for residential and rural consumption, should be continued.

61. Federal power marketing policy should be carried out flexibly to assure sound adaptation of Federal power supply responsibility to regional power resources and the most effective cooperation of all power systems, public and private, in the task of assuring ample supplies of power at the lowest possible rates.

62. Since private power systems will probably continue to provide a large share of the new capacity required to meet future needs, Federal arrangements for marketing power should where possible take full advantage of private power facilities, provided the contracts preserve the preferential rights of public bodies and cooperatives to a share of the power, or its equivalent, at the lowest possible rates.

63. Where the Federal Government assumes a major responsibility for the power supply to distribution systems, this should be recognized as a utility responsibility; requiring the construction of new generating capacity, whether hydroelectric or steam-electric, well in advance of expanding needs.

FISH, WILDLIFE, AND RECREATION

64. Preservation and enhancement of the Nation's fish and wildlife resources should be recognized as one of the important objectives of comprehensive river

basin planning. The requirements of this objective should be thoroughly investigated in connection with project proposals designed to serve other major purposes. Releases of water from multiple-purpose reservoir projects should be adequate, except where higher uses dictate otherwise, to guarantee continuous use of the river by wildlife and fish. All proposed basin projects should be studied to determine in advance their effect on waterfowl habitat.

65. The recreation potentialities of all water resources, whether natural or artificial, should be recognized, and expansion of outdoor recreation opportunities should be given full consideration in all comprehensive basin programs. To achieve this objective suitable lands adjacent to Federal water projects should be reserved for recreation use, and consideration should be given to minimizing water level fluctuations in storage reservoirs during vacation season, to improving low flows of rivers, and to pollution abatement. In densely populated areas and in regions where natural water recreation opportunities are limited, recreation may be a controlling factor in water resources programs.

66. Cooperative arrangements should be worked out with States and local governments for planning, developing, and maintaining recreation areas at government water projects, subject to the observance of specified standards to preserve general opportunity to enjoy the recreation resource under conditions in harmony with the natural environment.

67. Federal participation in recreation features of water resources programs should be determined in relation to Federal participation in other recreation programs. To this end, it is desirable that Congress authorize a study of the whole recreation field, having as its objective the development of a national recreation policy.

FUTURE POSSIBILITIES

68. The Federal Government should recognize that, with growth of population, urban concentration, industrialization, and the need for an expanding agricultural base, availability of fresh water may soon become a limiting factor in the expansion not only of the Nation's arid and semiarid regions but also of our entire civilization. The Government should, therefore, accept the responsibility for large investment in broad research programs designed to expand the available supplies of water. Such research programs will be directed toward:

(*a*) Exploring and developing the necessary techniques for utilizing the full possibilities of the Nation's ground water resources;

(*b*) Establishment of a sound national policy for control of artificial rainmaking activities and the application of science to devising methods which can be utilized in the public interest; and

(*c*) Exploration and experimentation, including pilot plant operation, in the general field of conversion of sea water to fresh water on an economical basis.

In terms of the Nation's future, such research and experimentation may well be found to rank with the development of atomic energy utilization.

69. The recommendations summarized above, and more fully explained in subsequent chapters, should provide the nucleus of a consistent national water resources policy to guide the Nation in the further development and use of its water potentialities.

70. The Commission recommends that the policy embodied in the above recommendations be incorporated in a single statute stating both principles and policies, together with provisions requiring their application to all Federal water resources activities irrespective of the agency or agencies concerned. Changes arising from these recommendations would, of course, not be applicable to existing contracts with project beneficiaries except upon their agreement. Nor do these recommendations contemplate a departure from the traditional recognition by Congress of rights to the use of water under State law as embodied in such legislation as the Reclamation Act of 1902.

THE SALINE WATER ACT*
July 3, 1952

A program for research into conversion of saline waters was authorized under this law.

An Act to provide for research into and development of practical means for the economical production, from sea or other saline waters, of water suitable for agricultural, industrial, municipal, and other beneficial consumptive uses, and for other purposes.

Be it enacted by the Senate and House of Representatives of the United States of America in Congress assembled, That, in view of the acute shortage of water in the arid areas of the Nation and elsewhere and the excessive use of underground waters throughout the Nation, it is the policy of the Congress to provide for the development of practicable low-cost means of producing from sea water, or from other saline waters, water of a quality suitable for agriculture, industrial, municipal, and other beneficial consumptive uses on a scale sufficient to determine the feasibility of the development of such production and distribution on a large-scale basis, for the purpose of conserving and increasing the water resources of the Nation.

SEC. 2. In order to carry out the purposes of this Act, the Secretary of the Interior, acting through such agencies of the Department of the Interior as he may deem appropriate, is authorized —

(a) by means of research grants and contracts as set forth in subsection (d) of this section to conduct research and technical development work, to make careful engineering studies to ascertain the lowest investment and operating costs, and to determine the best plant designs and conditions of operation;

(b) to study methods for the recovery and marketing of byproducts resulting from and incident to the production of water as herein provided for the purpose of ascertaining the possibilities of offsetting the costs of water production in any area by the commercial utilization of such products;

(c) to acquire, by purchase, license, lease, or donation, secret processes, technical data, inventions, patent applications, patents, licenses, land and any interest in land (including water rights, easements, and leasehold interests), plants and facilities, and other property or rights: *Provided,* That the land or other property acquired hereunder shall not exceed that necessary to carry on the experiments and demonstrations for the purposes herein provided;

*66 *Statutes at Large,* 328–29.

(d) to engage, by noncompetitive contract or otherwise, chemists, physicists, engineers, and such other personnel as may be deemed necessary, and any educational institution, scientific organization, or industrial or engineering firm deemed suitable to do any part of the research or other work, and to the extent appropriate to correlate and coordinate the research and development work of such educational institutions, scientific organizations and industrial and engineering firms; and

(e) to cooperate with any other Federal, State, or municipal department, agency, or instrumentality, and with any private person, firm, educational institution, or other organization in effectuating the purpose of this Act.

SEC. 3. Research undertaken by the Secretary of the Interior under the authority contained in this Act shall be coordinated or conducted jointly with the Department of Defense to the greatest practicable extent compatible with military and security limitations, to the end that research and developments under this Act which are primarily of a civil nature will contribute to the defense of the Nation and that research and developments in the same field which are primarily of a military nature and are conducted by the Department of Defense will be made available to advance the purposes of this Act and to strengthen the civil economy of the Nation.

SEC. 4. The Secretary of the Interior is authorized, for the sole purpose of this Act, to dispose of all water and other products produced as a result of his operations under this Act pursuant to regulations to be prescribed by him: *Provided,* That nothing in this Act shall be construed to alter existing law with respect to the ownership and control of water.

SEC. 5. All moneys received for products of the plants under this Act shall be paid into the Treasury as miscellaneous receipts.

SEC. 6. The Secretary of the Interior shall make reports to the President and the Congress at the beginning of each regular session of the action taken or instituted by him under the provisions of this Act. The report shall include suitable recommendations for further legislation.

SEC. 7. The Secretary of the Interior may issue rules and regulations to effectuate the purposes of this Act.

SEC. 8. There are authorized to be appropriated, from any funds in the Treasury not otherwise appropriated, such sums, not to exceed $2,000,000, for a five-year period, to carry out the provisions of this Act: *Provided,* That departmental expenses for the correlation and coordination of information over such five-year period shall not exceed the sum of $500,000: *Provided further,* That such departmental expenses shall be scheduled in equal amounts for each year of such period insofar as practicable.

Approved July 3, 1952.

After the Bureau of the Budget became the instrument of presidential coordination of natural resource projects, proponents of these programs often interpreted Bureau requirements as being aimed more at eliminating projects than coordinating them.

Bureau of the Budget Circular A-47 is the best known example of budgetary requirements. Proponents of public power development attacked A-47 as a barrier to future power programs, with its provisions in regard to "taxes foregone," but it also provided severe criteria for all types of resource projects.

Circular A-47 was actually approved by the Director of the Budget in the closing days of the Truman administration, but adherence to it during the Eisenhower administration brought the sharpest criticism. After the documer:t became a campaign issue in 1960, modifications were made in 1961 during the administration of John F. Kennedy.

TO THE HEADS OF EXECUTIVE DEPARTMENTS AND ESTABLISHMENTS

SUBJECT: Reports and budget estimates relating to Federal programs and projects for conservation, development, or use of water and related land resources.

1. *Purpose.* The policies of the President with regard to programs and projects for the development of water and related land resources have been established from time to time both as a part of the normal budget and legislative review process under Bureau of the Budget Circulars No. A-11, "Instructions for the preparation and submission of annual budget estimates," and No. A-19, "Reports and recommendations on proposed and pending legislation," and as a part of the review of project reports under Executive Order 9384, "Submission of reports to facilitate budgeting activities of the Federal Government." This Circular is intended to draw together certain of these policies for water resources programs and projects and to provide the agencies in advance with a better understanding of the considerations which will be used in determining the relationship of a proposed program or project, or budget estimate, to the program of the President.

The standards and procedures set forth in this Circular will be used by the Executive Office of the President in reviewing agency reports and budget estimates subject to its provisions, in order that uniform policies may be applied

*Executive Office of the President, Bureau of the Budget, *Circular A-47*, 1–22.

with a view towards (a) establishing priority for projects yielding the greatest value to the Nation, and (b) securing effective resources development at minimum necessary cost. The priority among programs or projects meeting the standards and procedures set forth in this Circular, and action upon budget estimates to initiate such programs or projects, necessarily will also depend on budget policies established from year to year to meet current economic conditions.

2. *Authority.* Executive Order 9384, October 4, 1943, requires submission to the Bureau of the Budget of reports relating to or affecting Federal public works and improvement projects. Bureau of the Budget Circular No. A-19, Revised, requires submission to the Bureau of agency reports on proposed and pending legislation. Bureau of the Budget Circular No. A-11, Revised, outlines the requirements for preparation and submission to the Bureau of annual budget estimates. This Circular, No. A-47, supplements the requirements of the Executive Order and Circulars referred to, and is issued pursuant to the authority cited therein.

3. *Coverage.* This Circular relates to Federal programs or projects for the conservation, development, or use of water and related land resources. It applies to any report and to any budget estimate to initiate construction of a program or project, which, by the terms of the Executive Order and Circulars referred to in paragraph 2, is required to be submitted to the Bureau of the Budget and which involves a program or project of the type referred to in the first sentence of this paragraph. It does not apply to budget estimates for electric transmission lines or steam electric generating plants required in connection with water resources projects.

4. *Compliance.*

   a. *Relation to existing law.* The standards and procedures set forth in this Circular shall not be regarded as authorizing any deviation from general or specific requirements of law. Whenever a report or budget estimate varies from such standards or procedures because of a requirement of existing law, the variation shall be indicated and reference made to the section of law imposing such requirement.

   b. *Application to budget estimates.* Except as provided in paragraph 4a, a budget estimate subject to this Circular shall conform to the standards and procedures set forth herein.

   c. *Variations from Circular.* This Circular shall not be regarded as requiring an agency to submit a report which is contrary to its views. However, any report which varies from the standards and procedures set forth herein because of agency policies shall, in the same manner as indicated in paragraph 4a, be accompanied by a statement of the reasons for the variation. Each report shall contain or be accompanied by appropriately documented information to indicate the exact extent to which the standards and procedures established herein have been followed in the preparation of the report. Where the preparation of the basic report is so far advanced on the date of issuance of this Circular that it would be impracticable to furnish the information required by this Circular, this fact will be taken into account in the consideration of the report. All reports submitted after July 1, 1953, however, must conform to the requirements of this Circular.

5. *Definitions.* For the purposes of this Circular:

a. "Project" means any integral physical unit or several component and closely related units or features, or any system of measures, undertaken or to be undertaken within a specified area for the control or development of water or related land resources, which can be considered as a separate entity for purposes of planning, evaluation, financing, construction, management, or operation. Separable units or features will generally be considered as separate projects.

b. "Program" means any combination or system of two or more interrelated projects.

c. "Benefits," as used for purposes of evaluation of proposed programs or projects, means all the identifiable gains, assets, or values, whether in goods, services, or intangibles, whether primary or secondary, and whether measurable in monetary or nonmonetary terms, which would result from the construction, operation, or maintenance of a program or project.

d. "Primary benefits" means the identifiable gains, assets, or values directly resulting from any program or project.

e. "Secondary benefits" means identifiable gains, assets, or values other than primary benefits of a program or project which are properly creditable to the program or project.

f. "Economic costs," as used for purposes of evaluation of proposed programs and projects, means all the financial costs of the program or project except investigating, surveying and planning costs incurred prior to authorization; and all the other identifiable expenses, losses, and liabilities, whether in goods, services, or intangibles, whether direct or induced, and whether measurable in monetary or nonmonetary terms, which are incurred as a result of constructing, operating, or maintaining a program or project.

g. "Financial costs" means all the monetary outlays made in connection with a program or project and interest costs connected therewith; i.e., the construction costs, the operation and maintenance costs, and interest on the unliquidated balance of the reimbursable construction costs. When applied to allocations made to *irrigation* for repayment purposes under paragraphs 7a and 18b, "financial costs" shall not include interest on the irrigation construction costs.

h. "Construction costs" means expenditures (amounts paid and payable) for the initial project construction and the net replacements and additions of significant units thereof, including contract work, materials and supplies, labor, and use of equipment; acquisition of lands, easements, rights-of-way, and water rights; costs of relocating facilities and the settlement of damage claims; interest during construction; any capital expenditures for protection of public health, for preventing loss of or damages to recreation, fish and wildlife and mineral resources, and scenic, archeological, and historical values; any capital expenditures for the replacement of recreation and fish and wildlife resources damaged or destroyed by the project; the appropriate portion of engineering, administrative and general expenses of the agency relating to the project; and all other amounts of expenditures specifically applicable to the investigations, surveys, plans, designs, and construction of the project. When applied to allocations made to *irrigation* for repayment purposes under paragraphs 7a and 18b, "construction costs" shall not include interest during construction on the costs allocated to irrigation.

i. "Operation and maintenance costs" means those expenditures for materials and supplies, labor, necessary services, equipment and operating facility use, and an appropriate portion of engineering, supervision and general expenses of the agency which are needed to operate a project once constructed and to make repairs, minor additions and replacements, and otherwise to maintain the project in sound operating condition for a maximum economic life. This includes any expenditures of the project, other than capital expenditures, for protection of public health, for preventing loss of or damages to recreation and fish and wildlife resources, and scenic, archeological and historical values; and any expenditures of the project, other than capital expenditures, for the replacement of recreation and fish and wildlife resources damaged or destroyed by the project.

j. "Net revenues" means the difference between the total revenues of the program or project or separable purpose thereof and the properly allocable financial costs of such program, project or purpose.

k. "Reclamation" means making land suitable for productive agricultural use or increasing or maintaining its productive agricultural use by means of (1) irrigation; (2) drainage, excluding drainage undertaken pursuant to Section 2 of the Act of December 22, 1944 (58 Stat. 887), and excluding drainage undertaken solely to counteract the effects of flood control works; and (3) recharging of ground waters.

6. *State, local, and Federal participation.* Agencies responsible for developing proposed programs or projects shall, as now provided under certain laws and administrative practices, consult with the people of the area primarily affected and with the State and local governments and Federal agencies concerned. This consultation should take place at the earliest feasible stage and should be continued throughout the investigation, survey, and planning stages, in order that the views of these groups and agencies may receive adequate consideration. Such consultation need not be repeated at the time budget estimates to initiate a program or project are being prepared; however, budget estimates shall include the latest information available on the views of Federal agencies, States, and interested local groups as to priorities of project development, scheduling of construction, and willingness to comply with requirements for local participation.

7. *Information for inclusion in, and criteria for review of, evaluation reports.*

a. The following categories of information, some of which are elaborated in later paragraphs of this Circular, shall be included in the evaluation report proposing authorization of a new water or related land resources program or project. Under certain of the categories of information listed below, there are indicated the criteria which will be used by the Executive Office in the review of proposed program or project reports:

(1) A description of the need for the production or services which would result from the program or project; the relation of the program or project to the other elements of the resource development program of the region in which the program or project is to be undertaken; the contribution of the program or project to balanced national conservation and development; and the efficiency of the program or project in meeting regional or national needs.

An important consideration in the review of evaluation reports will be whether execution of the program or project, and, within practical limits, execution of each separate part of a program or project, will be more economical than alternative means available in the region for meeting the same needs. Where a single-purpose alternative is available, inclusion in a multiple-purpose program or project plan of any purpose of resource development will be considered only if the purpose is accomplished more economically through the multiple-purpose program or project than through the single-purpose alternative. A further consideration in the review of evaluation reports will be the relative economy of alternative means available on a national basis for meeting the needs to be met by the program or project.

(2) A concise but complete estimate of all the benefits and all of the

economic costs of undertaking the program or project. In addition to comparing the total benefits of the program or project with its total economic costs, the estimate should also show separately the particular benefits and economic costs attributable to each purpose of the program or project. Wherever appropriate, benefits and economic costs shall be expressed in monetary terms. Where monetary estimates cannot reasonably be made, the relative significance of such benefits and costs shall be stated in as precise and quantitative terms as possible. Because any long-term estimates are subject to wide margins of error, the results should be expressed in ranges rather than in single figures. The estimate should be made from an over-all public or national viewpoint and should indicate any specifically identifiable groups, localities, or districts receiving program or project benefits.

While it is recognized that a comparison of estimated benefits with estimated costs does not necessarily provide a precise measure of the absolute merits of any particular program or project, one essential criterion in justifying any program or project will, except in unusual cases where adequate justification is presented, be that its estimated benefits to whomsoever they may accrue exceed its estimated costs. Inclusion in a multiple-purpose program or project plan of any purpose of resource development will, except in unusual cases where adequate justification is presented, be considered only if the benefits attributable to that particular purpose are greater than the economic costs of including that purpose in the program or project. Monetary computations will be most useful in arranging programs or projects, or parts thereof, serving the same purpose in the order of their economic desirability.

(3) All data relating to the financial feasibility and to the allocation and reimbursement of financial costs prepared in accordance with the standards set forth in paragraphs 11–21. This shall include a statement as to the financial feasibility of reimbursable features of the program or project and the net effect of the program or project on the Federal Treasury. For this purpose the project report shall show an analysis of the sources of repayment or sharing of the financial costs of each of the purposes involved in the program or project. Financial costs shall be converted to an annual basis to make possible a comparison of annual financial costs and annual revenues of any program or project or separable purpose thereof.

(4) A statement as to the source and nature of, and an appraisal of the adequacy of, the basic information available and used during the preparation of such program or project and the methods employed in the analysis and interpretation of such basic information.

b. Requests for funds for the initiation of construction of a program or project following authorization shall be accompanied by a statement indicating the changes which have occurred, if any, since submittal of the original report upon which authorization was based, affecting the total cost, the economic evaluation, or the purposes of the program or project. If substantial changes have occurred, the request shall be accompanied by a revised evaluation report.

8. *Benefits to be included in evaluation.* The evaluation report prepared in accordance with paragraph 7 shall include an estimate of the primary benefits of the program or project. Unless the report sets forth clear justification for considering other factors, main reliance in the review of project reports will be placed on the following categories of primary benefits:

a. Reduction of flood damage, including damage from water and sediment, to land and other public and private property; and prevention of loss of life.

b. Increases in the expected net income obtained directly from changed use of the property made possible by any form of flood control.

c. Increases in expected net income from lands on which watershed treatment measures are to be installed as part of the program or project.

d. Increase in expected net farm income from additional production or reduced cost of production of farm products as a result of reclamation of land.

e. In the case of navigation projects other than harbor improvements, the transportation savings resulting from:

(1) The differential between expected costs of movement by non-water transport and expected costs of movement by water transport for those commodities which will be carried by land transport if the project is not built, but which will move by water if the project is built.

(2) For traffic which will not move without the waterway improvement, but which will move by water if the project is built, the differential between the cost of transportation by waterway and the highest cost at which it would be feasible for the traffic to move.

(3) Where the project improves an already navigable waterway, the

differential between expected costs with and without the project of moving on the waterway traffic expected to move on the waterway even if the project is not built.

f. Direct benefits of shore protection.

g. Direct benefits from harbor improvements, including those for small boat traffic.

h. Value of electric energy to be produced. This is equal to the lower of two figures:

    (1) The cost of equivalent energy from the cheapest alternative source of energy—private, Federal, or other—that is available, or could be expected to develop in the absence of the project, to meet the same power needs. Taxes and interest charges for this alternative source should be computed on a basis comparable with the project.

        Note.—Where the project plan includes the cost of constructing and operating the necessary facilities to transmit and distribute the project power to load centers, the costs of the alternative source with which the project is compared should also include transmission and distribution costs to the same load centers. Where the project plan does not include transmission costs, the total costs incurred by the alternative source in providing power at load centers should, for purposes of determining power benefits, be reduced by the transmission costs incurred in bringing the project power to the same load centers.

    (2) Value of power to users (considered as the highest price they would pay and applicable especially where the cost of alternative power would be prohibitive for particular users).

i. Value of municipal, industrial, and domestic water supply to be furnished, measured by the cost of obtaining equivalent supply from the cheapest alternative source that would most likely be used in the absence of the project, including the cost of development of the same source of water by the water users themselves as one of the alternatives. Taxes and interest charges for the alternative source should be computed on a basis comparable with the project.

j. Increases in the value of recreation and fish and wildlife resources expected as a result of the project. Although such benefits are usually not subject to measurement in monetary terms, complete information, in terms of the amount and type of expected use of recreation and fish and wildlife developments is required as a basis for comparison of the incremental costs and benefits of such developments referred to in paragraphs 11c and 19b.

[665]

k. Savings in the cost of water treatment or gains in the value of streams for industrial, municipal, and domestic water supply, and other uses, through the abatement of water pollution; and reduction in the cost of pollution abatement by stream flow augmentation. Such benefits should be calculated as the residual benefit possible after allowing for all direct measures to control pollution at the source that would normally be required or considered necessary by the public health authorities concerned.

The evaluation prepared in accordance with paragraph 7 shall also include an estimate of any secondary benefits which the program or project will provide. The evaluation shall include a separate showing of total primary and total secondary benefits. Until standards and procedures for measuring secondary benefits are approved by the Bureau of the Budget, the evaluation shall be based mainly upon primary benefits.

The evaluation shall also include an appraisal of the general benefits which will accrue through such effects as safeguarding life and public health, stabilizing national and regional food and raw materials production, and contributing directly to the improvement of technically underdeveloped areas within the Nation's boundaries.

9. *Costs to be included in evaluation.* The evaluation prepared in accordance with paragraph 7 shall include an estimate of the total construction costs and the total operation and maintenance costs of the program or project, whether such costs are incurred by the Federal Government, State and local governments, or private interests.

Such an evaluation shall also include a statement of economic costs expected to be induced by the program or project, such as the costs of:

a. Displacement of people.

b. Decreased value of lands, minerals, water quantity or quality, and other water or related land resources, where not reflected in market values.

c. Rectifying adverse effects upon sanitation, transportation, highway construction or maintenance, or other activities reasonably foreseen as being affected by the program or project.

d. Business losses, such as disruption of trade or diversion of waterborne traffic from existing ports or channels.

e. Losses in State or local tax revenues, adjusted for changes in costs of State and local government services caused by the existence of program or project facilities.

f. Unprevented and uncompensated losses of or damages to fish and wildlife resources; recreation resources; and scenic, archeological or historical values.

g. Abandonment of economically useful structures, such as locks and bridges.

Such an evaluation shall also include an appraisal of other detriments to the general welfare, whether or not they can be measured in monetary terms, and the groups which will suffer any substantial injury should be identified so far as feasible.

10. *Comparison of benefits and economic costs.* Benefits to be obtained and economic costs to be incurred throughout the assumed economic life of a program or project, as limited by paragraph 14 of this Circular, where expressed in monetary terms, shall be converted to a common time basis to facilitate the comparison called for in paragraph 7a(2). Where benefits and economic costs are compared on an annual basis, interest on the construction costs should be included in the computation of average annual equivalents for total economic costs. Where the present net worth method of comparing benefits and economic costs is to be used, future benefits and economic costs should be discounted to present values. Using an interest rate to cumulate benefits and economic costs is necessitated where the net gain or loss at any given time during the operation of the program or project is to be computed. Determination of the applicable interest or discount rate shall be made in accordance with paragraph 15, except for the interest rate on project costs to be financed by non-Federal sources.

11. *Purposes to which costs may be allocated and criteria for allocation of costs.* The evaluation report prepared in accordance with paragraph 7 shall include a tentative allocation of the construction costs and operation and maintenance costs of the program or project to the several purposes to be served, which allocation shall serve as the basis for the proposed reimbursement and cost-sharing arrangements recommended in the report. Proposals for the allocation of costs will be reviewed in accordance with the following standards:

    a. Subject to the criteria set forth in paragraphs b and c following and paragraphs 19 and 20, costs of both separable and joint facilities shall be equitably allocated to the following purposes and to no other purposes:

        (1) Flood control
        (2) Reclamation
        (3) Navigation
        (4) Watershed management
        (5) Electric power and energy
        (6) Domestic, municipal, or industrial water supply
        (7) Recreation development
        (8) Fish and wildlife development
        (9) Pollution control or abatement

    b. Costs of programs or projects shall be allocated to the several purposes for which they are undertaken on the following basis:

        (1) The costs of facilities or features of a program or project used only for a single purpose of water resources development shall

[667]

be allocated to the respective purposes served by such facilities or features.

(2) The costs of facilities or features of a program or project used jointly by more than one purpose of water resource development shall be allocated among the purposes served in such a way that each purpose will share equitably in the savings resulting from combining the purposes in a multiple-purpose development.

c. Allocations of costs to items (8) and (9) of paragraph a above shall be governed by the following:

(1) Allocations of costs to fish and wildlife shall be limited to the following:

(A) Costs incurred for the development of fish and wildlife to the extent that such costs are to be borne by States, local governments, or local interests.

(B) The increment of additional costs of a project incurred for fish and wildlife development if the fish and wildlife resources to be developed are determined by the Secretary of the Interior in accordance with present law to be of national significance, and if either (a) the work is proposed to be authorized as a part of a national fish and wildlife program and financed under appropriations made for that purpose, or (b) the letter transmitting the proposed report to the Congress contains proposed authorizing language stating the maximum amount of such costs which would be borne by the Federal Government.

(2) Allocations of costs to pollution control or abatement shall be limited to those costs for that purpose which are to be fully reimbursed by the States, local governments, districts, or other interests concerned, including other Federal establishments.

12. *Responsibility for allocation of costs on multiple-purpose programs or projects.* For purposes of this Circular, the head of the agency responsible for construction of the program or project will be considered responsible for:

a. Making the initial tentative allocation of costs among the purposes to be served by a program or project.

b. Making a revised cost allocation prior to the submission of a budget estimate to initiate the program or project if the costs can be ascertained with greater accuracy at that time than at the time of submission of the project report, or if the designated use of the program or project is changed, or if the estimated costs have changed substantially. Where designated use is changed or estimated costs have changed substantially, the head of such agency shall also indicate the reasons therefor.

Other agencies having responsibilities with respect to various purposes of the project, such as power marketing, rate approval, reclamation, navigation, flood control regulation, etc., shall be afforded full opportunity to consult and make their views known at both these stages in the determination of the cost allocation.

13. *Reimbursement and sharing of costs.* For the purposes of this Circular, it is essential that definite determinations be made as to which part of the financial costs of a proposed program or project will be reimbursed to the Federal Government, which will be borne by others than the Federal Government, and which will not be reimbursed. With respect to financial costs to be reimbursed and cash contributions to be made, the proposed source of funds therefor shall be clearly indicated. Where cash contributions are required, such requirement shall be expressed as a percentage of the construction costs of the program or project, rather than in dollars. Where repayment is to be made over a period of time, a tentative schedule of payments to be made to the Federal Government shall be established. With respect to any further financial costs to be borne by others, such as contributions of property, the nature of the cost-sharing arrangements to be entered into by the Federal Government shall be indicated. With respect to nonreimbursable costs, the authority relied upon in declaring such costs to be nonreimbursable shall be clearly indicated; where no legislative authority exists, justification shall be presented for proposing that the costs be considered nonreimbursable.

14. *Length of repayment period.* Proposals for repayment of the Federal investment in a program or project will be reviewed in accordance with the following standards:

a. Rates and other charges for the products or services of a program or project shall be set so that repayment of the initial Federal investment in the program or project can be accomplished within a period equal to the useful economic life of the proposed program or project, but not longer than 50 years, following the date on which the head of the sponsoring agency determines that benefits from the program or project will be available to the beneficiaries. This same period of time with the same limitation shall be used for computing benefits and costs of the proposed program or project.

b. In the case of a major replacement, modification, or addition to a project, the cost thereof shall be reimbursed within (1) the estimated useful economic life of such replacement, modification, or addition, (2) the estimated remaining useful economic life of the project to which it is an addition, or (3) 50 years, whichever is least, following the date on which the head of the sponsoring agency determines that benefits from the replacement, modification, or addition will be available to the beneficiaries. In the case of a major replacement, modification, or addition to a project serving power or domestic, municipal, or industrial water supply, the unliquidated balance of the initial Federal investment allocated to such purpose, together with any unpaid interest or other expenses may be proposed for re-scheduling of repayment over the same period of time as is proposed for repayment of the cost of the major replacement, modification, or addition.

c. Where a major new power or domestic, municipal, or industrial water supply project or major portion thereof is to be operated in conjunction with, or as a part of, an existing system of projects serving the same purpose or purposes, the portion of the initial construction costs of the existing system allocated to that purpose which is unliquidated at the time such new project or portion of a project is to be added, together with any unpaid interest or other expenses, may be combined with those costs of the new project or portion thereof allocated to that purpose; and the rates and charges required for the repayment of the total combined costs may be computed so as to repay these costs over the useful economic life of the new project or portion thereof but in not to exceed 50 years, provided that the system to which the new project is to be added has a remaining useful economic life at least equal to that of the proposed new project. For each proposed addition to an existing system, there should be a separate estimate of the benefits, economic and financial costs, and the revenues from or attributable to the new project or portion thereof.

15. *Determination of interest rate on Federal investment.* Interest for purposes of estimating reimbursements shall be calculated at a rate based upon the average rate of interest payable by the Treasury on interest-bearing marketable securities of the United States outstanding at the end of the fiscal year preceding such computation which, upon original issue, had terms to maturity not more than 12 months longer or 12 months shorter than the economically useful life of the project or part thereof in which Federal investment is to be made. Where the economically useful life of the project is expected to be longer than 15 years, the rate of interest shall be calculated at a rate based upon the average rate of interest payable by the Treasury on obligations, if any, outstanding at the end of the fiscal year preceding such computation, which, upon original issue, had terms to maturity of 15 years or more.

If there are no such outstanding interest-bearing marketable securities of the United States with original terms to maturity not more than 12 months longer or 12 months shorter than the economically useful life of the project, or with original terms to maturity of 15 years or more, interest shall be calculated at a rate equal to the rate of interest payable by the Treasury on the issue of interest-bearing marketable securities of the United States outstanding at the end of the fiscal year preceding such computation which, upon original issue, had terms to maturity shorter than, but most nearly equal to, the economically useful life of the project.

Where the average rate calculated by the methods prescribed above is not a multiple of ⅛ of 1 percent, the rate of interest shall be the multiple of ⅛ of 1 percent next lower than such average rate.

16. *Additional standards relating to power.*

a. Proposals for the incorporation in a program or project of power features will be reviewed in accordance with the criterion that total financial costs allocated to power shall be fully reimbursable. For this purpose, the project report shall include an estimate of the revenues to be obtained from the sale and disposition of the program or project power and any other funds which may be derived from the generation, transmission, sale, and disposition of such power, or activities incidental thereto.

b. Where a program or project contemplating immediate or eventual construction of power facilities is proposed for legislative authorization, the report on such program or project shall include a statement of the views thereon of the Federal Power Commission, the agencies concerned with marketing power produced at Federal plants in the region, and other appropriate agencies. Agencies submitting such views shall be given reasonable notice by the agency proposing a program or project involving power facilities of the latter agency's intention to complete the evaluation of the program or project. If the views of the agencies referred to above are not made known to the agency proposing the project within 90 days after completion of the main program or project report, the head of the agency proposing the program or project may submit the report thereon to the Bureau of the Budget without an accompanying statement of the views of these agencies.

Such statements will be used in determining (1) the need for the additional power which such program or project would make available, (2) the cost of such additional power at load centers, compared with the cost of equivalent power from alternative sources in the same region, (3) the revenues which would be derived from the sale of the additional power, (4) the effect of the program or project on the rate of depletion of the fuel resources of the region or Nation, and (5) recommendations as to the timing of the installation of generating and other power facilities as part of, or incidental to, the program or project.

17. *Additional standards relating to flood control.*

a. In the preparation of any program or project report concerned with flood control, the head of the agency proposing such program or project shall give consideration in the report to all methods of preventing or reducing flood damage in each particular instance and shall include a report on the most effective and most economical choice or combination of one or more of the following methods of alleviating flood damage:

(1) Flood plain development and redevelopment, relocation, and zoning.

(2) Sedimentation and runoff control.

(3) Storage of flood waters on cultivated fields, other watershed lands, or underground through appropriate measures.

(4) Levee and flood wall construction.

(5) Reservoir storage.

(6) Channel improvement and rectification, bank stabilization, and floodways and diversions.

(7) Flood forecasting.

(8) Such other measures as will result in effective flood damage prevention or control.

If the head of the agency preparing such a report finds that flood damage can be prevented most effectively and economically through adoption by States, local governments, or districts of programs for flood plain development and redevelopment, relocation, and zoning, or other similar measures, either in substitution for, or as a supplement to, construction of flood control works, he shall include in his project report information as to the extent to which it may be feasible to enter into arrangements with such States, local governments, or districts providing for Federal assistance to them in carrying out such measures. Such information shall be included on the assumption that the State, local government, or district in question will be authorized to engage in such development, relocation or zoning. As a guide for proposing such arrangements, the share of the cost which may be borne by the Federal Government as assistance to States and local governments for such measures shall be no more than the share of costs which the Federal Government would bear in prosecuting the most economical alternative method of obtaining similar flood control benefits.

b. The report on any program or project having significant main stem flood control benefits, except for those of the Tennessee Valley Authority, shall include a statement of the views of the Secretary of the Army or the Chief of Engineers on such aspects of the program or project. The report on any main stem program or project having flood control benefits, except for those of the Tennessee Valley Authority, shall include a statement by the Secretary of Agriculture indicating the effect any existing or potential flood prevention programs in the tributaries and headwaters of the river would have on the economic justification and feasibility of the main stem program or project.

It would be expected that the views of the Corps of Engineers, the Department of Agriculture, and/or any other agency concerned would, ordinarily, be reconciled prior to the submission of a project report to the Bureau of the Budget.

c. Where benefits of the type described in paragraph 8b of this Circular are attributed to a local flood control project, the project report will be reviewed in accordance with the criterion that there shall be a payment or contribution toward the construction costs of the project equal to at least 50 percent of an amount determined by applying to the total construction costs of the project the ratio of the particular land enhancement benefits involved to total monetary primary benefits as estimated in the evaluation report. To the extent feasible, a payment or contribution toward the costs of the program or project shall also be made where benefits of the type described in paragraph 8b of this Circular are attributed to other flood control or flood prevention programs or projects. In determining the payment or contribution that should be required in these cases, the responsible agency should consider the value of benefits to local beneficiaries. The evaluation report shall explain how the portion of the cost to be borne by local beneficiaries was determined.

18. *Additional standards relating to reclamation.*

a. *Appraisal of reclamation benefits.* The report on any program or project having significant reclamation benefits shall include a statement of the views of the Secretary of Agriculture on the economic aspects of such phases of the program or project and his estimates of the effect of such reclamation benefits on the short-range and long-range agricultural needs of the Nation and the region in which the program or project is located, and the place of the program or project within the framework of a desirable long-range program to meet the Nation's and the region's estimated requirements for food, fiber, and other agricultural commodities.

The Secretary of Agriculture shall be given reasonable notice by the head of the agency proposing any program or project having significant reclamation benefits of the latter's intention to complete an evaluation of the program or project. If the report of the Secretary of Agriculture on the economic aspects of the reclamation phases of a program or project is not available within 90 days after the completion of the main program or project report, the head of the agency proposing the program or project may submit the report thereon to the Bureau of the Budget without an accompanying report from the Secretary of Agriculture.

b. *Repayment of irrigation costs.* Consistent with the standards of this Circular relating to repayment, irrigation project reports submitted for authorization by Congress may propose repayment of irrigation construction costs within 50 years, with allowance for an additional development period of not to exceed 10 years.

Note.—Where irrigation projects are authorized administratively by the Secretary of the Interior under present law, repayment of the construction cost is based on the ability of the water users to pay over a period of 40 years, with allowance for an additional development period of not to exceed 10 years, except that a longer period may be used where the costs are to be returned under contracts entered into pursuant to section 9(e) of the Reclamation Project Act of 1939. Projects in which the returnable allocations, together with non-returnable allocations permitted by existing law, do not equal construction costs may be authorized only by act of Congress.

Pending the enactment of general legislation dealing with the use of the interest component to show assistance in the retirement of construction costs allocated to irrigation, proposed irrigation project reports will be reviewed in accordance with the following criteria:

(1) Irrigation aspects of proposed projects shall meet a test of economic justification made in accordance with the principles, standards, and procedures set forth in this Circular.

(2) Net revenues from other purposes associated with the project may be proposed for use in helping to repay costs allocated to irrigation.

(3) Where the cost allocated to irrigation is in excess of the sum of the anticipated repayments by the water users and other identifiable irrigation beneficiaries, and any net revenues of any separable purposes of the project, the project report shall identify these excess costs and may propose that they be borne by the Federal Government as a subsidy to irrigation. Where a Federal subsidy is proposed, either by use of the interest component or otherwise, the project report shall clearly show the amount and composition of such subsidy, and the letter of transmittal to the Congress shall contain proposed authorizing language stating the maximum amount of such subsidy to irrigation which would be borne by the Federal Government. As soon as feasible, arrangements will be made to show any such subsidy in the annual Budget presentation to the Congress.

Note.—In determining financial feasibility of irrigation projects, the Department of the Interior has construed Federal reclamation laws to permit the use of interest payments on the construction cost allocated to power or water supply to show assistance in the retirement of construction costs allocated to irrigation that are in excess of the ability of the water users to repay. There has been no general legislation specifically dealing with this policy. The Bureau of the Budget, in clearance of project reports, has never specifically approved or disapproved the policy of applying the interest component to assist in the retirement of costs allocated to irrigation. The use of the interest component for this purpose raises several important policy problems: (a) the interest component represents an indefinite type of subsidy, (b) the interest component may be used to make a project appear to be financially feasible which is not economically sound, and (c) the size of the interest component necessarily varies with the size of the power or water supply investment, and therefore, the use of the interest component discriminates against irrigation projects which are not directly associated with power or water supply projects or in which such investments are small in relation to the size of the total projects.

19. *Additional standards relating to recreation.* Proposals for recreational aspects of Federal water resources development programs and projects will be reviewed in accordance with the following standards:

a. Recreation potentialities shall be given full consideration in the preparation and evaluation of proposed water resources programs and projects. The financial costs of those aspects of surveys, investigations, and planning required to provide a full and complete understanding of the recreation potentialities of these programs and projects shall be treated as a nonreimbursable Federal expense.

b. Recreation costs and benefits shall be dealt with on an incremental basis; i.e., costs specifically incurred for and benefits directly creditable to recreation shall be evaluated and considered apart from other project costs and benefits. Only the incremental costs expected to be incurred in providing recreational facilities as described in the following paragraphs e and f shall be allocated to recreation.

c. Potential damages to existing recreation areas, facilities, or values shall be recognized in planning for water resources programs and projects, and the financial costs of prevention of such damage, or the replacement of such areas or facilities, to the extent practicable, shall be clearly set forth. All such costs shall be considered as joint or common costs and equitably allocated among the major purposes served by the project.

d. Minimum basic facilities and services for protection of the program or project area and the accomodation or protection of the visiting public, usually at the location of the dam site, shall not be considered recreational facilities, but necessary adjuncts to the construction of Federal projects. The costs of these facilities and services shall be considered as joint or common costs and allocated to the major purposes for which such projects are constructed.

e. When modification in the design of a project or additional development in the project area, including access roads, is required in order to make recreational values available to the public, such modification or development shall be included in the project proposal only if:

(1) The States or local governments or other beneficiaries agree to repay the full cost thereof; or

(2) Such values are clearly indicated to be of national significance in accordance with criteria set forth in paragraph g following; and if either (a) the work is proposed to be authorized as a part of the national park or national forest programs for this area and is to be financed by appropriations made for these programs, or (b) the letter transmitting the proposed report to the Congress contains proposed authorizing language stating the maximum amount of such cost which would be borne by the Federal Government.

f. Where the public interest in the protection and preservation of recreation values of any water resources program or project require the purchase or the setting aside of a limited amount of additional land therefor, any costs thereof may properly be considered a Federal expense and allocated to recreation development. Where such recreation values are not of national significance, however, the costs of such purchase or setting aside of lands shall be recommended as a Federal expense only if State or local governments have, through an appropriate official, indicated an unwillingness or inability to protect and preserve such values. The acquisition of lands by the Federal Government to protect recreation values shall ordinarily be restricted to areas to which access roads are likely to be built. In cases where recreation values are of State or local significance, the lands acquired by the Federal Government shall be sold, leased or licensed, or (in exceptional cases) granted, under appropriate rules or regulations, to State or local governments for development as soon as possible. All funds derived from such sales or leases shall be deposited in the general fund of the Treasury.

There shall be provided a specific list and description of such lands recommended for acquisition or withdrawal and the reasons why their acquisition or withdrawal is required to protect or preserve recreation values.

g. In determining whether the recreation resources of a Federal water resources project area are of national significance, the following criteria shall be considered:

(1) The water resource project itself is such as to make it a subject of continuing Nation-wide public interest.

(2) The presence within or adjacent to the water resource area of outstanding scenic, historical, scientific, or archeological values of interest to the general public makes development of the recreation resource a matter of national interest.

(3) The recreation area, after development, will probably be used by a substantial number of residents of States other than the State or States in which the project area is located.

(4) The relation and proximity of the water resource project area to a national park, monument, national forest, or wilderness area is such that the recreation development will supplement the program on those federally administered areas.

20. *Additional standards relating to domestic, municipal, and industrial water supply.* Proposals for water supply aspects of Federal water resource development programs and projects will be reviewed in accordance with the following criteria:

a. Domestic, municipal, industrial, and other similar water supply shall be considered primarily a local and State responsibility. The needs of communities and industries for water supply shall, however, be given full consideration in the investigations, surveys, and preparation of plans for Federal river development programs and projects.

b. Proposals for the incorporation in a Federal program or project of provisions for domestic, municipal, or industrial water supply shall be made only if the total financial costs to be allocated to this purpose will be fully reimbursed by the States, local governments, districts, or persons served.

21. *Provision in Federal water resources programs and projects for future requirements.* Where a significant saving will result from inclusion in the original plan for a program or project of additional or enlarged structures, facilities, or parts thereof which will serve anticipated future non-Federal needs, as, for example, excess storage capacity in reservoirs for municipal or industrial water supply, provision for such inclusion may be made if:

a. The cost of including the facilities for anticipated future needs, including the properly allocable part of the joint costs of the program or project, represent not more than 15 percent of the total construction costs of the program or project.

b. All financial costs of such additions will be repaid within 50 years after the date on which initial use of such addition is begun, regardless of the degree to which the full capacity provided is utilized during that period.

[677]

In arriving at the financial costs of such additions, interest on the construction costs during the period of deferral of any use may be waived.

c. Reasonable assurance is given by local interests at the time the project report is prepared that initial use of the proposed addition to the program or project will begin within not more than 10 years, and a repayment contract is signed by local interests prior to the beginning of construction agreeing to start repayment within such 10-year period.

By direction of the President:

Frederick J. Lawton
Director

DWIGHT D. EISENHOWER

GREATER INITIATIVE TO STATES?*
1955

From the time of Theodore Roosevelt, Congress has rarely heeded the re-ports of special committees or commissions on conservation issues. This excerpt from the reports of the Commission on Intergovernmental Relations, headed by Meyer Kestenbaum, is an example of one which received little attention.

GREATER INITIATIVE TO STATES IN WATER DEVELOPMENT PROJECTS

The Commission recommends legislative action to extend to all water development projects initiated or proposed by the National Government the requirement now contained in the Flood Control Act of 1944—that the views and recommendations of State and local agencies be taken fully into account prior to the authorization of new projects.

The Commission further recommends that agencies of the National Government afford to the States a larger measure of initiative and responsibility in multipurpose, basinwide development of water resources. There should be a balanced division of activities between the National Government and the States moving toward individual State, interstate, National-State, or National responsibility. The Board of Coordination and Review and State advisory councils should be fully used for this purpose.[1]

In the entire field of water resource development, the views of State and local agencies should receive increased attention when projects proposed by the National Government are being appraised. Flood control legislation of the past

*U.S. Commission on Intergovernmental Relations, *A Report to the President for Transmittal to the Congress* (Washington, D.C.: Government Printing Office, June 1955), 241–42.

[1] Senators Humphrey and Morse comment:

"Encouragement of greater State initiative in water development should not be construed as mean-ing any lessening of the National Government's responsibility. We want to make it clear that we do not believe that all the self-liquidating and potentially profitable undertakings should be reserved for the States and private interests, thereby relegating the National Government's role to financing only such projects as others are unwilling or unable to finance. We do not believe that a willingness to finance such projects should be the only criterion in determining the extent of the national inter-est that may be involved."

decade directs Federal agencies and the Congress to weigh State and local views regarding contemplated projects. This principle is sound and should be extended to all water development programs.

The Commission favors participation of the National Government in water development projects where a clearly definable national interest exists. However, where such interest does exist, the Commission advocates a cooperative instead of unilateral approach, and suggests that even though State and local agencies should not have veto power, the Congress should withhold authorization of projects until the opinions and recommendations of all interested agencies at National, State, and local levels have been carefully reviewed and every effort has been made to bring all parties into reasonable agreement.

WATER SUPPLY*
July 3, 1958

An amendment to the Rivers and Harbors Act of 1958 established water supply as a firm purpose in the construction of federal water projects. Senator Robert S. Kerr of Oklahoma was one of the chief sponsors of the proposal.

TITLE III—WATER SUPPLY

SEC. 301. (a) It is hereby declared to be the policy of the Congress to recognize the primary responsibilities of the States and local interests in developing water supplies for domestic, municipal, industrial, and other purposes and that the Federal Government should participate and cooperate with States and local interests in developing such water supplies in connection with the construction, maintenance, and operation of Federal navigation, flood control, irrigation, or multiple purpose projects.

(b) In carrying out the policy set forth in this section, it is hereby provided that storage may be included in any reservoir project surveyed, planned, constructed or to be planned, surveyed and/or constructed by the Corps of Engineers or the Bureau of Reclamation to impound water for present or anticipated future demand or need for municipal or industrial water, and the reasonable value thereof may be taken into account in estimating the economic value of the entire project: *Provided,* That before construction or modification of any project including water supply provisions is initiated, State or local interests shall agree to pay for the cost of such provisions on the basis that all authorized purposes served by the project shall share equitably in the benefits of multiple purpose construction as determined by the Secretary of the Army or the Secretary of the Interior as the case may be: *Provided further,* That not to exceed 30 per centum of the total estimated cost of any project may be allocated to anticipated future demands where States or local interests give reasonable assurances that they will contract for the use of storage for anticipated future demands within a period of time which will permit paying out the costs allocated to water supply within the life of the project: *And provided further,* That the entire amount of the construction costs, including interest during construction, allocated to water supply shall be repaid within the life of the project but in no event to exceed fifty years after the project is first used for the storage of water for water supply purposes, except that (1) no payment need be made with respect to storage for future water supply until such supply is first used, and (2) no interest shall be charged on such cost until such supply is first used, but in no case shall the interest-free period exceed ten years. The interest rate used for pur-

*72 *Statutes at Large,* 319–20.

poses of computing interest during construction and interest on the unpaid balance shall be determined by the Secretary of the Treasury, as of the beginning of the fiscal year in which construction is initiated, on the basis of the computed average interest rate payable by the Treasury upon its outstanding marketable public obligations, which are neither due nor callable for redemption for fifteen years from date of issue. The provisions of this subsection insofar as they relate to the Bureau of Reclamation and the Secretary of the Interior shall be alternative to and not a substitute for the provisions of the Reclamation Projects Act of 1939 (53 Stat. 1187) relating to the same subject.

(c) The provisions of this section shall not be construed to modify the provisions of section 1 and section 8 of the Flood Control Act of 1944 (58 Stat. 887), as amended and extended, or the provisions of section 8 of the Reclamation Act of 1902 (32 Stat. 390).

(d) Modifications of a reservoir project heretofore authorized, surveyed, planned, or constructed to include storage as provided in subsection (b), which would seriously affect the purposes for which the project was authorized, surveyed, planned, or constructed, or which would involve major structural or operational changes shall be made only upon the approval of Congress as now provided by law.

SEC. 302. Title III of this Act may be cited as the "Water Supply Act of 1958".

Approved July 3, 1958.

JOHN F. KENNEDY

REPORT OF THE KENNEDY-JOHNSON NATURAL RESOURCES ADVISORY COMMITTEE*
February 18, 1961

To further stress the conservation and resource development issues, Senator Kennedy established the Kennedy-Johnson Natural Resources Advisory Committee, with members in every state. This campaign committee evolved into a policy advisory committee after the election. The final report of the committee was adopted at a meeting just prior to the inauguration of the President.

The Kennedy-Johnson Natural Resources Advisory Committee is proud of its opportunity to serve in the campaign of President John F. Kennedy. Because of the commitments for constructive resource development and conservation made by the President during his campaign, we look forward to an administration that will establish landmarks of achievement toward a constructive program of protection for the rightful heritage of all Americans.

We know that vigorous new leadership is essential if we are to conserve our renewable resources of water, soil, forests and wildlife, and that full development of these resources is necessary to make possible the economic growth essential to America's role in the free world. We believe that the widest enjoyment of benefits of our natural resources should be made available to the greatest number of people at the lowest possible cost.

An adequate water supply for our growing population will be a major domestic problem for many years to come. The physical needs of urbanism greatly accelerate this crisis. With these problems in mind, we recommend that the new resource challenges of urbanism be met by closely coordinated federal-state efforts. If a Department of Urban Affairs is created, it should include within its framework a team of experts who can work with the regular resource agencies in meeting some of these problems.

Existing federal agencies can do the work necessary for a meaningful conservation program. Conflicts between agencies can only serve to delay or defeat fulfillment of natural resource programs. Policy guidance can come from the

*"Kennedy-Johnson Natural Resources Advisory Committee Final Report, Including Amendments Adopted by the Advisory Committee at Its Meeting, Jan. 17, 1961, Washington, D.C.," 1–10.

President and a Council of Resource and Conservation Advisers in the Office of the President.

Growing water needs make imperative the development of long-range research programs for the conversion of saline and brackish waters. Improved recharging methods of ground water supply are also needed.

Research into improved methods for the construction of waterway projects should also be pressed. Full study should be given to the possibility of using nuclear devices for the construction of these projects and the recovery of minerals, including oil from shale.

BUDGETARY POLICY

We welcome the end of the "no new starts" policy. We believe that the national budget policy should distinguish between capital investment and operating expenditures in the natural resources field. The Bureau of the Budget should measure all the benefits of projects in relation to the national economy as a whole and the national goals of all the people.

The restrictive interpretations of Bureau of the Budget Circular A-47 should be ended at once. We believe that a re-study of the effect of this Circular should be ordered by the Bureau of the Budget and that all provisions inconsistent with the stated goals of the Kennedy administration should be eliminated or changed. The "taxes foregone" calculation added into feasibility studies by A-47 is an example.

Recreation benefits are becoming each year a more valuable part of every type of water project. Recreational features should be developed to the maximum in all federal water projects and these benefits should be included in calculating the value of these projects.

The tendency of the Bureau of the Budget in recent years to discourage project development by imposing excessive requirements on local interests should be modified to meet water needs realistically. Special consideration should be given to the problems of undeveloped and depressed areas.

The Department of Defense should furnish, on request by an agency engaged in evaluating any project pursuant to Congressional action, an opinion for transmission with the agency's report to Congress, as to the value of the project, if any, to the American defense potential, with particular reference to transportation, electric power, the production of human and animal food, and other factors.

FLOOD CONTROL AND RECLAMATION

Highest priority should be given to the early completion of urgently needed flood control projects already authorized and prompt action should be taken toward authorization of projects that have been often delayed because of unreasonable Bureau of the Budget restrictions. We cannot achieve full development of our national economy until we are assured of the flood protection necessary for all of our river valleys. These projects are income-producing, wealth-creating assets, in addition to protecting lives and property.

The reclamation of land should be restored as an essential part of our natural resources program under historic policies initiated by Theodore Roosevelt to control speculation and monopoly as a means of assuring the greatest good to the greatest number of people. The continued development of supplemental water supplies for existing irrigated acres and the opening of new lands for settlement through reclamation are entirely consistent with long-term national objectives. Such development provides a most important basic element to a successful regional economy, a stable diversified agriculture. The full development of our river basins carries with it not only flood control and reclamation benefits, but power, navigation and recreational dividends which contribute to the growing economy we seek.

SOIL CONSERVATION AND WATERSHED DEVELOPMENT

Renewed emphasis in our soil conservation program should be placed on permanent conservation practices. The program should treat the causes, rather than the symptoms, of destructive soil erosion. The soil conservation program of the Department of Agriculture should be symbolic of the dedicated conservation outlook of the new administration.

Few resource programs can directly benefit as many citizens in as many states at so small a relative cost as the small watershed program. Beneficiaries of this program are not merely farmers, but millions of people in towns and cities. The recreational potential, largely unmeasured, will be invaluable to many more millions in the large urban areas. It could be one of the prime forces in bringing lasting help to economically depressed areas.

Already local organizations have applied for help in some 1400 watersheds containing about 100 million acres of land. Applications are falling off, however, because of the long delay between the filing of the application and the time when the projects can be reached for consideration—a situation attributable to limited planning funds that have heretofore been allocated to this vital program.

Administration policy should include the following objectives:

(1) A goal of 2,000 watersheds completed or under construction by 1968.

(2) Completion by 1968 of the original pilot watersheds.

(3) Provision of adequate loan funds for local organizations.

(4) Organization of future years' budgets so that resource conservation programs will be separated from unrelated activities. The small watershed program has been handicapped by competing for funds with the many other activities of the Department of Agriculture. It should be considered in relation to related programs of the Corps of Engineers, reclamation, and other public works activities.

POWER

Long-range energy resource development objectives based upon forecasts of need and the public interest should be established by the federal government.

A national energy and fuels policy to guide federal agencies responsible for resource development should be enacted by Congress to provide:

(1) Progressive evaluation standards for multiple-purpose projects.

(2) Cost allocation formulae for multiple-purpose projects which are consistent with the principle of regulation by competition.

(3) Abundant electricity at minimum cost to the ultimate consumer, whether he is served by investor-owned, local public, or cooperative distribution systems.

(4) Fully adequate conservation of non-renewable energy sources.

The Department of the Interior, in cooperation with other agencies, must reassert its responsibility to provide long-range planning of generation and transmission facilities to meet future needs, with immediate attention to the economic necessity of inter-regional federal transmission ties. The so-called Keating amendment should be repealed.

Regional wholesale power supply systems should be made responsible for meeting the expanding wholesale power requirements of all retail electric systems at the lowest possible cost and supplied with as much hydroelectric capacity as is economically feasible for low-cost peaking power and reserve capacity.

Falling water, coal at the mine mouth, atomic energy, or even solar energy could supply the fuel, depending upon conditions in various regions. Because our supplies of coal are plentiful and often more useful when converted to electricity, an important part of the power should be "coal by wire" from the now-depressed mining areas in West Virginia and Pennsylvania and the coal and lignite deposits of the West.

Atomic power, developed and financed by the people, should be made available from federal nuclear power plants as soon as production costs can be materially reduced.

NAVIGATION

The waterways of the United States play a vital role in the economic strength and well-being of the nation. Their improvement and modernization constitute one of our most productive public investments, highly rewarding to the American free enterprise economy. The freedom of the waterways from tolls or toll-equivalent charges or taxes is fundamental to their continued contribution to an expanding national economy.

Availability of low-cost water transportation provides a foundation for economic growth which could not occur on a comparable scale in its absence. It has generated a major post-war industrial expansion along the nation's navigable waterways, providing abundant opportunity for private investment, affording employment of a high productive character for hundreds of thousands of our people, and generating greatly enlarged productive capability for economic welfare and the national defense.

Navigation improvements have exhibited their values most strikingly in stimulating development of resources in regions of the country where growth has heretofore lagged through lack of economic access to sources of raw materials and markets. The rapid increase in tonnages of farm crops shipped by water has been substantially reducing the disparity between central market prices and income realization on the farm. Stimulus to water-dependent industry provided by improvements to harbors and waterways has been of special benefit to regions suffering from the loss of traditional industries as a result of technological factors. By virtue of modernized water transportation, extensive areas of the nation have been contending successfully with the forces of economic stagnation and moving towards full participation in national standards of productivity and income.

The emerging problems of the future urgently demand a vigorous rededication to the philosophy of free waterways improvement. Considerations of national security involving encouragement to dispersal of strategic industry, capabilities for low-cost mass transportation of basic industrial commodities and fuels, economy in the consumption of fuels and scarce materials, and optimum recuperative power following heavy nuclear attack, also counsel an expanded program of waterways improvement.

The enormous growth of traffic on the waterway system in the post-war years is beginning seriously to over-tax its present capacity throughout extensive reaches. These deficiencies present a grave challenge to more purposeful direction of our national efforts. The demand for water transportation will probably double by 1980. Deficiencies in harbor and channel depths and inadequacies of locking facilities, many in advanced states of deterioration, are choking off development of water commerce and discouraging the more economic use of deeper-draft, more powerful, vessels. Many of our coastal harbors over the country are not prepared to handle deeper-draft vessels and a general program of modernization is needed.

Appropriate remedies for the consequences of past neglect and indifference call for full acceptance of federal responsibility for leadership in this vital area of the public domain, based on recognition of the true public values involved. Failure to move forward with decisiveness on the construction of sound and productive projects can only result in the wanton neglect of our national capabilities at a time when every consideration of national interest dictates the intelligent and effective marshalling of all our resources.

POLLUTION CONTROL

One of the earliest enactments of the 87th Congress should be the Blatnik Pollution Control Bill, vetoed in 1960. In addition to financial assistance to local communities in the construction of sewage treatment facilities, necessary federal enforcement and research and technical assistance programs should be strengthened.

The goal of our national pollution policy should be to protect and enhance the capacity of our water resources to serve the widest possible range of human needs. This goal can be approached only by adopting the positive policy of keeping waters as clean as possible, as opposed to the negative policy of attempting to crowd into a stream all the wastes it might possibly assimilate, regardless of the destruction of important watershed values.

The policy should formally recognize the recreation value of water resources as a full partner with domestic, industrial and agricultural values in water quality management and programs.

The administrative level of the water supply and pollution control activities in the Public Health Service and in the states should be commensurate with the importance of the problem.

Research into the effects of the use of highly toxic chemical pesticide detergents as a destructive pollutant of land, water and air should be greatly expanded.

FISH AND WILDLIFE CONSERVATION

We recommend enactment of legislation which will assure perpetuation of wilderness values. A sympathetic administration can help eliminate confusion and misconceptions which have blocked passage of this legislation in the past. We need to protect specimens of our old frontier just as we need to protect national shrines and art treasures.

Wildlife refuges and ranges must be protected to serve the purposes to which they are dedicated without interference by commercial exploitation. Immediate legislative authorization is needed to establish a loan fund advance on duck stamp revenue to permit immediate purchasing of wetlands before drainage destroys these areas. Cooperative programs should be developed to preserve extensive wildfowl breeding grounds in Canada.

More research is needed into the serious fish and wildlife problems being caused by expanding land use and the rapidly mounting pressures of the human population.

Production of fish in the lakes and wildlife on the perimeter of our reservoirs should become an integral part of reservoir management. Present land acquisition policies should be revised in the interest of full recreational opportunity.

Research into fish production in federal reservoirs is needed to maximize benefits from them.

The many needs for work in reforestation, soil conservation, park improvement and fish and wildlife development offer potential employment for several hundreds of thousands of idle young men between the ages of 16–21 years. Both federal and state projects could utilize the high school "drop-outs", in need of work experience and vocational training. Healthful outdoor work would improve the level of physical fitness, reduce juvenile delinquency and generally prepare more useful future citizens.

NATIONAL PARKS

Shorelines parks for public recreation are the most critically needed additions to our national park system. They must be acquired before all potential sites are lost to urban development and commercial exploitation.

There is still great need for improving and expanding our national park system to meet the needs of a greatly increasing population. One solution which should be considered is a program of assistance to states and local communities in the expansion of park resources.

FORESTRY

Increased attention to forestry—our great publicly-owned forests and our private forests—is one of the most meaningful investments we can make in achieving the economic strength essential to our national goals.

By the year 2000 we will have 275 million people in our nation. Since trees do not grow to crop size overnight, forestry is a long-time proposition and we must act now to assure our nation's timber future. There are 490 million timbered acres in our great land, 130 million acres in public ownership and 360 million acres in private holdings.

Small holdings and publicly owned forests predominate in forest ownership. If we are to meet our goals in wood fiber requirements in the next 40 years our total production must be doubled. The greatest opportunity for improvement is on our small private holdings—half our forest acreage—and on our public forests, which represent another quarter of our acreage.

For private forests we need a revitalized small woodland program including credit, grants-in-aid, management and forest development assistance, and in some cases expansion of public holdings. The key to progress is an adequately financed cooperative federal-state effort.

Investments in our national forests are of proven value yielding direct returns to the taxpayers, needed revenue to local governments, stabilization to area payrolls and long-range benefits to our over-all economy.

On the national forests and other federal forests the key to attaining resource goals is development by applying the principles of multiple use and sustained yield. Reforestation, access roads, forest protection, soil and water management and recreational development are examples of the field in which acceleration is of vital importance. Work on the national forests in distressed areas, and their expansion in these areas, are basic means of attacking chronic unemployment problems.

Of far-reaching importance is research. To be effective, it must be comprehensive. It must embrace wood utilization and marketing as well as all phases of forest management and use. There must be a rate of financing commensurate with the need to find solutions quickly to large unsolved problems.

We urge a forest resource development program—national in scope—that looks to tomorrow's needs, discharging fully our obligation to those yet unborn.

PUBLIC DOMAIN LANDS

Particular attention should be given to the 500,000,000 acres of public lands which are an important resource reserve providing grazing, timber, wildlife and water values. Renewed vigor is needed in the work of land classification, surveys, minerals exploration, range conservation, timber development and recreational use, with full protection of the public interest. We urge that a meaningful program sufficient to meet our growing population needs, be adopted for the Bureau of Land Management.

We urge that special recognition be given to increasing grazing opportunities upon the public lands, consistent with sound conservation practices and the protection of wildlife.

The Bureau of Land Management must be revitalized to fulfill its obligation in the protection and development of these valuable assets. The public domain lands must be administered with a view to full use of all benefits, in keeping with other natural resources.

This Committee recognizes that to give full effect to its recommendations will require maximum effort. The Committee also recognizes that anything less than maximum effort would be insufficient to meet the demands of our ever-growing natural resources needs, and that failure to meet those needs would have to stand as a betrayal of the future generations of Americans.

February 18, 1961

PRESIDENT KENNEDY'S NATURAL RESOURCE MESSAGE*
February 23, 1961

One of President Kennedy's first special messages to the Congress dealt with development and conservation of natural resources, and included both policy statements and recommendations.

To the Congress of the United States:

From the beginning of civilization, every nation's basic wealth and progress has stemmed in large measure from its natural resources. This Nation has been, and is now, especially fortunate in the blessings we have inherited. Our entire society rests upon—and is dependent upon—our water, our land, our forests, and our minerals. How we use these resources influences our health, security, economy, and well-being.

But if we fail to chart a proper course of conservation and development—if we fail to use these blessings prudently—we will be in trouble within a short time. In the resource field, predictions of future use have been consistently understated. But even under conservative projections, we face a future of critical shortages and handicaps. By the year 2000, a U.S. population of 300 million— nearly doubled in 40 years—will need far greater supplies of farm products, timber, water, minerals, fuels, energy, and opportunities for outdoor recreation. Present projections tell us that our water use will double in the next 20 years; that we are harvesting our supply of high-grade timber more rapidly than the development of new growth; that too much of our fertile topsoil is being washed away; that our minerals are being exhausted at increasing rates; and that the Nation's remaining undeveloped areas of great natural beauty are being rapidly preempted for other uses.

Wise investment in a resource program today will return vast dividends to-morrow, and failures to act now may be opportunities lost forever. Our country has been generous with us in this regard—and we cannot now ignore her needs for future development.

This is not a matter of concern for only one section of the country. All those who fish and hunt, who build industrial centers, who need electricity to light their homes and lighten their burdens, who require water for home, industrial, and recreational purposes—in short, every citizen in every State of the Union— all have a stake in a sound resources program under the progressive principles of national leadership first forged by Pinchot and Theodore Roosevelt, and backed by the essential cooperation of State and local governments.

*Natural Resources, H. Doc. 94, 87th Cong., 1st sess., 1-9.

This statement is designed to bring together in one message the widely scattered resource policies of the Federal Government. In the past, these policies have overlapped and often conflicted. Funds were wasted on competing efforts. Widely differing standards were applied to measure the Federal contribution to similar projects. Funds and attention devoted to annual appropriations or immediate pressures diverted energies away from long-range planning for national economic growth. Fees and user charges wholly inconsistent with each other, with value received, and with public policy have been imposed at some Federal developments.

To coordinate all of these matters among the various agencies, I will shortly issue one or more Executive orders or directives—

(1) Redefining these responsibilities within the Executive Office and authorizing a strengthened Council of Economic Advisers to report to the President, the Congress, and the public on the status of resource programs in relation to national needs;

(2) Establishing, under the Council of Economic Advisers, a Presidential Advisory Committee on Natural Resources, representing the Federal agencies concerned in this area and seeking the advice of experts outside of Government; and

(3) Instructing the Budget Director, in consultation with the departments and agencies concerned, to formulate within the next 90 days general principles for the application of fees, permits, and other user charges at all types of Federal natural resource projects or areas; and to reevaluate current standards for appraising the feasibility of water resource projects.

In addition, to provide a coordinated framework for our research programs in this area, and to chart the course for the wisest and most efficient use of the research talent and facilities we possess, I shall ask the National Academy of Sciences to undertake a thorough and broadly based study and evaluation of the present state of research underlying the conservation, development, and use of natural resources, how they are formed, replenished, and may be substituted for, and giving particular attention to needs for basic research and to projects that will provide a better basis for natural resources planning and policy formulation. Pending the recommendations of the Academy, I have directed my science adviser and the Federal Council for Science and Technology to review ongoing Federal research activities in the field of natural resources and to determine ways to strengthen the total Government research effort relating to natural resources.

I. WATER RESOURCES

Our Nation has been blessed with a bountiful supply of water; but it is not a blessing we can regard with complacency. We now use over 300 billion gallons of water a day, much of it wastefully. By 1980 we will need 600 billion gallons a day.

Our supply of water is not always consistent with our needs of time and place. Floods one day in one section may be countered in other days or in other sections by the severe water shortages which are now afflicting many eastern urban areas and are particularly critical in the West. Our available water supply must be used to give maximum benefits for all purposes—hydroelectric power, irrigation and reclamation, navigation, recreation, health, home, and industry. If all areas of the country are to enjoy a balanced growth, our Federal reclamation and other water resource programs will have to give increased attention to municipal and industrial water and power supplies as well as irrigation and land redemption; and I am so instructing the Secretary of the Interior, in cooperation with the Secretary of Agriculture and the Secretary of the Army.

1. PLANNING AND DEVELOPMENT

A. We reject a "no new starts" policy. Such a policy denied the resource requirements and potential on which our economic growth hinges; and took a heavy toll in added costs and even human life and homes by postponing essential flood control projects. I have requested the Director of the Bureau of the Budget, working with appropriate department and agency heads, to schedule a progressive, orderly program of starting new projects to meet accumulated demands, taking into account the availability of funds, and implementing with the agencies concerned, wherever possible, the very excellent and timely report of the bipartisan Senate Select Committee on National Water Resources issued 3 weeks ago.

B. This administration accepts the goal urged by the Senate select committee to develop comprehensive river basin plans by 1970, in cooperation with the individual States. I urge the Congress to authorize the establishment of planning commissions for all major river basins where adequate coordinated plans are not already in existence. These commissions, on which will be represented the interested agencies at all levels of government, will be charged with the responsibility of preparing comprehensive basic development plans over the next several years.

C. A major reason for such planning is the ability to identify both the need and the location of future reservoir sites far in advance of construction. This advantage will be dissipated in great measure if the selected sites are not preserved—for uninhibited commercial and residential development in such areas increase ultimate acquisition costs and may result in pressures against the project required. I urge the Congress to enact legislation permitting the reservation of known future reservoir sites by the operating agency whenever such protection is necessary.

D. The full development of the power and other water resource potentials of the Columbia Basin is a vision that must be fulfilled. The Columbia River Joint Development Treaty with Canada is before the Senate for approval. I urge the Senate to approve this treaty at the earliest possible time, to permit an immediate start on the immense efforts that can be jointly undertaken in power production and river control in that basin.

E. This administration is committed to strengthening and speeding up our flood control program as rapidly as our fiscal and technical capabilities permit. Unfortunately, efforts to reduce flood losses by constructing remedial works are being partially offset by rapid industrial and residential development of flood plain lands.

I am asking all Federal agencies concerned to provide data on flood hazards in specified areas to all 50 States, and to assist in their efforts for effective regulation or zoning of the flood plains. In addition, I have instructed the Federal agencies concerned with urban development—including the Housing and Home Finance Agency and the Bureau of Public Roads—to coordinate their activities with the flood control agencies to insure that their programs utilize flood information to advantage.

F. Complementing larger downstream reservoirs in the control of floodwaters are the small watershed projects which are an integral part of our soil and water conservation program, along with terracing, strip cropping, grass waterways and other erosion prevention measures. Nearly 300 million of our Nation's 460 million acres of farm croplands still need these basic practices for preserving our water and soil resources. I have asked the Secretary of Agriculture, in cooperation with other interested Federal agencies, to review the basic objectives of our soil conservation and watershed management programs, and to make certain that any Federal assistance is directed toward realizing maximum benefits for the Nation as a whole. In addition, there should be improved coordination of the various Federal and local activities in this field.

2. WATER AND AIR POLLUTION CONTROL

Pollution of our country's rivers and streams has—as a result of our rapid population and industrial growth and change—reached alarming proportions. To meet all needs—domestic, agricultural, industrial, recreational—we shall have to use and reuse the same water, maintaining quality as well as quantity. In many areas of the country we need new sources of supply—but in all areas we must protect the supplies we have.

Current corrective efforts are not adequate. This year a national total of $350 million will be spent from all sources on municipal waste treatment works. But $600 million of construction is required annually to keep pace with the growing rate of pollution. Industry is lagging far behind in its treatment of wastes.

For a more effective water pollution control program, I propose the following:

First, I urge enactment of legislation along the general lines of H.R. 4036 and S. 120 extending and increasing Federal financial assistance for the operation of State and interstate water pollution control agencies.

Secondly, I urge that this legislation increase the amount of Federal assistance to municipalities for construction of waste treatment facilities in order to stimulate water pollution construction in those cities with inadequate facilities.

Third, I urge that this legislation strengthen enforcement procedures to abate serious pollution situations of national significance.

Fourth, I propose an intensive and broadened research effort to determine the specific sources of water pollution and their adverse effect upon all water uses; the effects upon the health of people exposed to water pollution; and more effective means of preventing, controlling, or removing the contaminants—including radioactive matter—that now pollute our rivers and streams so that the water may be safely used.

Fifth, I propose the establishment of a special unit within the Public Health Service under the Department of Health, Education, and Welfare, where control measures to prevent and limit pollution of our water will be developed.

Sixth, This same unit should provide new leadership, research, and financial and technical assistance for the control of air pollution, a serious hazard to the health of our people that causes an estimated $7.5 billion annually in damage to vegetation, livestock, metals, and other materials. We need an effective Federal air pollution control program now. For although the total supply of air is vast, the atmosphere over our growing metropolitan areas—where more than half the people live—has only limited capacity to dilute and disperse the contaminants now being increasingly discharged from homes, factories, vehicles, and many other sources.

3. *SALINE AND BRACKISH WATER CONVERSION*

No water resources program is of greater long-range importance—for relief not only of our shortages, but for arid nations the world over—than our efforts to find an effective and economical way to convert water from the world's greatest, cheapest natural resources—our oceans—into water fit for consumption in the home and by industry. Such a breakthrough would end bitter struggles between neighbors, states, and nations—and bring new hope for millions who live out their lives in dire shortage of usable water and all its physical and economical blessings, though living on the edge of a great body of water throughout that parched lifetime.

This administration is currently engaged in redoubled efforts to select the most promising approaches to economic desalinization of ocean and brackish waters, and then focus our energies more intensively on those approaches. At my request, a panel of the President's Science Advisory Committee has been working with the Secretary of the Interior to assure the most vigorous and effective research and development program possible in this field.

I now pledge that, when this know-how is achieved, it will immediately be made available to every nation in the world who wishes it, along with appropriate technical and other assistance for its use. Indeed the United States welcomes now the cooperation of all other nations who wish to join in this effort at present.

I urge the Congress to extend the current saline water conversion research program, and to increase the funds for its continuation to a level commensurate with the effort our current studies will show to be needed—now estimated to be at least twice the level previously requested.

II. ELECTRIC POWER

To keep pace with the growth of our economy and national defense requirements, expansion of this Nation's power facilities will require intensive effort by all segments of our power industry. Through 1980, according to present estimates of the Federal Power Commission, total installed capacity should triple if we are to meet our Nation's need for essential economic growth. Sustained heavy expansion by all power suppliers—public, cooperative, and private —is clearly needed.

The role of the Federal Government in supplying an important segment of this power is now long established and must continue. We will meet our responsibilities in this field.

Hydroelectric sites remaining in this country will be utilized and hydroelectric power will be incorporated in all multiple-purpose river projects where optimum economic use of the water justifies such action.

The Tennessee Valley Authority will continue to use the financing authority granted it by the last Congress to meet the power needs of the area it serves.

Our efforts to achieve economically competitive nuclear power before the end of this decade in areas where fossil fuel costs are high will be encouraged through basic research, engineering developments, and construction of various prototype and full-scale reactors by the Atomic Energy Commission in cooperation with industry.

In marketing Federal power, this administration will be guided by the following basic principles which recognize the prior rights of the general public, consumer and taxpayer who have financed the development of these great national assets originally vested in them:

(1) Preference in power sales shall be given public agencies and cooperatives.

(2) Domestic and rural consumers shall have priority over other consumers in the disposal of power.

(3) Power shall be sold at the lowest possible rates consistent with sound business principles.

(4) Power disposal shall be such as to encourage widespread use and to prevent monopolization.

Finally, I have directed the Secretary of the Interior to develop plans for the early interconnection of areas served by that Department's marketing agencies with adequate common carrier transmission lines; to plan for further national cooperative pooling of electric power, both public and private; and to enlarge such pooling as now exists.

III. FORESTS

Our forest lands present the sharpest challenge to our foresight. Trees planted today will not reach the minimum sizes needed for lumber until the year 2000. Most projections of future timber requirements predict a doubling of current consumption within 40 years. At present cutting rates, we are using up our old growth timber in western stands. Because of the time requirements involved, we must move now to meet anticipated future needs, and improve the productivity of our nearly 500 million acres of commercial forest land.

Unfortunately, the condition of our forest land area is substantially below par: 45 million acres are in need of reforestation; more than 150 million acres require thinnings, release cuttings, and other timber stand improvement measures if growth rates are to be increased and quality timber produced; forest protection must be extended to areas now poorly protected. Losses in growth from insects and disease need to be reduced substantially by wider application of known detection and control measures.

(A) I urge the Congress to accelerate forest development on Federal public lands both as a long-term investment measure and as an immediate method of relieving unemployment in distressed areas.

(B) To make additional supplies of merchantable timber available to small businesses, I have directed the Secretaries of Agriculture and the Interior to accelerate the program of building approved access roads to public forests.

(C) A more difficult and unresolved forest situation lies in that half of our forest land held in small private ownerships. These lands, currently far below their productive potential, must be managed to produce a larger share of our future timber needs. Current forest owner assistance programs have proven inadequate. I am therefore directing the Secretary of Agriculture, in cooperation with appropriate Federal and State agencies, to develop a program to help small independent timber owners and processors attain better forest management standards and more efficient production and utilization of forest crops.

IV. PUBLIC LANDS

The Federal Government owns nearly 770 million acres of public land, much of it devoted to a variety of essential uses. But equally important are the vacant, unappropriated, and unreserved public domain lands, amounting to some 477 million acres—a vital national reserve that should be devoted to productive use now and maintained for future generations.

Much of this public domain suffers from uncontrolled use and a lack of proper management. More than 100 million acres of our Federal grazing districts are producing livestock forage well below their potential. We can no longer afford to sit by while our public domain assets so deteriorate.

I am, therefore, directing the Secretary of the Interior to—

(1) accelerate an inventory and evaluation of the Nation's public domain holdings to serve as a foundation for improved resource management;

(2) develop a program of balanced usage designed to reconcile the conflicting uses—grazing, forestry, recreation, wildlife, urban development, and minerals; and

(3) accelerate the installation of soil-conserving and water-saving works and practices to reduce erosion and improve forage capacity; and to proceed with the revegetation of rangelands on which the forage capacity has been badly depleted or destroyed.

V. OCEAN RESOURCES

The sea around us represents one of our most important but least understood and almost wholly undeveloped areas for extending our resource base. Continental shelves bordering the United States contain roughly 20 percent of our remaining reserves of crude oil and natural gas. The ocean floor contains large and valuable deposits of cobalt, copper, nickel, and manganese. Ocean waters themselves contain a wide variety of dissolved salts and minerals.

Salt (and fresh water) fisheries are among our most important but far from fully developed reservoirs of protein foods. At present levels of use, this country alone will need an additional 3 billion pounds of fish and shellfish annually by 1980, and many other countries with large-scale protein deficiency can be greatly helped by more extensive use of marine foodstuffs. But all this will require increased efforts, under Federal leadership, for rehabilitation of depleted stocks of salmon and sardines in the Pacific, ground fish and oysters in the Atlantic, lake trout and other desirable species in the Great Lakes, and many others through biological research, development of methods for passing fish over dams, and control of pollution.

This administration intends to give concerted attention to our whole national effort in the basic and applied research of oceanography. Construction of ship and shore facilities for ocean research and survey, the development of new instruments for charting the seas and gathering data, and the training of new scientific manpower will require the coordinated efforts of many Federal agencies. It is my intention to send to the Congress for its information and use in considering the 1962 budget, a national program for oceanography, setting forth the responsibilities and requirements of all participating Government agencies.

VI. RECREATION

America's health, morale, and culture have long benefited from our national parks and forests, and our fish and wildlife opportunities. Yet these facilities and resources are not now adequate to meet the needs of a fast-growing, more mobile population—and the millions of visitor-days which are now spent in federally owned parks, forests, wildlife refuges, and water reservoirs will triple well before the end of this century.

To meet the Federal Government's appropriate share of the responsibility for fulfilling these needs, the following steps are essential:

(A) To protect our remaining wilderness areas, I urge the Congress to enact a wilderness protection bill along the general lines of S. 174.

(B) To improve both the quality and quantity of public recreational opportunities, I urge the Congress to enact legislation leading to the establishment of seashore and shoreline areas such as Cape Cod, Padre Island, and Point Reyes for the use and enjoyment of the public. Unnecessary delay in acquiring these shores so vital to an adequate public recreation system results in tremendously increased costs.

(C) For similar reasons, I am instructing the Secretary of the Interior, in cooperation with the Secretary of Agriculture and other appropriate Federal, State, and local officials and private leaders to—

formulate a comprehensive Federal recreational lands program;

conduct a survey to determine where additional national parks, forests, and seashore areas should be proposed;

take steps to insure that land acquired for the construction of federally financed reservoirs is sufficient to permit future development for recreational purposes; and

establish a long-range program for planning and providing adequate open spaces for recreational facilities in urban areas.

I am also hopeful that consistent and coordinated Federal leadership can expand our fish and wildlife opportunities without the present conflicts of agencies and interests: One department paying to have wet lands drained for agricultural purposes while another is purchasing such lands for wildlife or waterfowl refuges—one agency encouraging chemical pesticides that may harm the songbirds and game birds whose preservation is encouraged by another agency —conflicts between private landowners and sportsmen—uncertain responsibility for the watershed and antipollution programs that are vital to our fish and wildlife opportunities.

I am directing the Secretary of the Interior to take the lead, with other Federal and State officials, to end these conflicts and develop a long-range wildlife conservation program—and to accelerate the acquisition of upper Midwest wet lands through the sale of Federal duck stamps.

CONCLUSION

Problems of immediacy always have the advantage of attracting notice— those that lie in the future fare poorly in the competition for attention and money. It is not a task which should or can be done by the Federal Government alone. Only through the fullest participation and cooperation of State and local governments and private industry can it be done wisely and effectively. We cannot, however, delude ourselves—we must understand our resources problems, and we must face up to them now. The task is large but it will be done.

John F. Kennedy

The White House
February 23, 1961

PRESIDENT KENNEDY'S WATER RESOURCES COUNCIL*
May 1962

This policy statement by President John F. Kennedy's Water Resources Council explains the use which the President planned for the council in coordinating water policy. Use of the council was one of the recommendations of the Kennedy-Johnson Natural Resources Advisory Committee. The statement includes the revisions in Budget Circular A-47 promised in the Kennedy campaign. In government terminology, these new criteria became known as "Document 97."

POLICIES, STANDARDS, AND PROCEDURES IN THE FORMULATION, EVALUATION, AND REVIEW OF PLANS FOR USE AND DEVELOPMENT OF WATER AND RELATED LAND RESOURCES

I. PURPOSE AND SCOPE

The purpose of this statement is to establish Executive policies, standards, and procedures for uniform application in the formulation, evaluation, and review of comprehensive river basin plans and individual project plans for use and development of water and related land resources. Problems of cost allocation and of reimbursement or cost sharing between the Federal Government and non-Federal bodies will be covered subsequently.

These provisions shall govern, insofar as they are consistent with law and other applicable regulations, all formulation, evaluation, and review of water and related land resources plans. Any proposed variation from these policies and standards shall be specified in planning reports and the reasons therefor indicated.

II. OBJECTIVES OF PLANNING

The basic objective in the formulation of plans is to provide the best use, or combination of uses, of water and related land resources to meet all foreseeable short- and long-term needs. In pursuit of this basic conservation objective, full consideration shall be given to each of the following objectives and reasoned choices made between them when they conflict:

A. DEVELOPMENT

National economic development, and development of each region within the country, is essential to the maintenance of national strength and the achieve-

*Policies, Standards, and Procedures in the Formulation, Evaluation, and Review of Plans for Use and Development of Water and Related Land Resources, Sen. Doc. 97, 87th Cong., 2nd sess., 1–13.

ment of satisfactory levels of living. Water and related land resources development and management are essential to economic development and growth, through concurrent provision for—

Adequate supplies of surface and ground waters of suitable quality for domestic, municipal, agricultural, and industrial uses—including grazing, forestry, and mineral development uses.

Water quality facilities and controls to assure water of suitable quality for all purposes.

Water navigation facilities which provide a needed transportation service with advantage to the Nation's transportation system.

Hydroelectric power where its provision can contribute advantageously to a needed increase in power supply.

Flood control or prevention measures to protect people, property, and productive lands from flood losses where such measures are justified and are the best means of avoiding flood damage.

Land stabilization measures where feasible to protect land and beaches for beneficial purposes.

Drainage measures, including salinity control where best use of land would be justifiably obtained.

Watershed protection and management measures where they will conserve and enhance resource use opportunities.

Outdoor recreational and fish and wildlife opportunities where these can be provided or enhanced by development works.

Any other means by which development of water and related land resources can contribute to economic growth and development.

B. PRESERVATION

Proper stewardship in the long-term interest of the Nation's natural bounty requires in particular instances that—

There be protection and rehabilitation of resources to insure availability for their best use when needed.

Open space, green space, and wild areas of rivers, lakes, beaches, mountains, and related land areas be maintained and used for recreational purposes; and

Areas of unique natural beauty, historical and scientific interest be preserved and managed primarily for the inspiration, enjoyment and education of the people.

C. WELL-BEING OF PEOPLE

Well-being of all of the people shall be the overriding determinant in considering the best use of water and related land resources. Hardship and basic needs of particular groups within the general public shall be of concern, but care shall be taken to avoid resource use and development for the benefit of a few or the disadvantage of many. In particular, policy requirements and guides established by the Congress and aimed at assuring that the use of natural resources, including water resources, safeguard the interests of all of our people shall be observed.

III. PLANNING POLICIES AND PROCEDURES

A. NATIONAL, REGIONAL, STATE, AND LOCAL VIEWPOINTS

1. All viewpoints—national, regional, State, and local—shall be fully considered and taken into account in planning resource use and development. Regional, State, and local objectives shall be considered and evaluated within a framework of national public objectives and available projections of future national conditions and needs. Similarly, available projections of future conditions and needs of regions, States, and localities shall be considered in plan formulation.

2. Significant departures from a national viewpoint required to accomplish regional, State, or local objectives shall be set forth in planning reports by those charged with their preparation. Such reports shall also describe the present economy of the locality, State, and region, changes which can be expected on the basis of current trends, specific economic problems of the area, and the manner in which the project is expected to contribute to the sound economic growth and well-being of the locality, State, and region.

3. Comprehensive plan and project formulation shall be based upon an analysis of the relationship of goods and services to be provided by a proposed resource use or development to available projections of national, regional, State, and local requirements and objectives. From a national point of view, the analysis shall include, within practical limits, a comparison of the proposed resource use and development with alternative means available for providing similar goods and services to the area and other areas and an indication of its relationship, if any, to specific considerations of national security.

B. MULTIPLE-PURPOSE PLANNING

Planning for the use and development of water and related land resources shall be on a fully comprehensive basis so as to consider—

(1) The needs and possibilities for all significant resource uses and purposes of development, including, but not limited to domestic, municipal, agricultural, and industrial uses of water; water quality control; navigation in relation to the Nation's transportation system; hydroelectric power; flood protection control or prevention; land and beach stabilization; drainage, including salinity control; watershed protection and management; forest and mineral production; grazing and cropland improvement;

outdoor recreation, as well as sport and commercial fish and wildlife protection and enhancement; preservation of unique areas of natural beauty, historical and scientific interest; and

(2) All relevant means (including nonstructural as well as structural measures) singly, in combination, or in alternative combinations reflecting different basic choice patterns for providing such uses and purposes.

C. RIVER BASIN PLANNING

River basins are usually the most appropriate geographical units for planning the use and development of water and related land resources in a way that will realize fully the advantage of multiple use, reconcile competitive uses through choice of the best combination of uses, coordinate mutual responsibilities of different agencies and levels of government and other interests concerned with resource use. Planning use of water and related land resources, therefore, shall be undertaken by river basins, groups of closely related river basins, or other regions, and shall take full cognizance of the relationships of all resources, including the interrelationship between surface and ground water resources. Despite this primary confinement to an area, the fact should be recognized that such planning also requires consideration of pertinent physical, economic, and social factors beyond the area.

D. INDIVIDUAL PROJECT PLANNING

To the extent feasible, programs and projects shall be formulated as part of a comprehensive plan for a river basin or other area, and the report proposing development shall indicate the relationship to the comprehensive plan. When a program or project has been formulated independently and not as part of a comprehensive plan, the report shall indicate, to the extent practicable, the relationship of the program or project to the probable later developments needed or to be undertaken in the basin and the reasons for proposing to proceed with the proposed program or project independently.

E. COORDINATION WITHIN THE FEDERAL GOVERNMENT AND WITH NON-FEDERAL INTERESTS

1. Federal planning shall be carried out on a coordinated basis from the earliest steps of investigation, survey, and planning through the entire planning and review process. When any Federal agency initiates an investigation or survey, it shall arrange for appropriate coordination and consideration of problems of mutual concern with other Federal agencies and with interested regional, State, and local public agencies and interests. When warranted, joint consideration of such problems shall be arranged. Full advantage is to be taken of all existing organizations and arrangements for coordination, such as river basin commissions, interagency committees, interstate bodies, and State and local agencies.

2. When plans for resource use or development affect the interests and responsibilities of other Federal agencies, the sponsoring agency shall, to the maximum extent practicable, consult with such agency or agencies in the field and at headquarters in conducting its investigation and preparing its report. When specific project proposals are contemplated, each affected agency shall be afforded an opportunity to participate in the investigations and surveys in an effort to develop fully coordinated proposals. Project reports shall include a statement of the extent of coordination achieved.

3. Before a report is submitted to the President and the Congress, each department or independent agency interested in the project and the concerned States shall be provided with copies of the proposed report, and given an opportunity to furnish a statement concerning the project proposal from the viewpoint of its interest and responsibility. Such statements shall be included in the reports submitted by a sponsoring agency. If such statements propose variations from the policies and standards specified herein, the reasons for each variation shall be stated. A sponsoring agency may submit a report without the views of any agency or State when a statement from that agency or State has not been received within 90 days after receipt of the project report or within such other period specified by law.

4. Planning by Federal agencies shall also be carried out in close cooperation with appropriate regional, State, or local planning and development and conservation agencies, to the end that regional, State, and local objectives may be accomplished to the greatest extent consistent with national objectives. When a proposed resource use or development affects the interest and responsibility of non-Federal public bodies, those bodies shall be furnished information necessary to permit them to evaluate the physical, economic, and social effects. Their views shall be sought, considered in preparation of reports and included in the final reports submitted to the President and the Congress or other approving authority.

F. RELATION TO EXISTING LAW AND EXECUTIVE ORDERS

The policies, standards, and procedures set forth herein shall not be regarded as authorizing any deviation from general or specific requirements of law or Executive order. Whenever a plan or proposal varies from such policies, standards or procedures because of a requirement of existing law or Executive order, the variation shall be indicated, and reference made to the section of law or Executive order imposing such requirements.

IV. REVIEW OF COMPREHENSIVE PLANS AND PROJECT PROPOSALS

With a view to arriving at general and specific independent judgments upon comprehensive plans, programs and project proposals, and parts thereof, as well as recommendations concerning such plans and proposals, review at all appropriate levels shall be based upon a thorough appraisal of planning reports and upon the following criteria:

(a) Compliance with the statement of purpose and scope, objectives of planning, and planning policies and procedures set forth herein.

(b) Compliance with law, legislative intent, and Executive policies and orders.

(c) Compliance with recognized technical standards.

(d) Compliance with standards for the formulation of plans and evaluation of tangible and intangible effects as set forth herein.

V. STANDARDS FOR FORMULATION AND EVALUATION OF PLANS

A. GENERAL SETTING, VIEWPOINT, AND PROCEDURES

1. Formulation of comprehensive and project plans, and evaluation of tangible and intangible effects shall reflect full consideration of, and adherence to the purpose and scope, objectives of planning, planning policies and procedures and criteria for review, as set forth herein.

2. Formulation and evaluation shall normally be based on the expectation of an expanding national economy in which increasing amounts of goods and services are likely to be required to meet the needs of a growing population, higher levels of living, international commitments, and continuing economic growth. Such an environment will necessitate relatively high and efficient levels of resource employment and a pattern of production in balance with the anticipated demand for goods and services.

3. Formulation and evaluation of plans or alternative plans shall be accomplished in such a way as to permit timely application of standards appropriate to conditions of: (a) Less than "full employment" nationally, and (b) chronic and persistent unemployment or underemployment in designated areas. Standards appropriate to (a) shall be those adopted at the time of existence of such condition and authorized by the President. Standards appropriate to condition (b) shall be used where an area has been so designated under the Area Redevelopment Act of 1961 (75 Stat. 47) or other authorized procedures relating to resource underemployment. In condition (b) project benefits shall be considered as increased by the value of the labor and other resources required for project construction, and expected to be used in project operation, project maintenance, and added area employment during the life of the project, to the extent that such labor and other resources would—in the absence of the project—be unutilized or underutilized. Such benefits should be clearly identified as redevelopment benefits for the purposes of cost allocation, cost-sharing procedures, and to indicate their significance for project justification.

4. A comprehensive public viewpoint shall be applied in the evaluation of project effects. Such a viewpoint includes consideration of all effects, beneficial and adverse, short range and long range, tangible and intangible, that may be expected to accrue to all persons and groups within the zone of influence of the proposed resource use or development. The adequacy of the coverage depends on how completely all effects can be traced and evaluated in comparable terms.

5. Full consideration shall be given to the opportunity and need for outdoor recreational and fish and wildlife enhancement in comprehensive planning for water and related land use and development, and project formulation and evaluation. Project plans shall include provision for public acquisition of lands and rights-of-way adjacent to proposed Federal or Federal-assisted water resource projects (additional to those needed for other uses and for public access) for administration by Federal, State, or local public bodies, as appropriate, to insure full ultimate realization of the outdoor recreational, fish and wildlife, and related resource enhancement opportunities of the project area. Plans shall indicate, in appropriate detail, all facilities needed for full development of the recreation and fish and wildlife potential, as well as specific indication of basic facilities required initially for access, health, safety, fire prevention, and use of the area.

6. Full consideration shall also be given in survey, investigation, and planning to the need for acquisition of lands necessary for all purposes of water resource development in advance of construction, so as to preserve these areas from encroachment by residential, commercial, industrial, and other development. Proposals to this end shall be set forth in special reports, or included in regular planning reports, when deemed necessary. Measures proposed should represent the minimum necessary action consistent with the objective of site preservation. Reliance should be placed, where feasible, on zoning and other measures by non-Federal authorities to keep lands on local tax rolls and control development until sites are needed for project purposes. Such measures should also include provisions for advance participation in construction or reconstruction of transportation facilities, when necessary, to avoid increased costs for relocation.

7. When there are major differences among technically possible plans conceived as desirable on the basis of consideration of intangible benefits and costs, in comparison with optimum plans based on tangible benefits and costs, alternative combinations of projects within a river basin or alternative projects, giving expression to these major differences, shall be planned. Comparison of their economic and financial costs shall be set forth in reports to provide a basis for selection among the alternatives by reviewing authorities in the executive branch and by the Congress. Minor differences, with regard to intangible considerations, shall be handled, to the extent practicable and economically feasible, by adjustments in plans. Planning reports shall clearly indicate alternatives, their

consequences, and adjustments made to take account of these minor differences.

8. When secondary benefits are included in formulation and evaluation of a project proposal, planning reports shall indicate—

(*a*) The amount of secondary benefits considered attributable to the project from a national viewpoint. Such benefits, combined with primary benefits, shall be included in the computation of a benefit-cost ratio.

(*b*) Secondary benefits attributable to the project from a regional, State, or local viewpoint. Such benefits shall also be evaluated, when this procedure is considered pertinent, and an additional benefit-cost ratio computed.

(*c*) Presentations in planning reports shall include an explanation of the nature of each type of secondary benefit taken into account from either viewpoint and the methods used in the computation of each of their values. The implications, from the national viewpoint, of considering secondary benefits of the project from a regional, State, or local viewpoint shall be set forth.

B. SPECIFIC SETTING FOR AREA UNDER CONSTRUCTION

1. Reports on proposed plans shall include an analysis of present and projected future economic conditions in the project area and the contribution that comprehensive or project development may be expected to make toward the alleviation of problems and the promotion of economic growth and well-being within the zone of influence. Economic projections will be made to provide a basis for appraisal of conditions to be expected with and without the plans under consideration, and an estimate of the contribution that comprehensive development may make to increased national income and welfare, and regional growth and stability. Such analyses will frequently require a general economic study of the area, a study of all of its resources, an assessment of their functional relationships, their development potentials, possible adverse effects, and the locational situation with reference to resources, markets, transportation, climate, and social factors. Analyses should indicate the significance of the locality and the region in producing increased goods and services to meet foreseeable needs.

2. These analyses should be as extensive and intensive as is appropriate to the scope of the project being planned. They should provide essential information for identifying both immediate and long-range needs in economic and social terms and these needs should be expressed in a form useful for program formulation. Presentations in reports should identify—

(*a*) The relationship between economic development needs and opportunities and potential water and related land resource use and development;

(*b*) The economic and social consequences of complete or partial failure to satisfy these needs; and

(*c*) The possible improvements in economic efficiency, alleviation of unemployment, stabilization of production and income, community well-being, and the quality of goods and services that will be forthcoming.

C. STANDARDS FOR FORMULATION OF PLANS

1. All plans shall be formulated with due regard to all pertinent benefits and costs, both tangible and intangible. Benefits and costs shall be expressed in comparable quantitative economic terms to the fullest extent possible.

2. Comprehensive plans shall be formulated initially to include all units and purposes which satisfy these criteria in quantitative economic terms:

(*a*) Tangible benefits exceed project economic costs.

(*b*) Each separable unit or purpose provides benefits at least equal to its costs.

(*c*) The scope of development is such as to provide the maximum net benefits.

(*d*) There is no more economical means, evaluated on a comparable basis, of accomplishing the same purpose or purposes which would be precluded from development if the plan were undertaken. This limitation refers only to those alternative possibilities that would be physically displaced or economically precluded from development if the project is undertaken.

3. Net benefits are maximized when the scope of development is extended to the point where the benefits added by the last increment of scale (i.e., an increment of size of a unit, an individual purpose in a multiple-purpose plan or a unit in a comprehensive plan) are equal to the costs of adding that increment of scale. The increments to be considered in this way are the smallest increments on which there is a practical choice of omission from the plan.

4. Reports or plans shall indicate the scale of development that would result from application of the foregoing criteria considering tangible benefits and project economic costs expressed in comparable terms. This will provide a baseline from which the effect of considering intangibles can be judged.

5. Reports and plans shall also indicate the extent to which departures from that scale of development are proposed in order to take into account intangibles or other considerations warranting a modification in scale not reflected in the tangible benefits and project economic costs. For example, a higher degree of flood protection, particularly in urban areas, than is feasible on the basis of tangible benefits alone may be justified in consideration of the threat to lives, health, and general security posed by larger floods. Also, when long-range water needs are foreseeable only in general terms and where alternative means of

meeting the needs are not available and inclusion of additional capacity initially can be accomplished at a significant savings over subsequent enlargement, such considerations may justify the additional cost required. Similarly, long-range power needs, in the light of generally expected economic growth of an area, may justify measures initially to insure later availability of the full power potential.

D. DEFINITIONS OF BENEFITS

1. Benefits: Increases or gains, net of associated or induced costs, in the value of goods and services which result from conditions with the project, as compared with conditions without the project. Benefits include tangibles and intangibles and may be classed as primary or secondary.

2. Tangible benefits: Those benefits that can be expressed in monetary terms based on or derived from actual or simulated market prices for the products or services, or, in the absence of such measures of benefits, the cost of the alternative means that would most likely be utilized to provide equivalent products or services. This latter standard affords a measure of minimum value of such benefits or services to the users. When costs of alternatives are used as a measure of benefits, the costs should include the interest, taxes, insurance, and other cost elements that would actually be incurred by such alternative means rather than including only costs on a comparable basis to project costs as is required when applying the project formulation criteria under paragraph V-C-2(d).

3. Intangible benefits: Those benefits which, although recognized as having real value in satisfying human needs or desires, are not fully measurable in monetary terms, or are incapable of such expression in formal analysis. Each type of benefit usually has a part which is readily measurable and may have a part which is not measurable or not readily measurable. The significance of this latter part shall be based upon informed judgment.

4. Primary benefits: The value of goods or services directly resulting from the project, less associated costs incurred in realization of the benefits and any induced costs not included in project costs.

5. Secondary benefits: The increase in the value of goods and services which indirectly result from the project under conditions expected with the project as compared to those without the project. Such increase shall be net of any economic nonproject costs that need be incurred to realize these secondary benefits.

E. TYPES OF PRIMARY BENEFITS AND STANDARDS
FOR THEIR MEASUREMENT

1. Domestic, municipal, and industrial water supply benefits: Improvements in quantity, dependability, quality, and physical convenience of water use. The

amount water users should be willing to pay for such improvements in lieu of foregoing them affords an appropriate measure of this value. In practice, however, the measure of the benefit will be approximated by the cost of achieving the same results by the most likely alternative means that would be utilized in the absence of the project. Where such an alternative source is not available or would not be economically feasible, the benefits may be valued on such basis as the value of water to users or the average cost of raw water (for comparable units of dependable yield) from municipal or industrial water supply projects planned or recently constructed in the general region.

2. Irrigation benefits: The increase in the net income of agricultural production resulting from an increase in the moisture content of the soil through the application of water or reduction in damages from drought.

3. Water quality control benefits: The net contribution to public health, safety, economy, and effectiveness in use and enjoyment of water for all purposes which are subject to detriment or betterment by virtue of change in water quality. The net contribution may be evaluated in terms of avoidance of adverse effects which would accrue in the absence of water quality control, including such damages and restrictions as preclusion of economic activities, corrosion of fixed and floating plant, loss or downgrading of recreational opportunities, increased municipal and industrial water treatment costs, loss of industrial and agricultural production, impairment of health and welfare, damage to fish and wildlife, siltation, salinity intrusion, and degradation of the esthetics of enjoyment of unpolluted surface waters, or, conversely, in terms of the advantageous effects of water quality control with respect to such items. Effects such as these may be composited roughly into tangible and intangible categories, and used to evaluate water quality control activities. In situations where no adequate means can be devised to evaluate directly the economic effects of water quality improvement, the cost of achieving the same results by the most likely alternative may be used as an approximation of value.

4. Navigation benefits: The value of the services provided after allowance for the cost of the associated resources required to make the service available. For commodities that would move in the absence of the project, the benefit is measured by the saving as a result of the project in the cost of providing the transportation service. For commodities that will move over the improved waterway but would not move by alternative means, the measure of the benefit is the value of the service to shippers; that is, the maximum cost they should be willing to incur for moving the various units of traffic involved. Navigation improvements may also provide benefits in other forms, such as reduction in losses due to hazardous or inadequate operating conditions and enhancement in land values from the placement of dredged spoil.

5. Electric power benefits: The value of power to the users is measured by the amount that they should be willing to pay for such power. The usual practice is

to measure the benefit in terms of the cost of achieving the same result by the most likely alternative means that would exist in the absence of the project. In the absence of economically feasible alternative means, the value of the power to users may be measured by any savings in production costs, increase in value of product that would result from its use, or its net value to consumers.

6. Flood control and prevention benefits: Reduction in all forms of damage from inundation (including sedimentation) of property, disruption of business and other activity, hazards to health and security, and loss of life; and increase in the net return from higher use of property made possible as a result of lowering the flood hazard.

7. Land stabilization benefits: Benefits accruing to landowners and operators and the public resulting from the reduction in the loss of net income, or loss in value of land and improvements, through the prevention of loss or damage by all forms of soil erosion including sheet erosion, gullying, flood plain scouring, streambank cutting, and shore or beach erosion, or, conversely in terms of advantageous effects of land stabilization.

8. Drainage benefits: The increase in the net income from agricultural lands or increase in land values resulting from higher yields or lower production costs through reduction in the moisture content of the soil (exclusive of excessive moisture due to flooding), and the increase in the value of urban and industrial lands due to improvement in drainage conditions.

9. Recreation benefits: The value as a result of the project of net increases in the quantity and quality of boating, swimming, camping, picnicking, winter sports, hiking, horseback riding, sightseeing, and similar outdoor activities. (Fishing, hunting, and appreciation and preservation of fish and wildlife are included under par. V-E-10.) In the general absence of market prices, values for specific recreational activities may be derived or estimated on the basis of a simulated market giving weight to all pertinent considerations, including charges that recreationists should be willing to pay and to any actual charges being paid by users for comparable opportunities at other installations or on the basis of justifiable alternative costs. Benefits also include the intangible values of preserving areas of unique natural beauty and scenic, historical, and scientific interest.

10. Fish and wildlife benefits: The value as a result of the project of net increases in recreational, resource preservation, and commercial aspects of fish and wildlife. In the absence of market prices, the value of sport fishing, hunting, and other specific recreational forms of fish and wildlife may be derived or established in the same manner as prescribed in paragraph V-E-9. Resource preservation includes the intangible value of improvement of habitat and environment for wildlife and the preservation of rare species. Benefits also result from the increase in market value of commercial fish and wildlife less the associated costs.

11. Other benefits: Justification of the recognition of any other benefits and of the standard used in their measurement shall be set forth in reports. Unless included under one or more of the above categories, reports should show the net economic effects of changes in transportation capability, or changes in productivity of forest, range, mineral, or other resources. A project's contribution toward meeting specific needs for servicing international treaties or for national defense may also be included.

F. DEFINITION OF COSTS

1. Project economic costs: The value of all goods and services (land, labor, and materials) used in constructing, operating, and maintaining a project or program, interest during construction, and all other identifiable expenses, losses, liabilities, and induced adverse effects connected therewith, whether in goods or services, whether tangible or intangible and whether or not compensation is involved. Project economic costs are the sum of installation costs; operation, maintenance, and replacement costs; and induced costs as defined below.

2. Installation costs: The value of goods and services necessary for the establishment of the project, including initial project construction; land, easements, rights-of-way, and water rights; capital outlays to relocate facilities or prevent damages; and all other expenditures for investigations and surveys, and designing, planning, and constructing a project after its authorization.

3. Operation, maintenance, and replacement costs: The value of goods and services needed to operate a constructed project and make repairs and replacements necessary to maintain the project in sound operating condition during its economic life.

4. Induced costs: All uncompensated adverse effects caused by the construction and operation of a program or project, whether tangible or intangible. These include estimated net increases, if any, in the cost of Government services directly resulting from the project and net adverse effects on the economy such as increased transportation costs. Induced costs may be accounted for either by addition to project economic costs or deduction from primary benefits.

5. Associated costs: The value of goods and services over and above those included in project costs needed to make the immediate products or services of the project available for use or sale. Associated costs are deducted from the value of goods and services resulting from a project to obtain primary benefits.

6. Taxes: Allowances in lieu of taxes or taxes foregone will not be included in project economic costs, except as required by law.

G. TIME CONSIDERATIONS

1. *Period of analysis.* — The economic evaluation of a project shall encompass the period of time over which the project will serve a useful purpose. Thus, the period of analysis should be the shorter of either the physical life or the eco-

nomic life of the structure, facility, or improvement. However, because of the difficulty in defining the more remote future conditions and the discount of long-deferred values, 100 years will normally be considered the upper limit of the period of analysis.

2. *Discount rate.* — The interest rate to be used in plan formulation and evaluation for discounting future benefits and computing costs, or otherwise converting benefits and costs to a common time basis shall be based upon the average rate of interest payable by the Treasury on interest-bearing marketable securities of the United States outstanding at the end of the fiscal year preceding such computation which, upon original issue, had terms to maturity of 15 years or more. Where the average rate so calculated is not a multiple of one-eighth of 1 percent, the rate of interest shall be the multiple of one-eighth of 1 percent next lower than such average rate.

This procedure shall be subject to adjustment when and if this is found desirable as a result of continuing analysis of all factors pertinent to selection of a discount rate for these purposes.

3. *Price levels.* — The prices used for project evaluation should reflect the exchange values expected to prevail at the time costs are incurred and benefits accrued. Estimates of initial project costs should be based on price relationships prevailing at the time of the analysis. Estimates of benefits and deferred costs should be made on the basis of projected normal price relationships expected with a stabilized general price level and under relatively full employment conditions for the economy. Pending development of mutually acceptable long-term price projections of this type, normalized current price relationships may be used in estimating deferred project effects. When benefits are measured in terms of the cost of an alternative, the prices should be those expected to prevail at the time such costs would have been incurred. Whenever project production is expected to influence prices significantly, the use of a price about midway between those expected with and without the project may be justified to reflect the public values involved. Appropriate price adjustments should be made where there is a limited foreseeable need or demand for the products or services to be provided by the project.

VI. RELATION TO COST ALLOCATION, REIMBURSEMENT AND COST-SHARING POLICIES, STANDARDS, AND PROCEDURES

Cost allocation, reimbursement and cost-sharing policies, standards, and procedures, as indicated in the section on "Purpose and Scope," above, are not generally included herein. Nevertheless, certain such matters of special importance in relation to the foregoing are included, as follows:

(*a*) All project purposes shall be treated comparably in cost allocation and each is entitled to its fair share of the advantages resulting from the multiple-purpose project or program. Project purposes to which costs may be allocated on a par with all other purposes, without restrictions regarding reimbursement or cost-sharing policies, shall include (but not be limited to) the following:

Domestic, municipal, or industrial water supply.

Irrigation.

Water quality control.

Navigation.

Hydroelectric power.

Flood control and prevention.

Land and beach stabilization.

Drainage, including salinity control.

Outdoor recreation development.

Fish and wildlife development.

Other purposes, such as area redevelopment and the servicing of international treaties and national defense when specific, quantifiable benefits are provided for such purposes by a project or program.

(*b*) Allocated costs, determined in accordance with principles and procedures to be established subsequently, shall provide a basis for consideration of reimbursement and cost-sharing arrangements.

(*c*) The period of analysis and discount rate established herein for purposes of formulation and evaluation of comprehensive plans and project plans (sec. V-G-1 and 2) shall not be construed as establishing the payout period or rate of interest to be used in reimbursement and cost-sharing arrangements.

(*d*) Planning reports of each department shall include appropriate recommendations covering reimbursement and cost-sharing arrangements and provide a detailed explanation of the basis used in arriving at the recommendations in consideration of the laws and administrative provisions in effect at the time.

LYNDON B. JOHNSON

THE WATER RESOURCES RESEARCH ACT*
July 17, 1964

This law, with the resulting grants to state universities, has greatly expanded water research in the nation. One of the chief purposes of the proposal was to stimulate state and local action on water resource problems.

An Act to establish water resources research centers, to promote a more adequate national program of water research, and for other purposes.

Be it enacted by the Senate and House of Representatives of the United States of America in Congress assembled, That (a) this Act may be cited as the "Water Resources Research Act of 1964."

(b) In order to assist in assuring the Nation at all times of a supply of water sufficient in quantity and quality to meet the requirements of its expanding population, it is the purpose of the Congress, by this Act, to stimulate, sponsor, provide for, and supplement present programs for the conduct of research, investigations, experiments, and the training of scientists in the fields of water and of resources which affect water.

TITLE I—STATE WATER RESOURCES
RESEARCH INSTITUTES

SEC. 100. (a) There are authorized to be appropriated to the Secretary of the Interior for the fiscal year 1965 and each subsequent year thereafter sums adequate to provide $75,000 to each of the several States in the first year, $87,500 in each of the second and third years, and $100,000 each year thereafter to assist each participating State in establishing and carrying on the work of a competent and qualified water resources research institute, center, or equivalent agency (hereinafter referred to as "institute") at one college or university in that State, which college or university shall be a college or university established in accordance with the Act approved July 2, 1862 (12 Stat. 503), entitled "An Act donating public lands to the several States and territories which may provide colleges

*78 *Statutes at Large,* 329–33.

for the benefit of agriculture and the mechanic arts" or some other institution designated by Act of the legislature of the State concerned: *Provided,* That (1) if there is more than one such college or university in a State, established in accordance with said Act of July 2, 1862, funds under this Act shall, in the absence of a designation to the contrary by act of the legislature of the State, be paid to the one such college or university designated by the Governor of the State to receive the same subject to the Secretary's determination that such college or university has, or may reasonably be expected to have, the capability of doing effective work under this Act; (2) two or more States may cooperate in the designation of a single interstate or regional institute, in which event the sums assignable to all of the cooperating States shall be paid to such institute; and (3) a designated college or university may, as authorized by appropriate State authority, arrange with other colleges and universities within the State to participate in the work of the institute.

(b) It shall be the duty of each such institute to plan and conduct and/or arrange for a component or components of the college or university with which it is affiliated to conduct competent research, investigations, and experiments of either a basic or practical nature, or both, in relation to water resources and to provide for the training of scientists through such research, investigations, and experiments. Such research, investigations, experiments, and training may include, without being limited to, aspects of the hydrologic cycle; supply and demand for water; conservation and best use of available supplies of water; methods of increasing such supplies; and economic, legal, social, engineering, recreational, biological, geographic, ecological, and other aspects of water problems, having due regard to the varying conditions and needs of the respective States, to water research projects being conducted by agencies of the Federal and State Governments, the agricultural experiment stations, and others, and to avoidance of any undue displacement of scientists and engineers elsewhere engaged in water resources research.

SEC. 101. (a) There is further authorized to be appropriated to the Secretary of the Interior for the fiscal year 1965 and each subsequent year thereafter sums not in excess of the following: 1965, $1,000,000; 1966, $2,000,000; 1967, $3,000,-000; 1968, $4,000,000; and 1969 and each of the succeeding years, $5,000,000. Such moneys when appropriated, shall be available to match, on a dollar-for-dollar basis, funds made available to institutes by States or other non-Federal sources to meet the necessary expenses of specific water resources research projects which could not otherwise be undertaken, including the expenses of planning and coordinating regional water resources research projects by two or more institutes.

(b) Each application for a grant pursuant to subsection (a) of this section shall, among other things, state the nature of the project to be undertaken, the period during which it will be pursued, the qualifications of the personnel who will direct and conduct it, the importance of the project to the water economy of the Nation, the region, and the State concerned, its relation to other known research projects theretofore pursued or currently being pursued, and the extent to which it will provide opportunity for the training of water resources scientists. No grant shall be made under said subsection (a) except for a project approved by the Secretary, and all grants shall be made upon the basis of the merit of the project, the need for the knowledge which it is expected to produce when completed, and the opportunity it provides for the training of water resources scientists.

Sec. 102. Sums available to the States under the terms of sections 100 and 101 of this Act shall be paid to their designated institutes at such times and in such amounts during each fiscal year as determined by the Secretary, and upon vouchers approved by him. Each institute shall have an officer appointed by its governing authority who shall receive and account for all funds paid under the provisions of this Act and shall make an annual report to the Secretary on or before the 1st day of September of each year, on work accomplished and the status of projects underway, together with a detailed statement of the amounts received under any of the provisions of this Act during the preceding fiscal year, and of its disbursement, on schedules prescribed by the Secretary. If any of the moneys received by the authorized receiving officer of any institute under the provisions of this Act shall by any action or contingency be found by the Secretary to have been improperly diminished, lost, or misapplied, it shall be replaced by the State concerned and until so replaced no subsequent appropriation shall be allotted or paid to any institute of such State.

Sec. 103. Moneys appropriated pursuant to this Act, in addition to being available for expenses for research, investigations, experiments, and training conducted under authority of this Act, shall also be available for printing and publishing the results thereof and for administrative planning and direction. The institutes are hereby authorized and encouraged to plan and conduct programs financed under this Act in cooperation with each other and with such other agencies and individuals as may contribute to the solution of the water problems involved, and moneys appropriated pursuant to this Act shall be available for paying the necessary expenses of planning, coordinating, and conducting such cooperative research.

Sec. 104. The Secretary of the Interior is hereby charged with the responsibility for the proper administration of this Act and, after full consultation with other interested Federal agencies, shall prescribe such rules and regulations as may be necessary to carry out its provisions. He shall require a showing that institutes designated to receive funds have, or may reasonably be expected to have, the capability of doing effective work. He shall furnish such advice and assistance as will best promote the purposes of this Act, participate in coordinating research initiated under this Act by the institutes, indicate to them such lines of inquiry as to him seem most important, and encourage and assist in the establishment and maintenance of cooperation by and between the institutes and between them and other research organizations, the United States Department of the Interior, and other Federal establishments.

On or before the 1st day of July in each year after the passage of this Act, the Secretary shall ascertain whether the requirements of section 102 have been met as to each State, whether it is entitled to receive its share of the annual appropriations for water resources research under section 100 of this Act, and the amount which it is entitled to receive.

The Secretary shall make an annual report to the Congress of the receipts and expenditures and work of the institutes in all States under the provisions of this Act. His report shall indicate whether any portion of an appropriation available for allotment to any State has been withheld and, if so, the reasons therefor.

SEC. 105. Nothing in this Act shall be construed to impair or modify the legal relation existing between any of the colleges or universities under whose direction an institute is established and the government of the State in which it is located, and nothing in this Act shall in any way be construed to authorize Federal control or direction of education at any college or university.

TITLE II—ADDITIONAL WATER RESOURCES RESEARCH PROGRAMS

SEC. 200. There is authorized to be appropriated to the Secretary of the Interior $1,000,000 in fiscal year 1965 and $1,000,000 in each of the nine fiscal years thereafter from which he may make grants, contracts, matching, or other arrangements with educational institutions (other than those establishing institutes under title I of this Act), private foundations or other institutions; with private firms and individuals; and with local, State and Federal Government agencies, to undertake research into any aspects of water problems related to the mission of the Department of the Interior, which may be deemed desirable and are not otherwise being studied. The Secretary shall submit each such proposed grant, contract, or other arrangement to the President of the Senate and the Speaker of the House of Representatives, and no appropriation shall be made to finance the same until 60 calendar days (which 60 days, however, shall not include days on which either the House of Representatives or the Senate is not in session because of an adjournment of more than three calendar days) after such submission and then only if, within said 60 days, neither the Committee on Interior and Insular Affairs of the House of Representatives nor the Committee on Interior and Insular Affairs of the Senate disapproves the same.

TITLE III—MISCELLANEOUS PROVISIONS

Sec. 300. The Secretary of the Interior shall obtain the continuing advice and cooperation of all agencies of the Federal Government concerned with water problems, of State and local governments, and of private institutions and individuals, to assure that the programs authorized in this Act will supplement and not duplicate established water research programs, to stimulate research in otherwise neglected areas, and to contribute to a comprehensive, nationwide program of water and related resources research. He shall make generally available information and reports on projects completed, in progress, or planned under the provisions of this Act, in addition to any direct publication of information by the institutes themselves.

Sec. 301. Nothing in this Act is intended to give or shall be construed as giving the Secretary of the Interior any authority or surveillance over water resources research conducted by any other agency of the Federal Government, or as repealing, superseding, or diminishing existing authorities or responsibilities of any agency of the Federal Government to plan and conduct, contract for, or assist in research in its areas of responsibility and concern with water resources.

Sec. 302. Contracts or other arrangements for water resources work authorized under this Act with an institute, educational institution, or non-profit organization may be undertaken without regard to the provisions of section 3684 of the Revised Statutes (31 U.S.C. 529) when, in the judgment of the Secretary of the Interior, advance payments of initial expense are necessary to facilitate such work.

Sec. 303. No part of any appropriated funds may be expended pursuant to authorization given by this Act for any scientific or technological research or development activity unless such expenditure is conditioned upon provisions determined by the Secretary of the Interior, with the approval of the Attorney General, to be effective to insure that all information, uses, products, processes, patents, and other developments resulting from that activity will (with such exceptions and limitations as the Secretary may determine, after consultation with the Secretary of Defense, to be necessary in the interest of the national defense) be made freely and fully available to the general public. Nothing contained in this section shall deprive the owner of any background patent relating to any such activity of any rights which that owner may have under that patent.

Sec. 304. There shall be established, in such agency and location as the President determines to be desirable, a center for cataloging current and projected scientific research in all fields of water resources. Each Federal agency doing water resources research shall cooperate by providing the cataloging center with information on work underway or scheduled by it. The cataloging center shall classify and maintain for general use a catalog of water resources research and investigation projects in progress or scheduled by all Federal agencies and by such non-Federal agencies of government, colleges, universities, private institutions, firms, and individuals as voluntarily may make such information available.

SEC. 305. The President shall, by such means as he deems appropriate, clarify agency responsibilities for Federal water resources research and provide for interagency coordination of such research, including the research authorized by this Act. Such coordination shall include (a) continuing review of the adequacy of the Government-wide program in water resources research, (b) indentification and elimination of duplication and overlaps between two or more agency programs, (c) identification of technical needs in various water resources research categories, (d) recommendations with respect to allocation of technical effort among the Federal agencies, (e) review of technical manpower needs and findings concerning the technical manpower base of the program, (f) recommendations concerning management policies to improve the quality of the Government-wide research effort, and (g) actions to facilitate interagency communication at management levels.

SEC. 306. As used in this Act, the term "State" includes the Commonwealth of Puerto Rico.

Approved July 17, 1964.

THE WILDERNESS ACT*
September 3, 1964

The Wilderness Act of 1964, climaxing a long campaign by conservationists, ranks as one of the major conservation achievements under President Lyndon Johnson, after an unqualified endorsement from President Kennedy.

The original Wilderness Bill, for which conservation groups campaigned, involved much larger land areas, but the final bill did add the force of law to administrative protection for 54 areas within the national forests. It also included a provision whereby other areas within national parks, monuments, and wildlife refuges could be added by the Secretary of the Interior with congressional approval.

Before passage the bill was carefully amended by western interests to see that it involved no real loss of valuable timber or mining potential.

An Act to establish a National Wilderness Preservation System for the permanent good of the whole people, and for other purposes.

Be it enacted by the Senate and House of Representatives of the United States of America in Congress assembled,

SHORT TITLE

SECTION 1. This Act may be cited as the "Wilderness Act".

WILDERNESS SYSTEM ESTABLISHED STATEMENT OF POLICY

SEC. 2. (a) In order to assure that an increasing population, accompanied by expanding settlement and growing mechanization, does not occupy and modify all areas within the United States and its possessions, leaving no lands designated for preservation and protection in their natural condition, it is hereby declared to be the policy of the Congress to secure for the American people of present and future generations the benefits of an enduring resource of wilderness. For this purpose there is hereby established a National Wilderness Preservation System to be composed of federally owned areas designated by Congress as "wilderness areas", and these shall be administered for the use and enjoyment of the American people in such manner as will leave them unimpaired for future use and enjoyment as wilderness, and so as to provide for the protection of these areas, the preservation of their wilderness character, and for the gathering and dissemination of information regarding their use and enjoyment as wilderness; and no Federal lands shall be designated as "wilderness areas" except as provided for in this Act or by a subsequent Act.

*78 Statutes at Large, 890–96.

(b) The inclusion of an area in the National Wilderness Preservation System notwithstanding, the area shall continue to be managed by the Department and agency having jurisdiction thereover immediately before its inclusion in the National Wilderness Preservation System unless otherwise provided by Act of Congress. No appropriation shall be available for the payment of expenses or salaries for the administration of the National Wilderness Preservation System as a separate unit nor shall any appropriations be available for additional personnel stated as being required solely for the purpose of managing or administering areas solely because they are included within the National Wilderness Preservation system.

DEFINITION OF WILDERNESS

(c) A wilderness, in contrast with those areas where man and his own works dominate the landscape, is hereby recognized as an area where the earth and its community of life are untrammeled by man, where man himself is a visitor who does not remain. An area of wilderness is further defined to mean in this Act an area of undeveloped Federal land retaining its primeval character and influence, without permanent improvements or human habitation, which is protected and managed so as to preserve its natural conditions and which (1) generally appears to have been affected primarily by the forces of nature, with the imprint of man's work substantially unnoticeable; (2) has outstanding opportunities for solitude or a primitive and unconfined type of recreation; (3) has at least five thousand acres of land or is of sufficient size as to make practicable its preservation and use in an unimpaired condition; and (4) may also contain ecological, geological, or other features of scientific, educational, scenic, or historical value.

NATIONAL WILDERNESS PRESERVATION SYSTEM— EXTENT OF SYSTEM

Sec. 3. (a) All areas within the national forests classified at least 30 days before the effective date of this Act by the Secretary of Agriculture or the Chief of the Forest Service as "wilderness", "wild", or "canoe" are hereby designated as wilderness areas. The Secretary of Agriculture shall—

(1) Within one year after the effective date of this Act, file a map and legal description of each wilderness area with the Interior and Insular Affairs Committees of the United States Senate and the House of Representatives, and such descriptions shall have the same force and effect as if included in this Act: *Provided, however,* That correction of clerical and typographical errors in such legal descriptions and maps may be made.

(2) Maintain, available to the public, records pertaining to said wilderness areas, including maps and legal descriptions, copies of regulations governing them, copies of public notices of, and reports submitted to Con-

gress regarding pending additions, eliminations, or modifications. Maps, legal descriptions, and regulations pertaining to wilderness areas within their respective jurisdictions also shall be available to the public in the offices of regional foresters, national forest supervisors, and forest rangers.

(b) The Secretary of Agriculture shall, within ten years after the enactment of this Act, review, as to its suitability or nonsuitability for preservation as wilderness, each area in the national forests classified on the effective date of this Act by the Secretary of Agriculture or the Chief of the Forest Service as "primitive" and report his findings to the President. The President shall advise the United States Senate and House of Representatives of his recommendations with respect to the designation as "wilderness" or other reclassification of each area on which review has been completed, together with maps and a definition of boundaries. Such advice shall be given with respect to not less than one-third of all the areas now classified as "primitive" within three years after the enactment of this Act, not less than two-thirds within seven years after the enactment of this Act, and the remaining areas within ten years after the enactment of this Act. Each recommendation of the President for designation as "wilderness" shall become effective only if so provided by an Act of Congress. Areas classified as "primitive" on the effective date of this Act shall continue to be administered under the rules and regulations affecting such areas on the effective date of this Act until Congress has determined otherwise. Any such area may be increased in size by the President at the time he submits his recommendations to the Congress by not more than five thousand acres with no more than one thousand two hundred and eighty acres of such increase in any one compact unit; if it is proposed to increase the size of any such area by more than five thousand acres or by more than one thousand two hundred and eighty acres in any one compact unit the increase in size shall not become effective until acted upon by Congress. Nothing herein contained shall limit the President in proposing, as part of his recommendations to Congress, the alteration of existing boundaries of primitive areas or recommending the addition of any contiguous area of national forest lands predominantly of wilderness value. Notwithstanding any other provisions of this Act, the Secretary of Agriculture may complete his review and delete such area as may be necessary, but not to exceed seven thousand acres, from the southern tip of the Gore Range-Eagles Nest Primitive Area, Colorado, if the Secretary determines that such action is in the public interest.

(c) Within ten years after the effective date of this Act the Secretary of the Interior shall review every roadless area of five thousand contiguous acres or more in the national parks, monuments and other units of the national park system and every such area of, and every roadless island within, the national wildlife refuges and game ranges, under his jurisdiction on the effective date of this Act and shall report to the President his recommendation as to the suitability or nonsuitability of each such area or island for preservation as wilderness.

The President shall advise the President of the Senate and the Speaker of the House of Representatives of his recommendation with respect to the designation as wilderness of each such area or island on which review has been completed, together with a map thereof and a definition of its boundaries. Such advice shall be given with respect to not less than one-third of the areas and islands to be reviewed under this subsection within three years after enactment of this Act, not less than two-thirds within seven years of enactment of this Act, and the remainder within ten years of enactment of this Act. A recommendation of the President for designation as wilderness shall become effective only if so provided by an Act of Congress. Nothing contained herein shall, by implication or otherwise, be construed to lessen the present statutory authority of the Secretary of the Interior with respect to the maintenance of roadless areas within units of the national park system.

(d) (1) The Secretary of Agriculture and the Secretary of the Interior shall, prior to submitting any recommendations to the President with respect to the suitability of any area for preservation as wilderness—

(A) give such public notice of the proposed action as they deem appropriate, including publication in the Federal Register and in a newspaper having general circulation in the area or areas in the vicinity of the affected land;

(B) hold a public hearing or hearings at a location or locations convenient to the area affected. The hearings shall be announced through such means as the respective Secretaries involved deem appropriate, including notices in the Federal Register and in newspapers of general circulation in the area: *Provided,* That if the lands involved are located in more than one State, at least one hearing shall be held in each State in which a portion of the land lies;

(C) at least thirty days before the date of a hearing advise the Governor of each State and the governing board of each county, or in Alaska the borough, in which the lands are located, and Federal departments and agencies concerned, and invite such officials and Federal agencies to submit their views on the proposed action at the hearing or by no later than thirty days following the date of the hearing.

(2) Any views submitted to the appropriate Secretary under the provisions of (1) of this subsection with respect to any area shall be included with any recommendations to the President and to Congress with respect to such area.

(e) Any modification or adjustment of boundaries of any wilderness area shall be recommended by the appropriate Secretary after public notice of such proposal and public hearing or hearings as provided in subsection (d) of this section. The proposed modification or adjustment shall then be recommended with map and description thereof to the President. The President shall advise the United States Senate and the House of Representatives of his recommendations with respect to such modification or adjustment and such recommendations shall become effective only in the same manner as provided for in subsections (b) and (c) of this section.

USE OF WILDERNESS AREAS

SEC. 4. (a) The purposes of this Act are hereby declared to be within and supplemental to the purposes for which national forests and units of the national park and national wildlife refuge systems are established and administered and—

(1) Nothing in this Act shall be deemed to be in interference with the purpose for which national forests are established as set forth in the Act of June 4, 1897 (30 Stat. 11), and the Multiple-Use Sustained-Yield Act of June 12, 1960 (74 Stat. 215).

(2) Nothing in this Act shall modify the restrictions and provisions of the Shipstead-Nolan Act (Public Law 539, Seventy-first Congress, July 10, 1930; 46 Stat. 1020), the Thye-Blatnik Act (Public Law 733, Eightieth Congress, June 22, 1948; 62 Stat. 568), and the Humphrey-Thye-Blatnik-Andresen Act (Public Law 607, Eighty-fourth Congress, June 22, 1956; 70 Stat. 326), as applying to the Superior National Forest or the regulations of the Secretary of Agriculture.

(3) Nothing in this Act shall modify the statutory authority under which units of the national park system are created. Further, the designation of any park, monument, or other unit of the national park system as a wilderness area pursuant to this Act shall in no manner lower the standards evolved for the use and preservation of such park, monument, or other unit of the national park system in accordance with the Act of August 25, 1916, the statutory authority under which the area was created, or any other Act of Congress which might pertain to or affect such area, including, but not limited to, the Act of June 8, 1906 (34 Stat. 225; 16 U.S.C. 432 et seq.); section 3(2) of the Federal Power Act (16 U.S.C. 796(2)); and the Act of August 21, 1935 (49 Stat. 666; 16 U.S.C. 461 et seq.).

(b) Except as otherwise provided in this Act, each agency administering any area designated as wilderness shall be responsible for preserving the wilderness character of the area and shall so administer such area for such other purposes for which it may have been established as also to preserve its wilderness character. Except as otherwise provided in this Act, wilderness areas shall be devoted to the public purposes of recreational, scenic, scientific, educational, conservation, and historical use.

PROHIBITION OF CERTAIN USES

(c) Except as specifically provided for in this Act, and subject to existing private rights, there shall be no commercial enterprise and no permanent road within any wilderness area designated by this Act and, except as necessary to meet minimum requirements for the administration of the area for the purpose of this Act (including measures required in emergencies involving the health and safety of persons within the area), there shall be no temporary road, no use of motor vehicles, motorized equipment or motorboats, no landing of aircraft, no other form of mechanical transport, and no structure or installation within any such area.

SPECIAL PROVISIONS

(d) The following special provisions are hereby made:

(1) Within wilderness areas designated by this Act the use of aircraft or motorboats, where these uses have already become established, may be permitted to continue subject to such restrictions as the Secretary of Agriculture deems desirable. In addition, such measures may be taken as may be necessary in the control of fire, insects, and diseases, subject to such conditions as the Secretary deems desirable.

(2) Nothing in this Act shall prevent within national forest wilderness areas any activity, including prospecting, for the purpose of gathering information about mineral or other resources, if such activity is carried on in a manner compatible with the preservation of the wilderness environment. Furthermore, in accordance with such program as the Secretary of the Interior shall develop and conduct in consultation with the Secretary of Agriculture, such areas shall be surveyed on a planned, recurring basis consistent with the concept of wilderness preservation by the Geological Survey and the Bureau of Mines to determine the mineral values, if any, that may be present; and the results of such surveys shall be made available to the public and submitted to the President and Congress.

(3) Notwithstanding any other provisions of this Act, until midnight December 31, 1983, the United States mining laws and all laws pertaining to mineral leasing shall, to the same extent as applicable prior to the effective date of this Act, extend to those national forest lands designated by this Act as "wilderness areas"; subject, however, to such reasonable regulations governing ingress and egress as may be prescribed by the Secretary of Agriculture consistent with the use of the land for mineral location and development and exploration, drilling, and production, and use of land for transmission lines, waterlines, telephone lines, or facilities necessary in exploring, drilling, producing, mining, and processing operations, including where essential the use of mechanized ground or air equipment and restoration as near as practicable of the surface of the land disturbed in performing prospecting, location, and, in oil and gas leasing, discovery work, exploration, drilling, and production, as soon as they have served their purpose. Mining locations lying within the boundaries of said wilderness areas shall be held and used solely for mining or processing operations and uses reasonably incident thereto; and hereafter, subject to valid existing rights, all

patents issued under the mining laws of the United States affecting national forest lands designated by this Act as wilderness areas shall convey title to the mineral deposits within the claim, together with the right to cut and use so much of the mature timber therefrom as may be needed in the extraction, removal, and beneficiation of the mineral deposits, if needed timber is not otherwise reasonably available, and if the timber is cut under sound principles of forest management as defined by the national forest rules and regulations, but each such patent shall reserve to the United States all title in or to the surface of the lands and products thereof, and no use of the surface of the claim or the resources therefrom not reasonably required for carrying on mining or prospecting shall be allowed except as otherwise expressly provided in this Act: *Provided,* That, unless hereafter specifically authorized, no patent within wilderness areas designated by this Act shall issue after December 31, 1983, except for the valid claims existing on or before December 31, 1983. Mining claims located after the effective date of this Act within the boundaries of wilderness areas designated by this Act shall create no rights in excess of those rights which may be patented under the provisions of this subsection. Mineral leases, permits, and licenses covering lands within national forest wilderness areas designated by this Act shall contain such reasonable stipulations as may be prescribed by the Secretary of Agriculture for the protection of the wilderness character of the land consistent with the use of the land for the purposes for which they are leased, permitted, or licensed. Subject to valid rights then existing, effective January 1, 1984, the minerals in lands designated by this Act as wilderness areas are withdrawn from all forms of appropriation under the mining laws and from disposition under all laws pertaining to mineral leasing and all amendments thereto.

(4) Within wilderness areas in the national forests designated by this Act, (1) the President may, within a specific area and in accordance with such regulations as he may deem desirable, authorize prospecting for water resources, the establishment and maintenance of reservoirs, water-conservation works, power projects, transmission lines, and other facilities needed in the public interest, including the road construction and maintenance essential to development and use thereof, upon his determination that such use or uses in the specific area will better serve the interests of the United States and the people thereof than will its denial; and (2) the grazing of livestock, where established prior to the effective date of this Act, shall be permitted to continue subject to such reasonable regulations as are deemed necessary by the Secretary of Agriculture.

(5) Other provisions of this Act to the contrary notwithstanding, the management of the Boundary Waters Canoe Area, formerly designated as the Superior, Little Indian Sioux, and Caribou Roadless Areas, in the Superior National Forest, Minnesota, shall be in accordance with regulations established by the Secretary of Agriculture in accordance with the general purpose of maintaining, without unnecessary restrictions on other uses, including that of timber, the

primitive character of the area, particularly in the vicinity of lakes, streams, and portages: *Provided,* That nothing in this Act shall preclude the continuance within the area of any already established use of motorboats.

(6) Commercial services may be performed within the wilderness areas designated by this Act to the extent necessary for activities which are proper for realizing the recreational or other wilderness purposes of the areas.

(7) Nothing in this Act shall constitute an express or implied claim or denial on the part of the Federal Government as to exemption from State water laws.

(8) Nothing in this Act shall be construed as affecting the jurisdiction or responsibilities of the several States with respect to wildlife and fish in the national forests.

STATE AND PRIVATE LANDS WITHIN WILDERNESS AREAS

SEC. 5. (a) In any case where State-owned or privately owned land is completely surrounded by national forest lands within areas designated by this Act as wilderness, such State or private owner shall be given such rights as may be necessary to assure adequate access to such State-owned or privately owned land by such State or private owner and their successors in interest, or the State-owned land or privately owned land shall be exchanged for federally owned land in the same State of approximately equal value under authorities available to the Secretary of Agriculture: *Provided, however,* That the United States shall not transfer to a State or private owner any mineral interests unless the State or private owner relinquishes or causes to be relinquished to the United States the mineral interest in the surrounded land.

(b) In any case where valid mining claims or other valid occupancies are wholly within a designated national forest wilderness area, the Secretary of Agriculture shall, by reasonable regulations consistent with the preservation of the area as wilderness, permit ingress and egress to such surrounded areas by means which have been or are being customarily enjoyed with respect to other such areas similarly situated.

(c) Subject to the appropriation of funds by Congress, the Secretary of Agriculture is authorized to acquire privately owned land within the perimeter of any area designated by this Act as wilderness if (1) the owner concurs in such acquisition or (2) the acquisition is specifically authorized by Congress.

GIFTS, BEQUESTS, AND CONTRIBUTIONS

SEC. 6. (a) The Secretary of Agriculture may accept gifts or bequests of land within wilderness areas designated by this Act for preservation as wilderness. The Secretary of Agriculture may also accept gifts or bequests of land adjacent to wilderness areas designated by this Act for preservation as wilderness if he has given sixty days advance notice thereof to the President of the Senate and the Speaker of the House of Representatives. Land accepted by the Secretary of

Agriculture under this section shall become part of the wilderness area involved. Regulations with regard to any such land may be in accordance with such agreements, consistent with the policy of this Act, as are made at the time of such gift, or such conditions, consistent with such policy, as may be included in, and accepted with, such bequest.

(b) The Secretary of Agriculture or the Secretary of the Interior is authorized to accept private contributions and gifts to be used to further the purposes of this Act.

ANNUAL REPORTS

SEC. 7. At the opening of each session of Congress, the Secretaries of Agriculture and Interior shall jointly report to the President for transmission to Congress on the status of the wilderness system, including a list and descriptions of the areas in the system, regulations in effect, and other pertinent information, together with any recommendations they may care to make.

Approved September 3, 1964.

MESSAGE BY MRS. LYNDON B. JOHNSON
ON THE BEAUTIFICATION PROGRAM*
May 24, 1965

Mrs. Lyndon B. Johnson will be remembered among First Ladies for the impetus which she gave governmental programs for the beautification of public grounds and the enhancement of natural beauty everywhere. An indifferent public, and an indifferent Congress, limited the achievements of the programs Mrs. Johnson advanced, such as highway beautification, but the general commitment to the beautification program will have important effect for years to come.

Mrs. Johnson's brief talk at the opening of the White House Conference on Natural Beauty is the most representative documentary of the program.

Mrs. LYNDON B. JOHNSON. Welcome to the White House Conference on Natural Beauty.

We are grateful that you have taken two days of your busy lives to come here and discuss ways to restore and increase the beauty of our land.

In the catalogue of ills which afflicts mankind, ugliness and the decay of our cities and countryside are high on America's agenda.

It seems to me that one of the most pressing challenges for the individual is the depression and the tension resulting from existence in a world which is increasingly less pleasing to the eye. Our peace of mind, our emotions, our spirit —even our souls—are conditioned by what our eyes see.

Ugliness is bitterness. We are all here to try and change that. This conference is a step towards the solution and I think a great one.

Our immediate problem is: How can one best fight ugliness in a nation such as ours—where there is great freedom of action or inaction for every individual and every interest—where there is virtually no artistic control—and where all action must originate with the single citizen or group of citizens?

That is the immediate problem and challenge. Most of the great cities and great works of beauty of the past were built by autocratic societies. The Caesars built Rome. Paris represents the will of the Kings of France and the Empire. Vienna is the handiwork of the Hapsburgs, and Florence of the Medici.

Can a great democratic society generate the concerted drive to plan, and having planned, to execute great projects of beauty?

I not only hope so—I am certain that it can.

All our national history proves that a committed citizenry is a mighty force when it bends itself to a determined effort. There is a growing feeling in this

---

*Beauty for America, Proceedings of the White House Conference on Natural Beauty, (Washington, D.C.: Government Printing Office, 1965), 17–18.

land today that ugliness has been allowed too long, that it is time to say "Enough," and to act.

During these two days you will discuss and originate plans and projects both great and small. Great must be the scope of the major projects to redesign our urban areas, renew and brighten the gateways to our cities, cleanse, set in order and dignify our riverfronts and our ports. Small, but equally important—perhaps most important—is the single citizen who plants a tree or tends his own front yard. There are 190 million of him. He is everybody.

Perhaps the most important part of this conference will be to help educate our people that the beauty of their land depends upon their own initiative and their will.

I have heard said—and many times—that among our greatest ills is the deep sense of frustration which the individual feels when he faces the complex and large problems of our century. Ugliness is not that sort of problem. Its vast scope will call for much coordination on the highest levels. But—and this is the blessing of it—it is one problem which every man and woman and child can attack and contribute to defeating. Natural beauty may be a national concern and there is much that government can and should do, but it is the individual who not only benefits, but who must protect a heritage of beauty for future generations.

There are no autocrats in our land to decree beauty, only a national will. Through your work, I firmly believe this national will can be given energy and force, and produce a more beautiful America.

The Conference Chairman, LAURANCE S. ROCKEFELLER. In calling us together, President Johnson set the tone for our endeavor. He said: I want new ideas. He said: I want to alert the American people to action. He cited concrete, specific problems for us to consider—not abstractions or theories.

In accordance with the President's directive, this conference is organized for action. It is not for philosophizing. As Mrs. Johnson said at the first meeting of her committee to beautify Washington, "We must not substitute the delight of debate for the art of action."

This is not to say that a social and moral basis for natural beauty is unnecessary. It is rather to say that we have such a foundation.

President Johnson has already affirmed it.

The people of this country, he has said, want not only a bigger America but a better and more beautiful America as well.

THE WATER RESOURCES COUNCIL*
July 22, 1965

The Water Resources Council was formally established by law in this act. The river basin commissions also authorized under the law have as yet not been fully implemented.

An Act to provide for the optimum development of the Nation's natural resources through the coordinated planning of water and related land resources, through the establishment of a water resources council and river basin commissions, and by providing financial assistance to the States in order to increase State participation in such planning.

Be it enacted by the Senate and House of Representatives of the United States of America in Congress assembled,

SHORT TITLE

SECTION 1. This Act may be cited as the "Water Resources Planning Act".

STATEMENT OF POLICY

SEC. 2. In order to meet the rapidly expanding demands for water throughout the Nation, it is hereby declared to be the policy of the Congress to encourage the conservation, development, and utilization of water and related land resources of the United States on a comprehensive and coordinated basis by the Federal Government, States, localities, and private enterprise with the cooperation of all affected Federal agencies, States, local governments, individuals, corporations, business enterprises, and others concerned.

EFFECT ON EXISTING LAWS

SEC. 3. Nothing in this Act shall be construed—

(a) to expand or diminish either Federal or State jurisdiction, responsibility, or rights in the field of water resources planning, development, or control; nor to displace, supersede, limit or modify any interstate compact or the jurisdiction or responsibility of any legally established joint or common agency of two or more States, or of two or more States and the Federal Government; nor to limit the authority of Congress to authorize and fund projects;

(b) to change or otherwise affect the authority or responsibility of any Federal official in the discharge of the duties of his office except as required to carry out the provisions of this Act with respect to the prepara-

*79 *Statutes at Large,* 244–54.

[733]

tion and review of comprehensive regional or river basin plans and the formulation and evaluation of Federal water and related land resources projects;

(c) as superseding, modifying, or repealing existing laws applicable to the various Federal agencies which are authorized to develop or participate in the development of water and related land resources or to exercise licensing or regulatory functions in relation thereto, except as required to carry out the provisions of this Act; nor to affect the jurisdiction, powers, or prerogatives of the International Joint Commission, United States and Canada, the Permanent Engineering Board and the United States Operating Entity or Entities established pursuant to the Columbia River Basin Treaty, signed at Washington, January 17, 1961, or the International Boundary and Water Commission, United States and Mexico;

(d) as authorizing any entity established or acting under the provisions hereof to study, plan, or recommend the transfer of waters between areas under the jurisdiction of more than one river basin commission or entity performing the function of a river basin commission.

TITLE I—WATER RESOURCES COUNCIL

SEC. 101. There is hereby established a Water Resources Council (hereinafter referred to as the "Council") which shall be composed of the Secretary of the Interior, the Secretary of Agriculture, the Secretary of the Army, the Secretary of Health, Education, and Welfare, and the Chairman of the Federal Power Commission. The Chairman of the Council shall request the heads of other Federal agencies to participate with the Council when matters affecting their responsibilities are considered by the Council. The Chairman of the Council shall be designated by the President.

SEC. 102. The Council shall—

(a) maintain a continuing study and prepare an assessment biennially, or at such less frequent intervals as the Council may determine, of the adequacy of supplies of water necessary to meet the water requirements in each water resource region in the United States and the national interest therein; and

(b) maintain a continuing study of the relation of regional or river basin plans and programs to the requirements of larger regions of the Nation and of the adequacy of administrative and statutory means for the coordination of the water and related land resources policies and programs of the several Federal agencies; it shall appraise the adequacy of existing and proposed policies and programs to meet such requirements; and it shall make recommendations to the President with respect to Federal policies and programs.

SEC. 103. The Council shall establish, after such consultation with other interested entities, both Federal and non-Federal, as the Council may find appropriate, and with the approval of the President, principles, standards, and procedures for Federal participants in the preparation of comprehensive regional or river basin plans and for the formulation and evaluation of Federal water and related land resources projects. Such procedures may include provision for Council revision of plans for Federal projects intended to be proposed in any plan or revision thereof being prepared by a river basin planning commission.

SEC. 104. Upon receipt of a plan or revision thereof from any river basin commission under the provisions of section 204(3) of this Act, the Council shall review the plan or revision with special regard to —

(1) the efficacy of such plan or revision in achieving optimum use of the water and related land resources in the area involved;

(2) the effect of the plan on the achievement of other programs for the development of agricultural, urban, energy, industrial, recreational, fish and wildlife, and other resources of the entire Nation; and

(3) the contributions which such plan or revision will make in obtaining the Nation's economic and social goals.

Based on such review the Council shall —

(a) formulate such recommendations as it deems desirable in the national interest; and

(b) transmit its recommendations, together with the plan or revision of the river basin commission and the views, comments, and recommendations with respect to such plan or revision submitted by any Federal agency, Governor, interstate commission, or United States section of an international commission, to the President for his review and transmittal to the Congress with his recommendations in regard to authorization of Federal projects.

SEC. 105. (a) For the purpose of carrying out the provisions of this Act, the Council may: (1) hold such hearings, sit and act at such times and places, take such testimony, receive such evidence, and print or otherwise reproduce and distribute so much of its proceedings and reports thereon as it may deem advisable; (2) acquire, furnish, and equip such office space as is necessary; (3) use the United States mails in the same manner and upon the same conditions as other departments and agencies of the United States; (4) employ and fix the compensation of such personnel as it deems advisable, in accordance with the civil service laws and Classification Act of 1949, as amended; (5) procure services as authorized by section 15 of the Act of August 2, 1946 (5 U.S.C. 55a), at rates not to exceed $100 per diem for individuals; (6) purchase, hire, operate, and maintain passenger motor vehicles; and (7) incur such necessary expenses and exercise such other powers as are consistent with and reasonably required to perform its functions under this Act.

(b) Any member of the Council is authorized to administer oaths when it is determined by a majority of the Council that testimony shall be taken or evidence received under oath.

(c) To the extent permitted by law, all appropriate records and papers of the Council may be made available for public inspection during ordinary office hours.

(d) Upon request of the Council, the head of any Federal department or agency is authorized (1) to furnish to the Council such information as may be necessary for carrying out its functions and as may be available to or procurable by such department or agency, and (2) to detail to temporary duty with such Council on a reimbursable basis such personnel within his administrative jurisdiction as it may need or believe to be useful for carrying out its functions, each such detail to be without loss of seniority, pay, or other employee status.

(e) The Council shall be responsible for (1) the appointment and supervision of personnel, (2) the assignment of duties and responsibilities among such personnel, and (3) the use and expenditures of funds.

TITLE II—RIVER BASIN COMMISSIONS

CREATION OF COMMISSIONS

SEC. 201. (a) The President is authorized to declare the establishment of a river basin water and related land resources commission upon request therefor by the Council, or request addressed to the Council by a State within which all or part of the basin or basins concerned are located if the request by the Council or by a State (1) defines the area, river basin, or group of related river basins for which a commission is requested, (2) is made in writing by the Governor or in such manner as State law may provide, or by the Council, and (3) is concurred in by the Council and by not less than one-half of the States within which portions of the basin or basins concerned are located and, in the event the Upper Colorado River Basin is involved, by at least three of the four States of Colorado, New Mexico, Utah, and Wyoming or, in the event the Columbia River Basin is involved, by at least three of the four States of Idaho, Montana, Oregon, and Washington. Such concurrences shall be in writing.

(b) Each such commission for an area, river basin, or group of river basins shall, to the extent consistent with section 3 of this Act—

> (1) serve as the principal agency for the coordination of Federal, State, interstate, local and nongovernmental plans for the development of water and related land resources in its area, river basin, or group of river basins;

> (2) prepare and keep up to date, to the extent practicable, a comprehensive, coordinated, joint plan for Federal, State, interstate, local and nongovernmental development of water and related resources: *Provided,*

That the plan shall include an evaluation of all reasonable alternative means of achieving optimum development of water and related land resources of the basin or basins, and it may be prepared in stages, including recommendations with respect to individual projects;

(3) recommend long-range schedules of priorities for the collection and analysis of basic data and for investigation, planning, and construction of projects; and

(4) foster and undertake such studies of water and related land resources problems in its area, river basin, or group of river basins as are necessary in the preparation of the plan described in clause (2) of this subsection.

MEMBERSHIP OF COMMISSIONS

SEC. 202. Each river basin commission shall be composed of members appointed as follows:

(a) A chairman appointed by the President who shall also serve as chairman and coordinating officer of the Federal members of the commission and who shall represent the Federal Government in Federal-State relations on the commission and who shall not, during the period of his service on the commission, hold any other position as an officer or employee of the United States, except as a retired officer or retired civilian employee of the Federal Government;

(b) One member from each Federal department or independent agency determined by the President to have a substantial interest in the work to be undertaken by the commission, such member to be appointed by the head of such department or independent agency and to serve as the representative of such department or independent agency;

(c) One member from each State which lies wholly or partially within the area, river basin, or group of river basins for which the commission is established, and the appointment of each such member shall be made in accordance with the laws of the State which he represents. In the absence of governing provisions of State law, such State members shall be appointed and serve at the pleasure of the Governor;

(d) One member appointed by any interstate agency created by an interstate compact to which the consent of Congress has been given, and whose jurisdiction extends to the waters of the area, river basin, or group of river basins for which the river basin commission is created;

(e) When deemed appropriate by the President, one member, who shall be appointed by the President, from the United States section of any international commission created by a treaty to which the consent of the Senate has been given, and whose jurisdiction extends to the waters of the area, river basin, or group of river basins for which the river basin commission is established.

ORGANIZATION OF COMMISSIONS

SEC. 203. (a) Each river basin commission shall organize for the performance of its functions within ninety days after the President shall have declared the establishment of such commission, subject to the availability of funds for carrying on its work. A commission shall terminate upon decision of the Council or agreement of a majority of the States composing the commission. Upon such termination, all property, assets, and records of the commission shall thereafter be turned over to such agencies of the United States and the participating States as shall be appropriate in the circumstances: *Provided,* That studies, data, and other materials useful in water and related land resources planning to any of the participants shall be kept freely available to all such participants.

(b) State members of each commission shall elect a vice chairman, who shall serve also as chairman and coordinating officer of the State members of the commission and who shall represent the State governments in Federal-State relations on the commission.

(c) Vacancies in a commission shall not affect its powers but shall be filled in the same manner in which the original appointments were made: *Provided,* That the chairman and vice chairman may designate alternates to act for them during temporary absences.

(d) In the work of the commission every reasonable endeavor shall be made to arrive at a consensus of all members on all issues; but failing this, full opportunity shall be afforded each member for the presentation and report of individual views: *Provided,* That at any time the commission fails to act by reason of absence of consensus, the position of the chairman, acting in behalf of the Federal members, and the vice chairman, acting upon instructions of the State members, shall be set forth in the record: *Provided further,* That the chairman, in consultation with the vice chairman, shall have the final authority, in the absence of an applicable bylaw adopted by the commission or in the absence of a consensus, to fix the times and places for meetings, to set deadlines for the submission of annual and other reports, to establish subcommittees, and to decide such other procedural questions as may be necessary for the commission to perform its functions.

DUTIES OF THE COMMISSIONS

SEC. 204. Each river basin commission shall—

(1) engage in such activities and make such studies and investigations as are necessary and desirable in carrying out the policy set forth in section 2 of this Act and in accomplishing the purposes set forth in section 201(b) of this Act;

(2) submit to the Council and the Governor of each participating State a report on its work at least once each year. Such report shall be trans-

mitted through the President to the Congress. After such transmission, copies of any such report shall be sent to the heads of such Federal, State, interstate, and international agencies as the President or the Governors of the participating States may direct;

(3) submit to the Council for transmission to the President and by him to the Congress, and the Governors and the legislatures of the participating States a comprehensive, coordinated, joint plan, or any major portion thereof or necessary revisions thereof, for water and related land resources development in the area, river basin, or group of river basins for which such commission was established. Before the commission submits such a plan or major portion thereof or revision thereof to the Council, it shall transmit the proposed plan or revision to the head of each Federal department or agency, the Governor of each State, and each interstate agency, from which a member of the commission has been appointed, and to the head of the United States section of any international commission if the plan, portion or revision deals with a boundary water or a river crossing a boundary, or any tributary flowing into such boundary water or river, over which the international commission has jurisdiction or for which it has responsibility. Each such department and agency head, Governor, interstate agency, and United States section of an international commission shall have ninety days from the date of the receipt of the proposed plan, portion, or revision to report its views, comments, and recommendations to the commission. The commission may modify the plan, portion, or revision after considering the reports so submitted. The views, comments, and recommendations submitted by each Federal department or agency head, Governor, interstate agency, and United States section of an international commission shall be transmitted to the Council with the plan, portion, or revision; and

(4) submit to the Council at the time of submitting such plan, any recommendations it may have for continuing the functions of the commission and for implementing the plan, including means of keeping the plan up to date.

POWERS AND ADMINISTRATIVE PROVISIONS
OF THE COMMISSIONS

SEC. 205. (a) For the purpose of carrying out the provisions of this title, each river basin commission may—

(1) hold such hearings, sit and act at such times and places, take such testimony, receive such evidence, and print or otherwise reproduce and distribute so much of its proceedings and reports thereon as it may deem advisable;

(2) acquire, furnish, and equip such office space as is necessary;

(3) use the United States mails in the same manner and upon the same conditions as departments and agencies of the United States;

(4) employ and compensate such personnel as it deems advisable, including consultants, at rates not to exceed $100 per diem, and retain and compensate such professional or technical service firms as it deems advisable on a contract basis;

(5) arrange for the services of personnel from any State or the United States, or any subdivision or agency thereof, or any intergovernmental agency;

(6) make arrangements, including contracts, with any participating government, except the United States or the District of Columbia, for inclusion in a suitable retirement and employee benefit system of such of its personnel as may not be eligible for or continuing in another governmental retirement or employee benefit system, or otherwise provide for such coverage of its personnel;

(7) purchase, hire, operate, and maintain passenger motor vehicles; and

(8) incur such necessary expenses and exercise such other powers as are consistent with and reasonably required to perform its functions under this Act.

(b) The chairman of a river basin commission, or any member of such commission designated by the chairman thereof for the purpose, is authorized to administer oaths when it is determined by a majority of the commission that testimony shall be taken or evidence received under oath.

(c) To the extent permitted by law, all appropriate records and papers of each river basin commission shall be made available for public inspection during ordinary office hours.

(d) Upon request of the chairman of any river basin commission, or any member or employee of such commission designated by the chairman thereof for the purpose, the head of any Federal department or agency is authorized (1) to furnish to such commission such information as may be necessary for carrying out its functions and as may be available to or procurable by such department or agency, and (2) to detail to temporary duty with such commission on a reimbursable basis such personnel within his administrative jurisdiction as it may need or believe to be useful for carrying out its functions, each such detail to be without loss of seniority, pay, or other employee status.

(e) The chairman of each river basin commission shall, with the concurrence of the vice chairman, appoint the personnel employed by such commission, and the chairman shall, in accordance with the general policies of such commission with respect to the work to be accomplished by it and the timing thereof, be responsible for (1) the supervision of personnel employed by such commission, (2) the assignment of duties and responsibilities among such personnel, and (3) the use and expenditure of funds available to such commission.

COMPENSATION OF COMMISSION MEMBERS

SEC. 206. (a) Any member of a river basin commission appointed pursuant to section 202 (b) and (e) of this Act shall receive no additional compensation by virtue of his membership on the commission, but shall continue to receive, from appropriations made for the agency from which he is appointed, the salary of his regular position when engaged in the performance of the duties vested in the commission.

(b) Members of a commission, appointed pursuant to section 202 (c) and (d) of this Act, shall each receive such compensation as may be provided by the States or the interstate agency respectively, which they represent.

(c) The per annum compensation of the chairman of each river basin commission shall be determined by the President, but when employed on a full-time annual basis shall not exceed the maximum scheduled rate for grade GS-18 of the Classification Act of 1949, as amended; or when engaged in the performance of the commission's duties on an intermittent basis such compensation shall be not more than $100 per day and shall not exceed $12,000 in any year.

SEC. 207. (a) Each commission shall recommend what share of its expenses shall be borne by the Federal Government, but such share shall be subject to approval by the Council. The remainder of the commission's expenses shall be otherwise apportioned as the commission may determine. Each commission shall prepare a budget annually and transmit it to the Council and the States. Estimates of proposed appropriations from the Federal Government shall be included in the budget estimates submitted by the Council under the Budgeting and Accounting Act of 1921, as amended, and may include an amount for advance to a commission against State appropriations for which delay is anticipated by reason of later legislative sessions. All sums appropriated to or otherwise received by a commission shall be credited to the commission's account in the Treasury of the United States.

(b) A commission may accept for any of its purposes and functions appropriations, donations, and grants of money, equipment, supplies, materials, and services from any State or the United States or any subdivision or agency thereof, or intergovernmental agency, and may receive, utilize, and dispose of the same.

(c) The commission shall keep accurate accounts of all receipts and disbursements. The accounts shall be audited at least annually in accordance with generally accepted auditing standards by independent certified or licensed public accountants, certified or licensed by a regulatory authority of a State, and the report of the audit shall be included in and become a part of the annual report of the commission.

(d) The accounts of the commission shall be open at all reasonable times for inspection by representatives of the jurisdictions and agencies which make appropriations, donations, or grants to the commission.

TITLE III—FINANCIAL ASSISTANCE TO THE STATES FOR COMPREHENSIVE PLANNING GRANT AUTHORIZATIONS

SEC. 301. (a) In recognition of the need for increased participation by the States in water and related land resources planning to be effective, there are hereby authorized to be appropriated to the Council for the next fiscal year beginning after the date of enactment of this Act, and for the nine succeeding fiscal years thereafter, $5,000,000 in each such year for grants to States to assist them in developing and participating in the development of comprehensive water and related land resources plans.

(b) The Council, with the approval of the President, shall prescribe such rules, establish such procedures, and make such arrangements and provisions relating to the performance of its functions under this title, and the use of funds available therefor, as may be necessary in order to assure (1) coordination of the program authorized by this title with related Federal planning assistance programs, including the program authorized under section 701 of the Housing Act of 1954 and (2) appropriate utilization of other Federal agencies administering programs which may contribute to achieving the purpose of this Act.

ALLOTMENTS

SEC. 302. (a) From the sums appropriated pursuant to section 301 for any fiscal year the Council shall from time to time make allotments to the States, in accordance with its regulations, on the basis of (1) the population, (2) the land area, (3) the need for comprehensive water and related land resources planning programs, and (4) the financial need of the respective States. For the purposes of this section the population of the States shall be determined on the basis of the latest estimates available from the Department of Commerce and the land area of the States shall be determined on the basis of the official records of the United States Geological Survey.

(b) From each State's allotment under this section for any fiscal year the Council shall pay to such State an amount which is not more than 50 per centum of the cost of carrying out its State program approved under section 303, including the cost of training personnel for carrying out such program and the cost of administering such program.

STATE PROGRAMS

SEC. 303. The Council shall approve any program for comprehensive water and related land resources planning which is submitted by a State, if such program—

(1) provides for comprehensive planning with respect to intrastate or interstate water resources, or both, in such State to meet the needs for

water and water-related activities taking into account prospective demands for all purposes served through or affected by water and related land resources development, with adequate provision for coordination with all Federal, State, and local agencies, and nongovernmental entities having responsibilities in affected fields;

(2) provides, where comprehensive statewide development planning is being carried on with or without assistance under section 701 of the Housing Act of 1954, or under the Land and Water Conservation Fund Act of 1965, for full coordination between comprehensive water resources planning and other statewide planning programs and for assurances that such water resources planning will be in conformity with the general development policy in such State;

(3) designates a State agency (hereinafter referred to as the "State agency") to administer the program;

(4) provides that the State agency will make such reports in such form and containing such information as the Council from time to time reasonably requires to carry out its functions under this title;

(5) sets forth the procedure to be followed in carrying out the State program and in administering such program; and

(6) provides such accounting, budgeting, and other fiscal methods and procedures as are necessary for keeping appropriate accountability of the funds and for the proper and efficient administration of the program.

The Council shall not disapprove any program without first giving reasonable notice and opportunity for hearing to the State agency administering such program.

REVIEW

SEC. 304. Whenever the Council after reasonable notice and opportunity for hearing to a State agency finds that—

(a) the program submitted by such State and approved under section 303 has been so changed that it no longer complies with a requirement of such section; or

(b) in the administration of the program there is a failure to comply substantially with such a requirement,

the Council shall notify such agency that no further payments will be made to the State under this title until it is satisfied that there will no longer be any such failure. Until the Council is so satisfied, it shall make no further payments to such State under this title.

PAYMENTS

SEC. 305. The method of computing and paying amounts pursuant to this title shall be as follows:

(1) The Council shall, prior to the beginning of each calendar quarter or other period prescribed by it, estimate the amount to be paid to each State under the provisions of this title for such period, such estimate to be based on such records of the State and information furnished by it, and such other investigation, as the Council may find necessary.

(2) The Council shall pay to the State, from the allotment available therefor, the amount so estimated by it for any period, reduced or increased, as the case may be, by any sum (not previously adjusted under this paragraph) by which it finds that its estimate of the amount to be paid such State for any prior period under this title was greater or less than the amount which should have been paid to such State for such prior period under this title. Such payments shall be made through the disbursing facilities of the Treasury Department, at such times and in such installments as the Council may determine.

DEFINITION

SEC. 306. For the purpose of this title the term "State" means a State, the District of Columbia, Puerto Rico, or the Virgin Islands.

RECORDS

SEC. 307. (a) Each recipient of a grant under this Act shall keep such records as the Chairman of the Council shall prescribe, including records which fully disclose the amount and disposition of the funds received under the grant, and the total cost of the project or undertaking in connection with which the grant was made and the amount and nature of that portion of the cost of the project or undertaking supplied by other sources, and such other records as will facilitate an effective audit.

(b) The Chairman of the Council and the Comptroller General of the United States, or any of their duly authorized representatives, shall have access for the purpose of audit and examination to any books, documents, papers, and records of the recipient of the grant that are pertinent to the determination that funds granted are used in accordance with this Act.

TITLE IV—MISCELLANEOUS

AUTHORIZATION OF APPROPRIATIONS

SEC. 401. There are authorized to be appropriated not to exceed $300,000 annually, to carry out the provisions of title I of this Act, not to exceed $6,000,-000 annually to carry out the provisions of title II, and not to exceed $400,000 annually for the administration of title III: *Provided,* That, with respect to title II, not more than $750,000 annually shall be available for any single river basin commission.

RULES AND REGULATIONS

Sec. 402. The Council is authorized to make such rules and regulations as it may deem necessary or appropriate for carrying out those provisions of this Act which are administered by it.

DELEGATION OF FUNCTIONS

Sec. 403. The Council is authorized to delegate to any member or employee of the Council its administrative functions under section 105 and the detailed administration of the grant program under title III.

UTILIZATION OF PERSONNEL

Sec. 404. The Council may, with the consent of the head of any other department or agency of the United States, utilize such officers and employees of such agency on a reimbursable basis as are necessary to carry out the provisions of this Act.

Approved July 22, 1965.

CONSERVATION IN 1968*
March 8, 1968

President Johnson's conservation message of 1968 reveals the first shift in emphasis on conservation issues since the turn of the century.

To the Congress of the United States:

Theodore Roosevelt made conservation more than a political issue in America. He made it a moral imperative.

More than half a century ago, he sounded this warning:

"To skin and exhaust the land instead of using it so as to increase its usefulness, will result in undermining in the days of our children the very prosperity which we ought by right to hand down to them amplified and developed."

The conservation work that Roosevelt began was protection of our natural heritage for the enjoyment and enrichment of all the families of the land. That is work which never ends. It must be taken up anew by each succeeding generation, acting as trustees for the next.

But the conservation problems Theodore Roosevelt saw are dwarfed by the new ones of our own day.

As unfolding technology has increased our economic strength and added to the convenience of our lives.

But that same technology—we know now—carries danger with it.

From the great smoke stacks of industry and from the exhausts of motors and machines, 130 million tons of soot, carbon and grime settle over the people and shroud the Nation's cities each year.

From towns, factories, and stockyards, wastes pollute our rivers and streams, endangering the waters we drink and use.

The debris of civilization litters the landscapes and spoils the beaches.

Conservation's concern now is not only for man's enjoyment—but for man's survival.

Fortunately, we have recognized the threat in time, and we have begun to meet it.

Through the landmark legislation of the past few years we are moving to bring a safe environment—both to this generation, and to the America still unborn.

> —The Water Quality Act of 1965 and the Clean Water Restoration Act of 1966 provide the foundation of our first major efforts to curb the pollution blighting America's waters.

*"The President's Message to the Congress on Conservation," *Weekly Compilation of Presidential Documents,* Mar. 11, 1968 (Washington, D.C.: Government Printing Office), 458–74.

—The Clean Air Act of 1965 and the Air Quality Act of 1967 build a strong base from which we can begin to clean the air.

—The Solid Waste Disposal Act of 1965 launched a new program to find the most efficient ways of disposing of millions of tons of solid wastes that clog the city and the countryside.

—The Highway Beautification Act of 1965 laid the groundwork for scenic roads and enjoyable travels.

—Over 2.2 million acres have been authorized for addition to the Nation's Park System—and for the first time in generations more land is being preserved for the people than is being developed for industrial or urban purposes.

But the work of the new conservation, too—like the task we inherited from an earlier day—is unending. Technology is not something which happens once and then stands still. It grows and develops at an electric pace. And our efforts to keep it in harmony with human values must be intensified and accelerated. Indeed, technology itself is the tool with which these new environmental problems can be conquered.

In this Message I shall outline the steps which I believe America must take this year to preserve the natural heritage of its people—a broad heritage that must include not only the wilderness of the unbroken forest, but a safe environment for the crowded city.

A PRIORITY CONSERVATION AGENDA

The dangers that threaten our environment are varied. To succeed in meeting their challenge requires a wide-ranging response, with special emphasis on the items of highest priority.

For Fiscal 1969, I propose a program to complete this vital agenda for action.

First, I recommend that we assure the people that their water supplies will be pure and plentiful now and in the years ahead by:

—Prosecuting the war on water pollution with conviction, combining Federal, State, and local efforts to finance the construction this year of $1.5 to $2 billion in community waste treatment plants.

—Creating a National Water Commission to plot the course of water resource management for the next century.

—Helping to assure the quality of community water supplies through the Safe Drinking Water Act of 1968.

—Meeting the water needs of one of America's fastest growing regions by authorizing that Central Arizona Project.

Second, I recommend that we guard the landscape against the waste products of modern life by:

- Protecting rivers, beaches and coastal areas against the devastation of oil spillage and other hazardous substances through strong legislation to control them.
- Preventing the future despoilment of thousands of acres of mining land through the Surface Mining Reclamation Act of 1968.
- Discovering efficient methods to dispose of the millions of tons of refuse and trash that threaten to engulf city and countryside, through an extension of the Solid Waste Disposal Act, and to accelerate the development of economical systems which will convert waste into useful by-products.
- Transforming our highways into corridors of beauty through prompt action to continue the Highway Beautification Program, and building new roadside parks for the traveling family.

Third, I recommend that we advance in the battle for clean air over America's cities by:

- Fully exploiting our vast technology to find new and effective pollution abatement methods.
- Investing $128 million as the Federal share in pollution control and research, more than has ever been committed in a single year before.
- Organizing for action, through the designation of Air Quality Control Regions under the landmark Air Quality Act of 1967.

Fourth, I recommend that we bring a sense of fulfillment, outdoor recreation and serenity to all Americans by:

- Bringing new national parks closer to the people who live crowded city lives by development of the redwood groves of California, the Northern Cascades of Washington and the historic Potomac River.
- Adding thousands of new acres of unspoiled and primitive lands to the wilderness system.
- Completing action on the nationwide networks of scenic rivers and trails.
- Focusing now on the problem of noise and its impact on our daily lives.

Fifth, I recommend that we explore the peaceful promise of the ocean's depths by:

—Beginning to plan now with other nations to launch an International Decade of Ocean Exploration.

—Putting our most advanced marine technology to work in the development of improved buoys for better prediction of weather and ocean conditions.

WATER POLLUTION CONTROL

America's rivers, lakes and coastal waters have nourished her growth: irrigated the farms, powered the dynamos, and provided transport for commerce.

But we have not used our waters well.

Our major rivers are defiled by noxious debris. Pollutants from cities and industries kill the fish in our streams. Many waterways are covered with oil slicks and contain growths of algae that destroy productive life and make the water unfit for recreation. "Polluted Water—No Swimming" has become a familiar sign on too many beaches and rivers. A lake that has served many generations of men now can be destroyed by man in less than one generation.

Only recently have we begun to reverse this trend—to undertake a program to preserve waters that are still clean, and purify those that have become infested with pollution.

The conditions have worsened through decades of neglect and indifference. They affect entire industries. They involve thousands of miles of waterways and thousands of communities that border them.

We have discovered not only that the problems of pollution are formidable, but that their solutions must be interlocking.

—Water quality standards must be set for entire bodies of water, varying from place to place depending on the water's use.

—Standards must be enforceable and they must apply to both municipalities and industries.

—Waste treatment plants must be constructed and other methods developed to prevent pollutants from reaching the water.

—New methods of cooperation and enforcement must be established at all levels, for waters bearing poisons do not stop at city, county or State boundaries. Clearing one part of a stream is no answer. Water bodies must be cleaned in their entirety.

America took strong action to combat the problem in 1965 with the Water Quality Act, and took another major step a year later with the Clean Water Restoration Act. Under those measures, the long and difficult task of cleaning the waters of our land has begun.

[749]

WATER QUALITY STANDARDS

Now, for the first time in our history, all the States have taken inventory of their water resources, considered their future needs, and developed quality standards.

As the law requires, these standards, and the plans to carry them out, have been submitted to the Secretary of the Interior for approval.

Many of the plans have already been approved. This is welcome news for communities and businessmen alike. Now they can take action because they know the standards they must all meet.

I have asked the Secretary of the Interior to speed the review of the remaining standards and plans so the Federal Government can more effectively help the States and communities turn their blueprints into action.

THE CONSTRUCTION OF TREATMENT PLANTS

The heart of a water pollution control program is the community waste treatment plant which prevents refuse, debris and filth from reaching the waters. To meet the Nation's critical needs calls for both the construction of new plants and the improvement of existing facilities.

Through the Clean Water Restoration Act, the Federal Government can provide financial help—from 30 to 55 percent of the cost—for the construction of municipal waste treatment works. Already, under that Act and earlier authority, 8,000 grants, totalling more than $1 billion, have been made. They have helped local communities build more than $4.5 billion worth of plants, to control the pollution in 67,000 miles of water on which almost 66 million Americans depend.

More is required, however. The problem is pressing and the backlog of needed plants is great.

With accelerated Federal help, we can stimulate the construction of $1.5 billion to $2 billion in waste treatment plants under the $700 million authorization approved by the Congress for Fiscal 1969.

This will be done in two ways.

First, I recommend an appropriation of $225 million for grants under the Clean Water Restoration Act. This should generate about $500 to $600 million of plant construction.

Second, I recommend legislation to allow the Secretary of the Interior to make annual installment payments in addition to the lump sum grants as is presently the practice. This would permit the Federal Government to make construction commitments up to a total of $475 million in Fiscal 1969.

Under this new financing method, the $475 million would generate a total of about $1 to $1.4 billion of construction. Communities would be able to build many of their urgently-needed plants without delay and get them into the fight against pollution now.

USER CHARGES

Capital and operating costs of treatment plants are expensive, and it is right that those costs be borne by those who receive the plant's benefits. Accordingly, the new financing program will require, as one criterion for assistance, that municipalities impose a system of user charges on those who use the plants.

A system of user charges would not only provide an equitable way of sharing costs, but would accomplish other desirable purposes, as well. Such charges would:

—Provide an incentive for industries to curb pollution through improved manufacturing techniques.

—Relieve the pressure on the overloaded tax bases of local governments.

SAFE COMMUNITY WATER SUPPLIES

As America's cities grew and developed their own water supply systems, cholera and typhoid posed a grim threat to health and safety.

That threat was countered long ago.

Now, we in America drink tap water without a thought as to its safety. And yet—that water is not always as safe as it should be.

We do not have enough information on the long-term health effects of substances in drinking water.

New hazards—chemical and industrial wastes, and other materials—are creating new problems.

The Nation's Public Health Service cannot respond fully to this danger. Its authority is limited by a law passed almost half a century ago.

A recent study has indicated that about 30 percent of the Nation's public drinking water systems may fall below Federal standards.

To help the cities and communities of America assure citizens that the water they drink is safe, I propose the Safe Drinking Water Act of 1968.

This measure will strengthen the authority of the Secretary of Health, Education, and Welfare to:

—Develop, adopt and enforce improved standards relating to chemical contaminants in drinking water.

—Conduct a comprehensive study of the safety of public drinking water supplies in the United States.

—Determine whether any additional steps are necessary in this area.

The new law will help move us toward this goal: That every glass of drinking water drawn from America's public water supply systems will meet proper health standards.

WATER MANAGEMENT AND PLANNING

NATIONAL WATER COMMISSION

We will not have served the water needs of Americans if we meet only the requirements of today's population. A prudent nation must look ahead and plan for tomorrow.

First, we must continue our sound programs of water management, research, and advance planning to solve supply problems and to prepare for the future needs of farms and factories, and growing city populations.

Second, we must establish a board to develop long-range policy for water resources.

Last year I asked the Congress to establish a National Water Commission to:
— Work with Federal, State and private agencies in a survey of our long-term water needs.
— Explore the effect of water development projects on regional growth.
— Identify alternative policies and programs to meet national and regional water resource objectives.

Both the Senate and the House of Representatives have passed legislation to establish this Commission. The measure is now in conference.

I urge the Congress to complete its action and authorize this much-needed Commission.

CENTRAL ARIZONA PROJECT

A vast area of the Western United States is arid. Thousands of acres are in danger of becoming a barren wasteland as underground sources of water are used up or depleted.

We have the techniques and know-how to overcome this problem.

Now legislation is required to authorize a program to bring water from the Colorado River to meet the urgent needs of the people of Arizona.

Proposals affecting the canyons and the gorges of this mighty and historic river have been the subject of searching national debate. Out of this discussion, a plan has evolved that will require no dams on the Colorado River, preserve its scenic values, and at the same time permit the immediate construction of essential water supply facilities.

I ask the Congress to authorize the Central Arizona Project this year.

LYNDON B. JOHNSON

OIL POLLUTION ABATEMENT

Last year, when the *Torrey Canyon* sank off the coast of Cornwall, the 30 million gallons of oil it was carrying spread destruction throughout the coastal waters, killing fish and birds, and then the refuse of this devastation swept onto the beaches.

Only this week, at home, tragedy struck again. The tanker *Ocean Eagle* broke in half at the mouth of San Juan Bay, spewing some 1½ million gallons of oil over some of the finest beaches in the Western Hemisphere.

Major disasters rarely occur. But minor oil spills are frequent—and their combined effect, although less dramatic, can also be harmful.

Last year, I asked the Secretary of the Interior and the Secretary of Transportation to study the problem of oil pollution in American waters. Their report warns us that we must protect the beaches, places of recreation, coastal and inland waters, and our fisheries from spillage not only of oil, but of other hazardous substances as well.

We need a comprehensive system to control oil pollution and to provide for prompt clean-up.

We also must be able to cope with the spillage of large quantities of such substances as chlorine.

Last year the Senate passed S. 2760 to deal with the problem of oil pollution.

I propose we build upon and strengthen that bill through the Oil Pollution and Hazardous Substances Control Act of 1968.

This Act, together with the earlier Senate legislation, would:

- As a general rule, make the discharge of oil unlawful if it occurs from a shore facility or a ship operating within 12 miles from shore. The 3-mile territorial and 9-mile contiguous zones are thus both covered. This greatly expands the previous standard of liability, which was limited to "gross or willful negligence" and to the 3-mile limit.
- Impose upon the oil pollutor responsibility for cleaning the beaches and waters.
- Empower the Federal Government to clean up oil spills whenever the owner or operator fails to act, but require the pollutor to reimburse the Government for the clean-up costs. Prior law limited the owner's liability to the salvage value of the ship. The proposal will make them liable for the full costs of clean-up.
- Authorize the Government to establish regulations for shipboard and related marine operations to reduce the possibility of oil leakage at the source.

[753]

—Provide protection against large and dangerous discharges of pollutants other than oil by requiring those responsible to take whatever clean-up or other action the Government considers necessary. If the pollutor fails to act, the Government will take the necessary steps, and hold the pollutor liable for the costs.

AIR POLLUTION

"Metals corrode, fabrics weaken and fade, leather weakens and becomes brittle, rubber cracks and loses its elasticity, paint discolors, concrete and building stone discolor and erode, glass is etched and paper becomes brittle."

This is not a description of the effects of a new weapon.

It is a sobering report on the results of pollution in the air we breathe.

And that air is not divisible into convenient shares. Polluted air affects the lungs of all—rich and poor, manager and worker, farmer and urban dweller.

Of all the problems of conservation, none is more urgent than the polluted air which endangers the American people. We have been fortunate so far. But we have seen that when winds fail to blow, the concentrations of poisonous clouds over our cities can become perilous.

Air pollution is a threat to health, especially of older persons. It contributes significantly to the rising rates of chronic respiratory ailments.

It stains our cities and towns with ugliness, soiling and corroding whatever it touches. Its damage extends to our forests and farmlands as well.

The economic toll for our neglect amounts to billions of dollars each year.

The Clean Air Act of 1963 gave the Federal Government authority to help States and local communities plan effective programs to combat pollution.

In 1965, at my request, the Congress strengthened that Act by empowering the Secretary of Health, Education, and Welfare to set standards controlling automobile exhaust pollution—a major and mobile source of air contaminants.

Last year we took a giant step with the Air Quality Act of 1967. That Act:

—Will help our States abate pollution in the only practical way—on a regional basis. For air knows no man-made boundary.

—Gives the Government standby power to impose Federal standards or enforce State standards, if the States do not act.

—Gives the Secretary of Health, Education, and Welfare new power to stop serious cases of pollution that present a clear hazard to the public's health.

—Through accelerated research and testing, will help provide the technological answers to this baffling problem: How can we most economically and effectively prevent pollution at its source—in the fuels, while those fuels are being burned, or before the fumes reach the air?

[754]

To carry out our efforts to fight air pollution, I am seeking some $128 million for Fiscal 1969—more than we have committed in any past year.

I have directed the Secretary of Health, Education, and Welfare to designate the Nation's principal Air Quality Control Regions within the next few months, and to publish Air Quality criteria and related information on control techniques. This information will give States, local governments and industry the cost and control data they need to carry out their responsibilities.

One day we will have clean air over America—but only if all-levels of Government and industry work closely and conscientiously. The legislation now on the books provides the framework for a partnership without precedent, matching the dimension of the need. The problem deeply affects us all, and all of us share the responsibility for solving it.

I am confident that those responsibilities will be carried out—and that we can return to the American people a fundamental right of their national heritage: the right to breathe clean air.

ASSISTANCE IN HARDSHIP CASES

We have looked carefully into the question whether water and air pollution control will have a serious economic impact on American industry.

According to recent studies, the cost should be small for most firms.

In some cases, however, pollution control costs may present undue financial hardships to both a business and a community. *I have asked the Secretary of Commerce and the Administrator of the Small Business Administration to give priority attention to providing assistance in these hardship situations.*

AIR AND WATER POLLUTION FROM FEDERAL INSTALLATIONS

In the field of pollution, it is not enough for an enlightened Federal government to stimulate the work of the States, localities and private industry. It must also set a good example for the Nation.

Across America, federal installations are adopting the latest air and water pollution control methods. During the coming year, that effort will be intensified.

We expect to devote $53 million to the task, for thirteen separate federal agencies and 360 air and water pollution abatement projects.

NOISE CONTROL

What was once critically described as "the busy hum of traffic" has now turned into an unbearable din for many city dwellers.

The crescendo of noise—whether it comes from truck or jackhammer, siren or airplane—is more than an irritating nuisance. It intrudes on privacy, shatters serenity and can inflict pain.

We dare not be complacent about this ever-mounting volume of noise. In the years ahead, it can bring even more discomfort—and worse—to the lives of people.

I am directing all departments of Government to take account of noise factors in choosing the location and design of buildings, highways and other facilities whose construction is assisted by Federal funds.

I also urge the Congress to take prompt action on legislation to strengthen the authority of the Secretary of Transportation to deal with aircraft noise. We need greater capacity to deal with the rapidly growing noise problem created by our expanding air transportation system.

SURFACE MINING

An air traveler over some of the richest country in America can look down upon deep scars gouging the earth, acres of ravaged soil stretching out on either side.

Advances in mining technology have allowed us to extract the earth's minerals economically and swiftly.

But too often these new techniques have been used unwisely and stripping machines have torn coal and other minerals from the surface of the land, leaving 2 million acres of this Nation sterile and destroyed. The unsightly scars of strip mining blight the beauty of entire areas, and erosion of the damaged land pours silt and acid into our streams.

Under present practices, only one-third of the land being mined is also being reclaimed. This start has been made by responsible individuals, by mining companies, and by the States that have already enacted laws to regulate surface mining.

America needs a nationwide system to assure that all lands disturbed by surface mining in the future will be reclaimed. This can best be achieved through cooperative efforts between the States and the Federal Government.

I propose the Surface Mining Reclamation Act of 1968. Under this Act:

- —Criteria will be established which the States will use in developing their own regulatory plans.
- —The States, assisted by Federal grants, will develop their own plans within two years and submit them to the Secretary of the Interior for review and approval.
- —The Secretary will impose Federal standards if the State plans are inadequate or if they are not submitted.

Surface mining also occurs on Federal lands. To enable Government to take

the lead in this important conservation effort, I have directed that:
- —Federal Agencies assure that their regulations require the reclamation of Federal lands leased for surface mining.
- —From now on, Federal contracts for the purchase of coal and other surface-mined minerals contain effective reclamation clauses.

SOLID WASTE DISPOSAL

In 1965, I recommended and the Congress approved a national planning, research and development program to find ways to dispose of the annual discard of solid wastes—millions of tons of garbage and rubbish, old automobile hulks, abandoned refrigerators, slaughterhouse refuse. This waste—enough to fill the Panama Canal four times over—mars the landscapes in cities, suburbia and countryside alike. It breeds disease-carrying insects and rodents, and much of it finds its way into the air and water.

The problem is not only to learn how to get rid of these substances—but also how to convert waste economically into useful materials. Millions of dollars of useful by-products may go up in smoke, or be buried under the earth.

Already scientists working under the 1965 Act have learned much about how soils absorb and assimilate wastes. States and local communities have drawn up their plans for solid waste disposal.

That Act expires in June, 1969.

To continue our efforts, I recommend a one-year extension of the Solid Waste Disposal Act.

In addition, *I am directing the Director of the Office of Science and Technology working with the appropriate Cabinet officers to undertake a comprehensive review of current solid waste disposal technology.* We want to find the solutions to two key problems:
- —How to bring down the present high costs of solid waste disposal.
- —How to improve and strengthen government-wide research and development in this field.

AGRICULTURAL WASTES

The new agricultural and land management techniques that increase the productivity of our farms have also brought new problems:
- —Soil and other substances polluting our streams are the result of the erosion of farmlands and other areas. This cause of pollution has never been fully controlled and rapidly expanding suburban development has aggravated it.
- —Added amounts of animal wastes are generated from the efficient concentration of cattle, hogs and sheep in feed lots.

[757]

We must not permit harmful effects on fish, other wildlife and on drinking water supplies of chemicals from fertilizer and pesticides—whatever their source.

Many of these problems can be dealt with through existing programs. But some will require new research and new approaches.

I am instructing the Secretary of Agriculture to conduct a government-wide review of these problems.

THE SPLENDOR OF A CONTINENT

Before anything else, Americans had the splendor of a continent. Behind the facade of our cities, beyond the concrete ribbons that connect them, much of that splendor remains.

It is there because men of vision and foresight—men like Gifford Pinchot, Theodore Roosevelt and Franklin Roosevelt—determined that the people's oldest legacy, the inheritance of a spacious land, must be preserved.

It is for each generation to carry on that work.

In our time, the task has become more difficult—but ever more urgent. Our numbers grow, our cities become more crowded, the pace of our lives quickens —but man's need to raise his spirits and expand his vision still endures.

A clear stream, a long horizon, a forest wilderness and open sky—these are man's most ancient possessions. In a modern society, they are his most priceless.

NATIONAL PARKS AND RECREATION AREAS

In the past several years, we have authorized the addition of more than 2.2 million acres to the Nation's Park System.

We are actually preserving more lands—over 1.7 million acres in 1967—for conservation and the recreational enjoyment of America's families than the bulldozer and power shovel are taking over.

A park, however splendid, has little appeal to a family that cannot reach it.

The magnificent areas preserved in the early days of conservation were remote from the cities—and many Americans had to travel half a continent to visit them.

The new conservation is built on a new promise—to bring parks closer to the people. The man who works hard all week—the laborer, the shopkeeper, the subway rider—deserves a chance to escape the city's crush and congestion. He should have the opportunity to give his children a weekend of recreation and beauty and fresh air.

To provide this chance is the purpose of our program.

In the last several years, 32 of the 35 areas set aside by the new conservation—seashores, lakeshores, and parks—were located near large urban centers

—North, West, East, and South. They are within easy driving distance of 120 million of our people. For example:

- The resident of New York City can within an hour or so reach the beaches and waters of the Fire Island National Seashore, established in 1965.
- A family living in the Washington, D.C. area has—since 1965—been able to enjoy the advantages and scenic wonders of Assateague Island National Seashore, only three hours away by car.
- Citizens of Chicago will soon be able to visit the conveniently located Indiana Dunes National Lakeshore, whose development began last year.
- A father in Kentucky can take his son hunting and camping in the new "Land Between the Lakes" recreation area, which will serve millions of Americans in the Southeast.
- Boy Scout troops in the Southwest can explore and hike through the Guadalupe National Park in Texas.
- People in North Carolina will have easy access to the Cape Lookout National Seashore, now underway.

In 1967, almost 140 million visits were made to National Park areas. These visits are increasing steadily—a tribute to the quality and importance of our parks. It is also a signal that more parks are needed.

Paramount among our last-chance conservation opportunities is the creation of a Redwood National Park in Northern California to preserve the tallest, most ancient sentinels of nature on the American continent. A park in this region would benefit millions of Americans living on the West Coast who could reach the park within an afternoon's drive.

I urge the House to seize this opportunity and complete action on a Redwood bill this year.

I also recommend that the House complete action on two other major additions to the Park System that we sought and the Senate approved last year:

- *North Cascades National Park* in Washington State, the American Alps, an unsurpassed spectacle of mountain beauty in the great Northwest.
- *Apostle Islands National Lakeshore,* along Wisconsin's most scenic water areas.

We can achieve a new concept in conservation—greater than a park, more than the preservation of a river—by beginning this year to make the Potomac a living part of our national life.

That great river, coursing through Maryland, Virginia and West Virginia, cradles much of our early history. Five million people live within 50 miles of its shores, and its legend beckons millions more from every part of the Nation. For the Potomac is truly the American River.

I urge the Congress to authorize the development of a uniquely historic area —the Potomac National River. Failure to act now will make us the shame of generations to come.

SCENIC TRAILS, RIVERS AND WILDERNESS AREAS

The urgent work of conservation leads us into three other areas.

A citizen should be able to leave his car behind and explore a scenic trail on foot, by bicycle or horse. He can do that if we establish a nationwide network of scenic trails, many near our large cities and through historic areas. *Once again, I urge the Congress—as I did last year—to authorize a network of scenic trails.*

"The time has come," I said in 1965, "to identify and preserve free-flowing stretches of our great scenic rivers before growth and development make the beauty of the unspoiled waterway a memory."

Let this be the session of Congress that grasps the opportunity.

Last year the Senate passed a bill to save seven wild rivers and five scenic rivers. *I urge the Congress to complete action this year on legislation which would establish a scenic rivers system.*

One of the greatest delights for an American is to visit a primitive area of his land in its natural splendor.

In 1964, the Congress passed the Wilderness Act—a milestone in conservation policy. It permits the Government to set aside, at little cost to the taxpayer, some of the truly unspoiled areas of our continent.

Last year I asked the Congress to add the first four wilderness areas to the system: San Rafael in California, Mount Jefferson in Oregon, San Gabriel in California, and Washakie in Wyoming.

I urge the Congress to complete action on these wilderness areas.

I am today recommending the addition of seven new areas to the wilderness system, embracing more than 400,000 acres of mountain and forest and lake. These new wilderness areas are:

- Mt. Baldy in Arizona's Apache National Forest.
- The Desolation Wilderness in California's Eldorado National Forest.
- The Flat Tops, in Colorado's Routt and White River National Forests.
- Pine Mountain in Arizona's Prescott and Tonto National Forests.
- The Spanish Peaks, in Montana's Gallatin National Forest.
- The Ventana Wilderness in California's Los Padres National Forest.
- Sycamore Canyon in Arizona's Coconino, Kaibab, and Prescott National Forests.

We are now surveying unspoiled and primitive areas in Arkansas, Oklahoma, Georgia, and Florida as further possible additions to the Wilderness System.

THE LAND AND WATER CONSERVATION FUND

The machinery to finance the acquisition of Federal recreation lands and to help the States plan, acquire and develop their own parks and forests is provided by the Land and Water Conservation Fund.

That Fund draws upon revenues from motorboat fuel taxes, Federal recreation area admission charges, and proceeds from the sale of surplus Federal lands.

For Fiscal 1969, I recommended new obligational authority of $130 million for the Land and Water Conservation Fund—an increase of $11 million over 1968.

But this alone may not be enough. The need for more recreation acreage to serve our growing population—along with rising land costs—requires that the Land and Water Conservation Fund be enlarged.

The longer we wait to acquire land for recreational purposes, the more those lands will cost.

A suitable addition to those sources of revenues now authorized can be found in the receipts from our mineral leases in the Outer Continental Shelf. That Shelf belongs to the people, and it is only right that revenues from it be used for the people's benefit. *I recommend that the Congress authorize the use of part of these revenues to augment the Land and Water Conservation Fund to raise it up to a level of $200 million a year for the next five years.*

THE NATION'S HIGHWAYS

More than any other mark we make upon the land, the signature of mid-20th Century America is found in the more than 3 million miles of highways that cross and link a continent.

It is not enough that those highways be roads of utility. They must also be safe and pleasant to travel.

We have embarked on a major campaign to make them safe, in the Highway and Traffic Safety Acts of 1966.

In 1965—in the Highway Beautification Act—we set out to make them attractive. In partnership with the States, we determined to remove and control the eyesores that mar the landscape—auto graveyards, unsightly billboards, junk heaps.

Early last year I asked the Congress to extend that Act—which expired on June 30, 1967—for two additional years. The Senate passed a one-year extension. It is still awaiting House action. The Highway Beautification Act represents an important item of unfinished business before the Congress. *I urge the Congress to complete action on the bill so that we can get on with the job of making America a more beautiful place to live.*

Our highways must be in harmony with the communities and countrysides of which they are part. Too often in the past, this need has received little more than lip service.

A distinguished Citizens' Advisory Committee on Recreation and Natural Beauty, under the Chairmanship of Mr. Laurance Rockefeller, has reported: "Highways have effects that reach far beyond those who drive on them; yet our present devices for choosing locations are still based mostly on requirements of the highway user rather than the community at large."

Under the new authority in the Department of Transportation Act, we are moving now to assure that natural beauty and recreational factors are woven into the highway and freeway planning process, along with traditional engineering and cost considerations.

> —The Secretary of Transportation is requiring States to give full consideration to the views of local groups—and private citizens in preparing their route selections for Federally-supported highways.
> —The Secretaries of Transportation, Housing and Urban Development, Interior, and Agriculture will review exceptional cases which raise questions concerning a proposed highway route's impact on scenic and historic values.

ROADSIDE PARKS

A highway should not be an unending ribbon of concrete from point to point.

American families traveling on their roads should be able to stop, to stretch their legs, to open a picnic lunch and relax before going on their way.

A park along the roadside—with landscaped grounds, an outdoor stove and tables, a path to explore—should be part of every travel experience. These way stations are not expensive. But they can add immeasurably to the comfort and enjoyment of a family on a trip.

I have directed the Secretary of Transportation to work with the Governors and Highway Commissioners of each State on a priority program to increase substantially the number and quality of rest and scenic areas along the Federal-aid Highway System.

VOLUNTEERS FOR CONSERVATION

All across America, men and women, boys and girls are making their cities and communities better places to live. In garden clubs and civic leagues, in Scout troops, 4-H clubs, and Junior Chambers of Commerce, they are planting and painting, cleaning and building, growing and repairing.

This is the army of conservation volunteers, and they number in the millions.

I propose this action program for volunteers to make America a place of beauty, enriching its communities and raising the spirits of their people, volunteers to:

- —Increase local conservation efforts in every community, through the full participation of all citizens.
- —Extend the National Paint-Up, Clean-Up, Fix-Up Week, now an annual event, to a seasonal event, four times a year.
- —Encourage every city to beautify its approaches, through the planting of trees, shrubs and flowers native to the area.
- —Impress upon every citizen the contribution he can make simply by observing the "No Litter" signs as he drives along the highway and walks along the street. Clean-up is costly. For example, it takes $2,000 of the taxpayers' money each year to keep each mile of highway leading into the Nation's capital free of refuse.
- —Call upon the news media to encourage the conservation work of local groups. Television and radio stations, which are granted the public airways, have a special obligation to highlight these worthy public events.

The volunteer work for conservation deserves recognition and honor. It deserves help in mobilizing for greater efforts in the years ahead.

Accordingly, I am asking the President's Council on Recreation and Natural Beauty and the Secretary of the Interior in cooperation with the Governors and Mayors to join with private organizations in sponsoring a series of regional workshops to focus attention on those areas where greater private conservation efforts would be particularly productive.

THE OCEANS

The seas are the world's oldest frontiers. As Longfellow observed, they not only separate—but unite—mankind.

Even in the Age of Space, the sea remains our greatest mystery. But we know that in its sunless depths, a richness is still locked which holds vast promise for the improvement of men's lives—in all nations.

Those ocean roads, which so often have been the path of conquest, can now be turned to the search for enduring peace.

The task of exploring the ocean's depth for its potential wealth—food, minerals, resources—is as vast as the seas themselves. No one nation can undertake that task alone. As we have learned from prior ventures in ocean exploration, cooperation is the only answer.

I have instructed the Secretary of State to consult with other nations on the

steps that could be taken to launch an historic and unprecedented adventure—
an International Decade of Ocean Exploration for the 1970's.

Together the countries which border the seas can survey the ocean's resources, reaching where man has never probed before.

We hope that those nations will join in this exciting and important work.

Already our marine technology gives us the ability to use the ocean as a new and promising source of information on weather and climate. We can now build and moor electronic buoys in deep water. Unattended, these scientific outposts can transmit to shore data for accurate long-range forecasts.

The benefits will be incalculable—to farmers, to businessmen, to all travelers.

This year we can begin development of improved ocean buoys. I urge the Congress to approve my request for $5 million in the Fiscal 1969 Coast Guard budget for this program.

As we turn more and more of our attention to the exploration and the promise of the seas, America must train more ocean scientists and engineers.

In 1966, I signed the National Sea Grant College and Program Act. This new partnership between the Federal Government and the Nation's universities will prepare men and women for careers in the Marine Sciences.

I recommend that the Congress appropriate $6 million in Fiscal 1969 to advance this program.

THE CRISIS OF CHOICE

Three years ago, I said to the Congress:

". . . beauty must not be just a holiday treat, but a part of our daily life."

I return to that theme in this message, which concerns the air we breathe, the water we drink and use, the oceans that surround us, the land on which we live.

These are the elements of beauty. They are the forces that shape the lives of all of us—housewife and farmer, worker and executive, whatever our income and wherever we are. They are the substance of The New Conservation.

Today, the crisis of conservation is no longer quiet. Relentless and insistent, it has surged into a crisis of choice.

Man—who has lived so long in harmony with nature—is now struggling to preserve its bounty.

Man—who developed technology to serve him—is now racing to prevent its wastes from endangering his very existence.

Our environment can sustain our growth and nourish our future. Or it can overwhelm us.

History will say that in the 1960's the Nation began to take action so long delayed.

But beginning is not enough. The America of the future will reflect not the wisdom with which we saw the problem, but the determination with which we saw it through.

If we fail now to complete the work so nobly begun, our children will have to pay more than the price of our inaction. They will have to bear the tragedy of our irresponsibility.

The new conservation is work not for some Americans—but for all Americans. All will share in its blessings—and all will suffer if the work is neglected. That work begins with the family. It extends to all civic and community groups. It involves city hall and State capitol. And finally it must engage the concern of the Federal Government.

I urge the Congress to give prompt and favorable consideration to the proposals in this Message.

Lyndon B. Johnson

The White House
March 8, 1968

INDEX

DATE DUE

GAYLORD			PRINTED IN U.S.A.